PROCESS AND PRACTICE
WITH READINGS

Acquisitions Editor: Ellen Schatz
Cover Design: Ruttle Graphics, Inc.
Electronic Production Manager: Angel Gonzalez Jr.
Publishing Services: Ruttle Graphics, Inc.
Electronic Page Makeup: Ruttle Graphics, Inc.
Printer and Binder: R. R. Donnelley & Sons Company
Cover Printer: The Lehigh Press, Inc.

**PROCESS AND PRACTICE WITH READINGS,
FIRST EDITION**

Argentine writer LUISA VALENZUELA is the author of several novels and collections of short stories, most of them translated into English. STRANGE THINGS HAPPEN HERE, Short stories and a novel, Harcourt Brace Jovanovich, 1979. THE LIZARD'S TALE, novel, Farrar Straus, 1987. OTHER WEAPONS, 3 novellas, North Point Press, 1986. HE WHO SEARCHES, novel, The Darlkey Archives, 1986. OPEN DOOR, short stories, North Point Press, 1988. THE CENSORS, short stories, North Point Press, 1992. BLACK NOVEL (with Argentines), novel, Simon and Schuster, 1992. Recently published in Spanish, SIMETRIAS, a collection of short stories, Editorial Sudamericana, Buenos Aires, 1994.

Library of Congress Cataloging-in-Publication Data

Eggers, Philip.
        Process and practice with readings / Philip Eggers.
        p.   cm.
        Includes bibliographical references (p.) and index.
        ISBN 0-673-46810-0 (PB)   0-673-46811-9 (IM)
        1. English language—Rhetoric. 2. English language—Grammar—
   Problems, exercises, etc. 3. College readers. I. Title.
  PE1408.E359 1995
  808'.0427—dc20   94-32172
                                    CIP

96 97 9 8 7 6 5 4 3

PROCESS AND PRACTICE
WITH READINGS

Philip Eggers

Borough of Manhattan Community College
The City University of New York

HarperCollins*CollegePublishers*

CONTENTS

UNIT 3   WRITING SHORT ESSAYS   77

UNIT 4 REVISING AND IMPROVING YOUR WRITING 133

UNIT 5 PROOFREADING YOUR WRITING AND REVIEWING GRAMMAR 175

UNIT 6   A COLLECTION OF READINGS   315

LIST OF READINGS BY RHETORICAL MODE

PREFACE

TO THE INSTRUCTOR

Process and Practice with Readings retains the purpose of the original *Process and Practice* but with a wider range and slightly altered format. The success of the original text indicates that its focus and intention matched the approaches of many writing teachers by concentrating on the two areas where students most need instruction: mastering the stages of the writing cycle and controlling the elements of grammar, particularly verb forms and sentence divisions. This edition continues to emphasize these elements of writing while including a variety of multicultural readings for teachers who want to enrich their writing courses with lively reading assignments as springboards for writing and discussion. No elements of the original text have been left out, though all of the first five units have been shortened somewhat to allow for the inclusion of readings without producing a ponderous volume. The book is built around the easily recognizable stages of the writing process, placing each activity or drill in its proper context as part of an organic whole. With this larger framework of the writing process made visible to them, students can practice separate skills with the knowledge that they are aiming at a larger goal, not doing isolated drills. The readings will enhance students' mastery of the writing process by illustrating some of the skills they are learning and by showing them the range of themes and techniques good writing encompasses.

Most writing teachers prefer to use samples of their own students' work as the primary basis for instruction, partly to demonstrate how to correct errors and improve style and usage and partly to instill a spirit of pride. Professional readings will not substitute for samples of our students' own work; they are not intended for that purpose. Instead, they provide a larger sampling of the wide range of strategies, topics, and stylistic techniques than any collection of student essays will do. Many writing teachers find some use of professional examples indispensable. The difficulty usually is, however, that assigning two books, a rhetoric and a reader, proves expensive and excessive; time seldom permits us to use both as extensively as we intend. To solve that problem, *Process and Practice with Readings* is designed to offer enough readings that the teacher has considerable choice and enough coverage of the writing process and grammar that nothing important has to be omitted.

Some teachers will, of course, continue to use the original *Process and Practice* without resorting to reading assignments. Writing courses vary considerably from one college to another. Increasingly, however, there has been a trend toward whole language instruction, of combining skills of listening, speaking, reading, and writing which too often have been taught in isolation. More and more teachers are discovering ways in which these learning processes reinforce one another. It is no accident that nearly all great writers have been voluminous readers—though, of course, not all voluminous readers turn out to be Nobel Prize-winning authors. Practicing reading aloud, both their own writing and passages from assigned readings, generally improves students' writing fluency along with their overall confidence in their ability to use language effectively. Certainly the inclusion of lively multicultural readings in a writing course will enrich the students' experience. One cannot tease out all of the ways in which students' writing gains from the discussion of prose models. Certainly we don't expect them to copy what they read in any simple sense. Probably the best explanation is to say that the readings draw them into a large world of discourse beyond the classroom—a world of voices even more varied than those in their classroom, and yet one in which they can find themselves very much at home. That process of reaching out, of joining, of inclusion, is probably what many pedagogical theorists mean when they use that familiar and possibly overused term, *empowerment.*

Like the original version of *Process and Practice,* this edition is designed to be useful, convenient, and modest in size and price. It continues to steer a middle course between the demands of an encyclopedic but intimidating and costly textbook and the constraints of a scaled-down, only-what-you-need-to-know workbook. Without being exhaustive or exhausting, the book omits nothing important in the stages of the writing process or the features of grammar that cause serious problems for developing writers. The readings are numerous enough and sufficiently varied in mode, topic, and writers' backgrounds to offer plenty of material for either a thematic or a modal approach. The readings also appeal to students of many age groups, since today's nontraditional students, especially in two-year colleges and large public four-year institutions, range from late adolescence to middle age and even older. The readings also are of moderate difficulty—on a college level of maturity in content but within the range of a first-year student's vocabulary and reading ability. Furthermore, the readings, like the content of the exercises in the earlier units, remain close to the interests of today's students, who come from many ethnic backgrounds. Like the writing activities in the other units, the readings contain educationally valuable material as well as insights into controversial issues.

Unit 6 has been designed to provide teaching aids along with the readings. The vocabulary exercises will help students concentrate on learning and remembering new words. The comprehension questions will help focus their attention on the meaning of the reading assignments and provide a basis for class discussions or collaborative learning. The writing assignments will allow for the use of readings as springboards for writing assignments, either as rhetorical models in various modes or as discussions of topics on which students may write.

Like the original *Process and Practice,* this edition assumes that much of the effort and inspiration must come from the students, but that you, the instructor, will provide the human link, the emotional stimulus, and the guidance that enable students to make writing an important part of their lives. This book is a teaching tool, not a self-help manual. Only by receiving attentive and authentic responses from you and from one another will your writing students experience their writing and reading as true communication. How you achieve this is up to you; this book is flexible enough to allow for a variety of pedagogical methods. The instructor's manual may further help expand your knowledge of teaching methods and research on writing pedagogy.

I want to thank the reviewers of this text for their critical remarks and helpful recommendations. They include Martha French, Fairmont State College; Lois Friesen, Butler County Community College; Marsha Groff, Texas A&M, Corpus Christi; Rosemary Hunkeler, University of Wisconsin-Parkside; and Michael Kimball, College of San Mateo. I appreciate also the editorial guidance of Ellen Schatz at HarperCollins and the careful scrutiny of the proofs by Carol Gardenier of Ruttle Graphics, Inc.

My colleagues and the students at Borough of Manhattan Community College continue to be the main source of what I know about writing, reading, and learning. Finally, to Jane, Tori, David, Wendy, and Michael I am boundlessly grateful for giving special meaning to the process and practice of living.

TO THE STUDENT

Perhaps you are one of the lucky students who can devour whole books in a few hours or who love to write poems, diaries, and term papers. Or you may be one of those who "hate English," or believe they do, and who would rather endure root canal therapy without anesthesia than write another 500-word theme. More likely, you are somewhere in the middle. Most people enjoy reading and writing at least once in a while, but even the best writers report a certain amount of struggle in their attempts to make the words come out right. Every writer is different, but whatever your writing and reading habits are, you will benefit from using this book.

Process and Practice with Readings is intended to draw you into the process of mental discovery that writing produces and to involve you in the discourse of many writers with many voices. By experiencing the varied opinions, styles, and viewpoints expressed in the readings, you will be prompted to develop your own style and opinions. As you improve your mastery of the writing process through units one through four, you will also be developing your individuality. Nothing is more individualistic than writing, but writing flourishes best as a social activity; reading and writing involve a continuous give and take. By writing as part of a group and a class, you will discover your powers as well as your weaknesses, your similarity to others as well as your uniqueness. As you share your writing with others, you will develop a distinctive voice and style. As you read the work of others, both classmates and professional writers, you will enlarge your vocabulary, range of knowledge, and grasp of writing techniques. The activities in Unit 1 will help you concentrate on developing fluency. In Units 2 and 3 you will explore paragraph and essay composition. Unit 4 will help you improve the word choice, sentence patterns, and style of your compositions.

Unit 5 is a workbook designed to help you with any catch-up work you need on grammar, usage, spelling, or punctuation. Although the *process* of discovery and expression is the goal, frequent *practice* is also necessary. Mastering the basics will not turn you into a conformist or make your writing dull, even though the same rules of grammar and spelling apply to everybody. In fact, a secure command of these basics will allow you greater freedom to develop your own voice and style. Use Unit 5 as you need it. Find out through the diagnostic test and your teacher's advice how much intensive work you need and in what areas.

The readings in Unit 6 will be assigned as your teacher decides. You may of course go ahead and read anything you want and work on the vocabulary and comprehension questions. Good writing will always repay several readings, so concentrate on the assigned readings with special care. If you find a writer who particularly appeals to you, look up other works she or he has written—novels, books of poems, or collections of short stories or essays. Read a biography of that writer and make his or her works a part of your life. Reading and writing go together; the more you enjoy good reading, the more thoughtful, fluent, and interesting your own writing will become.

Philip Eggers

U N 1 I T

PREWRITING

The first stage in the writing process includes prewriting activities. Some of these will limber up your mental muscles and get the ink flowing. Others will allow you to explore topics without pausing to worry about organization or corrections. Remember that your prewriting activities are for practice and exploration; in doing them you should concentrate on facts, ideas, and feelings more than on the language itself. You should be trying to discover as much as you can, not trying to avoid red marks on your paper. In prewriting activities, unlike the later stages of the writing process, more is always better, so keep your pen moving.

FREEWRITING

First of all, write. Write about anything on your mind, and let your mind wander. Write for five or ten minutes without letting your pen stop. If you can't think of anything, write the same word several times until you get moving again. There is no such thing as right or wrong in this activity, except for stopping before the time is up.

This kind of writing is called **freewriting** or automatic writing. Freewriting means writing without pausing for a given length of time or until you have written a certain amount, such as a full page. You can develop fluency in freewriting by doing it regularly. If you sometimes find yourself saying, "I can't get started," freewriting will make it easier for you to become unstuck. Some teachers have students do freewriting for five or ten minutes every day, whereas others assign it only at the beginning of the semester. If your teacher does not require you to do it, practice freewriting on your own, especially in the first weeks of your writing course.

If you become anxious about being timed when you write, you may want to aim for filling up a page when you freewrite. Writing at least a page at a time makes you better able to reach for the full paragraph and complete essay later, even though your freewriting sample may be very different from actual paragraphs and essays. For one thing, your sample may contain repetitions and mistakes, and may wander from one topic to another. Some of what you say may be nonsense; some of it may seem to come from left field. The main purpose of freewriting is to let your writing flow rhythmically and endlessly, like the current of a river. Sometimes it won't; there may be a few rocks in the river, and you may get stuck. With practice, however, your pauses will become brief, and the river will flow again.

Here is one example of freewriting done by a student:

> *Here we go again, writing about whatever came into my head. Last time I wrote it was raining outside, now I'm writing and it's raining again. Boy is it hot in here. I hope I finish this page without my hand getting tired. Yesterday I went to the movies with Barbara and Joanne, boy was it fun. I had a nice hamburger and some fries afterward. Sonya just came into the class late. Why is she always late? The teacher ought to do something about her, she's stuck on herself. Stuck. I'm stuck. This afternoon is the nursing quiz and I'm not ready for it. Nursing is easier than last term anyway. I hope I get to meet that guy named Kevin in the class next door. He tells funny stories and seems to like me. He's kind of funky though. I'm tired of going out with Marvin all the time because he thinks he's so cool. He always borrows money from me but forgets about it and never wants to pay me back. Some guys don't have any responsibility but Kevin is grown up. I talked to him last week about his job and he really impress me with his attitude.*

Try to develop a conversational ease in your freewriting: pick up a topic and stay with it as long as it interests you, the way people do in conversation. The benefits of freewriting usually come by accident. You learn to focus on an idea and develop it and to move from one idea to a related one. By doing freewriting every day in a journal you may find that you begin to sharpen your statements of ideas.

EXERCISE: Freewriting

Practice freewriting by writing without stopping for five minutes. Don't hurry; just keep the pen moving. Begin with a key word so that your mind is focused, but don't try to compose a formal essay. Here are some possible key words: *college, weekends, teachers, shopping, horror movies, traveling, sports, parents.* After five minutes of writing, stop. How much have you written? You will probably find that when you do not have to worry about grammar, spelling, organization, or your teacher's criticisms, you are able to write a whole page in a very short time.

Do a five-minute exercise like this every day for a week. When this routine becomes easy, try ten-minute writing sessions. Begin with some key word or idea in mind, but don't try to "stay on the topic"; just write naturally the way you talk in conversation. If you discover yourself writing so well that you actually want to read your freewriting sample to someone, go right ahead. But do not write with the intent of satisfying a critic. You may feel more confident and be more fluent writing just for yourself.

FOCUSED WRITING

After you have been freewriting for several weeks, you will develop a new attitude toward writing. Writing will become an everyday activity, like walking, conversing, and reading. You will stop regarding writing as a formal, specialized job that you can do only when wearing a suit. You will stop worrying about a teacher looking over your shoulder with a red pencil, poised to find your mistakes. You will write for yourself because you like to write—anywhere it is convenient, any time you feel like it, and about any subject on which you want to state your opinions.

This new positive attitude will make your writing better, but it will not produce finished, organized essays. The next step is **focused writing,** which will bring you a little closer to the process of composing organized paragraphs and essays. Focused writing is a not-quite-so-free exercise in which you write on a single topic during a chosen period of time. As in freewriting, you maintain a steady rhythm, concentrating on letting the words flow without being distracted by problems of grammar, spelling, or organization. In focused writing, however, you steer in one direction. In freewriting there is only one *don't*: Don't stop. In focused writing there are two: Don't stop and don't wander off the subject.

Naturally, you will do this better if you have become comfortable writing continuously for two pages or ten minutes in your freewriting. And of course you should phase in your focused writing by choosing subjects familiar to you. Here is one student's focused writing about subways:

> *The subway is a pain in the neck. It smells terrible down there. Bag ladies with infected feet and burns always begging, then the train takes so long to come. Sometimes I lean over the track and I wanna go down the track to meet it. When I get on the train sometimes I have to stand up usually when my feet are hurting and the train is shaking and its all hot and stuffy. You think you're just going to die! On the subway tracks sometimes you can see the rats walking around looking for food and they look real nasty. Some of them are big and fat like cats. During the summer the subway is hot and during the winter it's cold. It is like going down into hell. Boxes crushed from trampling feet, newspapers flying here and there. Coffee cups are placed on any convenient spots and cigarette butts are everywhere. Trains pulling in and out of the station sound like a volcano. If you try to speak to the person next to you, they can't hear a word you are saying.*

The student stayed on the topic very well and expressed some strong feeling about her experience with the subway. She did not plan to express a particular emotion; she simply explored the thoughts and feelings she already had. You may find yourself jumping from one thought to another, and making some writing errors. The important thing, however, is to discover how much you can say about the subject.

EXERCISE I: Focused Writing

Write, without stopping, a whole page on the subject of your family. Don't try to organize your thoughts first; just write everything that comes to mind.

EXERCISE II: Focused Writing

Do focused writing for ten minutes or two pages (whichever you find easier) on subjects from the following list:

1. The worst purchase you ever made
2. The kind of car you'd like to own
3. What you like to do on dates
4. The kinds of food you like to eat
5. Television programs you love and hate
6. Your friends' different attitudes toward marriage
7. How you like to dress
8. How computers make your life easier or harder

KEEPING A JOURNAL

In some college courses, not just English courses but also content courses in other subjects, you may be asked to keep a journal in which you write down your responses to assigned readings or class discussions. **Journal writing** will enhance your understanding of the course material by making you a more active participant. Your instructor may also intend these journals to be prewriting explorations from which you can draw ideas for essays and research paper topics. Even if you are not asked to keep journals in all courses, you can keep your own journals to help you focus your ideas and remember assigned material.

What should you enter in a journal? Your instructor may give you guidance on what she or he wants; otherwise, you will probably gain more from expressing your own thoughts about the course material than from trying to aim for the "right" ideas. Journals can help you develop critical thinking skills, express your preferences and dislikes, and relate course assignments to your personal experience. The freedom from fear of making mistakes, displeasing a grader, or leaving something out will allow you to pursue your own insights more fully than you can in formal term papers.

BRAINSTORMING: MAKING LISTS

Like freewriting and focused writing, **brainstorming**—spilling all the facts, ideas, examples, and feelings you have on a particular subject—is another prewriting activity. Brainstorming is much like focused writing except that you do not write continuously. You simply jot down everything you can in the form of a big list. Making lists conditions your mind for writing by improving your ability to explore a subject. The list can be a jumble of words, phrases, and statements. Don't censor anything at first. Selecting and organizing come later.

You have made plenty of lists before in your life—shopping lists, lists of things to do, lists of books to read and people to invite. When you made such lists, did you worry about how you put words together or how you spelled them? No, you just wanted to be sure you didn't miss anything or anyone important. Do that when you make lists as a prewriting activity.

Here is a list containing everything one student could think of about jobs:

pay scales	blue collar jobs
jobs in health care	military, government jobs
private industry	college training for jobs
I have had three jobs.	changing jobs and careers
computers changing many jobs	interviewing for jobs
discrimination against	jobs for immigrants
senior citizens	why people choose jobs

changes in future job market	temporary jobs
husband and wife both working	working while going to college
	boring jobs
jobs in socialist countries	jobs in entertainment
bilingual job opportunities	working mothers
women in "men's" jobs	forty hour week
unions	vacations
commuting to work	fringe benefits
health hazards on some jobs	counseling for jobs at college
unemployment	jobs for handicapped people
pensions	jobs that change locations often
jobs overseas	dangerous jobs
owning small businesses	minimum wage

EXERCISE I: Brainstorming

Make a list of everything you notice about a room you are in—a classroom, room at home, or office where you work. See how many details you can mention. Compete with another student to see whose list has more entries. Train yourself to be a sharp observer.

EXERCISE II: Brainstorming

Make lists of everything you can think of on the topics that follow. Try to cover every square inch of each subject, remembering that there is always one more idea or fact hidden somewhere. Spend ten minutes on each topic.

1. Television—jot down facts, ideas, personal opinions, and experiences.
2. Yourself—put down as many facts, descriptive details, and thoughts about yourself as you can.
3. An activity you engage in, such as martial arts, playing the guitar, cooking, using a computer.
4. A social issue like drug abuse, child abuse, divorce, poverty, street crime, unemployment, sexism, immigration.

ORGANIZING IDEAS

Before you do any serious composing of paragraphs or essays, practice grouping ideas. Get into the habit of seeing large patterns before you fill in details; make rough sketches of your subjects before you work out the fine points.

Learn to break down lists into a few main categories. After you compile lists, look them over to identify the large groups of ideas into which they can be divided. Some items may not fit and will have to be dropped. Look back at the student's list concerning jobs and divide the items into the categories below:

Types of jobs: Problems with jobs:

Rewards of jobs: Preparing for jobs:

Other (items that do not fit the previous categories):

EXERCISE I: Grouping

Identify the three main categories of items in the following list. The general subject is teenage problems. Two of the items do not belong in any of the three subgroups. List these two separately.

peer group's use of drugs
parents too strict about
    curfews
absenteeism from school
choosing courses in school
sharing family chores
talking to parents about sex
alcoholism among peers
competition with brothers
    and sisters
changing schools
sharing secrets with brothers
    and sisters
having to share a room with
    a brother or sister at home
fads in clothing and hair styles
    among peers
boredom with classes
dropping out of school
showing respect for parents
teenage gangs
organized crime

school guidance counselors
    not helpful
parents don't understand
not popular with peer group
jealousy among friends
foreign cars
too much academic pressure
getting respect from parents
danger from sexually
    transmitted diseases
ethnic differences among
    friends
younger brothers and sisters
    invading one's privacy
girls being interested in
    older boys
snobbishness among friends
too much emphasis placed
    on grades
athletes get all the attention
    in school
teenage pregnancy

Name the three categories:

1. _____

2. _____

3. _____

Name the two items that do not fit:

1. _____

2. _____

EXERCISE 11: Grouping

Choose one of your lists from the brainstorming exercises. Divide the items into categories as in the exercise above, eliminating any items that do not fit into your three or four main groups.

CLUSTERING

Another prewriting activity that many students and teachers find valuable is clustering: a way of making an unsystematic diagram of your thoughts on a subject and showing connections between ideas. Like brainstorming, clustering brings out many half-forgotten bits of information on a subject. Begin clustering by writing your main topic in the middle of the page and circling it:

Careers for Women

Next, develop a diagram spreading out like a spider in all directions, showing some of the related ideas:

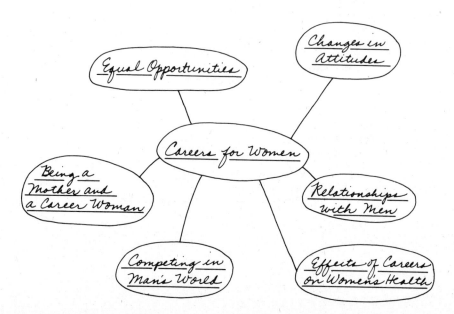

Each of these related ideas has many facts, thoughts, and examples connected to it. The diagram that follows shows how you fill in the map as much as you can.

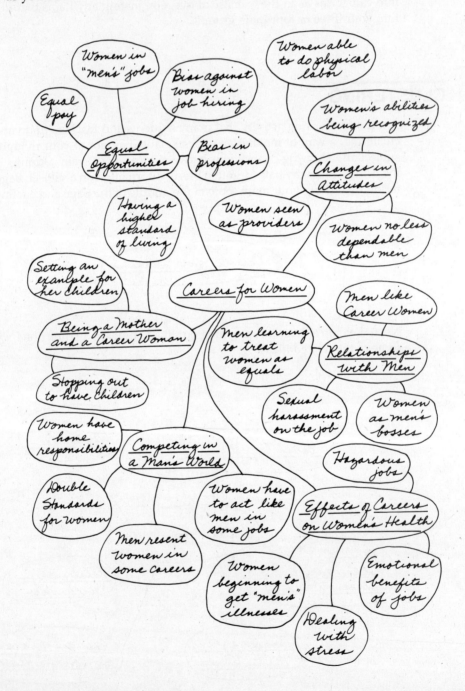

Don't worry if your cluster begins to spread out all over the page. The more ideas the better.

What can you do with a cluster?

A cluster helps to:

1. Discover new ideas on the topic.

2. See links between subtopics.

3. Identify supporting details.

4. Identify specific ideas that might provide a thesis if your main topic is too broad.

"Careers for Women" is obviously too broad a subject for a single essay. Looking at the cluster, you might decide that only one part of it would give you a better thesis.

How about "Women Are Beginning to Feel the Effect of Careers on Their Health"? Now make a more detailed cluster on that topic:

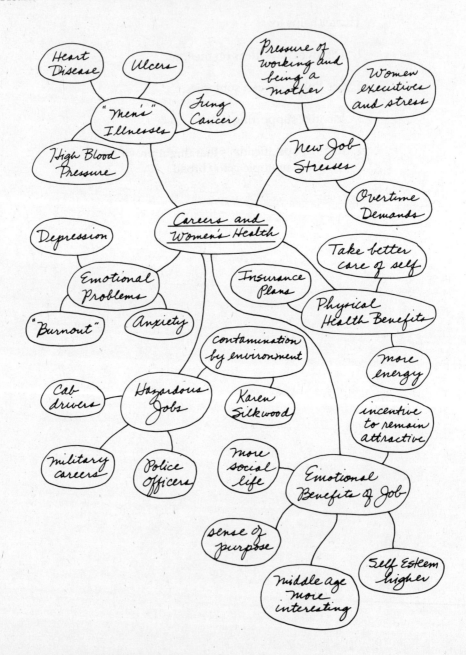

EXERCISE: Clustering

The following cluster has been partially filled in. Complete the cluster with items that relate to each of the subtopics in the cluster.

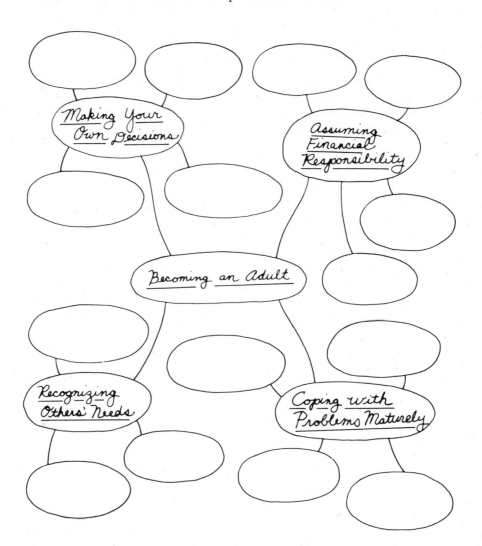

OTHER PREWRITING ACTIVITIES

No single prewriting technique is best for everybody. Each writer has to find the technique that is most helpful in exploring a topic and arranging material. Here are a few other methods often used by writers and teachers:

Ask Yourself Questions

Journalists for years have used the five W's—who, what, when, where, and why—to develop their material. Ask yourself these questions about your subject. Imagine that you are being interviewed about your topic. What questions would the interviewer ask you?

Use the Five Senses

Good writing makes imaginative use of all five senses, not just the eyes. Make a list of facts about a familiar object, such as a coin, a hat, a piece of jewelry, or a pear. Underline all facts that are *not* visual. Have you mentioned impressions of taste, hearing, smell, or touch?

Keeping a Learning Log

In classes that you find difficult, write for five minutes after every class session summing up what you have learned that day. This will give you a record to use for review before tests, and it will reinforce your memory of what you learned. It will sometimes also bring out what you failed to understand and need to ask the instructor or tutor about. If the class requires term papers, you may find the topics for papers in entries you made in your learning log.

Write Imaginary Letters

In addition to writing actual letters to friends and family members, you may find it stimulating to write letters to people in the news whose actions or opinions arouse your anger or enthusiasm. You need not send such letters; simply writing them serves a creative purpose. Once in a while, you may even decide to mail one.

READING ALOUD: GETTING FEEDBACK

At all stages of the writing process, you can benefit by reading your writing aloud to other people. Don't cringe! Once you become used to reading your writing aloud, you will enjoy it. Many people are a little self-conscious at first; if you are, try reading to just one person with whom you feel comfortable, and have that person read his or her work to you. The other person does not have to be an expert on grammar or even highly educated. The purpose of reading aloud at this stage is not to catch mistakes; it is to help you explore the subject further and discover whether your writing comes across the way you expect it to.

In the prewriting stage, getting feedback will chiefly help you discover the possibilities of your subject and clarify your attitude toward it. When other people tell you in their own words exactly what they think you have said and what you meant and felt, they help you form a clear picture of your own purpose. Sometimes what *they* think you meant is not what *you* really meant. In that case, you may have to state your ideas differently. Sometimes, too, other people detect your hidden feelings and intentions, which you should bring out more clearly. You never can predict what others will discover in your writing until you read it to them and hear what they have to say. You may also be surprised at how much they enjoy listening to you!

Types of Feedback to Get from Your Listeners

Here are some guidelines on getting feedback. When you have another person or group of persons listen to you read your writing aloud, have them give you these responses:

What You Said.   At first it may seem silly to have them merely repeat your ideas, but by doing this they help you recognize your own thoughts and feelings and discover whether you really communicated them.

What You Felt About the Subject.   When you do focused writing, you are not thinking much about your feelings—you are just expressing them. A listener can often recognize your feelings better than you can.

What Interested the Listener Most.   You may be surprised to find that some of your minor details excited the listener more than what you considered your important ideas. Be ready to open your mind to your listener's reactions; these reactions often give you hints on what to expand and emphasize.

What the Listener Wanted to Hear More or Less About.   While doing focused writing, you don't think much about the reader. Feedback from a listener afterward, however, can help you determine what is going to be interesting to readers and what will bore them. One listener may not give you a completely reliable indication, but if you get the same response from many people in a group, you had better consider it carefully!

What the Listener Did Not Understand.   One lesson all beginning writers need to learn (and advanced writers should never forget) is that there is no guarantee that the reader will know what you mean just because *you* know what you mean. A large part of the craft of writing is stating as clearly and simply as possible exactly what you mean. Only the listener can tell you what he or she does not understand.

INCLUDING YOUR AUDIENCE

Once you have become comfortable reading your writing aloud, especially if you have done it with a group, begin considering your audience as you write. Freewriting and focused writing do not require an audience; you are thinking only about the flow of language and the subject. Finished, organized writing, however, such as college term papers, business reports, letters, magazine articles, and so on, always includes an audience. The writer is communicating to someone or some group of people. The way you express yourself on paper is influenced by the person or group for whom you are writing. Although your style should always be your own, your audience determines in part what facts you choose to communicate, the difficulty of the words you select, the tone you adopt (serious, funny, casual, formal, etc.) and how much explaining you do.

Here are some guidelines to follow in writing for your audience:

Find the Right Voice

Your writing should sound authentic and should be appropriate for the subject, situation, and reader. Since most of your college writing will be read by the teacher and other members of the class, your tone should be natural and direct but not as personal as if you were writing to a close friend or family member. Don't strain to sound "intellectual" or "businesslike" either, or you may adopt a voice that sounds artificial. Here is a sample of writing that shows this kind of straining:

> *Accounting has often been considered by myself to provide the required remuneration and advancement potential necessary for me to further my goals in a professional career of my choice. Additionally, such a career possibility will enable me to enhance myself in my pursuit of fulfillment of my personal satisfaction.*

What's wrong with this? The writer is so busy trying to sound impressive that he or she winds up not saying much of anything. It's better not to be pompous. Write the way you would talk to other adults in a semiformal situation such as a job interview:

> *I have chosen to become an accountant for several reasons. Having above average ability in mathematics and a quick memory, I should be able to do the work well. I also enjoy being efficient and helping others improve the efficiency of their work. The high salaries earned by successful accountants appeal to me as well, and my parents will be pleased if I become the first C.P.A. in the family.*

This passage may be less "impressive" because it doesn't use many big words, but it has something to say and sounds like an actual person talking to someone else. Finding the right voice means using a tone somewhere between stilted, artificial language and the casual language of private conversation.

---

*See improving your choice of words in Unit 4.

Use the Appropriate Vocabulary

For most college writing, use adult vocabulary. Explore the range of word choices available, always trying to use the most precise words, not just the biggest ones.* If you are studying a technical field like nursing, remember that nonspecialists may not know the technical terms you have learned, so explain these terms if you use them. Slang and street talk, at the other extreme, should be used only for special effects such as humor or surprise. Writers who rely on slang for emphasis become lazy and choose the first slang term that comes to mind instead of considering more precise options. For example, a slang term that has been around a long time is *knock*—to "knock" something you don't like. Consider some of the alternatives many people never think of—*put down, belittle, disparage, minimize, denigrate,* and *ridicule.* Most slang terms, which began as colorful and imaginative inventions, quickly become stale; they are the mark of a careless writer or speaker. Using frequent slang will cause the reader to lose respect for your grasp of the subject and the seriousness of your intentions. Select the best words for your purpose. Use simple language if you write for children, adult language for adults, and technical language for specialists. And don't forget to look for synonyms (words that have similar meanings) in *Roget's Thesaurus.*

Respect Your Reader

Readers will be annoyed if you talk down to them or leave them no room to disagree. Give them the right to have their own opinions and feelings. Some writers prefer to antagonize their readers in order to provoke an angry exchange of opinion. In most college writing, however, your purpose is to weigh evidence and present ideas, not to propagandize or incite anger. If you wish to explain facts or persuade the reader to agree with your opinion, adopting a prejudiced attitude will weaken your effect. Blatant biases will usually cause the reader to stop reading entirely or to ignore your argument. Recognizing the reader's right to differ with you, on the other hand, may make it possible to win the reader to your side.

Recognize Your Reader's Knowledge of the Subject

If you are writing informatively for people who know very little about your subject, explain everything they need to know. If, however, you are writing about basketball and your readers are all basketball coaches, don't explain what a free throw is.

Write for the Same Audience Throughout

Sometimes students begin term papers with a general introduction that tells the reader facts any nine-year-old would know; then they suddenly jump into the most specialized, technical discussion imaginable. Decide whom you're writing for.

EXERCISE I: Including Your Audience

Read aloud with a group the following contrasting samples of writing and discuss the ways in which the two samples have been influenced by the audience for whom they were written.

Consider the differences in (a) facts selected, (b) use of language, and (c) attitudes or biases. Read:

1. a passage from a local newspaper intended to inform, and a passage from a tabloid such as *The National Enquirer* intended to entertain
2. a passage from a magazine intended mostly for women and a passage from a magazine intended mostly for men
3. a passage from an elementary or junior high school textbook and a passage from a college textbook

---

EXERCISE II: Including Your Audience

Write about the same subject for two widely different groups of readers. Do this as focused writing. Choose a subject that both groups would be interested in but would have different attitudes about. Don't *plan* to write differently in the two samples—just write *for* the particular audience, and notice afterward how your audience unconsciously affected what you said. Here are some suggestions:

1. college—for a group of high school students and a group of professors
2. marriage—for a group of divorced people and a group of children
3. jobs—for a group of politicians and a group of unemployed people
4. crime—for a group of prison inmates and a group of police officers
5. your home town—for people who live there and people who have never been there
6. your area of study—for a group of experts and people who are just beginning to study it

MAKING YOUR POINT

While practicing freewriting and focused writing, you thought only about putting plenty of words on the page without stopping. You probably discovered, however, that as you explored some subjects, you had strong opinions and feelings about them. You discovered purposes that you had not planned, such as "I want to complain about the subways" or "I want to tell you how interesting my family is." Perhaps when you read your work aloud, some of your listeners helped you to identify some of these unstated purposes by saying things like "You certainly are angry about the way they treated you on the job" or "You described your sister so well that I feel I've already met her."

Prewriting is a form of exploring what you think and feel. As you move into actual composing, however, you will begin writing with a *stated* main point. You will learn to tell the reader what you are going to say—not just what your topic is, but how you are going to write about it: defend it, attack it, describe it, compare it with something else, analyze its parts, define it, or persuade the reader to accept your opinion of it. Knowing your purpose is all-important. Many essays succeed or fail because the writer either did or did not have a strong point that was clear throughout the essay. Learn to recognize the difference between merely choosing a topic and knowing how you want to discuss it. "Women's Health Problems" is a topic; "Career Women Face Special Health Problems" is a main point.

EXERCISE I: Making Your Point

Make a point about each of the following topics. First write nonstop for a few minutes on each topic. Then find a point you have made about the topic and write it in the blank.

Example:

Topic: Professional basketball

Point: _____ *The three-point rule made basketball more exciting.* _____

1. Topic: Marriage

   Your point: _____

2. Topic: Cocaine

   Your point: _____

3. Topic: Diets

   Your point: _____

4. Topic: Television news

   Your point: _____

5. Topic: Pornography

   Your point: _____

EXERCISE II: Making Your Point

Read both of the following passages and tell which one starts with a clearly stated point and supports that point all the way through. Which one wanders in different directions and keeps bringing up new points instead of developing one main point?

Passage A:

College athletes deserve to be paid because they bring in money and prestige to their colleges. The benefits that top athletes bring to their schools are enormous. Many colleges like UNLV, Duke, and Notre Dame attract good students because athletes have made these colleges prestigious, yet these same athletes are not paid for their work. Furthermore, sports bring large amounts of money to the schools, but none of this income goes to the athletes in the form of salaries. Athletic coaches, faculty members, and administrators at these colleges are paid high salaries, while the athletes work just as hard for nothing. In the age of television, the financial benefits gained by colleges, commercial sponsors, and vendors from basketball tournaments and football bowl games add up to millions. If talk show hosts and newscasters can earn millions of dollars a year, the talents of college athletes also deserve high salaries.

Passage B:

Sports in college are exciting, but there is some controversy surrounding them. When I was a freshman I tried out for the baseball team, but I realized I would not have enough time for my studies, so I quit. Many of my friends decided to stay on either the baseball team or the football team, but some of them are having a hard time keeping up with their work. Most colleges in our conference give athletic scholarships, but they usually aren't enough to cover all your expenses. Our team came in second in the conference last year, but we have a chance to win first place this season. Our quarterback is thinking of signing a professional contract. If he does, we'll be lucky to come in third or fourth. The women's teams are much better since the school hired a new athletic supervisor two years ago. My favorite television sport is the Olympics. I wish I didn't have to wait four years for it to come back again every time. Some people like to watch pro football, but I think college sports are the best because the fans have more loyalty to their teams. What's really surprising, though, is that there aren't more injuries in gymnastics, because it looks so dangerous, but I guess if you're coached properly, you know how to avoid getting hurt.

Passage A starts with a clear purpose—to convince us that college athletes ought to be paid. Then it goes on to give reasons why this is true. Passage B, however, reads more like focused writing: it stays on the broad subject of sports, but it jumps from one idea to another, such as the writer's experience with baseball, the local college's chances of winning, women's teams, sports on television, and athletic injuries. Passage B would be useful as a warm-up exercise for exploring ideas, but Passage A is closer to a fully developed paragraph of the kind we will study in Unit 2.

SUPPORTING YOUR POINT

There are many ways to support a point, as you will learn in Unit 2 and Unit 3. Whatever method you are using, you should always follow one rule: *include enough details to support the point*. When you make a point, the reader expects you to explain what you mean and illustrate it with facts and examples. This part of writing means work for you, but it makes your writing much more enjoyable, interesting, and informative. Supporting your point does not mean restating the point in slightly different words. Remember to *show* rather than *tell* the reader what you mean. If your sister tells you, "I just met a terrific guy last night," you expect her to fill you in with facts about what he looks like, where he's from, and how he acts. The same thing applies to your writing: you lead off with a statement that arouses interest; then you follow up with specific evidence to support the statement.

E X E R C I S E I: Supporting Your Point

Read the passage below. In the first blank, write, in your own words, what the point of the passage is. Next list *five* supporting facts in the passage that illustrate the point.

It is evident to anyone watching television and reading the newspapers that relations between the police and urban teenagers are in trouble. One could mention the rap artists who have expressed hostility to police for using excessive force, or one could cite the growth of gangs that seem to consider the police just as much their enemy as other gangs. Articles appear frequently about the need for civilian review boards to study cases of alleged police brutality, and everyone knows about the Los Angeles riots in 1992 that were touched off by the acquittal of police officers who were videotaped beating Rodney King. Smaller disturbances occurring in other cities have been on the news as well, such as a riot in Washington Heights in Manhattan over the shooting of a young Hispanic man. Talk shows have featured police officers and commissioners explaining how difficult and dangerous their work is, and gang members have been interviewed expressing their frustration. Police face greater danger than ever because there are so many handguns in the possession of adolescents and even children, and inner city teenagers and young men face greater difficulty than ever finding good jobs and career opportunities.

Main Idea: _____

_____

Five Supporting Facts: 1. _____

2. _____

3. _____

4. _____

5. _____

EXERCISE 11: Supporting Your Point

Begin with the statement, "A college education will make my life better." Then write a passage in which you include at least five specific examples to support your point.

THINKING CRITICALLY

Once you have learned to identify your main point in prewriting exercises, you are well on the way toward composing more formally developed paragraphs and essays. A further skill that contributes to effective paragraph and essay writing is **critical thinking**. Although critical thinking is involved in almost all stages of writing and cannot be learned separately, you will be a better writer if you pay special attention to the main principles of critical thinking. Good writing, after all, is more than choice of words and correct grammar. It also involves clear and original thinking. Here are some of the goals to work toward as you practice paragraph and essay writing in Units 2 and 3:

Critical Thinking Guidelines:

1. Be Clear About Your Main Point.   Distinguish carefully between your main idea and subordinate ideas, and establish the boundaries of your discussion. Does this discussion include all educational institutions, all colleges, or just your college? Does it include men and women, just women, just single women, or just young single women?

2. Judge on the Evidence.   Get all the facts and base your main point on the evidence. A reader can always detect a closed-minded, dogmatic writer and will usually respond negatively.

3. Consider All Alternatives.   Choose your main point by first considering all the possible points of view and eliminating the others—not by jumping to conclusions. If you are suggesting a solution to a problem, consider all the possible solutions first. If you are analyzing a cause or effect, be aware that there may be a combination of causes and effects for most social problems.

4. Divide Your Topic into Parts.   Don't oversimplify; break your topic into components to discuss it carefully in all its complexity. If you are discussing an event that changed your life, tell about what led up to it, how it happened, and how it affected you afterward. If you are describing a place or person, discuss separate features of your subject in separate paragraphs.

5. Don't Judge by Appearances.   Discuss both what's obvious about your topic and the hidden issues, causes or personal motives involved. If you're making a comparison between two films, they may appear to be similar to most people, but when you think more carefully about them, you may begin to see important differences.

6. Be Aware of Biases, Especially Your Own.   Everyone has biases, some of them favorable, some unfavorable, and since we're human, we won't get rid of all of them. However, biases can get in the way of effective writing; they cause us to lose our grip on the truth and on our readers, whose biases may be different from ours.

7. Don't Confuse Strong Emotion or Strong Language with a Strong Argument.   Powerful writing often expresses strong emotion and uses powerful language, but some very bad writing does the same. Strong feelings and extreme words should be justified by the force of the points you make and the evidence you use to support them.

8. Be Observant.   See what others overlook. On many topics people pass along familiar comments that are partly true but not very original or precise. As a good writer, try to see beyond these clichés; either challenge them or show how they are inadequate.

9. Spend Time with Your Topic.   What you think about your subject may change after you have thought it over for a day or two. Unless you have to write an essay in class without knowing the topic ahead of time, don't try to throw the whole essay together in a hurry; you'll do a more intelligent job if you live with the topic and mull it over for a while.

10. Discuss the Topic with Others.   If you have a writing group in your class, use other students' opinions to help you develop all sides of the topic. If not, seek out others' views to test your own for areas where you have not thought carefully or thoroughly enough. This kind of discussion will not make you less original, just less superficial.

COMPUTERS AND THE PREWRITING PROCESS

More and more students today compose and edit their essays on computers. You probably have access to a word processing program at school or at home, at least for occasional use. If you are lucky enough to have one available frequently, don't wait to use it until you think of yourself as an advanced writer. Many students practice prewriting activities like brain-storming, arranging, and outlining on computers. Grammar and spelling drills are also available on software.

Advantages of Word Processing

As a beginning writer, you can benefit greatly from word processing technology. With a word processor you can create a document and change it easily in all sorts of ways before you consider it completed. Later units of this book take up the kind of composing, revising, editing, and proofreading that you will do in writing formal compositions. Many of the advantages of word processing involve these later stages of writing. However, word processing also offers advantages for prewriting activities. You will feel much freer to explore your ideas and feelings if you use a word processor, because you will worry less about making mistakes. After all, you can correct your mistakes without erasing or putting a fresh sheet of paper in a typewriter. Part of the trouble many beginning writers have with writer's block comes from their fear of messing up the neat page they are producing. With word processing, there is no page to mess up.

If you have not worked on a computer before, you may think of it as a machine to be used only after you have done much scribbling and scratching beforehand. Wrong: don't save the computer for the later stages. The chief advantage of word processing is that you can "scribble" and do as many rough drafts and make as many changes as you like until you are ready to consider your work completed. Only when you print out your document do you have a piece of paper with writing that cannot easily be altered.

Invisible Writing

You may find that freewriting and focused writing are more fun to do on a computer than on paper. Even if you cannot touch-type, you will be able to write an impressive amount in a short time using a word processor. One kind of prewriting activity that you can do on a computer but not on paper is called **invisible writing.** Some students find this even better than freewriting on paper for developing an uninhibited flow of words. To do invisible writing, turn the screen light down so you cannot see what you write, then write without stopping for a designated number of minutes. When you have finished, turn up the screen light and read your writing. Students who become blocked by their fear of errors sometimes write more freely this way—they seem to be carrying on a conversation with the machine rather than producing a text for someone to fill with corrections in red ink. You may find that invisible writing loosens you up. Like other prewriting activities, it is a skill-builder that works better for some writers than others.

Software Available

An enormous amount of software is available for writers. If you want to buy your own program, consider the cost as well as the kind of writing you expect to do. Some of the older programs, such as WordStar (MicroPro International) and Bank Street Writer (Broderbund Software), will serve most writers' needs. Q&A Write (Symantec) is highly rated as a program for individual use. Programs with more professional features are more expensive. Highly rated software such as Nota Bene (Dragonfly Software), Microsoft Word (Microsoft Corp.) and WordPerfect (WordPerfect Corp.) offer many advanced features that are useful for scholars, professional writers, and corporations, but they can be costly. Every year new programs for composing and editing appear, as well as specialized programs for teaching grammar, vocabulary, and spelling. Your college may have one or more of the latter programs available, and you will benefit from asking your instructor about the possibilities. Specialized teaching and editing programs include Writer's Workbench (Bell Labs), EPIS-TLE (IBM), WANDAH (UCLA), Proofreader (Random House), Grammatik (Aspen Software), and HOMER (UCLA). Certain outlining programs such as Think Tank, Kamas, and Framework may also prove helpful.

Getting Started

Nearly all third- and fourth-year college students now use word processing. Whether or not you are required to include it in your work as a beginning writer, take advantage of any opportunities you have to phase it into your college work. It may help you now and will certainly prove important later. If you are just beginning to learn about word processing, you may want to read a well-known author's account of his first attempts to use it (William Zinsser, *Writing with a Word Processor*, New York, Harper & Row, 1983).

If you have no experience at all with word processing, don't be afraid to try it when the opportunity arises. Once someone shows you how to use the keyboard commands with one word processing program, you will find it easier to learn another program. Although there are important differences among programs, getting started is more important than worrying about these differences. Learning to use whatever software is available will not be a mistake or waste of time. You will have taken a big step into the world of high technology.

2

PRACTICING PARAGRAPHS

In the first unit you practiced many kinds of prewriting activities. Usually you wrote a page or more at a time without thinking about organization or grammar. Continue to do prewriting, especially the kind that seems to work best for you—focused writing, brain-storming, clustering, writing journals. Think of prewriting exercise as warm-ups. An athlete, even a top professional, does warm-up exercises both during the off-season and before a game. In the same way, professional authors often write journals and use other prewriting techniques before they compose an article, chapter, or book.

Prewriting activities, however, are only warm-ups. To create a finished essay, you must learn to organize and develop your material so that it supports a main point. To acquire this skill, practice writing paragraphs. It is possible to start right out with whole essays, but most writers do better if they first master the chief building block of the essay: the paragraph. Paragraph writing practice will condition you to organize material around topic statements and to group your ideas into related units.

PARAGRAPH BASICS

This section covers key aspects of paragraphs—recognizing them, signaling where they begin, determining their length, creating topic sentences, and using key words in topic sentences. Bear in mind that what you are learning here and in the rest of this unit is only intended to help you write better essays, not to focus on paragraphs as finished products separate from essays. The skills you work on in creating paragraphs are the same skills you will use in a more extended way to create essays in Unit 3.

Recognizing Paragraphs

A paragraph is a medium-sized block of writing that discusses one topic, or idea, which is often stated in the first sentence. Although you will be creating paragraphs by themselves in this unit, think of the paragraph as part of a larger piece of writing—an essay, story, article, chapter, report, or business letter. You will be practicing paragraphs separately in order to concentrate more effectively on composition skills such as organization and development before you attempt to compose whole essays.

Signaling Paragraphs

Show your reader where your paragraphs begin by indenting—that is, by starting the first sentence about half an inch from the left margin (or five spaces when you type). (Exception: in some business letters the writer skips a line before every paragraph instead of indenting.) The last sentence in your paragraph may end anywhere on the line from left to right; leave the rest of the line blank, like this one.

In most ordinary writing, you will see about two or three paragraphs on every page. See the example on the following page.

Determining Paragraph Length

In this unit you will practice writing full paragraphs, the kind that make up the body of an essay. Such paragraphs usually contain one hundred to two hundred words, or about seven to twelve sentences. Introductory and concluding paragraphs are usually shorter, as are paragraphs used for making transitions and paragraphs in dialogue. In published writing, paragraphs may be very short, as in newspaper reports with narrow columns, or very long, as in dense technical articles. What makes a paragraph the right length is not merely the number of words but the way the words fulfill the writer's purpose.

Read the following sample paragraph, noticing its length and overall plan along with the structural details pointed out in the margin. This paragraph was written by a student who was experienced at developing ideas and tying them together.

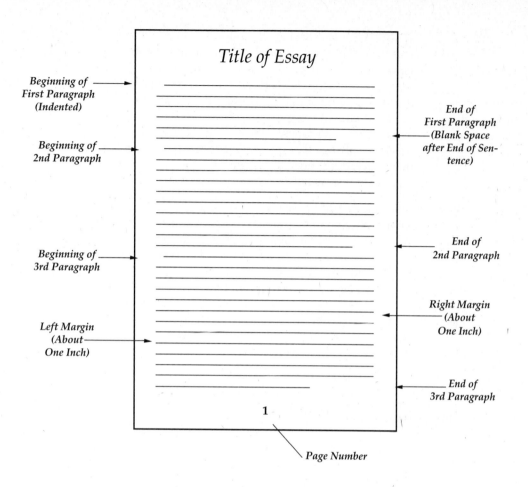

Title of Essay

Beginning of
First Paragraph
(Indented)

End of
First Paragraph
(Blank Space
after End of Sen-
tence)

Beginning of
2nd Paragraph

Beginning of
3rd Paragraph

End of
2nd Paragraph

Left Margin
(About
One Inch)

Right Margin
(About
One Inch)

End of
3rd Paragraph

1

Page Number

Sample paragraph:

*Topic sentence
states opinion.*

*Body of
paragraph
discusses
main idea.*

Mandatory drug testing on the job is *unfair* to individual workers. Many employers are considering the possibility of forcing their workers to take random drug tests. *These* employers understandably worry about the harm drugs can do in the workplace. Certainly drug testing is proper in jobs where the safety of the public is at stake, like piloting planes, but making all workers take drug tests is an invasion of their privacy. Employers never take drug tests themselves, and no one has proved that the tests are foolproof. *Therefore* it is *not fair* to make workers risk losing their jobs by taking *such* tests. If companies are worried about workers being unproductive because of drug use, they can check productivity directly and penalize

*Key word limits
main idea.*

*Transitional
words link
statements.*

anyone who isn't doing a good job, whether the reason is laziness, alcoholism, emotional problems, or drug abuse. As bad as drug abuse is, workers can be hooked on other problems just as much, and none of *these* are tested. It is no *fairer* to impose frequent drug testing on workers than to make them take weekly psychological examinations or marriage therapy or check their gambling debts. Invading individuals' privacy by any *such* mandated tests is *unfair.*

Length of this paragraph: 199 words, 10 sentences

This paragraph contains a topic: mandatory drug testing. The first sentence builds this topic into a topic sentence by adding a verb, *is,* and a descriptive phrase, *unfair to individual workers.* The rest of the paragraph discusses the idea stated in this topic sentence. To hold the paragraph together, the writer repeats key words like *unfair* and includes connecting words and reference words like *such, these,* and *therefore* to show links between statements. Finally, to avoid boring the reader, the writer varies her sentences, making some short and simple, others longer and more complicated. Above all, she never wanders off the point.

Using Topic Sentences*

Every effective paragraph has a main purpose. Usually this purpose is to express a single idea. In the preceding sample paragraph, the idea was that mandatory drug testing on the job is unfair. Your topics should be as clear and specific as this one. One way to be sure they are is to use precise **topic sentences.**

A topic sentence is the sentence, usually the first one in the paragraph, that states the main point of the paragraph. Experienced writers sometimes put topic sentences in the middle or at the end of a paragraph. Occasionally the topic may be so obvious throughout the paragraph that the writer does not need a topic sentence. Despite these exceptions, you should practice beginning your paragraphs with topic sentences. These help you to identify your main points and stick to them.

A topic sentence makes a promise to the reader. It says, "This is what this paragraph is going to discuss." It charts the direction and boundaries of the paragraph. *It should be broader than any other sentence in the paragraph—broad enough to include all the other sentences—but no broader.* If the topic sentence is too general, the topic it presents will not be discussed thoroughly in the paragraph. If the topic sentence is too narrow and factual, it will not cover everything that is in the paragraph.

---

*Review fragments, run-together sentences, and comma splices in Unit 5.

Can you tell the difference between a broad statement and a limited statement? Which of the following three statements is broadest? Which is most limited?

1. Several of my courses this term require a large amount of homework.
2. My sociology professor assigned a twenty-five-page report and five-hundred pages of reading.
3. College is very difficult.

Only one of these would make an effective topic sentence for a paragraph. Statement 3 is too broad for a single paragraph: discussing all the features of college work and college life that are difficult would take up many pages. Sentence 2 is merely a factual statement; it leads nowhere. Sentence 2 is the kind of statement that is useful to *support* a topic statement. Statement 1 might make a good topic sentence because it is broad enough to include a number of supporting examples (individual courses) but limited enough to be discussed in a paragraph. Furthermore, it serves as a guide, leading the reader to expect a discussion of how much homework each course demands.

EXERCISE I: Topic Sentences

If the following sentences were in the same paragraph, which one would make a good topic sentence that includes all the others? Which sentence is not on the topic and would not belong in the same paragraph with the others?

1. Violinists, singers, and flutists often perform on the sidewalk.
2. Readers of horoscopes tell people's futures.
3. The street life in Manhattan offers visitors a variety of distractions.
4. Dancers on roller blades display uncanny grace and virtuosity.
5. Most of the large stores are not open on Sunday.
6. Vendors hawk scarves, wallets, jewelry, handbags, and toys on many street corners.
7. Charitable organizations ask for contributions.
8. Political volunteers stop as many pedestrians as they can to gather signatures on their petitions.
9. Young men and women hand out free passes to live television shows, advertisements for new stores and massage parlors, and free samples of cigarettes and perfume.

Which sentence makes a guiding statement about a whole paragraph topic? _____

Which sentence is not on the topic at all? _____

How many sentences give factual support for the topic sentence? _____

EXERCISE II: Topic Sentences

Do a prewriting exercise of your own choosing (focused writing, clustering, brainstorming, and so on) about your own neighborhood. Then look over your material and find a key idea. Write this idea in the form of a topic sentence. List as many supporting details as you can.

WRITING ASSIGNMENT: Topic Sentences

Write a paragraph of about 150 words beginning with the topic sentence you composed in Exercise II. Be sure to stay on the specific topic!

Using Key Words in Topic Sentences

Remember that a topic sentence does more than just name a subject. It expresses an opinion about the subject; it points a direction, opens a discussion, and creates an impression of the subject. A simple statement of fact, such as "It was cold yesterday," does not make a useful topic sentence. Which of these two might make a good topic sentence?

    a.   I have a friend named Evelyn.
    b.   My friend Evelyn is very competitive.

Suppose you were going to write a paragraph beginning with sentence A. What would the paragraph say about Evelyn? Almost anything is possible, since the topic sentence gives no specific idea. Sentence B would make a better topic statement because it tells what the paragraph should say about Evelyn. Can you think of examples of behavior that would show how competitive someone is? *Competitive* is the key word in sentence B; it introduces a controlling idea. Most good topic sentences contain such a key word or phrase.

Compare these statements:

Mertz Rent-a-Car offers *rapid advancement* for ambitious employees.
Mertz Rent-a-Car is a *nice place to work*.

Nice is one of those catchall terms, like *good, bad, interesting, great,* and *unique,* that leads nowhere in particular. The first statement makes a sharp, clear point that the paragraph could support with specific facts.

EXERCISE I: Key Words

In the following five sentences, find and underline the key words or phrases that create specific impressions.

Example: For a twelve-year-old, running away from home is a *frightening* experience.

Frightening tells what impression the whole paragraph should create.

1. My first driving lesson was a hilarious experience.
2. Professional wrestling usually looks faked.
3. An effective job interview requires a manner that is appropriate for the job.
4. Dustin Hoffman has usually played unconventional film roles.
5. Adjusting to a new roommate requires a cooperative approach.

Explain how each key word or phrase gives you ideas about what the paragraph should include. Think of some examples or explanations of each topic statement.

EXERCISE 11: Key Words

Underline the key word or phrase in each of the following sentences and decide whether the statement would make an effective topic sentence. If it would, write ok in the blank. If the key word or phrase is too vague, write a more precise one in the blank.

Examples:

The first year of law school is *different*.   *more specialized than college*

Snorkel diving is very *expensive*.   *OK*

1. Hawaii is a good place to visit.   _____

2. My room is arranged efficiently for study.   _____

3. Psychotherapy made Esther more independent.   _____

4. Kung fu is a bad sport for some people.   _____

5. Parochial schools are better than public schools.   _____

6. Stamp collecting teaches you about a lot of things.   _____

7. Arranging a family reunion requires a logical plan.   _____

WRITING ASSIGNMENT I: Key Words

Compose a paragraph using one of the preceding statements as your topic sentence. (Use your version if you improved it.) Include specific details to support the point.

WRITING ASSIGNMENT II: Key Words

Think about someone you know who has an unusual way of behaving. Brainstorm for ten minutes, listing everything you can think of about how this person behaves. Then look over the list and find one main point that you can make about this person—a point that will include most of the details you have listed. Eliminate the details that do not fit this point. Write a topic sentence using a key word or phrase to describe this person's behavior, and compose an exploratory draft of a paragraph on this subject. Look over your draft to be sure that all sentences belong on the topic and that the whole paragraph reads smoothly. Make revisions and write a final draft.

Read the following sample paragraph after you have brainstormed your topic. Notice how the student who wrote this paragraph succeeded in stating a clear topic sentence and developing it in an interesting way. Try to make your final draft equally unified and interesting.

A Person with an Unusual Way of Behaving

My sister Maggie has a ridiculous way of reading signs. Every sign she sees in a store, on a wall, on a jacket, or even in a parking lot she reads by singing it out loud. When she went to the hospital last week to visit a friend, she started singing notices like Do Not Trespass, No Smoking, Only for Staff. Nurses looked at her as if she were crazy. Last Saturday we went to the movies, and when she began to read the movie's cast, of course she started singing it. I moved from my seat. She likes singing so much that even when she reads her school books at home, she sings the lessons aloud. Sometimes we're watching television and she begins to sing the little 800 number they put on the bottom of the screen. I really don't like her unique way of reading things.

WHAT MAKES A PARAGRAPH GOOD?

In learning to compose good paragraphs, you will also learn most of what it takes to compose good essays. Although you do not have to pay special attention to your paragraphs when you create exploratory drafts, your final drafts will need well-constructed paragraphs to be effective. In this section you will learn the qualities of good paragraphs so that you can create strong paragraphs yourself. The four main elements that combine to make effective purposeful paragraphs are **unity, coherence, transitions,** and **development.**

Paragraph Unity

The prefix *uni* means *one*. A unified paragraph has *one* clear purpose. The topic statement, as we have already discussed, is limited enough so that the rest of the paragraph can support it well; no statements should wander off the topic. In your prewriting exercises you first did freewriting, paying no attention to staying on a topic. Then you did focused writing, which meant staying on one topic. A short piece of focused writing is still not a unified paragraph (although it might be the basis for a good paragraph when revised). In your focused writing you may sometimes have had a brilliant new idea and wandered off the topic like a shopper after an unexpected bargain. In your focused writing as well, you did not compose a topic sentence that would fit exactly the amount of writing you were planning to do. Now you will concentrate on the paragraph as a finished product made from the raw materials of your ideas and statements in your focused writing. Above all you must know what your topic is and then stay on the topic. Every sentence in your paragraph should follow logically from the one before, and all sentences should give facts, ideas, or examples that support the topic statement.

E X E R C I S E: Paragraph Unity

The following paragraph is unified except for two sentences that wander off the topic stated in the first sentence. Underline these two irrelevant sentences.

> *Nutrition has at last become a professional career for well-trained specialists. People who work in nutrition, called nutritionists, have bachelor's degrees in biology and related subjects. Many of them have graduate degrees as well. They can earn the title of Registered Dietitian (R.D.) if they pass a certifying examination. There is intense competition for jobs by people with college degrees. Nutritionists work in a variety of high-level jobs in teaching institutions, government agencies, and private corporations that supply and process food. Some assist in health programs at schools and hospitals, and others provide material for television documentaries on health and fitness. Some people think that exercise is just as important to your health as the food you eat. Nutrition is one of the few careers that offer opportunities in all regions of the country and in both the public and private sectors.*

Now read the paragraph aloud with the two irrelevant sentences omitted. It reads more smoothly, doesn't it? Unrelated sentences interrupt the flow of thought and lead the reader off the path, destroying the unity of the paragraph.

Paragraph Coherence

Not only should all sentences in a paragraph support the topic statement, but they should be *arranged in a clear, recognizable order.* **Coherence** means that all the parts of something *cohere,* or hang together. To produce a car engine, you have to have all the right pieces, but you also have to fit the pieces together correctly so the engine can run. The main rule for fitting the pieces of a paragraph together coherently is to *make every sentence follow logically from the one before.* This is one of the important basic principles of good writing. The sentences in a paragraph should read in a natural sequence, like numbers in a row—1, 2, 3, 4, 5—not jump around unpredictably like random numbers—1, 7, 3, 8, 4, 9.

A paragraph with a natural sequence is much easier to read than one without any shape. A coherent paragraph will serve its purpose more effectively than an incoherent one, whether the purpose is to express a feeling, state an opinion, convey an experience or impression, or persuade the reader to agree.

Here is a paragraph that lacks coherence:

> *My first attempt to register for courses in my freshman year was one of the worst experiences of my life. I'll never go through that again! Most of the courses I planned to take were already closed, so I had to settle for whatever I could get. The first frustration came when I entered the gymnasium and was told that freshmen had to register in the student union. I discovered that I had to stand in not one line but six lines—one for each course I wanted. As I was heading back to my dorm room about ready to explode, I met a friend who told me that I was right in the first place, but now I was late and would have to wait in line because everyone was ahead of me. When I got to the student union, someone told me that freshmen couldn't register until the next day. After I finished five hours later, I found out that I could have done all my registering a week earlier just by seeing my adviser. Nobody had told me it would be difficult, so I was not prepared for five hours of waiting in six long lines, not being able to get the courses I wanted, and constantly receiving false information.*

Although the first sentence in the preceding paragraph is a fairly clear and specific topic sentence and all of the following statements support it, the paragraph is still confusing. That is because the order of sentences has been jumbled. Here is the paragraph arranged in a coherent order:

> *My first attempt to register for courses my freshman year was one of the worst experiences of my life. Nobody had told me it would be difficult, so I was not prepared for five hours of waiting in six long lines, not being able to get the courses I wanted, and constantly receiving false information. The first frustration came when I entered the gymnasium and was told that freshmen had to register in the student union. When I got to the student union, someone told me that freshmen couldn't register until the next day. As I was heading back to my dorm room about ready to explode, I met a friend who told me that I was right in the first place, but now I was late and would have to wait in line because everyone was*

ahead of me. I discovered that I had to stand in not one but six lines—one for each course I wanted. Most of the courses I planned to take were already closed, so I had to settle for whatever I could get. After I finished five hours later, I found out that I could have done all my registering a week earlier just by seeing my adviser. I'll never go through that again!

Coherence can be achieved in paragraphs by arranging the material according to time sequence, spatial sequence, or climactic sequence.

Time Sequence

The sample paragraph you just read is arranged in **time sequence.** It describes a series of actions taking place one after the other: the attempt to register at the gym, the wild-goose chase to the student union, the return to the gym, the five hours of waiting in line, and the discovery that all this could have been avoided. Time sequence is the easiest kind of arrangement of material in a paragraph. You have undoubtedly used it in writing about personal experiences. The main thing to keep in mind is to make the sequence of actions clear; don't leave out any steps that the reader needs to follow the action.

In the next paragraph several gaps occur in the sequence of statements. As a result, the action is difficult to follow. Find the places where something is left out. What belongs in these spaces?

When Sonya gets up in the morning, she is usually still sleepy because her alarm rings at 6 A.M. The first thing she does is head for the kitchen to start coffee and put on an egg to boil. When she is finished in the bathroom, she returns to her bedroom and looks over her wardrobe to choose a dress to wear. Then she gets dressed and goes back to the kitchen to eat her breakfast in a hurry because it is usually about 6:45 by this time. Once she has reached the bus stop, she knows that she will be late if the bus comes later than 7:15. Her subway ride usually takes about half an hour. If everything goes right, she gets to work by 8 A.M.

This student's paragraph came out easier to read when she revised it to include information missing from the first draft:

When Sonya gets up in the morning, she is usually still sleepy because her alarm rings at 6 a.m. The first thing she does is head for the kitchen to start coffee and put on an egg to boil. Next she goes to the bathroom to shower and fix her hair. When she is finished in the bathroom, she returns to her bedroom and looks over her wardrobe to choose a dress to wear. Then she gets dressed and goes back to the kitchen to eat her breakfast in a hurry because it is usually about 6:45 by this time. After breakfast, she rushes to the corner two blocks away to catch a bus. Once she has reached the bus stop, she knows that she will be late if the bus comes later than 7:15. The bus takes her to the subway station on the opposite side of the park. Her subway ride usually takes about half an hour. If everything goes right, she gets to work by 8 A.M.

EXERCISE I: Time Sequence

Write a paragraph like the one you have just read. First make a list of the things you do when you get up in the morning. Then compose your paragraph, using a smooth time sequence with no necessary information left out.

EXERCISE II: Time Sequence

Look through your prewriting exercises and find one that includes an experience that took place in time sequence. This can be either something that happened to you or some other event you described. You will need about half a page of writing to make a normal-sized paragraph. Choose an experience that can be described in this much space. Revise your writing to make a unified paragraph written in time sequence. Since you were not trying to compose neat paragraphs in your prewriting exercises, you may have to add steps that were left out, remove irrelevant sentences, and make other corrections.

Spatial Sequence

Another way of achieving coherence in your paragraphs is by arranging statements in **spatial sequence.** This means that your description follows the placement of items in space, for example, inside to outside, front to back, side to side, up to down, near to far. As with time sequence, be sure not to leave any confusing gaps, and use enough details so that the reader has a clear picture of what you are describing. The paragraph should move like a camera panning (as filmmakers call it) slowly over a scene. If you have ever tried making home videos, you know that if you move the camera too fast, the film will be hard to follow. In filmmaking and writing alike, the viewer or reader has to be given enough time with a few important details to recognize the arrangement, and the focus has to move gradually enough so the picture does not become a confusing blur.

The paragraph that follows is arranged in spatial sequence. What direction of movement does it use to achieve coherence?

> As he approached the town, Fred began to sense familiarity. The shopping mall he passed just inside the city limits seemed new to him, because all the buildings were fairly new. Just beyond it, however, he passed a used-car lot that he seemed to know, even though he didn't recognize the name. Soon he crossed some old railroad tracks, and now he knew he had driven this way before. He slowed down as he spotted Dom's service station on his left, and realized he had known it would be there. His memory told him there would be a high school just over the hill on his right as he entered the business section of town. There it was. As he drove past the high school from which he had graduated and nosed his car in anticipation toward the remodeled courthouse in the center of town, he knew he had accidentally returned to his hometown, modernized beyond recognition in the suburbs but still the same at its heart.

In describing a place, such as a building, a neighborhood, or a room, use spatial sequence to give coherence to the picture. Otherwise the details will add up to a jumbled mess. Here is a paragraph that lacks coherence because the descriptive details are not arranged in a recognizable order:

> *There was a huge pile of dirty laundry left near the door two weeks ago. One desk was barely visible under a mound of loose term papers, audio cassettes, books and magazines lying open, and camera equipment. One bed was made drum-tight like a marine recruit's bunk. Another desk lined up straight against the wall had every item in place, with pens and pencils positioned in parallel rows, books matched on the shelves above according to height, and papers stacked evenly on one corner. A broken stationary bicycle was lying on its side with a set of free weights scattered under and around it. The other bed looked as if a barroom fight had taken place on it—the torn and stained wool blanket was littered with cigarettes, crumpled soda cans, socks, and underwear. There was also a computer table with a monitor and printer polished to look like new, and a desk chair carefully placed one foot behind the table.*

This paragraph has plenty of descriptive details, but it is hard to follow because the details are not arranged in any pattern. The paragraph reads like a list from a brainstorming exercise. Arranged in spatial order, however, the details make a coherent paragraph with the addition of a clear topic sentence and some "spatial orientation" words:

> *Michael and Sean's dormitory room looked like an apartment for the odd couple. Everything on the left side showed Sean's incredible sloppiness; everything on the right showed Michael's obsessive tidiness. As you entered the room and looked to the left, you saw first a huge pile of dirty laundry two weeks old. Behind it was a broken stationary bicycle lying on its side with a set of free weights scattered under and around it. Behind that was a bed that looked as if a barroom fight had taken place on it—the torn and stained wool blanket was littered with cigarettes, crumpled soda cans, socks, and underwear. The desk in the far corner was barely visible under a mound of loose term papers, audio cassettes, books and magazines lying open, and camera equipment. By contrast, the right side of the room was geometrically perfect. The front was taken up by a bed made drum-tight like a marine recruit's bunk. The desk, lined up straight behind it against the wall, had every item in place, with pens and pencils positioned in parallel rows, books matched on the shelves above according to height, and papers stacked evenly on one corner. Standing in the far right corner was a computer table with a monitor and printer polished to look like new and a desk chair carefully placed one foot behind the table.*

EXERCISE I: Spatial Sequence

Imagine you are driving in a place that is familiar to you. Compose a paragraph describing your impressions as you draw nearer and nearer to a particular spot. Remember to include enough details to communicate the overall movement from far to near.

EXERCISE II: Spatial Sequence

Brainstorm to collect facts about your room. Do not think about composing or arranging. Once you have your list of facts, look it over and try to think of a topic statement that will make your description interesting. Find a key word—*mysterious, boring, messy, casual, neat, colorful*—to describe the overall impression of your room. Then write an exploratory draft in which you describe the room spatially, for example from front to back or left to right. Look over your draft to see if you left anything out or need to add details or make corrections. Write a final draft.

Climactic Sequence

A third kind of paragraph arrangement is called **climactic sequence.** In this arrangement, sentences build to a climax. They start with less important or less emphatic statements and end with the most important or most emphatic statements. Climactic sequence is effective in paragraphs that discuss ideas rather than tell stories or describe places. A paragraph in climactic sequence may give a series of facts, reasons, or examples to support a point. When you write such paragraphs, be sure to include enough facts and ideas to support your point, and make each sentence follow from the one before and build to a climax.

Here is a paragraph that follows a climactic sequence:

> *Crack is the most dangerous drug available. Compared with cocaine and heroin, it is inexpensive and easy to buy in most urban areas. Therefore many teenagers and even children ten or eleven years old are trying it and selling it. Crack is also very easy to use, so people who might hesitate to inject heroin or sniff cocaine may smoke crack. Still more important is its powerful high, which sets in very quickly and leads many people to use it a second time and third time. Worst of all, it is powerfully addictive in a short time, it often has devastating effects on the brain, and it can sometimes cause death through its sudden effect on the heart.*

This paragraph lists some of the dangers of crack. The writer puts them in a sequence that she believes builds from the somewhat less crucial facts about low cost and ease of use to the more important facts about effects.

Climactic sequence can also be useful in discussing personal topics. In the following paragraph, a student discusses the advantages of renting films and watching them on a VCR. Again, the order of sentences moves from the less important to the more important.

> *Renting films and watching them on my VCR has quite a few advantages. I don't have to wait until a particular time for a film to begin at a local theater and maybe even wait in line, taking the chance of not getting a ticket. I can also watch the film several times if I want to, or stop it in the middle and rerun part of it if I missed something. Instead of having to pay $7.50 or $8.00 to watch a film at a theater—twice as much if I take my girlfriend—I can rent a film for $2.71 at the video store where I am a member. The biggest advantage of all is that I can choose*

a film from hundreds of movies available at the video store instead of having to see one of the four showing at the theater near my home.

EXERCISE I: Climactic Sequence

Number the following statements in the order you would arrange them in climactic sequence, putting 1 first as the least important and 5 last as the most important.

Topic statement: Owning a car in a large city has several disadvantages. Supporting statements:

1. Parking in the city is always expensive. 1
2. In the city your car is likely to be stolen or broken into. 5
3. Insurance rates are highest for urban car owners. 4
4. Air pollution in the city tends to damage a car's paint. 3
5. Gasoline prices are higher in the city than elsewhere. 2

EXERCISE II: Climactic Sequence

Choose one of the topics below for a paragraph to be written in climactic sequence. First brainstorm or do focused writing on the topic. List as many supporting statements as you can, being sure to include only those that specifically support the topic. Using your list of supporting statements, write a first draft beginning with the topic sentence and including your supporting statements in order of increasing importance. You may want to number your statements as in the preceding exercise before writing the rough draft. Write a final draft, being sure that your sentences read smoothly and are correct.

Suggested topic sentences:

1. Waiting until about age 30 to have a baby has several advantages.
2. Current fashions are convenient.
3. State lotteries have a number of benefits for society.
4. Fraternities and sororities have several appealing features for college students.
5. Call-in radio talk shows entertain listeners in several ways.
6. I read personal advice columns for a number of reasons.

Paragraph Transitions*

Successful paragraphs move the reader along smoothly from beginning to end. Remember the main rule: *Every sentence should follow logically from the one*

---

* See correcting by subordinating and punctuation (semicolons, commas) and the use of pronouns in Unit 5.

before. Having a logical arrangement based on a recognizable order—time sequence, spatial sequence, or climatic sequence—is the most important way to achieve continuity. In addition, you should use **transitional expressions** to signal connections to the reader. Your overall plan is like an itinerary you have worked out for a trip. Transitional expressions are like the road signs you will need occasionally to be sure you are going in the right direction.

Tie your sentences together by repeating key words, but don't overdo this—remember that too much repetition makes for boring writing. Use *pronouns* (he, she, it, you, they, we) to refer to persons, places, and things already mentioned. Make sure the person or thing to which any pronoun refers is absolutely clear. Finally, learn to use transitional words and phrases like those listed here to show connections between statements. Each kind of writing has its own kind of transitional expressions. Look over your previous writing to see if you use some of these words occasionally. Which ones have you never used? Practice using these and develop new habits.

Caution: Some writers who discover they have not been using enough transitional expressions to show connections at first use too many. They may put a transitional word or phrase at the beginning of every sentence. As a result, their writing suddenly becomes mechanical and self-conscious. Remember that these transitional expressions are like road signs: you don't need them

---

Transitional Words and Phrases

For Adding Information	also, and, besides, first (second, third), furthermore, in addition, likewise, moreover, too
For Showing Opposites and Contrast	although, but, even though, however, nevertheless, on the other hand, yet, still
For Showing Time	after, afterward, at last, at that time, beforehand, earlier, later, meanwhile, soon, then, while
For Showing Place	above, adjacent to, behind, below, beyond, farther, here, nearby, next to, opposite to, to the left, to the right
For Showing Results or Conclusions	as a result, consequently, finally, hence, in conclusion, so, then, therefore, thus
For Showing Examples	chiefly, especially, first of all, for example, for instance, for one thing, in general, mainly, namely, particularly, specifically

at every point along the way, but you do need them at key points where the reader might otherwise lose the train of thought. What is missing from the following paragraph?

> *A term paper in physics submitted at Princeton University in the 1970s brought its author nationwide publicity. There was nothing extraordinary about the methods or sources John Aristotle Phillips used. He startled the public by proving that he could design his own atomic bomb. He had access to some books on physics and nuclear technology. He could not use any secret government material. His project showed that an ordinary undergraduate could design a nuclear bomb by using only information available to the public. He had to spend many hours studying these books. His project did not require special expertise or original discoveries. The extra information he needed was also available to the public. He bought some copies of documents in Washington, D.C. He telephoned the DuPont Company about explosives. He had no secret information. He worked on the project several months. He finished his research. He submitted a workable plan for an atomic bomb. He earned an A for the project. The government kept the paper as a classified document.*

The paragraph does not read smoothly because there are no transitional words in it. Sometimes you have to pause and figure out the connection between one sentence and the next. Now read the same paragraph with transitional words included:

> *A term paper in physics submitted at Princeton University in the 1970s brought its author nationwide publicity. Although there was nothing extraordinary about the methods or sources John Aristotle Phillips used, he startled the public by proving that he could design his own atomic bomb. He had access to some books on physics and nuclear technology, but he could not use any secret government material. Therefore, his project showed that an ordinary undergraduate could design a nuclear bomb by using only information available to the public. Even though he had to spend many hours studying these books, his project did not require special expertise or original discoveries. Furthermore, the extra information he needed was also available to the public. For instance, he bought some copies of documents in Washington, D.C., and he telephoned the DuPont Company about explosives, but he had no secret information. After working on the project several months, he finished his research and submitted a workable plan for an atomic bomb. He earned an A for the project, but the government later kept the paper as a classified document.**

EXERCISE I: Transitional Expressions

Circle the transitional words in the following paragraph. First look back at the list to remind yourself what they are.

---

*Information from John A. Phillips and David Michaels, *MUSHROOM: The Story of the A Bomb Kid.* Used by permission of William Morrow & Co., Inc. Copyright © 1978 by John Aristotle Phillips.

Fiction in the media can occasionally be too realistic. For example, a radio drama called The War of the Worlds *produced by Orson Welles in 1938 scared thousands of listeners into believing the world was coming to an end. In fact, some started to evacuate the cities and even planned suicide. The first thing that made the show realistic was that many people tuned in late and assumed it was a news report. What further added to the effect was that most of the drama was presented in unusually effective broadcast style. In addition, Orson Welles gave it unique realistic touches; for instance, he copied the fumbling and vomiting of the announcer who witnessed the explosion of the Hindenberg blimp. As a result, many listeners believed that the Martians were actually landing in New Jersey. Furthermore, many were carried away by the emotional excitement of the battles and disasters that followed. Although many listeners knew it was just a radio play, so many people across the continent were taken in by its realism that reports of suicides, traffic accidents, and stampeding crowds began occurring everywhere. Consequently, the program brought many threats of lawsuits; in fact, nearly a million dollars in damages was sought in actions against the network. None of the claims, however, could be backed up, so the network did not have to pay anything. Still they did settle one claim: a man who had spent his shoe money trying to escape the disaster received a new pair of shoes from the radio station.**

EXERCISE 11: Transitional Expressions

In the paragraph below, supply missing transitional words from the following list. Be sure to select words that make sense.

although	however
also	in addition
as well as	in fact
but	nevertheless
for instance	while

Most students have heard the name of Frederick Douglass. Some,

(1) _____, have not actually read his autobiography entitled

Narrative of the Life of Frederick Douglass, an American Slave. They

(2) _____ may not have learned about his later life as an abo-

litionist. (3) _____ his story makes exciting reading for its

own sake, it offers (4) _____ many glimpses into the lives

---

*Information from John Houseman, *Run-Through.* New York: Simon & Schuster, 1971.

of both black and white people during the period of slavery. (5) _____, it shows much about the family loyalties of slaves and their longing for freedom and upward mobility. The book (6) _____ describes vividly some of the atrocities Douglass witnessed. (7) _____ it is not a work of simple propaganda, (8) _____ a creative portrait of a people maintaining their humanity (9) _____ suffering hardship and cruelty. Douglass includes an account of his escape, (10) _____ his impressions of life in the North. (11) _____, the whole plot reads almost like a nonfiction novel. It does, (12) _____, leave out his later life as a famous orator, journalist, and diplomat.

WRITING ASSIGNMENT: Transitional Expressions

Write a paragraph on one of the following topics. Remember to develop your topic, use transitional expressions, and keep your ideas in order.

1. The career of a famous person who interests you. Remember to make the statements follow the sequence of important events in the person's career, and use words referring to time (*first, soon after, next, finally,* etc.) to hold the paragraph together.
2. A favorite possession. Use connecting words to show relationships between your statements; words of time (*when, first, later*) to tell about how you acquired it, words of cause and effect (*because, therefore*) to tell why you value it, and words of position (*on top, inside, on the left, underneath*) to describe what it looks like.
3. A goal you have set for yourself. Use transitional words of cause and effect (*because, therefore*) to tell why you are aiming for that goal, and use words of addition (*and, also, besides, in addition*) to explain the satisfactions this goal will bring you.
4. A place you would like to be right now. Use words of position (*nearby, right, left, on top*) to describe and identify the place, and use cause and effect words (*because, therefore*) to tell why you would like to be there.

Paragraph Development

Although well-developed paragraphs are usually longer than poorly developed ones, **paragraph development** does not depend on length. A long paragraph that wanders off the topic or is repetitious, for instance, is not well developed. Development means supporting the main point with examples, quotations, explanations, facts, statistics, descriptive details, and ideas. There are many kinds of paragraph development, as you will see in the next section of this unit. Some of them may come easily to you; others may require more practice.

The first step is to develop the habit of supporting all topic sentences adequately with interesting details and ideas. Some inexperienced writers give the impression of being lazy simply because they do not realize how much supporting material they need to put into their paragraphs. Be ambitious: do not underestimate. Most beginning writers produce paragraphs that are underdeveloped, not overdeveloped. Here, for instance, is the rough draft of a paragraph that gives only a sketchy idea of the topic:

> *The rock group Kiss gained popularity partly through its weird live performances. The people in it had a strange appearance because of their unusual faces and costumes. The total effect was uncanny.*

Although this paragraph stays on the topic, it does not say much about it. A reader is likely to feel cheated and to want more details. In this revised draft there is plenty of interesting detail:

> *The rock group Kiss gained popularity partly through its weird live performances. The members wore long frizzly wigs, jump suits, dragon boots with high heels, and psychedelic face makeup. Towering Gene Simmons would have blood dripping from his Dracula mouth, and fire would shoot out of the mouth of drummer Peter Criss. Kiss performed music in an atmosphere of horror and insanity that caused audiences to walk out on its first appearances in 1973, but soon the public became fascinated by the effect. Fans began to pack Kiss concerts and buy millions of its albums. Other rock groups were forced to provide more excitement on stage if they wanted to please their fans and compete with Kiss.*

Often you can tell whether your paragraphs are developed enough by reading your work aloud to other students. Remember that in the prewriting activities in Unit 1 you were advised to get feedback from classmates after they listened to you read your work aloud.

How much development is enough? There are no rules to tell you this. Every paragraph is different, and every paragraph is part of a larger piece of writing with its own purposes. The topic sentence and the curiosity of the reader partly determine how much detail you should put into the paragraph. The purpose of each paragraph within the whole essay sometimes affects paragraph development as well. Keeping these things in mind, remember that in this unit you are trying to master the skill of writing effective paragraphs of a normal length, about seven to twelve sentences. Because that is not a long piece of writing, you need to condense as much vivid detail and fresh thinking into each paragraph as you can.

EXERCISE: Paragraph Development

The following paragraph stays on the topic but the statements are broad and not supported by examples. Rewrite the paragraph, developing it by adding interesting details from your own experience.

Sample paragraph (undeveloped):

> *My clothes reflect my personality. When I am in informal situations, I wear casual clothes that suit my taste. When I dress for action, I wear whatever seems attractive and comfortable for doing my favorite activities. When I want to dress up, I put on clothes that give me the look I want on the job or at social occasions.*

WRITING ACTIVITY I: Paragraph Development

Study the picture above. First list as many items as you can identify. Then group the items into three or four categories. Next write an exploratory draft beginning with the topic sentence, "This shop window contains several kinds of groceries." Once you have completed the draft, look it over to see if you have achieved a smooth flow of language from one sentence to the next. Make any revisions needed, and correct any errors. Write a final draft.

WRITING ACTIVITY 11: Paragraph Development

For additional practice in paragraph development, choose topics from the list that follows. Before composing each paragraph, do whatever kind of prewriting activity works best for you—focused writing, brainstorming, clustering, and so on. Look over your prewriting and find a sentence that states a significant idea about the topic. Begin the paragraph with this statement as your topic sentence. Be sure to include plenty of supporting details.

1. The worst job you ever had
2. The craziest thing you ever did
3. The worst class you ever attended
4. The best movie you ever saw
5. The biggest challenge you ever faced
6. The most generous thing you ever did
7. Your favorite way to deal with problems
8. A lesson you learned by making a mistake
9. An older person you admire
10. The skill you perform best
11. The accomplishment you are most proud of
12. Where you want to live after college

TYPES OF PARAGRAPHS

Different kinds of writing require different kinds of paragraphs. If the purpose of an essay is to tell about an event, we call it a **narrative.** If its purpose is to create an impression of a person, place, or object, we call it a **descriptive essay.** If it is meant to help us understand something, we call it **expository** (i.e., explanatory). Patterns of expository writing include comparison, process analysis, definition, classification, and cause/effect analysis. A **persuasive** essay, on the other hand, tries to convince us of something. These four chief categories of writing—narration, description, exposition, and persuasion—are often called the **rhetorical modes.** Not every piece of writing, of course, fits neatly into one of these modes, but most belong primarily in one mode while making some use of other modes. You will notice that after you have practiced writing paragraphs in separate modes in Unit 2, you will develop whole essays that call on you to use the same skills of organization in Unit 3. Writing paragraphs in separate modes is a little like practicing separate skills in a sport: you can work on your forehand, backhand, net game, and service separately during tennis lessons, but when you play the game, you must be ready to use them all. When you compose paragraphs in this unit, you will be able to concentrate on each mode in pure form for practice, but in Unit 3, you will be composing essays in which you may combine modes of development at times. Thinking in paragraphs, however, is one of the crucial skills required in the writing process. In creating whole essays, you may not actually compose your paragraphs separately, but once you have practiced paragraph composition, you will be able to examine your paragraphs and revise, correct, and improve them to strengthen your essays.

Narration: Telling About an Event*

Telling about personal experiences or events that happened to yourself or other people is called **narrative writing.** Many short stories, novels, and history books are in this form. In narrative writing, paragraphs tell parts of a larger story and are written in time sequence. A narrative paragraph should (1) have enough details to give the reader a close-up of the events, (2) contain enough transitional expressions to help the reader follow the sequence of actions, and (3) be written in one tense, usually the past tense since the paragraph is usually about actions taking place in the past. Narrative paragraphs may seem the easiest kind to write, but for them to be good you may have to do quite a bit of revision. Try to include well-chosen words and interesting details, and be sure your sentences progress smoothly from beginning to end.

Here is a rough draft of a narrative paragraph written by a student:

> *First impressions can sometimes mislead you. Not very long ago I met a guy who impressed me a lot. He seem to be a real cool guy, he asked me out to dinner at a expensive restaurant. Was I angry when he left me with the check after we ate the highest priced dinner on the menu. He said he had to go to the men's room and never came back. Boy, was I furious. I just got my paycheck and had to spend a big chunk of it paying the bill. I'll never go out with a guy like him again!*

This student had an interesting story to tell, but she didn't arrange her facts effectively and, as you can see, she made some writing errors. The paragraph needed rearranging, developing, and correcting. Here is her revised revision:

> *First impressions can sometimes mislead you. Last October I met Richard, who impressed me with his sense of humor and warm, caring manner. Although he was very sophisticated, he also showed mature concern for his aging mother and his younger sister. Of course I was excited when he asked me out to an expensive French restaurant for dinner. The date was perfect at first; we carried on wonderful conversation about our favorite films and singers, and he insisted that I order the highest price á la carte items on the menu. I was even beginning to think*

---

*See verb tenses in Unit 5.

he was being too generous when he ordered a raspberry tart for my dessert and excused himself to visit the men's room. I waited for ten minutes. My raspberry tart came but my date did not. He disappeared and left me with a check for $87.

In telling about your own experiences, use the **first person** (*I, we*). In telling about an event that happened to someone else, use the **third person** (*she, he, it, they*). When you start a paragraph in the first person, stay in the first person; when you start in the third person, stay in the third person.* Choose one specific event and stick to it; a paragraph that tells about one limited action thoroughly is better than a paragraph that skims over a series of events. The sample narrative paragraph that follows is written in the third person and concentrates on one man's specific goal in 1948:

> *Preston Tucker tried to manufacture a dream car in the late 1940s but failed because he was ahead of his time. He hoped to see a low, modern-looking automobile with a one-piece windshield, an aluminum air-cooled engine, and safety features such as a collapsing steering column and a third headlight that turned with the wheels. He collected $25 million by selling stock and franchises, and he bought a huge war plant in Chicago to use as his factory. He worked hard to gain support and publicity, but he ran into difficulties with government agencies as well as newspaper columnists who claimed he was a fake. Furthermore, some of his new ideas could not be carried out with the technology of those days. After building only about fifty Tucker cars, he had to close his plant. Today, the Tucker cars still in existence are rare collectors' items.***

WRITING ASSIGNMENT I: Narrative Paragraphs

Start with a focused writing exercise in which you write everything that comes to mind about an incident that happened to you in the last week or two—recently enough for you to remember details and specific remarks. Write at least a full page without stopping; you want plenty of material so that you can select the most effective details. Read over your focused writing and think of a topic statement that sums up the meaning of the experience. Now write an exploratory paragraph beginning with the topic sentence and including only the most relevant and interesting material from your focused writing. Read your exploratory draft carefully for errors; if you can, read it aloud to someone else to get feedback on how to improve it. Write a final draft.

---

*See shifts of person in Unit 5.

**Information from Philip S. Egon, *Design and Destiny: The Making of the Tucker Automobile.* Orange, Cal.: Auto Quarterly, 1989.

WRITING ASSIGNMENT II: Narrative Paragraphs

Write a paragraph telling how a person you know (either a friend or a famous person) tried to achieve a specific goal and either succeeded or failed. Include only the facts related to his or her goal. Do not try to tell a whole life story. Notice that in the paragraph about Preston Tucker there are no details about his personal life, training, or experience after 1948. Stay on the specific topic.

Description: Telling About Persons, Places, and Objects*

Three Rules for Writing Good Descriptive Paragraphs
1. Limit your subject. 2. Include concrete details. 3. Arrange your sentences in a spatial sequence.

Rule 1: Limit Your Subject

A descriptive paragraph can be about a large or small subject. If you want to describe the subject thoroughly, you must choose a very small subject. If you want to describe a large subject, you must concentrate on one of its characteristics. Either way, you must limit your topic. Here are some examples of limiting a large subject by choosing a physical characteristic:

Large Subject	*Reduced Subject*
My sister	My sister's face
My favorite city	The business district in my favorite city
My favorite building	The entrance to my favorite building

Another way to limit is to select one characteristic of the subject rather than a physical part of it. The three large subjects could thus be limited in this way:

- My sister's taste in clothes
- The traffic problem in my favorite city
- The efficient use of space in my favorite building

---

*Review adjectives and adverbs in Unit 5.

E X E R C I S E: Limiting Descriptive Topics

Limit these topics in two ways—first by choosing a physical characteristic of the subject; second by selecting another characteristic.

General Subject	Physical Characteristic	Other Characteristic
Example:		
San Francisco	*Golden Gate Park*	*San Francisco Climate*
1. Rolls-Royce		
2. Miami		
3. Oprah Winfrey		
4. Puerto Rico		
5. Disney World		

Rule 2: Include Sensory Details*

As we have seen, not all description is physical, but descriptive paragraphs almost always include some physical details. Most effective description is rich in details that appeal to the five senses. Don't forget that you can describe not only what you see, but also what you taste, feel, smell, and hear. Read the following paragraph and find words that create sense impressions. Identify the sense that each word appeals to—touch, sight, hearing, taste, or smell.

Sample paragraph:

Thanksgiving at my grandparents' house was always a delicious, uproarious occasion. When we arrived, the house was filled with the aroma of turkey, mincemeat pies, and home-baked breads wafting from the oven. The shrieks of rowdy children tumbling over one another echoed through the downstairs rooms, and the bellow of a basset hound rang from the back steps. The antique armchairs and sofa were positioned with exquisite care, and the living room sparkled from hours of dusting, sweeping, and scrubbing. A familiar candelabra on the mantel added an extra light and warmth to the crackling fire in the fireplace. The dinner itself was a high point of the year, with bubbling conversation and laughter that never subsided long, with teasing of shy children by good-natured uncles, and the endless family gossip. The Thanksgiving turkey seemed more tender and juicy every year, and a child could wallow in mounds of mashed potatoes with huge dollops of gravy. Homegrown beans and peas, canned since the summer, along with tart

---

*See using specific language in Unit 4. For examples of writing that use the five senses, read Walt Whitman's poem, "There was a Child Went Forth," John Updike's story, "A & P," and Li-Young Lee's poem, "Persimmons," in Unit 6.

cranberry sauce, filled stomachs so full that the hot dessert pies sat cooling on plates while youngsters poked half-heartedly at them.

Think of description as a way of sharing a whole experience with the reader. Don't hold back on the details; remember that the reader doesn't know anything about the experience until you share it with him or her. Choose specific words instead of vague or general ones. Compare the two versions of the following paragraph, noticing how the general words in the first version have been replaced by specific, vivid ones in the second.

Original paragraph:

After the party the room was in a mess. The furniture was in disorder, and the walls and floor were messed up. Party decorations were lying all around. Some people had even left clothing here and there. In some places you could still see food and drink that hadn't been cleaned up.

Revised paragraph, details added:

After the party the room was a mess. Two overturned chairs huddled in a corner, one with both back legs broken off. The ivory couch, decorated with crimson blotches of spilled punch, protruded at a strange angle into the center of the room. Hand prints and graffiti in green, red, and yellow crayon had defaced the elegant wallpaper, and the beige carpet was beautified by three enormous pink stains. Rainbow-colored streamers hung limply from the ceiling; and paper hats and horns covered the floor, the table, and the television set. Several gloves had been left on the armchair, and a knit cap and scarf lay under the coffee table. Half-emptied paper cups, along with plates with remnants of hors d'oeuvres and sandwiches, had been abandoned on bookshelves, end tables, and stereo speakers.

The more detailed paragraph is much longer, of course. As soon as you begin including descriptive details, you will find that your paragraphs will become better developed.

EXERCISE: Details in Descriptive Paragraphs

The words in the following list are general and not very descriptive. In the blanks to the right, write specific substitutes for them—words that create sense impressions.

Example:

a large animal   *a rhinoceros*

1. small building   _____

2. a tall plant   _____

3. things to eat   _____

4. loud sounds   _____

5. a large vehicle   _____

6. bright colors   _____

7. something to wear   _____

Rule 3: Arrange Your Sentences in Spatial Sequence*

You have already practiced achieving coherence in your paragraphs using spatial sequence. In most descriptive paragraphs the details should be arranged in an order that follows some physical direction—inside to outside, far to near, top to bottom, and so on. Read the next paragraph and identify what kind of spatial sequence its sentences follow.

> *The Duesenberg car of the 1930s was truly elite, both inside and out. Its engine was one of the most powerful of its time, a straight eight-cylinder, 420-cubic-inch giant that delivered over three-hundred horsepower. On some models it could accelerate the car from a standstill to 100 miles per hour in seventeen seconds; lighter models could eventually reach 130 miles per hour. Special bearings, springs, and connecting rods enabled the engine to maintain exceptional speeds. The exterior was equally superior, with a wide, low look to its long body. The hood took up nearly half the length, giving it a racing car appearance but with the elegance of the most expensive touring cars. It had fine touches, like wire wheels, and was built on a chassis with a 142.5-inch wheelbase. The chassis alone cost over ten thousand dollars—in the 1930s! It's no wonder that for many years after this, when they saw anything outstanding, people would say, "It's a Doozie!"***

As you probably could tell, this paragraph is arranged on an inside/outside scheme—first a description of what was under the hood, then a description of the car's exterior.

Many other kinds of spatial sequence are possible. Your description could follow the eye's movement in some way—from left to right, bottom to top, and so on. Here is a paragraph describing a circus. In what direction does the eye travel?

> *In the ring to the right, a troop of clowns were carrying on their hilarious battle with a Volkswagen Beetle that seemed to run by itself. The Beetle chased the clowns around the ring, forward and back, backfiring like a cannon at every turn. In the center ring, four elephants were being led through their balancing act by the trainer while the ringmaster watched from the side. The ring to the left displayed a family of tumblers doing somersaults and leaping onto one another's shoulders from a seesaw. And at a frightening altitude overhead, acrobats were executing heart-stopping turns and twists in midair without the safety of a net.*

---

*See the discussion of spatial sequence in this unit.

**Information from Jan. P. Norbye, *The 100 Greatest American Cars.* Blue Ridge Summit, Pa.: TAB Books, 1981.

WRITING ASSIGNMENT: Spatial Sequence in Descriptive Paragraphs

Think of a place that is familiar to you, such as a bus or train station, a courtroom, a classroom, a shopping mall, a church, mosque, or synagogue, a supermarket, or a video arcade. Visualize the scene in your memory as specifically as you can, and brainstorm, making a list of all the descriptive details you can remember. Arrange the items in two or three spatial categories, such as front, middle, back, or left, middle, right. Then write an exploratory draft, remembering to begin with a topic sentence in which a key word or phrase identifies the overall quality of the place. Read over your draft to find gaps that need transitional expressions. Make any improvements in word choice or grammar that are needed. Write a final draft. Remember to include sensory details.

EXTRA WRITING ACTIVITY: Descriptive Paragraphs

Choose one of the following photographs. Imagine that you are the person in the picture and write a paragraph expressing the thoughts and feelings that you imagine yourself experiencing as you inhabit that person's body. Use the first person (I think, I feel, and so on) to express these feelings.

Next, give the person an imaginary name, and write a paragraph in the third person (Betty looks, Sam is talking), describing the person from the outside, how he or she looks, how he or she is positioned in the picture, and what he or she is probably thinking. (Remember to watch your *s* endings on verbs with a singular, third person subject: she looks.)

Exposition: Comparative Paragraphs*

Comparing people, objects, places, experiences, or ideas is an important writing exercise. Although few articles or essays do nothing but compare, many include some comparisons. The ability to make clear, thought-provoking comparisons is a skill every experienced writer needs. Practicing writing comparative paragraphs will develop both your powers of discussing a topic in paragraph form and your ability to think clearly.

Categories of Comparisons	
Parallels:	Pointing out the similarities between two people or things
Contrasts:	Pointing out the differences between two people or things
Comparison/contrast:	Pointing out both similarities and differences between two people or things.

---

*See adjectives and adverbs in comparisons in Unit 5. For an example of extended comparison, read Lester Thuraw's "New Competitors" in Unit 6.

When you compare, be sure to discuss both subjects together. Begin your paragraph with a topic sentence that mentions *both* persons or things, not just one. This way you will avoid the trap of discussing one, then the other, and leaving the reader to figure out how the subjects are similar or different. Which of these two sentences makes a better beginning for a comparison?

1. Ballet requires more stamina than basketball.
2. Ballet makes enormous demands on the body.

Either sentence might make a good topic sentence, but only the first sentence starts off with a comparison. We could expect the paragraph to discuss the demands of ballet *and* basketball.

EXERCISE I: Comparative Paragraphs

Choose the three sentences in the group below that would make good topic statements for comparative paragraphs.

1. Some people like snakes as pets.
2. Poodles are easier to train than dalmatians.
3. Last summer was unusually hot.
4. My brother is less reliable than I am.
5. Knowing Spanish is more useful in business than knowing Latin.
6. Students begin algebra in the ninth grade.

Attention to Detail

One important skill necessary in making good comparisons is the ability to *notice* many detailed similarities and differences. When beginning writers do not succeed in their efforts to compare, they often have not done enough brainstorming. They have found only a few similarities or differences and then given up. For practice, let's consider the similarities and differences between high school and college discovered by an imaginary student named Stanley. If Stanley really brainstormed, he might think of not two or three points of comparison, but many.

Stanley's Experience of High School vs. College

Similarities	*Differences*
many required courses in both	more elective courses in college
extracurricular activities in both, especially athletics	less time for extracurricular activities in college

lived at home in high school	live in an apartment near campus
both are coeducational (boys and girls in both)	worked only on weekends in high school; work two evenings in college
held a job while going to high school and college	more homework in college; not much time anymore for social life
much homework in both	
active social life in both	
liked science and math best in both	more specialized chemistry courses in college
both last four years	lost election in high school; just became vice president of sophomore class in college
both in Colorado	
ran for student government in both	
both had modern buildings and good gymnasium	college campus has seventeen buildings at two locations
high school was all in one building	

EXERCISE 11: Comparative Paragraphs

For practice, make a list of the similarities and differences between your own life as a college student and your life as a high school student. Then write a paragraph explaining why you like one of these situations better than the other. Be sure to begin with a comparative statement for your topic sentence.

Three Kinds of Comparison

The following three paragraphs illustrate the three main kinds of comparison. The first discusses the similarities between two countries, the second contrasts the differences between two sisters, and the third explores both the similarities and the differences between two jobs a student held. Notice that the topic sentences are focused and that they all make comparative statements.

Paragraph 1 (two similar subjects):

> *As island monarchies, Japan and Great Britain have much in common. Both are small in land area but heavily populated, and both rely on the sea for food and imports. Each has a huge capital city that has played a major role in world affairs, and each has been in the forefront of industrial development. Although the surrounding ocean has enabled both to remain culturally isolated during some periods in history, the nearness of the continent has been the source of many wars over the centuries. Both peoples, in fact, derive from their neighboring continents, and their languages have close ties to continental languages—Japanese to Chinese picture writing and English to German and French. Over the centuries both nations have presided over great empires, both of which have disintegrated.*

Paragraph 2 (two different or contrasting subjects):

> *My two sisters are so different in their attitude toward work that it is hard to believe they come from the same family. Jill has always been a workaholic, while*

Joy always wanted to have a good time. When they were little girls, Joy would be skinning her knees in rollerskate races and begging Dad for money to buy candy while Jill was earning Mom's approval for her help with cooking and cleaning. In school Jill studied diligently and brought home stacks of homework. Joy, on the other hand, discovered that school was a social whirl and considered high grades the sign of a boring personality. In high school she was the favorite cheerleader; Jill was president of the honor society. Although Joy dropped out of college after two months, she has joined a country music group and expects to have a career on television without needing any higher education. Jill, with an M.B.A. and piles of honors, is heading up the corporate ladder.*

Paragraph 3 (two subjects that are both similar and different):

My two jobs as coach of an amateur basketball team and as bartender required some of the same skills but offered different rewards. In both jobs I had to understand people and motivate them. The players needed cheering up when the team was losing, and customers at the bar told me their life stories, expecting me to be their psychoanalyst. Both jobs demanded cool control when tempers flared or fights broke out. Despite these similarities, the satisfactions from the two jobs were different. Besides the high pay, tending bar gave me the feeling that I had helped a few individuals and maybe given them a better outlook. Coaching, on the other hand, was volunteer work, but I received the satisfaction of inspiring teamwork and helping a whole group of kids grow together.

WRITING ASSIGNMENT: Comparative Paragraphs

Think of two jobs you have had, two members of your family, two places you have lived, or two schools you have attended. Brainstorm to make two lists. On the left write down all the similarities between the two; on the right list the differences. Write an exploratory draft beginning with a comparative topic sentence, such as "My sister and I are alike in our personal habits but very different in our career goals." Look over your work and read it aloud to someone else for feedback. Make revisions and corrections. Write a final draft.

Exposition: "How To" Paragraphs**

Explaining how something happens or works is called **process analysis.** Explaining how to do something on the job is called **procedural writing.** Paragraphs of this kind follow a step-by-step plan and are not difficult to organize.

---

*For another comparison of two persons, read "Sadie and Maud," a poem by Gwendolyn Brooks, in Unit 6.

**See shifts of person and use of pronouns in Unit 5. For an example of process analysis writing, read Gail Sheehy's "Predictable Crises of Adulthood" in Unit 6.

However, they do demand great care: you have to be unusually clear and thorough. If you are explaining how to hook up a stereo set, for instance, you cannot make confusing statements or leave anything out; otherwise the set will not work. We are used to giving instructions aloud, with the aid of gestures, tone of voice, and feedback from the listener. A writer can't use these devices. A writer's words have to say it all; he or she has no second chance to discuss what the reader does not understand. All the necessary details have to be included, but unnecessary ones will clutter the explanation and make it harder to follow.

You also have to make sure that the reader can understand all of your terms. If you are writing for experts, you will use specialized terms; if you are writing for general readers, your vocabulary will be no more technical than necessary and you must explain the meaning of all technical terms the first time you use them. Remember your reader. You cannot write the same paragraph for general readers that you would for specialists.

The following paragraph is about how an ordinary gasoline engine works. Is it written for laypersons (nonspecialists) or expert mechanics?

> *The engine used in most cars is called an internal combustion engine, meaning that it burns fuel inside the cylinders. The gasoline is mixed with air in the carburetor; then the mixture is drawn into the cylinders (most cars now have four or six cylinders). As the piston rises in each cylinder, it compresses the air-fuel mixture, which is ignited by the spark plugs. The small explosion drives the piston down again. On its return, it forces exhaust gases from the cylinder. The piston goes through a four-stroke cycle: first, the intake stroke; next, the compression stroke; third, the power stroke; and last, the exhaust stroke. The up-and-down motion of the piston is converted to circular motion by the crankshaft, from which it is eventually transmitted to the axles and wheels.*

Obviously, this paragraph is not written for experts, since it gives only introductory facts. However, the writer does assume that the reader has enough familiarity with the engine parts to know what pistons and cylinders look like.

Here is another paragraph explaining a process. This one is about how a particular emotional illness develops. This paragraph covers a few major stages rather than many small steps.

> *Anorexia nervosa is an emotional illness that leads some people, most often adolescent girls, to starve themselves. It develops in stages, beginning with normal dieting, often by people who are not much overweight in the first place. Social isolation leads to an obsession with food, weight, and exercise. If not treated at the beginning, the condition worsens to a stage in which victims may lose twenty percent of their weight, look like skeletons, have lowered pulse rate and body temperature, lose their menstrual periods, and have thinning hair. Next, in the acute stage, they may develop delusions about their bodies, imagining they are fat when they are terribly underweight, and go through rituals of excessive exercise and limited food intake. They become secretive and sometimes go on huge binges of overeating, after which they vomit the food to keep from gaining weight. Finally,*

some go into the chronic, or long-lasting stage, in which they can remain socially isolated and unhealthy for years. Some can even starve themselves to death if not given intensive psychiatric help.*

EXERCISE I: "How To" Paragraphs

The following diagram is extremely simple, isn't it? Write a paragraph describing it. Give your description to someone who has not seen the figure. See if that person can follow your instructions and produce a perfect copy. No coaching while the other person is drawing! Anything you want to say has to be in the paragraph. Not so easy, is it?

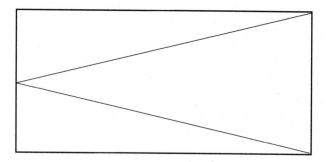

EXERCISE II: "How To" Paragraphs

"How to" paragraphs should be held together by transitional words that refer to steps in a sequence, such as *first, next, then, after,* and *finally.* Underline the transitional words in this paragraph.

> *Doing your best on an essay examination requires a systematic approach. Before you do any writing, read the instructions and topics carefully so that you know how many topics you are to discuss and how much time you have for each. Next, choose your topic or topics according to your preparation and knowledge. Then, before actually writing, jot down the main parts of the essay and some of the important facts to support each main point. Only at this point are you ready to write. When you do write, be sure that your introductory paragraph includes a plan or "map" for your whole essay so that you and the grader will know just what you intend to cover. At last it is time to write the main body paragraphs and show how much you know about the subject. Be sure to include plenty of facts. If possible, end with a concluding paragraph that restates your chief ideas without repeating the words of the introduction. Finally, read your paper twice: once for*

**Information from Steven Levenkron, *Treating and Overcoming Anorexia Nervosa.* New York: Scribner's, 1983.

errors in spelling, grammar, and phrasing, and once for revisions in content. If you have done all this, even if you do not earn an A, you can feel confident that you have done your best.

WRITING ASSIGNMENT: "How To" Paragraphs

Choose one of the following topics and write a "how to" paragraph. Remember to begin with a concise, clear topic statement and to develop your discussion step by step, using transitional words.

1. How to meet people at parties
2. How to tune an engine
3. How to behave during a job interview
4. How to choose a college
5. How to feed a dog
6. How to stop smoking
7. How to plan a wedding reception
8. How to earn high grades

WRITING ASSIGNMENT: Process Paragraphs

Write a paragraph explaining how some machine or apparatus works, how some condition like alcoholism or drug addiction develops, how children learn a certain skill, or how students change when they go to college. Remember your reader: write for the general reader, not the specialist.

Exposition: Definition Paragraphs*

Writing a paragraph defining a term means more than giving a dictionary definition. Instead, the writer really discusses the word—what it means and what it does not. More than that, the writer discusses the experience, relationship, object, or idea that the word refers to. Defining *love,* for instance, is a way of discussing how people relate to each other; defining *success* is a way of discussing what people try to achieve in our society. In a good definition the

*See subject-verb agreement in Unit 5. For an example of writing that develops an extended definition of a term, read Christopher Peterson's "Stress and Coping" in Unit 6. See also "Ambition" by Perri Klass.

writer includes examples, humor, or analysis to show the reader what the word really means. Erich Fromm wrote a whole book defining love, for example. In *The Art of Loving,* he spent many pages examining the meaning of love, giving examples, explaining types of love, identifying the true characteristics of love, and telling the difference between real love and other feelings. That is an unusually long definition. In fact, whole essays that do nothing but define a term are rare. However, it is important for any writer to be able to define terms, and writing paragraphs defining terms for practice is an important exercise for anyone who wants to have college-level writing skills.

When you define a term, be careful not to make a circular statement. What is wrong with this definition?

Love is the feeling you have when you are very fond of someone.

This is a true statement, but it does not amount to much. This is almost like saying, "Love is the feeling of loving someone," or "Love is love." Think about the *real* meaning of the term, what it is and what it isn't, how you see it applied to real people and situations. Here is how Erich Fromm defined love. He identified four of love's necessary elements:

*Beyond the element of giving, the active character of love becomes evident in the fact that it always implies certain basic elements, common to all forms of love. These are care, responsibility, respect, and knowledge.**

A definition usually places the term to be defined in a general category and then makes specific statements about its qualities or the things that it is made of.

Term	*Category*	*Description or Parts*
Love	Art	Care, responsibility, respect, knowledge

Here we can see how Dr. Fromm defined love: he said it is an *art* to be learned, like music, painting, or writing; then he identified its four main characteristics. Someone else might have called it a *feeling* or a *relationship* instead and described its parts differently. Here are two other definitions of love:

1. Love is a feeling that makes a person want to be with someone else in order to share that person's feelings and experiences.
2. Love is a relationship between two people in which both of them want to help each other grow and enjoy life.

Are these definitions different from Dr. Fromm's or do they agree with his? Write a sentence of your own defining love.

---

*Erich Fromm, *The Art of Loving.* New York: Harper & Row, 1956.

EXERCISE I: Definitions

Here are some one-sentence definitions of other words. Underline the word or phrase that tells what category the term belongs in.

Example: A *shortstop* is a <u>baseball player</u> who stands between second and third base and catches ground balls and short fly balls.

1. A *soft sell* is a sales technique in which the salesperson uses tricky psychological methods to persuade the customer.

2. A *bomber* is a divorce lawyer who overpowers the ex-spouse's attorney and wins a lot of money for his client.

3. A *deadbeat* is a borrower who never pays back the money he or she owes to another person or company.

4. *Hypertext* is a computerized information system that allows the user to work in a nonlinear fashion.

Definition paragraphs begin with one-sentence definitions and really discuss the characteristics or parts of the thing being defined. You can see how the definitions just given could easily become topic sentences for whole paragraphs. Each calls for examples or explanations to help the reader understand the term better. If we begin by defining *soft sell* as a sales technique in which the salesperson uses tricky psychological methods to persuade the customer, we would continue the paragraph by giving descriptions of some of these methods. We would tell how some salespeople flatter customers, pretend to agree with anything they say, or make them think their purchase will give them prestige.

Here is a paragraph written by the famous author of a book on baby and child care, Dr. Benjamin Spock. Read the paragraph carefully and underline the term that he is defining.

> *Much more dangerous than the open antagonism of one individual toward another . . . is the readiness of a majority of human beings to mistrust or hate whole groups of people with whom we have little or no acquaintance. Psychiatrists call this displaced hostility. It is derived from the antagonism that was first built up in all of us in early childhood toward family members. As we grew a bit older we sensed that since we were utterly dependent on them we must stay on the right side of them. And increasingly our parents and other teachers made us feel deeply guilty about hating them. So we learned to displace. In early childhood we are apt, in our society, to fear and hate witches, ogres, kidnappers, and*

other fiends that we hear about and that appear in our bad dreams. By the time we are six or eight we are ready to pick up and carry into adulthood the prejudices of the family and neighborhood against groups of real people. The less we know them in actuality the more easily we can imagine them as evil and fear and despise them.*

Dr. Spock's paragraph defines the term *displaced hostility* by explaining the feeling many people have toward groups, races, or nations they consider their enemies. He tells how this feeling comes about as a result of our hostility toward family members in childhood and our redirecting this hostility toward people we don't even know.

EXERCISE II: Definitions

Write one-line definitions for three of these terms:

punk	jock	robot
preppie	hip-hop	elective course
superstar	neurotic	gridlock

WRITING ASSIGNMENT: Definition Paragraphs

Use your imagination to write a good definition of one of the following terms. Write a paragraph in which you discuss the meaning of the term by analyzing, giving examples, expressing feelings, using personal experience, or identifying the sources or parts of the idea. Remember, this is not a one-line dictionary definition, but a *discussion* of the term.

art	heroism	love
beauty	intelligence	prejudice
courage	insanity	sophistication
friendship	liberated woman	success
happiness	marriage	wealth

---

*Benjamin Spock, *Decent and Indecent,* New York: Dutton Co., Saturday Review Press, 1969.

Exposition: Classification Paragraphs*

A paragraph can break down a large subject into categories. Writing paragraphs in which you classify subjects is good practice in clear thinking as well as organized writing. Your categories should not overlap but should have a common denominator. For example, students can be classified by their styles of dress: "grunge," "prep," athletes, etc. Aim for three or more groups. Two will be comparative, not classification. Try the following exercise to sharpen your powers of classifying.

EXERCISE I: Classification Paragraphs

Identify three main groups in which all the animals in the following list can be placed. List all of them under the appropriate headings.

bass	woodpecker	monkey
wolf	bear	wren
raccoon	horse	cow
mockingbird	canary	sparrow
trout	wildcat	ox
deer	goldfish	bison
parakeet	salmon	cod
carp	cardinal	catfish
fox	oriole	nightingale
pigeon	bluegill	antelope

EXERCISE II: Classification Paragraphs

Group each of the following subjects into three categories—that is, identify three types of colleges, cars, and so on. Do not let the categories overlap.

Example:

Colleges: 1. private four-year colleges 2. state universities 3. two-year community colleges

movies	professors
cars	stores
college students	television programs
friends	politicians
investments	vacations

*For an example of writing based on classification, read "Ducks vs. Hard Rocks" by Deairich Hunter in Unit 6.

WRITING ASSIGNMENT I: Classification Paragraphs

Write a paragraph explaining the three main categories of one subject in the preceding list. Read the following sample paragraph first, noticing the use of transitional words and the clear separation of categories.

> *There are three main kinds of addiction: dependency on chemical substances, on patterns of activity or behavior, and on people. Addiction of the first type is familiar to everyone in the form of drug addiction and alcoholism. However, it also includes dependency on such substances as tobacco, coffee, and sedatives. Addiction to patterns of behavior includes excessive television watching, playing video games, gambling, eating, exercising, and sleeping. The third form of dependency is the immature reliance on and need for another person or persons, as opposed to a productive relationship in which both partners gain and contribute out of free choice. What characterizes all forms of addiction is an inability to function well without the habit, along with a destructive effect on the person's life and social relationships.*

This paragraph explains that there are three kinds of addiction, but that they have certain things in common. The purpose of dividing a subject into categories is to understand it better. In this case, we understand what makes addiction undesirable, even when the addiction is to a good thing, like a relationship or exercise. Sometimes we can see something clearly only when we identify its different types. In biology, we divide animals and plants into many categories by a system called **taxonomy.** Biologists can name what species, genus, family, and so on a particular animal or plant belongs to. Only by such a system is it really possible to understand living things, including human beings.

Exposition: Cause and Effect Paragraphs*

Often in college writing you will have to analyze the causes of something. You will have to explore how some situation in society or world affairs got to be the way it is. In social science courses especially you will study the origins of criminal behavior, inflation, wars, drug addiction, urban decay, problems in the schools, marriage customs, attitudes toward morality, and so on. To do such analyses well, you will have to study the subjects. However, you can practice paragraphs in which you explore the cause of such things by using information from newspaper reports, personal experiences, and what you have learned from parents and teachers. You can explore most issues intelligently without being an expert in sociology, history, criminology, or psychology. Good analysis, however, requires you to do more than simply express your opinion. You must support your opinion with clear reasoning, facts, experience, and examples.

---

*See subordinate conjunctions and fragments in Unit 5. For examples of Cause and Effect writing, read Langston Hughes's "Salvation" and Alex Thio's "How Education Raises Our Income" in Unit 6.

In cause/effect analysis, good writing cannot be separated from clear thinking. Use your common sense and keep an open mind. Remember a few guidelines:

Rules for Cause and Effect Analysis

Rule 1. *Don't jump to conclusions.* Do focused writing on your topic; brainstorm. Instead of settling for the first explanation that pops into your mind (usually the one that everyone automatically comes up with), test it. Could it be wrong? Could it be only one explanation among others?

Rule 2. *Don't oversimplify.* Most important social problems and historical events have many origins. Consider indirect causes as well as direct causes. Remember that something that occurs after something else is not necessarily caused by it. Distinguish between a well–established fact and a controversial opinion.

Rule 3. *Avoid making scapegoats.* When discussing the causes of a problem, try not to blame everything on the same old convenient villains. Television, for instance, is blamed for everything from poor school performance to violence in the streets and sex crimes. How do we know that it really is the cause? Could it be one of many causes? Is it the most important one?

Rule 4. *Do your homework.* If you write an analytical paper for a specialized course such as sociology or history, back up your statements with facts from the assigned readings or research. The instructor is interested less in your personal *opinion* than in your *conclusions* based on an analysis of what you have read.

The following paragraph has a topic sentence and stays on the topic by discussing one cause of crime. In what way, however, does it fail to make a reasonable analysis of the problem?

Poverty is the cause of crime. Poor people steal because they can't get money any other way. How can the government expect to get rid of crime when there are so many people without jobs or a decent income to live on? The cost of living keeps going up for poor people, and they have to go out and commit crimes to pay the rent and put food on the table. All the government has to do to eliminate the crime problem is provide jobs and housing for the poor. It's the government's fault that the crime rate keeps rising. People who have decent housing, food, and clothing do not commit crimes.

After getting feedback from readers, this writer discovered that he needed to make revisions, since many readers disagreed with some of his points. He realized that he had oversimplified the problem and made a scapegoat of the government. Not that he was completely wrong; he simply had to focus his argument better and support it with better reasoning. Here is his revised paragraph:

> *Poverty is often said to be the chief cause of crime. But the real cause cannot be poverty alone, since some very poor communities have little crime and since most poor people are not criminals. The greater problem is poverty in the midst of a rich society, a society in which crime has become a means of making quick money. Some people who become accustomed to a life of drug peddling, car stripping, or working for organized crime syndicates believe that they can rise out of poverty faster and farther through crime than by doing legitimate work. They look around and see many prosperous and some extremely rich people who did not necessarily work hard for their money, and they want to grab the easiest money they can get. Crime has become a major "career," with a nationwide annual income of more than $100 billion. As long as this situation continues, and as long as people born into poverty believe that crime offers as promising an "occupation" as anything else, the United States will continue to have an enormous amount of crime.*

WRITING ASSIGNMENT: Cause and Effect Paragraphs

Do a page of focused writing on one of the topics from the list that follows. Use this exercise simply to explore the range of your ideas on the subject— don't censor yourself. Look over your page and try to identify the precise cause or effect involved. Create a cluster in which you place the main cause (or effect, depending on the topic) in the middle and some secondary causes (effects) in the balloons around the middle. Then identify specific details associated with the secondary causes and write them in smaller balloons.

For example:

Once you have explored the topic in this way, write an exploratory draft of a paragraph beginning with a precise topic sentence. Develop the paragraph in climactic sequence, using reasonable arguments and whatever facts you have. Reread the paragraph and, if you can, get feedback from others by reading it aloud. Revise and correct; write a final draft.

Suggested topics:

1. Why did a particular performer, performing group, or athletic team succeed?
2. Why did a particular product or program catch on with the public?
3. Why is the divorce rate higher now than it was thirty years ago?

4. Why do a large percentage of students drop out of high school (or college)?
5. Why do many people continue to smoke even though they know it will harm their health?
6. Why do people use slang?
7. Why are there so many abortions even though birth control methods are widely available?
8. Why do many people feel unhappy during holidays?
9. What is the effect of television violence on children?
10. How has the women's movement changed young people's attitudes toward marriage?
11. How does being rich affect people's behavior?
12. How does a college education improve the quality of a person's life?
13. How does immigrating to the United States affect a person's attitudes?
14. How does American society benefit from having immigrants from many countries?
15. What effect does being unable to read have on a person's life?

Persuasion: Writing to Convince*

Writing that explains why the reader should believe something or why society should do something is called **persuasive writing.** In this kind of writing you are trying to change someone's opinion or give reasons why the opinion is correct. Here are some places you will find persuasive writing and speaking outside the classroom:

- political speeches and debates
- advertisements on television and in magazines
- editorials in newspapers and editorial comments on television
- arguments in private life
- business reports that recommend new policies
- lawyers' speeches in court
- sales pitches in automobile showrooms and stores
- books that recommend changes in laws or public attitudes

These kinds of persuasive writing and talking can range from a few words to a whole book. In writing persuasive essays, you will develop skills that come into play in other forms of spoken and written communication.

Every attempt at persuasion can be boiled down to one topic sentence. The speaker or writer argues that something *should* or *ought* to be done. Persuasive paragraphs frequently use words like *should, ought, might, must, have to, could, probably, likely, possibly, certainly,* and *undoubtedly.* Such words measure what the writer thinks should be changed in people's attitudes or actions.

---

*See mixed sentences and pronouns and antecedents in Unit 5. For examples of persuasive writing, read Henry Louis Gales's "Delusions of Grandeur" and B. D. Calen, "What Real Families Are Like" in Unit 6.

These words signal *why* relationships—causes, effects, and consequences. They link motives and reasons to actions. Learn to use them correctly in your own paragraphs.

Here are some *why* statements and *should* statements that could serve as topic sentences for persuasive paragraphs.

1. People who witness a mugging should call the police but should not intervene if the muggers are armed.
2. Students who major in computer programming ought to acquire typing skills.
3. Child abuse must be prevented if we are to have a future generation of healthy parents.
4. It might be better to use the popular vote count than the electoral system in electing a president.
5. Too much emphasis on athletics could damage the academic reputation of a college.
6. Elementary schools should provide activities for children until five o'clock so that working mothers do not have to get afternoon baby-sitters.

Rules for Persuasive Writing

Rule 1. *Be logical and fair.* Don't oversimplify or exaggerate. If you level with your readers, they will respect you and more likely be persuaded.

Rule 2. *Support your opinion.* You won't convince anyone if you just keep restating your opinion. You have to give facts, reasons, examples, testimony (other people's opinions), and personal experience to make a convincing case.

Rule 3. *Remember your readers.* They have the right to disagree and are not necessarily stupid if they do, so don't insult them. Consider the objections they might have to your position and try to answer these objections.

Which of these two statements seems more persuasive?

a. Richard does well in calculus because he comes from Texas.
b. Richard does well in calculus because he had excellent mathematics courses in high school.

Sentence A violates rule 1. It is not a logical statement; the writer imagines a cause-and-effect connection that does not exist. Sentence B is logical. Excellent high school math courses often do prepare students to do well in college math.

Which of these statements is more persuasive?

a. Women can never be good police officers because police work is not women's work.
b. Women can be effective police officers. Commissioners' reports from five major cities state that female officers have performed as well as male officers.

Sentence A violates rule 2. The claim is not supported. The writer states an opinion but does not back it up with evidence. Sentence B makes a claim, then backs it up with a fact. Sentence B is more persuasive. (This does not mean that everyone will *agree* with it without further discussion, only that it goes further than sentence A in discussing the opinion.)

Which of these statements do you find more persuasive?

a. Foreign cars are usually more expensive to repair than American cars, because the imported parts cost a lot.
b. Anyone who buys a foreign car is not only stupid but disloyal to the American way of life.

Sentence B violates rule 3. The writer insults readers who already own foreign cars but does not provide any real support for the opinion. Sentence A makes a more careful claim and backs it up. The writer avoids the impression of knowing everything and giving no one else the right to an opinion.

Which of the following two paragraphs seems to provide more evidence to support the topic statement?

Paragraph A:

The mall on Palm Boulevard is a convenient place to shop. Last weekend my mother and I spent four hours there. We bought a pair of slacks for each of us, a clock radio, and a quartz watch. Then we had a terrific pizza at one of the restaurants. Later we just browsed around, looking at the boutiques and antique shops. There is a lovely indoor fountain with an artificial waterfall, into which we threw pennies for good luck. Mother felt really energetic that day because she had been down with the flu and was excited about getting out and enjoying the crowds for a while. After two hours, though, she began to get tired and so did I, because there was so much to do.

Paragraph B:

The mall on Palm Boulevard is a convenient place to shop. The wide variety of stores allows for one-stop shopping. There are two enormous supermarkets, a half dozen drug stores, fifteen clothing stores of different kinds, three furniture outlets, four sporting goods stores, a high-quality department store, two stationery shops, and fifty-three smaller retail shops of all kinds, from boutiques to coin and stamp shops. Parking is no problem, with a large free parking lot at each end of the mall and a small one with meters near the middle entrance. Benches are located every two hundred feet for the benefit of weary shoppers, and there is easy access to rest rooms. Customers who want to break for lunch have a choice of restaurants offering six different ethnic cuisines, and there are two fast food restaurants for those in a hurry. And if you run short of money, four bank branches with twenty-four-hour cash machines allow you to continue shopping without leaving the mall. Nothing is missing that could make for easy, convenient shopping.

The two preceding paragraphs should show the difference between casually expressing an opinion and really backing it up with evidence. Paragraph A relies on personal experience more than factual evidence and even goes off the topic a little. It reads like a personal letter. A reader who does not know the writer personally wants to know the kinds of information given in paragraph B, not gossip about the writer's personal life. The kind of evidence you include, then, depends on the point you are making and the sort of reader you hope to persuade.

E X E R C I S E: Persuasive Statements

Explain whether each of these sentences seems persuasive. If not, explain what is wrong with it.

1. Senator Sly cannot be trusted because he's a politician and all politicians are crooks.
2. You should get another doctor's opinion before having the operation, since it is major surgery and your doctor might be wrong.
3. It is always a mistake to get married young, because young people cannot cope with responsibility.
4. It would not be sensible to invest all of your money in a small business, since over ninety percent of small businesses fail.
5. The strange weather we've been having must be caused by the Russians; they are always trying to play dirty tricks on us with their satellites.
6. Governor Smiley would not make a good president because he looks too much like a television talk show host.
7. The film I saw last night was excellent: the acting was outstanding and the story held my interest.
8. The price you paid for that food processor was too high; it sells for ten dollars less in three other stores.
9. Sally must be smarter than Ellen because Sally went to a more expensive college.
10. I'll probably get a package in the mail tomorrow; it's supposed to rain tomorrow, and the last time I got a package it rained.

WRITING ASSIGNMENT: Persuasive Paragraphs

Read the following two case studies. Then choose one and write a paragraph explaining what you think the person or persons should do in this situation. Give convincing evidence to show why you recommend a particular course of action.

Case 1:

Ms. Cruz is the principal of a high school in a metropolitan area. A group of students has come to her requesting that the school begin to distribute free condoms and introduce candid discussions of contraception, teenage sexual behavior, homosexuality, and AIDS in the required health education course. Ms. Cruz herself believes that the course is behind the times because it says very little about these topics. She knows, however, that some students and their parents will object strongly. What should she do?

Case 2:

Shirley and Mark have been married two years and live in Los Angeles. Both have career ambitions: he is a social worker employed by the city and has a private practice as a therapist; she works for a large educational software company. Shirley's firm wants to promote her and move her to Boston, where she will be in charge of a new project and will have a much higher salary. Mark knows that if they move to Boston he will eventually be able to get a job and set up a new private practice, but the move will set him back in his career. Shirley really wants to accept her company's offer. What should they do?

COMPUTERS AND PARAGRAPH PRACTICE

Paragraph practice is especially well suited to word processing. Once you have learned the simpler commands of a word processing program, you become aware of the freedom you have to move large blocks of words anywhere you want. You can push phrases, sentences, and whole paragraphs around like hockey pucks. Like many students, however, you may at first feel bewildered by this power to rearrange your work and tend to concentrate instead on making smaller changes, such as correcting misspellings and grammatical mistakes. The prospect of reconstructing a whole essay by means of word processing commands may seem too much to handle while you are still learning the commands for deleting, inserting, backspacing, and so on.

For that reason, working with paragraphs can be excellent practice in learning to revise with computers. You can see the whole paragraph on the screen while you are tinkering with it. You can even compare two versions of the same paragraph on the screen, leaving one as the original for comparison while revising words, phrases, and sentences in the other. The important thing in revision (as you will learn in Unit 4) is to do more than make corrections of small errors and really change what you have written. Working with paragraphs by themselves, you are much more likely to feel confident about making changes than if you start with a whole essay.

Practicing Types of Paragraphs on a Computer

For extra practice in writing effective paragraphs, try revising some of the paragraphs you have composed while studying Unit 2. With each type of paragraph, try to improve your development by inserting additional relevant material. Try to rearrange the order of sentences whenever possible to improve effectiveness.

A. Narrative Paragraphs: Enter one of your narrative paragraphs on the screen; then insert additional sentences in the narrative in their proper chronological places. Next, delete one or two sentences from the narrative to see if you can improve the paragraph by removing less important details. Try to insert transition words like *then, next,* and *after that* where needed. Aim for the most effective sequence of sentences.

B. Descriptive Paragraphs: Enter one of your descriptive paragraphs on the screen. Identify vague, uninteresting, or inaccurate descriptive words and replace them with specific, vivid, and precise ones. Find phrases that lack descriptive words and insert effective ones. Add whole sentences if possible.

C. Expository Paragraphs: Enter on the screen one of the paragraphs you wrote in an expository pattern (comparison, definition, cause/effect, etc.). Try to revise your sentence patterns and sentence length. If all of your sentences are short, combine several of them (see Unit 4 for sentence combining). If some are too long, break them up. If most of them follow the same pattern, rewrite several of them to lend variety to your style, or insert additional ones to break up the monotony. Keep on experimenting.

D. Persuasive Paragraphs: Enter one of your persuasive paragraphs on the screen. Try adding more statements to strengthen your argument. Experiment with changing the order of your arguments to achieve greater emphasis, putting the clinching point at the end.

3

WRITING SHORT ESSAYS

Now that you have developed the ability both to write continuously for a page or two and to develop a specific point in paragraph form, you are ready to compose whole essays.

RECOGNIZING THE ESSAY

The **essay** is several pages of organized writing about one topic and on one main point about the topic. It can be very long, but the essays you will practice will be about five to eight paragraphs, or about five hundred to twelve hundred words. Every college student must be able to plan, compose, revise, and proofread such essays.

BUILDING ESSAYS OUT OF PARAGRAPHS

Paragraphs are the building blocks of essays. A successful essay contains the same elements as a good paragraph: *An essay should have a clear, limited main point; a logical arrangement; smooth, varied sentences; and correct spelling and grammar.* Like a paragraph, it should contain transitional words to signal relationships. It should have a recognizable beginning, middle, and end. However, it is not just a series of paragraphs strung together. The first paragraph makes a short introduction, the body paragraphs (there may be three, four, or five) discuss and illustrate separate supporting points, and the last paragraph briefly sums up and reaffirms the main point.

Here is a diagram of a two-page essay containing five paragraphs. This is a model you can use for many of your short essays. Notice its three main parts: the **introduction, body,** and **conclusion.**

ESSAY DIAGRAM

Title

Introductory paragraph arouses interest and states main purpose of essay. (3-4 sentences)

Body paragraph #1 discusses first subtopic. (5-12 sentences)

Body of paragraph #2 discusses second subtopic. (5-12 sentences)

1

Body paragraph #3 discusses third subtopic. (5-12 sentences)

Short concluding paragraph sums up main purpose. (3-4 sentences)

2

Study the following sample essay. It follows the five-paragraph diagram you just looked at, with an introduction, thesis statement, body, and conclusion. Answer the questions after the essay.

Trivia Aren't So Trivial: Sample Essay

Introduction

Many people think of fads as silly ways to waste time and money. This is true of some food and clothing crazes, but the explosion of interest in

Thesis Statement

so-called trivia has some real benefits. *People who spend their time and money on trivia games and books*

Three Subtopics Named

learn a lot about science, history, and the media.

Subtopic 1

You may not be able to earn a Ph.D. in nuclear physics by playing trivia games, but *you can pick up some interesting scientific knowledge.* Perhaps not everyone is fascinated to know that a caterpillar has six fully developed legs or that an expert on spiders is called an arachnologist. Maybe some people are not urgently waiting to learn that *robot* comes from a Czechoslovakian word for "work." Still, there are many interesting and useful facts to

Examples of Subtopic 1

discover about nature. Did you know, for instance, that the eye is the fastest healing organ in your body? Or that yogurt may help some groups of people live longer? How many people are aware that kangaroos never drink water? Only trivia experts possess such treasures of scientific fact.

Subtopic 2

In the history department, knowledge of trivia makes you more aware of world events. Without the benefit of trivia, most people would have only

Examples of Subtopic 2

vague ideas of famous people and events. Most people think that hundreds of women were burned in Salem, Massachusetts, as witches; the truth is that nineteen people were hanged and one pressed to death with stones, but none was burned. Some modern Catholics are not aware that at one time there were two popes, one in Rome and one in Avignon, France. And most Americans are surprised to learn that there were not one but three great civilizations in ancient Mexico—the Olmec, the Zapotec, and the Mayan. Another surprising fact is that at the time of the American Revolution, over eighty-five percent of the people who had come to the New World were Africans. Such bits of information make people

Subtopic 3

conscious that the real past was quite different from their picture of it.

Discussion of Subtopic 3

Although many people think they know a lot about the media, trivia games can sharpen and broaden their knowledge in that area, too. Most trivia questions in the categories of movies and television are much harder to answer than experienced viewers might expect, even though they are related to famous films, television stars, or series. While being an expert on such names and titles might appear to be useless, "useless" knowledge can keep people in touch with common feelings and experiences millions of Americans have enjoyed for half a century. Knowing the name of Ben Casey's hospital or Mr. Kotter's school won't be worth any money, but people who are curious about media facts usually make entertaining company and probably understand our society a little better than others.

Summary of Main Thesis

In conclusion, it is obvious that people who dedicate their time to the study of trivia get a lot of enjoyment and educational value out of what they are doing. Like most fads, books and games about trivia are sometimes silly, but they are not a waste of time.

Concluding Thought

Even if trivial facts are not the same as a serious education, they remind us how much we don't know and how different reality is from the way we imagine it. Trivia aren't so trivial!

1. In your own words, what is the main purpose of this essay? _____

    _____

2. What similarities are there between the introductory paragraph and

    the concluding paragraph? _____

    _____

3. What differences are there? _____

    _____

4. What method do paragraphs 2 and 3 use to develop their subtopics?

    _____

5. What method does paragraph 4 use to develop its subtopic? _____

_____

6. List five transitional words or phrases that are used to signal connec-

tions between statements or paragraphs. _____

_____

PRACTICING THESIS STATEMENTS*

The **thesis statement** is the sentence that explains the main purpose of an essay, much the way a topic sentence explains the purpose of a paragraph. Since the skills in writing thesis statements are similar to those used in writing topic sentences, this might be a good time to review the topic sentence in Unit 2, pp. 30–34. Like a topic sentence, a thesis statement can be just a short, simple sentence stating an opinion or attitude. A compound sentence with two main ideas may be confusing as a thesis statement. The thesis statement can, however, divide the main idea into two, three, or four parts. A thesis statement has to be broader than the topic sentence in a paragraph, since the thesis statement must cover the material for a whole essay.

Simple Thesis Statement:

People who spend their time and money on trivia games and books learn a lot.

Developed thesis statement:

People who spend their time and money on trivia games and books learn a lot *about science, history, and the media.*

Although a simple thesis statement is often satisfactory, a developed one provides a map for the rest of the essay and thus guides the reader more. Science, history, and the media are the subtopics for the body paragraphs in the sample essay. A simple thesis statement in this case would not guide the reader as clearly; it would not look forward to the topic sentences in the body paragraphs.

Thesis Statements Must Be Broad

Thesis statements must be broad enough to state the whole purpose of the essay. Why would the following sentence not make a good thesis statement for the sample essay?

_____

*Since thesis statements often contain two or three items in a series, this is a good time to review parallelism, colons, and the use of commas in a series in Unit 5.

Trivia games are available in more than ten areas of knowledge.

This is a specific factual statement. It does not provide a main idea or purpose for the total essay.

E X E R C I S E: Thesis Statements

Identify which sentence in each pair might make a thesis statement for an essay:

I. A. Los Angeles had a severe water shortage in 1977.
    B. In the long run, California will have to find artificial sources of water to meet the needs of its expanding population.

II. A. The Tigers won the game 3 to 1.
    B. The game between the Tigers and the White Sox was full of suspense and unexpected reversals.

III. A. The current prison system lacks adequate means for rehabilitation and psychiatric counseling.
     B. The state prison at Capital City contains 1400 inmates.

IV. A. Levels of alcohol in the blood can be tested by instruments.
    B. Drunken driving can be controlled better by strict enforcement than by new laws.

V. A. My vacation in Venezuela was wonderful, because I met some remarkable people and enjoyed delicious food.
    B. I visited Venezuela for two weeks in March 1994.

Thesis Statements Must Be Precise

Although thesis statements must be broad enough to state the essay's main purpose, they should never be fuzzy or confusing. Remember that catchall words like *bad, good, nice, great, interesting,* and *thing* are not precise. What is good to one person is bad to another; what one person finds interesting another finds tedious. Try to find more precise key words for your thesis statements. Compare these two thesis statements:

A. *Return of the Goat People* is a bad film.
B. *Return of the Goat People* is a noisy, violent film with stiff acting and overused camera techniques.

Sentence A does not guide the reader much. It says only that the writer is going to make negative remarks about the film. Sentence B states what kind of objections the writer is going to make to the film.

E X E R C I S E: Thesis Statements

Write precise, developed thesis statements for imaginary essays on these topics:

1. Teenagers and their parents

   Thesis statement: _____

   _____

2. Television watching

   Thesis statement: _____

   _____

3. College courses

   Thesis statement: _____

   _____

4. Choosing careers

   Thesis statement: _____

   _____

5. Children and divorce

   Thesis statement: _____

   _____

INTRODUCTORY PARAGRAPHS

The first paragraph in an essay serves several purposes. Its main purpose is to let the reader know what the essay is about, usually in the thesis statement. Most writers, however, find starting with the thesis statement too abrupt. Instead, they lead up to the thesis statement in various ways. The three-step design of **lead-in, tie-in,** and **thesis statement** is a useful device for beginning writers.

Starting with the Three-Step Design

Begin your paragraph with an effective **lead-in.** This attention-getter can be one of several types:

- A quotation or question
- A catchy remark
- A general, thought-provoking statement

- A surprising fact or statistic
- A problem or riddle

Be creative when you compose introductory paragraphs. Begin with a lively lead-in, to capture the reader's interest, then find a way to focus that interest on the subject. The two or three sentences in which you do this are your **tie-in.** Finally, move smoothly from your tie-in to your thesis statement. The three-step design—*lead-in, tie-in, thesis statement*—will help you begin your essays successfully. As you become more experienced, you will find other effective ways to arrange your introductions.

The paragraph that follows serves as an introduction to an essay on the subject of computer technology in the office. Notice how it follows the three-step design for introductory paragraphs.

> *"Future shock," a term from the title of a book by Alvin Toffler, means confusion caused by technological change. Nowhere is future shock more evident than in offices that have not kept up with recent advances in word and information processing. For the first time since the invention of the typewriter and the telephone, drastic changes in office procedures are occurring. Managers who hope to compete in today's business world must stay abreast of word processing software, electronic filing, and new methods of communication.*

Organized paragraphs like this do not result from your first efforts to write on a subject. First you must do plenty of prewriting to identify your main purpose and supporting details. Then you will need to write a rough draft of your introductory paragraph, perhaps even two or three, before you compose your final version.

How NOT to Begin

If you try to compose an essay without any prewriting warm-ups, your introductory paragraph may have severe problems. For instance:

1. You may begin by apologizing for not knowing what to write:

> *In this essay I am supposed to write about the effect of computers. I don't own a computer and I'm not very good at word processing because I don't type very well. All I can say is that computers are very important and are here to stay. Every time I go into a magazine store, I see whole racks of magazines about computers. I wish I could understand everything they write about in those articles.*

Compare this paragraph with the previous one about computers in the office. This one reads like a piece of focused writing; you can see the writer searching for something to say about the topic. The paragraph has no organization, no lead-in, and no thesis statement. Don't tell the reader what you don't know; explore what you *do* know through prewriting techniques until you find a good way to begin.

2. You may bore your reader by writing *too* much about what you are going to do in the essay:

> *I am going to discuss computers in this essay. First, I plan to talk about how important computers are in today's world. My next paragraph will be about how computers are used in the home. Then I will discuss how computers are used in different kinds of business. Finally, I will stress how important computers will be in the future.*

This writer has a clear plan but calls too much attention to it. No customer in a restaurant wants the chef to bring out all the recipes, pots, pans, and soup spoons used in preparing the food. Your reader also does not want to know the planning details. Leave the homework at home.

3. You may begin with grand, overblown statements that fail to lead into your thesis or contain any specific meaning:*

> *Since the beginning of time human beings have invented new technological advances that have helped and hindered the progress of society toward perfection. In modern times of today, nothing has had a bigger impact on the way people live than one single invention: a machine called the computer. This machine will be remembered for all time.*

E X E R C I S E: Introductory Paragraphs

Read the three sample paragraphs that follow. Identify the one that is carefully organized; find the *lead-in, tie-in,* and *thesis statement.* Explain why the other two would fail as introductory paragraphs.

Paragraph A:

> *Animals are one of the most important things on this earth. Animals have been around since human beings were created, and they come in millions of shapes and sizes. Most people could not live without animals, and many keep them for pets. If human beings ever get rid of the animals, it will be the worst crime in history. We should all be grateful for animals and learn all about them.*

Paragraph B:

> *Do animals have rights? In the past, we have heard about human rights, civil rights, and women's rights, but now for the first time we have groups demonstrating to protect the rights of animals. Such groups may strike some people as eccentric or silly, since we kill millions of animals for food and we must sometimes perform experiments on animals to save human lives. But we should take seriously what the animal rights supporters are telling us: that other species have*

---

*If you find yourself having difficulty with this problem, study the section on wordiness in Unit 4.

a right to exist and that we should stop unnecessary killing of animals and cru-elty to them.

Paragraph C:

In this essay I am going to talk about the topic of animals. I once had a dog named Florence. It was sort of a poodle but it had big floppy ears. Otherwise, I haven't had much experience with pets, so I talked to my uncle about animals be-cause he used to have a farm where he raised sheep and cows. He told me some funny stories about his animals that made me laugh out loud. Animals can be a lot more interesting than I realized, but I still don't know much about them.

WRITING ASSIGNMENT: Introductory Paragraphs

Practice writing an introductory paragraph. First choose an essay topic from the list below. Then create a thesis statement for the whole essay. Remember: an introductory paragraph usually does not begin with a topic sentence the way body paragraphs do. Instead it will contain the thesis statement for the whole essay at or near the end of the paragraph. Once you have written the thesis statement, think of a lead-in that will arouse interest—remember to keep that first sentence short and lively. Now write the whole paragraph, per-haps four to six sentences—shorter than most body paragraphs. Look over the first draft of your paragraph and check for words or phrases that need im-provement and for errors. Write a final draft. Identify your lead-in, tie-in, and thesis statement in the paragraph.

1. Extracurricular activities in college: A benefit or waste of time?
2. College curriculum: Should students be allowed to choose any courses they want?
3. Cheating on term papers and exams: Do many students do it, and why?
4. Safe sex: How can young adults protect themselves against sexually transmitted diseases?
5. Single parents: Can one parent raise children just as effectively as two?
6. Today's military: Why do young people join?
7. The etiquette of dating: Should women ask men for dates? Who should pay?

CONCLUDING PARAGRAPHS

Concluding paragraphs, like introductory paragraphs, are usually short. Al-though you can just stop when you run out of things to say in an essay, good writers usually make some concluding statements that leave the reader with a sense of completeness and a desire to think more about the subject. Like the opening, the ending of your essay should be dramatic, witty, imaginative, amusing, or thought provoking. It might be a question, a prediction, or a paradox. It should remind the reader of something you said at the beginning, but it should not merely repeat the information in the first paragraph. Think of the concluding paragraph as an upside-down version of the introductory paragraph. It may begin by reemphasizing the main idea (but not by restating the thesis sentence word for word) and end with statements that wrap up the discussion with humor, emotional appeal, or insight.

How NOT to Conclude

If you have not gone through the writing process sufficiently and really explored what you want to say on your subject, you may find yourself writing a concluding paragraph that is not a conclusion at all. Often you will need to write several pages in your exploratory draft before you discover your really original ideas. If you try to complete your essay in one hasty draft, your "concluding" paragraph may be the one in which these important new ideas finally come out. If this happens, either rethink the whole essay, using material from this "concluding" section as the main point of your essay, or rethink the concluding paragraph to make it fit the essay you have.

1. Do **not** use the concluding paragraph to introduce main ideas that are not supported in the essay. Consider this attempt at a conclusion to our imaginary essay on computers in the office:

   So we can see that computers have many benefits to offer businesses. This is why colleges should encourage students to take courses in computer programming and make sure all students have computer literacy. In fact, high schools ought to consider computer literacy a basic skill as important as reading, writing, and mathematics.

   This paragraph jumps off the track. The essay is about computers in the office, but at the end the writer suddenly becomes interested in the implications of computers in education. The concluding paragraph is a bad place to change your topic, just when you should be stressing the points already made.

2. Another kind of conclusion that does not succeed in a short essay is the mechanical summary. Sometimes a very long piece of writing such as a book or dissertation, especially if it is complicated, needs a summary to help the reader digest and remember the points made in it. In a short college essay, however, such a summary is an excellent way to bore the reader. Consider this paragraph as an ending to our essay on computers in the office:

   In summary, I have discussed in this essay some of the ways that computers make offices more efficient. The first way I discussed was electronic filing techniques. In the next paragraph I talked about word processing. Then I explained the advantages of high-technology editing. When you have read what I explained about these advantages, you will understand why it is important to know about computers if you work in an office.

This paragraph emphasizes the writer's plan when the focus should be on the topic itself. Give the reader a sense of order, and make some indirect reference to your opening, but don't overdo the repetition.

Model Concluding Paragraph

Here is a more successful concluding paragraph to our essay:

Reemphasis on Thesis

Broadening to Suggest Further Thought

Echo of Opening

> Knowing the equipment, filing techniques, and methods of writing and editing can be a great asset in today's office. Most offices across the country are rapidly replacing their out-moded procedures with computerized methods. Smaller companies may find the initial adjustment expensive, and some managers may feel anxious about giving up comfortable, old procedures. Nevertheless, the change pays off in the long run, and the pangs of change are easier to bear than the misery of suffering future shock while competitors hurry on ahead.

Note the use of the phrase *future shock* here. This phrase brings the essay full circle back to the beginning line of the essay (see page 84).

WRITING ASSIGNMENT: Concluding Paragraphs

Look over the introductory paragraph you composed in the previous exercise. Without actually writing a whole essay at this time, imagine that you have completed the body paragraphs on the topic. Now write an effective concluding paragraph that reaffirms your main thesis and broadens out to suggest directions for further thought on the subject. End with a lively, thought-provoking finale. Consider your first attempt at writing this paragraph to be an exploratory draft. Check it for errors and ineffective words or phrases; revise, then write a final draft.

MODES OF DEVELOPING SHORT ESSAYS

In Unit 2 you practiced writing paragraphs in the four rhetorical modes—narrative, descriptive, expository, and persuasive. Now you will apply the skills of development and organization you practiced in that unit in composing whole essays. Although the exercises in Unit 3 roughly parallel those in Unit 2, being grouped generally into the chief modes, you will not be merely repeating what you did in the previous unit. Essays not only require the writer to develop material much more extensively within a mode, they also may require the writer to borrow from one mode to develop another.

The Narrative Mode: Telling About an Event

As you know from practice with narrative paragraphs, narration means telling a story. Like narrative paragraphs, narrative essays are arranged in time sequence, each paragraph marking one stage of the action. If you are telling about a trip you have taken, for instance, one paragraph might tell about planning for the trip, the next about getting to your destination, the next about what you did there, and another about your return. Although personal experiences happen in a steady flow of time, your paragraphs mark off the important phases of the experience, giving shape to the whole story.

First Person Narration: Telling About a Personal Experience*

You may choose to write in the first person in your narrative essay (I, me, my), telling about your personal experience. When you plan the essay, brainstorm to collect interesting details about each phase of the experience. Narratives generally follow a before/during/after sequence; ask yourself questions about each stage to be sure you have included all the important facts. Here is an example of brainstorming done by a student as her first step in creating an essay about her family's trip to New York City. She arranged her material into questions and answers about each stage of the trip.

Before:

Question	*Answer*
Why did we go?	We have relatives—my father's cousin and his family—on Long Island. We wanted to visit them and see tourist attractions in Manhattan. I also wanted to check out some of the colleges in New York.
What was it like planning the trip?	Hysterical. My dad's cousin invited us to come in late June when school was out. That was June 15. We had to plan the trip, get clothes ready, and agree on what to do in about a week.

---

*Review narrative paragraphs in Unit 2. For examples of first person narrative, read Richard Wright's "Facing the Bullies" and Russell Baker's "My First Job" in Unit 6.

| How did we get there? | We drove all the way from Detroit. My brother Steve had just gotten his license, so he wanted to split the driving with Mom and Dad. We stayed overnight in Pennsylvania. |

During:

What was it like staying with our relatives?	Terrible at first. All they wanted to do was go bowling and rent home videos, and all we wanted to do was rush into Manhattan. After two days we went into Manhattan by ourselves.
What did we do in Manhattan?	Saw some of the tourist sights—Fifth Avenue, Wall Street, Rockefeller Center, the Statue of Liberty. Went shopping at Saks, saw the Trump Tower, tried to see a musical comedy (sold out). Then we split up. Dad took me to look at N.Y.U., Columbia, Hunter College, and Pace U. Mom and Steve saw a live television show. Went with relatives to a Mets game.
What did I like and dislike?	The people were fantastically varied; some were helpful and friendly but a lot of homeless people. The buildings and shopping were exciting, but too much noise and rushing.

After:

| What was the return trip like? | Not as much fun as going there. We argued a lot because each of us wanted to do something we didn't get to do and blamed the others. We also disagreed about what we liked and what we should do the next time. We drove all the way back without stopping overnight. |
| What did I get out of the trip? | I learned how different each one of us in the family is from the others. I got over my fear of New York and sometimes wish I had gone to college there. I also learned to discuss whatever you plan to do with other people you're going to do it with before you do it. |

Like most brainstorming, this exercise produced more ideas and facts than could be used in one unified essay. The next step was to write an exploratory draft that would use some of this material, leave out some of it, and add details where needed.

Exploratory draft:

Three years ago my family took a trip to New York. It was the longest trip we ever took together as a family, although I have been on longer trips by myself, to such places as Los Angeles and Florida. But this trip was especially important because it taught me a lot about myself and my family. The trip was sort of a surprise because we weren't really expecting to go to New York that summer, but my dad's cousin called from Long Island and insisted that we come visit his family at the end of June. That was only one week later. I'll say this about my family—they don't mind doing things at the drop of a hat!

We decided to drive because it would be too expensive to fly, and we would need the car in New York City. Our relatives couldn't be expected to squeeze us all into their car with them, after all. My brother Steve had just gotten his driver's license, and he was dying to prove he could drive better than Mom and Dad, so he got to take turns with them at the wheel. We took it easy driving and stayed overnight in a small town in Pennsylvania. When we finally got to New York, we had to drive through all that traffic to get to the Long Island Expressway and find our way to our relatives' house in Suffolk County, Long Island. We were really tired but eager to see the city. Were we in for a surprise when we found out that nobody in their family ever went to the city themselves! They expected us to stay at their house and go bowling or watch home videos.

This wasn't exactly what we came to New York for, so after two days we politely convinced them that we wanted to drive into Manhattan. That made the whole vacation better, but I wished we had discussed all this before we left. The same problem came up when we started going into Manhattan every day. We realized that each one of us had a different idea of what we wanted to do, and we all just assumed that everybody would agree.

We agreed on some things. We all wanted to see some of the tourist attractions, so we walked up and down Fifth Avenue, saw the Empire State Building, Saks Fifth Avenue, St. Patrick's Cathedral, Trump Tower, and Rockefeller Center. We also took the subway down to Wall Street and the World Trade Center and rode the Staten Island Ferry and saw the Statue of Liberty. Then we had to negotiate what to do next. Dad's idea was for me to visit some of the colleges in New York, so I agreed to go along to look at New York University, Columbia, Pace University, and Hunter College. I didn't really expect to go to college in the East, but I thought it might be interesting. Steve wanted to see a live television show, and Mom wanted to shop, so the two of them managed to see the Geraldo show live and spend an afternoon back on Fifth Avenue. We all wanted to see a musical comedy on Broadway. Kiss of the Spider Woman was showing then, but it was impossible to get tickets (more great planning ahead!), so we settled for Cats, *which was still running after many years.*

I liked the excitement of Manhattan, and the people were mostly a lot friendlier than I expected. They would always give directions if you asked them—although not always the right ones. I didn't like the noise of the traffic and the subways, and there were homeless people asking for money everywhere we went. But I think it would be interesting to live in New York, and sometimes I wish I had gone to college there the way my dad hoped I would. No other place has so many varied types of people.

Before we went back we did have one interesting outing with our relatives. We went to a Mets game at Shea Stadium, which they considered going into the city. Otherwise, not much happened before we headed back. I didn't enjoy the trip back as much as the trip to New York. For some reason, we seemed to argue about everything. Each one of us felt there was something we missed doing in New York, and each of us had a different attitude about the whole trip. I slept most of the way because we decided not to stay overnight anywhere on the way back.

I could say I learned two things from the trip. One is not to take other people's attitudes and wishes for granted, not even your own family's. The other is the importance of communication and planning. If you want to go on a trip or do some other important project with other people, be sure to plan ahead and discuss the plan with everybody else involved. You'll be glad you did.

On rereading this essay in rough draft, the writer decided that she wanted to keep many of the interesting details but needed to organize the story better. Although the rough draft had a loose before/during/after sequence, some paragraphs had too many topics and the main idea did not become clear until the end. She wanted to add more vivid details from her prewriting activities and make the main point clear from beginning to end. She decided to include in her revised essay a title, a thesis, and a clear paragraph arrangement.

An Unplanned Vacation

Lead-in

My family likes to do things at the drop of a hat. Therefore, when my father's cousin on Long Island called to invite us for a visit, it seemed perfectly natural to Dad that we would take off for New York on a week's notice. None of us had been to New York before, and we all wanted to go. The difficulty was that we made no real plans. We didn't discuss with Dad's relatives what we would do during the week and a half we would stay with them, and worst of all, we didn't discuss with one another what we wanted to see and do in Manhattan. The trip taught us the value of communication and planning.

Tie-in

Thesis Statement

Paragraph 2: Getting There

Our trip to New York wasn't exactly a disaster, but we learned as soon as we left Detroit what price you pay for not thinking ahead. The car was due for a tune-up, a brake job, and re-alignment. Of course there wasn't time to have any of that done, and of course we had to drive because there wasn't time to reserve a flight. The drive was going smoothly at first; my brother Steve had just gotten his license and was taking turns with Mom and Dad. With three drivers, we didn't plan on stopping over anywhere, but somewhere in a small town in Pennsylvania we had a flat tire. We got to a service station and found out that not only did the tire have to be replaced, but new brake shoes had to be installed and the front end had to be aligned or else we would ruin another set of tires. All that meant an overnight stay in a town that didn't even have a movie theater, far less any night life or tourist attractions.

Paragraph 3: Arrival

Once we were on our way again, the trip was easy except for driving all the way through metropolitan New York to get to Long Island. When we reached our relatives' house in Suffolk County, we were tired but eager to launch out on an exploration of the Big Apple the next day. Were we in for a surprise when we found out that they expected us to stay at their house the whole visit and spend the time going bowling or watching movies on their VCR! Once again, we realized the problems we had created for ourselves by not thinking ahead. We could have discussed our plans with them before we left, but now we had a problem— how to let them know that we were going to spend most of our time in Manhattan without hurting their feelings. Fortunately Mom is a gifted negotiator and managed to convince them politely that it would be better for everybody if we went into the city during the day several times. That made the whole vacation better, but I wished we had made the arrangement ahead of time.

Paragraph 4: What We Did There

Once we started our jaunts into Manhattan, the same problem of inadequate planning came up. We soon realized that each of us had a different idea of how to spend our short time in the city. Since we hadn't talked it over before, we had to begin each day with a round-table discussion. Amazingly, we did agree well enough to see most of the big tourist sights, including the Empire State Building, St. Patrick's Cathedral, Rockefeller Center, and Trump Tower. We also took the subway down to Wall Street and the World Trade Center and rode the Staten Island Ferry so we could see the Statue of Liberty. The rest we had to negotiate. Dad's idea was that I should see some of the colleges in New York, so I agreed to go along with him to look at New York University, Columbia University, Hunter College, and Pace University.

Although I didn't really expect to attend college in the East, I thought it would preserve family harmony if I cooperated. Steve wanted most of all to see a live television show, and Mom wanted to shop for gifts for friends and relatives, so the two of them managed to collaborate by spending an afternoon on Fifth Avenue and getting free tickets for the Geraldo show at Times Square in the evening. Our last unpleasant reminder of our lack of foresight came when we tried to get tickets for a musical comedy—something we all agreed on. Our first choice, *Kiss of the Spider Woman*, was sold out for months; the only tickets we could get to a really good Broadway show were for *Cats*, which had been around for more than ten years. And our seats were in the back row.

Conclusion   From beginning to end, this trip taught us the value of communication and planning. Although we enjoyed many experiences on the trip and liked our relatives very much, we decided that from then on, we would discuss any major plans with each other and not take each other so much for granted. The trip back involved a lot of arguing; we didn't agree on much of anything about the trip, but the whole experience forced us to understand one another better. Maybe our unplanned vacation benefited us all.

An unplanned essay is like an unplanned vacation: you can learn a lot from it, but it's not as good as a planned one. You may have noticed that in the final draft the writer added some interesting details that support the main idea, and she took out irrelevant details.* She also divided her paragraphs differently to give a clearer sense of the phases of the trip.

WRITING ASSIGNMENT: Narration

Think of a trip you have taken, either alone or with others. Follow the stages of the writing process to create an essay about the trip. First, brainstorm or do focused writing to explore the facts and impressions you remember and group the material into stages—before, during, and after. Then look over your prewriting activities. What did the trip teach you? Write an exploratory draft

---

*We have been emphasizing organization and main thesis here, but remember that revision also includes choice of details and improvement of language. At this point, you may want to look ahead to Unit 4, "First and Second Drafts."

in which you mainly try to tell the important facts and experiences. Put this rough draft away and look at it again a day or two later. Read it aloud to someone else; you and your listener together may be able to recognize your main idea and your attitude toward the experience. (The writer of "An Unplanned Vacation" was obviously somewhat annoyed over what happened, but she ended on a positive note.) Once you have a clear idea of your main point and your paragraph groupings, write the final draft.

Third Person Narration: Telling About a Public Event

Third-person narration means telling about an event from the outside, either as an observer or as a researcher who has collected facts about the event. Factual narratives of this kind include news reports, magazine articles about important events, and books of history and biography. Short stories and novels are also third person narratives in which the events are imaginary. As a college student, you will no doubt write essays and term papers that either tell about historical events or trace the lives of famous people.

As in first-person narration, third-person narration should be based on a clear arrangement of paragraphs. As always, you should have an interesting lead-in and conclusion, and each body paragraph should focus on a single stage of the action. Sentences should follow smoothly one after the other with occasional transitional expressions like *next, after, then, soon, later,* and *meanwhile.*

When doing a narrative essay on an event, be sure to collect your important facts first and do some focused writing to explore your thoughts about the event.

Sample Narrative: Writing About the Los Angeles Riots

Let us consider, as an example, writing a short essay that will tell about the riots in Los Angeles in early May 1992. Before trying to write a whole exploratory draft, let's collect some of the main facts about the event. All of us remember some of the main things that happened, but to be sure we are accurate and possibly discover a few details we didn't know about, we should always make use of available sources in the library, such as newspapers or magazines. If we look, for instance, at the reports by the *Los Angeles Times* during the period of May 1–5, 1992, we can collect some of the following information:

Brainstorming: The Facts

- The Rodney King trial ended on Wednesday, April 29, 1992, with a jury of six men and six women acquitting all four police officers charged with beating Mr. King.
- Within 24 hours over 1000 fires had been set and 25 people already killed.
- The police department, as even Chief Daryl Gates admitted, was slow to respond.

---

*For an example of third person narrative, read "Doctors and Doctorates" by White and Gribben in Unit 6.

- Unlike the Watts riots of 1965, these riots occurred all over town, from near downtown, into South Los Angeles, through Hollywood, and toward the Westside.
- Firefighters ran into threats and assaults from angry mobs, though in places some residents came out to protect firefighters.
- Members of the press, particularly those with television cameras, were likely to be attacked, beaten, and have their equipment stolen, almost without regard to their ethnic identity.
- Looters, including blacks, Hispanics, and whites, pillaged thousands of businesses, in an almost "carnival" atmosphere.
- Acts of heroism were seen along with lawless violence. Reginald Denny, the white truck driver who was seen being beaten almost to death on television, was rescued by two black women and two black men, who helped him to a hospital just in time to save his life. Similarly, a black family hid and protected a free-lance news reporter who had been shot four times and took him to the police, who summoned medical help.
- City services were halted or hampered for several days: bus service was canceled citywide; mail delivery ceased; baseball and basketball games were called off; schools were closed; college exams were postponed, and repair services of all kinds were unavailable.
- Korean businesses were especially hard hit by arson and looting; television viewers witnessed some Korean store owners trying to protect their property at gunpoint.
- Violence on a much lesser scale erupted in other cities, including San Francisco, Atlanta, Las Vegas, Brooklyn, Tampa, Seattle, Birmingham, Madison, San Diego, and even Toronto.
- The gangs, such as the Crips and Bloods, called off their war against each other and joined in ransacking the city together.
- The jurors, who thought they had rendered a fair verdict, were stunned by the reaction to their decision; some went into hiding.
- By Sunday, over 8500 federal troops, including marines and the national guard, had been brought in to maintain calm.
- When the riots had ended, cleanup operations brought out many volunteers of all ethnic backgrounds and occupations, including UCLA students, ministers, film professionals and actors like Edward James Olmos, retirees, and residents of all kinds who worked in a cooperative spirit together.
- Mayor Tom Bradley appointed Peter Ueberroth, who had organized the 1984 Olympics in L.A., to oversee rebuilding efforts.
- The riots proved to be the costliest in U.S. history in damage to property and the costliest in this century in human life.
- L.A. residents of all races strongly condemned both the jury's verdict and the riots (81 percent disagreed with the verdict, 71 percent strongly; 75 percent thought the violence totally unjustified).
- 30,000 people marched in Koreatown to show solidarity.
- The speaker of parliament in South Korea called for reparation payments by the U.S. Government to Korean Americans victimized by the riots.

- The final toll tallied just after the riots was 58 dead, 2383 injured, 5383 fires, 14,103 arrests, $785 million property damage, and 5273 buildings destroyed or damaged.*

There are obviously many interesting facts about the event. Before trying to create an essay out of them, we should group the facts into some related categories. For this purpose, a clustering diagram may be useful: See the clustering diagram on the next page. From the cluster exercise, we can see that the topic contains many aspects, some of which we do not want to explore in depth. And we still don't have a main point. Perhaps we can arrive at one by trying an exploratory draft.

Exploratory First Draft:

The Los Angeles riots began only a few hours after a jury in the Simi Valley courthouse turned in a not guilty verdict on the four officers charged with beating black motorist Rodney King. Looting, arson, destruction of property, shooting, and assaults on motorists went on in many sections of Los Angeles and continued on a huge scale through Thursday and Friday. Thousands of buildings were destroyed and hundreds of people injured or killed. The police, accused of overreacting against Rodney King, were criticized for acting too slowly in the face of violence. Firefighters and television cameramen were threatened and attacked by rioters. City services, including bus service, mail delivery, and repair services,

---

*Information from the following *Los Angeles Times* articles:

May 1, 1992: "South L.A. Burns and Grieves," by Jonathan Peterson and Hector Tobar; "Opportunists, Criminals Get Blame for Riots," by Victor Merina and John Mitchell; "LAPD Slow in Coping with Wave of Unrest," by David Freed and Ted Rohrlich; "Looting and Fires Ravage L.A.," by Greg Braxton and Jim Newton; "Beaten Driver a Searing Image of Mob Cruelty," by Laurie Berklund and Stephanie Chavez; "A View of Model Multi-ethnic City Vanishes in Smoke," by Stephen Braun and Ashley Dunn; "A Long Night of Anger, Anarchy," by Charisse Jones and Dean E. Murphy; "Jurors Rattled by Aftermath; Defend Verdicts," by Paul Lieberman and Stuart Silverstein; "Firefighters Feel the Raw Heat of Fear," by David Ferrell and Mathis Chazanov; "The Press Under Fire: Riot Targets Journalists," by Patt Morrison; "Free-Lance Reporter Shot Four Times, but Family in South L.A. Saves Him," by James Rainey; "Everyday Life Shattered in Many Ways," by Miles Corwin; "Violence Erupts in Other Cities," by David Treadwell.

May 2, 1992: "Looters, Merchants Put Koreatown Under the Gun," by Ashley Dunn; "When Right and Wrong Blur," by Amy Wallace and Nora Zamichow; "San Francisco Police Halt Demonstration Before It Starts," by Richard C. Paddock and Jennifer Warren; "Jackson Issues Call for Calm," by Paul Feldman; "Violence in Atlanta for 2nd Day," by David Treadwell and Edith Stanley.

May 3, 1992: "Shovels, Brooms Become Tools of Healing," by Edward J. Boyer and Marc Lacey; "Bush Sends Troops to L.A.," by Paul Lieberman and Louis Sahagun; "Korean Urges Compensation," from Times Wire Reports.

May 4, 1992: "Reaction Divided over Key Role for Ueberroth," by Jube Shiver, Jr. and James Rainey; "Los Angeles: A Great City That's Too Big to Fail," Editorial.

May 5, 1992: "L.A. Strongly Condemns King Verdicts, Riots," by Frank Clifford and David Ferrell.

The L.A. Riots

Events
- Firefighters attacked
- Shooting
- Fires
- Spread across city
- Different from Watts
- Acts of heroism

Looting
- Many groups
- Gangs together
- "Law-abiding" people

Causes
- Rodney King verdict
- Ethnic rivalries
- Gangs
- Lack of opportunity
- Joblessness
- Police brutality
- Family breakdown

Reactions
- Military
- Police
- Jury's reaction
- Riots in other cities
- Opinion polls
- Editors
- TV coverage
- Call for government attention to cities

Aftermath
- Rebuilding Czar, Peter Ueberroth
- Many ethnic groups
- Movie stars
- Cleanup
- People of different occupations
- Churches help racial reconciliation
- Effect on business
- Toll estimated
- L.A.'s image changed

were stopped; baseball and basketball games were cancelled, schools were closed, and college exams were postponed.

Violence spread throughout many areas of Los Angeles and surrounding areas. Violence and protests erupted across the nation with significant incidents in San Francisco, Atlanta, Las Vegas, Brooklyn, and other cities.

During the riots, some of the gangs, which had been deadly enemies, ignored their hatreds and joined together in ransacking the city. Korean businesses were especially hard hit by arson and looting; Korean store owners were seen on television trying to defend their property at gunpoint. A march through Koreatown later brought out 30,000 people into the streets to show solidarity.

Both the good and the bad sides of people were brought out by the emergency. At first, many of the rioters were expressing anger at the jury's verdict, but soon mob violence took its own course, and people of all ethnic groups, many who had been law-abiding before, threw themselves into the melée. One woman who was helping her daughter steal, confessed, "I'm really not like this." Terrible acts of brutality occurred against innocent bystanders, and whole sections of the city seemed bent on destroying themselves. Some commentators observed that the jury's verdict had appeared to create a climate in which right and wrong had almost disappeared. However, in the midst of the destructive and self-destructive nightmare, heroic acts were done by Good Samaritans. Television viewers saw white truck driver Reginald Denny being beaten almost to death, but they did not see the two young black women and two black men who helped Denny steer his truck to a hospital where quick medical attention barely saved his life. Similarly, a black family helped hide and protect a freelance reporter who had been shot four times and took him to the police, who summoned medical help. Sometimes, when fire fighters reached a scene and confronted armed residents, they found that these men had come out to protect them rather than attack them.

Reactions to the riots ranged from the few who supported the verdict and condemned the riots to the equally small percentage who thought the riots completely justified. A very large percentage of Los Angeles residents, however, condemned both the verdict and the violence. Eighty-one percent disagreed with the verdict (71 percent strongly); 75 percent thought the violence was totally unjustified. The jurors themselves, some of whom went into hiding, thought they had rendered a fair decision and were stunned by the explosion that it triggered. Many people feared that the image of Los Angeles as a leader in interracial cooperation had been destroyed for good. Some believed that the slow police action was intentional; Chief Daryl Gates said he thought quicker action might have caused even worse violence. But others pointed out that the faster action of Police Chief Richard Hongisto and Mayor Frank Jordan in San Francisco had kept violence at a much lower level in that city.

Federal troops were finally brought in—8500, including marines and national guard, by Sunday, May 3, but they were too late to prevent the major destruction that had already taken place. The riot proved to be the most destructive to property in United States history and the most destructive to life in the twentieth century (though not as much as the anti-draft riots by Irish immigrants in

New York in July 1863, in which 1000 people died). The final toll, as determined on May 5, 1992, was 58 deaths, 2383 injuries, 5383 fires, 14,103 arrests, $785 million in damage, and 5273 buildings damaged or destroyed.

In the aftermath of the riot, many people began to see some good coming out of the terrible events. People of all ethnic groups and occupations came out into the streets to join in the cleanup operation and help rebuild the city. Ministers, college students, retirees, celebrities like actor Edward James Olmos, and residents of all kinds formed cleanup brigades. Churches held interracial gatherings to promote racial harmony. Mayor Tom Bradley appointed Peter Ueberroth, the organizer of the 1984 Olympics in Los Angeles, to oversee the rebuilding efforts. One retired black auto mechanic said, "Everything that usually turns real, real bad flip-flops over and starts turning good." And the editors of the L.A. Times wrote on Monday, May 4, 1992, "Like a very large and famous bank that must be protected from trouble because 'it's too big to fail,' Los Angeles, too, is too big to fail. So we won't let it, will we?"

When we read over this draft, we realize that although we have put a lot of interesting material into it and have a general sequence that moves from the Rodney King verdict through the riots to the reactions and aftermath, the paragraphs are a little mixed up. Some are too small and undeveloped; others are very large and too cluttered with details. Even more important, we haven't stated a clear main idea. But, as often happens in an exploratory draft, we may have discovered one at the end: the idea that the riots almost destroyed Los Angeles' image as a leader in interracial cooperation, but the response of the community may have saved it.

Main Idea

The Los Angeles riots nearly destroyed the image of the city as a national leader in interracial cooperation, but the community's response afterward may eventually recapture it.

Now we can try for a revised final version in which each paragraph contributes clearly to this main idea, and all of the details are included for a purpose.

Revised Draft:

Too Big to Fail

Introduction: Leads into Main Idea

Before May 1992, Americans viewed Los Angeles as the most successfully interracial city in the United States. That image, however, was shattered and nearly destroyed by the riots that ravaged the city in the wake of the Rodney King trial. When the six men and six women in Simi Valley found the four officers not guilty of having unjustifiably beaten Mr. King, the city erupted in an explosion of arson, looting, destruction of property, and assaults on motorists. Unlike the Watts riots of 1965, the violence was not confined to a single area but reached from near downtown into South Los Angeles, through Hollywood, and toward the West

Side. As if suddenly shedding its facade of civilization and racial harmony, Los Angeles was nearly consumed in violence.

Paragraph 2: The Breakdown of Coordination

The breakdown, for several days, seemed total. Within hours of the verdict on Wednesday, April 29, 1992, violence broke out, and within twenty-four hours over one thousand fires were burning and twenty-five people had already been killed. City services halted: there was no mail delivery or bus service, schools were closed, college exams were postponed, and basketball and baseball games were called off. The police, criticized previously for overreacting, were now blamed for not responding quickly enough. Firefighters encountered rioters who threatened and assaulted them. Television cameramen became the special targets of attack. A city previously famous for its powers of coordination appeared to lie disorganized and helpless in the face of the firestorm.

Paragraph 3: The Breakdown of Racial Cooperation

Dispelled, too, was the illusion of Los Angeles as a model of interracial harmony. Respect and civility seemed lost altogether. Korean businesses were hit hard by arson and looting; television audiences watched Korean store owners trying to protect their property at gunpoint. Ethnic hatreds mixed with indignation over the jury's verdict found expression in random attacks on unlucky motorists. Television viewers saw a truck driver named Reginald Denny dragged from his truck and beaten almost to death. The only ethnic cooperation in evidence seemed to be the participation of whites, Hispanics and blacks in a free-for-all of looting; people who had otherwise been law-abiding carted off sneakers, television sets, computers, and even sofas. One woman who was helping her daughter steal, confessed, "I'm really not like this." Even the notorious gangs like the Crips and the Bloods ignored their hatreds and joined in ransacking the city.

Paragraph 4: Signs of Cooperation Still Evident

Yet, even in the worst hours of the riots, stirring examples of Good Samaritanism that transcended race proved that Los Angeles still had plenty of good people in it. Television viewers were unfortunately not able to watch two black women and two black men heroically rescue Reginald Denny by guiding his truck to a hospital just in time to save his life. Nor did television news show us the black family that hid and protected a free-lance reporter who had been shot four times, risking their own lives to take him to the police, who summoned medical help. And sometimes firefighters, alarmed to be confronted by armed men, discovered that they had appeared to protect the firefighters, not attack them.

Paragraph 5: The Cooperative Spirit of the Cleanup

Still more hopeful was the reaction of the city after the riots. Polls showed that a large majority of city residents, regardless of race, condemned both the verdict and the violence: 81 percent disagreed with the verdict (71 percent strongly), and 75 percent thought the violence was totally unjustified. People of all ethnic groups and occupations came out into the streets to join the cleanup operations and help rebuild the city. Ministers, college students, retirees, celebrities like actor Edward James Olmos, and residents of all kinds formed integrated cleanup brigades. Churches held gatherings to promote racial harmony. Mayor Tom Bradley appointed Peter Ueberroth, the organizer of the 1984 L.A. Olympics, to oversee the rebuilding efforts.

Conclusion: The Good That May Come from Tragic Events

Almost immediately after the riots had ended, this city of great heart and spirit was coming together to heal itself. As one retired black auto mechanic said, "Everything that usually turns real, real bad flip-flops over and starts turning good." And the editors of the *Los Angeles Times* wrote on Monday, May 4, 1992, "Like a very large and famous bank that must be protected from trouble because 'it's too big to fail,' Los Angeles too, is too big to fail. So we won't let it, will we?" Los Angeles had a lot to regain after these devastating riots, but those who knew the city well believed that somehow it would.

WRITING ASSIGNMENT: Third-Person Narration

Plan, compose, write, and revise an essay telling about a public event. Either collect material from newspapers or magazines, or write about an event that you already know many details about from recent news coverage. Brainstorm to put down on paper as many facts as you can, and use other prewriting activities to prepare. Then write an exploratory draft to discover your ideas about the event; look over your draft for a main idea and plans for arranging paragraphs. Write a final draft. Remember that when you use printed sources, you must not quote word for word unless you use quotation marks, as in the last paragraph of the previous essay. And when you write formal research papers in advanced courses, you will be expected to use the correct form for identifying your sources and to provide a list of sources at the end of your paper.

The Descriptive Mode: *Telling About a Place**

Descriptive essays, although they may contain elements of other kinds of writing, are intended chiefly to give a mental picture of a place, person, or object. As in descriptive paragraphs, be sure to use vivid, specific details and arrange your material in spatial sequence. This means that each paragraph, except the introduction and conclusion, will concentrate on one part or feature of the subject you are discussing. As in all essays, your thesis statement, preferably located near the end of the introductory paragraph, should state an idea that holds the whole description together. It will indicate what parts or features of the subject (the place, person, or object) the essay will discuss, and some point it makes.

Describing a place, whether it is a small area such as your room or a huge land mass such as the continent of Africa (as in the sample essay that follows), requires thought, organization, and supporting details. Therefore you should expect to go through the stages of the writing process. The details will not arrange themselves; you have to group them into spatial categories by either outlining, making lists, or clustering. You should expect to do one or two rough drafts before you get the arrangement and the details right. If you do not have an interesting main idea about the place you are discussing, try focused writing to explore your thoughts and impressions before you try to compose an organized essay. In the sample essay describing Africa, the writer first tried creating a cluster that helped him clarify his mental picture of the subject. In doing this, he also discovered his main thesis: that Africa is not really just one land mass, but three masses, each with a different ecology and climate.

The Three Africas: Sample Essay

Introduction: Creates Interest and Identifies Three Areas to Be Described

When many people hear the word *Africa*, they picture steaming jungles and gorillas. Hollywood films have shrunk the public image of this immense, varied continent into a small segment of its actual diversity. To have a more accurate picture of the whole continent, one should remember that there are, roughly, three Africas, each with its distinct climate and terrain, and with a style of life suited to the environment. The continent can be

*Review descriptive paragraphs in Unit 2.

divided into the northern desert areas, the south-eastern grasslands, and the tropical jungles to the southwest.

Paragraph 2: Northern Regions

The northern regions have the environment and living patterns of the desert. Egypt, Libya, Algeria, and Morocco have hot, dry climates with very little land suited to farming. Therefore, the population tends to be clustered into cities along rivers or the seacoast or into smaller settlements near oases. For thousands of years, people have lived in this vast region, subsisting partly on what crops and animals they could raise and partly on trade with Europe.

Paragraph 3: Southeastern Regions

The southeastern grasslands provide a better environment for animal life and for some kinds of crops. Many wild animals inhabit the plains in this region—elephants, giraffes, rhinoceros, antelopes, zebras, and lions. The people in this area have long been expert cattle raisers and hunters. Tea, coffee, cotton, cashew nuts, and tobacco are some of the main products grown in this region. Fishing also provides some food and income for people along the coast. The population here is less concentrated in cities and towns than in the north, but tends to be denser in areas where adequate rainfall and fertile soil make farming possible.

*Paragraph 4:
West Africa*

West Africa is the region closest to the Hollywood image of mysterious jungles. As in the other two regions, the way people subsist depends upon their environment. This does not mean that most of the people live in grass huts in the jungle. Such nations as Nigeria have become highly modernized by income from oil, timber, and minerals. Most of the western countries have some farming that provides food and income; sugar cane, coffee, and tobacco are the important cash crops, while bananas, rice, and corn are raised for food. Fishing in the rivers and along the coast also accounts for food and income, and precious stones, especially diamonds, enhance the economy of Angola and the Ivory Coast.

*Conclusion:
Restates Main
Idea*

Even a superficial look at the major regions of Africa shows that it is a varied continent with several environments. Although most of the continent is tropical in its range of temperature, the climate ranges from deserts to rain forests. Similarly, human life-styles vary from the simplest rural villages to industrial cities, both new and ancient. Contrary to the myth, however, jungle life makes up only a very small portion of the whole of Africa.

WRITING ASSIGNMENT I: Description*

Write a short essay describing one of the pictures on the following two pages. Divide your description into three parts: foreground, middle ground, and background; or left, middle, and right. Remember to brainstorm, noting as

*This is a good point at which to study the use of descriptive words such as adjectives and adverbs in Unit 5.

many details as you can before you actually write the essay. Try to use precise, vivid adjectives to describe what you see.

WRITING ASSIGNMENT I I: Description*

Write a short essay of about five paragraphs describing the town where you live or the college campus where you study. Remember that you must limit such a broad topic by focusing on one controlling idea about the place. (Notice how the essay on Africa concentrates on disproving the myth that Africa is merely a jungle.) Divide your description into two, three, or four body paragraphs, each one describing one section of the place you are writing about. Remember to practice what you have learned about introductory and concluding paragraphs.

---

*For examples of writing that describes a place, read Margaret Mead's "College: DePauw" and James Comer's "Medical School" in Unit 6.

*Portraying a Person**

Another important kind of descriptive essay is the portrait of a person. While resembling the one-paragraph description of a person that you have practiced, the essay portrait is longer and fuller. It will succeed best if you discuss several characteristics of the person, one in each body paragraph. The thesis statement should introduce these characteristics. A descriptive thesis statement might read, "Mary is one of the most sensible, ambitious, and resourceful members of the freshman class." One body paragraph would discuss how sensible she is, one would discuss how ambitious she is, and the final one would discuss how resourceful she is. Although the reader can follow your plan more easily if you name the subtopics in your thesis statement, it is not necessary to do so. You may sometimes prefer a simpler thesis statement such as "I admire Mary for three outstanding traits." Either way, be sure to have the two, three, or four subtopics in mind before you begin the body paragraphs. Also, remember to have a controlling central idea that all the subtopics will support, such as your admiration for the person in his or her successful pursuit of a career, or some such general concept. Notice how in the following sample essay the main idea, that Sam is a survivor, is supported by three subtopics—that he reacts quickly, that he is persistent, and that he has a sense

*For an example of writing that portrays a person, read Earl Shorris' essay, "Bienvenida," and Sherwood Anderson's "Discovery of a Father" in Unit 6.

of humor. To discover this arrangement of subtopics and to find supporting details for each one, the author developed the following cluster:

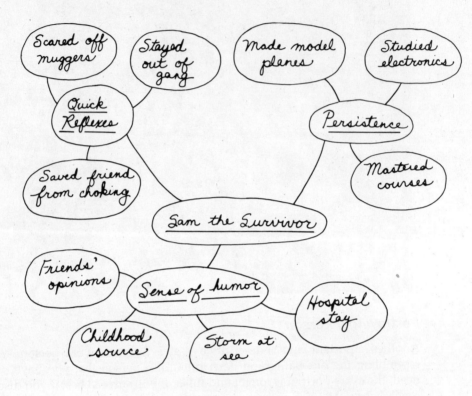

Sam the Survivor:
Sample Essay: Describing a Person

Introduction: States Main Idea and Three Supporting Points

Although many people admire personality, looks, or intelligence more, I think that the instinct for survival is one of the most valuable human traits. Having witnessed my cousin Sam pull through dangers, difficulties, and stresses, I have come to put a high value on the qualities that help people survive. I admire Sam particularly for his quick reflexes, his dogged persistence, and his sense of humor.

Paragraph 2: Discusses Sam's Quick Reflexes

Sam takes pride in being able to respond quickly in any crisis. Once as a teenager he escaped from two muggers by his quick thinking. When cornered on a dark side street by two young toughs with knives, he caught them off guard by leaping in the air, aiming a karate kick at them, and shouting as loudly as he could. This sudden action frightened them just long enough for him to make a getaway by dodging between parked cars. The same kind of quick thinking carried him through many situations later, such as talking his way out of a gang that was trying to force him to join them and sell drugs. Once he even saved a friend from choking to death in a restaurant by using the Heimlich maneuver.

Paragraph 3: Discusses Sam's Persistence

These exciting incidents are less important in the long run than his ability to keep going when others give up. Even though he is lazy about many ordinary tasks, when a goal matters to him he keeps working toward it with the endurance of a marathon runner. He trained himself in this ability years ago by constructing model airplanes and ships so intricate they would have driven most people to a nervous breakdown. From there he went on to absorb everything there was to know about electronics and computers. His professors in college were astonished at how thoroughly he mastered these subjects, while he was barely passing courses that did not interest him. He was never an outstanding student overall, but because of his determination to excel in electronics, he not only graduated but landed an excellent job.

Paragraph 4: Discusses Sam's Sense of Humor

In my opinion, Sam's most important strength as a survivor is his sense of humor, especially about himself. Whereas others tell jokes and laugh when they are relaxed, Sam's humor shines most brilliantly when he is under stress. Twice he has been close to death, and both times his humor kept him going. The first was an accident in which he was severely burned and had to spend two months in the hospital, where he entertained the other patients and even the staff with endless jokes and stories despite the pain he suffered. The other incident occurred aboard a fishing boat in the Gulf of Mexico. A tropical storm had driven the boat farther out from shore than it should have been, and the waves threatened to overturn it. Sam buoyed up the spirits of the other passengers, some of whom could not even swim, until a large steamer was able to reach them. Sam's friends could name dozens of smaller incidents where his humor, which hardly ever shows itself at parties or other social occasions, eased a stressful situation.

Those who know him best insist that this trait comes from his growing up in a poor family with an alcoholic father and learning to overcome troubles by means of humor.

Conclusion: Discusses Main Idea in New Words

Sam's three outstanding traits would not be evident to someone meeting him for the first time. He often strikes strangers as dull and ordinary, since he gives no impression of being particularly smart or entertaining. He is one of those precious individualists whom we eventually learn to value more than others born with more noticeable talents or good looks.

WRITING ASSIGNMENT I: Portraying a Person

Choose a person you have strong feelings about—someone you admire very much or someone you dislike strongly. This person may be someone close to you, such as a family member or friend you have known for a long time, or it may be a famous person. If you choose a celebrity, however, be sure you know a lot about the person, since you will have to back up whatever you say about him or her.

First do some focused writing beginning with the phrase: "I admire (or do not admire) _____ because. . . ." Continue writing nonstop about this person, trying to express all your feelings about him or her and your reasons for feeling that way. Next, make a list of ten qualities this person possesses. You will not discuss that many traits, but you should explore as many possibilities as you can. If you can't think of more than one or two traits you probably do not know this person well enough to write a good description. Start over with someone else.

Once you have a pretty good idea of your attitudes about the person and have a list of traits, do a cluster similar to the preceding one on Sam the Survivor. Then write an exploratory draft. Read it aloud to someone for feedback. Be sure you have a clear thesis: What is the overall point you wish to make about this person? Reorganize your draft if necessary for clear paragraph divisions. Write a final draft.

The Expository Mode: Discussing an Issue*

In English composition courses and in other college courses as well, you will have to write essays about social issues. These will allow you to make use of

*Review expository paragraphs in Unit 2.

what you know about writing "how" and "why" paragraphs. Such essays usually include several modes that you have practiced in your paragraph writing. Although chiefly expository, such essays may also contain narration, description, definition, comparison, and persuasion. You have been practicing these modes separately, but it is well to remember that in expository writing you will often combine several of them to support your points.

Expository essays on social issues may cover any number of topics, but they tend to fall into the following broad categories:

- Schools and education
- Crime and the justice system
- Children and child rearing
- Marriage, divorce, and living together without marriage
- The media and their effect on our lives
- Moral questions, for example, abortion, mercy killing
- Medical problems such as AIDS
- Alcoholism and drug abuse
- The economy
- Environmental issues (chemical and nuclear waste, air and water pollution)
- Conflicts between the older and younger generations
- College and professional sports
- Civil rights
- The women's movement
- Foreign policy
- Technological change and its effects

These are, of course, broad categories, not topics for essays. The topics you write about, whether you choose them or they are assigned to you, will be much more specific. You have been exposed to all of these general concerns through news broadcasts, editorials, television documentaries, magazine articles, books, and general conversation. In some advanced courses you will study such issues systematically and have to write about them using source material. For now, however, we are concerned with your ability to write intelligently about social issues using your knowledge from your own experience and your general knowledge as a concerned citizen.

A reasonably well-informed person should be able to write an effective essay on any one of the foregoing subjects without any specialized research. We are speaking here of the kind of article or letter to the editor that appears frequently in newspapers and magazines, not the heavily documented research paper that might appear in a scholarly magazine or be assigned in an advanced seminar. You do not need to be an expert to express an opinion and back it up with evidence. What you *do* need is a clear main point and the ability to organize your ideas effectively. How you organize depends on the kind of essay you are writing. There are several common patterns for explanatory essays; we will look at a few.

Essays Based on Examples* One of the simplest methods of developing and organizing expository essays is **multiple illustration,** or **enumeration.** This means supporting the main point in a series of examples that illustrate it. This method allows you to draw on your own experience or on the experience of people you know, or to furnish examples from your reading. Each example may be a small story or description of a situation that proves your main point. College examination questions often call on students to provide examples form their reading in the course to illustrate some thesis. In composition courses as well as popular magazines, lively personal essays may use multiple examples to discuss a social issue like single parenthood, computerized dating, forced retirement, or teenage runaways in an amusing or emotionally moving way.

Remember a few pointers when writing essays of this kind:

- Be sure that your examples all support the point—it is easy to get into an interesting story and lose the point you are making, ending up with a long piece of gossip.
- Think about the order of your examples, putting the most important, dramatic one last.
- Vary your examples—although they all support one *main* idea, the way they do it should differ in order to hold the reader's interest.
- Make connections between the examples by using transitional phrases like "another example," "a still more exciting case," "a third incident that illustrates the point," and so on.

Here is a short plan for an essay using multiple examples:

Main point: People sometimes achieve greatness by overcoming physical illnesses or handicaps.

Examples:

1. Demosthenes, the ancient Greek leader, became a great speaker by overcoming his speech handicap.
2. Theodore Roosevelt became a great military and political leader by overcoming his childhood asthma.
3. Helen Keller, though born deaf, mute, and blind, overcame these handicaps to become a great public figure.
4. Jim Abbott, although born with only one hand, became a pitcher for the California Angels and the New York Yankees.

E X E R C I S E: Multiple Examples

Write sentences about famous people whose lives make good examples of the main point.

Main point: Young celebrities such as rock stars, television actors, and athletes sometimes cannot handle sudden fame and destroy their careers through drug abuse, alcohol, or self-destructive behavior.

---

*For examples of writing that uses many examples to illustrate a point, read Howe and Strauss's "We Don't Even Have a Name" and Nash's "The Student Movement" in Unit 6.

Examples:

1. _____

2. _____

3. _____

4. _____

Problem/Solution Essays

Essays in which you propose solutions to problems involve careful thinking and require clear, organized writing. Such essays may propose solutions to personal problems, problems on the job, or large social or political problems. Writing successful essays of this kind requires critical thinking as part of your prewriting and composing process. While planning a problem/solution essay, be sure you have explored the whole range of the topic before writing. Ask yourself questions like these:

1. What kind of problem am I trying to solve? Is this an ethical, psychological, economic, social, or political problem?
2. Why does this problem have to be solved? What will happen if it is not?
3. What are all of the possible ways of trying to solve this problem?
4. Which solution do I think is the best?
5. Why will the other ones not be as effective?
6. Why will mine prove the most successful?

Here is a sample problem for you to analyze. First read the statement of the problem and offer your solution. Then read the analysis afterward and the model student essay. Which elements of the problem did you overlook when you first reacted to the problem? What possible solutions did not occur to you? Did you think of any not mentioned?

Statement of Problem: Andrea has been working for a year and a half in a clothing store. She has been happy with her working conditions, her co-workers, and her salary. About a month ago, however, she began to realize that the store's owner has been engaged in a major fraud: he buys cheap imitations of name brand dresses, jeans, shirts, and sweaters with false labels and sells them for genuine name brands at a huge mark-up. What should Andrea do?

Critical Thinking Analysis:

1. What kind of problem is this?
   This is mainly an ethical problem because Andrea knows that she is working for a partly criminal operation. There are possible economic and psychological implications for Andrea as well.

2. Why must this problem be solved?
    Andrea's conscience will not let her ignore this scam. Equally impor-
    tant, she is working her way through law school and wants to be-
    come a criminal attorney, so she doesn't want to be part of an illegal
    operation or have such a fact on her record.
3. What are the alternatives?
    There are many possibilities, some of which Andrea would not con-
    sider. She can ignore the problem and hope it won't be discovered.
    She can ignore the problem and quit her job, hoping to get another
    good one. She can quit her job and report the fraud to the police or
    the Better Business Bureau. She can keep her job and report the
    fraud, either anonymously or as a whistle-blower. She can confront
    her boss, either to demand that he stop or to blackmail him for more
    money. She can ask her co-workers for advice, or she can consult her
    friends, family, or religious counselor.
4. Which solution is the best?
    Your answer to this question depends partly upon your own values,
    priorities, and personality.

Read the sample essay below which expresses one student's opinion of
the best solution to Andrea's problem. Do you agree or disagree?

Speaking Up for What You Believe

Introduction:
Stresses
Importance of
the Topic

My friend Andrea taught me a lesson about having the courage to stand up and tell the truth no matter what. Most people would not have the nerve to do what she did, and when she told me about it, at first I thought she was crazy. After thinking about it, however, I decided that she did the right thing. She is a good role model that other people should imitate.

Paragraph 2:
Gives
Background

Andrea worked in a clothing store in her neigh-borhood until last year. She liked her job because she was getting a good salary and she liked the other salespeople. She was getting so good at rec-ommending the right sizes, styles, and colors to customers that they always came back to her for ad-vice. She earned two raises in a year and a half and was helping to pay her way through law school.

Paragraphs 3
and 4: Present
Problem

One day last March she was shocked to dis-cover that the owner of her store was a crook. While some name brand items were being deliv-ered, she admired some of them, and one of the delivery men laughed and told her confidentially that they were all cheap imitations. At first Andrea didn't believe him, but when she looked at them closely and saw the low prices the owner was paying, not to mention the huge mark-up he was getting, she realized it had to be true.

Right then she panicked because she didn't know what to do. She didn't want to be part of a big scam because she always tried to be honest, and she resented the owner for getting so much money by cheating customers. She was afraid that if she said anything he might take revenge against her, but if she didn't do anything, somebody might report the fraud and she could get caught up in the crime. As a future lawyer, she didn't want anything illegal or even suspicious on her record.

Paragraph 5: Considers Alternatives

She thought over some of her alternatives. She felt like quitting her job, but she needed the income. She wanted to confront the boss immediately, but she was sure he would fire her and make up a phony reason that would hurt her chances for getting other jobs. She thought of becoming a whistle-blower by taking the story to the local television station, but then she was afraid no other employers would want to hire her because she would look like a troublemaker.

She finally decided to talk to all the other salesworkers during their lunch hour and convince them that they should all go with her to the boss and demand that he stop cheating customers. Some of the other workers didn't want to do anything about it and got angry when she kept insisting that they join her. But finally she convinced them that if they didn't do anything, somebody would eventually find out and report the fraud, at which point the store would be closed down and they would all lose their jobs, maybe even be arrested.

Paragraphs 6 and 7: Explain Solution

So they all met with the boss and made their demands. At first he denied that he was doing anything illegal; then he tried to laugh it off, saying that everyone else was doing the same thing. Then he got angry because they wouldn't back down, and he told them that they were getting good salaries from the same money and had no right to complain. They still wouldn't let him have his way, so, to their surprise, he shrugged and said okay, he would stop doing it, but they would have to take a ten percent salary cut because he couldn't afford to keep paying them what they were making when he started losing some of his profits.

Conclusion: Reaffirms Rightness of Solution

So, the problem was solved, in a way. Some of the other workers were very angry with Andrea for a while because they had to take a pay cut, but a few others backed her up and praised her for standing up for what she believed in. A year later she got a better job as a clerk in a law firm. I still wonder where she got the nerve to stick her neck out. I told her she has a lot of courage and will make a good criminal lawyer.

E X E R C I S E: Thinking Critically About Problem Solving

Choose one of the problems below and write answers to the critical thinking questions on p. 113–114. Then write an essay explaining the problem and proposing the best solution to the problem.

a. Frank is looking out his apartment window one evening when he sees two men attacking an elderly woman across the street. Frank is an able-bodied young man; he does not have a gun. What should he do?

b. Audrey picks up her paycheck one Friday and notices that the amount is much too large—about twice as much as she is supposed to be getting. Her firm is very large and has hundreds of employees, so the error might not be noticed, if it is an error. What should Audrey do?

c. While John is working on his term paper for sociology, he overhears a friend, who is on the baseball team with him, bragging that he paid someone to write his term paper for him. John knows that his friend needs a very high grade in sociology to remain eligible for baseball and keep his scholarship. What should John do?

Solutions to Social Problems* Essays about social problems require a larger perspective than ones about personal problems. As a student you will certainly be asked at some time to write an essay proposing a solution to one of the many problems our society has. Assignments like this may be given not only in English courses but in the social sciences such as psychology or sociology. In such essays, you are expected to use critical thinking and display an understanding of the methods of analysis used in the social sciences. You may be expected as well to show knowledge of the facts related to the problem and even have to do research for the assignment.

The content of such essays may be more demanding than that of a more personal essay, but the writing process involved is similar. Again, you should do some prewriting activity, particularly asking yourself questions about the

---

*For an example of problem/solution writing, read Henry Louis Gates, Jr.'s "Delusions of Grandeur" in Unit 6.

problem and its possible solutions. Problem/solution essays of this kind often can be organized into three main parts:

1. Establishing the need for a solution
2. Considering various proposals
3. Stating and defending the best proposal

Leaving out any of these parts will inevitably weaken your essay.

An outline for a problem/solution essay might look like this:

I. Introductory paragraph stressing the urgency of the problem and indicating the kind of solution you will propose
II. Body paragraphs
    A. Paragraph explaining the need at length and possibly analyzing how the problem arose
    B. Paragraph discussing other proposed solutions and showing why they will not work
    C. Paragraph (or two) explaining your solution in detail and showing why it will work
III. Concluding paragraph reemphasizing the need for change and stressing the effectiveness of your solution, possibly warning what will happen if your proposal is not implemented

This, of course, is just one possible way to organize such an essay. Any outline should be the result of plenty of brainstorming about the subject. Do not try to set up an outline for your essay without first exploring the range of your knowledge and opinions on the problem you will discuss.

Read the following sample essay, noticing how the writer follows the above outline:

Hope for the Homeless

Introduction: Dramatizes Problem

Homeless people differ in many ways. Some are drug addicts or alcoholics; some are victims of personal catastrophes. Many are mentally ill. Nearly all are unemployed and some seem unemployable. Some are handicapped. A large number are literally homeless in that they have been evicted from their previous home and cannot find affordable shelter. For such a diverse group of people with such severe and differing problems, no one source of aid would seem to be enough. One attribute the group shares, however, is lack of hope. The only solution that will make a permanent difference is one that gives homeless people the hope that they can find a better life than that of sleeping in subway stations and panhandling on the streets.

Paragraph 2: Explains Need For New Approach

In most cities, efforts to aid the homeless have not reduced the numbers significantly. Shelters have been established in most large cities and many smaller communities, but people living in them remain as homeless as ever. Many of the shelters even add to the problem, by becoming centers for drug trafficking; homeless people may fear the crime and violence in the shelters. Attempts to round up, house, and care for homeless people who appear to be mentally ill have sometimes been foiled by civil libertarians who support the "rights" of the homeless to live in the streets and behave as they choose. Putting people in welfare hotels has proved an expensive disaster—local governments end up paying exorbitant rents to house families in dangerous and barely livable conditions. As a result of current policies, the homeless population seems to keep expanding, and their living conditions keep getting worse.

Paragraph 3: Discusses Other Proposals

Other solutions have been proposed. People often point to abandoned buildings in the inner cities and say they should be renovated to provide housing for the homeless. Certainly shelter is part of the problem, and any cities that can afford to renovate abandoned buildings that they own should do so. But many homeless people are also without hope. If they are just assigned apartments, their personal problems of joblessness, alcoholism, drug addiction, or mental illness remain. Some may go back to living in the streets, even when given a place to live. People need identities and self-confidence, not just four walls around them. Job-training programs also sound good, and should be available. But many of the homeless need much more than job training. In fact, some once had good jobs, and a few were even highly trained professionals. Any effective improvement in their lives can come only if they acquire real hope—not fanciful promises, but the realistic inner confidence that their lives are going somewhere.

Paragraph 4: Discusses Writer's Proposal

If we put ourselves in the position of the homeless, we can better understand what it will take to solve their myriad problems. To regain confidence about your life when you have reached the bottom, you need plenty of human contact. You need to know that somebody cares and is going to keep on caring. You also need to know that the fight for a better life is worth the effort—that there is a real possibility of a well-paid job, a decent home, and a safe social environment. To provide people with hope means to provide all of this— and no program for helping the homeless has yet gone this far. There must be much more help by social workers and psychologists, and treatment centers for alcohol abuse and drug abuse, to begin with. Nothing can be accomplished without this first step. Then there must be decent temporary housing that does not herd people together like animals. Finally, there must be job counseling, training, and placement, along with follow-up services so that those who get back on their feet do not give up at the first sign of difficulty.

Conclusion: Reemphasizes Urgency of Problem

Like anything, hope costs money. It is useless to pretend that we can even touch the problem of homelessness without spending more on housing, counseling services, and employment assistance than has been spent so far. Emergencies of this size demand emergency relief. The federal and state governments should treat the problem of homelessness the way they treat emergencies like floods, earthquakes, and droughts, and spend the money where it is needed. The cost will be high, but not as high as the cost of ignoring the problem. When we face hopelessness all around us—huddled in doorways, lying in train stations, reaching out for coins in the streets—we pay a price in the loss of hope for our own lives and our society.

WRITING ASSIGNMENT: Problem/Solution Essays

Identify a problem at your college, such as racism on campus, the rising cost of tuition, fraternity hazing, cheating on exams and term papers, snobbishness between different groups of students, a high dropout rate, problems with registration and financial aid, problems with course selection and curriculum, or problems with extracurricular activities or the athletic program. Discuss this problem with friends to explore the range of opinions about it. Do two pages of focused writing expressing your thoughts about the problem—what is causing it, who is responsible, and what should be done about it.

Once you have explored your thoughts, brainstorm the separate aspects of the problem. First, list everything you can about the problem itself—its causes, why it has to be dealt with, whom it affects, whether it is getting worse, and so on. Then list all the possible solutions, including any suggested by friends. Finally, identify the one solution that seems most likely to work, and write down everything you can about it.

At this point you should have the basis for a working draft of a problem/solution essay. Make a rough outline of your paragraph plan before you begin. You may not follow this outline exactly, because new ideas may come as you compose (always be open to new ideas even if they force you to reconsider your outline). Write your exploratory draft using the outline as a general guide only. Put the essay aside for a day or two; then look at it again. Read it aloud to friends for their feedback. If they disagree, use their disagreement as an opportunity to dig deeper into the subject, either to strengthen your point with better evidence or to modify your point. Revise your organization if revision is needed. Write a final draft.

Essays Based on Autobiographical Example*   Another method of developing an expository essay is by means of your own experience. An autobiography is a story you write about your own life. Development by autobiographical example means using experiences from your own life to support a point. If you have ever been the victim of discrimination because of race, sex, or religion, you could use the experience to illustrate how prejudice manifests itself in our society. If you have had experience with the courts, you could use it to discuss the legal system. Many topics are suited to this method. Adoption, divorce, immigration, upward mobility, hospital care, problems in the schools, and issues regarding jobs and unemployment can all be discussed effectively by means of autobiographical examples. Of course, you have to have enough experience to discuss the issue effectively. Everyone, for instance, has plenty of experience with the schools, but not everyone can use personal experience to discuss adoption or immigration.

Such essays can be vivid and forceful, sometimes humorous. However, it is easy to get off the track and forget that your main purpose is to discuss only one issue. *Be sure to state your main point early in the essay, and use topic sentences to focus your paragraphs on supporting points.*

Read the following essay, noticing how the writer states a clear main idea and develops it in separate paragraphs using facts from her own experience.

Working While Attending College
Sample Essay 1: Autobiographical Example

Introduction: With the cost of college nowadays, you almost
Arouses Interest   have to be rich to finish a degree without working
and States Thesis   at least part of the time. When I came to New York

---

*Review verb tenses in Unit 5. For examples of persuasive writing using autobiographical example, read Richard Rodriguez's essay, "Bilingual Education," in Unit 6.

City from Guyana, South America, I thought it would be easy to get a nursing degree and pursue the career of my choice. It turned out to be much harder than I expected, working full-time and taking classes at night. A two-year nursing degree is taking much more than two years, but I have discovered that you can turn the problem of working full-time while attending college into a big opportunity to improve your life.

Thesis Statement

First of all, you have to learn how to live with a double schedule. When I first came to this country, I got a full-time job in a bank, thinking that I would work only part-time when I began my studies. Instead, I quickly realized I could not afford to pay my rent and other expenses without working full-time. This meant I would have to maintain a forty-hour or more work week and fit my courses in whenever I could. Luckily, the community college I wanted to attend had just opened an evening nursing program that allowed me to take courses in the evenings and on weekends. On paper, this looked like a good schedule, but I was shocked to learn that I had no time for social activities or shopping, and very little for homework. The first semester I slept only five hours a night and became so tired that I thought I wouldn't make it. To make matters worse, I suffered stomach pains just before midterm exams and was afraid I would end up in the hospital. Fortunately, it was just heartburn, and I was able to take some medication and not have to drop out of college. By the end of the first term, I was sure that with enough determination I would reach my goal.

Paragraph 2:
Overcoming
Personal
Difficulties

A working student also has to overcome academic difficulties and make sensible choices. I didn't expect problems with my courses because I had always been good in school. Since English was the main language in my schools at home, I was able to pass proficiency tests in reading and writing, and I knew I would do all right in speech and writing courses. Math was never my strong point, however, and I found out that I would have to take a remedial math course before enrolling in the math course for nursing students. I also discovered that since I had not taken chemistry in high

Paragraph 3:
Overcoming
Academic
Obstacles

school, I would have to complete a college chemistry course before beginning the science courses like anatomy and physiology in the nursing sequence. Most working students also find out as I did that since they have very little time for homework, they have to reduce their course loads. The nursing degree that I had planned to complete in four semesters was obviously going to take four, maybe five or six years. But I was determined.

Paragraph 4: The Advantages of Being a Working Student

Here I am in my third year, not as far along as I had hoped. But I have discovered that many of my classmates also work full-time, and we see many advantages to being a working student. We are more mature and self-disciplined because we carry our work habits over to our studies. We concentrate harder than some of the younger, nonworking students, and teachers seem to show us more respect, partly because we are used to being serious and punctual and getting work done. We also have more life experiences to relate to our courses in sociology, literature, and psychology. Instead of cramming knowledge into our heads in a few overloaded semesters in an ivory tower situation, we continually relate what we study to our lives and work. By taking longer to earn degrees, we have time to assimilate what we learn and develop our awareness from one semester to the next. While it's true that we don't have much time for socializing or extracurricular activities, we do learn to make friends quickly in classroom situations and make the most of our social opportunities between classes.

Conclusion: Reasserts Main Idea and Looks to the Future

Most of us working students probably wouldn't have chosen to work full-time while attending college, but we didn't have that choice. Still, many of us have been able to turn a disadvantage into a big opportunity. When I finish my studies next year, I will enter the career of my choice better prepared to work in it than I could have been any other way. I have learned to use my time efficiently. Having balanced work and study, I will be able to balance work and child care when I have a family. I have acquired the attitude of lifelong learning instead of the get-it-over-with attitude of some nonworking students. Working full-time while going to college can make you a better learner, a better worker, and a better person.

WRITING ASSIGNMENT: Autobiographical Example

Basing your choice on your own experience, select one of the following topics for an essay using autobiographical example to support the main idea.

1. Discrimination in our society is still present.
2. Women still have to do most of the work around the house.
3. Military service changes people's lives.
4. The schools are not what they should be.
5. Hospitals are not as safe and efficient as we think.
6. Becoming a father (mother) changes your life.

Since this essay will be chiefly in narrative form, start with a focused writing exercise in which you tell everything that comes to mind about your experiences with this subject (hospitals, schools, parenthood, and so on). Once you have as much material as you can gather, think about what you want to say. What have you learned from your experience? Be as specific as you can. To say that the schools are bad, for instance, is an overgeneralization. In what way are they bad? Is your experience typical?

Once you have a thesis statement, write an exploratory draft. Try to stay on the point throughout the draft, and divide your experience or experiences into clearly identifiable phases or events. Put this draft away for a day or two. Then read it aloud to someone else to see if that person responds with similar experiences from his or her life. If that person disagrees with your point, perhaps you need to sharpen the point or modify it. If you have a strong point, you will probably get an "I know what you mean" response. Using feedback from your listener and your own critical eye, revise your draft as needed to make the main point clear and the paragraphs distinct and unified. Write a final draft.

The Persuasive Mode: Enumerating Reasons*

One reliable pattern of organization for argumentative essays is the series of reasons. You express your main idea in the thesis statement, then give three or four reasons why you hold that opinion. One reason should be discussed in each body paragraph. This method produces an extremely clear arrangement, but it is not necessarily simple. You may want to support each reason in a different way—a small story for one, facts for another, analysis of cause and effect for a third. The overall plan, in other words, is simple, but there is plenty of room for variety in the ways you develop the parts. As a result, you will need to be careful about making smooth transitions between body paragraphs and seeing to it that all three or four reasons really do support your thesis. A final concern is the sequence of reasons: which comes first? second? last? Usually, the most convincing reason should come last, in the most emphatic position.

---

*At this point you may want to review the discussion of persuasive writing in Unit 2. For an example of an essay enumerating reasons, read Nash's "The Student Movement" in Unit 6.

The following sample essay gives three reasons to back up the opinion expressed in the thesis statement. Can you explain the method used to develop each body paragraph?

Working Mothers
Sample Essay: Enumerating Reasons

Introduction:
Arouses Interest
and States
Main Thesis

A generation ago, any woman who went out to work and left her children with a babysitter felt guilty unless she had no other source of income. Attitudes have changed: now a large percentage of mothers with small children hold jobs, many of them full-time. Although there are problems involved in being a mother and career woman at the same time, I believe there are three good reasons why mothers who want to go out and work should do it.

Paragraph 2:
Discusses First
Reason by
Process Analysis

First, working outside the home is good for the mother herself. Motherhood is an exciting experience, but the endless hours of minding infants and small children can lead to depression. The mother needs another dimension to her life in order not to feel trapped in her home and buried under tons of baby food, diapers, and laundry. Furthermore, if she began a career before her children were born, an interruption of several years—which often stretches into many years—will set her progress back at a crucial time. In later years she will feel frustrated and insignificant when she tries unsuccessfully to regain the momentum she had at the beginning of her career. As the frustration builds, she may unconsciously blame her children or her husband for the lack of fulfillment in her life. If she continues to grow in her career, she will maintain a more positive attitude toward both herself and her family.

Paragraph 3:
Discusses
Second Reason
by Example

Another reason why she should continue working is that it can be good for her children. Of course, she must coordinate her work and her time with the children in the right way. My friend Anne, for example, has shown me how successful a working woman can be as a mother. Anne was a full-time nurse before she had children, and she continued her career after a son and daughter were born, two years apart. Her first step after the birth of the first child was to find a first-rate babysitter to look after the baby during the day.

She also worked out a schedule with her husband, who was a security guard during the afternoon and evening, so that he could watch the baby during part of the morning. Then she figured out many ways to keep up a close relationship with her children, calling them from work during the day, and planning evening and weekend activities that made the quality of the time spent with them very high. Her children are now seven and nine years old and appear to be healthy, well adjusted, and well behaved.

Paragraph 4: Discusses Third Reason by Use of Definition

Finally, it is good for society if women know that motherhood will not close off their options or force them to accept inferior status. A truly democratic society might be defined as one in which every person is able to achieve as much as his or her talents allow. The women's movement has done much to open doors that once were closed to women, thus creating a more democratic society. Women in a sense won participation in our political democracy when they won the constitutional right to vote in 1920, but social democracy is an ideal that includes more than the right to vote. It encompasses equal opportunities in careers, equal legal rights, and equal moral obligations. Giving women the opportunity to choose motherhood and a career without jeopardizing either is certainly a big step toward full democracy.

Conclusion: Summarizes Main Argument

For the good of the mothers themselves, their children, and society, women with small children should be encouraged to work outside the home. Current trends have been in the direction of more working mothers, and the change is mostly for the better. While we may have to give up some of the simpler, settled family styles of our grandparents' day, we should enjoy the advantages that go along with the change.

The Persuasive Mode: The Dialogue Pattern*

Still another effective method of developing an opinion on a social issue is the dialogue pattern. You will often see this method in editorials. The writer will state an opinion held by some person or group that he or she disagrees with;

---

*For an example of writing that follows the dialogue pattern, read Alex Thio's "How Education Raises Our Income" in Unit 6.

then the writer will use the rest of the editorial to reply to that opinion. The result is either a long answer to one opinion or a pro-and-con discussion in which the writer takes up several opinions of the opposition and answers them one by one.

This method is especially effective for the most controversial issues, ones that demand open-mindedness and fairness. By taking up the arguments of the other side, the writer demonstrates reasonableness and a grasp of the issue. To write this kind of essay well, you must be able to answer the best objections from the other side. It is tempting to use the "straw man" technique of mentioning only opinions that you can easily knock over, while ignoring really convincing ones.

Organizing an essay of this kind is not difficult if you include three or four opinions held by the other side. Include one in each body paragraph and refute each one effectively. The pattern is much like the series-of-reasons method: arrange the body paragraphs so that the arguments build up from the least to the most important. Each paragraph can be developed in its own way. When you answer one objection from the other side, you may find a personal example to be your best means of support; when you answer the next, you may use logical analysis, and so on.

WRITING ASSIGNMENT I: The Dialogue Pattern

Find a magazine or newspaper article, preferably an editorial, that expresses a strong opinion you disagree with. List the main point of the article and the supporting reasons. Across from these write your own opposing opinions on each point. Add to your list any further points you can think of on *your* side. If you have difficulty thinking of sufficient reasons to support your opinion, try a nonstop writing exercise to explore your thoughts on the subject.

Once you have sufficient ideas, write a first draft of an essay using the dialogue method. Begin with an introduction identifying the writer and article you are opposing, as well as its main point. State your opposing point. Base the body of your essay on a series of rebuttals to the main arguments given in the article. Add any important points on your side not considered in the article, and write an effective conclusion. As always, read your rough draft aloud to someone else, preferably a small group of other students, to get as much feedback as you can. Use the feedback to strengthen arguments that need more support and to better explain arguments that are unclear. Do not be afraid to modify your arguments if they contain errors—the point of dialogue, after all, is to seek the truth. Reread your first draft to be sure you have represented your opponent's opinion correctly and organized your material effectively, saving your strongest argument for the last. Write a final draft.

WRITING ASSIGNMENT II: The Dialogue Pattern

Each of these exercises contains a main thesis and some supporting points. Across from each point, write in arguments on the opposite side. After completing the exercise, choose *one* of them as the basis for an essay, following the same writing stages as in Writing Assignment I. You may take either side of the question.

1. Thesis Statement: Drugs should be legalized in the United States.

    Opposing Thesis Statement: Legalizing drugs would make the drug problem worse in the United States.

Supporting Points:

Opposing Points:

A. Legalizing drugs would reduce drug-related crimes and violence.

A. _____

_____

_____

B. We can't stop drug traffic—it is too widespread.

B. _____

_____

_____

C. People have a right to make their own choices, even harmful ones.

C. _____

_____

_____

D. Legalizing drugs would make drug use less exciting; there would be less addiction.

D. _____

_____

_____

E. We tried making alcohol illegal in the 1920s; that did not work, and keeping drugs illegal does not work either.

E. _____

_____

_____

F. The government would collect taxes on the legal sales of drugs.

F. _____

_____

2. Thesis Statement: Women should
    not serve in the military.

    Opposing Thesis Statement: Women
    improve the military significantly.

Supporting Points:

Opposing Points:

A. Women are not as strong as men
    in combat and other military work.

A. _____

    _____

    _____

B. Women are needed at home during
    wartime.

B. _____

    _____

    _____

C. Women would be more emotional
    in war situations.

C. _____

    _____

    _____

D. Women might get pregnant and
    drop out.

D. _____

    _____

    _____

E. Having women around would
    distract men from their duties.

E. _____

    _____

    _____

3. Thesis Statement: Pornographic
    videos, magazines, and telephone
    services are harmless forms of
    entertainment and should be
    permitted.

    Opposing Thesis Statement:
    Pornography promotes violence
    and harms society by degrading
    both sex and women.

Supporting Points:

Opposing Points:

A. People have a right to whatever forms of entertainment they choose.

A. _____

_____

_____

B. Pornography has not been proven to be harmful.

B. _____

_____

_____

C. Many serious films, books, and works of art are "pornographic."

C. _____

_____

_____

D. Denial and ignorance of sexuality does more harm than pornography, which helps educate people.

D. _____

_____

_____

4. Thesis Statement: Young people should not have sex before marriage.

Opposing Thesis Statement: Sexual experience before marriage is morally and socially acceptable today.

Supporting Points:

Opposing Points:

A. The only safe sex today is celibacy before marriage.

A. _____

_____

_____

B. Sex is right only with the person you want to spend your life with.

B. _____

_____

_____

C. The purpose of sex is to bear children, which should happen in marriage.

C. _____

_____

_____

D. Sex before marriage is often psychologically harmful, especially for young teenagers.

D. _____

_____

_____

E. Premarital sex tends to make marriages fail.

E. _____

_____

_____

Ten Current Topics for Additional Practice in Persuasive Writing

1. Should there be mandatory drug testing on all jobs?
2. Should people who have AIDS or are HIV positive be guaranteed the right to keep their jobs and not be turned down for new jobs?
3. Should high schools distribute condoms free to students?
4. Should smoking be banned in all public places?
5. Should surrogate motherhood be allowed by legal contract?
6. Should a teenager who gets pregnant have an abortion, keep her child, or put it up for adoption?
7. Should college athletes be paid salaries?
8. Should teenagers who commit serious crimes be tried and sentenced as adults?
9. Should colleges offer a three-year bachelor's degree to cut costs?
10. Should homosexual people be allowed to get married?

COMPUTERS AND ESSAY WRITING

In this book you have been encouraged to focus on the writing process, that is, to think of an essay as the result of many stages of development. When you write by hand or on a typewriter, this means you produce many *drafts*, each one better developed, organized, and written than the last. Every time you wrote something about the topic, whether you were doing focused writing, clustering, a rough draft, or a final draft, you left separate sheets of paper that could be looked at and compared with one another.

Writing on a computer is different. It is possible to do all your prewriting on the screen and all your composing on one document that you can keep revising, rearranging, and correcting as many times as you want. You can, if you wish, wait to print it out only when you have the final document exactly as you want it. This means that you no longer have separate drafts to compare in discussion with your tutor, teacher, or classmates. If your writing class meets in a room equipped with computers, you may have limited access to a printer; therefore, you may tend to avoid printing out your document until the point at which you do not want to revise it any more.

The trouble with that approach is that you will be closing yourself off from much important input from classmates and other readers, and possibly from your teacher. The teacher or tutor will probably confer with you as you work, giving advice over your shoulder and asking questions about words, phrases, or sentences in your essay. Discussing the whole essay with a small group, however, will be possible only if you print out a draft that you expect to revise and reorganize considerably. The physical arrangements of computers tend to encourage writers to mind their own business, unless they are working on a network that allows the students and the teacher to communicate with one another electronically. Even if you have this advantage, you may want to write a rough draft longhand or print out your first draft and, in either case, read your first draft aloud to a small group of classmates. The act of collaborative reading, listening, and responding is just as important if you write on a computer as if you write longhand or on a typewriter. No machine can take the place of human interaction in the writing process. Developing a voice in your writing and making your words arouse laughter, curiosity, anger, or enthusiasm is as difficult without peer feedback as it would be for a standup comedian to predict which jokes will work and which will fall flat without trying them on a live audience.

The computer can be a miraculous tool for helping you produce a perfect finished document, but don't expect it to do the creative work for you. Use it to the maximum for those aspects of your work where you find it helpful—the spelling check, the capacity for changing words or phrases, or the larger capacity for rearranging large chunks of text. When you find that it seems to get in your way—if, for instance, you simply *must* write your first draft longhand—remember that the computer is a tool, not an end in itself.

As an exercise in developing your relationship with the computer, try this comparison: Do one essay assignment entirely without using the computer; use longhand or a typewriter for the whole process from prewriting activities to final draft. Then do a similar assignment entirely on the computer, from prewriting activities through the final revised and proofread document. Ask yourself these questions:

1. When I did the assignment without the computer, at what points did I find myself frustrated and impatient, writing too cautiously for fear of making a mistake and having to redo a whole page or make messy corrections?
2. When I did the whole process on the computer, at what points did I feel out of touch with my own writing because the machine felt impersonal? Was there any point at which I wanted to tear out a sheet of lined paper and begin writing?

For you and all writers in today's world of electronic communications, the important question is, what combination of speaking, handwriting, composing on the computer screen, and working with printouts will allow you to produce your best essays?

Only you can discover the answer.

4

REVISING AND IMPROVING YOUR WRITING

You have now learned and practiced prewriting skills and have practiced writing paragraphs.

You have also composed short essays and have done minor revising. So far you have worked on

the plan, content, and organization of your work. Now we will turn to techniques for improving

the effectiveness of your language, especially your choice of words and your sentence patterns. To

write vividly and forcefully you must be able to turn monotonous, flat prose into writing that

catches and holds the reader's interest. This means taking what you thought was already a "final

draft" and making it still better.

FIRST AND SECOND DRAFTS

In the previous units you have learned to work with a topic through several phases of the writing process. Moving from prewriting to formal composition, you have written paragraphs and essays and have revised many of their features. In this unit you will concentrate on improving completed first drafts, one of the most difficult but crucial stages of the writing process.

Revising means more than making a neater copy in more legible handwriting. Neatness is not the goal; revision should be messy. You may go through several very messy drafts before you arrive at exactly what you want. Real revision means re–vision, or re–seeing—taking another look. Use the feedback from your listeners to guide you, just as you used it in prewriting to explore the topic. Now, however, think about cutting, adding, rephrasing, and polishing.

Write the best first draft that you can. Then assume that it is not good enough and make it better. Effective revision requires cutting for greater force and conciseness as well as adding details to develop your topic. If you want to write 500 words, aim for 700 and cut out the deadwood. Remember that *the difference between mediocre writing and superior writing usually lies in revision.* Treat your first draft as a rough, loose working model of the essay you want, and keep revising to bring it to perfection.

Here is an example of a reasonably good first draft that needs alterations to bring it to life. Where does it leave out facts? Where is it too vague? Where is the language not vivid enough?

First draft:

> *Moving out of my parents' house was a big problem. I had to find a place to live, look for a job, and take charge of my daily responsibilities. I never realized until then how much my parents had provided for me. Then I got a car since I couldn't use the family car anymore and I soon discovered how many expenses owning a car involves. Getting myself moved, which meant packing the stuff that I owned, was a huge mess. But once I was settled in my new life-style I was glad I decided to move.*

Revised draft:

> *Moving out of my parents' house was a big ordeal, but it helped me mature. I took on many new responsibilities. For instance, I found my own apartment in Queens, and I packed my clothes, books, and stereo equipment into a U-Haul van and transported all of it to my new residence. My next step was to apply for a job. I interviewed for a position as a security guard at a department store and began working the night shift. I also learned how to cook hamburgers, spaghetti, and steak for myself, and I took care of my own laundry. Since I could no longer use the family car, I bought a 1991 Plymouth Sundance and was suddenly shocked to find how much extra auto expenses are: $600 a year for insurance, $80 a month for parking, and $30 a week for gas. All of these adult responsibilities made me realize how much I had taken my parents for granted and how much they had pro-*

vided for me. Once I had made all these adjustments and was settled into my new life–style, I was proud of my adult responsibilities and glad I had made a mature decision. And of course my parents breathed a big sigh of relief!

What are the main differences between the first draft and the revised version? What makes the revision better than the first draft? What makes the revised version longer than the first? What could the writer do to improve the revised version?

Read the following draft. This short essay is on a subject the writer had been reading about and thus knew something about. It is much more developed than the first draft you just read; however, it too can be improved a great deal by revision.

Sample first draft:

Silicon Valley

Silicon Valley is an important place in modern America. Lots of companies have started there. Some of them began very small and became huge in a few years. Most of these companies make computers or things related to computers. Silicon Valley is in California, located between Palo Alto and San Jose. It got its name from the material silicon, which is used in making computer chips.

For the last twenty or thirty years, companies have been started there. Some of them became big and successful; and some of them didn't. This makes the place exciting to think about. California has always been the place for people with big dreams and ambitions. Nowadays, Hollywood isn't the place for such people the way it used to be. Now people with big ideas dream about starting a company in Silicon Valley and watching it grow into an enormous corporation.

Computers are important in our lives. This makes Silicon Valley important as a new capital of technology. The Japanese are also making computers. Silicon Valley is the place where the United States competes with the Japanese companies.

Now Silicon Valley is getting very crowded. So many companies have started there that there is not much room for new ones. Other places may begin to have a lot of computer companies being built there. If that happens, Silicon Valley may become just one of many high-technology areas. Or maybe it will be where the headquarters of these companies stay, while a lot of their other business is done somewhere else.

The writer of this essay has done a good job in many ways. She has found out a lot about her subject and has expressed some thought-provoking ideas about it. She has given the reader factual information and stayed on the general topic. Her sentences are clear and easy to read, and her vocabulary is college level, even including such phrases as "high technology."

Why is this not a first-rate finished essay? If this writer asked for readers' feedback on the essay, she would find that quite a few ideas are not developed with specific examples and that her organization is not very clear. Readers might tell her as well that her sentences tend to be rather short and choppy and that she repeats some words (especially Silicon Valley) and phrases too often. To make the essay better, she would have to revise her phrasing and organization, as well as dig up some interesting examples to support her important ideas.

Revised version:

Silicon Valley Fever

Between Palo Alto and San Jose, California, lies the high-technology capital of the world. In Silicon Valley, named after the material used in making computer chips, thousands of companies that design and manufacture computers, video games, software, and electronics equipment have sprung up. Giants like Apple Computer, Atari, Hewlett-Packard, and Intel have their main operations there.

From the Gold Rush of 1849 through the golden years of Hollywood, California has always lured dreamers to the West Coast with promises of wealth and success. So it is that in the last thirty years, Silicon Valley has held out the promise of fantastic success to young business people. Some have watched their small companies with a handful of employees mushroom in three or four years into corporations with annual sales above $100 million. Instead of the hundreds of small concerns that struggle every year and fail to compete in a field dominated by IBM, the public notices the big success stories like Apple and Intel. Silicon Valley has captured the imagination of Americans as a symbol of overnight success and as the competition with Japan's outstanding computer and electronics firms.

Now, however, some changes are occurring. So many companies have begun there that almost no building space remains. Other suburban areas may become the sites of high-technology complexes. The Boston area, with MIT and Harvard University nearby, and Austin, with the University of Texas, have already attracted many companies that design computers and related products. Silicon Valley could lose its leadership as the chief center of computer manufacturing. On the other hand, the large companies may decide to do their manufacturing, packaging, and marketing in areas where space is cheaper and more available, while keeping their headquarters in Silicon Valley. The application of computers to education, business, banking, the military, and scientific research has turned the area into the computer center of the world, and that's what it will probably remain.

This version is much better than the first draft in several ways. First, its organization is clearer: it has three paragraphs with clear topics:

Paragraph 1: Introduction tells about the importance of Silicon Valley
Paragraph 2: Explains how Silicon Valley has become the symbol of success
Paragraph 3: Predicts what may happen as a result of current changes

The writer has also included specific examples to illustrate important points:

General idea:	Many companies are located there.
Specific examples:	Apple Computer, Atari, Hewlett-Packard, and Intel
General idea:	These companies make things related to computers.
Specific examples:	computers, video games, software, and electronics equipment

First and Second Drafts 137

General idea:	Some companies were very successful.
Specific examples:	companies with a handful of employees that mushroomed in three or four years into corporations with annual sales of over $100 million (Apple and Intel)
General idea:	Other areas may compete with Silicon Valley.
Specific examples:	Boston, Austin
General idea:	Computers are important in our world.
Specific examples:	the application of computers to education, business, banking, the military, and scientific research

Furthermore, the sentences in this version are more developed and varied than the short, simple sentences in the first draft. Compare these sentences for their length and form:

First Draft: Lots of companies have started there. Some of them began very small and became huge in a few years. Most of these companies make computers or things related to computers.

Revised Version: In Silicon Valley, named after the material used in making computer chips, thousands of companies that design and manufacture computers, video games, software, and electronic equipment have sprung up.

First Draft: California has always been the place for people with big dreams and ambitions.

Revised Version: From the Gold Rush of 1849 through the golden years of Hollywood, California has always lured dreamers to the West Coast with promises of wealth and success.

First Draft: Other places may begin to have a lot of computer companies being built there.

Revised Version: The Boston area, with MIT and Harvard University nearby, and Austin, with the University of Texas, have already attracted many companies that design computers and related products.

Finally, the writer, in revising the first draft, has remembered that good writing depends on vivid, forceful, specific words instead of vague, weak ones. Notice the differences:

First Draft	*Revised Version*
is an important place	lies the technological capital
lots of companies	thousands of companies
things related to computers	video games, software, and electronics equipment
have been started	have sprung up
watching it grow	watched their companies . . . mushroom
other places	other suburban areas

EXERCISE I: Revision

The following essay contains weaknesses in organization, use of examples, sentence patterns, and choice of words. Rewrite the essay, improving it as many ways as you can.

Losing Weight

Everybody wants to lose weight. To lose weight successfully, you have to have the right attitude and the right system, losing weight the right way will make you feel better and look better.

You have to have the right attitude to lose weight. Also the right system. If you have the wrong attitude you probably won't succeed. If you have the wrong system, you may lose weight too fast or too slow or not keep it off. For example, there are many people who have the wrong attitude that all they have to do is starve theirselves for about a week or a month and they will be thin. There are many other dumb attitudes that some people have about dieting, they just don't understand how to make it work. Then they gain all the weight back if they lose any.

For example, the wrong system or no system at all won't help you lose weight. Some famous people, for example, used the wrong system and even when they lost a lot they got too heavy again in a short time.

In conclusion, the right system for losing weight and a successful attitude are necessary for people who want to take off weight. And keep it off.

Questions to Help You Revise:

1. How many recommendations does this essay include? How should the paragraphs be arranged to bring these out?
2. How well developed are the paragraphs? How would you develop them instead?
3. What specific examples would you add to make this a more informative, interesting essay?
4. How would you improve the introduction and conclusion?
5. What sentence errors should be corrected?

EXERCISE II: Revision

Rewrite the following essay to improve its organization, use of examples, sentence patterns, and choice of words.

Job Interviews

Job interviews are very important. Going for a job interview, it is important to know how to behave and how to look. Knowing how to take a good interview is important because you may get a good job.

When you go for an interview, you should look and act right, you shouldn't act too loose, like you just came off the street. You shouldn't dress wrong either. If you dress and act right, you may get the job, if you don't you won't get the job. Acting right means talking the right way and being polite. Friendly but not pushy. You should also be confident. Men should dress well, usually in suits and ties. Women should also dress well, not in jeans. Some people don't make a good impression because they are too shy or uninteresting. Some people don't know how to talk well. Most people don't know what to say to an employer and some people don't know how to dress right. The important thing is to make a good impression. Because that makes the employer feel that you are right for the job and the company.

IMPROVING YOUR CHOICE OF WORDS

In the process of revising paragraphs and essays, as in the previous exercises, concentrate above all on the whole shape and development of your revised draft. Once you are satisfied with the essay as a whole, it is time to improve it by concentrating on your diction, or choice of words. The most noticeable difference between an acceptable but uninteresting essay and one that makes the reader want to read it again and again is usually a powerful use of words. Choose words that are precise, appropriate in connotation, specific, economical, vivid, and idiomatic.

Being Precise

Legal, scientific, and medical writing must be precise for professional reasons, but all writing is more effective when the words convey exactly the right meaning. You know how infuriating it is when you ask for directions and someone tells you your destination is "down the road a piece" or "a few miles from here." You need more precise directions. Similarly, in writing, make careful statements. Be especially careful with words like *all, everybody, nobody, most, many, some,* and *a few.* In conversation we casually throw around remarks like "Everybody knows that song." We don't take such remarks literally, but you should not write casual statements about serious issues. "Everybody wants stricter enforcement of drug laws" is not a careful statement. "Most people" would probably be a safe phrase in this statement; "many people" or "some people" would be too weak.

Be careful also to choose the correct transitional expressions and connective words. Don't use *and* as a catchall connective instead of *but, therefore,* or some other connective. "Police sometimes react too quickly, *and* they don't have enough training" is less precise than "Police sometimes react too quickly *because* they don't have enough training." Avoid using *which* or *in which* vaguely in place of *and* or other connectives. "Teenagers face many temptations today, *in which* they often get into trouble" is awkward and imprecise. A better statement might be "Teenagers are often in difficult situations *in which* they suddenly need help." Some writers often misuse *whereas*, treating it as an all-purpose transitional word. The correct use of *whereas* is to show a contrast, as in the statement "The state law permits turning right on a red light, *whereas* the city ordinance prohibits it." Do not use it carelessly, as in "The government should do something about the homeless, *whereas* inexpensive public housing should be built and counseling should be provided."

As you learn new vocabulary, do not be afraid to use it in your writing. Just be sure to check the meaning in a dictionary first. When you begin noticing a particular new word in your reading, you may guess at the meaning— and guess wrong. "This will *exacerbate* the condition"; "This will *alleviate* the condition." Which word do you want? What is the difference between *uninterested* and *disinterested?* Between *discreet* and *discrete?* What does it mean to *defer* payment? What exactly do we refer to as a *story,* a *novel,* a *poem,* or a work of *prose?* What does it mean to *rationalize?* Is that different from *being rational?* When should you write *infer* and when should you write *imply?* What is the difference between *compose* and *comprise?* These are just some of the hundreds of fine distinctions made by careful writers. If you hope to be a careful writer, you must always have a dictionary at hand, especially when you edit.

EXERCISE I: Choosing Precise Words

The underlined words or phrases are imprecise or incorrect as used. Use common sense and a dictionary to help you determine more precise equivalents. Write them in the blanks.

Example:

___*consists of*___   The kit is comprised of three blank tapes, a film on video, and a head-cleaner tape.

_____ 1. The presence of heavily armed police only alleviated the crowd's anger.

_____ 2. Food served in fast-food restaurants is more nutritious than most people think, and the problem is that it is highly caloric.

_____ 3. Most people believe in astrology and witchcraft.

_____ 4. Both parties in the labor dispute agreed to submit the decision to an uninterested third party.

_____ 5. All of the members of Congress put their constituents' wishes before the needs of the nation.

_____ 6. Biology majors must take at least three courses in subjects not related to science, whereas two must be in the humanities.

_____   7. Lucile <u>rationalized</u> that she could afford to pay no more than $700 for rent.

_____   8. The writer is <u>inferring</u> that she really does not believe the government's statistics.

_____   9. When Donna pointed out his mistake, Frank <u>extracted</u> his statement.

_____   10. The patient's stomach was badly <u>extended</u> from the internal pressure.

EXERCISE 11: Choosing Precise Words

Read the following paragraph and choose more precise words for the ones in italics.

(1) *Nearly all* people who think they are no good at mathematics (2) *enjoy* a problem that experts call math anxiety. This problem comes more from fear and avoidance than from a lack of (3) *instinct*. (4) *Still and all,* people who suffer from it can overcome the problem. First, they need to develop positive feelings about math by joining groups of people who have similar (5) *disadvantages* in learning mathematics. Psychologically trained teachers (6) *in which they use* unconventional methods help members of such groups gain confidence. Teachers diagnose individual students' problems and help them break down advanced procedures (7) *as to* smaller steps that are easy to master. (8) *A few of* these students will not necessarily become experts in higher mathematics, (9) *and* they will be able to make ordinary math a part of their lives. They do not even have to like mathematics, but they will have a confident attitude toward it as a skill that they can (10) *accept* whenever they choose.

Using Correct Connotation

Connotation is what a word suggests; **denotation** is what it means literally. Blue, red, green, and gray denote certain colors, but they all connote something else—blue, sadness; red, radicalism or anger; green, envy or illness; and gray, indistinctness (a gray area). In effective writing one chooses words for their implied meanings and associations as well as for their factual meanings. *Love, adoration, affection, devotion, liking,* and *friendship* all mean about the same thing, but each word suggests a different emotional quality. *Debate, argue, quarrel,* and *clash* all refer to differences of opinion but suggest different degrees of feeling. Some words are more formal than others: *before, previously,* and *hitherto* all refer to the past, but each one is more formal than the one before. Most of us would never use *hitherto* in conversation.

In college writing, faulty connotation may result from not finding the right voice and tone. If your writing shuttles between casual street remarks and formal discussions, your word choice will be erratic. An essay that contains words such as *hitherto, reciprocal, charismatic,* and *extraneous* will sound funny if it also contains expressions like *cop out, cool, booze,* and *dude*. Some words may also have offensive connotations; *gal,* for instance, has a sexist connotation that *women* does not. *Spinster* used for a single woman has both sexist and old-fashioned connotations that *bachelor* used for a single man does not. Words may also have favorable or negative connotations. *Bureaucrat,* for example, may refer to an office worker in a large organization, but it can suggest a person who merely follows orders without being humanly involved in his or her work. *Government employee* does not have a negative connotation of this kind. Be sure that the words you choose have the connotations appropriate to your intention and tone.

EXERCISE I: Connotation

Explain why each of the words in italics has the wrong connotation for its use in the sentence. Write a more appropriate word in the blank.

Example:

__*assistants*__   I admire the mayor for appointing high quality *inferiors*.

_____ 1. After the refreshments were served, half of the executives decided to *split*.

_____ 2. The police commissioner told the officers to stop *griping* about the regulations.

_____ 3. The Senate *quarreled about* the bill for two hours.

_____ 4. The SWAT team approached with extreme caution so that the sniper would not suddenly go *wacko*.

_____ 5. Two female attorneys encouraged all the *ladies* in the audience to consider law as a profession.

_____ 6. Eddie Murphy starred in a *mirthful* film.

———————————————— 7. Martin Luther King, Jr., was America's most *notorious* civil rights hero.

———————————————— 8. Cooking a pot roast dinner made Stanley feel *homely.*

———————————————— 9. After the long wait, the diner *leered* at his salad angrily.

———————————————— 10. The ball-carrier *sidled* head-on into the pack of defensive linemen.

Using Specific Language

Whenever possible, use specific words instead of general ones and words that appeal to the five senses instead of abstract ones. Rather than "large," write "six feet four, weighing 300 pounds." Instead of "loud noise," write "a piercing car alarm." Use a more identifiable term like "1992 Oldsmobile" in place of the general word "car." In descriptive writing especially, choose specific adjectives and nouns that create sense impressions: a "blue spruce" can be visualized specifically, whereas the word "tree" conveys a vague impression at best. In expository writing, try to make statements that evoke a personal response through specific examples instead of statements that make impersonal generalizations. When you find yourself about to write, "The American family is less cohesive than it used to be," stop and think up a statement that the reader will respond to more personally, such as, "Most American children are lucky to see their parents one hour a day."

Compare the two paragraphs below. The first is written in vague language that does not show imaginative selection of words that appeal to the senses. The second, richer in specific, sensory words, was written by the well-known author Maya Angelou:

Vague:

> We lived in a big house. We had a lot of people renting rooms from us; they were all different from one another. Some were workers, and others were prostitutes. One couple talked with me until the husband went away. Then the wife became shy. There was also an old couple who were boring.

Specific:

> Our house was a fourteen-room typical San Franciscan postearthquake affair. We had a succession of roomers, bringing and taking their different accents, and personalities and foods. Shipyard workers clanked up the stairs (we all slept on the second floor except Mother and Daddy Clidell) in their steel-tipped boots and metal hats, and gave way to much-powdered prostitutes, who giggled through their makeup and hung their wigs on the door-knobs. One couple (they were college graduates) held long adult conversations with me in the big kitchen downstairs, until the husband went off to war. Then the wife who had been so charming and ready to smile changed into a silent shadow that played infrequently along the walls. An older couple lived with us for a year or so. They

*owned a restaurant and had no personality to enchant or interest a teenager, except that the husband was called Uncle Jim, and the wife Aunt Boy. I never figured that out.**

Recognize the difference between general, somewhat specific, and highly specific language:

General	Somewhat Specific	Highly Specific
vehicle	car	Porsche
animal	dog	bull terrier
medical worker	nurse	geriatric nurse
sports	track and field	400-meter hurdles

E X E R C I S E: General and Specific Language

Revise these sentences using specific, concrete words in place of general, abstract words:

1. Maxine lived in a large building and worked in a small business not far away. She took public transportation to work.

   _____

   _____

2. Ernie participated frequently in sports. He like several of them, but was outstanding in one. He won awards in that sport.

   _____

   _____

3. People who are addicted to various substances can do a number of things to get over their addictions.

   _____

   _____

4. Inez took a rather long vacation to several islands; she enjoyed a number of activities while she was there.

   _____

   _____

*Maya Angelou, *I Know Why the Caged Bird Sings*. New York: Random House, 1969.

5. When you live in a big city, you get used to a number of scary sights, loud noises, and unpleasant encounters.

_____

_____

Reducing Wordiness

In your prewriting and composing, you have worked hard to develop fluency, which means to be able to write many words without too much hesitation and awkwardness. Now it may seem like a step backward to try to *reduce* the number of words in your final drafts. Here we want to distinguish between effective words and wasted words. Well-chosen words add to the meaning and power of your essays; deadwood or clutter, as some editors call wasted words, gets in the way. Expert writers make words count more than beginners do; they improve their rough drafts by shortening them without changing the meaning or reducing the coverage. This is what you will do as your final step in learning to be a good editor of your own writing. If the instructor assigns a five-hundred word essay, aim for about seven hundred words first. In your prewriting and writing of a rough draft, you should not be concerned about wordiness; it will hamper your flow of words and ideas. When the time comes to edit, however, your essay should be long enough that you can pare down the excess words and still fulfill the assignment.

Wordiness is a loose, repetitious way of writing. It can have several causes. Carelessness may cause a writer to overlook repetitions and wasted phrases. Or trying too hard to sound impressive can lead to the use of formulated, wasted phrases. Quite often, wordiness comes from not recognizing effective writing through lack of experience in reading good writers. Many writing students, in fact, do not realize that good writing is *concise*. Just as an expert swimmer or runner knows how to get the most speed and distance with the least effort, an expert writer learns to get the most mileage out of each word and sentence.

Here is an example of wordy writing:

> *In modern times of today, the majority of Americans in our society, by and large, have come to recognize that our senior citizens are in need of quite a number of kinds of help and assistance that they are not receiving as of yet.*

The following would do much better:

> *Most Americans now realize that the elderly need many kinds of help that they are not receiving.*

This sentence has only 17 words, in contrast to the 44 words of the first sentence, and it makes the point much more clearly. If you look back at the wordy statement, you will find that none of the extra 27 words adds anything to the meaning. These words are like wood chips to be cut away from the block by the carver. You are the carver.

You will be a more concise writer and better editor if you learn to spot the common patterns of wordiness. Although editing, unlike grammar, cannot be reduced to rules to be learned and errors to be corrected, conciseness (the opposite of wordiness) can be learned through practice. Here are some of the common faults of wordiness:

- Useless repetitions, called **redundancies.** "Modern times of today" is a wordy way of saying "now." "Help and assistance" is saying "help" twice.

- Vague phrases and false connectors. "By and large" sounds like a transitional phrase but really serves no purpose.

- Roundabout substitutes for simple words. "As of yet" means "yet"; "on the basis of the fact that" means "because."

Writing clean, direct sentences does not necessarily mean writing short sentences or using short words. Sometimes using complicated sentences and long words is the best way, even the only way, to express particular ideas. But use these *only* if they are the best; otherwise, keep your sentences simple and straightforward.

Here is a list of wordy phrases commonly used by careless writers; more concise equivalents are on the right.

Wordy Phrase	*Concise Word or Phrase*
due to the fact that	because
with respect to	about
in terms of	about
in this day and age	nowadays
hurried quickly	hurried
in all probability	probably
at that point in time	then
conduct an investigation	investigate
blue in color	blue
circular in shape	circular
there are many students who join	many students join
it is my belief that	I believe that
inside of the house	inside the house
has a preference for	prefers
in my opinion I feel that	I think that

In Alice Walker's story "Everyday Use," she writes	In "Everyday Use," Alice Walker writes
he is the kind of person who *likes* to play chess	he likes to play chess

---

EXERCISE I: Wordiness

Read the paragraph below and underline the wordy phrase in each sentence. Then rewrite the paragraph with each wordy phrase omitted or replaced with a more concise one.

Of all the anxiety disorders, phobias are the most common of them all. More than one out of ten people will experience phobias at some point in time in their lifetimes. This is due to the fact that there are many objects and situations that can trigger phobias. People with phobias may, in point of fact, fear heights, airplane flights, driving, dogs, snakes, closed spaces, open spaces, shopping malls, or social situations. What causes the fear, by and large, is not immediate danger but something irrationally associated with the object or situation. In the opinion of most therapists, they believe that behavior therapy can usually help eliminate phobias. Therapists help people with phobias confront rather than avoid the situations in which they experience and feel anxiety. There are a number of people who have acute panic attacks. In these cases therapists have a tendency to prescribe medications to block the attacks. Although anxiety disorders do not endanger people's physical health, they can, as a matter of fact, limit their lives severely.

EXERCISE II: Wordiness

Look over your previous paragraph and essay assignments. Make a list of the ten most frequent wordy phrases you have used, and write next to them more concise equivalents. Then choose the assignment that seems wordiest and rewrite it. Try to reduce it by at least 20 percent.

Using the Active Voice for Strength*

Difference Between Active Voice and Passive Voice

In the **active voice**, the subject *does* the acting:

      s   *v*
The <u>radio</u> <u>blasted</u> hard rock music on the bus.

In the **passive voice**, the subject *receives* the action:

      s   *v*
Loud <u>rock</u> <u>music</u> <u>was heard</u> by everyone on the bus.

Both active and passive voice are correct English, but too-frequent use of the passive voice weakens writing. Sometimes in news reports and business writing, the passive voice may be best because who is doing the action is not important:

1. Three more <u>suspects</u> <u>were taken</u> into police headquarters for questioning in the continuing search for the mass murderer.
2. The <u>machines</u> <u>were shipped</u> to the Denver branch on Monday.

We do not need to know who took the suspects into custody or who shipped the machines. However, use of the passive is *not* effective in most writing.

Weak Writing	*Strong Writing*
<u>Kim</u> <u>was invited</u> by Raymond to model for him.	<u>Raymond</u> <u>invited</u> Kim to model for him.
The <u>truth</u> <u>was</u> suddenly <u>realized</u> by both contestants at once.	Both <u>contestants</u> suddenly <u>realized</u> the truth at once.

E X E R C I S E: Using the Active Voice

Convert these sentences from passive voice to active voice.
    Example:

The turnoff for Route 287 was finally reached by Carla.

Active voice: *Carla finally reached the turnoff for Route 287.*

---

*See the use of participles with passive voice in Unit 5.

1. The poem was read aloud in class by Margaret.

   Active voice: _____

2. The Yankees were beaten by the Tigers in the playoffs.

   Active voice: _____

3. The moon was landed on by the Apollo 11 crew in 1969.

   Active voice: _____

4. Her personal computer was given to Edith by her parents.

   Active voice: _____

5. Many letters have been sent by me to your office.

   Active voice: _____

Using Strong, Vivid Verbs*

One key to forceful writing is selecting verbs that do heavy work for you. All words count, but verbs are especially important. Pick your verbs as you would pick a pair of designer jeans. A flat, boring, vague verb can numb the reader. A vital, specific verb can make a sentence crackle, sing, or snarl. Be on the lookout for the flat, catchall verbs that do not create pictures—words like *move, look, go,* and of course *is.* Read some of your previous writing, circling the verbs. Do you come up with nothing but *has, have, are, does, do,* and *looks?* If so, you are still singing on one or two notes. Use the whole scale. Instead of *looks,* try *stares, gazes, gapes, ponders, peers, surveys, contemplates,* or *leers.* Notice the difference between flat, vague verbs and vivid ones in these examples:

1. The runner *moved* to the left, *went* to the right, and *went* through three tacklers for a first down.
2. The runner *feinted* to the left, *veered* to the right, and *ploughed* through three tacklers for a first down.

1. Eleanor *looked* at the photograph for five minutes, *looked* out the window, and then *watched* the other students writing.
2. Eleanor *studied* the photograph for five minutes, *glanced* out the window, and then *glared* at the other students writing.

---

*You may want to review finding verbs, subject-verb agreement, and verb tenses in Unit 5. See also the use of verbs in Richard Wright's "Facing the Bullies" in Unit 6.

1. Norman *said* hello to the new vendor, *said* good morning to the bus driver, and *said* a few words to the attractive girl sitting next to him on the bus.
2. Norman *greeted* the news vendor, *tossed* a "good morning" to the bus driver, and began *flirting* with the attractive girl sitting next to him on the bus.

Underline the verbs in the following passage. Notice how the writer has chosen specific verbs instead of repeating *is, does,* or *goes.*

> *Teenagers need privacy; it allows them to have a life of their own. By providing privacy, we demonstrate respect. We help them disengage themselves from us and grow up. Some parents pry too much. They read their teenagers' mail and listen in on their telephone calls. Such violations may cause permanent resentment. Teenagers feel cheated and enraged. In their eyes, invasion of privacy is a dishonorable offense. As one girl said: "I am going to sue my mother for malpractice of parenthood. She unlocked my desk and read my diary."**

E X E R C I S E: Using Effective Verbs

Rewrite these sentences, substituting vivid, precise verbs for vague, flat ones.
Example: Sandra *looked* at the dress with disgust.

Rewrite: _____*Sandra glowered at the dress with disgust.*_____

1. Robert *went* to the police station for help.
2. The students *were* in the lounge.
3. The van *moved slowly* through heavy traffic.
4. The announcement *said* that the prime minister of India had been killed.
5. A geriatric nurse *has* many responsibilities.
6. The dancers *moved* to the loud music.
7. One driver *said* that he would sue the cab driver who ran into his Porsche.
8. The half-conscious patient *looked* at the ceiling.
9. The ice hockey players *moved* across the ice.
10. Misty blue-green mountains *were* in front of them.

Using Idioms Correctly

Idioms are fixed phrases or combinations like "out of order," "keep an eye on," "take your time," or "out of the question." These phrases often do not make sense if you analyze them word by word, but people who grow up speaking English (all other languages have idioms, too) learn the meanings of idioms by habit. Careless writers may, however, occasionally write phrases

---

*Haim G. Ginott, *Between Parent and Teenager,* New York: Macmillan Publishing Co., 1965. Reprinted by permission of the publisher.

that are not idiomatic, and students who have learned English as a second language or as a foreign language often have some difficulties with idioms. When you edit your writing, check to see that your phrasing matches the natural phrasing of American speech. If you learned English as a second or foreign language, you may need extra practice with spoken English to become more secure in your grasp of idioms. A dictionary of American idioms may speed the process. All students, however, are likely to have a little trouble with idiomatic word combinations that involve advanced vocabulary. The most common problems occur in matching verbs with prepositions. For instance, we say that a person is accused *of* a crime, charged *with* a crime, convicted *of* a crime, and sentenced *to* ten years in jail. Here is a list of some common errors in idiom:

Not Idiomatic	*Idiomatic*
In the other hand.	On the other hand.
The horse is not capable to run.	The horse is not capable of running.
She was bored of the party.	She was bored with the party.
The discussion centered around politics.	The discussion centered on politics.
I am concerned for your grades.	I am concerned about your grades.
We went in search for the cat.	We went in search of the cat.
I differ from you on that subject.	I differ with you on that subject.
She was born at Denver.	She was born in Denver.
A cassette deck is preferable than a radio.	A cassette deck is preferable to a radio.
Fish is superior than red meat.	Fish is superior to red meat.
A cheetah has twice the speed as a dog.	A cheetah has twice the speed of a dog.
Sandra was not interested to go along.	Sandra was not interested in going along.
Poor health prevented him to do it.	Poor health prevented him from doing it.

EXERCISE: Idiomatic Usage

The paragraph below contains eight expressions that are not idiomatic. Circle these phrases and write the correct idiomatic phrases above them.

Plea bargaining is a method used by the courts to speed up the process of law enforcement. When a person is charged of a crime, he or she has the option to pleading guilty or not guilty. If the plea is not guilty, a trial must take place, and the person may receive a severe sentence or go free, according on the jury's decision. To avoid the time-consuming procedures of jury trials, judges often have defendants to plead guilty in exchange for a lighter sentence. Those who defend plea bargaining point out that holding complete trials for all persons accused with crimes would overwhelm the system and bring it to a halt. In the other hand, critics insist that plea bargaining never produces perfect justice. That is, if the defendant is guilty, he or she should not get off by a light sentence, whereas if he or she is innocent, pleading guilty for avoiding a harsher sentence is unjust. It is up to judges, prosecutors, and defense attorneys to make the system work as justly as possible.

IMPROVING SENTENCE EFFECTIVENESS

Have you ever read a story, article, or book that had a powerful effect on you—left you touched, delighted, angered, or convinced? What do you think made the writing come alive with feeling and purpose? In part, it may have been the mysterious element of originality. Each writer's imaginative gift is his or her own, and not everything about the best writing can be taught in a classroom. However, most stylistic effects boil down to choice of words, which you have been practicing, and sentence effectiveness, which you will be practicing next. Improving sentence form will make your style forceful and varied.

Avoiding Repetition

Although some repetition of words, phrases, and sentence patterns is necessary to good writing, too much repetition will set the reader snoring. Several techniques will help you achieve sentence variety: using pronouns to avoid repeating nouns, varying your sentence beginnings, and using all three basic sentence types.

*Using Pronouns to Avoid Repeating Nouns**

What is wrong with this passage?

> *Yvette is my next-door neighbor. Yvette has three children, ages six, eight, and twelve. I first met Yvette when I moved into the apartment house where*

---

*You may at this point want to review the use of pronouns in Unit 5.

> *Yvette lived. Yvette didn't wait for me to come over to introduce myself; instead Yvette showed up right there at my door with a present to welcome me to the new building. That's what I like about Yvette—Yvette always thinks of others first.*

In this passage, the writer always refers to her neighbor with one word, Yvette. She never uses the pronouns *she* or *her* instead. Read the passage again and say *she* or *her* wherever you think it would break up the repetition effectively. (Note: it is not a good idea to use only *she* or *he* in place of a person's name; pronouns can become boring too.)

Read the improved passage, with *she* and *her* substituted to avoid repeating *Yvette* too often:

> *Yvette, my next-door neighbor, has three children, ages six, eight, and twelve. I first met her when I moved into the apartment house where she lived. Yvette didn't wait for me to come over to introduce myself; instead she showed up right there at my door with a present to welcome me to the new building. That's what I like about her—she always thinks of others first.*

The original passage contained eight references to *Yvette*. How many does the revised passage contain? _____

E X E R C I S E: Using Pronouns

Read the following passage and underline references to *George*. Rewrite the passage, eliminating too much repetition by substituting *he, him,* or *his* in place of the name.

> *George is a student in my sociology class. No one would say that George is a model student. Whenever George arrives, the class winces as if expecting a scene. George always enters late, and George usually drops a pencil or book before flopping loudly into George's seat. George never expresses George's opinion during class discussion or answers a question when the teacher calls on George, but as soon as the teacher starts to lecture, George is sure to make a loud remark or ask an irrelevant question.*

Varying Sentence Beginnings*

One of the most common faults of beginning writers is to begin nearly all sentences the same way. Look over some of your previous writing—your paragraphs and essay exercises. Did you begin most of your sentences with the subject followed by the verb?

---

*You may at this point want to review the use of commas after introductory parts and subjects and verbs in Unit 5.

Sentences can begin many ways, not always with the main subject and verb. One of the most familiar patterns is the monotonous repetition of "I did," "I saw," "I went," and so on, in essays about a personal experience. Read this sample passage.

> *I used to live in a neighborhood where many of the kids committed minor crimes. I thought stealing fruit from an open stand or jumping turnstiles in the subway was a sign of courage and intelligence. I never worried much about what would happen if I got caught doing these things. I wanted to learn from the older kids how to get away fast and how to fool the police. I thought I was leading the life of a legendary outlaw until my cousin was arrested.*

It is easy to fall into this "I, I, I" pattern without noticing it. Remember that there are many other ways to begin a sentence.

Ways to Begin Sentences Other than with the Main Subject and Verb

1. Begin with an introductory phrase or clause:

   In my neighborhood, there were many kids who committed minor crimes.

   When my family moved to St. Louis, there were many kids in my neighborhood who committed minor crimes.

2. Begin with a participle (-ing or -ed verb form):

   Influenced by the example of my friends, I began to commit minor robberies.

   Ingnoring the possible consequences, I ventured into a life of minor robberies.

3. Begin with an appositive (a short identifying word or group):

   A skilled thief at the age of ten, I took pride in my daring and expertise.

Learn to use these sentence beginnings to break up monotonous patterns. Many of your sentences will begin with the ordinary subject/verb combination, but some variety will make your writing more lively and readable. Read the revised version of the original passage.

> *In my old neighborhood there were many kids who committed minor crimes. Influenced by their example, I ventured into an early career of robbery. I ignored*

the possible consequences of stealing fruit from open stands or jumping subway turnstiles. A skilled thief at the age of ten, I took pride in my daring and expertise. From older kids I learned how to get away fast and fool the police. Not until my cousin was arrested did I begin to question the wisdom of trying to become a legendary outlaw.

EXERCISE: Sentence Beginnings

Rewrite the following sentences so that they begin with an introductory phrase or clause, a participle, or an appositive.

Group I: Introductory Phrases and Clauses

Example: I found a wonderful Mexican restaurant two blocks away.
Rewrite: Two blocks away I found a wonderful Mexican restaurant.

1. Stephanie was lucky to find an apartment with two bathrooms near 94th Street.

   Rewrite:_____

2. Most of the jobs had already been filled by the time Steven applied.

   Rewrite:_____

3. The old grocery store began to lose business when a new supermarket opened across the street.

   Rewrite:_____

4. The price of gasoline is no longer exorbitant because the worldwide prices for oil have declined.

   Rewrite:_____

5. We will take a taxi home after the party.

   Rewrite:_____

*Group II: Participles**

Example: The driver noticed a problem with the engine while turning the corner.
Rewrite: While turning the corner, the driver noticed a problem with the engine.

---

*Review participles in Unit 5.

1. May did her math and Spanish homework after taking a shower.

   Rewrite:_____

2. Roberto, knowing that he had a good chance to win, pulled into the lead.

   Rewrite:_____

3. The boat, abandoned a year ago by its owner, was now half submerged.

   Rewrite:_____

4. Kimberly hurried home to her stepmother, elated by her test score.

   Rewrite:_____

5. Some of the patients, committed to the mental ward for false reasons, were eventually released.

   Rewrite:_____

Group III: Appositives*

Example: Mr. Rogers, who has been a popular television figure for many years, criticized some of the new commercials.

Rewrite: A popular television figure for many years, Mr. Rogers criticized some of the new commercials.

1. The candidate, a former member of the CIA, insisted on the importance of classified information.

   Rewrite:_____

2. My sister, who is an ardent supporter of children's rights, joined a new lobbying group.

   Rewrite:_____

3. The professor, a graduate of Purdue University, was an expert on agricultural technology.

   Rewrite:_____

4. Most of the actors, who were experienced professionals used to the unexpected, had no trouble coping with the emergency.

   Rewrite:_____

---

*See the use of oppositives in Unit 5.

5. The Great Lakes, a gigantic creation of the glaciers during the Ice Age, are a source of fresh water for the Midwest.

Rewrite: _____

Varying Sentence Length and Type

Good writing depends on sentence variety. Learn to vary both the length and pattern of your sentences. Some students try to "play it safe"—escaping grammatical errors by writing only short, simple sentences. As a result, their style becomes immature and blunt. Others have the opposite problem: they launch into sentences without much attention to form and create long, tangled, shapeless monstrosities that are too complicated to revise. Be realistic: you can't expect to compose sentences as complicated as those of Henry James or James Baldwin without planning or careful revision. Neither should you underestimate your ability and settle for short, flat, monotonous sentences.

Sentence *length* and *type* have to be studied together. In order to revise a passage written in short, choppy sentences, you have to know how to form longer sentences.

Here is an example:

> *Bungee jumping appeals to a lot of people. It is one of the most thrilling sports. It looks very dangerous. Some people have been killed at it. But this was caused by equipment failure. Many people claim it is perfectly safe. Some states have made it illegal. This seems unfair. After all, parachuting is legal. It is just as dangerous.*

This passage is written in very short sentences, all of which contain only one subject-verb combination. Such sentences are grammatically defined as *simple sentences.** To rewrite the passage in more varied sentences, some short and simple, others longer and more complicated, we must also include some *compound* and *complex* sentences. Compound sentences combine two main clauses joined by a semicolon or a comma and a short connective word like *and* or *but*. Complex sentences combine one main clause with one subordinate clause beginning with a word like *because, when, although,* or *which*.

Notice the difference:

> *Bungee jumping, which looks very dangerous, appeals to people because it is one of the most thrilling sports. Some people have been killed at it, but this was caused by equipment failure. Many people claim it is perfectly safe. For states to make it illegal, as some have done, seems unfair; after all, parachuting, which is just as dangerous, is legal.*

In this revised passage, the first sentence is complex, the second compound, the third simple, and the fourth compound-complex.

---

*See Unit 5 for more on simple, compound, and complex sentences.

E X E R C I S E: Varying Sentence Length and Type

The passage below is written in short, simple sentences. Rewrite it so that some of the sentences are a little longer and constructed in the form of compound or complex sentences.

> *Virtual reality is a computer term. It refers to a sense of three-dimensional reality. This is created by computer images. Usually these are seen through headsets. Virtual reality may be induced by different types of programs. They may be used for anything from video games to training for surgeons or astronauts.*

The opposite problem of writing long, tangled sentences usually comes from a lack of planning or revision. If you find yourself frequently getting lost in sentences that are much too long or complex, break them up into clearer statements of moderate length. Here, for example, is the kind of sentence it is easy to produce if you're not careful:

> *Of all the sightings of unidentified flying objects, many are not very believable, such as the ones about people being abducted by little creatures that look like E.T. and kidnap the people and take them into their space platforms and perform brain operations on them or impregnate them with sperm from outer space so that they will give birth to half-human, half-extraterrestrial babies, but some of the reports of seeing flying objects are hard to dismiss as just optical illusions or weather conditions because they come from level-headed people with scientific training.*

This sentence is much too long and overloaded. Rather than merely revise it a little, the writer should break it up into several shorter sentences:

> *Many of the sightings of unidentified flying objects are not very believable. For example, people have claimed that they were abducted by little creatures that looked like E.T. and taken to space platforms where they were subjected to brain surgery. Some women have even claimed that they were impregnated by extraterrestrials and gave birth to babies that were half-human and half from outer space. Other reports of UFOs, however, are hard to dismiss as mere optical illusions or weather conditions because they come from level-headed people with scientific training.*

This passage now has four sentences of varying length and type. Of course, many other revisions of the original passage are possible, but almost any good one would have to begin by breaking up the long, stringy sentence into several shorter ones.

E X E R C I S E: Avoiding Long, Tangled Sentences*

Rewrite the long sentence below as a more effective passage made up of three, four, or five sentences of varying length and type:

---

*Review run-together sentences, and comma splices in Unit 5.

"Beverly Hills, 90210" appeals to teenagers because it shows not only how many of the well-off families live in places like Beverly Hills where most of the families have expensive homes with pools and two-car garages not to mention a separate room for each child with plenty of high-tech equipment but also it shows the kinds of problems that most teenagers have to deal with such as being influenced by their peers to drink illegally and act wild even if they don't want to and wanting to fit in and be accepted, especially by the in-crowd which leads to getting into trouble like getting arrested for drunken driving.

COMBINING SENTENCES TO IMPROVE YOUR STYLE*

Sentence combining is something all writers do, often unconsciously, to show relationships between ideas and to make their writing more effective. Combining can be simple or complicated. It includes both adding elements to simple statements by using connecting words like *and* and inserting within simpler statements modifying words or phrases (a procedure called **embedding**). Advanced writers learn to pack much material into their clauses and sentences; beginners tend to write in short, simple statements or to string long ones together loosely.

Sentence-combining exercises can start you on the road to acquiring this density and complexity. In simple terms, *sentence combining means taking short kernel (or core) sentences and fitting their essential facts together into more developed statements.*

For example:	
Kernel Sentences:	The painter did a job
	The job was careless.
	The job was messy.
	The messiness and carelessness were embarrassing.
Developed Sentence:	The painter did an embarrassingly careless and messy job.

We have packed in the facts from the kernel sentences to make one mature statement. We embedded *careless* and *messy* as adjectives before the noun *job* and *embarrassing(ly)* as an adverb describing the adjectives *careless* and *messy.* Being able to do this kind of combining is indispensable to writing varied, mature, and readable English. Studying grammar alone will not give you this skill. It comes partly from your familiarity with the phrasing and rhythm of English, which you have gained from speaking, reading, and hearing the language. You can improve the skill you already possess by doing sentence-

---

*You may want to review fragments; run-together sentences; comma splices; and simple, compound, and complex sentences in Unit 5 to be sure you combine sentences grammatically.

combining exercises that help you recognize the varied possibilities for expressing a thought.

There is never just one way to combine a series of kernel sentences, although in some exercises one way may seem much better than the others and some possibilities may sound awkward. In the previous example, there are other possible combinations. Are these two as good as the first?

1. The painter did a job that was embarrassingly careless and messy.
2. The job done by the painter was careless and messy to the point of being embarrassing.

These took more words to say the same thing as the first sentence. While this does not necessarily mean that the first way was best, we all like economy. The shortest, most compact way is often the best, as long as it is not awkward or unclear.*

E X E R C I S E I: Combining Sentences

The following kernel sentences have been combined into pairs of developed sentences. Circle the letter of the sentence you prefer in each case. Explain to a classmate why you prefer it. Is it smoother, more condensed, or freer of grammatical errors than the other one?

1. The dancer gave a performance.
   The performance was graceful.
   The performance was skillful.
   The grace and skill were remarkable.

   Developed sentences:

   The dancer gave a remarkably graceful and skillful performance.
   The performance the dancer gave was graceful and skillful to the point of being remarkable.

2. The student wrote an essay.
   The student was ambitious.
   The essay was long.
   The essay was involved.
   The writing was rapid.

   Developed sentences:

   The student who was ambitious wrote an essay that was long, involved, and rapidly written.
   The ambitious student rapidly wrote a long, involved essay.

---

*You may want to review adjectives and adverbs in Unit 5 before doing the next exercises.

3. The road changed.
   The road was bumpy.
   The road was made of dirt.
   The change was unexpected.
   The change was into a broad highway.

   Developed sentences:

   The bumpy dirt road unexpectedly changed into a broad highway.
   The dirt road, which was bumpy, changes suddenly into a broad highway.

E X E R C I S E   I I: Combining Sentences

Write your own developed sentences using the kernel sentences given. Write two possible sentences for each group; circle the letter of the one you find reads more smoothly.

1. The teacher gave a test.
   The test was short.
   The test was easy.
   The shortness and easiness were surprising.

   Developed sentences:

   A. _____

   B. _____

2. The campers erected a tent.
   The tent was green.
   The tent was made of canvas.
   The tent was large.
   They erected it carefully.

   Developed sentences:

   A. _____

   B. _____

3. The story came to an end.
   The story was about ghosts.
   The story was thrilling.

The end was abrupt.
The end was shocking.

Developed sentences:

A. _____

B. _____

4. Travis learned rap music.
   He learned from other teenagers.
   The teenagers performed on television.
   They performed in films.
   Travis watched them perform.

   Developed sentences:

A. _____

B. _____

5. Jennifer selected an umbrella.
   She selected it carefully.
   The umbrella was beautiful.
   The umbrella was plaid.
   The umbrella looked expensive.

   Developed sentences:

A. _____

B. _____

In these exercises you have either *added* parts by joining them with *and* to the main sentences or *embedded* parts by fitting them tightly into the sentences as modifiers. You should also be able to use free modifiers sometimes to make your sentences more varied. A **free modifier** is a descriptive word or phrase that reads as an extra element, interesting and informative but not essential. The same descriptive elements can sometimes be used either way:

Embedded: The dancer gave a *remarkably graceful, skillful* performance.
Free: The dancer's performance, *remarkably graceful and skillful*, received tremendous applause.

The second way sounds more sophisticated, doesn't it? That does not mean that it is better, but by knowing how to use such options you can make your style more interesting.

For practice, convert the embedded modifiers to free modifiers in this sentence.

1. The *heavy, lumbering* dump truck rolled gradually to a stop.
2. The dump truck, _____, rolled gradually to a stop.

Free and Embedded Modifiers*

Free modifiers are groups of words—nouns, verbs, or adjectives—that can be placed in different parts of the sentence. They are called free because they are movable; the same cluster may be located before the main statement, in the middle of the main statement, or after the main statement. A free modifier is added to enliven or add color to the main statement.

Suppose we begin with a main statement:

Michael took extra courses in the summer.

Now we add a free modifier:

hoping to graduate in three years

This modifier can be placed at the beginning:

Hoping to graduate in three years, Michael took extra courses in the summer.

Or it can be placed in the middle:

Michael, hoping to graduate in three years, took extra courses in the summer.

It can also be placed at the end:

Michael took extras courses in the summer, hoping to graduate in three years.

E X E R C I S E: Combining Sentences with Modifiers

Write two developed sentences for each exercise. Use embedded modifiers in one sentence, free modifiers in the other.

Example:

Ted's girlfriend was waiting.
She was waiting at the cafe.

---

*See dangling and misplaced modifiers in Unit 5. Sometimes a free modifier will not fit correctly in one of its possible positions. See also correcting by subordinating in Unit 5.

His girlfriend was pretty.
His girlfriend was charming.
She waited patiently.

Embedded modifiers: Ted's *pretty, charming* girlfriend was waiting patiently at the cafe.

Free modifiers: Ted's girlfriend, *pretty and charming*, was waiting patiently at the cafe.

1. The poodle came running.
   The running was toward his owner.
   The poodle was trimmed.
   The trimming was exquisite.
   The poodle was perfumed.

Embedded modifiers: _____

Free modifiers: _____

2. The car was parked.
   The parking was near the school.
   The car had been stolen.
   The car had been stripped.
   The car was new.

Embedded modifiers: _____

Free modifiers: _____

3. The wedding took place.
   It was in a ballroom.
   The wedding was large.
   The wedding was planned.
   The planning was careful.

Embedded modifiers: _____

Free modifiers: _____

4. The sequoias towered.
   They were in the forest.
   They towered above the other trees.
   They were ancient.
   They were awesome.

Embedded modifiers: _____

Free modifiers: _____

Who, Which, and That Clauses*

Clauses that begin with *who, which,* or *that* are called **relative clauses,** meaning that they *relate to,* or describe, some person or thing just before them in the sentence. Two kernel sentences can sometimes be combined by turning one of them into a relative clause:

Kernel sentences:	Some people drive to work every day.
	These people don't want the price of gasoline to rise.
Developed sentence with relative clause:	People *who drive to work every day* don't want the price of gasoline to rise.
Kernel sentences:	A filmmaker has a limited budget.
	That filmmaker cannot afford to hire famous stars.
Developed sentence with relative clause:	A filmmaker *who has a limited budget* cannot afford to hire famous stars.

The same thing can be done with things instead of people using *which* or *that* instead of *who:*

Kernel sentences:	Some companies receive government contracts.
	These companies face bureaucratic regulations.
Developed sentence with relative clause:	Companies *that receive government contracts* face bureaucratic regulations.
Kernel sentences:	A bill passes both houses of Congress.
	That bill can be signed or vetoed by the President.
Developed sentence with relative clause:	A bill *that passes both houses of Congress* can be signed or vetoed by the President.

Some clauses use prepositions like *in, to, for, of,* and *from* before *which* or *whom.* Learn to use these patterns as well:

---

*You may want to review the use of commas to separate *who* and *which* clauses in Unit 5. See also use of verb forms in relative clauses and the use of *who* and *whom.*

Kernel sentences: You spoke to a woman in the elevator.
The woman is our Saturday afternoon newscaster.

Developed sentence with relative clause: The woman *to whom you spoke in the elevator* is our Saturday afternoon newscaster.

E X E R C I S E: Combining Sentences With Relative Clauses

Combine these kernel sentences into developed sentences using *who, which,* or *that* clauses:

1. Some students wait until the last minute to study for exams.
   These students rarely earn high grades.

   Developed sentence:

   _____

2. Some colleges have developed work-study programs.
   These colleges have flourished in a tight economy.

   Developed sentence:

   _____

3. Robert Frost is known as a New England poet.
   He was actually born in San Francisco.

   Developed sentence:

   _____

4. A person appears on television talk shows.
   That person often has a film or book to promote.

   Developed sentence:

   _____

5. For some people correct spelling is easy.
   These people often learned to read early.

Developed sentence:

_____

6. From some countries raw materials are exported to the United States.
   These countries suffer economic losses when the dollar increases in
   value.

   Developed sentence:

   _____

7. Brochures were sent to some customers.
   These customers can receive free six-month subscriptions.

   Developed sentence:

   _____

8. Some mayors have been in office for over ten years.
   These mayors have seen a change in urban policies.

   Developed sentence:

   _____

9. Some stars suddenly become intensely bright.
   Later they turn into black holes.

   Developed sentence:

   _____

10. The public places a lot of trust in a political leader.
    That leader should set an example of honesty.

    Developed sentence:

    _____

How, When, Where, and *Why* Combinations

You can often combine kernel sentences by **subordinating,*** which means
turning one kernel sentence into a **subordinate clause.** Here is an example:

_____

*Clauses using *who, which,* and *that* also subordinate by using these relative pronouns; they are
called **relative clauses.** To check your grammar while using subordinate clauses to combine sentences, you may want to review subordinate conjunctions and fragments in Unit 5.

Kernel sentences: Utility bills are high during the
                                      summer.
                                  Air conditioning consumes a large
                                      amount of electricity.

The first statement is the base sentence; the second explains *why* the first is true. Transform the second into a subordinate clause by using *because*.

Developed sentence: Utility bills are high during the
                                      summer *because* air conditioning
                                      consumes a large amount of
                                      electricity.

In such combinations, the base statement is a **main clause.** It contains a subject and verb (bills *are*) and stands by itself as a complete statement. The other statement becomes a **subordinate clause.** It also has a subject and verb (air conditioning *consumes*) but cannot stand by itself. Rather, it tells how, where, when, or why the main statement is true. Subordinate clauses begin with introductory words called **subordinate conjunctions** like these:

after	if
although	since
as	until
as if	when
because	where
before	while

Notice that more than one subordinate conjunction may be possible in the same combination:

Utility bills are high during the summer, *when* air conditioning consumes a large amount of electricity.
Utility bills are high during the summer, *since* air conditioning consumes a large amount of electricity.

E X E R C I S E: Combining Sentences by Subordinating

Combine these kernel sentences into developed sentences by subordinating.
    Example:

Kernel sentences: The original date of the performance
                                      was changed.
                                  The original date conflicted with
                                      commencement exercises.

Developed sentence: The original date of the performance
                                      was changed *because* it conflicted
                                      with commencement exercises.

1. Politicians lose their credibility with the public.
    Politicians make wild promises.

    Developed sentence:

    _____

2. Drivers should be especially alert.
    Drivers approach busy intersections.

    Developed sentence:

    _____

3. Actors in soap operas are sometimes attacked in public.
    The characters they play do ugly or immoral things on the screen.

    Developed sentence:

    _____

4. The marathon run is named after an ancient Greek city.
    The Athenians defeated the Persians at that place.

    Developed sentence:

    _____

5. This trampoline is not difficult to assemble.
    You follow the instructions step by step.

    Developed sentence:

    _____

6. Reading modern poetry is difficult.
    Its meaning is usually hidden.

    Developed sentence:

    _____

7. You can learn a lot about the process of your writing.
    Other people share their impression of it with you.

    Developed sentence:

    _____

8. Cordless telephones are very convenient.
   People nearby can sometimes listen in on your conversation.

   Developed sentence:

   _____

9. Sandra has decided to wait to get married.
   She will be thirty-five years old at that time.

   Developed sentence:

   _____

10. Most presidents lose popularity in the polls.
    They have been in office a year or two.

    Developed sentence:

    _____

EXTRA PRACTICE: Combining Sentences

Rewrite each set of kernel sentences as a single developed sentence, eliminating boring repetitions.

1. "User friendly" is a term.
   The term refers to computers.
   The term means that a computer or program is easy.
   The easiness is for the person using it.

   Developed sentence:

   _____

   _____

2. Alan Turing was a genius.
   He broke a code.
   The code was used by the Germans.
   It was used during World War II.

Developed sentence:

_____

_____

3. Absentee landlords own buildings.
   They live somewhere else.
   They do not have to live with problems.
   The problems come from poor maintenance.
   The maintenance is of the buildings they own.

   Developed sentence:

   _____

   _____

4. A pecking order is a system.
   The system is of status levels.
   This term comes from hens.
   Hens show dominance over other hens.
   They show dominance by pecking them.

   Developed sentence:

   _____

   _____

5. Subsidies are grants.
   They are given by the government.
   They are given by private organizations.
   These organizations want to foster improvement.
   The improvement is cultural or social.

   Developed sentence:

   _____

   _____

6. Bobby Fisher was a chess player.
   He became world champion.
   He defeated Boris Spassky.

This was in 1972.
He stopped playing chess.
He disappeared from sight.
He decided to make a comeback.
This was in 1992.

Developed sentence:

_____

_____

REVISING WITH A WORD PROCESSOR

Word processing is the biggest innovation in writing since the invention of the typewriter. Even the typewriter does not free us to make revisions or speed up the work of producing a neat, error-free copy as much as the computer does. For editing especially, the computer is, or can be, a great asset. This might not be apparent to someone who has used a typewriter for years. The difference between typewriter and computer lies, of course, in the vastly greater freedom to revise and edit that a computer provides. Most of us, no matter how often we are told that neatness is not the substance of writing, find it nearly impossible to hand in a paper that has visible corrections. This results in crippling us at the revision stage. Whether writing by hand or typing, we want *this* to be the final draft. If we realize too late that the sentence just written could have been worded better, we probably settle for it the way it is. Not so when we use a word processor: now we can try a sentence three or four ways and look at all the options before we decide which is best, and we don't have to rewrite the entire page to change a single line. As all writers who use word processing know, we can also shift sentences or paragraphs around—insert, delete, change, and correct without limit—before we put the document on paper.

All this, then, *is* an asset—but only for the person who knows how to revise. The computer only follows orders. You still have to decide which verb is more emphatic, which version of a sentence is more effective. Many people mistakenly think that the only skill needed for word processing is mastery of the commands. You do have to know how to delete, insert, move, and correct words and phrases before word processing can do you any good. The more important skill, however, is that of exploring options, especially word choice, sentence arrangement, and choice of content. Do not imagine that word processing by itself will make you a better writer; it will, however, help you learn the craft of revising. Only the rare writer who can write one draft quickly and not need to change it significantly will be satisfied with a typewriter.

To put it another way, word processing eliminates our main excuse for not revising—not wanting to retype the page. Therefore, if you are fortunate enough to have your own personal computer with a word processing program, or if your college enables you to use computers in the classroom, remember that extensive revision is the key to effective writing. Word processing will enable you to do the following with less frustration:

- Revise your overall plan, adding content to develop paragraphs more fully, eliminating material that seems irrelevant, and changing the sequence of sentences and paragraphs. If you want to arrange your body paragraphs in climactic sequence, for instance, you can actually rearrange them without having to retype them.
- Explore sentence options, using the skills practiced in sentence combining to try out several patterns based on the same kernel sentences. You can write three or four versions of a sentence, choose one, and delete the rest.
- *Really* consider your diction, looking at each verb, noun, adjective, and adverb to consider whether another might be more precise, concrete, vivid, or accurate in connotation. Use the skills you have practiced in this unit regarding word choice.
- Eliminate wordiness. Learn the pleasure of deleting wasted words and condensing wordy phrases to create a cleaner, more readable copy; it is one of the joys of writing.

In addition, it is now possible to get help with editing from word processing programs. Be cautious about what you expect, however. The state of the art in style checks is still not advanced enough for you to gain much from such checks unless you already have a strong command of grammar and revision skills. Most style checks will give you information only about the average length of your sentences and items like the frequency with which you use the passive voice. More sophisticated style checks will question your use of particular phrases, but you are the final authority. The computer will not improve your style; it will only help make you more conscious of your stylistic habits.

As programs become more sophisticated, however, these aids will become more and more useful as learning tools. If you have done any word processing, you probably know how to use a spelling check, and you probably also realize that, instead of making you a lazy speller, it forces you to notice the words that you habitually misspell, thus making you a better speller. So will it eventually be with style checks—they will give you some of the feedback that a good writing instructor might give you. At present, however, they fall far short of the kind of human response listeners and readers can give you about your ideas and attitudes and of the stylistic comments a good teacher will give you on your effectiveness.

5

PROOFREADING YOUR WRITING AND REVIEWING GRAMMAR

Proofreading and correcting grammatical slips involve the most basic elements of writing as well as the final polishing touches. Basic mistakes can destroy the effectiveness of an essay that has been created carefully through the stages of prewriting, composition, and revision. In this unit, practice until your grammar, proofreading, and spelling reach the same high level as the other writing skills you developed in the earlier units.

PROOFREADING AND CORRECTING THE REVISED ESSAY

Proofreading for errors in typing, punctuation, spelling, and grammar is most important on the next-to-last draft. The final copy that you turn in should be letter perfect and without correction marks. On the earlier drafts, you need not spend time making minor corrections, since you will probably change or remove many passages later. In fact, proofreading too soon may make you resist making revisions later, because you won't want to "ruin" your handiwork. Save the really detailed corrections for the late stages. Make a final draft as if you were going to hand it in; then proofread this draft and make final corrections for the one you *really* hand in. This way you will have an almost perfect copy of your own for safekeeping.

Proofreading requires extremely close attention, not the careless attention we usually give to television programs and advertisements. As you read your work slowly aloud, you will learn not to *mentally correct* errors—that is, to read the way you meant the passage to be without noticing little words left out, endings omitted, words repeated, apostrophes missing, letters reversed, and so on. As you do the grammatical exercises in this unit, you will become more expert at recognizing errors. However, even a writer whose grammar is flawless must pay close attention when proofreading. Everyone makes careless mistakes.

Try copying the following passage exactly as it is on the page:

> NOW IS THE TIME FOR
> FOR ALL GOOD MEN TO
> TO COME TO THE AID
> THEIR COUNTRY.

Did you notice the two repeated words and the one left out? When you read passages with which you are familiar, you tend to overlook slips like this. When you read your own writing, you are even more likely to overlook errors. In proofreading your own work, remember these pointers:

1. Read aloud slowly. Most writers are tempted to skim over their work silently. Force yourself instead to read carefully, word by word. Some professional writers even read their work backward to avoid rushing over mistakes. Try it.
2. Know yourself. What mistakes do you always make? Do you make certain spelling mistakes? Drop *ed* endings? Leave out small words? Run sentences together? Leave fragments? When you know your own habits, you will know the corrections your writing is most likely to need.
3. Proofread several times. When writing at home, proofread once carefully after you have written the essay. Then put the essay away for a day or two and proofread it again later. You will often catch mistakes that you overlooked the first time.

EXERCISE: Proofreading

The passage that follows contains simple writing mistakes: words left out, words accidentally repeated, wrong punctuation, simple misspellings. Circle the mistakes; then rewrite the passage, correcting as many mistakes as you can.

Teenage Pregnancies

In today's society they are many teenager who are sexual active. They get involved in sex because their friends push them into or because they afraid to be consider unpopular. In order to prevent teenage pregnancies parent should talk with their children. They can only give advices they cant make their children do do what they want them too. But at least showing concern give the teenagers a sense of responsibility.

Being a teenager isnt easy you are under alot of pressure and when it gets to much you may want to run away with the person you love. You hope you will escape the pressure but having a baby not going to be the answer. When you have a baby to soon, it mean taking on more pressure, not getting away from responsibility. The mature way to deal with the problem of an unwanted pregnancy is to avoid the problem altogether: take responsibility for birth control and wait to have child until your older and ready to become parent, or say no to sex.

REVIEWING BASICS

Correcting your writing does require knowledge of grammar. When many college students say they "are terrible with grammar," however, they are usually exaggerating. When you speak English correctly, you are following most of the important grammatical rules. Correcting your writing simply requires a keen sense of the occasional mistakes that can show up even in the writing of people who speak mostly correct English. Producing error-free writing is a goal that college students should expect to attain.

You do not have to relearn grammar from the ground up. Some review of basics, however, will probably help you recognize and correct errors that fall into familiar patterns. In this unit you will review the major kinds of writing errors and concentrate on learning how to correct them, especially the ones that give you the most trouble.

DIAGNOSTIC TEST

The following test will give you an idea of your strengths and weaknesses in grammar, punctuation, and spelling. You can then use Unit 5 for explanation and practice in the areas where you require the most improvement. Bear in mind, however, that correcting grammatical mistakes on a short-answer test is not the same as correcting them in your writing. Correct grammar must be incorporated into your whole writing process as a set of habits, especially in the final proofreading stage. Always notice your instructor's marks and comments on your writing, and listen to your classmates' feedback to identify your strengths and weaknesses.

Part One: Sentence Divisions

In each group of sentences, only *one* is correct—A, B, or C. Check the blank next to the correct sentence in each group.

1. _____ A. Four graduates signed up for interviews. Because the job offered exciting opportunities.

   _____ B. Four graduates signed up for interviews because the job offered exciting opportunities.

   _____ C. Four graduates signed up for interviews, the job offered exciting opportunities.

2. _____ A. When a team really works together. It has a better chance of winning.

   _____ B. When a team really works together; it has a better chance of winning.

   _____ C. When a team really works together, it has a better chance of winning.

3. _____ A. Julio learned to drive when he was seventeen, and his brother Hector learned when he was even younger.

_____ B. Before Julio learned to drive at the age of seventeen. His brother Hector had already learned.

_____ C. Because his brother Hector already knew how to drive; Julio learned to drive at the age of seventeen.

4. _____ A. Prospective officers must pass the required courses at the academy. Also meet the physical requirements for the police force.

_____ B. Prospective officers must pass the required courses at the academy they must also meet the physical requirements for the police force.

_____ C. Prospective officers must pass the required courses at the academy. They must also meet the physical requirements for the police force.

5. _____ A. Soap operas appeal to many television viewers. Because they combine suspense, glamor, and scandal.

_____ B. Soap operas, which combine suspense, glamor, and scandal, appeal to many television viewers.

_____ C. Soap operas appeal to many television viewers they combine suspense, glamor, and scandal.

6. _____ A. Learning French was easy for Marva. Being that she was able to use a language program on her computer.

_____ B. After she learned how to use the language program on her computer. Marva found it easy to learn French.

_____ C. Learning French was easy for Marva once she was able to use a language program on her computer.

7. _____ A. First year students usually have difficulty scheduling all the courses they want; by the second year registration becomes easier.

_____ B. First year students usually have difficulty scheduling all the courses they want. But find the process easier in their second year.

_____ C. First year students usually have difficulty scheduling all the courses they want; but finding the process easier in their second year.

8. _____ A. Owning a home has become increasingly difficult for young couples. Especially if they have only one income.

_____ B. Owning a home has become increasingly difficult for young couples, especially if they have only one income.

_____ C. Young couples, especially if they have only one income. Often find it difficult to own a home.

9. _____ A. The restaurant, which lowered its prices last week. Soon was crowded with customers.

    _____ B. The restaurant lowered its prices last week, soon it was crowded with customers.

    _____ C. The restaurant lowered its prices last week; soon it was crowded with customers.

10. _____ A. Excessive drinking is bad for your health; it harms your liver, pancreas, and nervous system.

    _____ B. Excessive drinking harms your liver, pancreas, and nervous system. Which is bad for your health.

    _____ C. Excessive drinking is bad for your health, it harms your liver, pancreas, and nervous system.

Part Two: Verb Forms, Endings, and Agreement

Write the correct forms in the blanks provided.

_____ 11. People who (give, gives) money to the homeless are kind-hearted.

_____ 12. One of the cases involving sexual harassment (was, were) brought before the Supreme Court.

_____ 13. Visiting Chicago was the most interesting thing that (happen, happens, happened) to Paulette last year.

_____ 14. Either a nurse or a physician's assistant (is, are) going to be assigned to the patient.

_____ 15. The registrar informed Shirley that she (has, have) twenty credits to complete before graduation.

_____ 16. A student who (ask, asks, asked) thoughtful questions will be more likely to succeed.

_____ 17. Last year this laptop computer (cost, costs, costed) more than it does today.

_____ 18. There (is, are) some employees still in the old pension system.

_____ 19. On the second shelf (was, were) a videotape and three compact disks.

_____ 20. Teachers are (suppose, supposed) to give homework three times a week.

_____ 21. A women's clothing store (use, used) to be located on this corner.

_____ 22. Last year the university (spend, spends, spent) three million dollars on a new dormitory.

_____ 23. All of the items on sale have price tags that (indicate, indicates) how much they have been marked down.

_____ 24. The first of the President's appointments (was, were) his
              Secretary of State.
_____ 25. Reading biographies and keeping a journal of her own
              (occupy, occupies) much of Marisol's time.

Part Three: Spelling

If the word or phrase is correct, write C in the blank; if not, write the correct form of the misspelled word in the blank.

_____ 26. definitly

_____ 27. recieved

_____ 28. separate

_____ 29. neccessary

_____ 30. supprise

_____ 31. its your turn

_____ 32. taller then her sister

_____ 33. responsibility

_____ 34. occurance

_____ 35. he past the exam

_____ 36. begining

_____ 37. adress

_____ 38. committment

_____ 39. minding there own business

_____ 40. Bring alot of paper.

Part Four: Punctuation

If the sentence is punctuated correctly, write C in the blank. If not, circle the spot where punctuation is wrong or missing and write the correct mark in the blank. No sentence has more than one error.

_____ 41. The reporters arrived at the scene about noon but no one seemed to know what had happened.

_____ 42. The city government took the following actions increasing the police force, hiring more teachers, and increasing transit fares.

_____ 43. A women's conference was scheduled to be held in Sacramento California in March 1995.

_____ 44. The number of available jobs has been increasing however, many of the new jobs do not pay very well.

_____ 45. The poet William Blake wrote "The road of excess leads to the palace of wisdom."

_____ 46. The monologue, filled with hilarious jokes about political celebrities was the best part of the talk show.

_____ 47. Good health habits, which include a good diet, exercise, and avoidance of substance abuse are as important as medical care.

_____ 48. Impressed by the students' abilities and hard work, the professor predicted that they would all pass the state licensing examination.

_____ 49. The language of the ancient Mayan civilizations is difficult to read, descendants of the Maya do, however, speak a similar language.

_____ 50. Although most of the drugs prescribed by the doctor have some side effects this one is least likely to cause problems.

Part Five: Pronouns, Parallelism, and Modifiers

If the sentence is correct, write C in the blank. If a word or phrase is wrong, circle it and write the correct word or phrase in the blank.

_____ 51. This computer is old, but it works as good as my brand new one.

_____ 52. Yolanda is kind, caring, and has a great deal of responsibility.

_____ 53. Most students find it more easier to write essays if their professors explain clearly what they want.

_____ 54. Women who work in corporations sometimes find that old-fashioned stereotypes will be applied to her.

_____ 55. Along with she and her roommate, seven students enrolled.

_____ 56. Some customers were afraid there wouldn't be no sale items left when they arrived.

_____ 57. While arriving at the beach, a thunderstorm appeared to be approaching from the north.

_____ 58. College athletes who become professionals sometimes make use of his college degree later in life.

_____ 59. The word processing program was easy to learn, flexible in its applications, and did not cost much.

_____ 60. The manager offered a refund to both my wife and me.

Possible Score: __60__   Your Score _____

SUBJECTS AND VERBS

To understand sentences, learn to spot subjects and verbs.

The Subject

The subject names the person or thing the sentence is about:
The whole *family* uses the new personal computer.
The *videotape* belonged to the school library.
Jay Leno became host of the "Tonight Show" in May 1992.

The Verb

The verb is the word that shows the action or being:
The whole family *uses* the new personal computer.
The videotape *belonged* to the school library.
Jay Leno *became* host of the "Tonight Show" in May 1992.

Every sentence must have at least one subject and verb that go together. A sentence states that someone or something does or is something. If the subject or verb is missing, the sentence is not complete. Underline the subjects and circle the verbs in these sentences:

1. The excited crowd waited for the singers to appear.

2. Seven students majoring in sociology traveled to Ghana.

3. The legal voting age in the United States is eighteen.

Finding Subjects

In most sentences, subjects appear at or near the beginning. Subjects can be nouns (words that name persons, places, or things):

the *campus*   *Detroit*   two *actresses*   my *car*   academic *subjects*

Sentences with Noun Subjects

The *space shuttle* orbited the earth before descending.
A *degree* in hotel management makes you eligible for the job.
Sex education in schools raises heated controversies.

Subjects can also be pronouns (words that stand for nouns):

I   *we*
you
she, he, it   *they*

Sentences with Pronoun Subjects

We discovered a new way to drive to New Orleans.
She entered a bicycle race.
You know the difference between discipline and child abuse.

EXERCISE I: Finding Subjects

Underline the subjects in these sentences. Two of the sentences have no subjects and are therefore incomplete; write *F* in the margin next to these two
fragments.

1. The first book on the list was about Latin America.

2. I know four people who have made their own films.

3. A few retired members contributed large sums of money.

4. Specially trained experts defused the incendiary bomb.

5. Reaching the warning track near the left field wall.

6. Next Monday you will have to pay $8.95 for the album.

7. Science fiction movies have set box office records this year.

8. We have introduced new pension regulations.

9. Latecomers to the theater will not be seated until the end of the first act.

10. During the search for a new university president.

EXERCISE 11: Finding Subjects

Underline the subject of each sentence in the following paragraph. One sentence is incomplete because it lacks a subject; circle the number in front of that fragment.

(1) We no longer stereotype people because of their sex. (2) Little girls do not have to limit their interests to paper dolls and toy sewing machines. (3) Little boys are not confined to toy guns, trucks, and erector sets. (4) Today's parents have become more concerned about the individuality of their children than about their children's conformity to stereotypes. (5) Teenagers, too, are less rigid in adopting "feminine" or "masculine" roles than in the past. (6) In most high schools, you will now find a large number of girls majoring in chemistry or mathematics. (7) And even playing aggressive sports, like lacrosse and basketball. (8) Furthermore, in most families, both parents share in wage earning as well as housework and caring for children. (9) In fact, few adult activities can be labeled "men's work" or "women's work" nowadays. (10) In the place of stereotyped roles, people are now adopting living patterns suited to their individual abilities and needs.

Multiple Subjects

Sentences may contain two subjects connected by *and* or *or*, or three or more subjects that form a list, or series. Writers often make mistakes in grammar if they fail to recognize these multiple subjects.

Sentences with Two Subjects

Betty and *David* went to see a horror film.
My *brother* and *I* bought tickets in the lottery.
You and *we* disagree about methadone treatment.

Sentences with Three or More Subjects

The *heart*, the *lungs*, and the *reproductive system* may be affected by the use of marijuana.
Buddhism, *Christianity*, and *Judaism* have much in common.
Cecil, *Marylou*, *Rachel*, and *I* eat lunch together.

Hard-to-Find Subjects

Some subjects are hard to identify:

Subjects in the Middle or End of the Sentence

a. Across from the diner was Sam's auto parts *store*.
    (This sentence begins with a descriptive phrase, "across from the diner" and ends with the subject, *store*.)
b. There are probably many *answers* to your question.
    (*There* is only a position word, never a subject; in sentences beginning with *there*, the subject usually comes after the verb.)

Verbal Subjects

Verbals are verb forms that can be used as subjects in place of nouns or pronouns; they may be infinitives (*to dance, to write*) or gerunds (*dancing, writing*).

a. *Moving* away from home was difficult for Sharon.
b. *To find* your sister in this crowd is going to be difficult.
    (In these sentences, *moving* and *to find* are verbals that serve as subjects.)

Whole-Clause Subjects

Sometimes whole groups of words, called *noun clauses,* can serve as subjects; they often begin with *what* or *that:*

a.   *What I would prefer* is a high-paying job with no responsibilities.
b.   *That you like rock* music is no secret to your friends.

You-Understood Subjects

In sentences that give commands or make requests, the subject is understood to be *you,* but is not included in the sentence:

a.   Tell me the rest of the story when we get home.
b.   Turn left at the light and follow Route 84.

In both these sentences, *you* is understood to be the subject.

EXERCISE I: Finding Subjects

Underline the subjects in the following sentences. If the sentence is a command or request, write *you* in the margin. Two of the sentences are incomplete because they lack subjects; write *F* in the margin next to these fragments.

1.   There is a fashion show in the student union this afternoon.

2.   Television, newspapers, and magazines compete for money from advertisers.

3.   Finish your A.A. degree before continuing on to a four-year college.

4.   A series that included documentaries on World War I, the Great Depression, and the rise of fascism.

5.   Located next to the drive-in bank was an electronics store.

6.   Later in the afternoon a wedding and reception are scheduled.

7.   Sonia, Stanley, and I belong to the same telephone shopping service.

8.   Angered by the news report, listeners bombarded the radio station with telephone calls.

9.   Lacrosse, racquetball, and rock climbing continue to be Ellen's favorite sports.

10. Having pleasant working conditions, good fringe benefits, and con-
genial coworkers.

E X E R C I S E 11: Finding Subjects

Compose a paragraph of seven to twelve sentences, keeping in mind what
you have learned about topic sentences, development, and unity. In this paragraph describe how people shop at some store or mall with which you are familiar. Tell how they decide on purchases, what they buy, and how they relate
to the employees. Remember to use vivid and precise words. After composing
the paragraph, underline the subject or subjects of every sentence, being sure
that no sentences are left incomplete because they lack subjects.

Finding Verbs

Action and Being Verbs

Verbs are the words that tell about action or being. In many sentences they
come directly after the subject:

$$\overset{s}{} \qquad \overset{v}{}$$

Both contestants <u>answered</u> the final question correctly. (action verb)

$$\overset{s}{} \quad \overset{v}{}$$

The challenger <u>was</u> ahead by $1500. (verb of being)*

Sometimes, however, verbs can come before subjects or they can be separated
from subjects; they can even appear at or near the ends of sentences:

$$\overset{v}{} \quad \overset{s}{}$$

Nearby <u>was</u> a store that sold comic books for collectors. (verb before subject at beginning of sentence)

$$\overset{s}{} \qquad\qquad\qquad\qquad\qquad\qquad \overset{v}{}$$

The audience, bored by the sloppy performance, <u>booed</u> loudly. (verb near
the end of the sentence, separated from the subject)

E X E R C I S E: Finding Verbs

Underline each subject and circle each verb in the following sentences. One
sentence in the paragraph lacks a verb; circle the number next to it.

---

*Forms of *be* are listed in Unit 5 under "Special Problems with Agreement."

(1) Smoking in public places is a nuisance. (2) Many smokers believe they have the right to fumigate restaurants, bars, trains, and offices. (3) Some even insist on chain-smoking in confined places like elevators. (4) Others smoke in nonsmoking train cars and rooms with no-smoking signs. (5) Some restaurants with special sections for nonsmokers. (6) Prohibiting smoking altogether in public places is unreasonable. (7) However, the nonsmoking public has a right to be free from concentrated fumes in most crowded rooms and waiting areas. (8) People with respiratory problems in particular need unpolluted air to breathe. (9) Infants and the elderly also suffer harmful consequences from cigarette smoke. (10) Those who breathe the air in a smoke-filled room are almost as vulnerable to the damage done by tar and nicotine as the smokers themselves.

Multiple Verbs

Many sentences have more than one verb matched with the same subject. To avoid errors, you must be able to identify all the main verbs:
Examples:

Mary *left* early and *took* a cab home.
Oscar *feinted* to the left, *crossed* rapidly to the right, and *fired* a jump shot from the foul line.

E X E R C I S E: Finding Multiple Verbs

Underline the verbs in these sentences; be sure not to ignore the second or third verb in the sentence. One sentence is incomplete because it lacks a verb; write *F* next to this fragment.

1. Cable television provides good reception and offers extra program choices.

2. Hot weather lures many people outdoors but produces sunburn.

3. Along with accounting and marketing, Susan wanted to take a course in word processing but eventually changed her mind.

4. I like foreign films and always see new ones when they open.

5. After the first game of the series but before the playoff.

Helping Verbs

Verbs often take **helpers** (*is* going, *should be* working, *has* applied, etc.), or **auxiliaries,** as they are called. Usually the helping verbs come right before the main verbs, but sometimes there are words separating them.

Be, Have, *and* Do: *The Most Common Helping Verbs*

Forms of *be* (is, are, was, were), *have* (have, has, had), and *do* (do, does, did) are the most common helping verbs.
Examples:

The prices of designer jeans *are* going wild.
Sally *has* gone to five aerobics classes this week.
Did you see the shell collection in the science building?

Fixed-Form Helpers

The many other helping verbs do not have changing forms like *be, have,* and *do*. These fixed-form (unchanging) helpers often appear next to main verbs:

can	might	should
could	must	will
may	shall	would

Examples:

The prices of personal computers *will* drop soon.
We *could* arrange to meet on Wednesday afternoons.
I *can* always give you a call tomorrow.

E X E R C I S E: Finding Verbs with Auxiliaries

Underline the complete verbs—both the main verbs and the helpers—in these sentences. One sentence is incomplete because it lacks a verb; write *F* next to this fragment. (Note: do not underline *not* and *never*; they are not verbs or helpers.)

1. Some students had never watched "Jeopardy."

2. The best party I ever attended was given by my boss.

3. After the first day of registration last semester.

4. Have you ever gone swimming in the nude?

5. A private school would cost more than a public school.

6. On the first page you will find a diagnostic quiz.

7. All lifeguards must learn cardiopulmonary resuscitation.

8. The space shuttle has already provided scientific benefits.

9. A calculator might help you find the error.

10. A smart investor should pay attention to interest rates.

Verbals: The Fake Verbs

Writers often leave sentences incomplete because they mistake verbals for main verbs.

The man in the back row *wearing* a yellow necktie.

Is this a complete sentence?

If you answered yes, you may need to review the difference between verbs and verbals. *Verbals* are forms made from verbs but used for other purposes. *Wearing* in this sentence is only a descriptive word; "wearing a yellow necktie" describes the man, but it doesn't say what he does.

The man in the back row wearing a yellow necktie *lives* in Utah.

Now we have a complete sentence with a verb telling what the man does.

Verbals can be verb forms ending in *ing* (called **present participles** or **gerunds**), forms ending in *ed* (called **past participles**), or forms with *to* in front of them (called **infinitives**).

Examples:

Fragment: The car *approaching* the intersection.
Sentence: The car approaching the intersection *slowed* down in time to avoid an accident. (verb added)
Fragment: The prices *listed* on the menu.
Sentence: The prices listed on the menu *do* not *include* dessert.
Fragment: *Pitching* against left-handed batters.
Sentence: Pitching against left-handed batters *is* his specialty.

Fragment: To *express* yourself effectively before an audience.
Sentence: To express yourself effectively before an audience, you *should*
            learn the techniques of public speaking.

E X E R C I S E: Finding Subjects and Verbs

Underline the subjects and circle the verbs in the following paragraph. One sentence has deliberately been left incomplete; circle the number next to it.

(1) There is no question about it. (2) Being a member of a successful New York basketball team is a mixed blessing. (3) The notoriety* forces one to look at the world differently from other people. (4) It provides money and access. (5) At the same time, it sets one apart from the rest of society and denies one the privilege of being an equal member of a crowd. (6) There is little chance, for example, for a public figure to fail without people knowing it, and no one grows without failing. (7) Many avoid the embarrassment of public failure. (8) By never placing themselves in positions where they might fail. (9) Therefore, they never grow. (10) My constant problem is to find places where I am allowed to fail in private. (11) Everyone does not thirst for fame. (12) For me, fame holds as much danger as it does benefit.**

FRAGMENTS

You have already been identifying some fragments, or incomplete sentences, in the previous exercises. Fragments are fake sentences; they begin with capital letters and end with periods, but lack some necessary part.

---

*Notoriety: public attention.

**Bill Bradley, *Life on the Run*. New York: *Time Books*, 1976.

Telling the Difference Between Fragments and Sentences

In the previous exercises, either the subject or the verb was missing from fragments. Some fragments, however, are incomplete because a word at the beginning turns them into subordinate clauses.

A whole sentence can be called a **main clause:**

$$s \qquad v$$
The <u>siren</u> <u>was making</u> an ear-splitting noise.

A **subordinate,** or **dependent, clause** also has a subject and verb but begins with a word like *because* or *when,* which makes the whole clause incomplete. It becomes a modifying part of a sentence:

Because the siren was making an ear-splitting noise

To make it complete, you must add a main clause:

Because the siren was making an ear-splitting noise, *the nearby residents evacuated the area.*

Subordinate Clauses and Subordinating Conjunctions

The **subordinating conjunctions** are words that turn main clauses into subordinate clauses. If you begin a sentence with one of these words, you must add a main clause to complete the sentence.

Subordinating Conjunctions			
after	even though	since	whenever
although	ever since	though	where
as	for as long as	unless	whereas
because	if	until	wherever
before	just as	when	while

Subordinate Clause Fragments

Remember that clauses beginning with these words are not sentences but fragments.

Because the bus splashed mud on Tina's jeans.

Although the three brothers grew up in different families.

To make such fragments complete, add a main clause.

Because the bus splashed mud on Tina's jeans, *she bought a new pair.*

Although the three brothers grew up in different families, *they attended the same school.*

EXERCISE: Subordinate Clause Fragments

All of the following sentences begin with subordinating conjunctions from the list on page 193. Five of them are complete sentences because they have main clauses as well as subordinate clauses. Five are fragments. Underline the main clause in each complete sentence; write *F* next to each fragment.

1. Many people do not understand how we elect a president because our electoral system is rather complicated.

2. Although many people believe they are voting for a presidential candidate on Election Day.

3. When they go to the polls, American voters actually choose members of the electoral college.

4. Unless members of the electoral college violate a long tradition, they all vote for the candidate who won the most votes in their state.

5. Because this system makes it possible in a close race for a candidate who got the most popular votes to lose the election.

6. If no candidate receives a majority of the electoral votes, the House of Representatives chooses a president.

7. Whenever the electoral system comes up for discussion, especially during a closely contested election.

8. After the election of 1824, for instance, in which no candidate won a majority, the House of Representatives chose John Quincy Adams, who had come in second in the popular vote.

9. Since the electoral system is not a perfect example of government "by the people."

10. For as long as we have been electing presidents in the United States.

Added-Clause Fragments

Subordinate clause fragments often occur as an afterthought, an incomplete statement added to complete the thought of a previous sentence but left to stand by itself:

Sentence Followed by Added-Clause Fragment

He was an entertaining teacher. Because he ran his sociology class like a television talk show.

Corrected Version with Two Complete Sentences

He was an entertaining teacher. He ran his sociology class like a television talk show.

Corrected Version with Parts Combined Into One Sentence

He was an entertaining teacher because he ran his sociology class like a television talk show.

When correcting added-clause fragments, first check to see whether the fragment can be combined with the sentence before it; usually it can. If not, rewrite the fragment as a complete sentence; this usually means removing the subordinate conjunction (*because, when, if,* etc.) or changing the *who, which,* or *that* to *he, she,* or *it*.

E X E R C I S E: Added-Clause Fragments

Each item below contains two statements. If both are complete sentences, write C in the blank. If one is a fragment, either rewrite the pair as a single combined sentence or rewrite the fragment as a complete sentence.

Example: I lost half my research paper. Because my computer was infected with a virus.

Correction: *I lost half my research paper because my computer was*

infected with a virus.

1. Computer viruses are just like biological viruses. Because they spread from one computer to another by contact.

_____

_____

2. Your computer could be described as getting "sick." When it picks up a virus carried by a floppy disk.

_____

_____

3. A famous virus is called the Michaelangelo virus. One which is designed to take effect on March 6, the birthday of the artist.

_____

_____

4. Such viruses can be carried from a floppy disk to your computer's hard disk. Where it corrupts or erases data, possibly causing you to lose large amounts of valuable material.

_____

_____

5. Viruses can lie hidden in your files. Until they become activated on predetermined days.

_____

_____

6. Protective software has been designed to detect and remove viruses. Although many of these programs are effective, they are seldom foolproof.

_____

_____

7. One problem is that new viruses keep appearing frequently. Many of which succeed in escaping the anti-virus programs.

_____

_____

8. The plague of computer viruses has brought an upsurge in sales of anti-virus programs. Which can be bought for several hundred dollars.

_____

_____

9. Well-known viruses have fanciful names like Michaelangelo, Jerusalem, Stoned, Azusa, and Dark Avenger. Names that suggest the devilish imaginations of the people who invent and spread them.

_____

_____

10. Anti-virus programs tend to have names like Vaccine, PC Doctor, Virus-Cure, and Flu-Shot. As if they were brands of medicine or first-aid kits.

_____

_____

Added-Phrase Fragments

Another kind of fragment that occurs frequently in student writing is the **added-phrase fragment.** This may be a phrase beginning with a verbal (an *-ing* word or infinitive such as *to go, to read,* etc.), or it may be a prepositional phrase, even a string of prepositional phrases.

-ing *Word Fragments*

The last three miles of the race proved to be hilly and dangerous. *Leaving only the most daring motorcyclists in the race.*

Sarah decided not to go to the party on Friday night. *Being exhausted by the overtime work she had put in at her job on Thursday.*

Fragment Beginning with *to*

Christopher knew the one thing he wanted most of all in life. *To establish his own computer retail outlet.*

Prepositional Phrase Fragment

Eileen had many happy memories of her summer experiences. *In the Caribbean, in Venezuela, and along the coast of Florida.*

Connecting the Fragment

In each of these examples, the added-phrase fragment really belongs to the sentence preceding it. Usually such writing can be corrected by connecting the fragment to the preceding sentence:

1. The last three miles of the race proved to be hilly and dangerous, *leaving only the most daring motorcyclists in the race.*

2. *Being exhausted by the overtime work she had put in at her job on Thursday,* Sarah decided not to go to the party on Friday night.
3. Christopher knew the one thing he wanted most of all in life: *to establish his own computer retail outlet.*
4. Eileen had many happy memories of her summer experiences *in the Caribbean, in Venezuela, and along the coast of Florida.*

Bear in mind that not all word groups beginning with *to,* with *-ing* words, or with prepositional phrases have to be fragments. A sentence may begin with one of these phrases and then have a main clause after it, forming a complete statement. We could even use one of the added-phrase fragments from the preceding examples as the beginning of a complete sentence:

To establish his own computer retail outlet, Christopher borrowed money from a commercial bank.

As with dependent-clause fragments, the beginning word or phrase may warn you that you *may* have a fragment, *but you must look at the whole sentence to see if it is complete.*

EXERCISE: Added-Phrase Fragments

If the sentence or sentence group is complete, write C next to it. If it contains a fragment, write *F.*

_____ 1. To dramatize the sufferings of Dust Bowl farmers during the Great Depression, John Steinbeck wrote a novel called *The Grapes of Wrath.*

_____ 2. Zora Neale Hurston wrote a novel called *Their Eyes Were Watching God.* To portray a young black woman's search for love in rural Florida.

_____ 3. Mark Twain ends *Huckleberry Finn* with his hero about to "light out for the territory." Leaving the reader to wonder what will become of Huck in later life.

_____ 4. In World War I, in the Spanish Civil War, and in World War II, Ernest Hemingway served as a war correspondent. Collecting material for his novels and short stories as well.

_____ 5. Observing wealthy upper-class New Yorkers with a realistic eye, Edith Wharton wrote novels that won acclaim in the early twentieth century.

_____ 6. Henry James portrayed the dilemmas of highly sophisticated, educated Americans. Striving to find a cultural identity while living and traveling in England, France, and Italy.

_____ 7. In *Invisible Man,* Ralph Ellison depicts the efforts of a young black man to adjust to, as well as to change, American society. With its many forms of obvious and subtle racism.

_____ 8. J. D. Salinger, in *The Catcher in the Rye,* portrays the hostilities, resentments, and insecurities of an adolescent in the 1950s.

_____ 9. F. Scott Fitzgerald's main character in *The Great Gatsby* embodies the wild life-style of the rich during the Jazz Age. Throwing lavish parties attended by movie stars and riding around in a chauffeur-driven Rolls-Royce.

_____ 10. Saul Bellow portrays the humorous but also sad and self-defeating lives of urban people in our time. Focusing especially on middle-class people in Chicago and New York.

Added-Verb Fragments

Our last category of fragments is the type created by adding a second or third verb to the same subject in a sentence—but without joining the extra verb or verbs to the sentence. One subject in a sentence can have two or more verbs (we call these compound verbs), but all verbs must be in the same sentence with their subject. If you break them off and try to start a new sentence with them, you will automatically create a fragment.

Example:

Fragment: Sharon glanced out the window at the park. *And shrieked as she spotted her boyfriend kissing another woman.*

Fragment corrected: Sharon glanced out the window at the park and shrieked as she spotted her boyfriend kissing another woman.

In this example, *shrieked* is a second verb that matches the subject *Sharon* (*glanced* is the first verb). Both *glanced* and *shrieked* belong in the same sentence with their subject *Sharon*. If a period is placed after *park,* as in the first example, the remaining words create a fragment that has no subject (who shrieked?). Remember that every sentence must have a subject and verb that go together. Therefore, to correct added-verb fragments, you can simply drop the period and join the fragment to the preceding sentence, where it belongs. It is also possible to correct the fragment by adding a subject to match the verb:

Sharon glanced out the window at the park. *She* shrieked as she spotted her boyfriend kissing another woman.

E X E R C I S E: Added-Verb Fragments

Some of the passages that follow contain fragments; others are complete. Write *F* next to the fragments, *C* next to those that are correct.

_____ 1. Many people nowadays are interested in space exploration. But do not know very much about outer space.

_____ 2. Most people cannot tell the difference between a planet and a star by looking at them over a period of time. They do not know that a planet changes its position continually.

_____ 3. Some people also underestimate the vastness of space. And imagine that we could travel to other stars in a week or two.

_____ 4. Comets and meteors also cause a lot of confusion. And lead people to think of them as the same.

_____ 5. Comets may appear small in the night sky. But can be millions of miles long.

_____ 6. Meteors are usually about the size of a pea. But they seem large because they burn up in our own atmosphere.

_____ 7. Some Americans think we should stop spending money on space exploration entirely. And use the money to improve our standard of living instead.

_____ 8. This may be partly because we did not come back with anything particularly valuable from the moon. Or definitely prove that life exists on Mars.

_____ 9. Many scientists are at work trying to communicate with extraterrestrial beings by means of radio and other technological devices. And hope to discover that we are not alone in the universe.

_____ 10. Telescopes in satellites will also help us learn more about outer space. They can peer at other stars and galaxies more clearly because they do not have to look through the earth's atmosphere.

Three Ways to Correct Fragments

1. Connect fragments to the sentences that precede or follow them.
2. Add subjects or verbs to make fragments complete.
3. Add main clauses to make fragments complete.

Connect the fragment to the preceding sentence:

Fragment: The students sat in small groups. And read their papers aloud to one another.
Correction: The students sat in small groups and read their papers aloud to one another.

Add a subject or verb to make the fragment complete:

Fragment: The shell of the missile fell to earth. And landed in a woods in Kentucky.
Correction: The shell of the missile fell to earth. *It* landed in a woods in Kentucky.

Add a main clause to make the fragment complete:

Fragment: After Stanley and Evelyn quarreled about her getting a job.
Correction: After Stanley and Evelyn quarreled about her getting a job, Stanley got one himself.

In your own paragraphs and essays, one of the easiest ways to correct fragments is to join them to sentences next to them. Fragments are often pieces of longer sentences that were mistakenly broken off; usually they can be reattached to the sentences in front of them. Just be sure that the resulting sentence is not too long and complicated. To check for fragments, read your essay carefully as if it were a list of sentence exercises, taking each sentence one at a time. Notice especially the *beginning* of each sentence.

REVIEW EXERCISE: Correcting Fragments

In each of the following passages, underline the fragment. Then rewrite the passage with the fragment attached to the sentence before or after it, whichever makes sense.

Example:

Courses in technical writing are useful. *If you become a skilled technical writer.* You will find many job openings, usually at high pay.

Rewrite, with fragments attached to the sentence after it:

Courses in technical writing are useful. If you become a skilled technical writer, you will find many job openings, usually at high pay.

1. Euthanasia, or mercy killing, has become increasingly controversial. Some people believe that it is justified. When a patient is terminally ill and in pain.
2. Some people object that any intentional taking of life is wrong. Because life is sacred even when a person is not happy. Therefore they support laws prohibiting euthanasia.
3. Before taking a simple-minded stand on the issue. We should study the difference between several types of euthanasia. We may then decide that we accept some forms and not others.
4. One type is ending the use of life-support machines. For patients in pain and beyond hope of recovery. Cases of this kind have already been disputed in courts.
5. If a patient's death is possible only through a direct act such as administration of a lethal drug. Euthanasia becomes much more controversial. Some people still will argue that it is morally better to relieve suffering than prolong it.
6. When a patient is not conscious, euthanasia is especially open to dispute. One way to simplify the problem is to use a "living will." Stating that if the person is injured or ill beyond recovery and is unconscious, death would be preferable to remaining in a coma.

7. The big moral question is whether life itself is the highest priority. Or whether life without hope or consciousness should be terminated. Obviously people with different philosophies will continue to disagree on the answer.

8. The issue should be discussed in public. Since families, doctors, and hospitals do face such decisions. New medical technology, in fact, makes it easier to prolong life when the patient is in a coma.

SIMPLE, COMPOUND, AND COMPLEX SENTENCES

To be able to recognize and correct the next groups of sentence errors, you should review the three main types of sentences. Sentences can be **simple, compound,** or **complex:**

Simple sentences have one main clause, with one subject-verb combination:

$\quad$ *s* $\qquad$ *v*

Tony works after school in a restaurant.

Compound sentences* have two main clauses joined together; each clause has its own subject-verb combination:

$\quad$ *s* $\qquad$ *v* $\qquad\qquad\qquad\qquad\qquad$ *s* $\qquad$ *v*

Stephanie buys lottery tickets every week, but Frank spends his money on compact disc recordings.

Complex sentences have one main clause and one (sometimes more than one) dependent clause. Each clause has its own subject-verb combination. The dependent clause can come before or after the main clause:

Main clause before dependent clause:

$\quad$ *s* $\qquad\qquad$ *v*

Irene usually gives money to the homeless people in her neighborhood

$\qquad$ *s* $\quad$ *v*

because she feels sorry for them.

Main clause after dependent clause:

$\qquad$ *s* $\quad$ *v*

Because Irene feels sorry for the homeless people in her neighborhood,

$\quad$ *s* $\qquad$ *v*

she usually gives them money.

---

*See commas before conjunctions in compound sentences later in Unit 5.

E X E R C I S E: Simple, Compound, and Complex Sentences

Identify each sentence that follows by writing *S* (simple), *CD* (compound) or *CX* (complex) in the blank next to it.

————— 1. The American family has gone through many changes in the last twenty years.

————— 2. When our grandparents were growing up, they lived in traditional nuclear families.

————— 3. The nuclear family includes the father, the mother, and their children.

————— 4. There are still many nuclear families, but many other kinds of nontraditional families also exist.

————— 5. Because the divorce rate has increased, many families are headed by one parent.

————— 6. Many families also include stepchildren; these are often called "blended families," like the Brady Bunch.

————— 7. The Huxtables, on "The Cosby Show," were a nuclear family, but both parents were wage earners.

————— 8. If current trends continue, most American families will be nontraditional in one way or another.

————— 9. Some people think that nontraditional families are healthy; others believe that traditional families are better for children.

————— 10. Most Americans still believe that their family is the most important element in their lives.

RUN-TOGETHER SENTENCES

Every sentence should end with a period, exclamation point, or question mark. A **run-together sentence** occurs when a writer goes right through the end of the sentence like a driver going through a red light.

> I watched the man enter the bank suddenly I realized he was planning a hold-up.

In this sentence, "enter the bank suddenly" looks like it goes together as a phrase, and it's easy to miss the cutoff point between sentences. Reading more carefully, we see that we have two sentences, not one:

> I watched the man enter the bank. Suddenly I realized he was planning a hold-up.

If two sentences are closely related, you may want to put them together in a compound sentence instead of separating them. Do not run them together, and *do not put just a comma between them*; use a semicolon, as in this sentence. Use a semicolon also in sentences joined together by long connectives like *however, therefore, meanwhile, consequently,* and *nevertheless*. These are called **conjunctive adverbs;** put semicolons before them when they connect main clauses in compound sentences.

Examples: Run-together Sentences Corrected Two Ways:

Run-together sentence:	A many-colored float rolled slowly toward midfield it was circled by cheerleaders and a marching band.
Corrected as two separate sentences:	A many-colored float rolled slowly toward midfield. It was circled by cheerleaders and a marching band.
Corrected with a semicolon:	A many-colored float rolled slowly toward midfield; it was circled by cheerleaders and a marching band.
Run-together sentence:	The tenants sent many letters to the landlord about the lack of heat and electricity however he did not reply for two weeks.
Corrected as two separate sentences:	The tenants sent many letters to the landlord about the lack of heat and electricity. However, he did not reply for two weeks.
Corrected with a semicolon:	The tenants sent many letters to the landlord about the lack of heat and electricity; however, he did not reply for two weeks.

EXERCISE I: Separating Run-Together Sentences

The following paragraph contains five run-together sentences. Rewrite the paragraph, separating the run-together statements with periods or semicolons, *not with commas*.

(1) *Lasers are now being used for many purposes for instance they serve as surgical tools in operations on the skin, eyes, and blood vessels.* (2) *Lasers also have many military uses they can guide bombs to their targets or pierce metal surfaces.* (3) *In communications, lasers are used in new types of photographic systems some sound devices, such as walkie-talkies, employ lasers.* (4) *Both art and industry now make extensive use of laser beams, and corporations have discovered countless industrial uses.* (5) *For instance, lasers have dramatically improved welding techniques, drilling, and cutting everything from gems and metals to fabric and paper can be cut with laser devices.* (6) *Lasers once seemed a*

remote form of new technology soon, however, we may have lasers in our appli-
ances at home. (7) Yesterday's miracle may become tomorrow's commonplace.

EXERCISE 11: Separating Run-Together Sentences

Separate the following run-together sentences by inserting periods or semi-colons (<u>not</u> commas) between the main clauses. Two sentences are not run-to-gether. Write *C* next to them.

1. A number of frauds have been committed in the pursuit of scientific discoveries some were done by famous scientists.
2. Galileo, for example, although universally admired for creating the modern scientific method, may have never been able to conduct some of the experiments he claimed he did.
3. Even Sir Isaac Newton may have been dishonest at times some scientists now believe he "adjusted" some of his calculations to support his theories.
4. The best-known scientific hoax was the Piltdown Man this was a skull that was attached to an ape jaw to look like the "missing link."
5. Gregor Mendel is known to all biology students as the father of genetics he too probably falsified some of his experimental data.
6. The British psychologist Sir Cyril Burt achieved worldwide recognition for his research on intelligence and heredity after his death, however, researchers concluded that he had made up most of his data.
7. Kepler's law, which describes the orbits of the planets, proved to be correct; nevertheless Kepler probably doctored some of his calculations when he couldn't get them to fit.
8. A number of Nobel Prize winners have either been suspected of falsifying research or have actually been proven guilty of it.
9. In one case an American researcher coauthored scientific articles with forty-seven colleagues not one of them spotted the fraudulent material in them.
10. The percentage of experiments involving fraud is probably quite small still, universities have had to develop better ways of detecting it.*

COMMA SPLICES

In previous exercises you have been warned not to put a comma between the two statements in a run-together sentence. This common mistake is called the **comma splice.**

---

*Information from Linda Marsa, "Scientific Fraud," *Omni,* June 1992.

Example:

Comma splice: We arrived at Danceteria before the main crowd, then we decided to look for a good film near Times Square.

Correct: We arrived at Danceteria before the main crowd. Then we decided to look for a good film near Times Square.

Correcting Comma Splices

Correct comma splices the same way you would correct run-together sentences. Separate the main clauses with a semicolon, or divide them into two separate sentences with a period.

A third way to correct either run-together sentences or comma-spliced sentences is by *joining the main clauses with a connecting word and a comma.* The connecting words to remember are called **coordinating conjunctions.**

Coordinating Conjunctions

Use these short connecting words, with commas before them, to join main clauses: *

, and
, but
, or
, nor
, yet
, so
, for

Example: Compare this comma-spliced sentence with the correct one using a comma with a conjunction.

Comma splice: The retail price of the dress is $41.95, the wholesale price is $25.

Correction: The retail price of the dress is $41.95, *but* the wholesale price is $25.

Ways to Correct Comma-Spliced and Run-Together Sentences

- Divide the two statements into separate sentences.
- Use a semicolon between the statements.
- Join the statements with a comma and connecting word.

---

*You may want to use a familiar memory device to remember this list of connecting words: the first letters of these words spell out FANBOYS (*For, And, Nor, But, Or, Yet, So*).

Here is an example of the same comma-spliced sentence corrected all three ways.

Comma splice: Sandra enjoys soap operas, she never misses an episode of *General Hospital.*

Correction: Sandra enjoys soap operas. She never misses an episode of *General Hospital.*

Sandra enjoys soap operas; she never misses an episode of *General Hospital.*

Sandra enjoys soap operas, and she never misses an episode of *General Hospital.*

EXERCISE I: Comma Splices

Correct the following sentence in three ways.

Emil attends the University of Texas, he is finding the work difficult but interesting.

1. Separate sentences: _____

_____

2. With semicolon: _____

_____

3. With connecting word and comma: _____

_____

EXERCISE II: Comma Splices

Each of the following sentences has a comma in the middle. If the sentence is correct, write C in the blank; if it contains a comma splice, divide it into two sentences or rewrite it using a semicolon or comma and connecting word.

1. Most Latin American countries became independent early in the nineteenth century, at that time the Spanish Empire had become weakened.

_____

_____

2. Because many Latin American cities refused to recognize Napoleon's brother Joseph as their leader, the control that Spain once held over the New World began to slip.

_____

_____

3. In 1817, Jose de San Martin helped Chile gain independence, he led his army in a heroic climb over the Andes.

_____

_____

4. Brazil became independent in 1828, it was still called an "empire" until 1889.

_____

_____

5. When Simon Bolivar defeated the Spanish at Boyaca in 1819, Colombia also joined the emerging group of independent nations.

_____

_____

6. In 1823, the United States proclaimed the Monroe Doctrine, this declaration warned European powers against further colonization in the Americas.

_____

_____

7. The United States, however, was not yet a great world power, the British navy actually did more than the United States to keep other countries out of Latin America.

_____

_____

_____

REVIEW EXERCISE: Comma Splices and Run-Together Sentences

Rewrite these sentences, separating the main clauses in one of these ways: (1) into two sentences, (2) with semicolons, or (3) with commas and short connectives. If a sentence is correct, write C next to it.

1. Most people have heard of the main laws of science and the social sciences, they should recognize, however, that the laws of nature are usually more precise than those of human behavior.
2. Kepler's law explains the motion of the planets around the sun, most students of astronomy master it early in their studies.
3. Darwin proposed the theory of evolution in 1859, then he explained its meaning for mankind in *The Descent of Man* in 1871.
4. Einstein's theory of relativity is generally known to be the basis for atomic energy, however, not many people understand it.
5. In 1798, the English economist Thomas Malthus proposed a theory of population he argued that population would increase geometrically (2, 4, 8, 16, etc.), while food supply would increase arithmetically (1, 2, 3, 4, etc.).
6. Another well-known theory in the social sciences is Gresham's law this law states that currency of low value drives currency of high value out of circulation.
7. There are also theories of linguistics Grimm's law and Verner's law, for instance, explain patterns of change in spoken language.
8. Some amusing "laws" have been concocted to explain social phenomena; Parkinson's law, for example, states that work expands to fit the manpower available.
9. The Peter Principle describes the workings of status levels, or hierarchies, it states that workers are promoted until they reach their "level of incompetence," where they remain in jobs they perform poorly.
10. Perhaps the most reliable principle describing modern society is Murphy's law, which states that whatever can go wrong will go wrong.

CORRECTING BY SUBORDINATING

A fourth way to correct run-together sentences and comma splices is to subordinate one statement to another. This means to turn one of the main clauses into a subordinate clause. Do this by adding one of the subordinate conjunctions like *because* or *when* to one of the main clauses or by beginning one of the main clauses with *who, which,* or *that* (making that clause a **relative** subordinate clause).

Run-together sentence:

The students felt nervous they had an examination that morning.

Correction by subordinating one clause:

The students felt nervous *because* they had an examination that morning.

The students, *who* had an examination that morning, felt nervous.

E X E R C I S E: Subordination

Correct the sentences that follow by making one main clause a subordinate clause. Use *although, because, if,* or *when* to subordinate one clause, or use *who, which,* or *that* to make it a relative clause.

1. Some experts once predicted that computers would make books obsolete, this has not happened so far.

   _____

   _____

2. The computer age began in the 1960s, this age has brought an increase in book publication.

   _____

   _____

3. The use of computers has actually increased the number of books many of them have been written about computers.

   _____

   _____

4. Books on word processing appear every month they have become too numerous to count.

   _____

   _____

5. Other areas of activity besides publishing expand as well, computer technology has an impact on them.

   _____

   _____

6. Teachers once feared they would be replaced by computers, they have discovered that their role is even more important than before.

_____

_____

7. Computers have enhanced rather than eliminated the teacher's job, teachers now can use computers to relieve them of meaningless drills.

_____

_____

8. A person doesn't know vocabulary like *software* and *spreadsheet programs* he or she is behind the times.

_____

_____

9. It may not be necessary to become a computer programmer, in tomorrow's world, all educated people will be familiar with computer language.

_____

_____

10. Home computers become as common as television sets the effect on our lives will be no less than a computer revolution.

_____

_____

SUBJECT-VERB AGREEMENT

In the **present tense,** use the correct form of the verb to match the subject. Singular subjects take singular verbs:

s v
Paula usually <u>arrives</u> on time.

Plural subjects take plural verbs:

   s   *s*   *v*

Paula and Richard usually arrive on time.

> **Hint**
>
> Verbs in the singular take the *s* ending in the present, unless *I* or *you* is the subject

	Singular	*Plural*
First person:	I write	We write
Second person:	You write	You write
Third person:	She, he, it *writes*	They write

Singular and Plural Subjects

Learn to tell the difference between singular and plural nouns. Most nouns form the plural by adding *s* or *es* to the singular.

Singular Nouns	*Plural Nouns*
one ticket	three tickets
a computer	both computers
my shoe	my shoes
Susan's typewriter	Susan's typewriters

Some nouns form their plurals in unusual ways. Some change their spelling instead of adding *s:*

Singular	*Plural*
a woman	four women
the man	those men
one child	all my children
your foot	both your feet
a mouse	two mice

Some stay the same in singular and plural:

one deer	a herd of deer
a big fish	a school of fish
a pet sheep	hundreds of sheep

Words ending in *f* or *fe* may change the *f* to *v* before adding *es:*

one half	both halves
one life	many lives
his wife	several wives

But in some words the *f* remains:

a steep roof	many roofs
definite proof	a number of proofs

Words ending in *o* sometimes take *s* and sometimes *es:*

hero	ten heroes
this tomato	ten tomatoes
one stereo	several stereos
my radio	our radios

Words ending in *y* usually change the *y* to *i* before *es:*

a large company	many companies
a new secretary	two new secretaries

But those with vowels before the *y* just add *s:*

a good play	three good plays
a new toy	some new toys

Hint

Use your dictionary to find the plural forms of nouns that you are uncertain about. If no plural is listed, you should add *s* or *es*.

E X E R C I S E I: Singular and Plural Subjects

Write *singular* or *plural* after each noun:

1. tests _____

2. scientists _____

3. bus _____

4. guitars _____

5. videodisc _____

6. hamburgers _____

7. professor _____

8. section _____

9. experiences _____

10. parent _____

E X E R C I S E I I: Singular Subjects

The following list contains *ten* subjects in the third person singular. Circle these ten. Then write ten sentences using them as subjects, remembering to use the *s* form of the verb in every sentence.

he	I
the store	your opinion
my shoes	her dress
that dog	our reasons
a test	seven women
two books	this corner
they	it
she	the game

Finding and Correcting Errors in Agreement

Most errors in subject-verb agreement involve missing *s* endings on nouns or verbs. Sometimes writers put *s* endings where they should not be.

Typical Errors:

Incorrect Singular Statement:	My sister Lucia *insist* on doing her best.
Corrected Form:	My sister Lucia *insists* on doing her best.
Incorrect plural statement:	Those people always *argues* with foreign visitors.
Corrected form:	Those people always *argue* with foreign visitors.

EXERCISE: Correcting Errors in Agreement

Some of the verbs in the following sentences agree with their subjects; some do not. If the verb is correct, write *C* in the blank; if not, write the correct form.

1. Wise investing depend upon several factors.   _____

2. It involves your income, needs, and willingness to take risks.   _____

3. Some people invests their money only in stocks.   _____

4. Other opportunities also exists.   _____

5. Municipal bonds, mutual funds, and term savings accounts all offer investment advantages.   _____

6. The right kind of investment for you mean considering several elements.   _____

7. Tax benefits from municipal bonds appeals to some investors.   _____

8. Stocks present possibilities for high income but with high risk.   _____

9. The investor who wants to avoid risks often choose mutual funds.   _____

10. Corporate bonds also offer high income possibilities but also with greater risk than municipal bonds.   _____

Special Problems with Agreement

Forms of Be, Have, *and* Do

The common helping verbs *be, have,* and *do* present special difficulties with agreement because they have more forms than other verbs. Instead of just adding an *s* ending, *be* has these forms:

	Singular	*Plural*
First person:	I *am*	We *are*
Second person:	You *are*	You *are*
Third person:	He, she, it *is*	They *are*

Note: In the **past tense,** *be* is the only verb that can cause agreement problems because it has two forms:

	Singular	*Plural*
	She was	They were

   Have has two forms in the present: *has* for third person singular and *have* for all other subjects.

   Do also has two forms: *does* for third person singular and *do* for all the others. Be careful about *don't* and *doesn't* as well.

EXERCISE I: *Be, Have,* and *Do*

Underline all 15 incorrect forms of be, have, and do in the following paragraph. Write the correct forms above the wrong ones.

   People has to face many pressures on holidays. Those who entertain a lot

has to send invitations to friends and relatives, prepare food, and decorate their homes. On some holidays, especially Christmas, giving gifts are in order, so many people does a lot of shopping and has to worry about choosing, wrapping, and mailing presents. On religious holidays, churches, synagogues, and mosques is full of worshippers practicing their religion. Loneliness and depression is widespread during major holidays, especially among the elderly, who is often far away from their relatives. Many families has to plan and pack for vacation trips during the holidays, and the crowded hotels and highways is usually a source of difficulty for them. Patients in hospitals, inmates in penitentiaries, and children in foster homes is likely to feel more isolated during holidays than at other times because they does not share the holiday festivities with their families. The financial and emotional pressures of the holidays has an effect on the rates of suicide, crime, and mental illness. Although most experts is likely to agree that the importance we place on holidays does great harm, few of us is going to stop observing and enjoying our favorite holidays. The pleasures of holiday parties and vacations is too great for us to abandon.

EXERCISE 11: *Be, Have,* and *Do*

Fill in the correct forms of *be, have,* and *do.*

1. Over the years, many theories about human origins _____ been posited.

2. Most scientists agree that the origin of pre-humans, called *Homo erectus,* _____ in Africa a million years ago.

3. Scientists _____ not agree, however, on where modern human beings, called *Homo sapiens,* _____ first found.

4. Some geneticists in recent years _____ proposed the Eve theory, which now _____ many distinguished supporters.

5. The main idea of this theory _____ that all modern human beings _____ descended from one woman who lived in Africa 200,000 years ago.

6. These scientists _____ their research by comparing the DNA of people from all parts of the world.

7. The evidence _____ prove one important fact: that all human beings _____ very closely related to one another.

8. Some scientists _____ not accept the Eve theory; they believe it _____ more probable that modern human beings developed in many parts of the world after pre-humans spread out from Africa.

9. If the Eve theory _____ prove correct, one important event _____ to be explained.

10. How _____ the new humans (*Homo sapiens*) from Africa replace all the pre-humans that _____ living in the Middle East, Europe, and Asia?

Subjects That Come After Verbs

Some of the sentences in the preceding exercises may have made you stop and think. You could not always just choose a verb that "sounded right." Such difficulty is likely to occur in sentences that do not follow the ordinary subject-verb-object order. Sometimes the verb comes before the subject; when it does, you can choose the right verb form only by finding the subject and matching the verb with it.

Verbs come before subjects in several kinds of sentences:

1. Questions usually contain reversed word order.

   v   *s*
   <u>Are</u> there any new <u>students</u> here today?

      v   *s*
   Why <u>have</u> the <u>lights</u> been turned off?

2. Sentences beginning with <u>there</u> or <u>here</u> place the verb before the subject:

      v   *s*
   There <u>have</u> to be many <u>reasons</u> for her decision.

      v   *s*
   Here <u>is</u> an exciting <u>picture</u> of her as a teenager.

3. Sentences beginning with descriptive phrases sometimes place the verb before the subject:

                  v   *s*
   Behind the door <u>were</u> three armed <u>men</u>.

                  v   *s*
   Sprayed on the walls <u>was</u> an angry <u>message</u>.

Notice that in such sentences you should not try to match the verb with the word right before it so that the combination sounds right. You must find the subject *after* the verb. In the last sentence, not the *walls were* but the *message was* sprayed on the walls.

EXERCISE I: Subjects That Come After Verbs

Underline the subject in each sentence and circle the correct verb form in parentheses:

1. There (is, are) several important terms used in economics.

2. Among the most familiar (is, are) *inflation* and *recession*.

3. What (has, have) been the primary cause of inflation?

4. There (has, have) to be several causes.

5. (Doesn't, Don't) a recession also have many possible causes?

6. Probably the simplest of all economic terms (is, are) the word *money*.

7. How simple, however, (do, does) the many conceptions of money prove to be?

8. (Is, Are) all forms of payment, including checks, credit cards, and traveler's checks, to be considered money?

9. Among other cultures (is, are) such kinds of currency as shells, beads, gold, and animals' teeth.

10. In the ancient world (was, were) still other forms of money, such as goods and services that people exchanged for other goods and services.

EXERCISE II: Subjects That Come After Verbs

Compose sentences beginning with the phrases below:

1. What is _____?

2. There are _____.

3. How does _____?

4. Along the fence are _____.

5. What have _____?

6. On the sidewalk were _____.

7. Where have _____?

Special Subjects

Some subjects are hard to match with verbs because they seem to be plural but are singular grammatically or because they are singular when used one way and plural when used another.

Singular Pronouns	*Singular/Plural Words*
everyone	all
anyone	half
someone	some
everybody	most
anybody	more
somebody	

Write *everyone has* some kind of special talent, not *have. Each, either,* and *one* are also singular, even though they are often followed by plural phrases. *Each* of the students *is* (not *are*). *Either* of the women *has* the right to participate (not *have*).

Some words are singular when they refer to amounts and plural when they refer to numbers.

All of the money *has* been spent (singular—an amount)
All of the visitors *are* required to wear passes (plural—a number)

E X E R C I S E: Special Subjects

Choose the correct form of each verb in parentheses; underline the subject before writing the verb in the blank.

1. Despite the enormous wealth in America, many still _____ (be) unemployed in the big cities.

2. According to federal reports, almost half of working-age residents in the largest cities _____ (be) neither employed nor looking for work.

3. Most of the young people in their late teens _____ (do) not have either part-time or full-time jobs.

4. In some cities only about one out of three men and women between sixteen and nineteen years of age _____ (be) in the labor force.

5. Each of the unemployed _____ (have) a reason for not working; it may be lack of skills, psychological problems, dependence on drugs or alcohol, or unavailability of jobs.

6. Some economists _____ (do) not give us hopeful predictions, because improved economic conditions do not seem to improve these unemployment figures.

7. All of the experts _____ (be) in agreement that the source of the problem is deeply rooted in our changing society.

8. Everyone who lives in or near a large city _____ (have) a stake in this problem.

9. Anyone who has been out of a job _____ (have) to realize what a serious problem unemployment is.

10. All of the money that has been spent on job programs _____ (have) not been able to solve the problem yet.

Group Nouns

Nouns that refer to groups of people present a special problem: Words like *army, family, team, jury, chorus, union, committee, company,* and *organization* seem to be plural because they refer to many people; however, they have plural forms (armies, families, etc.), so the singular forms should be used with singular verbs. An *army marches* on its stomach, or The *team has* won eleven games this season. When you refer to such words as single units, using the singular form, use singular verbs as well. However, when you use the word to refer to the individual members of the group, it is permissible to use a plural verb. Some writers find it awkward and not strictly correct to write, the team *are* taking their places on the field. It is less objectionable to write, the players *are* taking their places, or the members of the team are taking their places. Most experts agree that it is permissible, at least, to use group nouns as plurals in this way. Just be sure to tell the difference between the group as a unit (singular) and as separate individuals (plural).

E X E R C I S E: Group Nouns

Circle the correct verb form in each sentence.

1. The committee (has, have) reached its decision.

2. Our family (has, have) an unusual kind of annual reunion.

3. The army (has, have) just published a new training manual.

4. The band (don't, doesn't) usually leave their instruments in the rehearsal room.

5. The company (is, are) making its projections for the next year.

6. The union (schedule, schedules) a meeting every Wednesday.

7. The jury sometimes (disagree, disagrees) violently with one another.

8. The police force (include, includes) members of all minority groups.

9. The Polar Bear Club (hold, holds) meetings during the winter.

10. The chorus usually (arrive, arrives) at the church around seven o'clock.

Verbs Separated from Subjects by Prepositional Phrases

A verb will often be separated from its subject by a prepositional phrase. Do not be confused by such phrases. *A subject cannot be part of a prepositional phrase.* If you try to match the verb with a word next to it, sometimes you may miss the subject and choose the wrong verb form. Notice the difference:

       s   *v*
1. The <u>names</u> <u>are</u> in alphabetical order.

  s   *v*
2. <u>One</u> ~~of the names on the list~~ <u>is</u> out of place.

In sentence 2, the subject *one* is separated from the verb *is* by two prepositional phrases, "of the names" and "on the list." You must mentally cross out these phrases and match the subject with the verb: "One . . . is out of place."

What are prepositional phrases? They are phrases made out of the little relational words like *in, of, with,* etc. Some of the most common prepositions are listed below:

about	beneath	like	through
above	beside	next to	to
across	between	of	toward
along	by	off	under
among	for	on	with
at	from	onto	
before	in	over	
behind	into	past	

E X E R C I S E: Verbs Separated from Subjects

In the following sentences underline the subject, cross out the prepositional phrase or phrases between the subject and verb, and circle the verb that matches the subject.

Example: The <u>cars</u> ~~in the lot across the street~~ (is, (are)) for sale.

1. Some <u>students</u> in a difficult nursing program (find, finds) the science courses challenging.

2. One of the trails in the western section of the park (has, have) been closed to hikers.

3. Training for guidance counselors (include, includes) courses in psychology and sociology.

4. Detroit and Chicago, along with five other cities, (has, have) undergone changes in residential patterns.

5. Long-lasting parties with techno-music and funky clothes (is, are) called raves.

6. Conflicts in countries like Rwanda and Bosnia (has, have) caused unbelievable suffering.

7. A stimulating environment with objects that appeal to the five senses (is, are) necessary to an infant's development.

8. A woman with ambitious career plans (need, needs) a good tax accountant.

9. The money from the sales of the films (belong, belongs) to the corporation.

10. Running in hot weather (deplete, depletes) the body's store of water.

Compound Subjects: And *versus* Either/Or

Two or more subjects joined by *and* take a plural verb:

North Carolina and *Tennessee* have good teams this year.

Rhoda and *Richard* are my best friends.

Joining two subjects with *either . . . or,* however, does not make the subjects plural. A statement with *either . . . or* says that only one person does the action:

Either *Sandra* or *Ted* is going to drive.

This sentence takes a singular verb because it says that one person is going to drive. Notice, however, that *either . . . or* sometimes joins subjects that are already plural; then of course the verb is plural:

Either *parents* or *teachers* have to be notified.

A rare sentence may contain one singular and one plural subject joined by *either . . . or.* This is awkward, so try to avoid it; if you can't, the rule is to make the verb agree with the subject nearer to it:

Either *Fred* or his *brothers are* going to inherit a fortune.

E X E R C I S E: Compound Subjects

Underline the subjects and circle the correct verbs in these sentences.

1. Either Diane or Carla (know, knows) how to do that problem.

2. Either cocaine or heroin (was, were) found in their possession.

3. Either Syria or Jordan (send, sends) diplomats.

4. Coffee, tea, and orange juice (is, are) served during the break.

5. Either sociology or government (is, are) a prerequisite.

6. Accounting and business management (is, are) offered every semester.

7. Either Chinese or Italian food (seem, seems) to suit her taste.

8. Either President Clinton or his advisers (answer, answers) such letters.

9. Payments and receipts (show, shows) up on the same financial statement.

10. Either the C train or the downtown express (stop, stops) at that station.

Compound Verbs

Many sentences have two or more verbs that go with the same subject. Be sure to make all such verbs agree with their subjects; it is easy to slip and not notice that one of them, usually the last one, does not agree with the subject. Notice the error in this sentence:

> Derrick always gets up at seven, drives to work, and spend his whole morning at the office.

How many verbs go with the subject *Derrick?* Which one does not agree?

E X E R C I S E: Compound Verbs

Circle the incorrect verbs in these sentences and write the correct forms in the blanks. If a sentence is correct, write *C.*

1. Sociology, as an academic discipline, is
   fairly modern and have a less ancient tradition than history or philosophy.   _____

2. Although their methods are less rigid than those of chemists or physicists, sociologists apply scientific methods to social problems and uses mathematical analysis. _____

3. Their subject of study, human behavior, cannot be put on a microscope slide and are harder to predict than the weather. _____

4. The researchers themselves are susceptible to bias but tries to be as objective as biologists or astronomers. _____

5. The French sociologist Emile Durkheim is famous for his studies of suicide and are often named as the first to use scientific research methods in sociology. _____

6. Talcott Parsons' writings set a high standard of sophistication for American sociology but were difficult to read. _____

7. Symbolic interactionism, a sociological approach also created in the United States, identifies symbolic meanings in society and emphasize how people interpret what they see. _____

8. Sociology and psychology are closely related disciplines but has different approaches to similar problems. _____

9. Mental illness, for example, is studied by sociologists as well as psychologists and are not fully understandable without both kinds of analysis. _____

10. Social groups and social change are important to all sociological schools of thought and have to be explained systematically. _____

Verbs In Who, Which, *and* That *Clauses*

Verbs that come after *who, which,* or *that* are usually tricky because these relative pronouns can be either singular or plural. You cannot tell whether a clause should read "who is" or "who are" without knowing whether the *who* is singular or plural. You must identify the antecedent,* or preceding word that *who* represents. *Who, which,* and *that* are relative pronouns; that is, they *relate* to something earlier in the same sentence. The verb depends on the word that *who* or *which* represents. For instance, you would use a singular verb in the phrase "a student who *registers* for Spanish" but a plural verb in the phrase "students who *register* for Spanish." Use a singular verb in the phrase

_____

*See pronouns and antecedents later in Unit 5.

"a course that *requires* a term paper" but a plural verb in the phrases "courses that *require* term papers."

E X E R C I S E: Verbs in *Who, Which,* and *That* Clauses

Underline the antecedent of *who, which,* or *that* in each sentence and supply a verb form that agrees with it.

1. A person who _____ a lie detector test is being measured for certain bodily responses.

2. These responses, which _____ pulse rate, breathing, and skin sensitivity, may indicate whether the person is telling the truth.

3. A person suspected of a crime who _____ false information while taking a lie detector test may register sudden changes in heart rate, perspiration, or blood pressure.

4. Persons who _____ very anxious about the situation in which they take the test, however, may register such changes without lying.

5. Furthermore, experts who _____ been able to train themselves to control their reactions have succeeded in passing lie detector tests even when they were lying.

6. A defendant who _____ to strengthen his case in court may sometimes take a lie detector test to prove his innocence.

7. Attorneys who _____ ways to include results of lie detector tests in their defense cannot rely mainly on such evidence.

R E V I E W   E X E R C I S E   I: Subject-Verb Agreement

Underline the subject or subjects and write in a correct verb form in each sentence.

1. Parapsychology, which studies mental experiences outside the normal range of human perception, _____ controversy.

2. Supporters, who claim that it is a legitimate science, _____ that it will reveal exciting truths.

3. Opponents, who deride it as a pseudoscience, _____ it to be harmful because it encourages irrational thinking.

4. Among some of the parapsychological subjects _____ telekinesis (movement of objects with the power of thought alone) and telepathy (mind reading).

5. A belief in precognition, or the ability to tell the future, _____ widespread in many societies.

6. Extrasensory powers such as clairvoyance (the ability to perceive events and objects beyond the reach of the senses) _____ been claimed by some people and exhibited to the public.

7. Psychics who _____ been called in for assistance by the police _____ sometimes been helpful in solving crimes.

8. Throughout the ages, prophets in many countries _____ made predictions of cataclysmic events.

9. Rising to challenge the claims of psychics and prophets, however, _____ been a small army of professional magicians and skeptics who often _____ the tricks used by these alleged supernaturalists.

10. A further problem _____ : the believers in parapsychology _____ not yet explained any scientific laws that would account for the magical events they claim to observe.

REVIEW EXERCISE II: Subject-Verb Agreement

Rewrite the following paragraph, converting it from plural to singular. Remember to include *s* endings on singular verbs. Instead of beginning the paragraph with Ellen and Janet, begin with just Ellen. Use *she* instead of *they*. Change *daughters* to *daughter*.

    Ellen and Janet have teenage daughters who insist on dressing and behaving in ways that antagonize their mothers. They disapprove of their daughters' hairstyles, which usually are spiked and have shades of purple. They often get angry over their choice of clothes as well. Their daughters often wear their jeans with holes in the knees and wear dresses and skirts that are so short that their mothers think they look like prostitutes. Their daughters resent what they consider their mothers' bossiness and intolerance, especially when it comes to choice of friends. They think they should be able to choose their own friends, but their mothers believe they always cling to the wildest and most antisocial individuals among their peers. Both mothers are afraid that their daughters are going to become drug ad-dicts or get killed in a car accident caused by a drunken driver. They are also afraid that their daughters will drop out of school and become pregnant. Both Ellen and Janet have tried to involve their daughters in family counseling, but the results have been only temporarily successful. Both women hope they can survive their daughters' adolescence without any major catastrophes.

S ENDINGS: A REVIEW

Many writers have trouble with *s* endings. This happens because *s* endings can be added to words for different reasons. Some words, of course, already end in *s*, like *kiss* or *class*. There are four *s* endings that we *add* to words:

Adding *s* Endings

1. Add *s* or *es* to verbs in the third person singular, present tense: The dancer moves.
2. Add s or *es* to plural nouns: The dancers move.
3. Add *'s* to singular possessives: a dancer's movements.*
4. Add s' to most plural possessives: four dancers' movements.
   (Exception: Add *'s* to plural possessives: when the pural does not already end in *s*: women's opinions.)

EXERCISE I: S Endings

Identify which of the *s* endings listed in the box is underlined in each sentence and write the number from the box (1, 2, 3, or 4).

Example: __1__ The jury want<u>s</u> more evidence.

_____ 1. Most citizen<u>s</u> know their constitutional rights.
_____ 2. The public need<u>s</u> to be informed by the media.
_____ 3. Most state<u>s'</u> constitutions have similar features.
_____ 4. Changes in constitutions take the form of amendment<u>s</u>.
_____ 5. The first ten amendments to the Constitution of the United States are called the Bill of Right<u>s</u>.
_____ 6. Passing an amendment require<u>s</u> a three-fourths majority of the states.
_____ 7. Amendment<u>s</u> can also be repealed.
_____ 8. The prohibition amendment'<u>s</u> unpopularity caused it to be re-pealed in the early 1930s.
_____ 9. The most recent amendment to approach a three-fourths vote was the Equal Right<u>s</u> Amendment.

*See apostrophes later in this unit.

———— 10. The National Organization for Women still supports this amendment.

EXERCISE 11: *S* Endings

Proofread the paragraph that follows. Circle the *ten* errors in the use of *s* endings—either incorrect or missing endings. Write the correct endings above the errors.

Stacy's Pet Peeves

Stacy made a list of her pet peeves. She decided that the list would include only things that could be called annoyance, not serious dangers or threats. The first one that occurred to her was what she calls "fall-outs." These are the subscription cards that fall out every time she pick up a magazine to read. Another one is the ballpoint pen that is supposed to clip into her shirt or blouse pocket but falls on the floor every time she bend down. Outside Stacy building there are some more irritation. She particularly dislikes the scaffolds that are erected to renovate storefronts because they makes it impossible for two people to walk side by side. Many restaurant's noise levels also add to the nuisances in Stacy's life. She finds it hard to talk to friend over the hubbub of voices and pots and pans. Like many people she also object to people smoking in buses, airplanes, and other closed-in places. And she hates to go on very hot days to movie theaters, restaurants, or supermarket where the air-conditioning is so cold that she has to wear a sweater to keep from shivering.

SPECIAL PROBLEMS WITH VERB TENSES

Verb tenses present many special problems. We will consider the following nine.

- Recognizing past, present, and future tenses
- *D* endings in the past—regular verbs

- When *not* to use *d* endings
- The past tense of irregular verbs
- Forming past participles
- Past participles with helping verbs
- Past participles as adjectives
- Past participles of irregular verbs
- Avoiding shifts in verb tense

Recognizing Tenses

To use correct verb tenses and avoid awkward shifts in tense, you must know the verb tenses and what they mean. There are three basic verb tenses:

Present: Phyllis *enjoys* racquetball.
Past: Phyllis *enjoyed* racquetball.
Future: Phyllis *will enjoy* racquetball.

Present Tense

All verbs take *s endings* (singular, third person) or *no endings* (plural and first and second person singular) in the present.

	Singular	**Plural**
First person:	I succeed	We succeed
Second person:	You succeed	You succeed
Third person:	He, she, it succeeds	They succeed

All verbs follow these forms for the present tense.

Past Tense

In the past tense, verbs fall into two categories: regular verbs, which take *d* endings, and irregular verbs, which change their spelling and do not take *d* endings.

Past Tense for Regular Verbs	*Past Tense for Irregular Verbs*
succeeded	became
walked	bought
kissed	saw
stampeded	drank
murdered	sang
worshipped	took
doubted	drove
discussed	broke
wandered	spent

Future Tense

All verbs form the future tense by adding the helping verb *will* to the main verb with no ending.

will succeed   will study
will deliver   will purchase
will work   will spend
will register   will jog

D Endings in the Past Tense

One of the most common writing errors is dropping or forgetting to add *d* endings on regular verbs.

EXERCISE: *D* Endings in the Past Tense

Circle incorrect verb forms and write the correct forms in the blanks.

1. Many natural disasters have occur in the twentieth century. _____

2. Avalanches, floods, earthquakes, hurricanes, and mudslides have happen all over the world. _____

3. The San Francisco earthquake in 1906 was one of the most famous because it demolish hundreds of beautiful buildings. _____

4. The most lethal earthquake in recent years was the one in Armenia in 1988, in which over 55,000 people perish. _____

5. The worst flood in modern times and possibly in history occurred when the Hwang Ho River overflow in 1931, killing millions of people. _____

6. Hurricane Andrew pass through southern Florida in 1992 and caused billions of dollars' worth of property damage. _____

7. In 1959 Typhoon Vera nearly destroy Nagoya, Japan's third largest city. _____

8. In 1963, when Hurricane Flora almost wiped out the Cuban coffee crop, Fidel Castro apply to the United States for aid. _____

9. The volcano Mount Pelée erupted in Martinique in 1902; it spew forth lethal gas that killed 36,000 people.   _____

10. The famous Mount Vesuvius in Italy erupt several times in the twentieth century: in 1905, 1929, and 1944.   _____

When *Not* to Use *D* Endings

If you tend to omit *d* endings in the past tense, remember that there are a few places where *d* endings should not be used. No *d* endings:

1. After the helping word *did*. *Did* is already in the past tense and does not need another past tense form to go with it:

   Did you *discuss* (not *discussed*) the salary?

   It really *did happen* (not *happened*) that way.

2. After other helping verbs (except *be* and *have*): *may, might, can, could, will, would, must,* and *should*:

   We *will walk* (not *walked*) there together.

   He *could learn* (not *learned*) a lot from you.

3. After the word *to*. A verb with the word *to* in front of it is called an infinitive; it is not in the past tense and does not take a *d* ending:

   We used *to live* (not *to lived*) in Cincinnati.

   They tried *to reach* (not *to reached*) the turnoff.

E X E R C I S E: Using *D* Endings

Write the correct form of each verb in the blank. Keep in mind that regular verbs in the past tense need *d* endings and that verbs following helping verbs (other than *have* and *be*) do not.

1. Epics are long stories or poems that record heroic actions that

   _____ long ago.
   (happen)

2. The names of the writers who _____ the earliest folk epics are
   (compose)
   often unknown.

3. Folk epics _____ in many countries—for instance, the
   (appear)
   Mahabharata in India, the *Sundiata* in Mali, the *Iliad* in Greece, and

   Beowulf in England.

4. The heroes of these stories usually _____ superhuman strength
   (possess)
   or magical powers.

5. Epics also often _____ lessons and moral advice that the
   (contain)
   listeners were supposed to _____ in their own lives.
   (follow)

6. Stories of this kind _____ down religious traditions from
   (hand)
   century to century and were thought to _____ historical truths.
   (preserve)

7. Sophisticated writers in later times, such as Vergil and Dante,

   _____ the epic form to _____ more polished and artificial
   (imitate)   *(create)*
   poems, sometimes called art epics.

8. In modern times some poets have _____ to _____ long
   (attempt)   *(compose)*
   autobiographical works in this tradition called personal epics.

9. Walt Whitman's "Song of Myself," the best known example of this

   type, _____ many American poets to try this form.
   (influence)

10. Ezra Pound's *Cantos*, William Carlos Williams' *Paterson*, and Derek

    Walcott's *Omeros* _____ on this tradition and did _____
    (pass)   *(attract)*
    the attention of poets to this form, even though the general public

    does not _____ these works as often as they should.
    (enjoy)

The Past Tense of Irregular Verbs

Irregular verbs never take *d* endings. Instead, they change in different ways—
go changes to *went*, *think* to *thought*, and so on. Most of these verbs you know
by usage, but some do cause frequent mistakes. Look over this list to see if you
recognize the past tenses.

Present	*Past*	*Present*	*Past*
be (am, is, are)	was, were	make	made
become	became	meet	met
begin	began	pay	paid
bring	brought	put	put
buy	bought	quit	quit
choose	chose	rise	rose
cost	cost	seek	sought
do	did	sell	sold
cut	cut	send	sent
feel	felt	shine	shone
fly	flew	sing	sang
get	got	spend	spent
give	gave	stand	stood
go	went	steal	stole
have	had	swim	swam
hear	heard	take	took
keep	kept	teach	taught
know	knew	tear	tore
lay	laid	think	thought
lead	led	throw	threw
lie	lay	write	wrote
lose	lost		

EXERCISE I: Past Tense of Irregular Verbs

Without looking at the preceding chart, fill in the past tense of the following
verbs. After checking your answers, be sure to memorize any that you found
you did not know already.

Present	*Past*	*Present*	*Past*
1. I spend	I _____	19. I buy	I _____
2. I send	I _____	20. I bring	I _____
3. I go	I _____	21. I seek	I _____
4. I meet	I _____	22. I teach	I _____
5. I feel	I _____	23. I hear	I _____

6. I keep	I _____		24. I stand	I _____
7. I lead	I _____		25. I lay	I _____
8. I write	I _____		26. I do	I _____
9. I steal	I _____		27. I begin	I _____
10. I choose	I _____		28. I sing	I _____
11. I rise	I _____		29. I swim	I _____
12. I sell	I _____		30. I know	I _____
13. I become	I _____		31. I fly	I _____
14. I give	I _____		32. I throw	I _____
15. I lie	I _____		33. I quit	I _____
16. I make	I _____		34. I put	I _____
17. I pay	I _____		35. I cut	I _____
18. I think	I _____			

EXERCISE II: Past Tense of Irregular Verbs

Supply the correct past tense forms for the verbs in parentheses.

Abraham Maslow has done much to change our views of human nature.
He (1) _____ (begin) as an experimenter who (2) _____ (spend)
most of his time studying emotional illness. He (3) _____ (write) a book
on abnormal psychology but then (4) _____ (become) dissatisfied with
approaches that (5) _____ (seek) only to understand the disturbed person. Instead, he (6) _____ (choose) to examine the characteristics of the
unusually healthy person. He (7) _____ (make) many original contributions to modern psychology and (8) _____ (bring) a new emphasis on
health and potential rather than sickness. He (9) _____ (know) that many
mysteries still (10) _____ (lie) unsolved in the psychology of the healthy
personality. He (11) _____ (teach) for many years and (12) _____ (be)

so popular he was called the Frank Sinatra of Brooklyn College. He later (13)

_____ (go) to Brandeis University and finally to California. His many articles and influential books (14) _____ (do) much to win fame for him and his theories. Certain of his concepts, such as self-actualization and the hierarchy of needs, (15) _____ (take) their place among the leading ideas of modern psychology.

Past Participles

Past participles are used with forms of *be* and *have* for special purposes. Past participles of regular verbs are formed by adding *d* endings. Past participles of irregular verbs often differ from the past tense.

Regular Verbs

Present	Past	Past Participle
I believe	I believed	I have believed
I dance	I danced	I have danced
I study	I studied	I have studied

Irregular Verbs

Present	Past	Past Participle
I go	I went	I have gone
I sing	I sang	I have sung
I send	I sent	I have sent

Past participles cause some of the same problems in writing as the past tense does. You will need to avoid dropping *d* endings on participles formed from regular verbs, and you will have to know the correct participle forms of irregular verbs from memory.

Past Participles with Helping Verbs

Past participles are used with helping verbs in two ways.

1. With *have, has,* and *had* to form the perfect tenses:

   Past Perfect: I *had* already *given* a brilliant performance.
                      I *had* previously *entered* the competition.
   Present Perfect: I *have* always *done* my taxes by myself.
                      I *have* never *cheated* on an examination.
   Future Perfect: I *will have begun* by the time you arrive.
                      I *will have reached* Charleston by noon.

2. With forms of *be* (*is, are, was, were*) to form the passive voice. The passive voice is not a tense; it is an arrangement of words in which the subject receives the action. In the active voice, the way we usually make statements, the subject does the action.

> Active voice: Sharon admired Hector.
> Passive voice: Hector *was admired* by Sharon.

In the active voice, the subject, Sharon, does the admiring; in the passive voice, the subject, Hector, receives the admiration. Form the passive voice with forms of *be* and the past participle:

> Active voice: Sidney threw a party.
> Passive Voice: A party *was thrown* by Sidney.

Past Participles as Adjectives

Past participles are sometimes used as adjectives, either before or after the nouns they describe:

> Participle before noun: I sent a *registered* letter.
> Participle after noun: I sent a letter *registered* on March 5th.
> Participle before noun: A *frozen* daiquiri is tasty.
> Participle after noun: A daiquiri *frozen* properly is tasty.

EXERCISE I: Past Participles

In the following sentences, circle past participles with missing *d* endings. Remember that past participles may appear after *have, has* or *had;* after *is, are, was,* and *were;* and before and after nouns.

1. A close friend of mine name Henry just won the lottery.

2. Rachel was dress well for the interview.

3. The students were confuse by the examination questions.

4. Old people should not be force to retire.

5. It could have happen to you if you had been there.

6. If the real assailant had not confess, my friend might have been convicted.

7. The mayor was ask to preside over the ceremony.

8. The manager was face with a crucial decision.

9. Julia was divorce three years ago.

10. A young woman marry to an older man has to make adjustments.

EXERCISE 11: Past Participles

Write sentences using the following phrases. Don't forget the *d* endings!
1. got married   2. was named   3. were forced to   4. has happened   5. is finished   6. are convinced   7. is concerned   8. has been canceled   9. have promised   10. was placed

Past Participles of Irregular Verbs

The past participles of irregular verbs are usually different from the past tense. Do not use the past tense in place of the participle with *have* or *be*.

Not: I have drank all the tea you gave me.
Correct: I have drunk all the tea you gave me.
Not: The bicycle was stole while I was shopping.
Correct: The bicycle was stolen while I was shopping.

Here is a list of irregular past participles that often cause mistakes:

Present	Past	Past Participle
become	became	become
begin	began	begun
bring	brought	brought
choose	chose	chosen
come	came	come
cost	cost	cost
do	did	done
drink	drank	drunk
drive	drove	driven
eat	ate	eaten
fall	fell	fallen
forget	forgot	forgotten
get	got	gotten
give	gave	given
go	went	gone
have	had	had
hide	hid	hidden
hurt	hurt	hurt
keep	kept	kept
know	knew	known

Present	*Past*	*Past Participle*
lay	laid	laid
lead	led	led
lie	lay	lain
meet	met	met
pay	paid	paid
quit	quit	quit
ride	rode	ridden
rise	rose	risen
run	ran	run
see	saw	seen
send	sent	sent
shake	shook	shaken
shine	shone	shone
sing	sang	sung
speak	spoke	spoken
spend	spent	spent
steal	stole	stolen
take	took	taken
throw	threw	thrown
write	wrote	written

EXERCISE III: Past Participles

Write the correct past participles in the blanks.

1. Has he ever _____ (shake) hands with Arsenio Hall?

2. I have _____ (send) a postcard to you.

3. That accident could have _____ (cost) you a fortune.

4. The bill was _____ (pay) by my uncle.

5. The winner was _____ (choose) by three judges.

6. The grant money has been _____ (spend) by now.

7. The prices have _____ (rise) since August.

8. You should have _____ (take) a nap before you came.

9. The message was _____ (write) on yellow paper.

10. She has not _____ (come) here to argue with you.

REVIEW EXERCISE: Past Tense and Past Participles

Write the correct form of the verb in the blank.

1. Many kinds of special words and phrases, which are _____ (call) figures of speech, are _____ (use) to express ideas vividly.

2. Poets have _____ (invent) thousands of metaphors; Shakespeare, for instance, _____ (write) that "All the world's a stage."

3. Through such imaginative comparisons, writers have _____ (give) us means of perceiving our lives in new ways.

4. Similes, comparisons using like or as, have also _____ (appear) frequently in literature. When Christina Rossetti wrote, "My heart is like a singing bird," she _____ (choose) a simile to express joy.

5. Synecdoche, referring to something by naming part of it, has also _____ (take) its place in literature.

6. You have probably _____ (hear) someone ask, "Do you have wheels?" He or she really wants to know if a car is available.

7. Metonymy, naming something by referring to an idea or fact associated with it, has also _____ (play) its part in writing.

8. For instance, you may have _____ (notice) the term "grandfather clause" in labor agreements. It refers to rules that apply to people who have _____ (work) for the company a long time, associating time with the age of grandfathers.

9. A euphemism, a mild term used in place of a blunter one, may be _____ (use) to avoid offending readers, but some writers have always _____ (consider) it better to be direct.

10. Prostitutes, for instance, _____ (use) to be _____ (call)

"ladies of the evening."

Avoiding Shifts in Verb Tense

Once you can recognize verb tenses and use the correct verb forms, learn to write without shifting awkwardly between tenses.

What's wrong with this passage?

> When I *got* up this morning, I *felt* excited. I *know* I *have* an exam at eleven o'clock, but I *was* ready for it because I *study* hard the night before.

If you are writing in the past, *stay in the past tense:*

> When I *got* up this morning, I *felt* excited. I *knew* I *had* an exam at eleven o'clock, but I *was* ready for it because I *had studied* hard the night before.

What's wrong with this description of a story?

> This story *is* about two girls who *lived* in the South. Although they *are* sisters, one of them *was* bright while the other *is* slow and simple. The mother *tries* to be a good parent to both, but she *couldn't* treat them the same way.

When discussing a story, *stay in the present tense:*

> This story *is* about two girls who *live* in the South. Although they *are* sisters, one of them *is* bright while the other *is* slow and simple. The mother *tries* to be a good parent to both, but she *can't* treat them the same way.

Verb Tenses in Writing: Some Guidelines

1. Stay in the same tense as long as the time you are writing about does not change.
2. If the time changes, the verb tense *should* change, even in the same paragraph or sentence.

    > I once *believed* that money *makes* people happy, but now I *realize* that happiness *depends* on your inner self and your relationships.

3. Tell about the plot of a play, novel, or story in the present tense.
4. Statements about eternal truths may be in the present even when you are telling about past events:

    > The child *learned* quickly that not all people in this world *can* be trusted.

5. If you are writing about experiences that you remember, statements like "I recall" or "I remember" are in the present. The events happened in the past, but you are recalling them now:

> I *remember* (not remembered) how cold the winters *used* to be in Wisconsin when I *was* a child.

6. Use helping words correctly: *may, can,* and *will* in present and future tenses and *might, could,* and *would* in the past.

EXERCISE I: Shifts in Verb Tense

Rewrite the following paragraph so that it stays entirely in the past tense. Underline the verbs you have changed from present to past.

> *David Bowie was born in Brixton, a lower-middle-class section of London, on January 8, 1947. His father did odd jobs, and his mother is an usherette at a movie theater. As a teenager, he began playing saxophone in a band. In his late teens he becomes a singer, and, after a number of not-so-successful records and a change of managers, he produced* Space Oddity, *his first successful album. He makes a few more albums in both England and America; then he posed as "Ziggy Stardust" in elaborate stage performances. In 1973 he decides to retire, but he reappeared a year later with another character known as "Aladinsane." In 1976 he retires again as "The Thin White Duke." About this time he made his film debut as a space visitor in* The Man Who Fell to Earth. *After spending several years in Berlin being rehabilitated from a serious drug problem, he reemerges as an actor in the 1980s. He played the Elephant Man on Broadway and a series of bizarre film roles, including the Goblin King in the puppet epic* Labyrinth, *a vampire in* The Hunger, *and Pontius Pilate in* The Last Temptation of Christ. *Although not all his films are box office successes, he was possibly the best actor of all the rock stars who performed in films. By the early 1990s, having discontinued his heavy drug use and bisexuality of the seventies, he turns his ambitions toward writing and directing films. He also won worldwide attention on April 24, 1992 by his marriage to the famous model Iman from Somalia.*

EXERCISE II: Shifts in Verb Tense

Rewrite the following paragraph so that it remains entirely in the present tense, with no shifts to the past. Underline the verbs you change from past to present.

> *Shirley Jackson's short story, "The Lottery," shows real human behavior in a fantasy setting. The story takes place in an imaginary village that resembled a New England or midwestern town in modern times. Although the villagers were*

just like real small town people, with their gossip and chatter about tractors and taxes, the town has an annual custom that was not at all like everyday life. Every June the people held a lottery in which the "winner" was stoned to death by friends, neighbors, and even family members. The lottery itself is a fantasy, but the way people behaved toward it was realistic. They conformed to a tradition without questioning its harmful effect. No one protests even though they knew they were being cruel to someone they loved. "The Lottery" taught a valuable lesson about how people were able to hang onto worn-out customs and conform to the behavior of their peers even when they should have known better.

ADJECTIVES AND ADVERBS

People often confuse adjectives with adverbs, and vice versa.

Telling the Difference Between Adjectives and Adverbs

The most common mistake people make with adjectives and adverbs is to write *good* when they mean *well*.

> *Not:* This car runs good.
> *But:* This car runs well.

Good is an adjective; *well* is an adverb. What is the difference?

Adjectives tell *which, what kind of,* or *how many;* they modify nouns or pronouns:

a *violent* storm	a *busy* street
the *first* exit	*five* drinks

Adverbs tell *how, when,* and *where;* they modify verbs, adjectives, and other adverbs:

She talks *brilliantly.*	He will write *soon.*
an *extremely* tall man	They played *very* skillfully.
We are parked *nearby.*	

Another common mistake is to omit the *-ly* ending on adverbs. Many adjectives can be converted into adverbs by adding *-ly.*

Adjective	*Adverb*
a *quick* meal	We ate the meal *quickly*
a *real* diamond	a *really* fine diamond
a *bad* feeling	They arranged it *badly.*
The answer was *correct.*	They answered *correctly.*

Remember to use *adjectives* after forms of *be* (*is, are, was, were*); adjectives modify the subject. Also use adjectives after verbs of the senses such as *feel, smell, sound,* and *taste*.

1. The novel sounds *exciting*. (*Exciting* modifies *novel*.)
2. The quiche smells *delicious*. (*Delicious* modifies *quiche*.)
3. I feel *good* this morning. (*Good* modifies *I*.)
4. The fish tastes *stale*. (*Stale* modifies *fish*.)

Do not confuse these adjectives (called predicate adjectives because they come after the verb, not before the noun) with adverbs that come after verbs.

1. The novel reads *smoothly*. (*Smoothly* modifies *reads*.)
2. The chef makes quiche *expertly*. (*Expertly* modifies *makes*.)
3. I dress *quickly* in the morning. (*Quickly* modifies *dress*.)
4. She catches fish *frequently*. (*Frequently* modifies *catches*.)

Do not confuse *well*, the adverb, with *well*, the adjective:

1. You certainly can swim *well*. (*Well* [adv.] modifies *swim*.)
2. You look *well* now that you've recovered. (*Well*, meaning healthy, is an adjective modifying *you*.)
3. You look *good* in that skirt. (*Good* is an adjective modifying *you*.)

Some Tricky Adverbs

Certain adverbs are often confused with adjectives. Be on the lookout for:

Adjective	*Adverb*
most people	*almost* always
She feels *bad*.	She sings *badly*.
an *easy* job	He does it *easily*.
an *everyday* task	He swims *every day*. (two words)
a *smooth* landing	We landed *smoothly*.
a *slow* pace	Drive *slowly*. (*Slow* is also accepted as an adverb.)

E X E R C I S E I: Adjectives and Adverbs

Circle the correct form in each sentence.

1. Television newscasters have to be (real, really) articulate.

2. Educational programs help children learn (easy, easily).

3. Some people feel (bad, badly) after watching too much television.

4. Soap operas have become an (everyday, every day) activity for many people.

5. Commercials are (most, almost, mostly) always louder than the programs.

6. Some children behave (violent, violently) after watching (violent, violently) programs.

7. To choose programs (careful, carefully), you should read reviews of the programs first.

8. Commercials lead customers to decide too (quick, quickly) about buying products.

9. Some sports fans react (wild, wildly) to athletic events.

10. Most viewers respond (emotional, emotionally) to soap operas.

EXERCISE I I: Adjectives and Adverbs

Compose sentences using the following words and phrases:

1. feels good	5. bad	9. every day
2. feels well	6. badly	10. everyday
3. especially	7. probable	
4. special	8. probably	

Adjectives in Comparisons

Besides their simple forms, adjectives have two forms that are used in comparisons. The comparative form is used to compare two unequal things, and the superlative form is used to set one thing off from all the others.

Simple Form	*Comparative Form*	*Superlative Form*
good	better	best
young	younger	youngest
strange	stranger	strangest
gentle	gentler	gentlest
happy	happier	happiest

Adjectives with three or more syllables always take *more* and *most* rather than the *er* and *est* endings.

beautiful	more beautiful	most beautiful
exciting	more exciting	most exciting

Your dictionary will show that some two-syllable words take *er* and *est* while others take *more* and *most*.

heavy	heavier	heaviest
friendly	friendlier	friendliest
subtle	subtler	subtlest
cheerful	more cheerful	most cheerful
precise	more precise	most precise

Use the comparative form when comparing two things or people:

She is wealthier than her cousin.
She is the wealthier of the two cousins.

(Remember to use th*a*n, not th*e*n, in making comparisons.)

Use the superlative form to set off one from a whole group:

She is the wealthiest woman in the group.
She is the wealthiest of the three cousins.

Adverbs in Comparisons

Adverbs also have comparative and superlative forms. Nearly all adverbs take *more* and *most*. The only exceptions are the few that serve as both adjectives and adverbs—*early, late, hard, fast, low,* and *straight*. These take *er* and *est: earlier, earliest.*

Simple Form	*Comparative Form*	*Superlative Form*
easily	more easily	most easily
violently	more violently	most violently
recently	more recently	most recently
happily	more happily	most happily

We also make negative comparisons, using adjectives and adverbs in combination with *less* or *least*.

expensive	less expensive	least expensive
difficult	less difficult	least difficult
safely	less safely	least safely
forcefully	less forcefully	least forcefully

Do not use both the *er* or *est* ending and the helping words *more, most, less,* or *least.*

Wrong: You are *more better* than the last shortstop.
They are *less healthier* than they should be.

Right: You are *better* than the last shortstop.
They are *less healthy* than they should be.

Wrong: This was the *most saddest* film I have seen.
            This was the *least richest* pastry on the menu.

Right: This was the *saddest* film I have seen.
            This was the *least rich* pastry on the menu.

EXERCISE I: Adjectives in Comparisons

Write the correct form of the adjective or adverb in the blank.

1. Most people enjoy films that are _____ (long) than ordinary ones.

2. Being longer, of course, does not make a film _____ (good).

3. Some of the _____ (fine) films ever made have been rather short.

4. Still, audiences often expect a longer film to provide a _____ (rich) experience than a short one.

5. One of the _____ (great) efforts of all time in filmmaking was the Russian version of *War and Peace.*

6. This was the _____ (accurate) of all film adaptations of Tolstoy's novel.

7. The original Russian version runs eight hours, twenty-seven minutes, a _____ (big) block of time than three or four normal films would require.

8. A Japanese film company made a still _____ (ambitious) film called *The Human Condition,* which lasted nine hours and twenty-nine minutes.

9. Much _____ (early), in 1925, a seven-hour, fifty-eight-minute silent film called *Sparks of the Flame* was made in the Soviet Union.

10. Two years _____ (late) a French filmmaker, Abel Gance, created a six-hour, eighteen-minute epic on Napoleon.

EXERCISE II: Adjectives and Adverbs in Comparisons

After each sentence, write a sentence using the same adjective or adverb in comparing two persons or things. Study the examples on the next page.

Lead is *heavy.*
Lead is heavier than tin.

John ran *fast.*
John ran faster than the moped.

1. This laptop computer is *easy* to use.

_____

2. Algebra is *difficult.*

_____

3. President Clinton jogs *frequently.*

_____

4. Working in a nuclear power plant is *dangerous.*

_____

5. Magazine models have to be *slender.*

_____

6. The Huxtables lived *happily.*

_____

7. The language in that film was *strange.*

_____

8. This ice cream tastes *good.*

_____

9. Sam always walks *noisily.*

_____

10. The dancer looked *young.*

_____

Misplaced and Dangling Modifiers

Modifiers are adjectives, adverbs, or phrases that function as adjectives or adverbs. Modifiers describe or change the meaning of other words in the sentence, so they should be close to the words that they modify. If they are too far away from the words they modify and cause confusion, we call them

misplaced modifiers. If the words they modify are not really in the sentence, we call them **dangling modifiers.**

Misplaced Modifiers

As a child, my grandmother took me to see a bullfight.

Standing on a curb, a bicyclist whizzed by and almost knocked Joyce over.

The italicized phrases in both sentences are out of place. If we take them to be describing the words next to them, the meaning is confused. It sounds as if the grandmother were a child and the bicyclist were standing on the curb. Rearrange sentences like these to say what you mean.

Better:

When *I* was a child, my grandmother took me to see a bullfight.

While *Joyce* was standing on the curb, a bicyclist whizzed by and almost knocked her over.

Another way:

As a child, I went to see a bullfight with my grandmother.

Standing on the curb, Joyce was almost knocked over by a bicyclist.

Dangling Modifiers

While drying her hair, the clock radio suddenly began blasting.

As a teenager, school became boring and homework was a drag.

These dangling modifiers are not much different from misplaced modifiers, except that in these sentences there is no word at all that the modifiers describe. Who was drying her hair? Who was a teenager? The reader has to guess. Add the necessary words.
Better:

While *Karen* was drying her hair, the clock radio suddenly began blasting.

As a teenager, I found school boring and homework a drag.

Identifying Misplaced and Dangling Modifiers

Many students who have good control of grammar in other areas still have trouble finding and correcting misplaced and dangling modifiers. The meaning may seem clear to them while it is not to the reader. Misplaced and dangling modifiers are often introductory phrases, so watch for them at the beginning of your sentences. However, they can occur in the middle or at the end of sentences:

Sergio reached for the drawer *filled with anger and resentment.*

A hurricane was moving slowly up the coast *while at Cape Cod.*

In the first sentence, the underlined phrase is misplaced: it should describe Sergio, but appears to describe the drawer.

Better:

Filled with anger and resentment, Sergio reached for the drawer.

In the second sentence, the modifying phrase would be dangling no matter where we put it; the sentence must say *who* was at Cape Cod.

Better:

A hurricane was moving slowly up the coast *while we were at Cape Cod.*

EXERCISE I: Misplaced and Dangling Modifiers

Underline the misplaced word or phrase and rewrite the sentence with the modifier in the right place.

Example: He will pick up the car that was wrecked <u>tomorrow morning</u>.

Tomorrow morning he will pick up the car that was wrecked.

1. She will have to repair the radio that was damaged with a screwdriver.

2. Sitting on the top shelf I discovered a copy of *The Catcher in the Rye.*

3. She wanted an apartment that would be large enough for two children with plenty of light.

4. Nearly starved, the helicopter pilot spotted the hikers shivering in the snow.

5. Decorated with rhinestones, the salesman placed the sweater back in the display case.

_____

_____

6. Puffed up with air, the scientist placed the bag over the flame.

_____

_____

7. Sketches of the suspect were drawn by an artist that looked like photographs.

_____

_____

8. Several people in Arizona reported seeing flying saucers in the newspapers.

_____

_____

9. Scratching his nose against an oak, Robert at last found his pony.

_____

_____

10. Joking with news reporters, we watched the president join his staff.

_____

_____

EXERCISE II: Misplaced and Dangling Modifiers

Rewrite these sentences, adding or changing words so that the modifying phrases are not misplaced or dangling.

Example:

Proud of America's new importance in the world, the 1920s were entered by the younger generation with enthusiasm.

Proud of America's new importance in the world, the younger

generation entered the 1920s with enthusiasm.

1. Often called the Jazz Age, many people now think of the 1920s as a period of wealth, entertainment, and reckless high living.

_____

_____

_____

2. Aware of the complexities of that decade, however, many social problems such as poverty and racism are evident to historians of the period.

_____

_____

_____

3. Government officials launched an irrational attack on unions, political outsiders, and members of minority groups, afraid of the government being overthrown by "Reds."

_____

_____

_____

4. A period of sudden blossoming by black writers, musicians, and artists, historians often refer to the 1920s as the Harlem Renaissance.

_____

_____

_____

5. Afraid of a threat to traditional values, immigration was restricted by a series of laws in the 1920s.

   _____

   _____

6. After introducing the Model T Ford, excitement over owning a car prevailed in the 1920s.

   _____

   _____

7. Americans were also excited about film stars and athletic celebrities whom they read about in newspapers that earned fabulous salaries.

   _____

   _____

8. Expanded dramatically by the convenience of commuting by automobile, the 1920s brought new importance to metropolitan areas.

   _____

   _____

9. The 1920s began with the prohibition of alcohol, after passing the Volstead Act and the Eighteenth Amendment in 1919.

   _____

   _____

10. This exciting decade was brought to an end by the stock market crash of October 12, 1929, remembered fondly by some as the Roaring Twenties.

    _____

    _____

PRONOUNS

Pronouns cause several kinds of writing difficulties.

Types of Pronouns

Pronouns are of several types.

Personal Pronouns Used as Subjects	*Reflexive Pronouns*
I	myself
you	yourself, yourselves
she	herself
he	himself
it	itself
we	ourselves
they	themselves

Personal Pronouns Used as Objects of Verbs and Prepositions	*Impersonal Pronouns*
me	one
you	each
her	either
him	anyone
it	anybody
us	everybody
them	everyone
	somebody
	someone
	none
	no one
	nobody

Pronoun Case

Probably the most frequent difficulty people have with pronouns lies in choosing the correct case for personal pronouns. This means knowing whether to use *I* or *me*, *we* or *us*, *she* or *her*, and *he* or *him*. When one of these pronouns occurs by itself, we can usually pick the correct form by the sound. However, when there are two pronouns or a pronoun occurs with a noun, choosing may be more difficult.

Which is correct?

Between you and me, the boss plans to promote Carol.

Between you and I, the boss plans to promote Carol.

Are you surprised to find out that the *first* one is correct? Both *you* and *me* are the objects of *between*.

Which is correct?

My brother and I tried out for a professional soccer team.

Me and my brother tried out for a professional soccer team.

The first one is correct again, because both *I* and *brother* are the subjects of the verb *tried*.

How can you tell which is right? The easiest way is not to analyze the grammar but to take out the other word, whether noun or pronoun, and read the sentence without it:

I tried out for a professional soccer team.

EXERCISE I: Pronoun Case

Circle the correct pronoun(s) in each sentence. (Read the sentence in your mind without the other word.)

1. Send applications to (she and I, her and me).

2. Wait until the neighbors hear about you and (I, me).

3. (Me and my sister, My sister and I) live a block from each other.

4. The proceeds will go to Bob and (he, him).

5. After (she and I, me and her) save enough money we will visit Cuba.

6. (We, Us) students should organize a bridge team.

7. Ted and (I, me) are learning to operate a small business.

8. After the bank has trained you and (I, me) to be managers, we can afford new cars.

9. The neighbors asked (he and she, him and her) about it.

10. According to Brenda and (she, her), the examination was easy.

EXERCISE 11: Pronoun Case

Write sentences using the following combinations correctly. Remember to read your sentences with each pronoun separately to be sure they are correct.

1. you and I	5. we and they	9. he and she
2. Robert and me	6. him and her	10. us and them
3. she and her brother	7. us Americans	
4. we undergraduates	8. you and him	

Pronoun Case: Using *Who* and *Whom*

Using *who* and *whom* correctly is a tricky business. Few speakers get the distinction right every time in conversation, and only the most careful grammarians always use the correct form in writing. In conversation, you can get away with using *who* when you aren't sure, but in college writing, you are expected to know when to use *whom*.

Remember that *who* is the form to use as a subject, and *whom* is the form to use as the object of a verb or preposition. To most people, it sounds right to say "to whom," "for whom," and "with whom." In more complicated phrases, however, you have to begin by identifying the main clause in the sentence and separating it in your mind from the relative clause (the *who* or *whom* clause). The relative clause determines whether you should write *who* or *whom*: write *who* if it is the subject of the verb; write *whom* if it is the object of the verb or of a preposition:

$$s \quad v \qquad\qquad s \quad v$$
1. Allison is the student <u>who</u> sits in the front row.
   (*who* as sub. of vb.)

$$s \quad v \qquad\qquad\quad o \qquad\qquad v$$
2. Allison is the student <u>whom</u> the teacher likes.
   (*whom* as obj. of vb. in rel. clause)

$$s \quad v \qquad\qquad pr. \quad o \qquad s \qquad v$$
3. Allison is the student with <u>whom</u> the tutor is speaking.
   (*whom* as obj. of prep.)

In conversation, we might phrase sentence 3 differently: "Allison is the student *whom* the tutor is speaking with." Strict grammarians may tell you not to end a sentence with a preposition this way, but even if you do, *whom* is still the object of *with* in the sentence.

EXERCISE 1: Using *Who* and *Whom*

In each of these sentences, circle the entire relative clause; then write *who* or *whom* in the blank. Explain how the pronoun functions, as subject or object, in the relative clause.

Example: Raoul named the person ___*who*___ he thought was harassing him.

1. Bill Gates is a young man _____ built a fortune on computer software.

2. He and his partners _____ created Microsoft Corporation became billionaires within a decade.

3. People with _____ he has worked find him to be an obsessive worker.

4. Users of personal computers, to _____ the initials MS-DOS are familiar, recognize the importance of Microsoft.

5. Starting as a young computer hacker _____ grew up in Seattle and dropped out of Harvard, Gates began creating software for personal computers in the 1970s.

6. Gates, _____ IBM helped enormously in the early 1980s by contracting with Microsoft to provide basic operating software for IBM's personal computers, now competes with IBM and Apple.

7. Gates is seen as a genius and visionary by those _____ he helped make rich.

8. He is seen as ruthless by those _____ he has defeated in the competition for control of the software market.

9. Gates was the child of a lawyer and a teacher _____ were both active in civil affairs.

10. He will continue to be a corporate figure about _____ there will be controversy.

EXERCISE 11: Using *Who* and *Whom*

Compose sentences modeled on the form of the following sentences.

Example: The couple whom you met last night are moving to Delaware.

Your sentence: _*The students whom you saw in the bookstore are seniors.*_

1. The player who scores the most points will return next week.

   Your sentence: _____

   _____

2. The article referred to three people who tested positive for HIV.

   Your sentence: _____

   _____

3. The voters preferred the candidate who they thought would create jobs.

   Your sentence: _____

   _____

4. The children whom the article described all grew up in other countries.

   Your sentence: _____

   _____

5. The personnel officer by whom you will be interviewed is a psychologist.

   Your sentence: _____

   _____

6. From whom were the packages sent?

   Your sentence: _____

   _____

7. Whom would she prefer to see marry her son?

   Your sentence: _____

   _____

Pronouns and Antecedents

Since pronouns are words that take the place of nouns, they always have nouns called **antecedents,** usually in the same sentence or the one just before it, to which they refer. Pronouns must agree with their antecedents in number, person, and gender.

1. Pronouns and antecedents agree in number:

   The *book* lost *its* cover. (*Book* and *its* are both singular.)

   Most *people* enjoy *their* birthdays. (*People* and *their* are both plural.)

2. Pronouns and antecedents agree in person:

The *company* changed *its* name. (*Company* and *its* are both in the third person.)

You must wear *your* tuxedo. (*You* and *your* are both in the second person.)

3. Pronouns and antecedents agree in gender:

Inez had *her* diploma framed. (*Inez* and *her* are feminine.)

James found *his* diskette. (*James* and *his* are masculine.)

Most mistakes in agreement of pronouns and antecedents have to do with number. Do not shift from a singular noun to a plural pronoun, or vice versa. Awkward shifts:

The *college* changed *their* financial aid rules this year. (*College* is singular; *their* is plural.)

People who use *drugs* often underestimate how harmful *it* is. (*Drugs* is plural; *it* is singular.)

Better:

The *college* changed *its* financial aid rules this year.

People who use *drugs* often underestimate how harmful *they* are.

Note: Indefinite pronouns like *everyone, everybody, anyone, someone,* and *nobody* are singular. Use singular forms like *he* or *she* to agree with them:

Anyone who does that is putting *his* or *her* life at stake.

EXERCISE I: Pronouns and Antecedents

Circle the correct pronoun in each sentence.

1. Every woman in the audience knows this is true for (them, her, she).

2. All of the people who voted in the last election expressed (his, her, their) preferences.

3. A law that is not enforced loses (their, his, its) validity.

4. Steps are being taken to prevent looting because (they, it) causes enormous damage.

5. The standard of living has risen slightly, but (they, he, it) may rise faster in the next year.

6. Mothers and fathers have recently pooled (her, his, their) knowledge in writing this book.

7. A firefighter who stays on the force for twenty years receives (his, her, his or her, their) retirement benefits.

8. Students of astronomy find that (he, she, they) need mathematics.

9. A father of small children often finds (their, his, its) time taken up with domestic responsibilities.

10. Songs are often presented to the public in video clips that express (its, his, their) feeling visually.

EXERCISE II: Pronouns and Antecedents

Rewrite the first five sentences by changing the pronouns and antecedents from singular to plural. In the last five, change them from plural to singular. Be sure that all verbs agree with their subjects.

Example: An ambitious entertainer usually has an agent to look after his or her interests.

Plural: Ambitious entertainers usually have agents to look after their interests.

1. Singular: An undergraduate who hopes to pursue a graduate degree has to earn high grades in his or her major subject.

   Plural: Undergraduates who _____

   _____

2. Singular: The last job at which I worked offered too few rewards for its difficulties.

   Plural: The last jobs _____

   _____

3. Singular: A child who writes poetry often develops his or her imagination and language skills at the same time.

   Plural: Children who _____

   _____

4. Singular: A man who wants to become a professional chef can pursue his career at a college of culinary arts.

   Plural: Men who _____

   _____

5. Singular: A company that uses computers effectively can increase its efficiency and maximize its profits.

   Plural: Companies that _____

   _____

6. Plural: Women who run for public office often make their way against opposition from their peers.

   Singular: A woman who _____

   _____

7. Plural: Pedestrians who refuse to obey the lights are risking their lives.

   Singular: A pedestrian who _____

   _____

8. Plural: Men who attend colleges that were once for women only sometimes find themselves in a minority group.

   Singular: A man who _____

   _____

9. Plural: Newspapers that sensationalize the news they print and use simple language are called tabloids.

   Singular: A newspaper that _____

   _____

10. Plural: Children who skip grades in school have to adjust to finding themselves in more mature social groups.

    Singular: A child who _____

    _____

SHIFTS OF PERSON

When you write a paragraph or essay, you may choose to write it in the first, second, or third person.

First Person

The *first person* refers to the writer or speaker (I) or to the group including the writer or speaker (we). Stories and essays are often written in the first person, meaning that the writer or narrator (an imaginary speaker) refers throughout the story to himself or herself by using *I, me, my,* and *mine.* Editorials in newspapers and company reports sometimes use the first person plural, the "editorial we." Such editorials and reports sound as if they are expressing the opinions of a whole group.

Second Person

The *second person* means the reader or listener (you). Whole essays are seldom written entirely in the second person. Procedural writing, which contains a series of instructions to the reader, often is. Personal letters usually contain many statements in the second person because the writer is addressing a specific reader whom he or she knows.

Third Person

The *third person* means any person or thing written about. Most college writing is in the third person because most of it is about topics studied in college courses, not about the personal life of the writer or reader. A statement that someone does something ("James writes country music") is in the third person. It may be singular (she, he, it) or plural (they).

Shifts of Person

Do not shift awkwardly from one person to another in your writing. Watch especially for the temptation to slip *you* into an essay that is supposed to be in the third person:

> *A person who wants to learn how to sing well has to think about several elements at once. He or she has to learn to open and relax the throat. You also have to use the diaphragm to support your breathing.*

This sort of shift from *he* or *she* to *you* is awkward and confusing. Either write the whole set of instructions in the second person, using *you* throughout, or keep it in the third person, using either *he* (or *she*) or *one.* (Note: You may shift between *one* and *he* or *she,* since you are remaining in the third person.)

Writers also sometimes make the mistake of shifting into the first person (I) when it is not appropriate:

Before you go out to run or participate in a vigorous sport, you should warm up with some stretching exercises. Before jogging, I always do leg stretching exercises and touch my toes several times.

This whole passage should remain in the second person, *you should* instead of *I.* Remember that when you give commands or instructions, the word *you* is often understood and does not have to be repeated frequently: "Always do leg stretching exercises" is shorter than "You should always do leg stretching exercises."

EXERCISE I: Shifts of Person

Underline the words containing shifts of person and write the correct words above them.*

    Example: When you look at the statistics, <u>one</u> might think twice about getting married. *(you)*

1. Many people think that marriage patterns haven't changed much since <u>your</u> parents' generation. *(their)*

2. However, statistics show that our parents tended to marry younger than <u>my</u> generation. *(our)*

3. Men in our parents' era usually got married at twenty-two; now <u>he</u> usually gets married at twenty-six. *(they)*

4. A typical woman in the 1950s got married at twenty; now <u>we get</u> married at twenty-four. *(she gets)*

5. This means that women today wait longer to get married than men did in <u>her</u> parents' generation. *(their)*

6. <u>One</u> often has to become launched in a career before <u>they get</u> married. *(we getting)*

7. A black man is especially likely to wait many years before <u>they</u> get married for the first time. *(he / she)*

---

*Information from Felicity Barringer, "Rate of Marriage Continues to Decline," *New York Times,* 17 July 1992, sec. A, p. 20.

8. In 1991, about a third of black men between the ages of thirty-five and thirty-nine reported that he had not been married yet.

9. Economic trends such as unemployment are related to the rate of
   People
   marriage; ~~you~~ are less likely to get married if ~~one does~~ *they do* not have a job.

10. Nowadays, we are all trying to get more college education than in the
    we   *delay*
    past, so ~~he or she~~ often ~~delays~~ marriage more than people used to.

E X E R C I S E 11: Shifts of Person

The following paragraph should be in the second person throughout. Sometimes, however, it awkwardly shifts to the first or third person. Underline all the pronouns that erroneously appear in the first or third person, and write the correct pronouns above them. Change verb forms if necessary.

To write an effective essay, you have to consider at least three elements: content, organization, and correctness. He or she has to have a clear main idea and develop it. Your content includes your main thought as well as the specific material you use to support it. I should have plenty of examples to illustrate my main idea. Sometimes it helps to jot down more examples than you will ever use. Organization is important too. One should not just state facts in any order without thinking of how I am going to arrange them. Your first example should be a powerful one; your last should be the most important of all. And we should not forget to make transitions between examples. Finally, I should always proofread my essay to find mistakes in grammar or phrasing. Never assume that the first draft needs no corrections or revisions. Always be ready to make any small corrections or improvements the essay needs. As the last step, you should give your essay an interesting title. Good titles will often occur to me when I am composing an essay, not beforehand. The title should suggest the topic and arouse interest but not necessarily declare the main point. Often the conclusion of his or her essay will echo a word or phrase used in the title. Our first impression and our last should be closely connected by this means.

PARALLELISM

Parallelism in sentences means that certain parts fit together smoothly—nouns matched with nouns, adjectives with adjectives, prepositional phrases with prepositional phrases, and so on. Parallelism is necessary when two parts of a sentence are joined by *and* or when three or more parts are listed in a series with commas separating them.

Examples of Parallel Combinations

1. We found a Sony Walkman, a skateboard, and a basketball in the schoolyard.
   noun   *noun*   *noun*

2. The marathon went along the avenue, over the suspension bridge, and into the park.
   prep. phrase   *prep. phrase*   *prep. phrase*

3. The party was noisy, wild, and hilarious.
   adj.   *adj.*   *adj.*

Examples of Combinations that Are Not Parallel

1. We discovered a battery, a radio, a generator, and looked for a hubcap.
   noun   *noun*   *noun*   *verb phrase*

2. Both women were attractive, worked in publishing houses, ambitious, and talented.
   adj.   *verb phrase*   *adj.*   *adj.*

3. The schools need newer equipment, smaller classes, and the dropout rate needs to be lowered.
   noun   *noun*   *whole clause*

Parallel and Nonparallel Sentences Compared

Nonparallel	*Parallel*
1. She is tall, athletic, and has skill.	1. She is tall, athletic, and skillful.
2. They wanted to advance in their jobs, earn a lot of money, as well as enjoying their work.	2. They wanted to advance in their jobs, earn a lot of money, and enjoy their work.
3. The visit to Eastern Europe left her better informed, more tolerant, and an optimist.	3. The visit to Eastern Europe left her better informed, more tolerant, and more optimistic.
4. Jason studied before school, after work, and he read assignments during lunch break.	4. Jason studied before school, after work, and during lunch break.
5. I got a headache from too little sleep and because I was anxious about the examination.	5. I got a headache from too little sleep and anxiety over the examination.

EXERCISE I: Parallelism

It helps to think of parallel elements as lists. When you number the parts, you can see more easily which one may not fit. In the following lists, circle the part that does not fit. Then rewrite it in the blank in a form that is parallel with the others.
 Example:

1. well-coordinated
2. quick
3. (has a lot of accuracy)
4. strong

                                                          accurate
_____

1. knows several languages
2. sings country music
3. acquainted with foreign countries
4. understands computers

_____

1. famous
2. wealthy
3. unusually talented
4. good voice

_____

1. over the bridge
2. the highway
3. under the viaduct
4. around the museum   _____

1. knee bends
2. doing pushups
3. lifting weights
4. jumping rope   _____

1. willingly
2. rapidly
3. efficiency
4. calmly   _____

1. who lived many years
2. working for the post office
3. who belonged to a union
4. who founded a political party   _____

1. to participate in sports
2. to build electronic gadgets
3. how to draw blueprints
4. to develop photographs   _____

1. afternoon
2. in the evening
3. before lunch
4. at bedtime   _____

EXERCISE 11: Parallelism

Circle the nonparallel part in each sentence and rewrite the sentence so that all parts are parallel.

Example: She was tall, ambitious, and (had a lot of talent.)

She was tall, ambitious, and talented.

1. He is stocky, athletic, and has a lot of poise.

_____

_____

2. We searched in the restaurant, in the parking lot, and even tried to find it under the car.

_____

_____

3. Shirley knows how to make films, choreograph musicals, and can even play the clarinet.

_____

_____

4. When you are shopping for a home computer, be sure to compare prices, talk with friends who own computers, read company brochures, and asking advice of people who work with computers.

_____

_____

5. As a child, Belinda was adventurous, had a sense of humor, and imaginative.

_____

_____

6. The camera stopped, was starting again, and suddenly raced forward.

_____

_____

7. Gracefully, easily, and moving with rapidity, he slipped through the defensive line.

_____

_____

MIXED SENTENCES

Some writers have problems putting the words of their sentences together. They may leave out necessary words, phrase ideas awkwardly, put words in the wrong order, or use words in the wrong form—as nouns instead of adjectives, for example. Such problems either make the sentences hard to understand or make them read awkwardly. What is wrong with these sentences?

1. In trying to swim with her clothes on was difficult.
2. I wondered was she the right girl for me.
3. Tim was a quarterback belonged on a professional team.
4. Our society is too militarism.

Each of these sentences contains a familiar kind of mistake.

Sentence 1 contains a phrase that does not match the rest of the sentence: "In trying to swim" cannot be the subject of "was difficult." The sentence should read:

Trying to swim with her clothes on was difficult.

Or

In trying to swim with her clothes on, she had difficulty.

Sentence 2 contains words in the wrong order. The sentence begins as a statement, then switches to a question. The sentence should read:

I wondered if she was the right girl for me.

Or

Was she the right girl for me?

Sentence 3 has a word missing. The sentence should read:

Tim was a quarterback *who* belonged on a professional team.

Sentence 4 contains a word used in the wrong form. *Militarism* is a noun when the word needed is an adjective. The sentence should read:

Our society is too *militaristic.*

EXERCISE I: Mixed Sentences

Each of the following sentences contains a phrase that does not fit. Rewrite the sentence so that all parts fit together.

1. By giving in to her demands was a sure way to make her bossier.

_____

_____

2. In repeating the answers to himself helped him do well on the test.

_____

_____

3. While driving with the brake on caused a burning smell.

_____

_____

4. After living in a big city was why she liked excitement.

_____

_____

5. By wearing their seat belts saved them from serious injuries.

_____

_____

Each of these sentences contains mixed-up word order. Rewrite the sentence with the phrasing straightened out.

6. She wondered, should she join her sister at the video arcade.

_____

_____

7. I asked my father was there any unemployment compensation in his day.

_____

_____

8. Tina asked did they have any watches for sale.

_____

_____

9. The police officer questioned had he been drinking.

_____

_____

10. A student wanted to know did psychologists agree about homosexuality.

_____

_____

EXERCISE II: Mixed Sentences

Each of the following sentences has a word or set of words missing. Indicate where the word is missing with a caret (∧) and write the missing word or words above the line.

Example: She was a worker *who* never shunned a difficult task.

1. The Rolls-Royce is a car never loses its value.

2. After the downpour was too muddy to have the class outdoors.

3. Because of inflation isn't any way for many families to finance a college education.

4. A heavy cocaine user needs a lot of money may resort to crime.

5. There too many players who care more about money than basketball.

6. When the sun is setting is difficult to drive on Route 30.

7. While it was raining in Philadelphia, was snowing in Cleveland.

8. A student in California wants to transfer to an Eastern college can expect to pay higher tuition.

9. They found the records been scratched.

10. Yvette be in Houston next month when you visit.

EXERCISE III: Mixed Sentences

In the following sentences, a word appears in the wrong form. Cross out the word and write the correct form above it.

Example: The lyrics were not very ~~interested.~~ *interesting.*

1. Some people insist that America is still a sexism society.

2. Cristina found it hard to be interesting in the slides.

3. How you dress for a job interview is very importance.

4. The assailant was not presence when the police arrived.

5. The traffic on the Beltway was worst today than it was yesterday.

6. Working with children takes a lot of patients.

7. A religion belief sometimes gives hope to terminal patients.

8. In his day there were few education opportunities.

9. Pluralistic is one of the most important features of our society.

10. His absent made the vote invalid.

REVIEW EXERCISE: Mixed Sentences

Rewrite each sentence, eliminating any mixed phrases, adding missing words, correcting words in the wrong form, or putting words into correct order.

1. They questioned should there be a traffic light on the corner.

   _____

2. One problem in the company's management is too much authoritarian.

   _____

3. While studying with the television set on is hard to concentrate.

   _____

4. A museum does not include a section on technology is out of date.

   _____

5. Janet asked her mother's helper could she be there on Friday.

   _____

6. *Waiting to Exhale* was a very interested novel.

   _____

7. By using too much water made the dough sticky.

———————————————————————

8. When the award is announced, is likely to be some objections.

———————————————————————

9. Driving a truck all night is very tired.

———————————————————————

10. The interviewer asked the students were they planning to get married right after graduation.

———————————————————————

PUNCTUATION

The major elements of punctuation are commas, apostrophes, end of sentence marks, semicolons, and colons.

Commas

Know the rules for commas, and use commas only according to the rules. Putting in too many commas does more harm than leaving some out.
Use commas:

1. in dates and place names
2. in a series and between several adjectives in a row
3. after introductory phrases and clauses
4. before and after interrupters
5. before and after nonrestrictive *who* and *which* clauses
6. before and after appositives
7. before short conjunctions in compound sentences
8. before and after persons spoken to
9. before and after contrasting parts
10. before and after direct quotations
11. in correspondence
12. to prevent confusion

Commas in Dates and Place Names

Put commas between the day of the week, the date, and the year. Most writers use a comma after the year as well when it is not at the end of the sentence.

He was born on Wednesday, January 6, 1910, and grew up in Ohio.

Most writers do not put a comma between the month and year:

The Chicago fire occurred in October 1871.

Separate a street address from the city and the city from the state or country, but do not put a comma before the zip code:

He worked at 199 Chambers Street, New York, New York 10007.

E X E R C I S E: Commas in Dates and Place Names

Insert commas where they are needed.

1. Jackie Robinson was born in Cairo Georgia on January 31 1919.

2. President Kennedy was assassinated on November 22 1963 in Dallas Texas.

3. Richard Nixon left the White House on August 8 1974.

4. Astronauts landed on the moon in July 1969.

5. The address is 1600 Broadway New York New York 10019.

6. She was born on Wednesday October 10 1968.

7. On May 6 1974 they were married in Cincinnati Ohio.

Commas in a Series and Between Several Adjectives in a Row

Place a comma after each element in a series except the last one; the comma before *and* is preferred:

They ate sandwiches, potato salad, and pie for lunch.

Do not use commas if *and* separates all elements in the series:

They ate sandwiches and potato salad and pie for lunch.

A series can contain any kind of words or phrases.

Nouns:	Books, records, and magazines lay on the table.
Verbs:	We ate, drank, sang, and danced at the party.
Pronouns:	I think that you, we, and they all look alike.
Adjectives:	The letters were terse, hard-hitting, and factual.
Adverbs:	The Jets played aggressively, efficiently, and shrewdly.

Prepositions:	The detective looked in, around, over, and under the safe.
Phrases:	The company preferred sales managers who were cordial with employees, knew the business, and demonstrated loyalty to the organization.

E X E R C I S E: Commas in Series

Put commas where they belong in these series. One sentence does not need commas. Write *C* next to it.

1. We toured China Japan and the Philippines.

2. The invitations were sent the presents were bought and the house was decorated for the party.

3. The child ran and ran and finally caught up with the dog.

4. Slowly delicately thoughtfully and thoroughly she explained the problem.

5. Separation from home from parents from a spouse or from friends produces anxiety.

6. Pay attention to the rhythm the notes and the dynamics at the same time.

7. Make your essays concise fluent and cohesive.

Commas Separating Coordinate Adjectives

Several adjectives in a row modifying the same noun are called **coordinate adjectives.** They should be separated by commas if you could put *and* between the adjectives in place of the comma: a large, comfortable room (compare with a large *and* comfortable room). Do not put a comma between the last adjective and the noun.

an intimidating, overpowering defense
an enchanting, imaginative, subtle performance
a squat, talkative official
a large, hairy, playful sheepdog

In these examples you could put *and* between the adjectives: a large and hairy and playful sheepdog. When you cannot put *and* between the adjectives, do not use commas:

a fine old chair (not a fine *and* old chair)
a navy blue beach towel (not a navy *and* blue *and* beach towel)

EXERCISE: Commas Between Coordinate Adjectives

Put commas where they are needed. Remember to test each series of adjectives by putting *and* between them.

1. She always wrote prompt courteous lively notes.

2. An ambitious young woman joined the faculty.

3. The counselor was prepared for a quarrelsome rebellious student.

4. A well-polished 1980 Corvette was parked next to a tired-looking overloaded Ford pickup.

5. Talkative entertaining vital people attended the meeting.

Commas After Introductory Phrases and Clauses

Put commas after most introductory words, phrases, and clauses:

Well, you can never be sure.
No, that is not a good idea.
Otherwise, the plan will work.
A few hours later, she began to cry.
When you have finished reading the article, may I borrow the magazine?

Interjections (single words at the beginning like *well, yes, oh,* and *ah*) are followed by commas. Interrupting words like *however, otherwise, meanwhile, first, nevertheless,* and *consequently,* when they begin a sentence, should be followed by a comma. Interrupting phrases (also called parenthetical phrases) like *of course, by the way, after all,* and *in a sense* normally take commas as well when they begin a sentence. Short descriptive phrases like *in a minute, after the game, next to the produce, along the railing,* and *during the performance* are usually followed by commas. Sometimes, however, they fit smoothly into the sentence and do not need them. Compare these two examples:

After a thirty-minute wait, she saw the doctor.
In the fifth problem there was a typographical error.

In the first sentence, the introductory phrase has a pause after it and should be followed by a comma. In the second sentence, the introductory phrase is necessary to the statement and reads better without a comma after it.

Whole clauses (word groups containing subject-verb combinations) normally are followed by commas when they begin sentences:

Although the pay was good, the job was unsatisfactory.
When he thought about the past year, he felt pleased.
Since you joined the faculty, the students have been ecstatic.
Because the message was translated, we could understand it.

E X E R C I S E: Commas After Introductory Parts

Put commas where they are needed after introductory parts in these sentences. If the sentence is correct without a comma, write C after it.

1. Yes this segment of *As the World Turns* is certainly absorbing.

2. Upset by what Darryl has told her about his financial needs and his trip to see Arthur Frannie is just beginning to lose trust in him.

3. Having grown too close to Emma Rosanna cries because her past has made her afraid of becoming attached to people.

4. Unaware of Lily's problem pregnancy Lucinda remains home and does not communicate.

5. When Margo asks Scott why John Eldridge left Thomas's estate to Lisa Lisa begs her son not to tell the truth.

6. Convinced that the difficulties caused by their interracial relationship have strengthened them Jessica and Duncan plan to marry in August.

7. The news of her daughter's miscarriage devastates Lucinda and causes her to rush to the hospital to comfort Lily.

8. After returning home in despair Lily remains very depressed, and no one can cheer her up.

9. Knowing that Kirk has been spending too much time with Ruth Ellie has become furious.

10. When Lucinda offers Scott a job on a trial basis for six months Margo urges him to take it.*

---

*Adaptation of "As the World Turns," *Soap Opera Digest* 17 (July 7, 1992): 82–83. Reprinted by permission of K-III Magazine Corporation.

Commas Before and After Interrupters

Sentence interrupters, or parenthetical expressions (think of *parentheses* before and after a phrase), are separated from the rest of the sentence by commas. When they appear in the middle of a sentence, put commas *before* and *after* them. Of course, when they come at the beginning, you can't put a comma before them; when they come at the end, you put a period after them.

Here are some of the common interrupters:

however	of course	as a matter of fact
consequently	by the way	for example
nevertheless	in a sense	in fact
to be sure	in my opinion	in the first place

These interrupters are usually set off by *pairs* of commas:

She knew, *by the way*, that the television set didn't work.
The subway, *in my opinion*, is too noisy.
The check, *however*, will not be honored at this bank.

Descriptive phrases containing past participles (-*ed* verb forms) and present participles (-*ing* verb forms) after a noun often serve as interrupters as well:

The captain, *puzzled by the strange blips on the radar screen*, cut the speed of the craft.

An immigrant stonemason, *hoping for steady work*, appeared in the office.

Adjective phrases that come after nouns are also set off by pairs of commas.

The instructions, *dense and hard to read*, gave them little aid.

Two fathers, *anxious about their sons' grades*, called the principal.

E X E R C I S E : Commas Around Interrupters

Put commas *before* and *after* the interrupting phrases in these sentences.

1. The income tax laws complicated and confusing take up volumes.

2. The causes of alcoholism in my opinion are both psychological and physiological.

3. Students without courses in chemistry will however have to fulfill their science requirements later.

4. Professional sports according to many fans have changed from a religion to show business.

5. Some people as a matter of fact still believe in exorcism.

6. Investors cautious about the latest changes in the prime rate did little trading on Thursday.

7. Some new cars for example have too much fiberglass.

Commas Before and After Relative Clauses

Descriptive clauses beginning with *who, which,* or *that* are called **relative clauses.** Relative clauses beginning with *who* or *which* are sometimes set off by commas. Here are the rules:

> **Do not** set off restrictive clauses with commas.
> **Do** set off nonrestrictive clauses with commas.

What are restrictive clauses? Restrictive clauses contain information necessary to the meaning of the sentence and therefore should not be separated from the rest of the sentence by any marks of punctuation.
Example 1:

> Students who receive A grades may skip the second course.

The clause *who receive A grades* should not be separated by commas because without it the sentence "Students . . . may skip the second course" means something completely different.
Example 2:

> The essay that won the prize was about illiteracy.

The clause *that won the prize* is restrictive; without it, the sentence does not specify which essay was about illiteracy.
Example 3:

> The town in which the research took place was in California.

The clause *in which the research took place* is restrictive because the sentence has no specific meaning without it.
What are nonrestrictive clauses? Nonrestrictive clauses are relative clauses beginning with *who* or *which* (clauses beginning with *that* are always restrictive). Nonrestrictive clauses add extra details to the sentence but are not crucial to the meaning.
Example 1:

> Fax machines, which send messages and graphics instantaneously, are beginning to replace the postal service.

The clause *which send messages and graphics instantaneously* is nonrestrictive because it merely adds information but is not crucial to the meaning of the sentence.

Example 2:

Philip Johnson, who designed some of America's most interesting buildings, failed the New York State licensing examination.

The clause *who designed some of America's most interesting buildings* is nonrestrictive because it adds information but is not necessary to identify the subject, Philip Johnson, whose name is already given.

E X E R C I S E: Commas with Relative Clauses

Put commas before and after the relative clauses in these sentences if the clauses add descriptions of subjects that are already specific. Do not add commas if the subjects are vague and need the clause to identify them.

(Note: A relative clause at the end of a sentence, of course, ends with a period.)

1. Dorothy Day who was a famous journalist and creative writer supported the cause of American socialism.

2. A person who lives in luxury may have a misunderstanding of poverty and unemployment.

3. Acronyms which are short words formed by the initials of other words have become widely used.

4. CREEP which stood for Committee to Reelect the President was an acronym used during the Nixon administration.

5. An acronym that is familiar to most people is SNAFU, a combination that stands for "situation normal; all fouled up."

6. CINCUS is an acronym that had to be abandoned after Pearl Harbor; it means Commander in Chief, U.S. Fleet.

7. A person who specializes in pediatrics needs patience and humor.

8. Alfred Kinsey who was a pioneer in sex research was known in high school as the boy who never had a girlfriend.

9. Elvis Presley who was to become the most famous popular singer in his era failed his first audition for the Arthur Godfrey show.

10. The population of the world which is now more than 5.5 billion is increasing rapidly.

Commas Before and After Appositives

Appositives are phrases that come after nouns or pronouns and describe or identify them. They are usually set off by pairs of commas:

Peter Arno, *the great cartoonist,* was voted America's best-dressed man in 1941.

Neil Armstrong, *the first man to step on the moon,* earned his pilot's license when he was 16.

Some very short appositives are not separated by commas:

The Emperor Nero was a psychopath.
My sister Karen will join us.

E X E R C I S E: Commas with Appositives

Put commas before and after the appositives in these sentences unless they are very short and read without a pause.

1. Samuel Taylor Coleridge the romantic poet of the nineteenth century was a heavy user of opium.

2. My uncle Ted used to be an opera singer.

3. Sandra the youngest member of the board voted for the proposal.

4. Dr. Benjamin Spock the author of the famous book on baby care joined the peace movement in the 1960s.

5. Malcolm X the Black Muslim political leader studied languages and history in prison.

6. Jason the smartest student in his biology class explained how to dissect a frog.

7. A. Philip Randolph the great labor leader organized a union of Pullman car workers.

Commas Before Short Conjunctions in Compound Sentences

Use a comma plus a short conjunction to link independent clauses in compound sentences. The short conjunctions are *and, but, or, for, nor,* and *so.* Remember to put commas *before* them but not *after.*

Independent clause   *Independent clause*

1. The location was desirable, *and* the price was reasonable.
2. Efforts were made by the police, *but* no suspects were found.
3. You may pay by check today, *or* you may have the store bill you later.
4. The first group stayed in the city, *for* they came from urban environments themselves.
5. The passengers were not injured, *nor* was the boat seriously damaged.
6. Sally had visited Puerto Rico before, *so* she knew where to eat in San Juan.

Remember that these short connectives are used in other ways and often do not have commas before them when they connect shorter parts such as words or phrases:

Ted *and* Mary took a walk along the shore. (*And* joins two subjects.)

The prizes went to Sam *and* Alice, *and* the awards for leadership went to Beverly. (The first *and* connects two nouns; the second *and* joins two independent clauses.)

The engine *but* not the suspension system was rebuilt. (*But* joins two subjects.)

I suggest the veal *or* the shrimp. (*Or* joins two nouns.)

Neither the acting *nor* the script was exceptional. (*Nor* joins two subjects.)

The beach was *so* beautiful that they went swimming as soon as they arrived. (*So* used with *that* is an adverb—no comma.)

EXERCISE I: Commas Before Conjunctions

Put commas before short conjunctions that join independent clauses in these sentences. Do not put commas before them if they join shorter elements. If the sentence is correct, write *C* next to it.

1. I like to study with the radio on but this music makes me nervous.

2. Buying lottery tickets gives me a sense of adventure and I always expect to win a million dollars next time.

3. You can turn left at the next light or you can follow the main highway for three blocks.

4. The history of World War II and the history of socialism are both special interests of Professor Jones.

5. My cat is ill so I plan to take her to the veterinarian.

6. The college has room for 900 freshmen but 1500 high school seniors have applied for admission.

7. The view was so breathtaking that they stared at it for hours.

EXERCISE 11: Commas Before Conjunctions

Compose your own compound sentences using the following short connectives. Put commas before the connectives.

1. and

_____

2. but

_____

3. or

_____

4. for

_____

5. so

_____

6. nor

_____

Commas Before and After Persons Spoken to (Direct Address)

When you speak directly to a person, using his or her name in a sentence, separate the name from the rest of the sentence. Use commas in *pairs* unless the name comes at the beginning or end of the sentence:

I remember, *Martha,* how you looked in high school.
Martha, I remember how you looked in high school.
I remember how you looked in high school, *Martha.*

Many writers omit these commas and ignore the difference in meaning:

"I remember Martha" is not the same as "I remember, Martha."

EXERCISE: Commas with Direct Address

Put commas in these sentences to separate the names of persons spoken to from the rest of the sentence.

1. You know Steve that the rest of us agree with you.

2. Barbara will you please give me some advice.

3. These are the photos that you took in Arizona Richard.

4. You may find Gladys that you like the other therapist better.

5. Herman can we send you a brochure about life insurance?

6. Here is good news cardholders for those of you planning to travel.

7. Tony please describe the area.

Commas Before and After Contrasting Parts

Use commas before and after contrasting phrases beginning with *not:*

The Yankees, not the Dodgers, won that series.
The weather was cooler, not warmer, than predicted.
The capital of Pennsylvania is Harrisburg, not Philadelphia.

EXERCISE: Commas with Contrasting Elements

Put commas in these sentences to separate contrasting elements.

1. The women not the men supported the action.

2. Arkansas not Tennessee was the first state to open a branch.

3. Lessons are available in karate not kung fu.

4. The clocks should be set forward not back.

5. Drive through the intersection not onto the service road.

6. Ham and cheese not liverwurst is what I ordered.

7. These sweaters come in blue not green.

Commas Before and After Direct Quotations

Before quoting a whole statement, put a comma after the introductory word *said, stated, asked,* and so on:

> He said, "This is the road to Seattle."
> She asked, "Will this book explain how to sell real estate?"
> The catalog stated, "This course includes intermediate algebra."

Put commas after quotations when the quotations come at the beginning of sentences. Commas belong inside quotation marks:

> "After dinner, let's play Scrabble," Sue suggested.
> "Don't leave any questions blank," the instructor said.

Short quoted phrases often fit smoothly into the sentence and should not be set off by commas:

> Trevor called his brother a "universal genius."
> Joanne was often called the "Whitney Houston look-alike."
> Shakespeare called music the "food of love."

EXERCISE I: Commas with Quotations

Use commas to separate the following quotations. Do not use commas when a short quoted phrase fits smoothly into the sentence. If the sentence is correct, write *C* next to it.

1. Sheila said "You have the same opinion I do."

2. "Let's meet in the cafeteria for lunch" Harry suggested.

3. They termed the procedure "a computerized approach to gambling on sports."

4. "I admire your determination" the manager said. "However, there are some errors in the reports."

5. The author stated "Few crime statistics reveal the source of the problem."

6. "The first day may be difficult" she explained.

7. Sandra asked "Why should we wait for them to call us?"

EXERCISE 11: Commas with Quotations

Write three sentences of your own. In the first, put the *he* or *she said* before the quotation; in the second, put the quotation first. In the third, fit a short quoted phrase into your sentence without a comma.

Your sentences:

1. _____

2. _____

3. _____

Commas in Correspondence

In business letters and personal letters, the closing is always followed by a comma:

Business Letters	*Personal Letters and Notes*
Sincerely yours,	Yours truly,
Yours very truly,	Yours,
Yours truly,	As always,
Cordially yours,	Best wishes,
	Love,

In personal letters, put commas after the greeting:

Dear Janet,	Dear Mom,
Dear Tom,	Dear Grandpa,

Commas to Prevent Confusion

Occasionally, you may need a comma to separate words that might appear to belong together when the meaning requires that they be separated. Watch especially for prepositions (in, around, over, through, etc.) that appear to go with the words after them when they do not:

Inside, the room looked bright and airy. (*Inside the room* is not a phrase to be read together.)

Not long after, the candidates gave speeches. (*After the candidates gave speeches* is not a clause.)

All around, the landscape looked lush and mysterious. (*Around the landscape* should not be read as a phrase.)

E X E R C I S E: Commas to Prevent Confusion

Put commas in these sentences to prevent confusion.

1. Far and near the house and the whole property were snow-bound.

2. I knew that when he thought it over the top figure would not seem very high.

3. The board decided that if the company ever went under the margin of profit among the competitors would increase.

4. It appeared that when the auditors were through the office would be more relaxed.

5. People who can usually buy cars on credit.

6. Those who should always win early promotions.

7. Joe thought that since he had enough to get by the funds that remained in the trust were not necessary to him.

Apostrophes

Apostrophes are used for two purposes:

Uses of Apostrophes

1. Use apostrophes in contractions, where letters have been left out:

   do not = don't
   should not = shouldn't

2. Use apostrophes to indicate possession:

   's for singular possessives: Karen's dress
   s' for plural possessives: four students' grades
   ' or 's for proper nouns ending in s: Keats' poems or Keats's poems

Exception: plurals that do not take s, such as *men* or *children*, take 's in the possessive:

   men's hats
   children's games

Some common mistakes:

- Carelessly leaving apostrophes out of contractions: dont, instead of don't; shes, instead of she's; wouldnt, instead of wouldn't
- Writing possessives without apostrophes: Karens dress, instead of Karen's dress; womens opinions, instead of women's opinions
- Putting apostrophes in the wrong place: my mothers' attitudes, instead of my mother's attitudes; its' cold, instead of it's cold
- Using apostrophes with personal pronouns: write hers, not her's; yours, not your's (Impersonal pronouns do take apostrophes: everyone's opinions; somebody's car.)

EXERCISE: Apostrophes

Circle the correct form in parentheses.

1. The English language (doesn't, dosen't, doesnt) go back as far in history as Latin and Greek.

2. According to most (experts, expert's, experts') opinions, Old English, or Anglo-Saxon, (didnt, did'nt, didn't) exist in the time of the ancient Greeks.

3. Old English, in any case (couldn't, could'nt, couldnt) really be called English as we speak it.

4. Many influences altered the way English was spoken over the centuries, but English (hasnt, has'nt, hasn't) lost its basic structure.

5. After the Norman Conquest in A.D. 1066, the biggest change in English came from the French (aristocrats', aristocrat's, aristocrats) speech.

6. Consequently, most languages (cant, can't, cann't) compete with English for richness of vocabulary.

7. Still, people in (Shakespeare, Shakespeares', Shakespeare's) time (would'nt, wouldnt, wouldn't) have guessed how widespread their language would become.

End Punctuation: Periods, Question Marks, and Exclamation Points

Use periods to end statements and indirect questions:

Statement: The store had a sale on January 2.
Indirect question: Sam asked whether the store was having a sale.

Use question marks after direct questions:

Is this book overdue?

When will you be back?

Why, if no one objects to the proposal, are we waiting until March to begin?

Don't forget to put the question mark at the end of long, complicated questions like the last one.

Use periods, not questions marks, after requests:

Would you please send me an application form.

Would you please let me know if you are interested.

Use exclamation points after sentences that express excitement or strong feeling:

Get out of my sight!

Watch out for that elephant!

That was a fabulous performance!

Use exclamation points after single words or phrases that express astonishment or strong emotion:

Help!

Stop!

No more war!

E X E R C I S E: End Punctuation

Put the correct end punctuation after these sentences.

1. The instructor asked whether the class had read the assignment

2. If you want help, why don't you ask one of us for it

3. Get out of that van It's going to explode

4. Would you please send me travel literature and maps of Florida

5. Will you be spending your vacation in Greece

6. Ask for the color and size that you want

7. If the restaurant is open, shall I make a reservation

Semicolons

Use semicolons to separate independent clauses in compound sentences when there are no short connectives.

Children of illegal aliens often attend public schools; some states have asked the federal government to pay for the cost of their education.

Buying on credit has disadvantages; one may overestimate one's ability to pay.

Semicolons, not commas, should also be used to separate independent clauses when there is a long connective word (a conjunctive adverb) like *however, therefore, meanwhile, nevertheless, consequently,* or *moreover* between the clauses. Use a comma *after* the connecting word:

Separate conference rooms are available for the two meetings; *however,* you may convene together afterward if you like.

We have already sent you a brochure; *meanwhile,* we are awaiting your request.

Use semicolons to separate independent clauses with the word *then* between them. *Then* is not a short connecting word like *and;* do not put a comma before it:

Not: We always swim at four o'clock, *then* we do aerobics.
But: We always swim at four o'clock; *then* we do aerobics.

Use semicolons to separate parts of a series when the individual parts have commas within them:

She had lived in Dallas, Texas; San Mateo, California; and Stamford, Connecticut.

You will have to pass three examinations: a reading test, in multiple-choice format; a writing test, in the form of a one-hour essay; and a mathematics test, given on a computer.

E X E R C I S E: Semicolons

Put semicolons between independent clauses in all of the following sentences except those with short connectives. Put commas before these connectives (*and, but, or, for, yet,* and *so*).

1. The legal profession attracts top students in many countries there are now about two million lawyers in the world.

2. Of these, about a third are practicing in the United States in fact the number of American lawyers has tripled since 1960.

3. Hollywood and television have popularized the legal profession "L.A. Law," *Presumed Innocent,* and *Reversal of Fortune* portray the excitement and challenge of lawyers' careers.

4. The United States has more lawyers per 100,000 people than any other Western country but Pakistan and Singapore have even more.

5. Japan, however, has a remarkably small number of lawyers even there, however, the profession is beginning to expand.

6. In America, seventy percent of law graduates pass the bar exam in Japan the passing rate is only three percent.

7. One cause of the explosion of lawsuits in the United States is the juries' huge awards in torts these are lawsuits in which someone claims injury from a faulty product or medical malpractice.

8. American lawyers in such cases are often paid contingency fees this means that they collect a percentage of the award if they win.

9. Another problem in many countries is that poor people cannot get adequate legal representation and many reforms have been proposed to solve the problem.

10. Some other countries have begun to regard America's litigation explosion as a disease someone invented the term "hyperlexis" to identify it.*

Colons

The colon (:) is used to introduce something. Use colons after *as follows* or *the following* to introduce lists:

> She called out the following names: Roberta, Carl, Tracy, Janice, and Lamont.

> Open the bottle as follows: press down on the lid, align the arrows, and turn lid to the left.

Use colons when you introduce a list formally:

> The ceremony will proceed in this order: first the procession into the auditorium, next the speeches, and finally the presentation of degrees.

> A reader can enjoy the book except for a few shortcomings: its unrealistic plot, its difficult style, and its improbable ending.

---

*Information from "A Survey of the Legal Profession," *The Economist* 324 (July 18, 1992): 1–8.

Use colons to separate main clauses in compound sentences when the second clause explains the first:

> Joan approached the interview with only one thought in mind: she intended to show them that she understood the job.

Do not use colons after informal introductory expressions (*like, such as, including,* or the abbreviation *e.g.*):

Not:	We ordered five books including: *The Color Purple.*
Better:	We ordered five books, including *The Color Purple.*
Not:	You need three liberal arts electives, such as: sociology, history, and literature.
Better:	You need three liberal arts electives, such as sociology, history, and literature.
Not:	You need to eat more nutritious food, e.g.: oat bran and citrus fruit.
Better:	You need to eat more nutritious food, e.g., oat bran and citrus fruit.

EXERCISE: Colons

Insert colons in any of the following sentences where they belong. If the sentence is correct, write C next to it.

1. Human sexuality has been studied by experts from all of the following disciplines psychology, sociology, biology, and women's studies.
2. Biologists have found interesting ways of interpreting human sexuality such as observing the sexual behavior of other species.
3. Previous studies had been done of these well-known primate species gorillas, orangutans, and chimpanzees.
4. Such studies proved disappointing for one chief reason the sexual habits of these animals did not resemble the practices of human beings.
5. One species, however, remained to be studied the bonobos, or so-called pygmy chimpanzees of Zaire.
6. The bonobos had not been studied for a very good reason they are difficult to find.
7. The bonobos' sexual behavior turned out to be a lot like that of humans in several ways they enjoy sex for pleasure and not just to reproduce, they engage in intercourse face-to-face, and the females have sex whether or not they are ovulating.
8. Some researchers think they have made important discoveries in watching the bonobos, such as a pattern of behavior that resembles that of prehistoric human beings.
9. Others, however, are disturbed by the following "naughty" practices of the bonobos sex between related individuals, sexual activity between individuals regardless of gender, and sexual activity between juveniles and adults.

10. Whatever we learn from watching other species in the wild, one thing is certain we are both very much like our biological relatives and very different from them.*

CAPITALIZATION

Learn the rules for using capital letters.

Rules for Using Capital Letters

Capitalize:

- The first word of every sentence and the first word of every quoted sentence: He said, "The tape is missing."
- The word *I* and the proper name of every person: John Smith, Meg Ryan, Mr. Jones, Jay Leno.
- The name of every city, state, country, and other specific place name: San Juan, Puerto Rico; Yankee Stadium; Golden Gate Park.
- The name of every day of the week, month, holiday: Monday, October, Thanksgiving Day (but *not* spring, summer, fall, and winter).
- The title of every book, play, magazine, short story, film, song, or television show: *The Oprah Winfrey Show, Time Magazine, A Raisin in the Sun, Gone with the Wind.* Note: Little words like *of, the,* and *a* are not capitalized unless they begin the title.
- The name of a company, organization, religion, school, or college: The Ford Motor Company, Livingston High School, Carleton College, St. Luke's Church. Note: Do not capitalize words like *church, high school, company,* or *college* if they are not part of a specific name.
- The name of a specific product: Coca Cola, Wheaties, Rolls-Royce. Note: Do not capitalize the word for the category of a product: A Mack truck, Smirnoff vodka, English toffee.
- A person's nationality: a French woman, a Japanese student, a Canadian hockey player, an American Indian.
- The title of a specific course: Sociology 101, Mathematics 104, American History 110. Note: Do not capitalize subjects like sociology or mathematics when not used to name specific courses.

---

*Information from Meredith F. Small, "What's Love Got to Do with It?" *Discover* 13 (June 1992): 46–51.

E X E R C I S E: Capital Letters

Proofread the following passage and circle the *ten* errors in capitalization.

Timothy's Least Favorite Courses

Although Timothy likes most of his courses, he took some in high school and College that he did not enjoy. In high school he took a course in History that bored him to death because the teacher, Mr. postlethwaite, demanded that the students learn one hundred dates from the discovery of America to the War in vietnam. then in college Timothy took a course called statistics 110, which was taught by a Professor from Harvard university. This course was so hard he withdrew after the first week and decided to take General Math 101 in the Spring. Next he took a course in russian and barely passed it. In his second year he decided to become a psychology major. He declared, "at last I've found the right subject for my talents."

SPELLING

To become a better speller, attack the problem from several directions at once. And don't expect to improve rapidly without really concentrating and memorizing. Only a few rare people can spell correctly without effort; the rest of us need a many-sided strategy, along with old-fashioned study and repetition.

What should you do to improve your spelling?

- Learn the patterns and rules. Although English spelling is irregular, with most rules having exceptions, you will do well to learn the rules.
- Master the look-alikes/sound-alikes. A large percentage of misspellings come from words being confused with others that look or sound almost like them.
- Drill on frequently misspelled words. Study tricky words, or spelling "demons," especially those in your area of work or study. A corporate employee should never misspell *business* or a nurse misspell *medicine*.
- Take personal responsibility for your spelling. Don't expect any book, course, or teacher to work magic for you. It's up to you; make lists of your own most often misspelled words—and study them.

Spelling Rules

The first step toward spelling competence is to learn the few main patterns—even though they may have exceptions.

Rule 1: Position of i and e

You probably have heard, and may know, the old rule:

> *i* before *e*
> except after *c*
> or when sounded like *a*
> as in *neighbor* or *weigh.*

Learn the jingle if you do not already know it. But be prepared to run into many exceptions. Study the patterns.

1. *i* before *e:* Bel*ie*ve. Most words with an *e* sound do follow the rule when there is no *c* before the combination:

   ach*ie*ve (ch, but not c)
   fr*ie*nd (even though pronounced eh)
   f*ie*nd
   gr*ie*ve
   l*ie*n
   n*ie*ce (the c comes *after* ie)
   p*ie*ce
   p*ie*rce
   pr*ie*st
   rel*ie*ve
   repr*ie*ve
   retr*ie*ve
   shr*ie*k
   th*ie*f

2. Except after *c:* Rec*ei*ve. Despite exceptions, this pattern usually holds true, too:

   c*ei*ling
   conc*ei*ted
   conc*ei*ve
   dec*ei*ve
   perc*ei*ve
   rec*ei*pt

3. Or when sounded like *a:* W*ei*gh. Combinations that are sounded like *a* or *i* are usually *ei:*

   *ei*ght
   fr*ei*ght

height
neighbor
vein
weight

4. Some exceptions to the rule: A few words take *ie* even though it comes after *c:*

financier
society
species

A few *ei* words with the *e* sound and no *c* before them can fool you, too:

either
leisure
neither
seize
weird

Rule 2: Keeping or Dropping the Final e

When adding an ending to a word with a final *e,* keep the *e* if the ending starts with a consonant:

arrange + ment = arrangement
hope + ful = hopeful
nine + ty = ninety
sincere + ly = sincerely
face + less = faceless
manage + ment = management

Drop the *e* if the ending starts with a vowel:

give + ing = giving
have + ing = having
erase + ure = erasure
locate + ion = location
guide + ance = guidance

Exceptions: To keep a *g* or *c* soft before a vowel, we sometimes keep the *e:*

age + ing = ageing *or* aging
manage + able = manageable
service + able = serviceable

The word *judgment* does not keep the *e* except in British spelling. *Dyeing* keeps the *e* to prevent confusion with *dying.*

Rule 3: Doubling Final Consonants

This rule is somewhat complicated, but it does not have many exceptions and it includes many common words. Learn the pattern.

The rule applies to words like *begin, control,* and *occur.* When you add an *ed, ing,* or *er* ending to these words, do you double the final consonant? Yes: begi*nn*ing, contro*ll*ed, and occu*rr*ed.

What do these words have in common? The rule says that they *end with a single consonant* (not *ck* as in shock, or *st* as in post) *preceded by a single vowel* (not a double vowel, as in br*ea*k or m*ee*t). And the accent must be on the last syllable (not earlier, as in *travel,* where the *l* does not have to be doubled, or *pivot,* where the *t* is not doubled).

To sum up: These words contain

- A single final consonant: begi*n*
- A single vowel preceding the final consonant: beg*i*n
- An accent on the last syllable: be*gin*

Many common words follow this pattern. When you become familiar with it, the rule is extremely useful. Here are only some of the examples:

begi*nn*ing	forge*tt*ing	refe*rr*ed
commi*tt*ed	occu*rr*ing	sto*pp*ed
contro*ll*ing	omi*tt*ed	thro*bb*ing
exce*ll*ing	prefe*rr*ing	

(The rule applies to one-syllable words as well.)

E X E R C I S E: Spelling Rules

Some of the following words are correct, and some are misspelled. Write *C* next to the correct ones, and spell the others correctly in the blanks. Review the rules first; try not to guess.

1. belief	_____		6. percieve	_____
2. occurance	_____		7. writeing	_____
3. placing	_____		8. definitly	_____
4. arrangment	_____		9. achieve	_____
5. weight	_____		10. commited	_____

11. stately   _____   16. refering   _____

12. noticeable   _____   17. replacment   _____

13. hopful   _____   18. removing   _____

14. movement   _____   19. permiting   _____

15. chief   _____   20. strokeing   _____

Common Mix-ups

The following words are often misspelled because they contain combinations that are easily confused with those in similar words. Study the groups carefully, looking for the trouble spots.

1. ability
   responsibility
   possibility
   (The last two do *not* contain *ability*.)

2. accumulate
   accommodate
   recommend
   (Study the *c*'s and *m*'s in these common words.)

3. across
   address
   (Both are often misspelled; notice the single *c* and double *d*.)

4. alone
   along
   (Two simple words but often carelessly mixed up)

5. amount
   among
   (Be careful not to write amo*u*ng, even though it rhymes with yo*u*ng.)

6. arithmetic
   athletics
   mathematics
   (Not ath*e*letics or ath*e*lete, and don't forget the *e* in mathematics.)

7. believe
   receive
   (These two most common *ie/ei* words do follow the rule.)

8. committee
   committing
   commitment
   (Note the single *t* in commitment.)

9. definitely
   immediately
   (Don't confuse *-itely* with *-ately* words.)

10. develop
    developed
    envelope
    (There is no such word as *develope*.)

11. divide   (Not d*e*vide)
    decide

12. familiar   (The extra *i* in *familiar* gives it an extra syllable.)
    similar

13. fulfill   (Don't spell it *for*fill or *fore*fill.)
    foretell

14. necessary   (Only one *c* in necessary, one *s* in occasionally, and
    occasionally   one *f* in professional)
    professional

15. pastime   (Don't double that *t* in pastime.)
    part-time

16. accidentally   (Not public*a*lly)
    publicly

17. relevant   (Two difficult words; notice the *e*'s and *a*'s and the
    prevalent   *l*'s and *v*'s.)

18. separate   (*Not* sep*e*rate)
    desperate

19. surprise   (Do not write *su*prise or *sur*pose.)
    suppose

20. strictly   (Not stric*k* or stric*k*ly)
    stick
    quickly

21. till   (Not unti*ll*)
    until

EXERCISE I: Spelling Mix-ups

The following paragraph contains fifteen misspelled words. Underline them and write the correct spellings above them.

Writing well is definately a marketable skill that you should develope. In business, law, and medicine, effective writing is neccessary. Students who do not beleive this is true are often supprised to discover too late that they lack this important proffesional requirement. Not untill they learn the hard way— by recieving criticism of their work—do many employees realize how prevelant the demand for good writing is. Amoung executives it is understood that the committment to writing goes alone with the strickly technical aspects of a job. Colleges accross the country are publically declaring their dedication to effective career writing.

EXERCISE 11: Spelling Mix-ups

Write these misspelled words correctly.

1. accidently   _____

2. immediatly   _____

3. past-time   _____

4. comittment   _____

5. develope   _____

6. athelete   _____

7. beleive   _____

8. reccomend   _____

9. occassionally   _____

10. seperate   _____

Pronoun Mix-ups

Forms of the common pronouns—*I, you, he, she, they,* and *we*—are often confused with other words. Study the groups below; these are simple words you should know perfectly.

1. He, his, he's

   His means belonging to him; *he's* is short for *he is. He's* looking for *his* wallet.

2. Its, it's, its'

   Its shows possession; *it's* is short for *it is* or *it has.* The jury made *its* decision. *It's* a cool day for July. *It's* (it has) been an entertaining evening. There is no such word as *its'.*

3. Mine, mind, mines

   Don't confuse *mine* (belonging to me) with *mind* (a smart mind). Although *mines* is widely spoken in dialect, there is no such pronoun in standard written English. (That pen is *mine*, not *mines*.)

4. Our, are, or

Our is possessive—belonging to us: *our* schedules. Don't confuse it with the verb *are*: Sally and Timothy *are* married. *Or* is a connective word: Either Tom *or* Randy will wait for you.

5. They, their, they're, there, there's, theirs

The word *they* is used as a subject, referring to a number of people or things: *They* belong to the gang.

Their means belonging to them: *Their* ideas are right.

They're is short for *they are*: *They're* going to be rich.

There means at that place, or it may be just a structure word: *There* is a new hair style this year.

There's is short for *there is* or *there has*: *There's* a noisy party upstairs.

Theirs means belonging to them: *Theirs* is the best pizza in town.

6. We're, were, where, wear, ware

We're is short for *we are*: *We're* the first people here.

Were is a verb: *Were* those books expensive?

Where asks about the place something happens: *Where* did you go last night? Don't mix up *where* and *were*. They look similar but don't sound alike.

Wear, as a verb, means to clothe: *Wear* your designer jeans. The noun *wear* also refers to clothing: Men's *wear* is sold here.

Ware refers to equipment and utensils: hardware, software, silverware. Don't confuse this with formal *wear* or evening *wear*, the noun, referring to clothing.

7. Who's, whose

Who's is short for *who is* or *who has*: *Who's* the manager of the store? *Who's* been making long distance calls?

Whose asks about ownership: *Whose* book is this?

8. You're, your, yours, yours'

You're is short for *you are*: *You're* never home when I call.

Your shows possession: *Your* contract is in
the mail.

Use *yours*, not *yours'*: That idea was *yours*.

EXERCISE I: Pronoun Mix-ups

The following paragraph contains fifteen misspellings. Underline them and
write the correctly spelled pronouns above them.

If your having trouble remembering names and facts, its very likely that

you can benefit from using memory tricks called mnemonic devices. Their the

little gimmicks, like rhymes, that help people remember names, words, num-

bers, and spellings. Theirs a familiar device for recalling names, for instance,

that is often used at parties. Each person tries to remember all the names of the

people their by joining there names with crazy adjectives—Ferocious Fran,

Studious Stu, and so on. Most of us find that are memories work better when

we associate new names or facts this way with familiar words or traits. Sup-

pose you meet a new acquaintance who's name is Richard, and suppose that

his expensively dressed. You're easiest way to remember his name is to think

of him as "rich." Its also easier to remember spelling words by using tricks.

Notice were the problem letters are, and exaggerate the pronunciation: say

Feb *roo* ary, for instance. Unless you're memory is sharper than mines, your

going to need such mnemonic devices now and then.

EXERCISE II: Pronoun Mix-ups

In each pair of sentences, one sentence is correct (write C in the blank) and the
other contains a misspelled word. Write the corrected word in the blank.

1. They're going to join the society next week. _____
   The teacher is reading there scores. _____

2. Its been a wonderful visit.
   The tree lost all of its bark.

   _____

   _____

3. Theirs a riot going on in the suburbs.
   There's a new way to solve those equations.

   _____

   _____

4. We rented are house to a young couple.
   Our vacation this year was exciting.

   _____

   _____

5. Whose been making those crank calls?
   Do you know whose sneakers these are?

   _____

   _____

6. Where have all the customers gone?
   Some of them where at the parade.

   _____

   _____

7. Would you mind giving me a hand?
   That idea was mind, not yours.

   _____

   _____

8. I think his not as smart as he looks.
   Let him have his way.

   _____

   _____

9. Don't wear boring clothes to the party.
   This is the place wear it happened.

   _____

   _____

10. Their is a beautiful beach on the sound.
    The neighbors took their dog with them.

    _____

    _____

Look-alikes/Sound-alikes

This list contains words that are often confused with each other because they look or sound alike. Say each word aloud in its example in order to hear the differences. Since these are common words, you should master all of them.

1. a, an, and, any

Use *a* before consonants, *an* before vowels: *a* computer, but *an* old computer. Use *an* before words beginning with silent *h*: *an* honest worker. Use *a* before *u* words that start with a *y* sound: *a* union leader. Use *a* before *one* because of the *w* sound: *a* one-cylinder motor. The rule is to use *a* before consonant *sounds* and *an* before vowel *sounds*. *And* is the connective word: Sam *and* his wife. *Any* refers to an amount or unit: We do not have *any* new employees.

2. advice, advise

Pronounce them correctly and you will spell them correctly: *Advice* contains the word *ice:* You give *advice* (a noun). *Advise* rhymes with *wise* and is a verb: You *advise* someone.

3. affect, effect

Affect is the verb: This *affects* all of us.
Effect is the noun: What is the *effect* of crime? (Exception: *effect* can sometimes be a verb, which means to bring about or create: Let's *effect* an improvement in communications.)

4. a lot, alot

Always write this as two words: We need *a lot* of financial backing. There is no such word as *alot*.

5. already, all ready

Already means now; *all ready* means prepared: It is *already* two o'clock; we are *all ready* to leave.

6. always, away

These do not sound alike, but because they look similar, many writers mistakenly write *alway*. Don't drop the *s*.

7. bought, brought

Be sure to write these as they sound: *bought* is the past tense of *buy:* We *bought* a surfboard. *Brought* is the past tense of *bring:* I *brought* it to the beach.

8. breath, breathe

Pronounce them: *Breath* is the noun, rhyming with *death:* I took a deep *breath*. *Breathe* is the verb, rhyming with *seethe:* Try to *breathe* through your nose.

9. buy, by

To *buy* is to purchase: We *buy* merchandise. *By* is usually a preposition: We pass *by* the museum.

10. choose, chose

The present form is *choose*—rhymes with *news:* I *choose* a different program each week. *Chose* is the past tense—rhymes with *rose:* Last month we *chose* the spot for our vacation.

11. conscience, conscious

Your *conscience* (pronounce it: kon shuntz) is your sense of right and wrong: Let your *conscience* be your guide. To be *conscious* (kon shuss) is to be aware: She was *conscious* of someone approaching.

12. convenience, convince

Listen to the sound: *convenience* (kun veen yuntz). I'll do it at your *convenience*. I'll *convince* (kun vintz) you to buy it.

13. does, dose

Notice the spelling and the sound: *does* sounds like *duzz:* She *does* everything. *Dose* rhymes with *close:* a *dose* of medicine. Notice the spelling of *doesn't* (*not* dosen't).

14. fine, find, fined

Fine means excellent: She was a *fine* dancer. To *find* means to locate: *Find* a date for your cousin. *Fined* (pronounced the same as *find*) means to be ordered to pay a fine: She was *fined* for double parking.

15. have, of

Don't write, I would *of* enjoyed that. It should be, I would *have* enjoyed that. Watch all those combinations—should have, might have, must have, could have. *Have* sounds like *of* in some phrases: she should've been here—short for *should have*.

16. know, no, now

Know and *no* sound alike and are often confused. Remember the word *knowledge*—that which you *know*. Don't write, I *no* how to swim. *Now* (rhymes with *cow*) means at present: We are *now* in the fourth act.

17. lead, led

Lead (or *leads*)—rhymes with *need*—is present tense: I usually *lead* the trumpet section. *Led* is the past tense: She *led* (rhymes with *red*) the parade last year. However, the metal *lead*, as in a *lead* pipe, is pronounced the same as *led*.

18. loose, lose, loss, lost

Pronunciation is the key again. *Loose*, meaning not tight, rhymes with *moose*: The nails had come *loose*. *Lose* is the verb, rhyming with *fuse*: Don't *lose* your temper. *Loss* is a noun: One *loss* won't affect your league standings. (*Loss* rhymes with *boss*.) *Lost* (rhymes with *cost*) means gone: They were *lost* in the forest.

19. pass, passed, past

The verb is *pass* (present tense) and *passed* (past tense): I *pass* the store every day; I *passed* all my courses last semester. Use *past* as the noun or the preposition: She lives in the *past;* we drove *past* her house.

20. principal, principle

Remember that *principle* (it has *le* like *rule*) means a rule or law: the *principle* of gravity. *Principal* means important: the *principal* of the school, the *principal* part in a play.

21. personal, personnel

Personal means private: a *personal* letter. *Personnel* (accent on the last syllable, rhymes with *shell*—and notice the double *n*) means employees: a *personnel* manager.

22. quiet, quit, quite

Notice the extra syllable in *quiet*, meaning silent: the room was *quiet*. (*Quiet* rhymes with *diet*.) To *quit* (rhymes with *hit*) means to stop: He *quit* his job. *Quite* (rhymes with *white*) means very: She is *quite* talented.

23. rise, raise

Both are verbs, but only *raise* takes an object: the sun will *rise* by itself, but you *raise* the blinds. Past tense: the sun *rose*; you *raised* the blinds.

24. since, sense

Since is the connecting word: It has been lonely *since* you left. *Sense* means understanding. She has good business *sense*.

25. sit, set

Sit means to take a seat: She always *sits* in the front row. Past tense: She always *sat* there. *Set* means to place something: He *set* the cans on the shelf. Past tense: He *set* the cans there.

26. sort, sought

Sort can be a noun or a verb: A *sort* of all-around athlete; They *sort* the pastries in rows. *Sought* is the past tense of *seek*: They *sought* everywhere for an apartment. Don't write, "It was *sought* of cold today."

27. suppose, supposed

Remember the *d* ending in statements like "You are supposed to attend." Use *suppose* without the *d* only as a verb in the present tense: "I *suppose* you agree with her."

28. than, then

Use *than* for comparisons—funnier *than* Eddie Murphy. Use *then* for time: *Then* we started dancing.

29. taught, thorough, though, thought, threw, through, throughout, tough

Master this difficult group by pronouncing each word carefully.

Taught (rhymes with *fought*) is the past tense of *teach*: She *taught* calculus.

Thorough (rhymes with *borough*) means complete: a *thorough* investigation.

Though (rhymes with *go*) is a connective word: *Though* he was nervous, he performed well.

Thought (rhymes with *bought*) is the past tense of *think*: We *thought* it was a good restaurant.

Threw (rhymes with *new*) is the past tense of *throw*: We *threw* a big party. Don't mix up *threw* and *through*; they sound the same.

Through (sounds the same as *threw*) means finished (when they were *through* eating) or inside (*through* the tunnel).

Throughout (pronounced throo owt) means everywhere within an area: *throughout* the whole state of Ohio.

Tough (rhymes with *puff*) as in "rough and *tough*"—means hard or difficult.

30. to, too, two

Two, the number, is usually spelled right: There were *two* cars in the garage. The trick is to know when to use *too*. Remember that *too*, with *more than one o*, means *more than enough*: There is *too* much noise here. It also means in addition: You come *too*. All the other meanings take *to*: travel *to* Cuba; *to* win at poker.

31. use, used

Remember the *d* ending in statements like "We used to live in Arkansas" or "She is used to working late." *Use* without the *d* ending is a verb in the present tense: "I *use* my microwave oven frequently."

32. worse, worst

Both are forms of *bad*: bad, worse, worst. Use *worse* to compare two things, persons, or situations: Her illness became *worse*. This film is *worse* than the other one. *Worst* is the superlative form; it describes one thing that stands out from the rest: the *worst* dinner I ever ate; the *worst* car in the lot.

EXERCISE I: Look-alikes/Sound-alikes

Choose the correct word in each sentence and circle it.

1. Many people give (advice, advise) without being asked.

2. The (principles, principals) of economics are complex.

3. Do you (no, know) how to check a patient's vital signs?

4. This proposal has too many (loose, lose) ends.

5. Students who have (past, passed) the test will take English 2.

6. Have you ever (taught, thought, through) about buying a condominium?

7. Banks nowadays have (too, to, two) many kinds of checking accounts.

8. Cholesterol has an (affect, effect) on the circulation.

9. All hospital (personnel, personal) were warned about a case of cerebrospinal meningitis.

10. See if you can (find, fine) an advertisement for a used motorcycle.

EXERCISE II: Look-alikes/Sound-alikes

Circle the correct phrase in each group.

1. alot of money
   a lot of money

2. alway prepared
   away prepared
   always prepared

3. a loss treasure
   a lost treasure
   a lose treasure

4. hotter then the Sahara
   hotter than the Sahara

5. quit intelligent
   quite intelligent
   quiet intelligent

6. the personnel office
   the personal office

7. two much attention
   to much attention
   too much attention

8. worse than a tornado
   worst then a tornado

9. an original taught
   an original thought
   an original though

10. the total effect
    the total affect

11. sensible advice
    sensible advise

12. an hour later
    a hour later
    and hour later

13. should of remembered
    should have remembered

14. brought at Macy's
    bought at Macy's

15. She past the test
    She pass the test
    She passed the test

16. sit the table
    set the table

17. plenty of common sense
    plenty of common since

18. raise the flag
    rise the flag

19. a find performance
    a fine performance

20. a clear conscious
    a clear conscience

REVIEW TEST

Name _____

This test may help confirm that you have learned the grammatical rules presented in Unit 5. If you find after taking this test that there remain areas of grammar or spelling on which you need further work, return to those sections of Unit 5 that cover those topics.

Part One: Sentence Divisions

In each group of sentences, only *one* is correct—A, B, or C. Check the blank next to the correct sentence in each group.

1. ____ A. Three members of the audience left the studio. Because the panelists had made offensive remarks.
   ____ B. Three members of the audience left the studio because the panelists had made offensive remarks.
   ____ C. Three members of the audience left the studio, the panelists had made offensive remarks.

2. ____ A. If you really study the statistics, you will find that the state's economy has improved.
   ____ B. If you really study the statistics. You will find that the state's economy has improved.
   ____ C. You will find that the state's economy has improved. If you really study the statistics.

3. ____ A. Brenda learned to speak Spanish when she was in high school, and her sister learned in college.
   ____ B. After Brenda learned to speak Spanish in high school. Her sister learned in college.
   ____ C. Brenda learned to speak Spanish in high school. Her sister in college.

4. ____ A. Prospective nurses must complete the required college courses. Also pass the state board examination.
   ____ B. Prospective nurses must complete the required college courses they must also pass the state board examination.
   ____ C. Prospective nurses must complete the required college courses. They must also pass the state board examination.

5. ____ A. Romance novels appeal to many readers. Because they combine suspense, glamor, and love.

   ____ B. Romance novels, which combine suspense, glamor, and love, appeal to many readers.

   ____ C. Romance novels appeal to many readers they combine suspense, glamor, and love.

6. ____ A. Learning algebra was difficult for Brian. Being that he changed schools in the middle of the term.

   ____ B. Because he changed schools in the middle of the term. Learning algebra was difficult for Brian.

   ____ C. Learning algebra was difficult for Brian because he changed schools in the middle of the term.

7. ____ A. Honor students receive letters of commendation from the dean; students who receive three letters earn special scholarships.

   ____ B. Honor students receive letters of commendation from the dean. And earn special scholarships if they receive three letters.

   ____ C. Honor students receive letters of commendation from the dean; and earning special scholarships if they receive three letters.

8. ____ A. Raising children has become increasingly expensive for young parents. Especially when the children reach school age.

   ____ B. Raising children has become increasingly expensive for young parents, especially when the children reach school age.

   ____ C. Young parents, especially when their children reach school age. Often find raising children increasingly expensive.

9. ____ A. The theater raised its ticket prices last week, soon it began losing customers

   ____ B. The theater, which raised its ticket prices last week. Soon began to lose customers.

   ____ C. The theater raised its ticket prices last week; soon it began to lose customers.

10. ____ A. Writing a journal enhances your academic performance; it helps you record and organize your best ideas.

   ____ B. Writing a journal helps you record and organize your best ideas. Which enhances your academic performance.

   ____ C. Writing a journal enhances your academic performance, it helps you record and organize your best ideas.

Part Two: Verb Forms, Endings, and Agreement

Write the correct forms in the blanks provided.

_____ 11. Students who (write, writes) two papers are eligible to earn an A for the course.

_____ 12. One of the films in the course (was, were) too long to view during the class period.

_____ 13. You never know what may (happen, happens, happened) if you go to one of June's parties.

_____ 14. Either a tax increase or a reduction in spending (is, are) likely to be requested by the governor.

_____ 15. Luisa knows that she (has, have) responsibilities to her family as well as her job.

_____ 16. A driver who stops and (ask, asks, asked) for directions is not likely to get lost.

_____ 17. A new medicine often (cost, costs, costed) more because of the extensive testing required.

_____ 18. There (is, are) many new books on the reading list this semester.

_____ 19. Next to the bodega (was, were) three clothing stores and a laundromat.

_____ 20. Students are (use, used) to taking semester exams in early January.

_____ 21. The last person out of the office is (suppose, supposed) to turn off the machine.

_____ 22. Amelia hopes to (spend, spends, spent) three weeks in Venezuela next February.

_____ 23. Anyone who (insist, insists) that dieting is easy should try losing twenty pounds.

_____ 24. One of Yolanda's favorite pastimes (is, are) long distance bicycling.

_____ 25. The topic of the essay (doesn't, don't) have to be on the list.

Part Three: Spelling

If the word or phrase is correct, write C in the blank; if not, write the correct form of the misspelled word in the blank.

_____ 26. necessary

_____ 27. beleive

_____ 28. it's time to begin

_____ 29. occassionaly

_____ 30. give them there reward

_____ 31. committment

_____ 32. richer then Donald Trump

_____ 33. responsability

_____ 34. occuring

_____ 35. alot of money

_____ 36. definitly

_____ 37. accross

_____ 38. seperate

_____ 39. received

_____ 40. similiar

Part Four: Punctuation

If the sentence is punctuated correctly, write C in the blank. If not, circle the spot where punctuation is wrong or missing and write the correct mark in the blank. No sentence has more than one error.

_____ 41. The government subsidizes theater, dance, and opera but corporations donate much more money to such artistic activities.

_____ 42. The store sells the following items compact disk players, video camcorders, and personal computers.

_____ 43. The travel agency has offices in Bogota Colombia and Kingston, Jamaica.

_____ 44. The new exhibit is being prepared for an opening in March meanwhile, the current exhibit will remain for another two months.

_____ 45. "That is the last time I will ever try to park on campus" Norman remarked when he saw the parking ticket.

_____ 46. Urged by his friends to make use of his talent Dwayne sang at the Apollo Theater.

_____ 47. The Articles of Confederation, which were adopted in 1781 attempted to unite the early American colonies.

_____ 48. The insurance was paid for by the employer not the workers.

_____ 49. The high schools have improved dramatically over the last decade nevertheless, parents must become more involved.

_____ 50. Michael Jordan, the greatest player of his time in the National Basketball Association, unexpectedly announced his retirement in 1993.

Part Five: Pronouns, Parallelism, and Modifiers

If the sentence is correct, write C in the blank. If a word or phrase is wrong, circle it and write the correct word or phrase in the blank.

_____ 51. Herbert writes very good when he puts effort into it.

_____ 52. The film was suspenseful, visually exciting, and provoked a lot of thought.

_____ 53. Children are more happier if adults pay close attention to what they think and feel.

_____ 54. Police officers now know that he cannot expect to get away with the use of excessive force.

_____ 55. Between you and I, this project will cost a lot more money than predicted.

_____ 56. When the car wouldn't run no more, they gave up and took a bus.

_____ 57. After looking everywhere for the letter, it was finally found in the wastebasket.

_____ 58. If they know they will receive stiff sentences, would-be criminals will think twice before he commits a felony.

_____ 59. The interviews were thorough, polite, and took a lot of time.

_____ 60. The social worker with whom you spoke yesterday is very experienced.

Possible Score: __60__ Your Score _____

6

A COLLECTION OF
READINGS

Most expert writers read eagerly and widely. Although reading will not give you rules for writing, exploring what other writers have done will give you a larger sense of how varied good writing can be. You shouldn't try to copy what other writers do but acquire instead a more developed "feel" for the range of styles, themes, and techniques employed by writers of different cultural backgrounds. Above all, enjoying good reading will inspire you to enjoy your own writing.

INTRODUCTION TO READING SELECTIONS

The readings in this unit have been chosen and arranged to help you appreciate many kinds of writing—essays, poems, stories, and chapters from textbooks. The writers represent diverse cultural backgrounds and express many points of view on many subjects. They are men and women, ranging in age from high school students to the elderly; they may be white, African-American, Latino, Native American, or Asian. Their differences are as interesting as what they share—a common ambition to write well and to express their humanity in powerful language.

Your teacher will probably assign many of these readings, some for the sake of discussion and some as a basis for writing assignments. You may want to go further and read more of the selections, and you may want to strengthen your vocabulary by studying the word list after each reading. Think about the "Reading for Understanding" questions after each reading, even when they are not assigned.

The four categories of readings are designed to help you develop your critical thinking powers. Reading selections on the same concept by writers of different backgrounds will give you experience balancing differing opinions and perspectives. Your own will probably resemble some of those you find in the readings, but try always to recognize the differences between your opinions, which are just as important as anyone else's, and those of these writers. And remember that differences of opinion, experience, or perception do not always mean that one is better than another, or that one is entirely right and another all wrong. Because we learn through experiencing differences and sharing opinions, keep your mind open to the possibilities of altering your opinions and expanding your understanding of issues.

The four categories here come directly out of human experience—yours, mine, and the writers'. Life changes happen to everyone, and we learn to endure, and sometimes enjoy them. We all have learning experiences within school and without; similarly, all of us work, both at our place of employment and in other situations. And for all of us, our families, however we identify them, are at the core of our lives. Many of these readings and the accompanying writing assignments are close to personal experiences; others are more general, and a few are formal, academic readings. This range from the personal to the intellectual will help you explore the kinds of writing you will be doing yourself—some based on your own experiences and some requiring you to draw on your powers of logical analysis and your reading. No one can explain exactly how extensive reading will help you write better, but nearly all experienced writers are convinced that it will. Certainly learning to enjoy and appreciate good reading will help you enjoy and appreciate good writing, especially your own.

LIFE CHANGES

Can you remember a time when your life was very different than it is now? Perhaps you lived in another city or town, or even another country. Perhaps you had a very different set of friends and a different school and neighborhood. Possibly you had to begin speaking a new language. Probably your family has changed, and certainly, in both large and small ways, you have changed. Every one of these changes has brought with it gains and losses: for every new friend you've taken into your life, another one has somehow drifted out of touch. For every disappointing date or athletic defeat there has been some wonderful surprise or hard-earned victory. Life is full of changes; one might almost say that life *is* a series of changes. Therefore, writers of all ethnic backgrounds, both men and women, make their vivid memories of life changes the heart of their work. Changes of age, place, status, health, and outlook call up our strongest emotions and reveal truths about ourselves and others. Reading what others say about the changes in their lives and writing about changes in your own will help you experience language as a vehicle of discovery.

Childhood

When the poet William Wordsworth wrote that the "child is father of the man," he acknowledged that the incidents and feelings of our childhood shape the adult we become. Childhood is a special time of intense joys and fears, of extreme vulnerability and great openness to wonder and experience. Many of the changes that take place in our childhoods violate the innocence we possess at that stage, but they also toughen us so that we can interact later with the adult world. If you recall some of the most memorable events of your childhood, they will probably involve both happy and sad occasions, moments of joy as well as embarrassment. Those moments also tend to mark turning points in the growth of your emotions and attitudes, often more than you were aware at the time. In the readings that follow, look for the turning points that occurred in these writers' lives as a result of the incidents, sometimes ones that would seem unimportant to adults, which they relive for us. Notice also the ideas they express, both positive and negative, about the inevitable changes all children endure in the process of growing up. What experiences of your own do the writers remind you of? What ideas can you put into your own words to explain the experiences of your childhood?

Richard Wright (1908–1960)

Despite his lack of formal education and the many obstacles he faced growing up in a racist environment, Richard Wright became one of the foremost twentieth-century American writers of fiction and autobiography. In *Black Boy*, the autobiography he first published in 1945 from which this excerpt is taken, Wright tells about growing up in Mississippi and Memphis and enduring racism, family violence, poverty, and the pressure to conform. Eventually, he would leave for Chicago in pursuit of dignity and freedom. Wright also wrote two well-known novels, *Native Son* (1940) and *The Outsider* (1950).

Facing the Bullies*

My mother finally went to work as a cook and left me and my brother alone in the flat each day with a loaf of bread and a pot of tea. When she returned at evening she would be tired and dispirited and would cry a lot. Sometimes, when she was in despair, she would call us to her and talk to us for hours, telling us that we now had no father, that our lives would be different from those of other children, that we must learn as soon as possible to take care of ourselves, to dress ourselves, to prepare our own food; that we must take upon ourselves the responsibility of the flat while she worked. Half frightened, we would promise solemnly. We did not understand what had happened between our father and our mother and the most that these long talks did to us was to make us feel a vague dread. Whenever we asked why father had left, she would tell us that we were too young to know.

One evening my mother told me that thereafter I would have to do the shopping for food. She took me to the corner store to show me the way. I was proud; I felt like a grownup. The next afternoon I looped the basket over my arm and went down the pavement toward the store. When I reached the corner, a gang of boys grabbed me, knocked me down, snatched the basket, took the money, and sent me running home in panic. That evening I told my mother what had happened, but she made no comment; she sat down at once, wrote another note, gave me more money, and sent me out to the grocery again. I crept down the steps and saw the same gang of boys playing down the street. I ran back into the house.

"What's the matter?" my mother asked.

"It's those same boys," I said. "They'll beat me."

"You've got to get over that," she said. "Now, go on."

"I'm scared," I said.

"Go on and don't pay any attention to them," she said.

I went out of the door and walked briskly down the sidewalk, praying that the gang would not molest me. But when I came abreast of them someone shouted.

"There he is!"

They came toward me and I broke into a wild run toward home. They overtook me and flung me to the pavement. I yelled, pleaded, kicked, but they wrenched the money out of my hand. They yanked me to my feet, gave me a few slaps, and sent me home sobbing. My mother met me at the door.

"They b-beat m-me," I gasped. "They t-t-took the m-money."

I started up the steps, seeking the shelter of the house.

"Don't you come in here," my mother warned me.

I froze in my tracks and stared at her.

"But they're coming after me," I said.

"You just stay right where you are," she said in a deadly tone. "I'm going to teach you this night to stand up and fight for yourself."

She went into the house and I waited, terrified, wondering what she was about. Presently she returned with more money and another note; she also had a long heavy stick.

"Take this money, this note, and this stick," she said. "Go to the store and buy those groceries. If those boys bother you, then fight."

I was baffled. My mother was telling me to fight, a thing that she had never done before.

"But I'm scared," I said.

"Don't you come into this house until you've gotten those groceries," she said.

"They'll beat me; they'll beat me," I said.

"Then stay in the streets; don't come back here!"

I ran up the steps and tried to force my way past her into the house. A stinging slap came on my jaw. I stood on the sidewalk, crying.

"Please, let me wait until tomorrow," I begged.

"No," she said. "Go now! If you come back into this house without those groceries, I'll whip you!"

She slammed the door and I heard the key turn in the lock. I shook with fright. I was alone upon the dark, hostile streets and gangs were after me. I had the choice of being beaten at home or away from home. I clutched the stick, crying, trying to reason. If I were beaten at home, there was absolutely nothing that I could do about it; but if I were beaten in the streets, I had a chance to fight and defend myself. I walked slowly down the sidewalk, coming closer to the gang of boys, holding the stick tightly. I was so full of fear that I could scarcely breathe. I was almost upon them now.

"There he is again!" the cry went up.

They surrounded me quickly and began to grab for my hand.

"I'll kill you!" I threatened.

They closed in. In blind fear I let the stick fly, feeling it crack against a boy's skull. I swung again, lamming another skull, then another. Realizing that they would retaliate if I let up for but a second, I fought to lay them low, to knock them cold, to kill them so that they could not strike back at me. I flayed with tears in my eyes, teeth clenched, stark fear making me throw every ounce of my strength behind each blow. I hit again and again, dropping the money and the grocery list. The boys scattered, yelling, nursing their heads, staring at me in utter disbelief. They had never seen such frenzy. I stood panting, egging them on, taunting them to come on and fight. When they refused, I ran after them and they tore out for their homes, screaming. The parents of the boys rushed into the streets and threatened me, and for the first time in my life I shouted at grownups, telling them that I would give them the same if they bothered me. I finally found my grocery list and the money and went to the store. On my way back I kept my stick poised for instant use, but there was not a single boy in sight. That night I won the right to the streets of Memphis.

QUESTIONS

Reading for Understanding

1. Name at least two experiences that Richard had for the first time in this episode. How do you think these experiences changed his attitude about himself?

2. Richard's father had just left the family. How do you think this fact influenced his mother's way of talking and behaving toward Richard and his brother? Would his incident with the bullies probably have been handled the same if his father had been still living at home there?

3. Richard was pushed by his mother to do something he didn't want to do. What did he want to do instead? Why do you think he obeyed her?

4. Why do you think the bullies ran away even though they outnumbered Richard and probably could have beaten him up again?

5. Do you think Richard's mother handled the situation well? Why or why not? Can you suggest other ways she could have dealt with the problem?

Noticing Writing Techniques

1. Richard Wright concentrates on describing his own feelings and thoughts. How did this affect your response to the reading? Did Wright's method of telling the story make you laugh? Feel sorry for Richard? Become alarmed? Get excited?

2. List at least ten vivid verbs of action Wright uses to express the intensity of the action in the story. Review the use of vivid verbs for strength in Unit 4. How do these verbs make you react differently to the story?

Noticing Vocabulary

_____ 1. *Dispirited* means
A. enthusiastic
B. religious
C. discouraged
D. uninformed.

_____ 2. To come *abreast* of someone means to
A. confront them face to face
B. come alongside them
C. stand behind them
D. move quickly ahead of them.

_____ 3. To *retaliate* means to
A. strike back
B. repay a loan
C. remember something
D. reach backward.

Writing Topics

1. Using the last paragraph in the reading (beginning "They closed in") as a model, create your own paragraph describing a scene filled with action. Remember to use vivid verbs and to vary your sentence length and form, as well as your sentence beginnings the way Wright does in his paragraph. Review Unit 4 for a discussion of effective word choice and sentence variety.

2. Compose an essay telling about a time when you faced a situation that you dreaded and how you triumphed over your fears and the obstacles themselves. This may be a situation of physical danger, as in Wright's story, or one involving fear of embarrassment or failure. Explain how coping with this situation changed the way you felt about yourself. For further writing topics and exercises, see Narrative Writing in Units 2 and 3.

Amy Tan (1952–   )

Amy Tan was born in Oakland, California, in 1952, her parents having just arrived in America. Her mother had left behind in China the daughters from her previous marriage. Amy did not learn about these half sisters until she was a teenager but now has a close relationship with her half-sisters. In *The Joy Luck Club* (1989), from which the following story is taken, she tells about four Chinese women whose daughters, like herself, were born in the United States. Although the stories are fictitious, they include many actual details and situations from her own life.

from *Rules of the Game**

My older brother Vincent was the one who actually got the chess set. We had gone to the annual Christmas party held at the First Chinese Baptist Church at the end of the alley. The missionary ladies had put together a Santa bag of gifts donated by members of another church. None of the gifts had names on them. There were separate sacks for boys and girls of different ages.

One of the Chinese parishioners had donned a Santa Claus costume and a stiff paper beard with cotton balls glued to it. I think the only children who thought he was the real thing were too young to know that Santa Claus was not Chinese. When my turn came up, the Santa man asked me how old I was. I thought it was a trick question; I was seven according to the American formula and eight by the Chinese calendar. I said I was born on March 17, 1951. That seemed to satisfy him. He then solemnly asked if I had been a very, very good girl this year and did I believe in Jesus Christ and obey my parents. I knew the only answer to that. I nodded back with equal solemnity.

Having watched the other children opening their gifts, I already knew that the big gifts were not necessarily the nicest ones. One girl my age got a large coloring book of biblical characters, while a less greedy girl who selected a smaller box received a glass vial of lavender toilet water. The sound of the box was also important. A ten-year-old boy had chosen a box that jangled when he shook it. It was a tin globe of the world with a slip for inserting money. He must have thought it was full of dimes and nickels, because when he saw that it had just ten pennies, his face fell with such undisguised disappointment that his mother slapped the side of his head and led him out of the church hall, apologizing to the crowd for her son who had such bad manners he couldn't appreciate such a fine gift.

As I peered into the sack, I quickly fingered the remaining presents, testing their weight, imagining what they contained. I chose a heavy, compact one that was wrapped in shiny silver foil and a red satin ribbon. It was a twelve-pack of Life Savers and I spent the rest of the party arranging and rearranging the candy tubes in the order of my favorites. My brother Winston chose wisely as well. His present turned out to be a box of intricate plastic parts; the instructions on the box proclaimed that when they were properly assembled he would have an authentic miniature replica of a World War II submarine.

Vincent got the chess set, which would have been a very decent present to get at a church Christmas party, except it was obviously used and, as we discovered later, it was missing a black pawn and a white knight. My mother graciously thanked the unknown benefactor, saying, "Too good. Cost too much." At which point, an old lady with fine white, wispy hair nodded toward our family and said with a whistling whisper, "Merry, merry Christmas."

When we got home, my mother told Vincent to throw the chess set away. "She not want it. We not want it," she said, tossing her head stiffly to the side with a tight, proud smile. My brothers had deaf ears. They were already lining up the chess pieces and reading from the dog-eared instruction book.

I watched Vincent and Winston play during Christmas week. The chessboard seemed to hold elaborate secrets waiting to be untangled. The chessmen were more powerful than old Li's magic herbs that cured ancestral curses. And my brothers wore such serious faces that I was sure something was at stake that was greater than avoiding the tradesmen's door to Hong Sing's. "Let me! Let me!" I begged between games when one brother or the other would sit back with a deep sigh of relief and victory, the other annoyed, unable to let go of the outcome. Vincent at first refused to let me play, but when I offered my Life Savers as replacements for the buttons that filled in for the missing pieces, he relented. He chose the flavors: wild cherry for the black pawn and peppermint for the white knight. Winner could eat both.

As our mother sprinkled flour and rolled out small doughy circles for the steamed dumplings that would be our dinner that night, Vincent explained the rules, pointing to each piece. "You have sixteen pieces and so do I. One king and queen, two bishops, two knights, two castles, and eight pawns. The pawns can only move forward one step, except on the first move. Then they can move two. But they can only take men by moving crossways like this, except in the beginning, when you can move ahead and take another pawn."

"Why?" I asked as I moved my pawn. "Why can't they move more steps?"

"Because they're pawns," he said.

"But why do they go crossways to take other men? Why aren't there any women and children?"

"Why is the sky blue? Why must you always ask stupid questions?" asked Vincent. "This is a game. These are the rules. I didn't make them up. See. Here. In the book." He jabbed a page with a pawn in his hand. "Pawn. P-A-W-N. Pawn. Read it yourself."

My mother patted the flour off her hands. "Let me see book," she said quietly. She scanned the pages quickly, not reading the foreign English symbols, seeming to search deliberately for nothing in particular.

"This American rules," she concluded at last. "Every time people come out from foreign country, must know rules. You not know, judge say, Too bad, go back. They not telling you why so you can use their way go forward. They say, Don't know why, you find out yourself. But they knowing all the time. Better you take it, find out why yourself." She tossed her head back with a satisfied smile.

I found out about all the whys later. I read the rules and looked up all the words in a dictionary. I borrowed books from the Chinatown library. I studied each chess piece, trying to absorb the power each contained.

I learned about opening moves and why it's important to control the center early on; the shortest distance between two points is straight down the middle. I learned about the middle game and why tactics between two adversaries are like clashing ideas; the one who plays better has the clearest plans for both attacking and getting out of traps. I learned why it is essential in the endgame to have foresight, a mathematical understanding of all possible moves, and patience; all weaknesses and advantages become evident to a strong adversary and are obscured to a tiring opponent. I discovered that for the whole game one must gather invisible strengths and see the endgame before the game begins.

I also found out why I should never reveal "why" to others. A little knowledge withheld is a great advantage one should store for future use. That is the power of chess. It is a game of secrets in which one must show and never tell.

I loved the secrets I found within the sixty-four black and white squares. I carefully drew a handmade chessboard and pinned it to the wall next to my bed, where at night I would stare for hours at imaginary battles. Soon I no longer lost any games or Life Savers, but I lost my adversaries. Winston and Vincent decided they were more interested in roaming the streets after school in their Hopalong Cassidy cowboy hats.

On a cold spring afternoon, while walking home from school, I detoured through the playground at the end of our alley. I saw a group of old men, two seated across a folding table playing a game of chess, others smoking pipes, eating peanuts, and watching. I ran home and grabbed Vincent's chess set, which was bound in a cardboard box with rubber bands. I also carefully selected two prized rolls of Life Savers. I came back to the park and approached a man who was observing the game.

"Want to play?" I asked him. His face widened with surprise and he grinned as he looked at the box under my arm.

"Little sister, been a long time since I play with dolls," he said, smiling benevolently. I quickly put the box down next to him on the bench and displayed my retort.

Lau Po, as he allowed me to call him, turned out to be a much better player than my brothers. I lost many games and many Life Savers. But over the weeks, with each diminishing roll of candies, I added new secrets. Lau Po gave me the names. The Double Attack from the East and West Shores. Throwing Stones on the Drowning Man. The Sudden Meeting of the Clan. The Surprise from the Sleeping Guard. The Humble Servant Who Kills the King. Sand in the Eyes of Advancing Forces. A Double Killing Without Blood.

There were also the fine points of chess etiquette. Keep captured men in neat rows, as well-tended prisoners. Never announce "Check" with vanity, lest someone with an unseen sword slit your throat. Never hurl pieces into the sandbox after you have lost a game, because then you must find them again, by yourself, after apologizing to all around you. By the end of the summer, Lau Po had taught me all he knew, and I had become a better chess player.

A small weekend crowd of Chinese people and tourists would gather as I played and defeated my opponents one by one. My mother would join the crowds during these outdoor exhibition games. She sat proudly on the bench, telling my admirers with proper Chinese humility, "Is luck."

A man who watched me play in the park suggested that my mother allow me to play in local chess tournaments. My mother smiled graciously, an answer that meant nothing. I desperately wanted to go, but I bit back my tongue. I knew she would not let me play among strangers. So as we walked home I said in a small voice that I didn't want to play in the local tournament. They would have American rules. If I lost, I would bring shame on my family.

"Is shame you fall down nobody push you," said my mother.

During my first tournament, my mother sat with me in the front row as I waited for my turn. I frequently bounced my legs to unstick them from the cold metal seat of the folding chair. When my name was called, I leapt up. My mother unwrapped something in her lap. It was her *chang*, a small tablet of red jade which held the sun's fire. "Is luck," she whispered, and tucked it into my dress pocket. I turned to my opponent, a fifteen-year-old boy from Oakland. He looked at me, wrinkling his nose.

As I began to play, the boy disappeared, the color ran out of the room, and I saw only my white pieces and his black ones waiting on the other side. A light wind began blowing past my ears. It whispered secrets only I could hear.

"Blow from the South," it murmured. "The wind leaves no trail." I saw a clear path, the traps to avoid. The crowd rustled. "Shhh! Shhh!" said the corners of the room. The wind blew stronger. "Throw sand from the East to distract him." The knight came forward ready for the sacrifice. The wind hissed, louder and louder. "Blow, blow, blow. He cannot see. He is blind now. Make him lean away from the wind so he is easier to knock down."

"Check," I said, as the wind roared with laughter. The wind died down to little puffs, my own breath.

My mother placed my first trophy next to a new plastic chess set that the neighborhood Tao society had given to me. As she wiped each piece with a soft cloth, she said, "Next time win more, lose less."

"Ma, it's not how many pieces you lose," I said. "Sometimes you need to lose pieces to get ahead."

"Better to lose less, see if you really need."

At the next tournament, I won again, but it was my mother who wore the triumphant grin.

"Lost eight piece this time. Last time was eleven. What I tell you? Better off lose less!" I was annoyed, but I couldn't say anything.

I attended more tournaments, each one farther away from home. I won all games, in all divisions. The Chinese bakery downstairs from our flat displayed my growing collection of trophies in its window, amidst the dust-covered cakes that were never picked up. The day after I won an important regional tournament, the window encased a fresh sheet cake with whipped-cream frosting and red script saying "Congratulations, Waverly Jong, Chinatown Chess Champion." Soon after that, a flower shop, headstone engraver, and funeral parlor offered to sponsor me in national tournaments. That's when my mother decided I no longer had to do the dishes. Winston and Vincent had to do my chores.

"Why does she get to play and we do all the work," complained Vincent.

"Is new American rules," said my mother. "Meimei play, squeeze all her brains out for win chess. You play, worth squeeze towel."

By my ninth birthday, I was a national champion. I was still 429 points away from grand-master status, but I was touted as the Great American Hope, a child prodigy and a girl to boot. They ran a photo of me in *Life* magazine next to a quote in which Bobby Fischer said, "There will never be a woman grand master." "Your move, Bobby," said the caption.

The day they took the magazine picture I wore neatly plaited braids clipped with plastic barrettes trimmed with rhinestones. I was playing in a large high school auditorium that echoed with phlegmy coughs and the squeaky rubber knobs of chair legs sliding across freshly waxed wooden floors. Seated across from me was an American man, about the same age as Lau Po, maybe fifty. I remember that his sweaty brow seemed to weep at my every move. He wore a dark, malodorous suit. One of his pockets was stuffed with a great white kerchief on which he wiped his palm before sweeping his hand over the chosen chess piece with great flourish.

In my crisp pink-and-white dress with scratchy lace at the neck, one of two my mother had sewn for these special occasions, I would clasp my hands over my chin, the delicate points of my elbows poised lightly on the table in the manner my mother had shown me for posing for the press. I would swing my patent leather shoes back and forth like an impatient child riding on a school bus. Then I would pause, suck in my lips, twirl my chosen piece in midair as if undecided, and then firmly plant it in its new threatening place, with a triumphant smile thrown back at my opponent for good measure.

I no longer played in the alley of Waverly Place. I never visited the playground where the pigeons and old men gathered. I went to school, then directly home to learn new chess secrets, cleverly concealed advantages, more escape routes.

But I found it difficult to concentrate at home. My mother had a habit of standing over me while I plotted out my games. I think she thought of herself as my protective ally. Her lips would be sealed tight, and after each move I made, a soft "Hmmmmph" would escape from her nose.

"Ma, I can't practice when you stand there like that," I said one day. She retreated to the kitchen and made loud noises with the pots and pans. When the crashing stopped, I could see out of the corner of my eye that she was standing in the doorway. "Hmmmph!" Only this one came out of her tight throat.

My parents made many concessions to allow me to practice. One time I complained that the bedroom I shared was so noisy that I couldn't think. Thereafter, my brothers slept in a bed in the living room facing the street. I said I couldn't finish my rice; my head didn't work right when my stomach was too full. I left the table with half-finished bowls and nobody complained. But there was one duty I couldn't avoid. I had to accompany my mother on

Saturday market days when I had no tournament to play. My mother would proudly walk with me, visiting many shops, buying very little. "This is my daughter Wave-ly Jong," she said to whoever looked her way.

One day after we left a shop I said under my breath, "I wish you wouldn't do that, telling everybody I'm your daughter." My mother stopped walking. Crowds of people with heavy bags pushed past us on the sidewalk, bumping into first one shoulder, then another.

"Aiii-ya. So shame be with mother?" She grasped my hand even tighter as she glared at me.

I looked down. "It's not that, it's just so obvious. It's just so embarrassing."

"Embarrass you be my daughter?" Her voice was cracking with anger.

"That's not what I meant. That's not what I said."

"What you say?"

I knew it was a mistake to say anything more, but I heard my voice speaking, "Why do you have to use me to show off? If you want to show off, then why don't you learn to play chess?"

My mother's eyes turned into dangerous black slits. She had no words for me, just sharp silence.

I felt the wind rushing around my hot ears. I jerked my hand out of my mother's tight grasp and spun around, knocking into an old woman. Her bag of groceries spilled to the ground.

"Aii-ya! Stupid girl!" my mother and the woman cried. Oranges and tin cans careened down the sidewalk. As my mother stooped to help the old woman pick up the escaping food, I took off.

I raced down the street, dashing between people, not looking back as my mother screamed shrilly, "Meimei! Meimei!" I fled down an alley, past dark, curtained shops and merchants washing the grime off their windows. I sped into the sunlight, into a large street crowded with tourists examining trinkets and souvenirs. I ducked into another dark alley, down another street, up another alley. I ran until it hurt and I realized I had nowhere to go, that I was not running from anything. The alleys contained no escape routes.

My breath came out like angry smoke. It was cold. I sat down on an upturned plastic pail next to a stack of empty boxes, cupping my chin with my hands, thinking hard. I imagined my mother, first walking briskly down one street or another looking for me, then giving up and returning home to await my arrival. After two hours, I stood up on creaking legs and slowly walked home.

The alley was quiet and I could see the yellow lights shining from our flat like two tiger's eyes in the night. I climbed the sixteen steps to the door, advancing quietly up each so as not to make any warning sounds. I turned the knob; the door was locked. I heard a chair moving, quick steps, the locks turning—click! click! click!—and then the door opened.

"About time you got home," said Vincent. "Boy, are you in trouble."

He slid back to the dinner table. On a platter were the remains of a large fish, its fleshy head still connected to bones swimming upstream in vain escape. Standing there waiting for my punishment, I heard my mother speak in a dry voice.

"We not concerning this girl. This girl not have concerning for us."

Nobody looked at me. Bone chopsticks clinked against the inside of bowls being emptied into hungry mouths.

I walked into my room, closed the door, and lay down on my bed. The room was dark, the ceiling filled with shadows from the dinnertime lights of neighboring flats.

In my head, I saw a chessboard with sixty-four black and white squares. Opposite me was my opponent, two angry black slits. She wore a triumphant smile. "Strongest wind cannot be seen," she said.

Her black men advanced across the plane, slowly marching to each successive level as a single unit. My white pieces screamed as they scurried and fell off the board one by one. As her men drew closer to my edge, I felt myself growing light. I rose up into the air and flew out the window. Higher and higher, above the alley, over the tops of tiled roofs, where I was gathered up by the wind and pushed up toward the night sky until everything below me disappeared and I was alone.

I closed my eyes and pondered my next move.

QUESTIONS

Reading for Understanding

1. How did Waverly Jong's success as a chess player change her personality and her relation to the rest of the family?

2. Would you say that her mother helped her to succeed or got in her way?

3. How did the fact that Waverly was a girl affect the way people reacted to her as a chess player?

4. How does her mother's advice apply to her chess playing? How does it give her an outlook toward life?

5. At the end of the story, Waverly is pondering her next move in her life. What do you think it will be? Has she become closer to her family as a result of her experience or farther from it?

Noticing Writing Techniques

1. Explain how Amy Tan's title, "Rules of the Game," applies to both chess playing and living. Notice the places in the story where the author refers to rules.

2. Try to find all the references to the wind in the story and explain how the author uses this repeated theme, or *motif.*

3. The mother, who was born and raised in China, cannot speak English as well as her daughter, who grew up in America. Why do you think the author frequently quotes the mother speaking in her incomplete and incorrect English? Do you find her statements funny, wise, thoughtful, or hard to understand? How would the story be different if she always spoke in standard English?

Noticing Vocabulary

_____ 1. *Solemnity* means
    A. noisiness   B. curiosity
    C. wisdom   D. formality.

_____ 2. A *benefactor* is one who
    A. steals something   B. bestows gifts or favors
    C. commits crimes   D. runs a business.

_____ 3. An *adversary* is
    A. a close friend   B. a relative
    C. an opponent   D. a mathematician.

_____ 4. *Obscured* means
    A. hidden from view   B. heavily insured
    C. easily seen or heard   D. twisted or bent.

_____ 5. A *malodorous* suit is
    A. dark   B. well-fitted
    C. bad-smelling   D. old-fashioned.

_____ 6. To make *concessions* is to
    A. object strongly   B. yield or make allowances
    C. give contributions to charity   D. make corrections.

Writing Topics

1. Think of some skill you have, like Waverly Jong's chess playing. Write a paragraph in which you tell what it's like to do this activity (e.g., dancing, driving a car, using a computer, singing, acting, or cooking). See Unit 2, Exposition: "How-To" Paragraphs for further advice and writing topics.

2. Write an essay in which you tell about how you surprised those around you by your unexpected attitudes, interests, or skills. Explain how this new perception of you changed both yourself and your relation to others who knew you well.

Langston Hughes (1902–1967)

Born in Joplin, Missouri, Langston Hughes grew up in the Midwest and later attended Columbia University in New York and Lincoln University. He became one of the leading figures of the Harlem Renaissance in the 1920s and one of America's most important poets. "Salvation" is from his autobiography *The Big Sea* (1940).

Salvation*

I was saved from sin when I was going on thirteen. But not really saved. It happened like this. There was a big revival at my Auntie Reed's church. Every night for weeks there had been much preaching, singing, praying, and shouting, and some very hardened sinners had been brought to Christ, and the membership of the church had grown by leaps and bounds. Then just before the revival ended, they held a special meeting for children, "to bring the young lambs to the fold." My aunt spoke of it for days ahead. That night, I was escorted to the front row and placed on the mourner's bench with all other young sinners, who had not yet been brought to Jesus.

My aunt told me that when you were saved you saw a light, and something happened to you inside! And Jesus came into your life! And God was with you from then on! She said you could see and hear and feel Jesus in your soul. I believed her. I have heard a great many old people say the same thing and it seemed to me they ought to know. So I sat there calmly in the hot, crowded church, waiting for Jesus to come to me.

The preacher preached a wonderful rhythmical sermon, all moans and shouts and lonely cries and dire pictures of hell, and then he sang a song about the ninety and nine safe in the fold, but one little lamb was left out in the cold. Then he said: "Won't you come? Won't you come to Jesus? Young lambs, won't you come?" And he held out his arms to all us young sinners there on the mourner's bench. And the little girls cried. And some of them jumped up and went to Jesus right away. But most of us just sat there.

A great many old people came and knelt around us and prayed, old women with jet-black faces and braided hair, old men with work-gnarled hands. And the church sang a song about the lower lights are burning, some poor sinners to be saved. And the whole building rocked with prayer and song.

Still I kept waiting to *see* Jesus.

Finally all the young people had gone to the altar and were saved, but one boy and me. He was a rounder's son named Westley. Westley and I were sur-

---

rounded by sisters and deacons praying. It was very hot in the church, and getting late now. Finally Westley said to me in a whisper: "God damn! I'm getting tired o' sitting here. Let's get up and be saved." So he got up and was saved.

The I was left all alone on the mourner's bench. My aunt came and knelt at my knees and cried, while prayers and songs swirled all around me in the little church. The whole congregation prayed for me alone, in a mighty wail of moans and voices. And I kept waiting serenely for Jesus, waiting, waiting—but he didn't come. I wanted to see him, but nothing happened to me. Nothing! I wanted something to happen to me, but nothing happened.

I heard the songs and the minister saying: "Why don't you come? My dear child, why don't you come to Jesus? Jesus is waiting for you. He wants you. Why don't you come? Sister Reed, what is this child's name?"

"Langston," my aunt sobbed.

"Langston, why don't you come? Why don't you come and be saved? Oh, Lamb of God! Why don't you come?"

Now it was really getting late. I began to be ashamed of myself, holding everything up so long. I began to wonder what God thought about Westley, who certainly hadn't seen Jesus either, but who was now sitting proudly on the platform, swinging his knickerbockered legs and grinning down at me, surrounded by deacons and old women on their knees praying. God had not struck Westley dead for taking his name in vain or for lying in the temple. So I decided that maybe to save further trouble, I'd better lie, too, and say that Jesus had come, and get up and be saved.

So I got up.

Suddenly the whole room broke into a sea of shouting, as they saw me rise. Waves of rejoicing swept the place. Women leaped in the air. My aunt threw her arms around me. The minister took me by the hand and led me to the platform.

When things quieted down, in a hushed silence, punctuated by a few ecstatic "Amens," all the new young lambs were blessed in the name of God. Then joyous singing filled the room.

That night, for the last time in my life but one—for I was a big boy twelve years old—I cried. I cried, in bed alone, and couldn't stop. I buried my head under the quilts, but my aunt heard me. She woke up and told my uncle I was crying because the Holy Ghost had come into my life, and because I had seen Jesus. But I was really crying because I couldn't bear to tell her that I had lied, that I had deceived everybody in the church, that I hadn't seen Jesus, and that now I didn't believe there was a Jesus any more, since he didn't come to help me.

QUESTIONS

Reading for Understanding

1. What lesson do you think this story tells about how adults should treat children? Why do the great efforts of his aunt, the minister, and the

congregation to save him not succeed? Why does Hughes choose the title "Salvation" if he wasn't saved?

2. How is Langston's attitude toward the church different from that of his friend Westley? Why does Westley find it easier to pretend to be saved? Westley is the son of a "rounder" (a drunkard or good-for-nothing); could this have influenced his attitude?

3. How might Langston's aunt have used a different method to persuade him to become religious? Could another method have worked better?

4. Does Langston's age of twelve make any difference in how he reacted? Would the story have ended differently if he had been five or sixteen?

5. Why doesn't Langston tell his aunt or anyone else about what he really thinks and feels? What does the fact that he cried about lying show about his character?

Noticing Writing Techniques

1. Langston Hughes was a poet. In this story he uses some poetic techniques even though he is not writing poetry. What metaphors can you find in the following passages: "the whole building rocked with prayer and song"; "the whole room broke into a sea of shouting"; "waves of rejoicing swept the place"? Find other passages where Hughes uses poetically vivid description or rhythmic language.

2. Why does Hughes use a number of exclamation points in the second paragraph? Why does he include two paragraphs that are only one sentence long?

3. Look up the word *irony* in the dictionary. Find words, phrases, or statements in "Salvation" that are meant to be ironic. In what way is the title ironic?

4. Hughes quotes the minister's words many times and tells us what his aunt said to him. Why does he never say anything himself? What point does Hughes make by never having his twelve-year-old self speak?

Vocabulary

_____ 1. A *revival* meeting is intended to
A. teach first aid techniques
B. create religious awakening
C. reduce crime and violence
D. teach young people to control their emotions.

_____ 2. Waiting *serenely* means waiting
A. with excitement   B. angrily
C. nervously   D. calmly.

_____ 3. *Dire* pictures are
   A. threatening   B. wonderful
   C. colorful   D. imaginative.

_____ 4. The description of Westley's *knickerbockered* legs means that he was wearing
   A. blue jeans   B. long, striped dress pants
   C. short pants   D. country overalls.

_____ 5. *Ecstatic* amens are said in a spirit of
   A. anger   B. sadness
   C. great confusion   D. great joy.

Writing Topics

1. Compose a descriptive paragraph in which you create a vivid picture of a crowd situation that you have experienced, such as a sporting event, rock concert, large party, college classroom, club meeting, graduation, or wedding reception. Try to bring in details appealing to the five senses, as Hughes does in describing the church congregation. See if you can use a simile or metaphor for imaginative effect. Review descriptive writing in Unit 2 for further pointers.

2. Write an essay telling about something that happened to you that marked a turning point between childhood and adolescence. This may be either an experience of disillusionment, like Hughes' experience, or one of gaining maturity and self-confidence. Combine descriptive details with an effective narrative organization. Explain how this experience helped to create the person you are as an adult. For further exercises and pointers, see the Narrative Mode and its autobiographical example in Unit 3.

Poems on Childhood

Walt Whitman (1819–1892)

Although Walt Whitman never had children himself, he is a sort of father figure to all modern American poets, and he expresses better than anyone else the spirit of American individualism and independence. In the poem below, which was included in his first collection of poems entitled *Leaves of Grass* (1855), he expresses the child's openness to experience and the way a child is formed by the varied elements of his environment.

There Was a Child Went Forth

There was a child went forth every day,
And the first object he look'd on, that object he became,
And that object became part of him for the day or a certain part of the day,
Or for many years or stretching cycles of years.

The early lilacs became part of this child,
And grass and white and red morning-glories, and white and red clover,
    and the song of the phoebe-bird,
And the Third-month lambs and the sow's pink-faint litter, and the mare's
    foal and the cow's calf,
And the noisy brood of the barnyard or by the mire of the pond-side,
And the fish suspending themselves so curiously below there, and the
    beautiful curious liquid,
And the water-plants with their graceful flat heads, all became part of him.

The field-sprouts of Fourth-month and Fifth-month became part of him,
Winter-grain sprouts and those of the light-yellow corn, and the esculent
    roots of garden,
And the apple-trees cover'd with blossoms and the fruit afterward, and
    wood-berries, and the commonest weeds by the road,
And the old drunkard staggering home from the outhouse of the tavern
    whence he had lately risen,
And the schoolmistress that pass'd on her way to the school,
And the friendly boys that pass'd, and the quarrelsome boys,
And the tidy and fresh-cheek'd girls, and the barefoot Negro boy and girl,
And all the changes of city and country wherever he went.

His own parents, he that had father'd him and she that had conceiv'd him
    in her womb and birth'd him,
They gave this child more of themselves than that,
They gave him afterward every day, they became part of him.

The mother at home quietly placing the dishes on the supper-table,
The mother with mild words, clean her cap and gown, a wholesome odor
    falling off her person and clothes as she walks by,
The father, strong, self-sufficient, manly, mean, anger'd, unjust,
The blow, the quick loud word, the tight bargain, the crafty lure,
The family usages, the language, the company, the furniture, the yearning
    and swelling heart,
Affection that will not be gainsay'd, the sense of what is real, the thought
    if after all it should prove unreal,
The doubts of day-time and the doubts of night-time, the curious
    whether and how,
Whether that which appears so is so, or is it all flashes and specks?

Men and women crowding fast in the streets, if they are not flashes and
 specks what are they?
The streets themselves and the facades of houses, and goods in the windows,
Vehicles, teams, the heavy-planked wharves, the huge crossing at the ferries,
The village on the highland seen from afar at sunset, the river between,
Shadows, aureola and mist, the light falling on roofs and gables of white
 or brown two miles off,
The schooner near by sleepily dropping down the tide, the little boat
 slack-tow'd astern,
The hurrying tumbling waves, quick-broken crests, slapping,
The strata of color'd clouds, the long bar of maroon-tint away solitary by
 itself, the spread of purity it lies motionless in,
The horizon's edge, the flying sea-crow, the fragrance of salt marsh and
 shore mud,
These became part of that child who went forth every day, and who now
 goes, and will always go forth every day.

QUESTIONS

Reading for Understanding

1. How was the child's environment different in Walt Whitman's time
 than it is now? Explain how the physical surroundings of the city have
 changed and how the family roles have changed.

2. Most of the details of the child's environment are pleasant, but which
 ones does he name that are unpleasant? What is the child's relationship
 to nature?

3. Which of the five senses does Walt Whitman use the most in describing
 the child's environment? List as many details as you can that appeal to
 each of the five senses.

4. Walt Whitman grew up in Long Island and New York City. What details in the poem could be used to identify this location? Is it possible to
 imagine the poem taking place in Texas or California or Minnesota?

5. Some people believe that children's personalities are inborn, the result
 of genetic traits inherited from the parents. Others believe that children's personalities are mostly the result of influences from their environments as they grow up. Which opinion does this poem seem to support? Which opinion seems more believable to you? How has your
 personality been shaped by your surroundings? What traits do you
 think you inherited from either of your parents?

Noticing Writing Techniques

1. Whitman writes *free verse,* which has no rhyme, regular meter, or set line length. How can poetry still be called poetry if it does not use any of these verse techniques? What is there about this poem that makes it different from a piece of prose writing such as an essay or short story?

2. What words and phrases does Whitman repeat many times? Do you find this repetition boring or does it communicate meaning and feeling to you?

3. This poem is about children, but do you think a child could understand and enjoy it? Do Whitman's vocabulary and phrasing require an adult's grasp of language?

4. Why do you think Whitman includes so many lists of objects, impressions, animals, plants, and people? What do these lists make you feel about the child's environment? About the child's sense of wonder at his surroundings?

Noticing Vocabulary

_____ 1. A *foal* is a
   A. baby pig   B. female goat
   C. baby horse   D. male horse.

_____ 2. *Mire* is
   A. jewelry   B. woodland
   C. grass   D. mud.

_____ 3. *Esculent* roots
   A. can be eaten   B. smell good
   C. grow only in spring   D. grow only in very wet
                                 climates.

_____ 4. *Gainsay* is an old-fashioned word for
   A. approve   B. deny
   C. analyze   D. estimate.

_____ 5. The *facades* of houses are their
   A. roofs   B. fronts
   C. front lawns and trees   D. surrounding buildings
                                 such as sheds or
                                 garages.

_____ 6. An *aureola* is a
   A. pleasant smell   B. pleasant sound
   C. dark thundercloud   D. halo.

Writing Topics

1. Create a paragraph describing a scene in nature that you remember from your childhood. Try to use all five senses in your description and choose specific words to create a vivid sense of the experience in the reader's mind. To make it easier to get started, first draw a sketch of the scene; then explain to a friend or classmate exactly what each detail in your drawing is and how you experienced the setting. You might want to review Description: Telling About Persons, Places, and Objects in Unit 2.

2. Write an essay enumerating the influences on your childhood that made you the person that you are. To what extent did you inherit your basic personality from your parents? How did your family environment affect you? How were you influenced by your physical surroundings, including both your neighborhood and nature? How did your social environment affect your personality? For further ideas, look up the Expository Mode: Essays Based on Examples in Unit 3.

Kahlil Gibran (1883–1931)

Born in Lebanon of Syrian extraction, Kahlil Gibran emigrated to the United States in 1895 with his family. He later returned to Beirut to study and also studied art in Paris. He wrote poems and plays in Arabic and combined poetic elements of the Arabic tradition with influences of Western poets. *The Prophet* (1923), his best-known work, is a sort of philosophical poem expressing the power of love; it has been translated into many languages.

On Children* from *The Prophet*

And a woman who held a baby against her bosom said,
Speak to us of Children.
   And he said:
   Your children are not your children.
   They are the sons and daughters of Life's longing for itself.
   They come through you but not from you,
   And though they are with you yet they belong not to you.

   You may give them your love but not your thoughts,
   For they have their own thoughts.
   You may house their bodies but not their souls,

---

*Copyright 1923 by Kahlil Gibran renewed 1951 by Administrators C.T.A. of Kahlil Gibran Estate and Mary G. Gibran. Reprinted by permission of Alfred A. Knopf, Inc.

For their souls dwell in the house of tomorrow, which you cannot visit,
   not even in your dreams.
You may strive to be like them, but seek not to make them like you.
For life goes not backward nor tarries with yesterday.

You are the bows from which your children as living arrows are sent forth.
The archer sees the mark upon the path of the infinite, and He bends
   you with His might that His arrows may go swift and far.
Let your bending in the archer's hand be for gladness;
For even as He loves the arrow that flies, so He loves also the bow that
   is stable.

QUESTIONS

Reading for Understanding

1. What does the prophet mean by saying, "Your children are not your children"? What is the difference between loving your children and treating them as property that you own?

2. Do you agree that it is wrong for parents to try to make their children turn out just like themselves? Why does the prophet insist that to do so is wrong?

3. If children do not truly "belong" to their parents, to whom does the prophet think they belong? Do you agree or disagree?

Noticing Writing Techniques

1. Like Whitman, Kahlil Gibran uses *free verse*, which means that he does not use regular meter, rhyme, or a set line length. In this poem, what is there that makes it a poem and sets it apart from the language of an essay, article, or short story?

2. When reading poetry, you have to read *figuratively*, or imaginatively; some statements may not be literally true but true in a different, poetic sense ("Your children are not your children"). You also may have to read *figures of speech*, such as *similes* and *metaphors*. What is Gibran saying about parents and children when he uses the metaphor of a bow and arrows at the end of the poem? Why does he speak of the future as the "house of tomorrow"?

Noticing Vocabulary

_____ 1. A person who *tarries* is
   A. hurrying
   C. fighting

   B. delaying
   D. searching.

_____ 2. Something that is *infinite* is

    A. amusing   B. difficult to read

    C. difficult to hear   D. limitless.

Writing Topics

1. Write a paragraph telling about a situation in which as a child you had your own thoughts and your parents wanted you to accept theirs. Explain why this difference arose and how it turned out. You might want to review Exposition: Comparative Paragraphs in Unit 2, especially Categories of Comparison.

2. Write an essay distinguishing between what you consider the right way for parents to guide, discipline, and protect their children and the wrong way for them to behave toward them, such as abusing, overprotecting, or neglecting them. Is behavior that is good at one age bad at another? Should boys be treated differently from girls? Should fathers relate differently than mothers to their children? For further pointers and writing topics, see the Expository Mode in Unit 3.

Adolescence

If you are a "traditional" college student, adolescence may be just behind you, or you may be young enough that some adults still consider you an adolescent. If you, like a growing number of college students nowadays, are entering college or returning to college at a later age, you will still remember your teenage years vividly. No one ever forgets his or her adolescence: for most people it is the most intense period of change and turbulence of their lives. Their bodies are changing, their social relationships are constantly in doubt, their futures are uncertain, and their feelings soar and plunge from exhilaration to suicidal despair. Most teenagers feel embarrassed at times over matters that adults see as insignificant; they get carried away by fads and styles, friendships and jealousies with an intensity that may bewilder them when they recall them years later. Teenagers defy their parents but feel a deep anxiety about having to leave their protection in a few years. At the same time, teenagers demand independence and fear it; they insist on their right to individualism in all things while copying the latest styles from their friends. Nothing can be more painful than rejection or loss during adolescence, but never again will the thrill of anticipation be so keen. Because of this double quality of adolescence, its heightened excitement as well as its dangers, writers have found it a fertile subject for drama, fiction, poetry, and social analysis, from *Romeo and Juliet* to *West Side Story* and *The Catcher in the Rye*. Modern American culture, especially rock and rap music, could almost said to *be* adolescent culture. Although many of our worst social problems, particularly crime, violence, and unwanted pregnancy, are notably adolescent problems, America has fallen in love with adolescence, because adolescence, above all, is a time of change.

Deairich Hunter (1965–   )

The following essay was written by Deairich Hunter when he was a high school student in Wilmington, Delaware; it was later printed in *Newsweek* magazine (August 18, 1980). He lived in Brooklyn for four months and attended an inner-city high school troubled by drugs, violence, and absenteeism. He observed three main categories of teenagers there. See if you believe that these three types are still to be found in most high schools today.

Ducks Vs. Hard Rocks*

Although the chaos and viciousness of the Miami riot happened months ago, the chaos and viciousness of daily life for many inner-city black people go on and on. It doesn't seem to matter where you are, though some places are worse than others. A few months ago I left my school in Wilmington, Delaware, moved to Brooklyn, New York, and really began to understand.

After you stay in certain parts of New York for awhile, that chaos and viciousness gets inside of you. You get used to seeing the younger guys flashing pistols and the older ones shooting them. It's not unusual to be walking down the street or through the park and see somebody being beaten or held up. It's no big deal if someone you know is arrested and beat up by the cops.

In my four months in Brooklyn I was mugged three times.

Although such events may seem extraordinary to you, they are just a part of life to almost any minority neighborhood. It seems like everybody knows how to use some kind of weapon, whether it's a pair of nun-chucks (two round sticks attached by a chain) or an ice pick. As long as it will do the job, you can use it.

In Brooklyn you fall into one of two categories when you start growing up. The names for the categories may be different in other cities, but the categories are the same. First, there's the minority of the minority, the "ducks," or suckers. These are the kids who go to school every day. They even want to go to college. Imagine that! School after high school! They don't smoke cheeb (marijuana) and they get zooted (intoxicated) after only one can of beer. They're wasting their lives waiting for a dream that won't come true.

The ducks are usually the ones getting beat up on by the majority group— the "hard rocks." If you're a real hard rock you have no worries, no cares. Getting high is as easy as breathing. You just rip off some duck. You don't bother going to school; it's not necessary. You just live with your mom until you get a job—that should be any time a job comes looking for you. Why should you bother to go look for it? Even your parents can't find work.

---

*"Ducks Vs. Hard Rocks" by Dearich Hunter. First published by NEWSWEEK, August 18, 1980.

I guess the barrier between the ducks and the hard rocks is the barrier of despair. The ducks still have hope, while the hard rocks are frustrated. They're caught in the deadly, dead-end environment and can't see a way out. Life becomes the fast life—or incredibly boring—and death becomes the death that you see and get used to every day. They don't want to hear any more promises. They believe that's just the white man's way of keeping them under control.

Hard rocks do what they want to do when they want to do it. When a hard rock goes to prison it builds up his reputation. He develops a bravado that's like a long, sad joke. But it's all lies and excuses. It's a hustle to keep ahead of the fact that he's going nowhere.

Actually, there is one more category, but this group is not really looked upon as human. They're the junkies. They all hang together, but they don't actually have any friends. Everybody in the neighborhood knows that a drug addict would cut his own throat if he could get a fix for it. So everybody knows junkies will stab you in the back for a dollar.

A guy often becomes a junkie when he tries to get through the despair barrier and reach the other side alone. Let's say a hard rock wants to change, to better himself, so he goes back to school. His friends feel he's deserting them, so they desert him first. The ducks are scared of him and won't accept him. Now this hard rock is alone. If he keeps going to school, somebody who is after him out of spite or revenge will probably catch him and work him over. The hard rock has no way to get back. His way of life is over; he loses his friends' respect, becoming more and more of an outcast. Then he may turn to drugs.

I guess the best way to help the hard rocks is to help the ducks. If the hard rocks see the good guy making it, maybe they will change. If they see the ducks, the ones who try, succeed, it might bring them around. The ducks are really the only ones who might be able to change the situation.

The problem with most ducks is that after years of effort they develop a negative attitude, too. If they succeed, they know they've got it made. Each one can say he did it by himself and for himself. No one helped him and he owes nobody anything, so he says, "Let the hard rocks and the junkies stay where they are"—the old every–man–for–himself routine.

What the ducks must be made to realize is that it was this same attitude that made the hard rocks so hard. They developed a sense of kill or be killed, abuse or be abused, take it or get taken.

The hard rocks want revenge. They want revenge because they don't have any hope of changing their situation. Their teachers don't offer it, their parents have lost theirs, and their grandparents died with a heartful of hope but nothing to show for it.

Maybe the only people left with hope are the only people who can make a difference—teens like me. We, the ducks, must learn to care. As a fifteen-year-old, I'm not sure I can handle all that. Just growing up seems hard enough.

QUESTIONS

Reading for Understanding

1. What are the three types of teenagers Hunter observed in the Brooklyn high school? To which type does he belong?

2. Which group is most likely to be able to change the situation? Why is it difficult even for them to make changes?

3. What does he think is the main cause of the negative attitudes of these teenagers?

4. He seems to be speaking chiefly about the young men; do you believe that the young women could also be grouped into these three categories? If not, what different categories would apply to them?

5. What does he believe the ducks ought to do to help the situation? If that fails, does he imply that anything could be done from the outside to improve the situation? What strategy does he suggest for this help?

Noticing Writing Techniques

1. This essay could be described as a comparison/contrast or a classification essay. Its larger aim, however, is that of a problem/solution essay. What is the problem that the author sees, and what solution or solutions does he tentatively suggest?

2. Do you think that Hunter's use of slang words helps put his point across or weaken the essay? Are some of these words out of date by now? Which ones are you familiar with, and which are strange to you? What slang words do you know for the types of teenagers he calls "ducks" and "hard rocks"? Do you know any slang words for other types of teenagers, including young women?

3. Hunter's tone is matter-of-fact, as if he didn't have any feelings about the subject he is deciding, even though he obviously does. Where in the essay can you tell that he does reveal his attitude toward these teenagers and their problems? Would the essay have been more effective if he had expressed rage or other emotions directly?

Noticing Vocabulary

_____ 1. Mathematically, a *minority* means
   A. the largest number
   C. any number less than half
   B. a tiny number
   D. at least seventy-five percent.

_____ 2. To show *bravado* is to act
   A. bravely
   C. with great skill
   B. timidly
   D. with a show of false courage.

Writing Topics

1. Write a paragraph describing one type of person in your neighborhood. Try to invent an imaginative term for this type, comparable to the "ducks" and "hard rocks" of the preceding essay. Develop your description by showing how appropriate this term is for this group. Avoid falling into stereotypes; try to observe carefully and originally. You may want to review Description under Types of Paragraphs in Unit 2.

2. Write an essay classifying at least three types of undergraduates at your college and labeling each group with an imaginative term. After writing a first draft describing these groups, identify your thesis statement that holds the entire essay together; write a final draft that uses these descriptions to support your main point. For further material and exercises, see the Expository Mode in Unit 3, especially Problem/Solution Essays.

Sandra Cisneros (1954–   )

Born in Chicago to a Mexican-American mother and a Mexican father, Sandra Cisneros portrays the lives of Chicano Americans in her fiction and poetry. She has taught in universities and public schools and has won awards for her stories in *Woman Hollering Creek* and her poems in *My Wicked Wicked Ways*. The following stories are from *The House on Mango Street* (1984).

Sally* from *The House on Mango Street*

Sally is the girl with eyes like Egypt and nylons the color of smoke. The boys at school think she's beautiful because her hair is shiny black like raven feathers and when she laughs, she flicks her hair back like a satin shawl over her shoulders and laughs.

Her father says to be this beautiful is trouble. They are very strict in his religion. They are not supposed to dance. He remembers his sisters and is sad. Then she can't go out. Sally I mean.

Sally, who taught you to paint your eyes like Cleopatra? And if I roll the little brush with my tongue and chew it to a point and dip it in the muddy cake, the one in the little red box, will you teach me?

I like your black coat and those shoes you wear, where did you get them? My mother says to wear black so young is dangerous, but I want to buy shoes just like yours, like your black ones made out of suede, just like those. And one day, when my mother's in a good mood, maybe after my next birthday, I'm going to ask to buy the nylons too.

Cheryl, who is not your friend anymore, not since last Tuesday before Easter, not since the day you made her ear bleed, not since she called you that name and bit a hole in your arm and you looked as if you were going to cry and everyone was waiting and you didn't, you didn't, Sally, not since then, you don't have a best friend to lean against the schoolyard fence with, to laugh behind your hands at what the boys say. There is no one to lend you her hairbrush.

The stories the boys tell in the coatroom, they're not true. You lean against the schoolyard fence alone with your eyes closed as if no one was watching, as if no one could see you standing there, Sally. What do you think about when you close your eyes like that? And why do you always have to go straight home after school? You become a different Sally. You pull your skirt straight, you rub the blue paint off your eyelids. You don't laugh, Sally. You look at your feet and walk fast to the house you can't come out from.

Sally, do you sometimes wish you didn't have to go home? Do you wish your feet would one day keep walking and take you far away from Mango Street, far away and maybe your feet would stop in front of a house, a nice one with flowers and big windows and steps for you to climb up two by two up-stairs to where a room is waiting for you. And if you opened the little window latch and gave it a shove, the windows would swing open, all the sky would come in. There'd be no nosy neighbors watching, no motorcycles and cars, no sheets and towels and laundry. Only trees and more trees and plenty of blue sky. And you could laugh, Sally. You could go to sleep and wake up and never have to think who likes and doesn't like you. You could close your eyes and you wouldn't have to worry what people said because you never belonged here anyway and nobody could make you sad and nobody would think you're strange because you like to dream and dream. And no one could yell at you if they saw you out in the dark leaning against a car, leaning against somebody without someone thinking you are bad, without somebody saying it is wrong, without the whole world waiting for you to make a mistake when all you wanted, all you wanted, Sally, was to love and to love and to love, and no one could call that crazy.

What Sally Said

He never hits me hard. She said her mama rubs lard on all the places where it hurts. Then at school she'd say she fell. That's where all the blue places come from. That's why her skin is always scarred.

But who believes her. A girl that big, a girl who comes in with her pretty face all beaten and black can't be falling off the stairs. He never hits me hard.

But Sally doesn't tell about that time he hit her with his hands just like a dog, she said, like if I was an animal. He thinks I'm going to run away like his sisters who made the family ashamed. Just because I'm a daughter, and then she doesn't say.

Sally was going to get permission to stay with us a little and one Thursday she came finally with a sack full of clothes and a paper bag of sweetbread her mama sent. And would've stayed too except when the dark came her father, whose eyes were little from crying, knocked on the door and said please come back, this is the last time. And she said Daddy and went home.

Then we didn't need to worry. Until one day Sally's father catches her talking to a boy and the next day she doesn't come to school. And the next. Until the way Sally tells it, he just went crazy, he just forgot he was her father between the buckle and the belt.

You're not my daughter, you're not my daughter. And then he broke into his hands.

Linoleum Roses

Sally got married like we knew she would, young and not ready but married just the same. She met a marshmallow salesman at a school bazaar, and she married him in another state where it's legal to get married before eighth grade. She has her husband and her house now, her pillowcases and her plates. She says she's in love, but I think she did it to escape.

Sally says she likes being married because now she gets to buy her own things when her husband gives her money. She is happy, except sometimes her husband gets angry and once he broke the door where his foot went through, though most days he is okay. Except he won't let her talk on the telephone. And he doesn't let her look out the window. And he doesn't like her friends, so nobody gets to visit her unless he is working.

She sits at home because she is afraid to go outside without his permission. She looks at all the things they own: the towels and the toaster, the alarm clock and the drapes. She likes looking at the walls, at how neatly their corners meet, the linoleum roses on the floor, the ceiling smooth as wedding cake.

QUESTIONS

Reading for Understanding

1. Sally in these stories feels a great need to escape from a home environment that is harmful to her. Do believe that by getting married she has escaped?

2. Sally is described by the young woman telling the story as a dreamer. Do you think her constant dreaming has anything to do with her getting married so young? Do you think the marriage will fulfill her dreams?

3. Sally's father is very strict with her because he doesn't want her to embarrass the family the way his sisters did. Do you think his strictness, which includes beating Sally up, succeeds in making her behave the

way he wants? Do you think he is justified in being worried about her behavior? Can you suggest any other way he might have related to her that would have had different results?

Noticing Writing Techniques

1. The author speaks through the voice of a teenage woman named Esperanza, a friend of Sally. At what points in these stories does Esperanza's language sound like that of a teenager? Does she ever use language that is not quite standard, correct English?

2. How does Esperanza's language show creativity and imagination? Can you find *figures of speech* such as *similes* or *metaphors* in her description of Sally?

3. The author has a knack for choosing unusual details to communicate her ideas. What importance is there in such details as linoleum roses, a marshmallow salesman, and Sally's black hair, coat, and shoes?

Writing Topics

1. Write a paragraph describing a person you have known who seemed different from those around him or her. Try to explain what made that person act differently. See Description: Telling About Persons, Places, and Objects in Unit 2.

2. Write a long letter to Sally explaining what you think about her life so far and recommending what she should do to make her life better at this stage. You may want to review Problem/Solution Essays under the Expository Mode in Unit 3.

John Updike (1932–   )

John Updike has been one of the foremost writers of American fiction in recent generations. He grew up in Pennsylvania, attended Harvard University, and wrote for the *New Yorker*. His novel *Rabbit, Run* (1960) won critical praise and fame, and he wrote a series of novels based on life of the same character, who started off as a star athlete in high school. "A&P" first appeared in 1962.

A&P*

In walks these three girls in nothing but bathing suits. I'm the third checkout slot, with my back to the door, so I don't see them until they're over by the

---

*From PIGEON FEATHERS AND OTHER STORIES by John Updike. Copyright © 1962 by John Updike. Reprinted by permission of Alfred A. Knopf, Inc. Originally appeared in "The New Yorker."

bread. The one that caught my eye first was the one in the plaid green two-piece. She was a chunky kid, with a good tan and a sweet broad soft-looking can with those two crescents of white just under it, where the sun never seems to hit, at the top of the backs of her legs. I stood there with my hand on a box of HiHo crackers trying to remember if I rang it up or not. I ring it up again and the customer starts giving me hell. She's one of these cash-register-watchers, a witch about fifty with rouge on her cheekbones and no eyebrows, and I know it made her day to trip me up. She'd been watching cash registers for fifty years and probably never seen a mistake before.

By the time I got her feathers smoothed and her goodies into a bag—she gives me a little snort in passing, if she'd been born at the right time they would have burned her over in Salem—by the time I get her on her way the girls had circled around the bread and were coming back, without a pushcart, back my way along the counters, in the aisle between the checkouts and the Special bins. They didn't even have shoes on. There was this chunky one, with the two-piece—it was bright green and the seams on the bra were still sharp and her belly was still pretty pale so I guessed she just got it (the suit)—there was this one, with one of those chubby berry-faces, the lips all bunched together under her nose, this one, and a tall one, with black hair that hadn't quite frizzled right, and one of these sunburns right across under the eyes, and a chin that was too long—you know, the kind of girl other girls think is very "striking" and "attractive" but never quite makes it, as they very well know, which is why they like her so much—and then the third one, that wasn't quite so tall. She was the queen. She kind of led them, the other two peeking around and making their shoulders round. She didn't look around, not this queen, she just walked straight on slowly, on these long white prima-donna legs. She came down a little hard on her heels, as if she didn't walk in her bare feet that much, putting down her heels and then letting the weight move along to her toes as if she was testing the floor with every step, putting a little deliberate extra action into it. You never know for sure how girls' minds work (do you really think it's a mind in there or just a little buzz like a bee in a glass jar?) but you got the idea she had talked the other two into coming in here with her, and now she was showing them how to do it, walk slow and hold yourself straight.

She had on a kind of dirty-pink—beige maybe, I don't know—bathing suit with a little nubble all over it and, what got me, the straps were down. They were off her shoulders looped loose around the cool tops of her arms, and I guess as a result the suit had slipped a little on her, so all around the top of the cloth there was this shining rim. If it hadn't been there you wouldn't have known there could have been anything whiter than those shoulders. With the straps pushed off, there was nothing between the top of the suit and the top of her head except just *her*, this clean bare plane of the top of her chest down from the shoulder bones like a dented sheet of metal tilted in the light. I mean, it was more than pretty.

She had sort of oaky hair that the sun and salt had bleached, done up in a bun that was unravelling, and a kind of prim face. Walking into the A&P with your straps down, I suppose it's the only kind of face you *can* have. She held her head so high her neck, coming up out of those white shoulders, looked kind of stretched, but I didn't mind. The longer her neck was, the more of her there was.

She must have felt in the corner of her eye me and over my shoulder Stokesie in the second slot watching, but she didn't tip. Not this queen. She kept her eyes moving across the racks, and stopped, and turned so slow it made my stomach rub the inside of my apron, and buzzed to the other two, who kind of huddled against her for relief, and then they all three of them went up the cat-and-dog-food-breakfast-cereal-macaroni-rice-raisins-season-ings-spreads-spaghetti-soft-drinks-crackers-and-cookies aisle. From the third slot I look straight up this aisle to the meat counter, and I watched them all the way. The fat one with the tan sort of fumbled with the cookies, but on second thought she put the package back. The sheep pushing their carts down the aisle—the girls were walking against the usual traffic (not that we have one-way signs or anything)—were pretty hilarious. You could see them, when Queenie's white shoulders dawned on them, kind of jerk, or hop, or hiccup, but their eyes snapped back to their own baskets and on they pushed. I bet you could set off dynamite in an A&P and the people would by and large keep reaching and checking oatmeal off their lists and muttering "Let me see, there was a third thing, began with A, aspargus, no, as, yes, applesauce!" or what-ever it is they do mutter. But there was no doubt, this jiggled them. A few houseslaves in pin curlers even looked around after pushing their carts past to make sure what they had seen was correct.

You know, it's one thing to have a girl in a bathing suit down on the beach, where what with the glare nobody can look at each other much anyway, and another thing in the cool of the A&P, under the fluorescent lights, against all those stacked packages, with her feet paddling along naked over our checker-board green-and-cream rubber-tile floor.

"Oh Daddy," Stokesie said beside me. "I feel so faint."

"Darling," I said. "Hold me tight." Stokesie's married, with two babies chalked up on his fuselage already, but as far as I can tell that's the only dif-ference. He's twenty-two, and I was nineteen this April.

"Is it done?" he asks, the responsible married man finding his voice. I forgot to say he thinks he's going to be manager some sunny day, maybe in 1990 when it's called the Great Alexandrov and Petrooshki Tea Company or something.

What he meant was, our town is five miles from the beach, with a big summer colony out on the Point, but we're right in the middle of town, and the women generally put on a shirt or shorts or something before they get out of the car into the street. And anyway these are usually women with six chil-dren and varicose veins mapping their legs and nobody, including them, could care less. As I say, we're right in the middle of town, and if you stand at our front doors you can see two banks and the Congregational church and the newspaper store and three real-estate offices and about twenty-seven old free-loaders tearing up Central Street because the sewer broke again. It's not as if we're on the Cape; we're north of Boston and there's people in this town haven't seen the ocean for twenty years.

The girls had reached the meat counter and were asking McMahon some-thing. He pointed, they pointed, and they shuffled out of sight behind a pyramid of Diet Delight peaches. All that was left for us to see was old McMahon patting his mouth and looking after them sizing up their joints. Poor kids, I began to feel sorry for them, they couldn't help it.

Now here comes the sad part of the story, at least my family says it's sad, but I don't think it's so sad myself. The store's pretty empty, it being Thursday afternoon, so there was nothing much to do except lean on the register and wait for the girls to show up again. The whole store was like a pinball machine and I didn't know which tunnel they'd come out of. After a while they come around out of the far aisle, around the light bulbs, records at discount of the Caribbean Six or Tony Martin Sings or some such gunk you wonder they waste the wax on, sixpacks of candy bars, and plastic toys done up in cellophane that fall apart when a kid looks at them anyway. Around they come, Queenie still leading the way, and holding a little gray jar in her hands. Slots Three through Seven are unmanned and I could see her wondering between Stokes and me, but Stokesie with his usual luck draws an old party in baggy gray pants who stumbles up with four giant cans of pineapple juice (what do these bums *do* with all that pineapple juice? I've often asked myself) so the girls come to me. Queenie puts down the jar and I take it into my fingers icy cold. Kingfish Fancy Herring Snacks in Pure Sour Cream: 49¢. Now her hands are empty, not a ring or a bracelet, bare as God made them, and I wonder where the money's coming from. Still with that prim look she lifts a folded dollar bill out of the hollow at the center of her nubble pink top. The jar went heavy in my hand. Really, I thought that was so cute.

Then everybody's luck begins to run out. Lengel comes in from haggling with a truck full of cabbages on the lot and is about to scuttle into that door marked MANAGER behind which he hides all day when the girls touch his eye. Lengel's pretty dreary, teaches Sunday school and the rest, but he doesn't miss much. He comes over and says, "Girls, this isn't the beach."

Queenie blushes, though maybe it's just a brush of sunburn I was noticing for the first time, now that she was so close. "My mother asked me to pick up a jar of herring snacks." Her voice kind of startled me, the way voices do when you see the people first, coming out so flat and dumb yet kind of tony, too, the way it ticked over "pick up" and "snacks." All of a sudden I slid right down her voice into her living room. Her father and the other men were standing around in icecream coats and bow ties and the women were in sandals picking up herring snacks on toothpicks off a big glass plate and they were holding drinks the color of water with olives and sprigs of mint in them. When my parents have somebody over they get lemonade and if it's a real racy affair Schlitz in tall glasses with "They'll Do It Every Time" cartoons stencilled on.

"That's all right," Lengel said. "But this isn't the beach." His repeating this struck me as funny, as if it had just occurred to him, and he had been thinking all these years the A&P was a great big dune and he was the head lifeguard. He didn't like my smiling—as I say he doesn't miss much—but he concentrates on giving the girls that sad Sunday-school-superintendent stare.

Queenie's blush is no sunburn now, and the plump one in plaid, that I liked better from the back—a really sweet can—pipes up. "We weren't doing any shopping. We just came in for one thing."

"That makes no difference," Lengel tells her, and I could see from the way his eyes went that he hadn't noticed she was wearing a two-piece before. "We want you decently dressed when you come in here."

"We *are* decent," Queenie says suddenly, her lower lip pushing, getting sore now that she remembers her place, a place from which the crowd that runs the A&P must look pretty crummy. Fancy Herring Snacks flashed in her very blue eyes.

"Girls, I don't want to argue with you. After this come in here with your shoulders covered. It's our policy." He turns his back. That's policy for you. Policy is what the kingpins want. What the others want is juvenile delinquency.

All this while, the customers had been showing up with their carts but, you know, sheep, seeing a scene, they had all bunched up on Stokesie, who shook open a paper bag as gently as peeling a peach, not wanting to miss a word. I could feel in the silence everybody getting nervous, most of all Lengel, who asks me, "Sammy, have you rung up their purchase?"

I thought and said "No" but it wasn't about that I was thinking. I go through the punches, 4, 9, GROC, TOT—it's more complicated than you think, and after you do it often enough, it begins to make a little song, that you hear words to, in my case "Hello (*bing*) there, you (*gung*) happy *pee*-pul (*splat*)!"—the *splat* being the drawer flying out. I uncrease the bill, tenderly as you may imagine, it just having come from between the two smoothest scoops of vanilla I had ever known were there, and pass a half and a penny into her narrow pink palm, and nestle the herrings in a bag and twist its neck and hand it over, all the time thinking.

The girls, and who'd blame them, are in a hurry to get out, so I say "I quit" to Lengel quick enough for them to hear, hoping they'll stop and watch me, their unsuspected hero. They keep right on going, into the electric eye; the door flies open and they flicker across the lot to their car, Queenie and Plaid and Big Tall Goony-Goony (not that as raw material she was so bad), leaving me with Lengel and kind in his eyebrow.

"Did you say something, Sammy?"

"I said I quit."

"I thought you did."

"You didn't have to embarrass them."

"It was they who were embarrassing us."

I started to say something that came out "Fiddle-de-doo." It's a saying of my grandmother's, and I know she would have been pleased.

"I don't think you know what you're saying," Lengel said.

"I know you don't," I said. "But I do." I pull the bow at the back of my apron and start shrugging it off my shoulders. A couple customers that had been heading for my slot begin to knock against each other, like scared pigs in a chute.

Lengel sighs and begins to look very patient and old and gray. He's been a friend of my parents for years. "Sammy, you don't want to do this to your Mom and Dad," he tells me. It's true, I don't. But it seems to me that once you begin a gesture it's fatal not to go through with it. I fold the apron, "Sammy" stitched in red on the pocket, and put it on the counter, and drop the bow tie on top of it. The bow tie is theirs, if you've ever wondered. "You'll feel like this for the rest of your life," Lengel says, and I know that's true, too, but remembering how he made that pretty girl blush makes me so scrunchy inside I punch the No Sale tab and the machine whirs "pee-pul" and the drawer splats out. One advantage to this scene taking place in summer, I can follow this up with a clean exit, there's no fumbling around getting your coat and galoshes, I just saunter into the electric eye in my white shirt that my mother ironed the night before, and the door heaves itself open, and outside the sunshine is skating around on the asphalt.

I look around for my girls, but they're gone, of course. There wasn't anybody but some young married screaming with her children about some candy they didn't get by the door of a powder-blue Falcon station wagon. Looking back in the big windows, over the bags of peat moss and aluminum lawn furniture stacked on the pavement, I could see Lengel in my place in the slot, checking the sheep through. His face was dark gray and his back stiff, as if he'd just had an injection of iron, and my stomach kind of fell as I felt how hard the world was going to be to me hereafter.

QUESTIONS

Reading for Understanding

1. Why do you think Sammy quit his job? Did you think that Lengel did an unreasonable thing, or was he just doing his job properly? How would you have behaved if you were Sammy? What would you have done if you were in Lengel's place?

2. What details in the story seem to show that Sammy has no respect for girls? What details seem to show that he has a lot of respect for them? How do you explain this confusion on Sammy's part?

3. What does Sammy mean at the end by saying that the world was going to be hard on him in the future?

4. Do you think Sammy's attitudes and behavior are typical of adolescents, or is he unusual for any age?

Noticing Writing Techniques

1. John Updike tells this story from Sammy's point of view and through Sammy's language. How would the story be different if it were told from Lengel's point of view or from Queenie's point of view? Would it be less funny? Would different details be mentioned? Would it have a different meaning?

2. How would you characterize Sammy's language? Does he use a lot of slang or street language? Does he sound educated? Why does he like to label people, calling the young woman Queenie and the customers sheep?

3. What does the story have to say about the attitudes of young people? About work? About individualism and conformity to rules and policies? Do you think the store should allow people to shop in bathing suits and barefoot? Do you think a college or high school should have a dress code?

Noticing Vocabulary

_____ 1. *Crescents* are shaped like
A. moons   B. stars
C. squares   D. figure eights.

_____ 2. A *prima donna* is
A. a humble person   B. a celebrated female performer
C. a brilliant female scientist   D. a bathing beauty.

_____ 3. A *fuselage* is a
A. large container for dumping   B. device for lighting fires
C. body of an airplane   D. connecting rod.

_____ 4. To look *prim* is to look
A. sloppy   B. extremely stylish
C. angry   D. extremely neat.

Writing Topics

1. Write a paragraph explaining what you did in a job you once held. Explain specifically and clearly as if you were giving instructions to someone who had to take over the job herself. Review Exposition: "How-To" Paragraphs in Unit 2.

2. Write an essay in which you explain why you agree or disagree with the following statement: Companies have the right to tell their employees how to dress, wear their hair and makeup, speak, and behave on the job. You may want to review Persuasive Essays in Unit 3.

Neil Howe and Bill Strauss

Neil Howe, an economist and historian, and Bill Strauss, a writer and political satirist, wrote the book called *13th Gen* (1993) to describe and define the current generation of teenagers and young adults, which are the thirteenth generation of Americans since the Declaration of Independence. If you are in that age group, do you recognize your generation in their description?

We Don't Even Have a Name*
from *13th Gen: Abort, Retry, Ignore, Fail?*

News clips document a young adult wasteland of academic nonperformance, disease–ridden sex, date–rape trials, wilding, and hate crimes. Today's youngish sports figures often look to elders like American Gladiators, athletically proficient but uncerebral, uncivic, lacking nuance. To older eyes, the Neon Deions differ from the Namaths and Aarons partly in their size, speed, and muscularity, but also in their in-your-face slam dunks, end-zone boogies, and weak team loyalties. Those who, like Mary Lou Retton, do succeed in capturing our hearts invariably set off to "rettonize" themselves and capture our product endorsements. Team logos, once sources of local pride, now mark territory for inner-city gangs. But the Ickey Shuffle, Shark jacket, and Air Jordon high-top aren't the only sporting icons new to this generation: There's also one-armed Jim Abbott pitching in the major leagues, America's world-champion soccer players, and second-generation black student-athletes like Duke's basketball star Grant Hill (the son of Yale and Dallas Cowboy football star Calvin Hill).

Yes, this is a generation with a PR problem. Its collective reputation comes from young celebrities and criminals, from the biggest stories of success and failure. Yet most in their teens and twenties are quick to insist that *People* cover stories and police blotters tell little about them personally, about their circles of friends, about their lives in school or on the job, about what it means to come of age in 1990s America. And, they insist, their generation will remain a mystery until elders take the trouble to block out the iconography and look more discerningly at the young men and women in daily American life.

In polyglot American cities—New York and Los Angeles especially—we see them as the reckless bicycle messengers (who, like *Bicycle Days* author John Schwartz, like to "live a little faster"), the rollerblading commuters, the pizza and package-delivery drivers, the young Koreans helping their fathers at grocery stores, the local-access cable TV producers, the deal making wannabees whom trader-turned-writer Michael Lewis says "age like dogs" before making their fortunes—or going broke trying. Other times, we notice them as the directionless college "slackers": the non-voters, the wandering nomads of the temp world, the store clerks whose every declaration sounds like it ends with a question mark, the women in tennis shoes lunching at the gym, the computer jockeys loading games onto their office PCs when the boss isn't looking.

---

*From THE 13TH GENERATION by Neil Howe and Bill Strauss. Coypright © 1993 by Neil Howe and Bill Strauss. Reprinted by permission of Vintage Books, a division of Random House, Inc.

In the inner city, they're the unmarried teen mothers and the unconcerned teen fathers. They're the lethal gangsters, the Crips and Bloods—and the innocent hiphoppers who have no illusions about why older white guys cross the street to avoid them. Across the landscape of urban youth, we see more millionaires and more hopelessly poor, more immigrants and more nativist skinheads, more social fractures and cultural fissures than today's 40-, 60-, or 80-year-olds could possibly remember from their own younger days.

In 'burb and town life, they are kids at the mall. Kids buying family groceries for busy moms and dads. Kids doing the wave at the ballpark. Kids of divorce. (Omigosh, it's Saturday, and I'm supposed to be with Dad, and I have, like, *so* much homework this weekend.) Kids battling back against drugs and alcohol. Kids in mutual protection circles of friends, girding against an adolescent world far more dangerous than anything their parents knew. Kids struggling to unlink sex from date-rape, disease, and death.

In school, the diversity of student bodies has never been greater—not just in ethnicity, but also in attitude, performance, and rewards. Asian-Americans (and immigrant children generally) are achieving at a tremendous clip, and black and Hispanic aptitude test scores are rising, while Anglo aptitude test scores remain below levels seen one, even two generations ago. On campus, women outperform men and soar into graduate programs, while collegians of both sexes struggle with a faculty-fueled debate over how to undo their various alleged insensitivities. Their handbills are more likely to promote products than ideologies, their protests more against the immediate scourges of their world—hikes in tuition, cuts in library hours, the hiring of teaching assistants who can't speak English—than against injustice in the world beyond. Most of them support global causes but don't have the money or time to contribute. Besides, they figure, what difference could they possibly make? . . .

When they look to the future, they see a much bleaker vision than any of today's older generations ever saw in their own youth. Even the hard-pressed youths of the Great Depression saw a path (albeit difficult) to a bright future, under the guidance of wise and determined older adults. But today's teens and twenties aren't singing about any "over the rainbow" reward and see precious little wisdom and determination up the age ladder. They have trouble identifying any path that does not lead to decline for them and their nation. Instead, they sense that they're the clean-up crew, that their role in history could be sacrificial—that, whatever comeuppance America has to face, they'll bear more than their share of the burden. It's a new twist, and not a happy one, on the American Dream.

Are they a "generation"? Yes, with a personality that reaches across the board—rich and poor, black and white, Hispanic and Asian, male and female, celebrity and everyman. Whatever a 15- or 25-year-old's individual circumstances, he or she can sense a composite personality, a generational core. It's something each individual can help define, "slack" within, or fight against—but cannot easily ignore. The simple fact of ethnic and socioeconomic diversity (in contrast to the far greater homogeneity found in older generations) is an essential part of this persona.

QUESTIONS

Reading for Understanding

1. This reading claims that today's younger generation has a far more pessimistic outlook toward the future than their parents' or grandparents' generations did. What are some of the reasons for this pessimism? Do you share this pessimism?

2. What are some of the examples of greater diversity in this generation?

3. How is this generation different in the schools and colleges than earlier generations of students?

4. How do the roles and images of women seem to have changed?

Noticing Writing Techniques

1. These authors are very *allusive,* meaning that they frequently *allude to,* or refer to, names and facts that the reader is expected to know. What kinds of people do they most often refer to? Can you identify all of the names to which they refer?

2. The style and vocabulary of this essay could be described as modern. What words, including slang terms, are so recent that a reader 20 years ago would not have been able to recognize them?

3. This essay is chiefly a series of examples. (See the Expository Mode: Essays Based on Examples in Unit 3 for a discussion of this writing mode.) What is the main point, or thesis, that all these examples support? Do you agree with the thesis?

Noticing Vocabulary

_____ 1. An *uncerebral* person is lacking in
    A. physical skills   B. health
    C. attractiveness   D. brains.

_____ 2. *Logos* are
    A. symbols identifying organizations or products
    B. very smart computer technicians
    C. extremely logical approaches to new problems
    D. computer languages.

_____ 3. To look *discerningly* means to look
    A. rapidly   B. perceptively
    C. carelessly   D. angrily.

_____ 4. In *polyglot* cities,
   A. many people are crowded together
   B. many forms of entertainment are available
   C. many languages are spoken
   D. many kinds of buildings are built.

_____ 5. *Fissures* are
   A. food supplies   B. cracks
   C. medicines   D. types of skin.

_____ 6. *Ideologies* are
   A. systems of ideas or belief B. well-trained scholars
   C. reference books   D. new methods of
                                     computation.

_____ 7. *Homogeneity* means
   A. variety
   B. belonging to different groups
   C. containing nutritious elements
   D. having the same characteristics.

Writing Topics

1. Write a paragraph describing the diversity present in your college. Be sure to include specific examples to show that your generation includes varied types of students.

2. This reading showed that the world for today's young men and women has more difficulties and pressures than in the past. Write an essay explaining what difficulties young people face in today's society and how this has affected their attitudes, their career choices, and their outlook on the future. For further pointers and exercises, review Cause and Effect Paragraphs in Unit 2 and Expository Essays in Unit 3.

Poems on Adolescence and Young Adulthood

Gwendolyn Brooks (1917–   )

The first African-American to win the Pulitzer Prize (in 1950), Gwendolyn Brooks has been awarded countless honorary degrees, fellowships, and awards. Nevertheless, she has always kept her focus as a poet on the lives of ordinary people, the people, as she put it, "of the taverns and the homes and the streets." Born in Topeka, Kansas, she grew up in Chicago, where she graduated from Wilson Junior College. She married Henry

Blakely II in 1939; they have a son and daughter. In "We Real Cool" Brooks captures the language and attitudes of risk-taking, rebellious teenagers.

We Real Cool

The Pool Players
Seven at the Golden Shovel

We real cool. We
Left School. We

Lurk late. We
Strike straight. We

Sing sin. We
Thin gin. We

Jazz June. We
Die soon.

QUESTIONS

Reading for Understanding

1. What do you think the main idea of this poem is? How would you describe the attitudes of the adolescents speaking in the poem? Could they be expressing more than one attitude at the same time?

2. This poem appeared in 1960. If Gwendolyn Brooks were to write it today, would the same idea still apply to the way teenagers live? Would any details have to be changed to keep up with the times? Would substances other than or in addition to gin be included?

Noticing Writing Techniques

1. Brooks reads this poem with an unusual, jazzy rhythm. How do you think she wants you to read the poem, as suggested by her placing the word *we* at the end of each line instead of the beginning? How does it sound if you pause slightly after the "we" in each line?

2. *Alliteration* is the repetition of sounds at the beginnings of words. Find examples of alliteration in this poem.

3. The language of this poem copies the patterns of the high school dropouts who are speaking in the poem. What examples can you find of ungrammatical phrases, slang, or street talk? Are today's street words much different from the words in the poem?

4. Would you say the tone of this poem is meant to sound like bragging, joking, or complaining? How would you compare this tone with the tone of today's rap albums?

5. How does the name of the pool hall, *The Golden Shovel*, tie in with the meaning of the poem? What does the word *golden* suggest about their experience of the place? What does the word *shovel* suggest about their possible future lives? Is the name an example of oxymoron (the combining of opposite terms)?

Writing Topics

1. Write a paragraph enumerating some of the reasons why teenagers drop out of high school nowadays. Review Cause and Effect Paragraphs in Unit 2.

2. Write an essay comparing the attitudes of teenagers nowadays who lead successful, happy lives with those who do not. What are the common traits of the "winners," and what common attitudes cause the others to be self-defeating? Review Exposition: Comparative Paragraphs in Unit 2.

Audre Lorde (1934–1993)

Perhaps because, as an African-American, a lesbian, and a feminist, Audre Lorde felt herself to be an outsider and identified with other outsiders, she was especially sensitive to the feelings of teenagers. Most adolescents feel excluded at some time or other; many, like the young woman in "Hanging Fire" (1978), feel alienated from social groups and even from their families. Although born of immigrant parents from the island of Cariacou in the Caribbean and raised in New York, Audre Lorde manages to express anxieties familiar to teenagers in many cultures.

Hanging Fire*

I am fourteen
and my skin has betrayed me
the boy I cannot live without
still sucks his thumb
in secret

---

how come my knees are
always so ashy
what if I die
before morning
and momma's in the bedroom
with the door closed.

I have to learn how to dance
in time for the next party
my room is too small for me
suppose I die before graduation
they will sing sad melodies
but finally
tell the truth about me
There is nothing I want to do
and too much
that has to be done
and momma's in the bedroom
with the door closed.

Nobody even stops to think
about my side of it
I should have been on Math Team
my marks were better than his
why do I have to be
the one
wearing braces
I have nothing to wear tomorrow
will I live long enough
to grow up
and momma's in the bedroom
with the door closed.

QUESTIONS

Reading for Understanding

1. Why does this young woman mix together thoughts about trivial things with thoughts about death? What does this reveal about teenagers' feelings? Which details might seem unimportant to an adult? Why are they so important to the young woman?

2. Would you describe the young woman's feelings as typical of fourteen-year-olds? What words would best describe her feelings?

3. What does the title "Hanging Fire" have to do with the poem? Why does the author choose a military term for the title?

4. The young woman imagines that if she died, someone would finally "tell the truth" about her. What truth do you think she is referring to?

5. What thoughts or feelings belong especially to a young woman? What thoughts are common to both young men and women?

Noticing Writing Techniques

1. Audre Lorde uses no punctuation. Instead she indicates pauses by her line endings. What effect does this have when you read the poem?

2. What effect does Lorde create by repeating certain phrases and thoughts in the poem? Does this repetition add to the meaning of the poem? Does it reveal anything about the young woman?

Writing Topics

1. Write a paragraph in which you reminisce about the attitudes, feelings, and problems that most concerned you when you were about fourteen years old. Try to arrange the paragraph in climactic order, building toward the most important concerns at the end. You may want to review Paragraph Coherence: Climactic Sequence in Unit 2.

2. Interview one of your parents or another adult of your parents' generation. Ask this person about what it was like for them to be teenagers. Get plenty of details about how they dressed, wore their hair, socialized, related to the opposite sex, behaved in school, and related to their parents. Then write an essay comparing teenage experience in your generation with that of your parents. You may want to review Exposition: Comparative Paragraphs in Unit 2.

Changes in Adult Life: Growth and Aging

After the rapid changes and emotional turmoil of adolescence, adult life seems calm and stable. But we never stop changing and we need never stop growing. Adult life includes both gradual development and crises; no two lives are identical, but all adults endure the difficulties of the aging process and enjoy the excitement of new challenges and opportunities. Nearly every life change from early adulthood to senility brings with it new perspectives and enjoyments as well as new problems. No matter how many billion people have lived on this earth, every person must encounter these changes like an explorer entering unmapped territory. Since each life is unique, no guidebook can tell us how to live our lives. At the same time, most of us can find it reassuring to know that the phases we go through are shared by other adults and that the stresses we feel are common to all people undergoing the same experience of gaining or losing a job, getting married or divorced, raising children, changing residence, retiring, becoming ill, or facing a death in the family.

Writers often focus on the crisis points of adult life, the times of conflict between people and within psyches. Whether in drama, fiction, psychology textbooks, or news reports, writers call our attention to the major life changes, making us aware of both the dangers they present and the opportunities for growth they offer. Writing and reading about life changes makes us aware of the limitless variety of individual experiences as well as the patterns of growth and decay common to all members of the human species.

Gail Sheehy (1937–   )

A well-known New York journalist, editor, and author, Gail Sheehy has written fiction, political biographies, and social analysis. Her best-known and most influential book has been *Passages* (1976), from which the following essay has been taken. Sheehy describes in this book what she believes are the six major periods of change modern adults go through from late adolescence to middle age. When reading it, see if her descriptions of these stages match your own stages of development and those of people you know well.

Predictable Crises of Adulthood* from *Passages*

We are not unlike a particularly hardy crustacean. The lobster grows by developing and shedding a series of hard, protective shells. Each time it expands from within, the confining shell must be sloughed off. It is left exposed and vulnerable until, in time, a new covering grows to replace the old.

With each passage from one stage of human growth to the next we, too, must shed a protective structure. We are left exposed and vulnerable—but also yeasty and embryonic again, capable of stretching in ways we hadn't known before. These sheddings may take several years or more. Coming out of each passage, though, we enter a longer and more stable period in which we can expect relative tranquillity and a sense of equilibrium regained.

Everything that happens to us—graduations, marriage, childbirth, divorce, getting or losing a job—affects us. These *marker events* are the concrete happenings of our lives. A developmental stage, however, is not defined in terms of marker events; it is defined by changes that begin within. *The underlying impulse toward change will be there regardless* of whether or not it is manifested in or accentuated by a marker event.   .   .   .

Although I have indicated the ages when Americans are likely to go through each stage, and the differences between men and women where they

---

*From PASSAGES by Gail Sheehy. Copyright © 1974, 1976 by Gail Sheehy. Used by permission of Dutton Signet, a division of Penguin Books USA Inc.

are striking, do not take the ages too seriously. The stages are the thing, and most particularly the sequence.

Here is the briefest outline of the developmental ladder.

Pulling Up Roots

Before 18, the motto is loud and clear: "I have to get away from my parents." But the words are seldom connected to action. Generally still safely part of our families, even if away at school, we feel our autonomy to be subject to erosion from moment to moment.

After 18, we begin Pulling Up Roots in earnest. College, military service, and short-term travels are all customary vehicles our society provides for the first round trips between family and a base of one's own. In the attempt to separate our view of the world from our family's view, despite vigorous protestations to the contrary—"I know exactly what I want!"—we cast about for any beliefs we can call our own. And in the process of testing those beliefs we are often drawn to fads, preferably those most mysterious and inaccessible to our parents.

Whatever tentative memberships we try out in the world, the fear haunts us that we are really kids who cannot take care of ourselves. We cover that fear with acts of defiance and mimicked confidence. For allies to replace our parents, we turn to our contemporaries. They become conspirators. So long as their perspective meshes with our own, they are able to substitute for the sanctuary of the family. But that doesn't last very long. And the instant they diverge from the shaky ideals of "our group," they are seen as betrayers. Rebounds to the family are common between the ages of 18 and 22.

The tasks of this passage are to locate ourselves in a peer group role, a sex role, an anticipated occupation, an ideology or world view. As a result, we gather the impetus to leave home physically and the identity to *begin* leaving home emotionally.

Even as one part of us seeks to be an individual, another part longs to restore the safety and comfort of merging with another. Thus one of the most popular myths of this passage is: We can piggyback our development by attaching to a Stronger One. But people who marry during this time often prolong financial and emotional ties to the family and relatives that impede them from becoming self-sufficient.

A stormy passage through the Pulling Up Roots years will probably facilitate the normal progression of the adult life cycle. If one doesn't have an identity crisis at this point, it will erupt during a later transition, when the penalties may be harder to bear.

The Trying Twenties

The Trying Twenties confront us with the question of how to take hold in the adult world. Our focus shifts from the interior turmoils of late adolescence—"Who am I?" "What is truth?"—and we become almost totally preoccupied with working out the externals. "How do I put my aspirations into effect?"

"What is the best way to start?" "Where do I go?" "Who can help me?" "How did *you* do it?"

In this period, which is longer and more stable compared with the passage that leads to it, the tasks are as enormous as they are exhilarating: To shape a Dream, that vision of ourselves which will generate energy, aliveness, and hope. To prepare for a lifework. To find a mentor if possible. And to form the capacity for intimacy, without losing in the process whatever consistency of self we have thus far mustered. The first test structure must be erected around the life we choose to try.

Doing what we "should" is the most pervasive theme of the twenties. The "shoulds" are largely defined by family models, the press of the culture, or the prejudices of our peers. If the prevailing cultural instructions are that one should get married and settle down behind one's own door, a nuclear family is born. If instead the peers insist that one should do one's own thing, the 25-year-old is likely to burn up Route 66 in the commitment to have no commitments.

One of the terrifying aspects of the twenties is the inner conviction that the choices we make are irrevocable. It is largely a false fear. Change is quite possible, and some alteration of our original choices is probably inevitable.

Two impulses, as always, are at work. One is to build a firm, safe structure for the future by making strong commitments, to "be set." Yet people who slip into a ready-made form without much self-examination are likely to find themselves *locked in.*

The other urge is to explore and experiment, keeping any structure tentative and therefore easily reversible. Taken to the extreme, these are people who skip from one trial job and one limited personal encounter to another, spending their twenties in the *transient* state.

Although the choices of our twenties are not irrevocable, they do set in motion a Life Pattern. Some of us follow the locked-in pattern, others the transient pattern, the wunderkind pattern, the caregiver pattern, and there are a number of others. Such patterns strongly influence the particular questions raised for each person during each passage, and so the most common patterns will also be traced throughout the book.

Buoyed by powerful illusions and belief in the power of the will, we commonly insist in our twenties that what we have chosen to do is the one true course in life. Our backs go up at the merest hint that we are like our parents, that two decades of parental training might be reflected in our current actions and attitudes.

"Not me," is the motto, "I'm different."

Catch-30

Impatient with devoting ourselves to the "shoulds," a new vitality springs from within as we approach 30. Men and women alike speak of feeling too narrow and restricted. They blame all sorts of things, but what the restrictions boil down to are the outgrowth of career and personal choices of the twenties. They may have been choices perfectly suited to that stage. But now the fit feels different. Some inner aspect that was left out is striving to be taken into account. Important new choices must be made, and commitments altered or deepened. The work involves great change, turmoil, and often crisis—a simultaneous feeling of rock bottom and the urge to bust out.

One common response is the tearing up of the life we spent most of our twenties putting together. It may mean striking out on a secondary road toward a new vision or converting a dream of "running for president" into a more realistic goal. The single person feels a push to find a partner. The woman who was previously content at home with children chafes to venture into the world. The childless couple reconsiders children. And almost everyone who is married, especially those married for seven years, feels a discontent.

If the discontent doesn't lead to a divorce, it will, or should, call for a serious review of the marriage and of each partner's aspirations in their Catch-30 condition. The gist of that condition was expressed by a 29-year-old associate with a Wall Street law firm:

"I'm considering leaving the firm. I've been there four years now; I'm getting good feedback, but I have no clients of my own. I feel weak. If I wait much longer, it will be too late, too close to that fateful time of decision on whether or not to become a partner. I'm success-oriented. But the concept of being 55 years old and stuck in a monotonous job drives me wild. It drives me crazy now, just a little bit. I'd say that 85 percent of the time I thoroughly enjoy my work. But when I get a screwball case, I come away from court saying, "What am I doing here?" It's a *visceral* reaction that I'm wasting my time. I'm trying to find some way to make a social contribution or a slot in city government. I keep saying, "There's something more.""

Besides the push to broaden himself professionally, there is a wish to expand his personal life. He wants two or three more children. "The concept of a home has become very meaningful to me, a place to get away from troubles and relax. I love my son in a way I could not have anticipated. I never could live alone."

Consumed with the work of making his own critical life-steering decisions, he demonstrates the essential shift at this age: an absolute requirement to be more self-concerned. The self has new value now that his competency has been proved.

His wife is struggling with her own age-30 priorities. She wants to go to law school, but he wants more children. If she is going to stay home, she wants him to make more time for the family instead of taking on even wider professional commitments. His view of the bind, of what he would most like from his wife, is this:

"I'd like not to be bothered. It sounds cruel, but I'd like not to have to worry about what she's going to do next week. Which is why I've told her several times that I think she should do something. Go back to school and get a degree in social work or geography or whatever. Hopefully that would fulfill her, and then I wouldn't have to worry about her line of problems. I want her to be decisive about herself."

The trouble with his advice to his wife is that it comes out of concern with *his* convenience, rather than with *her* development. She quickly picks up on this lack of goodwill: He is trying to dispose of her. At the same time, he refuses her the same latitude to be "selfish" in making an independent decision to broaden her own horizons. Both perceive a lack of mutuality. And that is what Catch-30 is all about for the couple.

Rooting and Extending

Life becomes less provisional, more rational and orderly in the early thirties. We begin to settle down in the full sense. Most of us begin putting down roots and sending out new shoots. People buy houses and become very earnest about climbing career ladders. Men in particular concern themselves with "making it." Satisfaction with marriage generally goes downhill in the thirties (for those who have remained together) compared with the highly valued, vision-supporting marriage of the twenties. This coincides with the couple's reduced social life outside the family and the in-turned focus on raising their children.

The Deadline Decade

In the middle of the thirties we come upon a crossroads. We have reached the halfway mark. Yet even as we are reaching our prime, we begin to see there is a place where it finishes. Time starts to squeeze.

The loss of youth, the faltering of physical powers we have always taken for granted, the fading purpose of stereotyped roles by which we have thus far identified ourselves, the spiritual dilemma of having no absolute answers—and or all of these shocks can give this passage the character of crisis. Such thoughts usher in a decade between 35 and 45 that can be called the Deadline Decade. It is a time of both danger and opportunity. All of us have the chance to rework the narrow identity by which we defined ourselves in the first half of life. And those of us who make the most of the opportunity will have a full-out authenticity crisis.

To come through this authenticity crisis, we must reexamine our purposes and reevaluate how to spend our resources from now on. "Why am I doing all this? What do I really believe in?" No matter what we have been doing, there will be parts of ourselves that have been suppressed and now need to find expression. "Bad" feelings will demand acknowledgment along with the good. . . .

Renewal or Resignation

Somewhere in the mid-forties, equilibrium is regained. A new stability is achieved, which may be more or less satisfying.

If one has refused to budge through the midlife transition, the sense of staleness will calcify into resignation. One by one, the safety and supports will be withdrawn from the person who is standing still. Parents will become children; children will become strangers; a mate will grow away or go away; the career will become just a job—and each of these events will be felt as an abandonment. The crisis will probably emerge again around 50. And although its wallop will be greater, the jolt may be just what is needed to prod the resigned middle-ager toward seeking revitalization.

On the other hand . . .

If we have confronted ourselves in the middle passage and found a renewal of purpose around which we are eager to build a more authentic life structure, these may well be the best years. Personal happiness takes a sharp turn upward for partners who can now accept the fact: "I cannot expect *anyone* to fully understand me." Parents can be forgiven for the burdens of our childhood. Children can be let go without leaving us in collapsed silence. At 50, there is a new warmth and mellowing. Friends become more important than ever, but so does privacy. Since it is so often proclaimed by people past midlife, the motto of this stage might be "No more bullshit."

QUESTIONS

Reading for Understanding

1. Does Gail Sheehy seem optimistic or pessimistic about the chances of finding happiness in the different stages of life? What attitudes does she think will cause people to end up unhappy? What attitudes will help them find happiness?

2. At what stages do marriages tend to be happier? At what stage or stages do they tend to be troubled?

3. Does Sheehy's description of these life stages match the life patterns of people you know well? Does it match your own life, up to the stage where you are right now?

4. Does Sheehy seem to be writing about one particular ethnic, cultural, or economic group? Do you believe that people from other cultures or economic backgrounds tend to go through these same stages?

5. What does Sheehy believe will happen to people who somehow fail to progress through these stages of development? Can you think of people you know who have not adjusted to life's changes? What has happened to them?

Noticing Writing Techniques

1. Sheehy begins with a metaphor comparing human beings to lobsters. Can you explain what this metaphor means? Why did she choose to begin with a comparison between human development and that of another animal? Can you think of any other possible metaphors for human life?

2. Sheehy writes in the *first person plural*, using the pronoun *we* rather than *I, you, he,* or *she*. How does that make you feel toward what she is saying? Would you respond differently if she described all these changes by saying "*You* begin Pulling Up Roots" instead of "*We* begin Pulling Up Roots"?

3. This essay falls into the general category of *process analysis*, which is a form of *expository* writing discussed in Units 2 and 3. How does Sheehy

divide her main idea into categories? What methods does she use to keep you aware of her main point through the whole essay? Do her titles of sections of the essay help you understand her point?

4. What specific details or examples does she use to make her point clearer and easier to identify with? How does she use quotations to illustrate her point?

Noticing Vocabulary

_____ 1. A *crustacean* is
    A. a stone-age person   B. a language
_____   C. a form of breakfast food   D. a shellfish.

_____ 2. The *embryonic* stage of development is
    A. the last stage before dying   B. the period of puberty
    C. the period before birth   D. the stage after growth has been completed.

_____ 3. A *tentative* action is
    A. decisive   B. indecisive
    C. well thought out   D. rapid.

_____ 4. A *sanctuary* is a place of
    A. safety   B. danger
    C. excitement   D. wealth.

_____ 5. To *facilitate* something is to make it
    A. more difficult   B. more complicated
    C. easier   D. better funded.

_____ 6. The purpose of a *mentor* is to
    A. cure diseases   B. guide and teach
    C. solve technical problems   D. give financial advice.

_____ 7. A *transient* state is
    A. permanent   B. exciting
    C. full of difficulties   D. temporary.

_____ 8. *Simultaneous* means
    A. in agreement
    B. placed next to each other
    C. sudden and unexpected
    D. happening at the same time.

_____ 9. A *visceral* reaction comes from the
    A. brain   B. guts
    C. habits learned in   D. sense of duty.
       childhood

_____ 10. When life becomes *provisional,* it becomes more

    A. satisfying

    B. based on temporary arrangements

    C. unsatisfying

    D. orderly.

_____ 11. *Stereotyped* roles

    A. conform to familiar patterns

    B. result from new ideas

    C. apply only to the elderly

    D. apply only to married people.

_____ 12. *Revitalization* means

    A. loss of abilities

    B. use of new medical procedures

    C. coming back to life

    D. feeding through a tube.

Writing Topics

1. Write a paragraph telling about how you feel toward your career and personal life at your age. Use the *first person singular* ("I feel," "I plan to . . ." etc.). Then rewrite the paragraph in the *third person singular,* beginning "A woman my age . . ." or "A man my age. . . ." Review Shifts of Person in Unit 5.

2. Write an essay telling about a major change that occurred in your life. First, explain how your situation was before the change; then explain what event occurred that brought about the change. Finally, explain how your life was different afterward and how the whole change affects you now. This will be a kind of *narrative essay* in its *chronological* plan, but you will also be doing a considerable amount of *analysis of cause and effect.* Some of the possible life changes to consider are the following: going off to college, entering the military, getting married, undergoing a health crisis, experiencing a death in the family, having a child, getting divorced, starting a job, changing jobs, immigrating from one country to another. Be sure to tell not merely the facts about what happened but also the meaning of what happened. Review Narrative Essays and Expository Essays in Unit 3, and Cause and Effect Paragraphs in Unit 2.

Christopher Peterson

Christopher Peterson is a professor at the University of Michigan and the author of numerous articles and books on psychology. The following piece, which is from his standard textbook on psychology, explains, in language aimed at college students, one of the key elements of life changes, stress. It describes ways we cope with stress and identifies some of the events that cause the most stress in our lives.

Stress and Coping*
from *Introduction to Psychology*

Some terms prove more difficult to define than others, and *stress* is one of these terms. Although there is general agreement that stress is what occurs when demands are made on someone, there is much less agreement when we try to be more precise. Sometimes we talk as if stress were a property of the environment: "That place was a pressure cooker; I couldn't wait to leave." Sometimes stress is attributed to a particular societal role, like being an emergency room nurse, a police officer, or an air traffic controller. Other times stress refers to the bodily changes that result from environmental demands: "My back is tied up in knots, just like my life!" And sometimes stress means one's psychological response: "I'm all stressed out". . . .

Individuals are not usually passive victims of the stressors they happen to encounter. They will often try to decrease stress by thinking, feeling, or acting in particular ways. That is, they cope. What makes coping an interesting topic for psychologists is that people cope in a variety of ways, some successful and some not. Being able to predict which way of coping someone chooses as well as the success of his or her choice has long been a goal of psychologists working in this area.

Defense Mechanisms.   Psychoanalytic theory ushered in an influential perspective on coping by introducing the notion of **defense mechanisms.** These are unconscious strategies that we use to defend ourselves against threat. Freud and other psychoanalytic theorists described a variety of defense mechanisms that people may use, some familiar and some bizarre (see table on page 370). In *projection,* for example, people attribute unacceptable characteristics of their own to other folks. Some types of prejudice involve projection, as when sexually preoccupied individuals criticize the behavior of other groups. In *repression,* we actively keep an upsetting memory out of our conscious minds. Repression is the process responsible for cases of amnesia that have a psychological basis.

Defense mechanisms rank as one of the major contributions of psychoanalytic theory. Note how many of the defenses described in the following table have become part of everyday vocabulary. These coping strategies were there all along for someone to see, but it took the genius of Freud to recognize them and offer a single explanation. . . .

Life Events and Hassles.   Another viewpoint in stress research looks at the role of environmental events in producing stress. Pioneering investigators Thomas Holmes and Richard Rahe (1967) created the Social Readjustment

---

*From INTRODUCTION TO PSYCHOLOGY by Christopher Peterson. Copyright © 1991. Reprinted by permission of HarperCollins College Publishers.

Defense Mechanism	Characterization and Example
Compensation	Investing one's energies in some activity to offset difficulties in another area; for example, working out or studying after a disappointing date
Denial	Acting as if something bad did not happen; for example, continuing to attend class after flunking out of school
Displacement	Directing one's impulses toward a substitute object or person; for instance, kicking the dog or yelling at the children after a difficult day at work
Fantasy	Engaging in wishful thinking or daydreaming when feeling stressed; for example, fantasizing about winning the lottery when taking final examinations
Intellectualization	Discussing a traumatic event without experiencing any emotions, as when a patient with a serious illness calmly discusses the chances of survival
Projection	Attributing one's own unacceptable characteristics to others; for example, a hostile person who sees everyone else as belligerent
Rationalization	Rewriting history after a disappointment, like the fox in Aesop's fables who decided that the grapes he couldn't have were probably sour anyway
Reaction formation	Replacing one impulse with its opposite; for example, acting hatefully toward a person one finds attractive
Regression	Acting like an infant or child in stressful circumstances; for example, throwing a tantrum during an argument
Repression	Forcing a threatening memory from awareness, as might happen when someone ``forgets'' the details of an assault
Sublimation	Channeling undesirable impulses into socially acceptable activities; for example, an aggressive individual might become a fire ``fighter'' or a police officer

Major Life Events

Event	"Life Change Unit" Score
1. Death of spouse	100
2. Divorce	73
3. Marital separation	65
4. Jail term	63
5. Death of a close family member	63
6. Major personal injury or illness	53
7. Marriage	50
8. Being fired at work	47
9. Marital reconciliation	45
10. Retirement	45
11. Major change in health of family member	44
12. Pregnancy	40
13. Sexual difficulties	39
14. Gaining a new family member	39
15. Major business readjustment	39
16. Major change in financial state	38
17. Death of a close friend	37
18. Changing to a different line of work	36
19. Major change in number of arguments with spouse	35
20. Taking out a mortgage or loan for a major purchase	31
21. Foreclosure on a mortgage or loan	30
22. Major change in responsibilities at work	29
23. Son or daughter leaving home	29
24. Trouble with in-laws	29
25. Outstanding personal achievement	28
26. Spouse begins or ceases work outside the home	26
27. Beginning or ending school	26
28. Major change in living conditions	25
29. Revision of personal habits	24
30. Trouble with boss	23
31. Major change in working hours or conditions	20
32. Change in residence	20
33. Changing to a new school	20
34. Major change in usual type and/or amount of recreation	19
35. Major change in church activities	19
36. Major change in social activities	18
37. Taking out a mortgage or loan for a minor purchase	17
38. Major change in sleeping habits	16
39. Major change in number of family get-togethers	15
40. Major change in eating habits	15
41. Vacation	13
42. Christmas	12
43. Minor violations of the law	11

Source: Holmes & Rahe, 1967

Rating Scale to gauge the *quantity* of stress a person had experienced in recent months. In responding to this scale, a research subject indicates which of forty-three major life events occurred in the past year (see table below). The more the event in question disrupts ongoing life and requires readjustment, as judged by research subjects, the higher the "life change unit" score assigned to the event. When total scores on the Social Readjustment Rating Scale are correlated with subsequent psychological and physical problems, a positive relationship is found. The more stressful life events you have recently experienced, the more likely you are to be depressed or anxious or sick.

It's not just major life events that create stress for us. Indeed, Kanner, Coyne, Schaefer, and Lazarus (1981) created a measure that parallels the Social Readjustment Rating Scale, except that it asks about hassles: small but annoying events in the course of daily life, such as losing one's car keys, being interrupted at dinner, making a mistake while balancing the checkbook, and having to take care of a pet. As hassles accumulate, so does stress, taking a toll on psychological and physical well-being. In their sheer numbers, hassles may be even more stressful than major life events.

QUESTIONS

Reading for Understanding

1. According to this passage, what exactly is stress? What causes stress? How do people cope with stress?

2. What life changes cause the most stress? Why do you think this is so?

3. From the list of defense mechanisms (also called coping mechanisms), how many of these terms are already familiar to you? How many of these mechanisms can you remember using in your own life? What has been your most successful method of coping with stress?

4. If you were a student in a psychology course given this reading as a class assignment, what term paper topic could you think of on the subject of stress? What possible questions about stress might you expect in a class discussion or examination?

Noticing Writing Techniques

1. Textbooks often use tables and charts to illustrate important points. Explain in your own words what each of these tables illustrates and what details in each table interested you. What do these tables add to the author's explanation of stress?

2. For what audience is this textbook written? What details—choice of vocabulary, examples, style, or tone—tell you that this is part of a college textbook? How do you know that the material is meant to be studied and remembered, not just read quickly for entertainment?

3. Can you identify any words, phrases, or examples that make the writing seem livelier than we sometimes expect textbooks to be? What sort of writing do you like in the textbooks you study in your major subject?

Noticing Vocabulary

_____ 1. *Stressors* are things that
    A. result from stress   B. make us stronger
    C. cause stress   D. make us weaker.

_____ 2. To be *preoccupied* by something is to be
    A. engrossed in it   B. angry about it
    C. likely to gain something   D. sad about it.
       from it

_____ 3. Things that are *correlated* are
    A. added together
    B. not related to each other
    C. covered with a rough surface
    D. matched together.

_____ 4. A *subsequent* event happens
    A. earlier   B. afterward
    C. at the same time   D. slowly.

Writing Topics

1. Write a paragraph telling about an incident in which you observed someone coping with stress by using one of the *defense mechanisms* defined in the essay. This person may be yourself or someone you know well.

2. Write an essay giving advice on how to cope with stress successfully. Mention several methods of coping with stress, and use examples from your own life or what you know of other people's experiences. Review "How-To" Paragraphs in Unit 2 and Problem/Solution Essays under the Expository Mode in Unit 3.

Poems on Life Changes

William Shakespeare (1564–1616)

Although not much is known for certain about the life of England's greatest poet and playwright other than that he grew up in the town of Stratford-upon-Avon and joined the theater world of London as an actor, playwright, and part owner of a theater, his works remain for us to enjoy. His sonnets, his long poems, and 37 of his plays continue to offer us the most comprehensive picture by a single author of life's variety, humor, and tragedy. In the following famous passage from *As You Like It*, he describes life as a theater and the stages of life as a series of roles played by actors.

All the World's a Stage
from *As You Like It*, (Act II, Scene 7)

All the world's a stage,
And all the men and women merely players.
They have their exits and their entrances,
And one man in his time plays many parts,
His acts being seven ages. At first the infant,
Mewling and puking in the nurse's arms.
Then the whining schoolboy, with his satchel
And shining morning face, creeping like snail
Unwillingly to school. And then the lover,
Sighing like furnace, with a woeful ballad
Made to his mistress' eyebrow. Then a soldier,
Full of strange oaths and bearded like the pard,
Jealous in honor, sudden and quick in quarrel,
Seeking the bubble reputation
Even in the cannon's mouth. And then the justice,
In fair round belly with good capon lined,
With eyes severe and beard of formal cut,
Full of wise saws and modern instances;
And so he plays his part. The sixth age shifts
Into the lean and slippered pantaloon,
With spectacles on nose and pouch on side,
His youthful hose, well saved, a world too wide
For his shrunk shank; and his big manly voice,
Turning again toward childish treble, pipes
And whistles in his sound. Last scene of all,
That ends this strange, eventful history,
Is second childishness and mere oblivion,
Sans teeth, sans eyes, sans taste, sans everything.

QUESTIONS

Reading for Understanding

1. Students often find Shakespeare's language difficult to read. Sometimes, however, they find that once the old-fashioned words are

explained, his plays are not so difficult to understand, especially when acted or read aloud. Most young people, for instance, find Mel Gibson's film version of *Hamlet* easy to follow. In the passage above, several words may not be familiar to today's American readers. *Mewling* means crying with a catlike sound. *Bearded like the pard* means having a mustache like a leopard. *Jealous in honor* means quick to anger when shown disrespect, or *dissed*, to use today's slang. A *capon* is a tasty fowl often given to judges in those days as a bribe. *Saws* are wise sayings. *Modern instances* are current examples. A *pantaloon* is a pair of trousers; the word came to refer to a ridiculous old man in plays. The *shank* is the calf. *Mere oblivion* means complete forgetfulness. *Sans* is the French word for *without*.

2. Does this poetic picture of life's stages seem optimistic or pessimistic about life? Does Shakespeare describe certain phases as happier than others? Shakespeare died at 52; would his portrayal of old age have been different if he had lived to be very old?

3. This is obviously a picture of the changes in a man's life. How might the changes have been different for a woman?

4. Are the changes in people's lives nowadays, as described, for example, in Gail Sheehy's *Passages,* similar to the changes Shakespeare describes?

Noticing Writing Techniques

1. Shakespeare's plays are written predominantly in *blank verse.* This verse form is not rhymed but has a regular line length and meter. Each line has five *feet,* or syllable combinations, and is called *pentameter.* Each foot is *iambic,* meaning that the first syllable is unaccented, the second accented. Most lines do not follow this pattern of *iambic pentameter* strictly because that would be too monotonous. One line that does is "With **eyes** se**vere** and **beard** of **for**mal **cut**." Read this line aloud with heavy emphasis on the accented syllables and you can recognize the pattern of iambic pentameter used with more variety throughout the passage.

2. Shakespeare uses the metaphor of life as a theater in which people change roles as they get older. Compare this to Gail Sheehy's metaphor of people as lobsters casting off outer shells and growing new ones. What does each metaphor make you feel about life's changes? Which one seems closer to your experience of change? Can you think of a different metaphor for life's changes?

Writing Topics

1. Write a paragraph describing a typical person of a certain age—young adult, middle-aged person, or elderly person. Try to describe familiar,

recognizable features without *stereotyping*. Decide whether you want to make your description amusing, sad, respectful, admiring, or pleasant, and be sure that all your details help create the same impression. Note: would you say Shakespeare is describing his subject sympathetically or making fun of him, or both? Review Descriptive Paragraphs in Unit 2 and Using Specific Language in Unit 4.

2. Write an essay about *stereotypes*. Give examples of some of the common stereotypes you have seen in films and on television. Explain the effects of stereotypes in books, films, and television programs. Do they harm the quality of the work itself? Do they harm individuals and society? Can there be positive stereotypes? Review Expository Essays in Unit 3 and Thinking Critically in Unit 1.

Edgar Lee Masters (1869–1950)

Raised in Petersburg, Illinois, Edgar Lee Masters strove to write truly American poetry in the tradition of Walt Whitman. He was a lawyer by profession and wrote in the language of ordinary people about the ordinary events of small town life—but found in these lives poetic meaning and intense feeling. *Spoon River Anthology* (1915), his best-known work, is a collection of poems that are imaginary epitaphs of common people who died in the small town of Spoon River. "Lucinda Matlock," in contrast to Shakespeare's passage, describes the stages of a woman's life rather than a man's.

Lucinda Matlock* from *Spoon River Anthology*

I went to the dances at Chandlerville,
And played snap-out at Winchester.
One time we changed partners,
Driving home in the moonlight of middle June,
And then I found Davis.
We were married and lived together for seventy years,
Enjoying, working, raising the twelve children,
Eight of whom we lost
Ere I had reached the age of sixty.
I spun, I wove, I kept the house, I nursed the sick,
I made the garden, and for holiday

---

*"Lucinda Matlock" from SPOON RIVER ANTHOLOGY by Edgar Lee Masters, Copyright 1992 University of Illinois Press.

Rambled over the fields where sang the larks,
And by Spoon River gathering many a shell,
And many a flower and medicinal weed—
Shouting to the wooded hills, singing to the green valleys.
At ninety-six I had lived enough, that is all,
And passed to a sweet repose.
What is this I hear of sorrow and weariness,
Anger, discontent and drooping hopes?
Degenerate sons and daughters,
Life is too strong for you—
It takes life to love Life.

QUESTIONS

Reading for Understanding

1. What attitude toward her life does this woman express in looking back on it? Would you call her optimistic or pessimistic? How did her life experiences create this attitude in her? Do you admire her attitude? Do you agree with it?

2. Why does she refer to the younger generation of men and women as "degenerate"? Would she describe today's younger generation that way? Is her attitude fair? Her life obviously had many difficulties and tragedies; is it possible, however, that she is insufficiently sensitive to new difficulties faced by younger generations? What new problems do today's young people face that she did not?

3. Which of her experiences could have happened only to a woman? How are most women's lives different now? Are they better or worse?

Noticing Writing Techniques

1. Edgar Lee Masters intended to write in plain American English as spoken by ordinary people. Does the language of this poem fit that description? Is anything in the language old-fashioned?

2. This poem is written in the *first person singular,* meaning the writer uses the pronoun *I* frequently. However, the speaker is Lucinda Matlock, a woman who died at 96, not the poet, who is a much younger man. Why did Edgar Lee Masters tell the story of this woman's life in her own words through the first person singular? How is the effect of the poem different from that of Shakespeare's, which refers to "each man" in the third person? Do you identify more easily with writing in the first person or third person?

3. This poem is written in plain language, uses no metaphors, and contains neither rhyme nor regular meter. Should it still be called a poem? If so, what makes it a poem?

Noticing Vocabulary

_____ 1. A state of *repose* means a state of
    A. excitement   B. thoughtfulness
    C. rest   D. change.

_____ 2. *Degenerate* sons and daughters are
    A. fun-loving   B. rebellious
    C. outspoken   D. morally degraded.

Writing Topics

1. Write a paragraph describing a very old person you know; try to give an impression of the person's attitude toward life as well as how he or she looks and behaves. Review Descriptive Paragraphs in Unit 2 and Portraying a Person under the Descriptive Mode in Unit 3.

2. Write an essay expressing your opinion about how we treat old people in this society. Use examples from your own life or from what you have seen on television or in the movies to illustrate your points. If you have lived in another country, compare the American way of treating old people with the way younger people treat the elderly in the country of your origin. Review Expository Essays in Unit 3.

LEARNING EXPERIENCES

Writing and learning go together. Writing is one of the best ways of learning a subject we are studying, and writing can reinforce our understanding of a subject we have already studied. Writing can also help us comprehend more fully the learning experiences that we have had outside school. Finally, the writing process is a learning experience in itself because while creating a paragraph or essay we explore, organize, and analyze facts and ideas stored in our minds. By working with materials that we already know, we create something we didn't know before. Learning and language go together in an activity that links reading, writing, listening, and speaking.

The readings in this section emphasize these linkages. They center on learning experiences and the way language makes learning possible. Learning, however, is not limited to classrooms and books, though both are important. The authors of these essays, stories, and poems recognize that as long as we are alive we are learning. What matters is what we learn and how strongly we respond to the learning opportunities life offers, both in school and out.

For a person who is capable of learning, some of the most powerful lessons come from experiences that were never intended to be lessons and people who never thought of themselves as teachers. What we learn in school should help us understand life experience, and life experience sheds light on what we study in school. If you entered college at the traditional age of 18, you already have a lot of life experience to enrich your understanding of course material you study in sociology, history, psychology, and literature. If, like many of today's students, especially at two-year colleges, you entered college at a later stage in your life, you can take advantage of the much larger range of adult experiences you bring to your courses.

Jamaica Kincaid (1949–   )

Born and educated in the Caribbean island of Antigua, Jamaica Kincaid emigrated to the United States in 1966. She wrote many stories for the *New Yorker,* including "Girl," which she later included in her collection *At the Bottom of the River* (1983). Her novel *Annie John* (1985) gained critical praise and remains popular.

Girl*

Wash the white clothes on Monday and put them on the stone heap; wash the color clothes on Tuesday and put them on the clothesline to dry; don't walk barehead in the hot sun; cook pumpkin fritters in very hot sweet oil; soak your little cloths right after you take them off; when buying cotton to make yourself a nice blouse, be sure that it doesn't have gum on it, because that way it won't hold up well after a wash; soak salt fish overnight before you cook it; is it true that you sing benna[1] in Sunday school?; always eat your food in such a way that it won't turn someone else's stomach; on Sundays try to walk like a lady and not like the slut you are so bent on becoming; don't sing benna in Sunday school; you mustn't speak to wharf-rat boys, not even to give directions; don't eat fruits on the street—flies will follow you; *but I don't sing benna on Sundays at all and never in Sunday school;* this is how to sew on a button; this is how to make a buttonhole for the button you have just sewed on; this is how to hem a dress when you see the hem coming down and so to prevent yourself from looking like the slut you are so bent on becoming; this is how to iron your father's khaki shirt so that it doesn't have a crease; this is how you grow okra[2]— far from the house, because okra tree harbors red ants; when you are growing

---

1. calypso or rock and roll

2. plant with edible green pods

*"Girl" from AT THE BOTTOM OF THE RIVER by Jamaica Kincaid. Copyright © 1978, 1983 by Jamaica Kincaid. Reprinted by permission of Farrar, Straus & Giroux, Inc.

dasheen,[3] make sure it gets plenty of water or else it makes your throat itch when you are eating it; this is how you sweep a corner; this is how you sweep a whole house; this is how you sweep a yard; this is how you smile to someone you don't like too much; this is how you smile to someone you don't like at all; this is how you smile to someone you like completely; this is how you set a table for tea; this is how you set a table for dinner; this is how you set a table for lunch; this is how you set a table for breakfast; this is how to behave in the presence of men who don't know you very well, and this way they won't recognize immediately the slut I have warned you against becoming; be sure to wash every day, even if it is with your own spit; don't squat down to play marbles—you are not a boy, you know; don't pick people's flowers—you might catch something; don't throw stones at blackbirds, because it might not be a blackbird at all; this is how to make a bread pudding; this is how to make doukona[4]; this is how to make pepper pot; this is how to make a good medicine for a cold; this is how to make a good medicine to throw away a child before it even becomes a child; this is how to catch a fish; this is how to throw back a fish you don't like, and that way something bad won't fall on you; this is how to bully a man; this is how a man bullies you; this is how to love a man, and if this doesn't work there are other ways, and if they don't work don't feel too bad about giving up; this is how to spit up in the air if you feel like it, and this is how to move quick so that it doesn't fall on you; this is how to make ends meet; always squeeze bread to make sure it's fresh; *but what if the baker won't let me feel the bread?*; you mean to say that after all you are really going to be the kind of woman who the baker won't let near the bread?

QUESTIONS

Reading for Understanding

1. What sort of woman does this mother want her daughter to become? Does she seem to trust her daughter? Does her advice suggest that her daughter is a small child, a teenager, or a young adult?

2. What sort of relationship does the mother expect to have with her daughter? Is this typical of most mother-daughter relationships in the United States today?

3. What categories of advice does this story contain? See Exposition: Classification Paragraphs in Unit 2.

4. Do you think the daughter learned most of this advice and followed her mother's guidance? Why or why not? Do you find the advice wise,

---

3. tropical plant with edible root

4. spicy pudding often made from plantain

foolish, valuable, or funny? Which statements do you agree with? Disagree with?

5. What does the mother want to teach her daughter about the role of women in society?

Noticing Writing Techniques

1. Why does Jamaica Kincaid write all of this advice as one long sentence connected by semicolons in a single long paragraph? What does this technique suggest about her mother's way of talking to her daughter? What does the mother's response to the daughter's two remarks show?

2. Why does the author jumble up very serious pointers about life with very minor advice on practical matters?

3. How does the author's writing technique create humor while still showing respect for her mother's teaching?

Writing Topics

1. Write a paragraph explaining how to perform specific duties you have done in a job you have had recently. Imagine you are giving advice to a substitute who is going to take over your job temporarily. Alternative topic: Write a paragraph advising a prospective student how to succeed in one of the courses you have taken in college. Review "How-To" Paragraphs in Unit 2.

2. Write an essay explaining what you have learned from your parents. Group your material into several parts based either on categories of knowledge you have gained or on different ways you learned from them (what they told you, what you learned from their actions, what they said to others, what they avoided saying, etc.). Review Enumerating Examples in Unit 3 under the Expository Mode.

Richard Rodriguez (1944–   )

Like many of today's students, Richard Rodriguez learned English as a second language. Born in San Francisco of Mexican parents, he went through a painful effort to acquire perfect English by having to give up speaking Spanish at home. He went on to higher education, attending Stanford University, Columbia University, and the University of California at Berkeley. His autobiography, *Hunger of Memory: The Education of Richard Rodriguez*

(1982), remains one of the important books on education, immigration, and language.

Bilingual Education* from *Hunger of Memory*

Supporters of bilingual education today imply that students like me miss a great deal by not being taught in their family's language. What they seem not to recognize is that, as a socially disadvantaged child, I considered Spanish to be a private language. What I needed to learn in school was that I had the right—and the obligation—to speak the public language of *los gringos.* The odd truth is that my first-grade classmates could have become bilingual, in the conventional sense of that word, more easily than I. Had they been taught (as upper-middle-class children are often taught early) a second language like Spanish or French, they could have regarded it simply as that: another public language. In my case such bilingualism could not have been so quickly achieved. What I did not believe was that I could speak a single public language.

Without question, it would have pleased me to hear my teachers address me in Spanish when I entered the classroom. I would have felt much less afraid. I would have trusted them and responded with ease. But I would have delayed—for how long postponed?—having to learn the language of public society. I would have evaded—and for how long could I have afforded to delay?—learning a great lesson of school, that I had a public identity.

Fortunately, my teachers were unsentimental about their responsibility. What they understood was that I needed to speak a public language. So their voices would search me out, asking questions. Each time I'd hear them, I'd look up in surprise to see a nun's face frowning at me. I'd mumble, not really meaning to answer. The nun would persist, "Richard, stand up. Don't look at the floor. Speak up. Speak to the entire class, not just to me!" But I couldn't believe that the English language was mine to use. (In part, I did not want to believe it.) I continued to mumble. I resisted the teacher's demands. (Did I somehow suspect that once I learned public language my pleasing family life would be changed?) Silent, waiting for the bell to sound, I remained dazed, diffident, afraid. Because I wrongly imagined that English was intrinsically a public language and Spanish an intrinsically private one, I easily noted the difference between classroom language and the language of home. At school, words were directed to a general audience of listeners. ("Boys and girls.") Words were meaningfully ordered. And the point was not self-expression alone but to make oneself understood by the others. The teacher quizzed: "Boys and girls, why do we use that word in this sentence? Could we think of a better word to use there? Would the sentence change its meaning if the words were differently arranged? And wasn't there a better way of saying much the same thing?" (I couldn't say. I wouldn't try to say.)

Three months. Five. Half a year passed. Unsmiling, ever watchful, my teachers noted my silence. They began to connect my behavior with the difficult progress my older sister and brother were making. Until one Saturday morning three nuns arrived at the house to talk to our parents. Stiffly, they sat on the blue living room sofa. From the doorway of the other room, spying the visitors, I noted the incongruity—the clash of two worlds, the faces and voices of school intruding upon the familiar setting of home. I overheard one voice gently wondering, "Do your children speak only Spanish at home, Mrs. Rodriguez?" While another voice added, "That Richard especially seems so timid and shy."

That Rich-heard!

With great tact the visitors continued, "Is it possible for you and your husband to encourage your children to practice their English when they are home?" Of course, my parents complied. What would they not do for their children's well-being? And how could they have questioned the Church's authority which those women represented? In an instant, they agreed to give up the language (the sounds) that had revealed and accentuated our family's closeness. The moment after the visitors left, the change was observed. "*Ahora,* speak to us *en ingles,*" my mother and father united to tell us. At first, it seemed a kind of game. After dinner each night, the family gathered to practice "our" English. (It was still then *ingles,* a language foreign to us, so we felt drawn as strangers to it.) Laughing, we would try to define words we could not pronounce. We played with strange English sounds, often overanglicizing our pronunciations. And we filled the smiling gaps of our sentences with familiar Spanish sounds. But that was cheating, somebody shouted. Everyone laughed. In school, meanwhile, like my brother and sister, I was required to attend a daily tutoring session. I needed a full year of special attention. I also needed my teachers to keep my attention from straying in class by calling out, *Rich-heard*—their English voices slowly prying loose my ties to my other name, its three notes, *Ri-car-do.* Most of all I needed to hear my mother and father speak to me in a moment of seriousness in broken—suddenly heartbreaking—English. The scene was inevitable: One Saturday morning I entered the kitchen where my parents were talking in Spanish. I did not realize that they were talking in Spanish however until, at the moment they saw me, I heard their voices change to speak English. Those *gringo* sounds they uttered startled me. Pushed me away. In that moment of trivial misunderstanding and profound insight, I felt my throat twisted by unsounded grief. I turned quickly and left the room. But I had no place to escape to with Spanish. (The spell was broken.) My brother and sisters were speaking English in another part of the house.

Again and again in the days following, increasingly angry, I was obliged to hear my mother and father: "Speak to us *en ingles.*" (*Speak.*) Only then did I determine to learn classroom English. Weeks after, it happened: One day in school I raised my hand to volunteer an answer. I spoke out in a loud voice. And I did not think it remarkable when the entire class understood. That day, I moved very far from the disadvantaged child I had been only days earlier. The belief, that calming assurance that I belonged in public, had at last taken hold.

Shortly after, I stopped hearing the high and loud sounds of *los gringos*. A more and more confident speaker of English, I didn't trouble to listen to how strangers sounded, speaking to me. And there simply were too many English-speaking people in my day for me to hear American accents anymore. Conversations quickened. Listening to persons who sounded eccentrically pitched voices, I usually noted their sounds for an initial few seconds before I concentrated on what they were saying. Conversations became content-full. Transparent. Hearing someone's tone of voice—angry or questioning or sarcastic or happy or sad—I didn't distinguish it from the words it expressed. Sound and word were thus tightly wedded. At the end of a day, I was often bemused, always relieved, to realize how "silent," though crowded with words, my day in public had been. (This public silence measured and quickened the change in my life.)

At last, seven years old, I came to believe what had been technically true since my birth: I was an American citizen.   .   .   .

My awkward childhood does not prove the necessity of bilingual education. My story discloses instead an essential myth of childhood—inevitable pain. If I rehearse here the changes in my private life after my Americanization, it is finally to emphasize the public gain. The loss implies the gain. The house I returned to each afternoon was quiet. Intimate sounds no longer rushed to the door to greet me. There were other noises inside. The telephone rang. Neighborhood kids ran past the door of the bedroom where I was reading my schoolbooks—covered with shopping-bag paper. Once I learned public language, it would never again be easy for me to hear intimate family voices. More and more of my day was spent hearing words. But that may only be a way of saying that the day I raised my hand in class and spoke loudly to an entire roomful of faces, my childhood started to end.

QUESTIONS

Reading for Understanding

1. What is Richard Rodriguez's main point about bilingual education? Do you agree or disagree with it? What does he believe is the main purpose of school?

2. What personal experience does he use to support his point? Can you think of any personal experiences of your own or of people you know that support or challenge Rodriguez's main point?

3. Do you think there is any way for a child like Richard to learn English as well as he did without the painful experiences he endured?

4. As a child, Rodriguez experienced Spanish as a very different language from English. What was the difference? Was this a real difference be-

tween the languages or was it just a difference in the way he experienced the two languages?

Noticing Writing Techniques

1. This essay uses autobiographical narrative to support a persuasive main point. How strongly do you think Rodriguez supports his opinion by using his own experience? Would his point have been stronger if he had brought in facts, statistics, and examples from other people's experience?

2. Does he have any purpose other than stating an opinion about bilingual education? What does his experience show about education and schooling in general? About childhood in general?

3. Why does Rodriguez frequently put words, phrases, and statements in parentheses? How does this affect you as a reader? Why does he use occasional Spanish words or phrases? Would it have been better if he had used more?

Noticing Vocabulary

_____ 1. *Diffident* means
    A. frightening   B. friendly
    C. timid   D. strange.

_____ 2. *Intrinsically* means
    A. by its nature   B. frequently
    C. infrequently   D. harmoniously.

_____ 3. An *incongruity* is
    A. a mistake   B. an inconsistency
    C. an accident   D. a stroke of good luck.

_____ 4. Something that is *accentuated* is
    A. desired   B. searched for
    C. made smaller   D. emphasized.

Writing Topics

1. Write a paragraph telling about your first day in school. Describe your feelings about it, your school itself, and your impression of your classmates and teacher. Review Paragraphs of Narration and Description in Unit 2.

2. Write an essay explaining how schools could be improved so that all students would learn better and enjoy learning. Use examples from

your own school experiences and those of people you know. Make realistic proposals, not ones that would be impossible to consider (some
might be too expensive, for instance, or violate state laws that required
public schools to admit all students in their districts). Review Prob-
lem/Solution Essays under the Expository Mode in Unit 3.

Zora Neale Hurston (1891–1960)

One of the premier talents of the Harlem Renaissance, Zora Neale Hurston has recently become
world famous for her novels, short stories, and
nonfiction. During her lifetime, however, she
rarely received the attention her writing deserved.
It remained for Alice Walker and others to redis-
cover Hurston's humor, originality, and vivid style.
In this passage from her autobiography, *Dust Tracks
on a Road* (1942), she tells about a period when, as a
young woman, she worked for a musical theater
company. Although she was not in school at the
time, the stint turned out to be one of the richest
learning experiences of her life and ended with her
going off to school. Later she was to attend Morgan
Academy (later called Morgan State University),
Howard University, and Barnard College in New
York. As she makes clear, however, she responded
to and learned from every situation.

Backstage* from *Dust Tracks on a Road*

The company, a Gilbert and Sullivan repertoire, had its own coach. That was
another glory to dazzle my eyes. The leading man had a valet, and the con-
tralto had an English maid, both white. I was the only Negro around. But that
did not worry me in the least. I had no chance to be lonesome, because the
company welcomed me like, or as, a new play-pretty. It did not strike me as
curious then. I never even thought about it. Now, I can see the reason for it.

In the first place, I was a Southerner, and had the map of Dixie on my
tongue. They were all Northerners except the orchestra leader, who came
from Pensacola. It was not that my grammar was bad, it was the idioms. They
did not know of the way an average Southern child, white or black, is raised
on simile and invective. They know how to call names. It is an everyday affair
to hear somebody called a mullet-headed, mule-eared, wall-eyed, hog-nosed,

'gator-faced, shad-mouthed, screw-necked, goat-bellied, puzzle-gutted, camel-backed, butt-sprung, battle-hammed, knock-kneed, razor-legged, box-ankled, shovel-footed, unmated so-and-so! Eyes looking like skint-ginny nuts, and mouth looking like a dish-pan full of broke-up crockery! They can tell you in simile exactly how you walk and smell. They can furnish a picture gallery of your ancestors, and a notion of what your children will be like. What ought to happen to you is full of images and flavor. Since that stratum of the Southern population is not given to book-reading, they take their comparisons right out of the barnyard and the woods. When they get through with you, you and your whole family look like an acre of totem poles.

First thing, I was young and green, so the baritone started out teasing me the first day. I jumped up and told him to stop trying to run the hog over me! That set everybody off. They teased me all the time just to hear me talk. But there was no malice in it. If I got mad and spoke my piece, they liked it even better. I was stuffed with ice-cream sodas and Coca-cola.

Another reason was that it was fun to them to get hold of somebody whom they could shock. I was hurt to my heart because the company manager called me into his dressing-room and asked me how I liked my job. After I got through telling him how pleased I was, he rushed out with his face half-made up screaming, "Stop, oh, Zora! Please stop! Shame on you! Telling me a dirty story like that. Oh! I have never been so shocked in all my life!"

Heads popped out of dressing-rooms all over. Groans, sad head-shakings and murmurs of outrage. Sad! Sad! They were glad I had not told them such a thing. Too bad! Too bad! Not a smile in the crowd. The more I tried to explain the worse it got. Some locked their doors to shield their ears from such contamination. Finally Miss M____ broke down and laughed and told me what the gag was. For a long while nobody could get me inside a dressing-room outside of Miss M____'s. But that didn't stop the teasing. They would think up more, like having one of the men contrive to walk down the aisle with me and then everybody lift shocked eyebrows, pretend to blush and wink at each other and sigh, "Zora! Zora! What would your mother say!" I would be so upset that I wouldn't know what to do. Maybe they really believed I wasn't nice!

Another sly trick they played on my ignorance was that some of the men would call me and with a very serious face send me to some of the girls to ask about the welfare and condition of cherries and spangles. They would give me a tip and tell me to hurry back with the answer. Some of the girls would send back word that the men need not worry their heads at all. They would never know the first thing about the condition of their cherries and spangles. Some of the girls sent answers full of double talk which went over my head. The soubrette spoke her mind to the men about that practice and it stopped.

But none of this had malice in it. Just their idea of good backstage gags. By the time they stopped, it seemed that I was necessary to everybody. I was continually stuffed with sweets, nut meats, and soft drinks. I was welcome in everybody's coach seat and the girls used to pinch pennies to see who carried me off to their hotel rooms. We played games and told stories. They often ordered beer and pretzels, but nobody offered me a drink. I heard all about their love affairs and troubles. They were all looking forward to playing or singing

leads some day. Some great personage had raved about all of their performances. The dirty producers and casting directors just hadn't given them
their chance. Miss M___ finally put a stop to my going off with the others as
soon as she was ready for bed. I had to stay wherever she stayed after that.
She had her own affairs to talk about.

She paid for a course for me in manicuring and I practiced on everybody
until I became very efficient at it. That course came in handy to me later on.

With all this petting, I became as cocky as a sparrow on Fifth Avenue. I got
a scrapbook, and everybody gave me a picture to put in it. I pasted each one
on a separate page and wrote comments under each picture. This created a
great deal of interest, because some of the comments were quite pert. They
egged me on to elaborate. Then I got another idea. I would comment on daily
doings and post the sheets on the call-board. This took on right away. The result stayed strictly mine less than a week because members of the cast began
to call me aside and tell me things to put in about others. It got to be so general
that everybody was writing it. It was just my handwriting, mostly. Then it got
beyond that. Most of the cast ceased to wait for me. They would take a pencil
to the board and set down their own item. Answers to the wisecracks would
appear promptly and often cause uproarious laughter. They always started off
with either "Zora says" or "The observant reporter of the Call-board as-
serts"—Lord, Zora said more *things!* I was continually astonished, but always
amused. There were, of course, some sly digs at supposedly secret love affairs
at times, but no vicious thrusts. Everybody enjoyed it, even the victims.

When the run came to an end, Miss M___ had a part in another show all
set, but rehearsals would not start for two weeks, so she took me to her home in
Boston and I found out some things which I did not want to know, particularly.

At times she had been as playful as a kitten. At others, she would be
solemn and moody. She loved her mother excessively, but when she received
those long, wordy letters from her, she read them with a still face, and tore
them up carefully. Then she would be gloomy, and keep me beside her every
minute. Sometimes she would become excessively playful. It was puzzling to
see a person cry awhile and then commence to romp like a puppy and keep it
up for hours. Sometimes she had to have sherry before she went to bed after a
hard romp with me. She invented a game for us to play in our hotel room. It
was known as "Jake." She would take rouge and paint her face all over a most
startling red. Then I must take eye shadow and paint myself blue. Blue Jake
and Red Jake would then chase each other into closets, across beds, into bathrooms, with our sheet-robes trailing around us and tripping us up at odd moments. We crouched and growled and ambushed each other and laughed and
yelled until we were exhausted.

Then maybe next day she hardly said a word.

While I was with her, she met a wealthy business man of Newark, and I
could tell that she was sunk. It all happened very suddenly, but gloriously.
She told me that now that she was going to get married and leave the stage,
she did not want me to work for anyone else in the business. In fact, she
thought that I should not be working at all. I ought to be in school. She said

she thought I had a mind, and that it would be a shame for me not to have any further training. She wished that she herself could go abroad to study, but that was definitely out of the question, now. The deep reservoir of things inside her gave off a sigh.

We were in northern Virginia then, and moving towards Baltimore. When we got there, she inquired about schools, gave me a big bearful hug, and what little money she could spare and told me to keep in touch with her. She would do whatever she could to help me out.

That was the way we parted. I had been with her for eighteen months and though neither of us realized it, I had been in school all that time. I had loosened up in every joint and expanded in every direction.

I had done some reading. Not as much as before, but more discriminate reading. The tenor was a Harvard man who had traveled on the Continent. He always had books along with him, and offered them to me more and more. The first time I asked to borrow one, he looked at me in a way that said "What for?" But when he found that I really read it and enjoyed it, he relaxed and began to hand them to me gruffly. He never acted as if he liked it, but I knew better. That was just the Harvard in him.

Then there was the music side. They broke me in to good music, that is, the classics, if you want to put it that way. There was no conscious attempt to do this. Just from being around, I became familiar with Gilbert and Sullivan, and the best parts of the light-opera field. Grand opera too, for all of the leads had backgrounds of private classical instruction as well as conservatory training. Even the bit performers and the chorus had some kind of formal training in voice, and most of them played the piano. It was not unusual for some of the principals to drop down at the piano after a matinee performance and begin to sing arias from grand opera. Sing them with a wistfulness. The arias which they would sing at the Metropolitan or La Scala as they had once hoped actively, and still hoped passively even as the hair got thinner and the hips got heavier. Others, dressed for the street, would drift over and ease into the singing. Thus I would hear solos, duets, quartets and sextets from the best-known operas. They would eagerly explain to me what they were when I asked. They would go on to say how Caruso, Farrar, Mary Garden, Trentini, Schumann-Heink, Matenzauer, and so forth had interpreted this or that piece, and demonstrate it by singing. Perhaps that was their trouble. They were not originators, but followers of originators. Anyway, it was perfectly glorious for me, though I am sure nobody thought of it that way. I just happened to be there while they released their inside dreams.

The experience had matured me in other ways. I had seen, I had been privileged to see folks substituting love for failure of career. I would listen to one and another pour out their feelings sitting on a stool backstage between acts and scenes. Then too, I had seen careers filling up the empty holes left by love, and covering up the wreck of things internal. Those experiences, though vicarious, made me see things and think.

And now, at last it was all over. It was not at all clear to me how I was going to do it, but I was going back to school.

QUESTIONS

Reading for Understanding

1. What does Zora Hurston mean when she says that she had actually been in school during the whole year and a half working in the theater company? What are some of the things she learned? Who taught them to her?

2. How might what she learned from this experience have helped her become a writer of novels and stories later? What did she do at this time that might hint that she would become a novelist later?

3. Zora Hurston is both praised and criticized for her extremely positive view of what happened to her and of people's motives. Did you at any time feel that she was too favorable or optimistic about the situation she was in? How did her positive attitude help her enjoy the experience and learn from it?

4. This passage gives a picture of actors who never made the big time (compare this description with films like *Bull Durham* and others about minor league athletes). What does Hurston make you feel and understand about such people? What are their good traits? What are their weaknesses? Does she seem to be like them or different from them?

5. At the end of this experience Hurston decided to go back to school. What in this experience might have led her to seek higher education?

Noticing Writing Techniques

1. Hurston is often praised for her imaginative, original style, in particular her poetic touches. What examples can you find of similes (poetic comparisons), unusual and original phrasing, and vivid choice of descriptive words?

2. Hurston calls this episode a maturing experience and she is telling it years later from the point of view of a more mature woman. How is her tone or attitude different in telling the story than it might have been if she were telling about it at the time it was happening?

Noticing Vocabulary

_____ 1. *Idioms* are
   A. stupid people   B. familiar phrases
   C. scientific laws   D. rules of grammar.

_____ 2. A *simile* is

    A. a poetic comparison   B. a happy statement

    C. a set of instructions   D. a difficult lesson.

_____ 3. *Invective* is

    A. high praise   B. foreign phrases

    C. medicine for a fever   D. insulting language.

_____ 4. A social *stratum* is a

    A. form of employment   B. method of analysis

    C. social level or class   D. form of religious belief

_____ 5. A *soubrette* is a

    A. lady's maid   B. female manager

    C. prostitute   D. leading actress.

_____ 6. *Discriminate* reading means

    A. interesting   B. highly selective

    C. inexpensive   D. full of insights and information.

Writing Topics

1. Write a paragraph describing a person from whom you learned something. This may be a teacher whose job was to instruct you, or it may be someone from whom you learned by example. Review Types of Paragraphs: Description in Unit 2 and and Portraying a Person in the Descriptive Mode of Unit 3.

2. Hurston calls her stint in the theater company a maturing experience. Write an essay about an experience of your own that helped you to grow up and to have mature attitudes and insights. Although Hurston analyzes the meaning of her experience after telling the story, you can also, if you prefer, analyze the meaning of your experience while you are telling about it. Choose, if possible, an experience in which you had to relate to people different from you in race, religion, age, or economic level. Review Narrative Essays and Autobiographical Example in Unit 3.

Helen Keller (1880–1968)

Stricken with a disease that left her both deaf and blind in her infancy, Helen Keller was one of the most astonishing learners in history. Aided by Anne Sullivan, her dedicated teacher, she not only learned to communicate through touch, but went on to achieve a higher education at Radcliffe College and become a celebrity and author. In this part of her autobiography, she tells about the day when Anne Sullivan entered her life.

The Most Important Day*
from *The Story of My Life*

The most important day I remember in all my life is the one on which my teacher, Anne Mansfield Sullivan, came to me. I am filled with wonder when I consider the immeasurable contrast between the two lives which it connects. It was the third of March, 1887, three months before I was seven years old.

On the afternoon of that eventful day, I stood on the porch, dumb, expectant. I guessed vaguely from my mother's signs and from the hurrying to and fro in the house that something unusual was about to happen, so I went to the door and waited on the steps. The afternoon sun penetrated the mass of honeysuckle that covered the porch and fell on my upturned face. My fingers lingered almost unconsciously on the familiar leaves and blossoms which had just come forth to greet the sweet southern spring. I did not know what the future held of marvel or surprise for me. Anger and bitterness had preyed upon me continually for weeks and a deep languor had succeeded this passionate struggle.

Have you ever been at sea in a dense fog, when it seemed as if a tangible white darkness shut you in, and the great ship, tense and anxious, groped her way toward the shore with plummet and sounding-line, and you waited with beating heart for something to happen? I was like that ship before my education began, only I was without compass or sounding-line, and had no way of knowing how near the harbor was. "Light! give me light!" was the wordless cry of my soul, and the light of love shone on me in that very hour.

I felt approaching footsteps. I stretched out my hand as I supposed to my mother. Someone took it, and I was caught up and held close in the arms of her who had come to reveal all things to me, and, more than all things else, to love me.

The morning after my teacher came she led me into her room and gave me a doll. The little blind children at the Perkins Institution had sent it and Laura Bridgman had dressed it; but I did not know this until afterward. When I had played with it a little while, Miss Sullivan slowly spelled into my hand the word "d-o-l-l." I was at once interested in this finger play and tried to imitate it. When I finally succeeded in making the letters correctly I was flushed with childish pleasure and pride. Running downstairs to my mother I held up my

---

hand and made the letters for doll. I did not know that I was spelling a word or even that words existed; I was simply making my fingers go in monkeylike imitation. In the days that followed I learned to spell in this uncomprehending way a great many words, among them pin, hat, cup and a few verbs like sit, stand and walk. But my teacher had been with me several weeks before I understood that everything has a name.

One day, while I was playing with my new doll, Miss Sullivan put my big rag doll into my lap also, spelled "d-o-l-l" and tried to make me understand that "d-o-l-l" applied to both. Earlier in the day we had a tussle over the words "m-u-g" and "w-a-t-e-r." Miss Sullivan had tried to impress it upon me that "m-u-g" is mug and that "w-a-t-e-r" is water, but I persisted in confounding the two. In despair she had dropped the subject for the time, only to renew it at the first opportunity. I became impatient at her repeated attempts and, seizing the new doll, I dashed it upon the floor. I was keenly delighted when I felt the fragments of the broken doll at my feet. Neither sorrow nor regret followed my passionate outburst. I had not loved the doll. In the still, dark world in which I lived there was no strong sentiment or tenderness. I felt my teacher sweep the fragments to one side of the hearth, and I had a sense of satisfaction that the cause of my discomfort was removed. She brought me my hat, and I knew I was going out into the warm sunshine. This thought, if a wordless sensation may be called a thought, made me hop and skip with pleasure.

We walked down the path to the well-house, attracted by the fragrance of the honeysuckle with which it was covered. Some one was drawing water and my teacher placed my hand under the spout. As the cool stream gushed over one hand she spelled into the other the word water, first slowly, then rapidly. I stood still, my whole attention fixed upon the motions of her fingers. Suddenly I felt a misty consciousness as of something forgotten—a thrill of returning thought; and somehow the mystery of language was revealed to me. I knew then that "w-a-t-e-r" meant the wonderful cool something that was flowing over my hand. The living word awakened my soul, gave it light, hope, joy, set it free! There were barriers still, it is true, but barriers that could in time be swept away.

I left the well-house eager to learn. Everything had a name, and each name gave birth to a new thought. As we returned to the house every object which I touched seemed to quiver with life. That was because I saw everything with the strange, new sight that had come to me. On entering the door I remembered the doll I had broken. I felt my way to the hearth and picked up the pieces. I tried vainly to put them together. Then my eyes filled with tears; for I realized what I had done, and for the first time I felt repentance and sorrow.

I learned a great many new words that day. I do not remember what they all were; but I do know that mother, father, sister, teacher were among them—words that were to make the world blossom for me, "like Aaron's rod, with flowers." It would have been difficult to find a happier child than I was as I lay in my crib at the close of that eventful day and lived over the joys it had brought me, and for the first time longed for a new day to come.

QUESTIONS

Reading for Understanding

1. What does Helen Keller mean by the "immeasurable contrast" between her life before Anne Sullivan came and her life afterward? What new elements came into her life?

2. What change in her attitude toward life occurred when she found she was able to use words and to learn?

Noticing Writing Techniques

1. How does Helen Keller use a visual comparison, one that she knows her reader will recognize even though she herself cannot see it? What physical sensations does she evoke that she was actually able to experience? Which of the five senses were important in the experience?

2. Keller tells about two days' events; one was the day Anne Sullivan arrived, and the second is a day several weeks later. What is the difference in what happened each time? Why does she skip from the one day to the other rather than tell a continuous story?

Noticing Vocabulary

_____ 1. To be in a state of *languor* is to be
    A. weak and tired   B. energetic
    C. curious   D. sad and bored.

_____ 2. A *tangible* object can be
    A. seen   B. heard
    C. touched   D. tasted.

_____ 3. A *plummet* is something that is
    A. cooked for dinner   B. served for dessert
    C. dropped into the water   D. used to catch fish.
       to measure depth

Writing Topics

1. Write a paragraph telling about the moment you overcame some difficulty, solved some problem, or mastered some skill for the first time. Review "How-To" Paragraphs and Narrative Paragraphs in Unit 2.

2. In our time, sufficient attention to the needs of handicapped people and planning to accommodate those needs is just beginning to be con-

sidered in most cities. Write an essay enumerating suggestions about what further arrangements should be made for the handicapped. Explain what kinds of accommodations can reasonably be expected and what kinds cannot. Review Problem/Solution Essays (pages 113–123) in Unit 3.

David Raymond (1959–   )

In 1976, when this piece appeared in the *New York Times*, David Raymond was a high school student. Like many students, he suffered from severe dyslexia, and, like millions of Americans, knew what it was like to be illiterate. Since then, much greater awareness of learning disabilities exists and schools tend to help students with them better than they used to. But anyone who has had trouble learning any skill can identify with his distress.

On Being 17, Bright, and Unable to Read*

One day a substitute teacher picked me to read aloud from the textbook. When I told her "No, thank you," she came unhinged. She thought I was acting smart, and told me so. I kept calm, and that got her madder and madder. We must have spent 10 minutes trying to solve the problem, and finally she got so red in the face I thought she'd blow up. She told me she'd see me after class.

Maybe someone like me was a new thing for that teacher. But she wasn't new to me. I've been through scenes like that all my life. You see, even though I'm 17 and a junior in high school, I can't read because I have dyslexia. I'm told I read "at a fourth-grade level," but from where I sit, that's not reading. You can't know what that means unless you've been there. It's not easy to tell how it feels when you can't read your homework assignments or the newspaper or a menu in a restaurant or even notes from your own friends.

My family began to suspect I was having problems almost from the first day I started school. My father says my early years in school were the worst years of his life. They weren't so good for me, either. As I look back now, I can't find the words to express how bad it really was. I wanted to die. I'd come home from school screaming, "I'm dumb. I'm dumb—I wish I were dead!"

I guess I couldn't read anything at all then—not even my own name—and they tell me I didn't talk as good as other kids. But what I remember about those days is that I couldn't throw a ball where it was supposed to go, I couldn't learn to swim, and I wouldn't learn to ride a bike, because no matter what anyone told me, I knew I'd fail.

---

*Copyright © 1975 by the New York Times Company. Reprinted by permission.

Sometimes my teachers would try to be encouraging. When I couldn't read the words on the board they'd say, "Come on, David, you know that word." Only I didn't. And it was embarrassing. I just felt dumb. And dumb was how the kids treated me. They'd make fun of me every chance they got, asking me to spell "cat" or something like that. Even if I knew how to spell it, I wouldn't; they'd only give me another word. Anyway, it was awful, because more than anything I wanted friends. On my birthday when I blew out candles I didn't wish I could learn to read; what I wished for was that the kids would like me.

With the bad reports coming from school, and with me moaning about wanting to die and how everybody hated me, my parents began looking for help. That's when the testing started. The school tested me, the child-guidance center tested me, private psychiatrists tested me. Everybody knew something was wrong—especially me.

It didn't help much when they stuck a fancy name onto it. I couldn't pronounce it then—I was only in second grade—and I was ashamed to talk about it. Now it rolls off my tongue, because I've been living with it for a lot of years—dyslexia.

All through elementary school it wasn't easy. I was always having to do things that were "different," things the other kids didn't have to do. I had to go to a child psychiatrist, for instance.

One summer my family forced me to go to a camp for children with reading problems. I hated the idea, but the camp turned out pretty good, and I had a good time. I met a lot of kids who couldn't read and somehow that helped. The director of the camp said I had a higher I.Q. than 90 percent of the population. I didn't believe him.

About the worst thing I had to do in fifth and sixth grade was go to a special education class in another school in our town. A bus picked me up, and I didn't like that at all. The bus also picked up emotionally disturbed kids and retarded kids. It was like going to a school for the retarded. I always worried that someone I knew would see me on that bus. It was a relief to go to the regular junior high school.

Life began to change a little for me then, because I began to feel better about myself. I found the teachers cared; they had meetings about me and I worked harder for them a while. I began to work on the potter's wheel, making vases and pots that the teachers said were pretty good. Also, I got a letter for being on the track team. I could always run pretty fast.

At high school the teachers are good and everyone is trying to help me. I've gotten honors some marking periods and I've won a letter on the cross-country team. Next quarter I think the school might hold a show of my pottery. I've got some friends. But there are still some embarrassing times. For instance, every time there is writing in the class, I get up and go to the special education room. Kids ask me where I go all the time. Sometimes I say, "to Mars."

Homework is a real problem. During free periods in school I go into the special ed room and staff members read assignments to me. When I get home my mother reads to me. Sometimes she reads an assignment into a tape recorder, and then I go into my room and listen to it. If we have a novel or something like that to read, she reads it out loud to me. Then I sit down with her and we do the assignment. She'll write, while I talk my answers to her. Lately I've taken to dictating into a tape recorder, and then someone—my father, a private tutor or my mother—types up what I've dictated. Whatever homework I do takes someone else's time, too. That makes me feel bad.

We had a big meeting in school the other day—eight of us, four from the guidance department, my private tutor, my parents and me. The subject was me. I said I wanted to go to college, and they told me about colleges that have facilities and staff to handle people like me. That's nice to hear.

As for what happens after college, I don't know and I'm worried about that. How can I make a living if I can't read? Who will hire me? How will I fill out the application form? The only thing that gives me any courage is the fact that I've learned about well-known people who couldn't read or had other problems and still made it. Like Albert Einstein, who didn't talk until he was 4 and flunked math. Like Leonardo da Vinci, who everyone seems to think had dyslexia.

I've told this story because maybe some teacher will read it and go easy on a kid in the classroom who has what I've got. Or, maybe some parent will stop nagging his kid, and stop calling him lazy. Maybe he's not lazy or dumb. Maybe he just can't read and doesn't know what's wrong. Maybe he's scared, like I was.

QUESTIONS

Reading for Understanding

1. What does David Raymond hope might happen if many people read his story of his problems? What was done wrong in his schooling?

2. Would you say he has a positive or negative attitude toward his life? Has his attitude changed over the years?

3. Why are learning disabilities like his often not recognized, either by those who have them or by parents and teachers?

Noticing Writing Techniques

1. This essay sounds like a high school student speaking. See if you can identify sentences, phrases, or particular words that make the article sound like a young adult talking informally.

2. David Raymond tells us his different feelings about what happened to him, but he never dwells at length on his feelings or describes them in great detail. What impression does he create of himself by avoiding lengthy explanations of his feelings? Does he come across to you as

modest, arrogant, friendly, hostile, thoughtful, or a mixture of different attitudes?

Writing Topics

1. Write a paragraph describing a person you know who had trouble learning in school. Explain why you believe he or she had difficulty and what that student or the teachers could have done about it. Review Descriptive Paragraphs in Unit 2.

2. Write an essay explaining some of the reasons why students with good abilities do poorly in school. Review the Persuasive Mode: Enumerating Reasons in Unit 3.

Margaret Mead (1901–1978)

Beginning with her classic *Coming of Age in Samoa* (1928), Margaret Mead wrote a series of studies of other cultures that made her the most famous American anthropologist. She took particular interest in the roles of women in different societies and analyzed American social patterns from the perspective of an anthropologist. In this section of her autobiography *Blackberry Winter* (1972) she recalls her first experience of college at DePauw University in Indiana, where she had come from the East Coast. Her experiences, particularly of the sorority system in American colleges, become the subject of a sort of anthropological analysis.

College: DePauw*
from *Blackberry Winter: My Earlier Years*

And so, even though it was decided that I was to go to DePauw rather than Bryn Mawr or Wellesley, I approached the idea of college with the expectation of taking part in an intellectual feast. I looked forward to studying fascinating subjects taught by people who understood what they were talking about. I imagined meeting brilliant students, students who would challenge me to stretch my mind and work instead of going skating with my lessons done well enough so that I led my classmates who hated what they were studying. In college, in some way that I devoutly believed in but could not explain, I expected to become a person.

At DePauw in 1919 I found students who were, for the most part, the first generation to go to college and whose parents appeared at Class Day poorly

---

*From BLACKBERRY WINTER by Margaret Mead. Copyright © 1972 by Margaret Mead. Reprinted by permission of William Morrow and Company, Inc.

dressed while their daughters wore the raccoon or the muskrat coats that were appropriate to the sorority they had made. It was a college to which students had come for fraternity life, for football games, and for establishing the kind of rapport with other people that would make them good Rotarians in later life and their wives good members of the garden club.

I arrived with books of poetry, portraits of great personalities to hang on the wall, and the snobberies of the East, such as the expectation that one dressed in the evening for the members of one's own family. And I was confronted by the snobbery and cruelty of the sorority system at its worst, with rules against rushing that prevented the women who had gone to college with my father and who had married my father's fraternity brothers from ever speaking to me or inviting me to their home—rules made by the Panhellenic Association in order to control competition that was so harsh and so unashamed that the very rules designed to control it made it even worse. This was my first and only real experience of discrimination—mild enough in all conscience.

It is very difficult to know how to evaluate how essential it is to have one's soul seared by the great injustices of one's own time—being born a serf or slave, a woman believed to have no mind or no soul, a black man or woman in a white man's world, a Jew among Christians who make a virtue of anti-Semitism, a miner among those who thought it good sport to hire Pinkertons to shoot down miners on strike. Such experiences sear the soul. They make their victims ache with bitterness and rage, with compassion for fellow sufferers or with blind determination to escape even on the backs of fellow sufferers. Such experiences can breed the desire to fight unrelentingly against the injustice that has let one's mother die because no doctor would attend her or let one's brother work in a mine because there was no school to recognize his talents—an injustice that substitutes arbitrary social categories for the recognition of humanity. Injustice experienced in the flesh, in deeply wounded flesh, is the stuff out of which change explodes. But the passionate fight for humanity—the fight to free slaves, free colonies, free women and children—also has been carried on by those who have never experienced, and in the case of whites fighting for blacks or men for women, never could experience in their own persons the depths of injustice against which they have fought. . . .

During the year I studied at DePauw, I did not deny that I was hurt, nor did I pretend to myself that I would have refused the chance to be accepted by a sorority. The truth is, I would not have known enough to refuse. And once inside, it is quite possible that I would have been as unseeing as the rest. As it was, what particularly offended me as the year wore on was the contrast between the vaunted democracy of the Middle West and the blatant, strident artificiality of the Greek-letter societies on that midwestern campus, the harshness of the rules that prevented my father's classmates from ever addressing a hospitable word to me, and, more than anything else, the lack of loyalty that rejection engendered among the chosen.

I discovered, too, that simple rejection was not enough. It had to be rubbed in. At that time it was fashionable for girls to wear what were called

Peter Thompson suits—tailored middy suits in dark-colored wool or pastel-colored linen. In the spring, when I too acquired a Peter Thompson suit, a prominent Theta, meeting me on the campus, roughly turned down my collar to look at the label, certainly expecting to find that my new dress was not authentic—as it was.

My unusual clothing was not all that was held against me. There was my room with its carefully planned color scheme, my books and pictures, and, above all, my tea set. And I did not chew gum. Then, as if these things were not enough, there was my accent. The big Freshman English Literature course was taught by a New Englander who conceived it to be his principal task to educate provincial Americans. The very first day he glared around the room and asked, "Does anyone in this class know how to pronounce c-a-l-f?" I volunteered, and when I used the broad *a* he commented, "Oh, you come from the East, don't you? Out here they say 'calf,'" and mockingly drew out the flat *a* sound. A third of the freshman class heard that doubtful compliment. There were two other students from the East. One was the daughter of a Methodist bishop who had formerly been the president of DePauw; the other was her close friend. That saved them. But I was branded. After a while some of my friends thought it was fun to get me to say, "I have been there," using the Bryn Mawr pronunciation, "bean," instead of the Midwestern "*bin.*" This usually happened when mothers came to visit and the girls wanted to show off the local curiosities.

And, although the sorority rejection was the sharper blow, there was another. I found out that I was also ineligible to belong to the Y.W.C.A. because, as an Epicscopalian, I did not belong to an Evangelical religion. There were five of us at DePauw who were religious rejects—myself, one Roman Catholic, one Greek Orthodox, one Lutheran, and one Jew. The Jew was David Lilienthal. On one occasion he was asked to give a talk to the Methodist Sunday School on the Jewish conception of Jesus. The rest of us were simply beyond the pale.

So I was confronted, for the first time in my life, with being thoroughly unacceptable to almost everyone and on grounds in which I had previously been taught to take pride. I responded by setting out to see what I could do within this system, which I found sufficiently uncongenial so that I spent no time lamenting my exclusion.

I wrote a stunt that was performed by the freshman dormitory, Mansfield Hall, as part of a competition in which we challenged the senior dormitory and the sororities—the first time this was done. I set to work to make the English honors society, Tusitala, which was the Samoan name that had been given Robert Louis Stevenson. I wrote and directed the pageant that the entire feminine student body, under the direction of the Department of Physical Education, gave each year. I also designed the freshman float for this occasion. And finally, I went into the political arena and succeeded in getting Katharine Rothenberger selected vice-president of the class by setting the sororities against one another. I was satisfied that by the end of the year I would have received a bid to join a sorority—probably at least two. For although no sorority might want to have me, each one would be afraid that I might become the property of a rival.

The teaching at DePauw was far less disappointing than the college social organization. In my catalogue I had marked courses totaling over 200 hours, even though 120 hours was all that a student could take in four years. I thoroughly enjoyed the magnificent teaching given by men who were first and foremost teachers, interested in their students and unharassed by the demand that they "publish or perish," an attitude that later came to haunt even small colleges like DePauw. The training in writing given me by Professor Pence was never equaled by anyone else. At DePauw I was introduced to discussions of the Old Testament prophets and the Social Gospel, and this firmly established association between the Old and the New Testament and the demands of social justice provided me with an ethical background up to the time of the development of ecumenicism and Vatican II. These courses were taught by deeply religious men who regarded it a privilege to be teaching where they were.

At DePauw, too, I took a course in History as Past Ethics, to which I still refer. However, there were only two girls and a couple of dozen boys in that class, and the two girls received the highest marks. As long as I was in high school, the greater maturity of adolescent girls had not struck me. But in the setting of this coeducational college it became perfectly clear both that bright girls could do better than bright boys and that they would suffer for it.

This made me feel that coeducation was thoroughly unattractive. I neither wanted to do bad work in order to make myself attractive to boys nor did I want them to dislike me for doing good work. It seemed to me that it would be much simpler to go to a girl's college where one could work as hard as one pleased.

This preference foreshadowed, I suppose, my anthropological field choices—not to compete with men in male fields, but instead to concentrate on the kinds of work that are better done by women. Actually, there are two kinds of field work that women can do better than men. One is working with women and children in situations in which male investigators are likely to be suspected and resented by the men of a society. The other is working with both men and women as an older woman, using a woman's postmenopausal high status to achieve an understanding of the different parts of a culture, particularly in those cultures in which women past the reproductive period are free from the constraints and taboos that constrict the lives of younger women. The first choice can be effectively exercised only in a situation in which the culture is being studied by a male-female pair or a team. For when a woman explicitly classifies herself with excluded women and uninitiated children, she does not have access to the rest of the culture. The second role is very practical for an older woman who is working alone in a culture that has already been explored by a male and female pair.

Nevertheless, as long as I remained at DePauw, I felt I was an exile. I used to sit in the library and read the drama reviews in *the New York Times*. Like so many other aspiring American intellectuals and artists, I developed the feeling that American small towns were essentially unfriendly to the life of the mind and the senses. I believed that the center of life was in New York City, where Mencken and George Jean Nathan were publishing *Smart Set,* where *The Freeman, The New Republic,* and *The Nation* flourished, where F.P.A. and Heywood Broun were writing their diatribes, and where the theater was a living world of contending ideas.

And Luther Cressman was in New York. I had had enough of the consolation of knowing that I was engaged, so that all the nonsense about having dates—or not having dates—was irrelevant. I wanted a life that demonstrated in a more real and dramatic form that I was not among the rejected and unchosen. And so, at the end of the year, I persuaded my father to let me leave DePauw and enter Barnard College.

What did I learn from this essentially very mild experience of being treated as an outsider and a reject from my own society? Just enough to know more clearly than ever that this is not the way to organize society—that those who reject or those who are rejected, and usually both, suffer irreversible character damage. It is true that sometimes one or the other may show magnificent character traits. I believe that the ideal of the English gentleman, embodied in the belief that he alone—and no one else—can destroy his position, is valuable. Equally, the position of the Jews, steadily persecuted but sustained by their conception of themselves as a chosen people, has produced an enormous number of highly intelligent, humanly sensitized, valuable men and women. But the reciprocal, the belief of the Nazis that they were the proper heirs of European civilization, from which all whom they regarded as lesser men should be excluded, was an evil that the world cannot face again. Whatever advantages may have arisen, in the past, out of the existence of a specially favored and highly privileged aristocracy, it is clear to me that today no argument can stand that supports unequal opportunity or any instrinsic disqualification for sharing in the whole of life.

By the very contrast that it provided, DePauw clarified my picture of the kind of college at which I wanted to be a student—a place where people were intellectually stirred and excited by ideas, where people stayed up all night talking about things that mattered, where one would meet one's peers and, still more important, people with different and superior minds, and, not least, where one would find out what one could do in life.

QUESTIONS

Reading for Understanding

1. Even though Margaret Mead came from a prosperous and educated family, she felt excluded during her first year at college. What caused her to be excluded? What did this make her begin to realize about groups of people who had been socially excluded?

2. What did she hope to experience at college? In what way was she disappointed? In what way was she pleased?

3. How did she adjust to her unsatisfactory situation? What did she learn from her courses?

4. What did she learn about the difference between men's and women's experiences in college? Why did she develop a negative attitude toward coeducational colleges?

5. How did her college experience influence her work later as an anthropological researcher?

Noticing Writing Techniques

1. Margaret Mead interrupts the story of her college experience to talk about large social problems like racism, anti-Semitism, and labor disputes. What is her reason for doing this? Do you find these general discussions relevant to her experience with snobbishness in college sororities? What connection does she draw?

2. Mead was later to make her career as an anthropologist. In what way does her writing reflect the professional methods of analysis of someone who compares cultures? How does her account of her college experience differ from the way the same story might have been told by a seventeen-year-old who had just finished her first year in college?

Noticing Vocabulary

_____ 1. Having *rapport* with groups of people means
A. getting along well with them
B. disliking them
C. coming from the same background
D. being related to them.

_____ 2. To *sear* something is to
A. rub it   B. burn it
C. slice it   D. see it.

_____ 3. To fight *unrelentingly* means to fight
A. carelessly   B. for a good cause
C. without knowing what   D. without giving up.
you're doing

_____ 4. *Vaunted* means
A. expensive   B. insulted
C. highly praised   D. exaggerated.

_____ 5. *Blatant* means
A. obvious   B. hard to find
C. in bright colors   D. confusing.

_____ 6. A *strident* sound is
   A. shrill
   C. melodious
   B. soft
   D. sudden.

_____ 7. *Provincial* people are
   A. well-informed
   C. foreign
   B. limited and unsophisticated
   D. highly cultivated.

_____ 8. *Ecumenicism* is a movement that seeks to
   A. keep groups true to their cultural roots
   B. introduce religious teaching in the schools
   C. achieve global unity among religions
   D. separate religion from government.

_____ 9. *Diatribes* are
   A. verbal attacks
   C. expressions of gratitude
   B. compliments
   D. prophecies of doom.

_____ 10. A *reciprocal* relationship is one that
   A. works only one way
   B. always turns out unhappily
   C. is based on a healthy matching of personalities
   D. works both ways.

Writing Topics

1. Write a paragraph comparing your college experience with your high school experience; narrow the topic to one aspect only, such as grades, tests, some extracurricular activity, or social life. Review Exposition: Comparative Paragraphs in Unit 2.

2. In our time, there is much controversy over different ethnic groups having separate proms, separate fraternities and sororities, and separate theme dormitories. Some people say that this practice gives students emotional and social support from others in their group. Opponents say that this practice destroys the gains made through the fight for desegregation and civil rights. Write an essay stating and supporting your opinion on the topic. Review the Persuasive Mode in Unit 3.

Michael White and John Gribben

Stephen Hawking is one of the most remarkable scientific geniuses of modern times. Stricken with Lou Gehrig's Disease early in his career and eventually immobilized by it, he nevertheless continued to pursue a career in theoretical physics and

write a best-selling book on the nature of the cosmos entitled *A Brief History of Time* (1988). The following reading, taken from a biography of Hawking written by two leading science writers, tells
about how he finished his education just after
being stricken with the disease.

Doctors and Doctorates*
from *Stephen Hawking: A Life in Science*

When Stephen returned to St. Albans for the Christmas vacation at the end of
1962, the whole of southern England was covered in a thick blanket of snow.
In his own mind he must have known that something was wrong. The strange
clumsiness he had been experiencing had occurred more frequently but had
gone unobserved by anyone in Cambridge. Sciama remembers noticing early
in the term that Hawking had a very slight speech impediment but had put it
down to nothing more than that. However, when he arrived at his parents'
home, because he had been away for a number of months, they instantly noticed that something was wrong. His father's immediate conclusion was that
Stephen had contracted some strange bug while in the Middle East the previous summer—a logical conclusion for a doctor of tropical medicine. But they
wanted to be sure. They took him to the family doctor who referred him to a
specialist.

On New Year's Eve, the Hawkings threw a party at 14 Hillside Road. It
was, as might have been expected, a civilized affair with sherry and wine;
close friends were invited, including schoolfriends John McClenahan and
Michael Church. The word passed around that Stephen was ill, the exact nature of the disease unknown, but something picked up in foreign climes was
the general impression. Michael Church remembers that Stephen had difficulties pouring a glass of wine and that most of the liquid ended up on the table-
cloth rather than in the glass. Nothing was said, but there was an atmosphere
of foreboding that evening.

A young woman called Jane Wilde, whom Stephen had previously known
only vaguely, had also been invited to the party. He was formally introduced
to her by a mutual friend during the course of the evening. Jane also lived in
St. Albans and attended the local high school. As the dying hours of 1962
trickled away and 1963 began, the two of them began to talk and to get to
know each other. She was in the upper sixth and had a place at Westfield College in London to begin reading modern languages the following autumn.
Jane found the twenty-one-year-old Cambridge postgraduate a fascinating
and slightly eccentric character and was immediately attracted to him. She recalls sensing an intellectual arrogance about him, but "There was something

lost, he knew something was happening to him of which he wasn't in control." From that night their friendship blossomed.

He was due back in Cambridge to begin the Lent term later in January, but instead of resuming his work there he was taken into hospital to undergo a series of investigatory tests. Hawking recalls the experience vividly:

> *They took a muscle sample from my arm, stuck electrodes into me, and injected some radio-opaque fluid into my spine, and watched it going up and down with X-rays, as they tilted the bed. After all that, they didn't tell me what I had, except that it was not multiple sclerosis, and that I was an atypical case. I gathered, however, that they expected it to continue to get worse, and that there was nothing they could do except give me vitamins. I could see that they didn't expect them to have much effect. I didn't feel like asking for more details, because they were obviously bad.*

The doctors advised him to return to Cambridge and his cosmological research, but that, of course, was easier said than done. Work was not going well and now the ever-present possibility of imminent death hung over his every thought and action. He returned to Cambridge and awaited the results of the tests. A short time later he was diagnosed as having a rare and incurable disease called amyotrophic lateral sclerosis, or ALS, known in the United States as Lou Gehrig's Disease after the Yankee baseball player who died from the illness. In Britain it is usually called motor neuron disease. . . .

During his first two years at Cambridge, the effects of the ALS disease rapidly worsened. He was beginning to experience enormous difficulty in walking, and was compelled to use a stick in order to move just a few feet. His friends helped him as best they could, but most of the time he shunned any assistance. Using walls and objects as well as sticks, he would manage, painfully slowly, to traverse rooms and open areas. There were many occasions when these supports were not enough. Sciama and his colleagues remember clearly that on some days Hawking would turn up at the office with a bandage around his head, having fallen heavily and received a nasty bump.

His speech was also becoming seriously affected by the disease. Instead of being merely slurred, his speaking voice was now rapidly becoming unintelligible, and even close colleagues were experiencing some difficulty in understanding what he was saying. Nothing slowed him down, however; in fact, he was just getting into his stride. Work was progressing faster and more positively than it had ever done in his entire career, and this serves to illustrate his attitude to his illness. Crazy as it may seem, ALS is simply not that important to him. Of course he has had to suffer the humiliations and obstructions facing all those in our society who are not able-bodied, and naturally he has had to adapt to his condition and to live under exceptional circumstances. But the disease has not touched the essence of his being, his mind, and so has not affected his work.

More than anyone else, Hawking himself would wish to underplay his disability and to concentrate on his scientific achievements, for that is really what is important to him. Those working with him, and the many physicists around the world who hold him in the highest regard, do not view Hawking as anything other than one of them. The fact that he cannot now speak and is immobile without the technology at his fingertips is quite irrelevant. To them he is friend, colleague and, above, all, great scientist.

Having come to terms with ALS and found someone in Jane Wilde with whom he could share his life on a purely personal level, he began to blossom. The couple became engaged, and the frequency of weekend visits increased. It was obvious to everyone that the two of them were sublimely happy and immensely important to each other. Jane recalls, "I wanted to find some purpose to my existence, and I suppose I found it in the idea of looking after him. But we were in love." On another occasion she said, "I decided what I was going to do, so I did. He was very, very determined, very ambitious. Much the same as now. He already had the beginnings of the condition when I first knew him, so I've never known a fit, able-bodied Stephen."

For Hawking his engagement to Jane was probably the most important thing that had ever happened to him: it changed his life, gave him something to live for and made him determined to live. Without the help that Jane gave him, he almost certainly would not have been able to carry on, or had the will to do so.

From this point on his work went from strength to strength, and Sciama began to believe that Hawking might, after all, manage to bring together the disparate strands of his Ph.D. research. It was still touch and go, but another chance encounter was just around the corner.

Sciama's research group became very interested in the work of a young applied mathematician, Roger Penrose, who was then based at Birkbeck College in London. The son of an eminent geneticist, Penrose had studied at University College in London and had gone on to Cambridge in the early fifties. After research in the United States he had begun in the early sixties to develop ideas of singularity theory which interfaced perfectly with the ideas then emerging from the DAMTP (Department of Applied Mathematics and Theoretical Physics).

The group from Cambridge began to attend talks at King's College in London where the great mathematician and cocreator of the steady state theory, Hermann Bondi, was Professor of Applied Mathematics. King's acted as a suitable meeting-point for Penrose (who travelled across London), those from Cambridge, and a small group of physicists and mathematicians from the college itself. Sciama took Carter, Ellis, Rees and Hawking to the meetings with the idea that the discussions might spark off applications to their own work. However, there were times when Hawking almost failed to make it to London.

Brandon Carter remembers one particular occasion when the group arrived late at the railway station and the train was already drawing in. They all ran for it, forgetting about Stephen, who was struggling along with his sticks. It was only after they had installed themselves in the carriage that they were aware he was not with them. Carter recalls looking out of the window, seeing a pathetic figure struggling towards them along the platform and realizing that Stephen might not make it before the train pulled away. Knowing how

Hawking was fiercely against being treated differently from others, they did not like to help him too much. However, on this occasion Carter and one of the others jumped out to help him along the platform and on to the train.

It would have been an odd twist of fate indeed if Hawking had not made it to at least one of those London meetings because it was through them that his whole career took another positive turn. Over the course of the talks at King's, Roger Penrose had introduced his colleagues to the idea of a space-time singularity at the center of a black hole, and naturally the group from Cambridge were tremendously excited by this.

One night, on the way back to Cambridge, they were all seated together in a second-class compartment and had begun to discuss what had been said at the meeting that evening. Feeling disinclined to talk for a moment, Hawking peered through the window, watching the darkened fields stream past and the juxtaposition of his friends reflected in the glass. His colleagues were arguing over one of the finer mathematical points in Penrose's discussion. Suddenly, an idea struck him, and he looked away from the window. Turning to Sciama sitting across from him, he said, "I wonder what would happen if you applied Roger's singularity theory to the entire Universe." In the event it was that single idea that saved Hawking's Ph.D. and set him on the road to science superstardom.

Penrose published his ideas in January 1965, by which time Hawking was already setting to work on the flash of inspiration that had struck him on the way home from London to Cambridge that night after the talk. Applying singularity theory to the Universe was by no means an easy problem, and within months Sciama was beginning to realize that his young Ph.D. student was doing something truly exceptional. For Hawking, this was the first time he had really applied himself to anything. As he says:

> I . . . started working hard for the first time in my life. To my surprise, I found I liked it. Maybe it is not really fair to call it work. Someone once said, "Scientists and prostitutes get paid for doing what they enjoy."

When he was satisfied with the mathematics behind the ideas, he began to write up his thesis. In many respects it ended up as a pretty messy effort because he had been in something of a wilderness for much of the first half of his time at Cambridge. The problems he and Sciama had experienced in finding him suitable research projects left a number of holes and unanswered questions in the thesis. However, it had one saving grace—his application of singularity theory during his third year.

The final chapter of Hawking's thesis was a brilliant piece of work and made all the difference to the awarding of the Ph.D. The work was judged by an internal examiner, Dennis Sciama, and an expert external referee. As well as being passed or failed, a Ph.D. can be deferred, which means that the student has to resubmit the thesis at a later date, usually after another year. Thanks to his final chapter, Hawking was saved this humiliation and the examiners awarded him the degree. From then on the twenty-three-year-old physicist could call himself Dr. Stephen Hawking.

QUESTIONS

Reading for Understanding

1. Why was Stephen Hawking able to make great discoveries and earn a Ph.D. even though the disease destroyed his ability to walk, talk, and use his hands? How did other people help make his success possible?

2. How did Hawking reveal personal pride in the way he reacted to his difficulty?

3. Why are we able to understand and appreciate this essay even if we do not understand technical terms like *singularity theory*?

4. Why did Jane Wilde fall in love with Stephen even though he was already becoming disabled by the disease? In what way was she important to him?

Noticing Writing Techniques

1. The writers of this biography combined details of Stephen Hawking's personal life with other details about his career. Does this combination confuse you or are the two sides of his life related?

2. This biographical portrait is told in the *third person singular* except for a few quotations by Stephen and his wife, which are in the *first person singular.* How are these quotations different in their tone and effect from the rest of the narrative? If Stephen had told the whole story, how might it have been different?

Noticing Vocabulary

_____ 1. An *atypical* case is one that is
A. just like the others B. not like the others
C. easily treated D. extremely serious.

_____ 2. *Cosmological* research is about
A. military technology B. history
C. plant and animal life D. the universe.

_____ 3. An *imminent* event is
A. never going to happen B. very important
C. about to happen D. mysterious.

_____ 4. To *traverse* something is to
A. destroy it B. understand it
C. carry it D. move across it.

_____ 5. *Disparate* strands of research are
A. different and separate B. closely related

_____ C. pointing in the same   D. difficult.
              direction

_____ 6. The *juxtaposition* of objects means they are
              A. placed next to one   B. placed far apart
                 another
              C. placed in a circle   D. placed in a row.

_____ 7. For an event to be *deferred* means for it to be
              A. cancelled   B. planned in advance
              C. moved to a new location D. delayed.

Writing Topics

1. Write a paragraph telling about a visit to the hospital. Describe in detail what happened, how you felt, and, using the five senses, what you remember of the place itself. If you have never been a patient yourself, tell about visiting someone in the hospital. Review Descriptive Paragraphs in Unit 2 and Using Specific Language in Unit 4.

2. People often say that love is a mystery. Obviously people are attracted to each other for different reasons. Write an essay enumerating some of the reasons people are romantically attracted to each other. Give examples of the different reasons from your own experience or what you have observed of other people's lives. Review the Persuasive Mode: Enumerating Reasons in Unit 3.

James P. Comer, M.D. (1934–   )

Dr. James P. Comer, a psychiatrist at Yale University, is the creator of the "Comer Process," a method of improving public schools that involves both the resources of universities and the participation of parents. His concern for education grows out of his own experience with schooling as an African American man pursuing higher education in the 1950's. In his autobiography, *Maggie's American Dream* (1988), he links his success in education and career to his mother's dreams for her family. In this section he tells about choosing to attend a predominantly black medical school.

Medical School* from *Maggie's American Dream*

Being black in America is often like playing your home games on the opponents' court. Instead of cheers you get jeers—and worse. By the time I was a

_____

*From MAGGIE'S AMERICAN DREAM by James P. Comer, M.D. Copyright © 1988 by James P. Comer M.D. Used by permission of Dutton Signet, a division of Penuin Books USA Inc.

senior in college, I felt good about Indiana University. I had overcome, and a number of people had helped me. But I was tired. Why did I have to fight? I just wanted to be a student, not a black student who had to prove something every step of the way. I wanted to feel that the school was my place—home court. For this reason I elected to go to the predominantly black Howard University College of Medicine in Washington, D.C., rather than to Indiana University.

In 1956 the nation's capital had only recently desegregated downtown stores, movie houses, and other facilities. I could not believe the rundown housing conditions only a few blocks from the White House. On the taxi ride from the railroad station to my dormitory room at Carver Hall, I saw children playing in squalor. Adult men sat on doorsteps, apparently without work. Everywhere buildings were abandoned or stood in advanced stages of deterioration.

Even then the two black worlds that are nowadays more visible existed, but the gap was less apparent. The walk from the medical school to Carver Hall was through a heavily populated housing project. Barefoot children stood in open doors. Some begged us for money. The Washington Senators were still playing baseball in Griffith Stadium right next to the medical school, and the more entrepreneurial kids "protected" the cars of fans for a small fee.

On the other hand, Carver Hall was a future "Who's Who in Black America." Vernon Jordon, former president of the National Urban League, lived on the first floor. Doug Wilder, the first black lieutenant governor of Virginia, and his roommate Henry Marsh, the first black mayor of Richmond, lived across the hall from me on the second floor. Andrew Young's brother, then a dental student, also lived at Carver. One of my classmates left medicine for law after the first year and became one of the country's most successful black businessmen. The place was crammed full of future doctors, lawyers, and leaders who would make a name for themselves across the country in years to come.

One of my classmates' uncle was dean of the chapel. He had us out to dinner early in the semester. He was one of the most brilliant people I've ever met. I visited the home of a surgeon who was one of the early black graduates of Indiana University Medical School. He lived on the northwest Black Gold Coast with row after row of black middle and upper income homes—large, beautiful structures with well-kept lawns. I had never seen a black neighborhood like that. It was like the Park Addition in my hometown, where only white people lived.

During the first week I was swept up in the whirl of "the hill"—the home of the undergraduates. I could not believe it. It was like being in a candy store with every color of chocolate from white to dark. I had never met so many attractive black women at one time in all my life. I got lost trying to find the infirmary and asked a coed for directions. She was so beautiful I lost my concentration. I thanked her and a block away I had to ask somebody else.

Many of my classmates were also refugees from predominantly white schools, and most of them had elected to go to Howard for the same reasons that I had. Some were from small black schools that I had never heard of, but most were from the best-known black schools—Howard, Lincoln, Morehouse. One black student who was from Tougaloo, a small black college in Alabama, did average work for the first year and then became a top student in the class in the second. He told me that he was intimidated by the comptetition from big-name schools. Being among so many attractive, intelligent, affluent, high-achieving blacks was just what the doctor ordered for me. But again I had to struggle. And in the struggle I came to realize that not all the problems in life are black and white.

I arrived on campus with a middle-ear infection. I also had a then undiagnosed allergy to fall pollen. My eyes were red, my ears were plugged and aching, and I felt like my head was in a fishbowl. During orientation I heard one of the deans tell us that one out of three students wouldn't make it. I looked to my left and to my right, and both people looked smarter than me. Suddenly I was scared. I flunked the first round of quizzes in almost everything. To make matters worse, I was allergic to the formaldehyde used to preserve the cadavers in anatomy. I had a hacking dry cough the entire first year.

Also, there were cliques at Howard, just as at Indiana—middle income, low income; light-skinned, dark skinned; "good" (white) hair, "bad" hair; Northeastern, Midwestern, Southern and West Indian. I was a low-income, in-between skin, "bad" hair kid from the Midwest—not a winner. Even so, the sense of belonging seemed to be based more on ability than on membership in these particular groups.

I had come too far to lose out now. I heard my mother's admonition: "You can learn just as well as anybody else . . . and you'd better!" September turned to October and hayfever season was over. I rallied. By the second round of exams I was doing average work, and by the third I was doing very well.

At Howard I discovered that I did not want to be a leader. I did not have to lead; there were plenty of good leaders in my class. I gradually became aware of the bind I had been in on the predominantly white Indiana campus. I had been trying to carry the race. I had tried to disprove the myths and stereotypes—blacks are poor in math, they are overly emotional, they are inarticulate. Too much of my motivation for learning had been negative: "I'll show them."

At Howard I was free from all this. I had been playing the role of acceptable Negro. I began to relax and swing with a group of fellows who were comfortable being black. Class parties were like none I had ever been to before. There was a real sense of belonging. I met many teachers who had a special dedication to black education and a sensitivity born of shared experience.

Sometimes, though, I found just the opposite. Some of the professors were bright, aggressive people who had never achieved the recognition they were due because they were black. Their choice of employment had been limited; professional societies had barred them; professional organizations had failed to recognize important work. Perhaps as a result, the spark had gone out of several once dynamic teachers. Their frustration was taken out on the students.

On one occasion I lost twenty-five points on an exam because I didn't use the problem-solving formula the professor claimed he discovered. All of the calculations that gained me the correct answer were on the paper. When I showed him he said angrily, "When you get a laboratory and a National Institute of Health research grant you can use your formula. Until then, you use mine."

One professor teased us about having it so easy, being on scholarships and loans. When he had been in medical school he had had a full-time job and sent half of his earning home to support his impoverished family in Baltimore. Many of my professors had worked, often full-time, while going to school. When I was growing up, I had read that Abraham Lincoln walked miles to school each day—an example of the will to succeed among the "builders of our nation"—while I was taught in many subtle and not-so-subtle ways that black people were too lazy to expend any energy to improve themselves.

The summer before medical school, I had worked as an orderly at St. Catherine's Hospital in my hometown. Because I was planning to become a general practitioner in East Chicago, I felt that I should get to know people and patients at the hospital. I had been told that I could not serve as an extern (similar to an intern) until after my first two years of medical school. But early in the summer after my first year, Dr. Steen, the director of training, overheard me telling a former high school classmate that I was a medical student, and immediately accepted me into the externship program. I learned a great deal as an orderly—medicine from the bedpans up.

For example, there was an extern who was very bright but very arrogant. He chewed out nurses twice his age and with ten times more experience. Finally they decided to let him hang himself. He made a treatment error on a patient a couple of nurses knew about, but wouldn't tell him. The extern's pride was wounded; the patient paid with pain and suffering. I vowed that when I became a doctor I would treat all my coworkers—professionals and nonprofessionals—with respect.

The notion was probably easier for me to hold than some. One of my non-professional coworkers was the lady on the elevator—Mom. She told every-body about her son, "the doctor." Some who didn't know us thought the ele-vator lady must surely be kidding. She had a great rapport and great respect for most of the doctors, but she saw some things she didn't like and made it clear that she didn't want that behavior from me. "When you get to be a doc-tor, I don't want you talking about 'the heart case' in room 202. That's a person with a name, family, and friends."

I began clinical clerkships in my third year, and I enjoyed all of them except psychiatry. I began to think about specializing in each one—surgery, obstetrics and gynecology, internal medicine, dermatology, opthalmology—all except psy-chiatry. I was amused by the theories. I laughed during the clinical lectures and joked that it was witch doctoring. I was assigned to a catatonic schizophrenic patient for four weeks. She didn't speak to me the entire time, *maybe* a faint smile when I said good-bye. And the next summer while an extern at St. Catherine's a patient developed acute paranoid symptoms and threatened me and his doctor, temporarily trapping us in his room. I knew that this specialty was not for me.

Late in my junior year I began to struggle with the question of whether I wanted to be a general practitioner or a specialist, even whether I wanted to be a doctor or not. True, I was Hugh and Maggie's son, the doctor. But I was a people person, and medical training seemed to be carrying me further away from my interests than toward them. These doubts would not solidify, though, until later.

My senior year, one of the most rewarding I have ever had, was marred only by one incident. During my pediatric clerkship I worked with an intern trying to save an infant who had been burned by hot water knocked off the stove in her congested apartment. Several times it looked like the baby was going to make it. Then she died. I was devastated and I thought the mother would be. I dreaded facing her. But when she heard, she stoically said, "Well, it was God's will." I wanted to scream out that God had nothing to do with it, that the conditions they lived under were man-made. But I looked at the peace and comfort that faith gave her—and remembered that I was a medical student—and held my tongue.

Mom and Mr. Robinson came down for graduation. It was a glorious graduation day. When I stood to take the Hippocratic Oath, I was in another world. It was the culmination of my greatest hope, my highest aspiration; all thereafter would be icing on the cake. As I took my seat, even though he couldn't be there, I could see Dad beaming with pride.

Norman finished college in 1958, Thelma and Charles in 1959. We would all obtain additional graduate degrees later on, but the major hurdle was over. Mom's dream, Dad's dream, our dream had come true.

QUESTIONS

Reading for Understanding

1. What was James Comer's reason for choosing a predominantly black medical school? Was he satisfied with his choice?

2. What social distinctions did he notice among the student body? How was his attitude toward his own role different from what it had been at Indiana University?

3. What was his attitude toward psychiatry, which later became his specialty? What caused this attitude?

4. What did he find unsatisfying about his medical studies? What had he intended to do as a doctor?

5. What do you think this essay says about race relations in the 1950s in the United States? Would his experience in college or medical school probably be different nowadays?

Noticing Writing Techniques

1. What does Dr. Comer mean by his metaphor at the beginning of the essay about basketball courts? What simile does he use to convey his excitement at being in this new social world?

2. Dr. Comer tends to mention the good and bad sides of nearly all his experiences. Try to list the good and bad sides of the following: his undergraduate experience at Indiana University; the social world at

Howard University; his experiences with the course work in medical school; his hospital experience; his senior year; his graduation.

Noticing Vocabulary

————— 1. *Entrepreneurial* people
A. like to study
B. are political activists
C. have the spirit of free enterprise
D. are cultivated and well read.

————— 2. To be *intimidated* is to be
A. frightened   B. inspired
C. persuaded   D. told something secretly.

————— 3. *Affluent* people are
A. poor   B. well-educated
C. intelligent   D. rich.

————— 4. A *clique* is a
A. business club   B. study group
C. snobbish group   D. form of business arrangement.

————— 5. *Inarticulate* means unable to
A. paint well   B. speak well
C. sing well   D. read well.

————— 6. To be *impoverished* is to be
A. lacking in good nutrition   B. unable to read and write
C. poor or deprived   D. lacking in growth.

————— 7. *Obstetrics* has to do with
A. old people's illnesses   B. childbirth
C. bone diseases   D. problems with the stomach.

————— 8. *Gynecology* deals with
A. women's diseases   B. infants' diseases
C. treatment of old people   D. problems with the eyes and ears.

————— 9. *Dermatology* deals with
A. skin diseases   B. problems with the nervous system
C. heart disease   D. problems with the feet.

————— 10. *Ophthalmology* treats the
A. teeth   B. bones
C. eyes   D. muscles.

Writing Topics

1. Write a paragraph comparing a social environment where you felt comfortable with one in which you felt uncomfortable. Review Exposition: Comparison Paragraphs in Unit 2.

2. Many colleges and graduate and professional institutions practice affirmative action in their admissions policies. That is, they give special preference to members of minority groups or to women in order to increase the number of college graduates or professionals in those groups. Some people say that this is a fair and effective way to achieve diversity and racial balance. Others say that such policies are reverse discrimination. Write an essay explaining why you support or oppose affirmative action policies. If you approve of them in some cases and not in others, explain the reason for these differences. Bring in examples to illustrate your point, and respond to some of the arguments made by those who disagree with you. Review Persuasive Essays in Unit 3.

Gary B. Nash, et al.

The following selection from a well-known history textbook is the kind of brief assignment you might read in an American history course. It tells about events in the 1960s that involved college students. Many of the groups and individuals are probably familiar to you, but you may not have read about what actually happened to make the sixties such a controversial time. Colleges have never been the same since, and youth culture as well was transformed permanently during that period.

The Student Movement and the Counterculture*
from *The American People: Creating a Nation and a Society*

The Student Movement

Members of the baby boom generation came of age in the 1960s, and many more of them, especially from the large middle class, moved on to some form of higher education than in any previous generation. By the end of the 1960s, college enrollment was more than four times what it had been in the 1940s.

In college, some students joined the struggle for civil rights. Hopeful at first, they gradually became discouraged by the limitations of the government's commitment, despite the rhetoric of Kennedy and the New Frontier.

---

*From THE AMERICAN PEOPLE: CREATING A NATION AND A SOCIETY by Nash et al. Copyright © 1992. Reprinted by permission of HarperCollins College Publishers.

Out of that disillusionment arose the radical spirit of the New Left. Civil rights activists were among those who in 1960 organized Students for a Democratic Society (SDS). In 1962, SDS issued a manifesto, the Port Huron Statement, written largely by Tom Hayden of the University of Michigan, and calling for the creation of a "New Left." "We are people of this generation, bred in at least modest comfort, housed now in universities, looking uncomfortably at the world we inherit," it began. It went on to deplore the vast social and economic distances separating people from each other and to condemn the isolation and estrangement of modern life. The document called for a better system, "a democracy of individual participation."

The first blow of the growing student rebellion came at the University of California in Berkeley. There civil rights activists became involved in a confrontation that quickly became known as the free speech movement. It began in September 1964 when the university refused to allow students to distribute protest material outside the main campus gate. The students, many of whom had worked in the movement in the South, argued that their tables were off campus and therefore not subject to university restrictions on political activity. When police arrested one of the leaders, students surrounded the police car and kept it from moving all night.

The university regents brought charges against the student leaders, including Mario Savio. When the regents refused to drop the charges, the students occupied the administration building. Then as in the South, police stormed in and arrested the students in the building. A student strike, with faculty aid, mobilized wider support for the right to free speech.

The free speech movement at Berkeley was basically a plea for traditional liberal reform. Students sought only the reaffirmation of a long-standing right, the right to express themselves as they chose, and they aimed their attacks at the university, not at society as a whole. The attack broadened as the ferment at Berkeley spread to other campuses in the spring of 1965. Students sought a greater voice in university affairs, argued for curricular reform, and demanded admission of more minority students. Their success in gaining their demands changed the shape of American higher education.

The mounting protest against the escalation of the Vietnam War fueled and refocused the youth movement. Confrontation became the new tactic of radical students, and protest became a way of life. Between January 1 and June 15, 1968, hundreds of thousands of students staged 221 major demonstrations at more than 100 educational institutions.

The next year, in October 1969, the Weathermen, a militant fringe group of SDS, sought to show that the revolution had arrived with a frontal attack on Chicago, scene of the violent Democratic convention of 1968. The Weathermen, taking their name from a line in a Bob Dylan song—"You don't need a weatherman to know which way the wind blows"—came from all over the country. Dressed in hard hats, jackboots, work gloves, and other padding, they rampaged through the streets with clubs and pipes, chains and rocks. They ran into the police, as they had expected and hoped, and continued the attack. Some were arrested, others were shot, and the rest withdrew to regroup. For the next two days, they plotted strategy, engaged in minor skirmishes, and prepared for the final thrust. It came on the fourth day, once again pitting agressive Weathermen against hostile police.

Why had the Weathermen launched their attack? "The status quo meant to us war, poverty, inequality, ignorance, famine and disease in most of the world," Bo Burlingham, a participant from Ohio, reflected. "To accept it was to condone and help perpetuate it. We felt like miners trapped in a terrible poisonous shaft with no light to guide us out. We resolved to destroy the tunnel even if we risked destroying ourselves in the process." The rationale of the Chicago "national action" may have been clear to the participants, but it convinced few other Americans. There and elsewhere, citizens were infuriated at what they saw.

The New Left was, briefly, a powerful force. Although activists never composed a majority, radicals attracted students and other sympathizers to their cause until the movement fragmented. But while it was healthy, the movement focused opposition to the Vietnam War and challenged inequities in American Society.

The Counterculture

In the 1960s, many Americans, particularly young people, lost faith in the sanctity of the American system. "There was," observed Joseph Heller, the irreverent author of *Catch-22* (1961), "a general feeling that the platitudes of Americanism were horseshit." The protests exposed the emptiness of some of the old patterns, and many Americans, some politically active, some not, found new ways to assert their individuality and independence, often drawing on the example of the beats of the 1950s.

Surface appearances were most visible and, to older Americans, most troubling. The "hippies" of the 1960s carried themselves in different ways. Men let their hair grow and sprouted beards; men and women both donned jeans, muslin shirts, and other simple garments. Stressing spontaneity above all else, some rejected traditional marital customs and gravitated to communal living groups. Their example, shocking to some, soon found its way into the culture at large.

Sexual norms underwent a revolution as more people separated sex from its traditional ties to family life. A generation of young women came of age with access to "the pill"—an oral contraceptive that was effortless to use and freed sexual experimentation from the threat of pregnancy. Americans of all social classes became more open to exploring, and enjoying, their sexuality. Scholarly findings supported natural inclinations. In 1966, William H. Masters and Virginia E. Johnson published *Human Sexual Response,* based on intensive laboratory observation of couples engaged in sexual activities. Describing the kinds of response that women, as well as men, could experience, they destroyed the myth of the sexually passive woman.

Nora Ephron, author and editor, summed up the sexual changes in the 1960s as she reflected on her own experiences. Initially she had "a hangover from the whole Fifties virgin thing," she recalled. "The first man I went to bed with, I was in love with and wanted to marry. The second one I was in love with, but I didn't have to marry him. With the third one, I thought I *might* fall in love."

The arts reflected both the sexual revolution and the mood of dissent. Federal courts ruled that books like D.H. Lawrence's *Lady Chatterley's Lover,* earlier considered obscene, could not be banned. Many suppressed works, long available in Europe, now began to appear. Nudity became more common on stage and screen. "Op" artists painted sharply defined geometric figures in clear, vibrant colors, starkly different from the flowing, chaotic work of the abstract expressionists. "Pop" artists like Andy Warhol, Roy Lichtenstein, and Jasper Johns made ironic comments on American materialism and taste with the representations of everyday objects like soup cans, comic strips, or pictures of Marilyn Monroe. Their paintings broke with formal artistic conventions. Some used spray guns and fluorescent paints to gain effect. Others even tried to make their pictures look like giant newspaper photographs.

Hallucinogenic drugs also became a part of the counterculture. One prophet of the "drug scene" was Timothy Leary, who, with Richard Alpert, was doing scientific research at Harvard University on LSD. Fired from their research posts for violating a pledge to the University Health Service not to experiment with undergraduates, the two promoted the cause of LSD nationally. As Alpert drifted into a commune in New Mexico, Leary aggressively asserted that drugs were necessary to free the mind. Working through his group, the League for Spiritual Discovery, he dressed in long robes and preached his message, "Tune in, turn on, drop out."

Drug use was no longer confined to an urban subculture of musicians, artists, and the streetwise. Soldiers brought experience with drugs back from Vietnam. Young professionals began experimenting with cocaine as a stimulant. Taking a "tab" of LSD became part of the coming-of-age ritual for many middle-class college students. Marijuana became phenomenally popular in the 1960s.

Music became intimately connected with these cultural changes. The rock and roll of the 1950s and the gentle strains of folk music gave way to a new kind of rock that swept the country—and the world. The Beatles were the major influence, as they took first England, then the United States, by storm. Other groups enjoyed enormous commercial success while attacking materialism and other bourgeois values. Mick Jagger of the Rolling Stones was an aggressive, sometimes violent showman on stage whose androgynous style showed his contempt for conventional sexual norms. Janis Joplin, a hard-driving, hard-drinking woman with roots in the blues, reflected the intensity of the new rock world until her early death by drugs.

The music was most important on a mid-August weekend in 1969 when some 400,000 people gathered in a large pasture in upstate New York for the Woodstock rock festival. There, despite intense heat and torrential rain, despite inadequate supplies of water and food, the festival unfolded in a spirit of affection. Some people shed their clothes and paraded in the nude, some engaged in public lovemaking, and most shared whatever they had, particularly the marijuana that seemed endlessly available, while major rock groups provided ear-splitting, around-the-clock entertainment for the assembled throng. The weekend went off without a hitch. Supporters hailed the festival as an example of the new and better world to come.

Other Americans, however, viewed the antics of the young with distaste. Their fears seemed vindicated at another festival four months later in Altamont, California. Some 300,000 people gathered at a stock car raceway to attend a rock concert climaxing an American tour by the immensely popular Rolling Stones.

Woodstock had been well planned; the Altamont affair was not. In the absence of adequate security, the Stones hired a band of Hell's Angels to maintain control. Those tough motorcyclists, fond of terrorizing the open road, prepared to keep order in their own way.

The spirit at Altamont was different from the start. "It was a gray day, and the California hills were bare, cold and dead," wrote Greil Marcus, a music critic. An undercurrent of violence simmered, Marcus observed, as "all day long people .   . speculated on who would be killed, on when the killing would take place. There were few doubts that the Angels would do the job."

With the Stones on stage, the fears were realized. As star Mick Jagger looked on, the Hell's Angels beat a young black man to death. A musician who tried to intervene was knocked senseless. Other beatings occurred, accidents claimed several more lives, and drug-overdosed revelers found no adequate medical support.

Altamont revealed the underside of the counterculture. That underside could also be seen in the Haight-Ashbury section of San Francisco, where runaway "flower children" mingled with "burned-out" drug users and radical activists. Joan Didion, a perceptive essayist, wrote of American society in 1967: "Adolescents drifted from city to city, sloughing off both the past and the future as snakes shed their skins, children who were never taught and would never now learn the games that had held the society together." For all the spontaneity and exuberance, the counterculture's underside could not be ignored.

QUESTIONS

Reading for Understanding

1. Although perfect objectivity may be impossible, textbooks usually try to give a balanced picture of events. How do these authors give both good and bad sides of the student movement and the counter culture? Do you find them to be neutral, or do you think they show more approval or disapproval of the sixties movements?

2. Does this account agree with what you already think of the sixties? Did you clearly disagree with the authors at any point?

3. In what way do you think the student movement permanently shaped American higher education, as the authors assert? In what ways do you think colleges have gained from the changes? In what ways have they been harmed?

4. In what way did music play an important part in the sixties counterculture? How were drugs important? How has popular music changed since then? How have the use of drugs and the attitude toward them changed?

Noticing Writing Techniques

1. Would you categorize this selection as primarily narrative, descriptive, or expository? Does it have a persuasive purpose? In what way does it tell a narrative? What does it describe, and what descriptive details are included to supports the authors' points? Where do the authors analyze their topic?

2. This writing assumes that you already know quite a few facts about the 1960s, such as names of famous rock stars. Was there any point at which you were unfamiliar with the examples being offered or the experts being quoted?

3. Would you describe the tone of the selection as highly emotional or unemotional? Formal or informal? Serious or humorous? Respectful or sarcastic? What do you think the tone of a textbook should be?

4. How did the authors try to make their writing livelier than many textbooks tend to be? Do you think they succeeded?

Noticing Vocabulary

_____ 1. *Disillusionment* means
    A. loss of money
    B. loss of energy and health
    C. loss of trust or ideals
    D. loss of self-esteem.

_____ 2. A *manifesto* is
    A. a set of laws
    B. a declaration of principles
    C. a collection of fancy books
    D. an oil painting.

_____ 3. To *condone* something is to
    A. oppose it
    B. invent it
    C. pardon it
    D. delay it.

_____ 4. To *perpetuate* something is to
    A. prolong it
    B. end it
    C. change it to a new location
    D. translate it into another language.

_____ 5. *Materialism* means placing importance on
    A. religion   B. the past
    C. wealth and property   D. marriage and the
                                     family.

_____ 6. *Bourgeois* values are those of
    A. the middle class   B. the poor
    C. women   D. religious institutions.

_____ 7. *Androgynous* styles
    A. copy the styles of the rich
    B. are loud and flashy
    C. suggest both sexes
    D. combine styles from different cultures.

_____ 8. *Exuberance* means having a lot of
    A. energy and joy   B. money
    C. intelligence and insight   D. influence.

Writing Topics

1. Write a paragraph summarizing what this textbook says about the student movement. Write a second paragraph summarizing what it says about the counterculture. This is just an exercise in summarizing and paraphrasing (putting someone else's ideas into your own words); therefore, do not analyze or give your personal opinions at this time. When paraphrasing, be sure to use only your own words; do not borrow whole phrases or sentences from the article.

2. Many of the examples of counterculture in this article are now mainstream, such as rock music. Write an essay on the question, "Is there a counterculture today?" Describe the attitudes, music, activities, and lifestyles of those who nowadays reject the mainstream, middle class lifestyle. Is there more than one counterculture group? Do you like or dislike this counterculture? Use specific examples to support your points. Review the Expository Mode: Essays Based on Example in Unit 3.

Poems About Learning Experiences

Gwendolyn Brooks (1917–   )

In this poem, written in 1945, Gwendolyn Brooks raises a question asked in her short poem "We Real Cool": what is the place of school and education in the lives of people who are not privileged and middle class? In "Sadie and Maud" we see two sisters who take different routes in their learning experiences. What are the results?

Sadie and Maud

Maud went to college.
Sadie stayed at home.
Sadie scraped life
With a fine-tooth comb.

She didn't leave a tangle in.
Her comb found every strand.
Sadie was one of the livingest chits
In all the land.

Sadie bore two babies
Under her maiden name.
Maud and Ma and Papa
Nearly died of shame.
Everyone but Sadie
Nearly died of shame.

When Sadie said her last so-long
Her girls struck out from home.
(Sadie had left as heritage
Her fine-tooth comb.)

Maud, who went to college,
Is a thin brown mouse.
She is living all alone
In this old house.

QUESTIONS

Reading for Understanding

1. What did Maud apparently get out of her college education? What comment does Gwendolyn Brooks, who graduated from college and taught in colleges, make about college in this poem?

2. What did Sadie learn about life without going to college? Would she have gained from going to college? Would Maud have gained from going out into the world?

3. Why do the parents and everyone take Maud's side? Do you take Maud's side and disapprove of Sadie's way of living? Which sister do you identify with?

Noticing Writing Techniques

1. Gwendolyn Brooks uses two metaphors in the poem. The most important one is the "fine-tooth comb," which is mentioned several times.

What does it mean that Sadie "scraped life/With a fine-tooth comb"? What does it mean that the comb was the only heritage she left to her daughters? What is the other metaphor connected to Maud in the last stanza? What does it mean?

2. What effect does Brooks's verse form have? It has a regular rhyme and a meter slightly like that of "Mary Had a Little Lamb," but this is clearly not a nursery rhyme.

3. Why does Brooks spend most of the poem talking about Sadie, when Maud seems to have done the more remarkable thing—going to college as a black woman in the 1940s?

Writing Topics

1. Write a paragraph comparing yourself with one of your siblings. Review Comparative Paragraphs in Unit 2.

2. Write an essay explaining some of the reasons why brothers and sisters in the same family can turn out very differently even though they seem to have similar influences in their lives. Use examples from your own family or the lives of people you know, as well as public figures in well-known families. Review the Persuasive mode: Enumerating Reasons in Unit 3.

Stephen Spender (1909–   )

Stephen Spender is an English poet who has always been concerned with political and social causes. Although much of his poetry is personal and emotional, he is always concerned with the possibilities of imagining a better society. In this poem he sees and feels the difference between the pathetic lives of slum children, with their hopeless futures, and the unrealistic promises that seem to be offered by the pictures and maps on the school-room walls. Yet he can imagine a different future for these children if those in charge care enough.

An Elementary Classroom in a Slum*

Far far from gusty waves, these children's faces.
Like rootless weeds the torn hair round their paleness.
The tall girl with her weighed-down head. The paper-

---

*From COLLECTED POEMS 1928–1985 by Stephen Spender Copyright © 1942 and renewed 1970 by Stephen Spender. Reprinted by permission of Random House, Inc.

seeming boy with rat's eyes. The stunted unlucky heir
Of twisted bones, reciting a father's gnarled disease,
His lesson from his desk. At back of the dim class
One unnoted, mild and young: his eyes live in a dream
Of squirrels' game, in tree room, other than this.

On sour cream walls, donations. Shakespeare's head
Cloudless at dawn, civilized dome riding all cities.
Belled, flowery, Tyrolese valley. Open-handed map
Awarding the world its world. And yet, for these
Children, these windows, not this world, are world,
Where all their future's painted with a fog,
A narrow street sealed in with a lead sky,
Far far from rivers, capes, and stars of words.

Surely Shakespeare is wicked, the map a bad example
With ships and sun and love tempting them to steal—
For lives that slyly turn in their cramped holes
From fog to endless night? On their slag heap, these children
Wear skins peeped through by bones, and spectacles of steel
With mended glass, like bottle bits in slag.
Tyrol is wicked; map's promising a fable:
All of their time and space are foggy slum,
So blot their maps with slums as big as doom.

Unless, governor, teacher, inspector, visitor,
This map becomes their window and these windows
That open on their lives like crouching tombs
Break, O break open, till they break the town
And show the children to the fields and all their world
Azure on their sands, to let their tongues
Run naked into books, the white and green leaves open
The history theirs whose language is the sun.

QUESTIONS

Reading for Understanding

1. The poem seems to be calling on authorities such as the "governor, teacher, inspector, visitor" to do something for these slum children. What does the poet suggest should be done? What is wrong with what the picture of Shakespeare, the picture of a valley in Tyrol (Austria), and the maps all seem to offer the children?

2. How much hope for upward mobility does the poem see in the lives of these children? How are they marked by the conditions of their lives?

3. Why does the poem describe the children and the donations of pictures and maps on the walls but say nothing about what they are studying?

4. Would a poem describing an inner-city classroom in today's America resemble this poem? What differences would there be?

Noticing Writing Techniques

1. How does the poet use images of nature in the poem? What do the images of windows mean? What does he mean by the metaphor of the children's future as "A narrow street sealed in with a lead sky"?

2. How would you describe the tone of the poem? Is it amusing, gloomy, angry, compassionate, or sad? Give examples to support your answer.

Writing Topics

1 Write a paragraph describing a room you see frequently—your dormitory room, your room at home, or a classroom. Use all five senses to convey the right impression of the room, and use a key word to unite all the details. Review Description: Telling About Persons, Places, and Objects in Unit 2.

2. Write an essay comparing the best teacher you ever had with the worst teacher you ever had. Explain in detail how they were different and why they were different. Review Comparative Paragraphs in Unit 2.

Langston Hughes (1902–1967)

Langston Hughes was one of the most productive and versatile writers of twentieth-century America. He was best known for his 12 volumes of poetry but also wrote fiction, drama, essays, and works of history. His formal education, however, was limited, including graduation from high school in Cleveland and a year at Columbia University—an experience reflected in the following poem.

Theme for English B*

The instructor said,

> Go home and write
> A page tonight.
> And let that page come out of you—
> Then, it will be true.

---

*"Theme for English B." from MONTAGE OF A DREAM DEFERRED. Copyright 1951 by Langston Hughes. Copyright renewed 1979 by George Houston Bass.

I wonder if it's that simple?
I am twenty-two, colored, born in Winston-Salem.
I went to college there, then Durham, then here
to this college on the hill above Harlem.
I am the only colored student in the class.
The steps from the hill lead down into Harlem,
through a park, then I cross St. Nicholas,
Eighth Avenue, Seventh, and I come to the Y,
the Harlem Branch Y, where I take the elevator
up to my room, sit down, and write this page:

It's not easy to know what is true for you or me
at twenty-two, my age. But I guess I'm what
I feel and see and hear, Harlem, I hear you:
hear you, hear me—we two—you, me, talk on this page,
(I hear New York, too.) Me—who?

Well, I like to eat, sleep, drink, and be in love.
I like to work, read, learn, and understand life.
I like a pipe for a Christmas present,
or records—Bessie, bop, or Bach.
I guess being colored doesn't make me *not* like
the same things other folks like who are other races.
So will my page be colored that I write?

Being me, it will not be white.
But it will be
a part of you, instructor.
You are white—
yet a part of me, as I am part of you.
That's American.
Sometimes perhaps you don't want to be a part of me.
Nor do I often want to be a part of you.
But we are, that's true!
As I learn from you,
I guess you learn from me—
although you're older—and white
and somewhat more free.

This is my page for English B.

QUESTIONS

Reading for Understanding

1. Langston Huges became somewhat disillusioned with formal education; does this poem give any indication why he became impatient
   with formal academic activities?

2. Does Hughes reveal his identity in this poem, or does he seem to be searching for his identity? What does he mean by questioning the instructor's words ("I wonder if it's that simple")?

3. What is his relation to the instructor? What does he mean by calling that relationship American?

Noticing Writing Techniques

1. How does Hughes use rhyme in the poem? How does he make the poem sound like matter-of-fact conversation?

2. As an assignment for an English class, how does this poem express Hughes' thoughts and feelings differently than a typical college essay would have done?

Writing Topics

1. Write a paragraph explaining why you chose to attend the college in which you are currently enrolled. Tell about what other options you had and what pros and cons you considered in making your choice. Review Cause and Effect Paragraphs in Unit 2.

2. Some people believe college students should be allowed to choose whatever subjects they want to study and sign up for any courses for which they are qualified. Others say that the college faculty should determine what knowledge students should have in order to be awarded a degree and should therefore prescribe a curriculum of specific course requirements to see that all graduates are fully educated. What is your opinion? Write an essay supporting your position on this issue with logical analysis, examples, and experience of your own and your friends. Review the Persuasive Mode in Unit 3.

Li-Young Lee (1957–   )

Li-Young Lee's family, of Chinese background, escaped from Indonesia during the dictatorship of Sukarno and eventually migrated to the United States. Currently a resident of Chicago, he has written several volumes of poetry, including *Rose* (1986), from which "Persimmons" is taken.

Persimmons*

In sixth grade Mrs. Walker
slapped the back of my head

---

and made me stand in the corner
for not knowing the difference
between *persimmon* and *precision.*
How to choose

persimmons. This is precision.
Ripe ones are soft and brown-spotted.
Sniff the bottoms. The sweet one
will be fragrant. How to eat:
put the knife away, lay down newspaper.
Peel the skin tenderly, not to tear the meat.
Chew the skin, suck it,
and swallow. Now, eat
the meat of the fruit,
so sweet,
all of it, to the heart.

Donna undresses, her stomach is white.
In the yard, dewy and shivering
with crickets, we lie naked,
face-up, face-down.
I teach her Chinese.
Crickets: *chiu chiu.* Dew: I've forgotten.
Naked: I've forgotten.
Ni, wo: you and me.
I part her legs,
remember to tell her
she is beautiful as the moon.

Other words
that got me into trouble were
fight and *fright, wren* and *yarn.*
Fight was what I did when I was frightened,
fright was what I felt when I was fighting.
Wrens were small, plain birds,
yarn is what one knits with.
Wrens are soft as yarn.
My mother made birds out of yarn.
I loved to watch her tie the stuff;
a bird, a rabbit, a wee man.

Mrs. Walker brought a persimmon to class
and cut it up
so everyone could taste
a *Chinese apple.* Knowing
it wasn't ripe or sweet, I didn't eat
but watched the other faces.

My mother said every persimmon has a sun
inside, something golden, glowing,
warm as my face.

Once, in the cellar, I found two wrapped in newspaper,
forgotten and not yet ripe.

I took them and set both on my bedroom windowsill,
where each morning a cardinal
sang, *The sun, the sun.*

Finally understanding
he was going blind,
my father sat up all one night
waiting for a song, a ghost.
I gave him the persimmons,
swelled, heavy as sadness,
and sweet as love.

This year, in the muddy lighting
of my parents' cellar, I rummage, looking
for something I lost.
My father sits on the tired, wooden stairs,
black cane between his knees,
hand over hand, gripping the handle.

He's so happy that I've come home.
I ask how his eyes are, a stupid question.
All gone, he answers.

Under some blankets, I find a box.
Inside the box I find three scrolls.
I sit beside him and untie
three paintings by my father:
Hibiscus leaf and a white flower.
Two cats preening.
Two persimmons, so full they want to drop from the cloth.

He raises both hands to touch the cloth,
asks, *Which is this?*

This is persimmons, Father.

*Oh, the feel of the wolftail on the silk,
the strength, the tense
precision in the wrist.*

I painted them hundreds of times
eyes closed. These I painted blind.
Some things never leave a person:
scent of the hair of one you love,
the texture of persimmons,
in your palm, the ripe weight.

QUESTIONS

Reading for Understanding

1. What errors did Li-Young Lee make in school? Were these errors in the use of language or lack of knowledge? What knowledge did he actually have about persimmons? Why did he appear to the teacher to be less knowledgeable than he was?

2. What did he learn from his parents? What could the teacher have done to bring out the knowledge he already had?

3. What part did persimmons play in his life?

4. Why is Donna mentioned in the poem? What does she have to do with the theme of learning?

Noticing Writing Techniques

1. Persimmons are a kind of symbol in the poem. What do they represent?

2. How does the author relate the words he misused in school to experiences in his own life? How does the word *precision* come in again at the end?

3. Why does he bring in Chinese words? Why has he forgotten some? What does he remember better than words?

Writing Topics

1. Write a paragraph describing an object that has played an important part in your life, like the persimmons in Li-Young Lee's experience. Explain how and why it has meant so much to you. Review Descriptive Paragraphs and Cause and Effect Paragraphs in Unit 2.

2. Many students in American schools are learning English as their second language and, as a result, sometimes have difficulties learning as easily as they would like. Write an essay suggesting some of the ways such students can learn more easily, succeed in school, and have good

relationships with classmates. Review How-To Paragraphs in Unit 2 and Problem/Solution Essays in the Expository Mode of Unit 3.

Linda Pastan (1932–   )

Linda Pastan was born in New York City, attended Radcliffe College and Brandeis University, and lives near Washington, D.C. She has written numerous books of poetry, including *PM/AM: New and Selected Poems (1982)*, which was nominated for the American Book Award and from which the following poem was taken.

Marks*

My husband gives me an A
for last night's supper,
an incomplete for my ironing,
a B plus in bed.
My son says I am average,
an average mother, but if
I put my mind to it
I could improve.
My daughter believes
in Pass/Fail and tells me
I pass. Wait 'til they learn
I'm dropping out.

QUESTIONS

Reading for Understanding

1. What is the mother's attitude toward what her family seems to expect of her?

2. What sort of roles is she expected to perform? Does the family want her to be a traditional housewife or a career woman?

3. What do you suppose she means by saying she's "dropping out"?

---

*Reprinted from PM/AM: *New and Selected Poems* by Linda Pastan, with the permission of W.W. Norton & Company, Inc. Copyright © 1982 by Linda Pastan.

4. How does it make her feel to be "graded" all the time? Could this poem also be used to make us think about how students themselves feel about being graded on everything they do in school and college?

Noticing Writing Techniques

1. This poem is not about a schoolroom situation; instead it uses the evaluation of students by means of grades and categories (average) as a metaphor for the mother's relation to her husband and children. By seeing herself as a "student" evaluated by "teachers," what sort of self-image does she create?

2. How does Linda Pastan create humor in this poem? How do we know that there is a serious message, even though the language of grades, etc., does not literally apply to her?

3. What does the surprise ending add to the poem? Imagine the poem without it or with a different ending.

Writing Topics

1. Write a paragraph telling about a grade you received that you thought was unfair. Explain what the grade was for (the course, exam, or term paper), why you thought it was unfair, and what you did about it. Review Persuasion in Unit 2.

2. Most schools give letter grades to evaluate students. A few, however, give only written evaluations without numbers or letter grades. Many people insist that grades are necessary and useful because they provide an incentive and indicate the level of students' achievement. Others, however, argue that grades create an unrealistic view of reality and an atmosphere not conducive to learning, emphasizing competition instead of real achievement and collaboration. Write an essay supporting your opinion of grades, based on your own experience, that of others you know, and general analysis. Be sure to respond to some of the opinions argued by those who disagree with you. Review Persuasive Essays in Unit 3.

CAREER OPTIONS

Choosing a career is one of the biggest decisions most people make. Some choose one career and stay with it their entire life; others flit from one career direction to another, never committing themselves to a single choice. Most young people nowadays will settle on a single career area (usually *not* one connected to their undergraduate major) but will move through five or six jobs within that area during their lifetimes. Some people identify themselves totally by their work; others work only to make money and feel little attachment to their work. Most people probably fall in the middle, finding meaning in their work but needing other sources of meaning in their families, social lives, cultural activities, political commitments, or religions.

Reading about other people's job experiences and career decisions tells us a lot about ourselves and what it means to be human. Such reading may help students clarify their ambitions and values and make choices. It also reveals much about society, and about the way people cope with major life problems.

The use of language, especially reading and writing, is as crucial to the world of work as it is to education. The following readings show how important language skills are in achieving success in most careers and in understanding the purpose of work in our lives.

Russell Baker (1925–   )

Although Russell Baker is known to many readers nowadays as a Pulitzer-Prize-winning commentator for the *New York Times*, he actually was born in Virginia and grew up there, in New Jersey, and in Baltimore. The story of his childhood, adolescence, and early adult life up to the point of getting his first job as a journalist with the *Baltimore Sun* he tells in *Growing Up*, a book that won the Pulitzer Prize for biography in 1983.

My First Job*
from *Growing Up*

I began working in journalism when I was eight years old. It was my mother's idea. She wanted me to "make something" of myself and, after a levelheaded appraisal of my strengths, decided I had better start young if I was to have any chance of keeping up with the competition.

The flaw in my character which she had already spotted was lack of "gumption." My idea of a perfect afternoon was lying in front of the radio rereading my favorite Big Little Book, *Dick Tracy Meets Stooge Viller*. My mother despised inactivity. Seeing me having a good time in repose, she was powerless to hide her disgust. "You've got no more gumption than a bump on a log," she said. "Get out in the kitchen and help Doris do those dirty dishes."

My sister Doris, though two years younger than I, had enough gumption for a dozen people. She positively enjoyed washing dishes, making beds, and cleaning the house. When she was only seven she could carry a piece of short-weighted cheese back to the A&P, threaten the manager with legal action, and come back triumphantly with the full quarter-pound we'd paid for and a few

---

*Reprinted from GROWING UP by Russell Baker. © 1982. Used with permission of Congdon & Weed, Inc. and Contemporary Books, Chicago.

ounces extra thrown in for forgiveness. Doris could have made something of herself if she hadn't been a girl. Because of this defect, however, the best she could hope for was a career as a nurse or schoolteacher, the only work that capable females were considered up to in those days.

This must have saddened by mother, this twist of fate that had allocated all the gumption to the daughter and left her with a son who was content with Dick Tracy and Stooge Viller. If disappointed, though, she wasted no energy on self-pity. She would make me make something of myself whether I wanted to or not. "The Lord helps those who help themselves," she said. That was the way her mind worked.

She was realistic about the difficulty. Having sized up the material the Lord had given her to mold, she didn't overestimate what she could do with it. She didn't insist that I grow up to be President of the United States.

Fifty years ago parents still asked boys if they wanted to grow up to be President, and asked it not jokingly but seriously. Many parents who were hardly more than paupers still believed their sons could do it. Abraham Lincoln had done it. We were only sixty-five years from Lincoln. Many a grandfather who walked among us could remember Lincoln's time. Men of grandfatherly age were the worst for asking if you wanted to grow up to be President. A surprising number of little boys said yes and meant it.

I was asked many times myself. No, I would say, I didn't want to grow up to be President. My mother was present during one of these interrogations. An elderly uncle having posed the usual question and exposed my lack of interest in the Presidency, asked, "Well, what *do* you want to be when you grown up?"

I loved to pick through trash piles and collect empty bottles, tin cans with pretty labels, and discarded magazines. The most desirable job on earth sprang instantly to mind. "I want to be a garbage man," I said.

My uncle smiled, but my mother had seen the first distressing evidence of a bump budding on a log. "Have a little gumption, Russell," she said. Her calling me Russell was a signal of unhappiness. When she approved of me I was always "Buddy."

When I turned eight years old she decided that the job of starting me on the road toward making something of myself could no longer be safely delayed. "Buddy," she said one day, "I want you to come home right after school this afternoon. Somebody's coming and I want you to meet him."

When I burst in that afternoon she was in conference in the parlor with an executive of the Curtis Publishing Company. She introduced me. He bent low from the waist and shook my hand. Was it true as my mother had told him, he asked, that I longed for the opportunity to conquer the world of business?

My mother replied that I was blessed with a rare determination to make something of myself.

"That's right," I whispered.

"But have you got the grit, the character, the never-say-quit spirit it takes to succeed in business?"

My mother said I certainly did.

"That's right," I said.

He eyed me silently for a long pause, as though weighing whether I could be trusted to keep his confidence, then spoke man-to-man. Before taking a crucial step, he said, he wanted to advise me that working for the Curtis Publishing Company placed enormous responsibility on a young man. It was one of the great companies of America. Perhaps the greatest publishing house in the world. I had heard, no doubt, of the *Saturday Evening Post?*

Heard of it? My mother said that everyone in our house had heard of the *Saturday Post* and that I, in fact, read it with religious devotion.

Then doubtless, he said, we were also familiar with those two monthly pillars of the magazine world, the *Ladies Home Journal* and the *Country Gentleman.*

Indeed we were familiar with them, said my mother.

Representing the *Saturday Evening Post* was one of the weightiest honors that could be bestowed in the world of business, he said. He was personally proud of being a part of that great corporation.

My mother said he had every right to be.

Again he studied me as though debating whether I was worthy of a knighthood. Finally: "Are you trustworthy?"

My mother said I was the soul of honesty.

"That's right," I said.

The caller smiled for the first time. He told me I was a lucky young man. He admired my spunk. Too many young men thought life was all play. Those young men would not go far in this world. Only a young man willing to work and save and keep his face washed and his hair neatly combed could hope to come out on top in a world such as ours. Did I truly and sincerely believe that I was such a young man?

"He certainly does," said my mother.

"That's right," I said.

He said he had been so impressed by what he had seen of me that he was going to make me a representative of the Curtis Publishing Company. On the following Tuesday, he said, thirty freshly printed copies of the *Saturday Evening Post* would be delivered at our door. I would place these magazines, still damp with the ink of the presses, in a handsome canvas bag, sling it over my shoulder, and set forth through the streets to bring the best in journalism, fiction, and cartoons to the American public.

He had brought the canvas bag with him. He presented it with reverence fit for a chasuble.[1] He showed me how to drape the sling over my left shoulder and across the chest so that the pouch lay easily accessible to my right hand, allowing the best in journalism, fiction, and cartoons to be swiftly extracted and sold to a citizenry whose happiness and security depended upon us soldiers of the free press.

The following Tuesday I raced home from school, put the canvas bag over my shoulder, dumped the magazines in, and, tilting to the left to balance their weight on my right hip, embarked on the highway of journalism.

---

[1]an outer garment worn by a priest at Mass

We lived in Belleville, New Jersey, a commuter town at the northern fringe of Newark. It was 1932, the bleakest year of the Depression. My father had died two years before, leaving us with a few pieces of Sears, Roebuck furniture and not much else, and my mother had taken Doris and me to live with one of her younger brothers. This was my Uncle Allen. Uncle Allen had made something of himself by 1932. As salesman for a soft-drink bottler in Newark, he had an income of $30 a week; wore pearl-gray spats, detachable collars, and a three-piece suit; was happily married; and took in threadbare relatives.

With my load of magazines I headed toward Belleville Avenue. That's where the people were. There were two filling stations at the intersection with Union Avenue, as well as an A&P, a fruit stand, a bakery, a barber shop, Zucarreli's drug store, and a diner shaped like a railroad car. For several hours I made myself highly visible, shifting position now and then from corner to corner, from shop window to shop window, to make sure everyone could see the heavy black lettering on the canvas bag that said THE SATURDAY EVENING POST. When the angle of the light indicated it was suppertime, I walked back to the house.

"How many did you sell, Buddy?" my mother asked.

"None."

"Where did you go?"

"The corner of Belleville and Union Avenues."

"What did you do?"

"Stood on the corner waiting for somebody to buy a *Saturday Evening Post*."

"You just stood there?"

"Didn't sell a single one."

"For God's sake, Russell!"

Uncle Allen intervened. "I've been thinking about it for some time," he said, "and I've decided to take the *Post* regularly. Put me down as a regular customer." I handed him a magazine and he paid me a nickel. It was the first nickel I earned.

Afterwards my mother instructed me in salesmanship. I would have to ring doorbells, address adults with charming self-confidence, and break down resistance with a sales talk pointing out that no one, no matter how poor, could afford to be without the *Saturday Evening Post* in the home.

I told my mother I'd changed my mind about wanting to succeed in the magazine business.

"If you think I'm going to raise a good-for-nothing," she replied, "you've got another thing coming." She told me to hit the streets with the canvas bag and start ringing doorbells the instant school was out next day. When I objected that I didn't feel any aptitude for salesmanship, she asked how I'd like to lend her my leather belt so she could whack some sense into me. I bowed to superior will and entered journalism with a heavy heart.

My mother and I had fought this battle almost as long as I could remember. It probably started even before memory began, when I was a country child in northern Virginia and my mother, dissatisfied with my father's plain workman's life, determined that I would not grow up like him and his people, with calluses on their hands, overalls on their backs, and fourth-grade educations in their heads. She had fancier ideas of life's possibilities. Introducing me to the *Saturday Evening Post*, she was trying to wean me as early as possible from my father's world where men left with their lunch pails at sunup, worked with their hands until the grime ate into the pores, and died with a few sticks of mail-order furniture as their legacy. In my mother's vision of the better life there were desks and white collars, well-pressed suits, evenings of reading and lively talk, and perhaps—if a man were very, very lucky and hit the jackpot, really made something important of himself—perhaps there might be a fantastic salary of $5000 a year to support a big house and a Buick with a rumble seat and a vacation in Atlantic City.

And so I set forth with my sack of magazines. I was afraid of the dogs that snarled behind the doors of potential buyers. I was timid about ringing the doorbells of strangers, relieved when no one came to the door, and scared when someone did. Despite my mother's instructions, I could not deliver an engaging sales pitch. When a door opened I simply asked, "Want to buy a *Saturday Evening Post?*" In Belleville few persons did. It was a town of 30,000 people, and most weeks I rang a fair majority of its doorbells. But I rarely sold my thirty copies. Some weeks I canvassed the entire town for six days and still had four or five unsold magazines on Monday evening; then I dreaded the coming of Tuesday morning, when a batch of thirty fresh *Saturday Evening Posts* was due at the front door.

"Better get out there and sell the rest of those magazines tonight," my mother would say.

I usually posted myself then at a busy intersection where a traffic light controlled commuter flow from Newark. When the light turned red I stood on the curb and shouted my sales pitch at the motorists.

"Want to buy a *Saturday Evening Post?*"

One rainy night when car windows were sealed against me I came back soaked and with not a single sale to report. My mother beckoned to Doris.

"Go back down there with Buddy and show him how to sell these magazines," she said.

Brimming with zest, Doris, who was then seven years old, returned with me to the corner. She took a magazine from the bag, and when the light turned red she strode to the nearest car and banged her fist against the closed window. The driver, probably startled at what he took to be a midget assaulting his car, lowered the window to stare, and Doris thrust a *Saturday Evening Post* at him.

"You need this magazine," she piped, "and it only costs a nickel."

Her salesmanship was irresistible. Before the light changed half a dozen times she disposed of the entire batch. I didn't feel humiliated. To the contrary. I was so happy I decided to give her a treat. Leading her to the vegetable store on Belleville Avenue, I bought three apples, which cost a nickel, and gave her one.

"You shouldn't waste money," she said.

"Eat your apple." I bit into mine.

"You shouldn't eat before supper," she said. "It'll spoil your appetite."

Back at the house that evening, she dutifully reported me for wasting a nickel. Instead of a scolding, I was rewarded with a pat on the back for having the good sense to buy fruit instead of candy. My mother reached into her bottomless supply of maxims and told Doris, "An apple a day keeps the doctor away."

By the time I was ten I had learned all my mother's maxims by heart. Asking to stay up past normal bedtime, I knew that a refusal would be explained with, "Early to bed and early to rise, makes a man healthy, wealthy, and wise." If I whimpered about having to get up early in the morning, I could depend on her to say, "The early bird gets the worm."

The one I most despised was, "If at first you don't succeed, try, try again." This was the battle cry with which she constantly sent me back into the hopeless struggle whenever I moaned that I had rung every doorbell in town and knew there wasn't a single potential buyer left in Belleville that week. After listening to my explanations, she handed me the canvas bag and said, "If at first you don't succeed . . . "

Three years in that job, which I would gladly have quit after the first day except for her insistence, produced at least one valuable result. My mother finally concluded that I would never make something of myself by pursuing a life in business and started considering careers that demanded less competitive zeal.

One evening when I was eleven I brought home a short "composition" on my summer vacation which the teacher had graded with an A. Reading it with her own schoolteacher's eye, my mother agreed that it was top-drawer seventh grade prose and complimented me. Nothing more was said about it immediately, but a new idea had taken life in her mind. Halfway through supper she suddenly interrupted the conversation.

"Buddy," she said, "maybe you could be a writer."

I clasped the idea to my heart. I had never met a writer, had shown no previous urge to write, and hadn't a notion how to become a writer, but I loved stories and thought that making up stories must surely be almost as much fun as reading them. Best of all, though, and what really gladdened my heart, was the ease of the writer's life. Writers did not have to trudge through the town peddling from canvas bags, defending themselves against angry dogs, being rejected by surly strangers. Writers did not have to ring doorbells. So far as I could make out, what writers did couldn't even be classified as work.

I was enchanted. Writers didn't have to have any gumption at all. I did not dare tell anybody for fear of being laughed at in the schoolyard, but secretly I decided that what I'd like to be when I grew up was a writer.

QUESTIONS

Reading For Understanding

1. Why did Russell Baker's mother consider it so important for him to go to work when he was only eight years old?

2. What circumstances made it hard to get a job or earn any money in those times?

3. How did Russell's sense of his own ambitions and abilities differ from his mother's idea of the sort of boy he should be?

4. What made his mother finally change her attitude toward him?

5. How did his personality differ from his sister's?

6. How did Russell's outlook change as a result of his experience selling magazines?

Noticing Writing Techniques

1. Which moments in this essay did you find funny? How does Russell Baker create humor by his use of language in these moments?

2. Although this essay is about himself, Baker focuses mostly on the statements and attitudes of others. How would the essay be different if he had spent most of his time telling about his own feelings and opinions instead of his mother's, his uncle's, his sister's, and his employer's?

3. Why does Baker tell so much of the story by means of direct quotation? Does a lot of quotation make it easier for you to understand the personalities and behavior being described? What rules of punctuation and paragraph division do you have to follow when you quote conversations between two people?

Noticing Vocabulary

_____ 1. *Allocated* means
A. placed in a different location
B. assigned
C. discovered
D. thrown out of joint.

_____ 2. *Interrogations* are
A. methods of curing disease
B. methods of watering crops
C. sessions of questioning
D. interruptions.

_____ 3. *Accessible* means
A. able to be used or reached
B. too much of something
C. frightening
D. too expensive.

_____ 4. *Extracted* means
A. confused
B. combined with something else
C. forgotten
D. pulled out.

_____ 5. The *Depression* was the period of
A. rapid technological change
B. very high prices
C. joblessness
D. the war over slavery.

_____ 6. To *intervene* is to
  A. come between
  C. bring to an end
  B. join
  D. call together for a meeting.

_____ 7. *Surly* people are
  A. self-confident
  C. sure of their opinions
  B. rude and bad-tempered
  D. polite and well-dressed.

Writing Topics

1. Write a paragraph in narrative form telling about some project you undertook as a child—building something, selling something, or taking on some other responsibility.

2. Write an essay telling how one of your parents or another adult used to give you advice and try to direct your life when you were a child. Explain their attitudes and quote some of their favorite sayings. Tell how you responded to this attempt to guide your life and how you changed in the process. Review Narrative Writing in Units 2 and 3 for further topics and ideas.

Henry Louis Gates, Jr. (1951–   )

Henry Louis Gates, Jr. is the chairman of the African-American Studies Program and W.E.B. DuBois Professor of the Humanities at Harvard University. He has published many articles and books, including *The Signifying Monkey,* on African-American subjects. In the article below from *Sports Illustrated* he asks questions about the career dreams of young people and questions whether the schools and the media serve them responsibly.

Delusions of Grandeur*

Standing at the bar of an all-black VFW post in my hometown of Piedmont, W. Va., I offered five dollars to anyone who could tell me how many African-American professional athletes were at work today. There are 35 million African-Americans, I said.

"Ten million!" yelled one intrepid soul, too far into his cups.

"No way, more like 500,000," said another.

_____

*"Delusions of Grandeur" by Henry Louis Gates, Jr. First appeared in *Sports Illustrated.* Copyright © 1991 by Henry Louis Gates, Jr. Reprinted by permission of Brandt & Brandt Literary Agents, Inc.

"You mean all professional sports," someone interjected, "including golf and tennis, but not counting the brothers from Puerto Rico?" Everyone laughed.

"Fifty thousand minimum," was another guess.

Here are the facts:

There are 1,200 black professional athletes in the U.S.

There are 12 times more black lawyers than black athletes.

There are 2.5 times more black dentists than black athletes.

There are 15 times more black doctors than black athletes.

Nobody in my local VFW believed these statistics; in fact, few people would believe them if they weren't reading them in the pages of *Sports Illustrated*. In spite of these statistics, too many African-American youngsters still believe that they have a much better chance of becoming another Magic Johnson or Michael Jordan than they do of matching the achievements of Baltimore mayor Kurt Schmoke or neurosurgeon Dr. Benjamin Carson, both of whom, like Johnson and Jordan, are black.

In reality, an African-American youngster has about as much chance of becoming a professional athlete as he or she does of winning the lottery. The tragedy for our people, however, is that few of us accept that truth.

Let me confess that I love sports. Like most black people of my generation—I'm 40—I was raised to revere the great black athletic heroes, and I never tired of listening to the stories of triumph and defeat that, for blacks, amount to a collective epic much like those of the ancient Greeks: Joe Louis's demolition of Max Schmeling; Satchel Paige's dazzling repertoire of pitches; Jesse Owens's in-your-face performance in Hitler's 1936 Olympics; Willie Mays's over-the-shoulder basket catch; Jackie Robinson's quiet strength when assaulted by racist taunts; and a thousand other grand tales.

Nevertheless, the blind pursuit of attainment in sports is having a devastating effect on our people. Imbued with a belief that our principal avenue to fame and profit is through sport, and seduced by a win-at-any-cost system that corrupts even elementary school students, far too many black kids treat basketball courts and football fields as if they were classrooms in an alternative school system. "O.K., I flunked English," a young athlete will say. "But I got an A plus in slam-dunking."

The failure of our public schools to educate athletes is part and parcel of the schools' failure to educate almost everyone. A recent survey of the Philadelphia school system, for example, stated that "more than half of all students in the third, fifth and eighth grades cannot perform minimum math and language tasks." One in four middle school students in that city fails to pass to the next grade each year. It is a sad truth that such statistics are repeated in cities throughout the nation. Young athletes—particularly young black athletes—are especially ill-served. Many of them are functionally illiterate, yet they are passed along from year to year for the greater glory of good old Hometown High. We should not be surprised to learn, then, that only 26% of black athletes at the collegiate level earn their degrees. For every successful educated black professional athlete, there are thousands of dead and wounded. Yet young blacks continue to aspire to careers as athletes, and it's no wonder why; when the University of North Carolina recently commissioned a sculptor to create archetypes of its student body, guess which ethnic group was selected to represent athletes?

Those relatively few black athletes who do make it in the professional ranks must be prevailed upon to play a significant role in the education of all of our young people, athlete and nonathlete alike. While some have done so, many others have shirked their social obligations: to earmark small percentages of their incomes for the United Negro College Fund; to appear on television for educational purposes rather than merely to sell sneakers; to let children know the message that becoming a lawyer, a teacher or a doctor does more good for our people than winning the Super Bowl; and to form productive liaisons with educators to help forge solutions to the many ills that beset the black community. These are merely a few modest proposals.

A similar burden falls upon successful blacks in all walks of life. Each of us must strive to make our young people understand the realities. Tell them to cheer Bo Jackson but to emulate novelist Toni Morrison or businessman Reginald Lewis or historian John Hope Franklin or Spelman College president Johnetta Cole—the list is long.

Of course, society as a whole bears responsibility as well. Until colleges stop using young blacks as cannon fodder in the big-business wars of so-called nonprofessional sports, until training a young black's mind becomes as important as training his or her body, we will continue to perpetuate a system akin to that of the Roman gladiators, sacrificing a class of people for the entertainment of mobs.

QUESTIONS

Reading for Understanding

1. How does Dr. Gates want young black students to change their career ambitions? What is causing them to have the ambitions they now have?

2. What does he want professional black athletes to do to change the situation?

3. What does he want other black professionals to do? How does he, as the leading black scholar in the country, set an example by writing this article?

4. Do you believe that his arguments apply just as well to young people of other ethnic groups?

Noticing Writing Techniques

1. How does Dr. Gates use statistics to support his point? Were you surprised and convinced by the statistics?

2. At what point in the article does he show an awareness of those who might disagree with him, especially those whose chief interest is sports?

3. What personal experience does he use to arouse interest in his opening paragraphs? What does he create emphasis in his concluding paragraph without merely repeating himself?

4. What method other than statistics does he use to support his main point?

Noticing Vocabulary

_____ 1. An *intrepid* person is
A. fearless
B. unintelligent
C. loud
D. crazy.

_____ 2. An *epic* is a
A. cure for disease
B. tool for repairing electrical problems.
C. heroic tale or poem
D. detective story.

_____ 3. A *repertoire* is a
A. closet for storing formal clothes
B. collection of performing skills.
C. concert hall
D. stand-up comedian

_____ 4. To be *imbued* with something is to be
A. impressed by it
B. tired of it
C. filled with it
D. changed by it.

_____ 5. *Archetypes* are
A. forms of architecture
B. sculptures
C. machines for transmitting typescript
D. original models.

_____ 6. To serve as a *liaison* is to
A. plan and give orders
B. form communication links
C. lead an investigation
D. protect from attack.

_____ 7. To *emulate* others is to
A. seek to be like them
B. criticize them
C. teach them
D. create idealized fantasies of them.

Writing Topics

1. Write a paragraph describing your career goal and how you came to choose it. Be as specific as you can in telling about the career you would like to be pursuing 15 or 20 years from now. Review Descriptive Paragraphs in Unit 2.

2. Write an essay defending one of the following statements:

   a. College sports bring many benefits to colleges and to students and therefore should be supported by the entire college community.

   b. College sports should no longer be considered amateur sports. Athletes should be given contracts and salaries just like professionals.

   c. College sports have gotten too big and commercialized. They should be eliminated or reduced to a minor place in campus life.

Be sure to show an awareness of arguments from the opposing side and to use facts and examples in supporting your own opinion. Review the Persuasive Mode: the Dialogue Pattern in Unit 3.

Perri Klass (1958–   )

Perri Klass is a pediatrician, novelist, and author of nonfiction, as well as a mother of two children. Although admitting to a large quantity of ambition herself, she asks, in this article, which was first published in *Self* (June 1990), whether too much ambition can cause problems.

Ambition*

In college, my friend Beth was very ambitious, not only for herself but for her friends. She was interested in foreign relations, in travel, in going to law school. "I plan to be secretary of state someday," she would say matter-of-factly. One mutual friend was studying literature, planning to go to graduate school; he would be chairman of the Yale English department. Another friend was interested in political journalism and would someday edit *Time* magazine. I was a biology major, which was a problem: Beth's best friend from childhood was also studying biology, and Beth had already decided *she* would win the Nobel Prize. This was resolved by my interest in writing fiction. I would win *that* Nobel, while her other friend would win for science.

It was a joke; we were all smart-ass college freshmen, pretending the world was ours for the asking. But it was not entirely a joke. We were *smart* college freshmen, and why should we limit our ambitions?

I've always liked ambitious people, and many of my closest friends have had grandiose dreams. I like such people, not because I am desperate to be buddies with a future secretary of state but because I find ambitious people entertaining, interesting to talk to, fun to watch. And, of course, I like such people because I am ambitious myself, and I would rather not feel apologetic about it.

Ambition has gotten bad press. Back in the seventeenth century, Spinoza thought ambition and lust were "nothing but species of madness, although they are not enumerated among diseases." Especially in women, ambition has often been seen as a profoundly dislikable quality; the word "ambitious" linked to a "career woman" suggested that she was ruthless, hard as nails, clawing her way to success on top of bleeding bodies of her friends.

Then, in the late Seventies and the Eighties, ambition became desirable, as books with titles like *How to Stomp Your Way to Success* became bestsellers. It was still a nasty sort of attribute, but nasty attributes were good because they helped you look out for number one.

But what I mean by ambition is dreaming big dreams, putting no limits on your expectations and your hopes. I don't really like very specific, attainable ambitions, the kind you learn to set in the career-strategy course taught by the author of *How to Stomp Your Way to Success.* I like big ambitions that suggest that the world could open up at any time, with work and luck and determination. The next book could hit it big. The next research project could lead to something fantastic. The next bright idea could change history.

Of course, eventually you have to stop being a freshman in college. You limit your ambitions and become more realistic, wiser about your potential, your abilities, the number of things your life can hold. Sometimes you get close to something you wanted to do, only to find it looks better from far away. Back when I was a freshman, to tell the truth, I wanted to be Jane Goodall, go into the jungle to study monkeys and learn things no one had ever dreamed of. This ambition was based on an interest in biology and several *National Geographic* television specials; it turned out that wasn't enough of a basis for a life. There were a number of other early ambitions that didn't pan out either. I was not fated to live a wild, adventurous life, to travel alone to all the most exotic parts of the world, to leave behind a string of broken hearts. Oh well, you have to grow up, at least a little.

One of the worst things ambition can do is tell you you're a failure. The world is full of measuring tapes, books and articles to tell you where you should be at your age, after so-and-so many years of doing what you do.

Almost all of us have to deal with the tremendous success of friends (or enemies), with those who somehow started out where we did but are now way in front. My college-alumni magazine arrives every two months without fail, so I can find out who graduated two years *after* I did but is now running a groundbreaking clinic at a major university hospital (and I'm only just finishing my residency!). Who is restoring a fabulous mansion in a highly desirable town by the sea. Who got promoted yet again, due to natural brilliance and industry.

I read an article recently about how one's twenties are the decade for deciding on a career and finishing your training, and the thirties are for consolidating your success and rising within your chosen job (and here I am in my thirties, not even sure what I want to do yet!). With all these external yardsticks, the last thing anyone needs is an internal voice as well, whispering irritably that you were supposed to do it better, get further and that all you've actually accomplished is mush, since you haven't met your own goals.

The world is full of disappointed people. Some of them probably never had much ambition to start with; they sat back and waited for something good and feel cheated because it never happened. Some of them had very set, specific ambitions and, for one reason or another, never got what they wanted. Others got what they wanted but found it wasn't exactly what they'd expected it to be. Disappointed ambition provides fodder for both drama and melodrama: aspiring athletes (who coulda been contenders), aspiring dancers (all they ever needed was the music and the mirror).

The world is also full of people so ambitious, so consumed by drive and overdrive that nothing they pass on the way to success has any value at all. Life becomes one long exercise in delayed gratification; everything you do, you're doing only because it will one day get you where you want to be. Medical training is an excellent example of delayed gratification. You spend years in medical school doing things with no obvious relationship to your future as a doctor, and then you spend years in residency, living life on a miserable schedule, staying up all night and slogging through the day, telling yourself that one day all this will be over. It's what you have to do to become a doctor, but it's a lousy model for life in general. There's nothing wrong with a little delayed gratification every now and then, but a job you do only because of where it will get you—and not because you like it—means a life of muttering to yourself, "Someday this will be over." This is bad for the disposition.

As you grow up, your ambitions may come into conflict. Most prominently nowadays, we have to hear about Women Torn Between Family and Career, about women who make it to the top only to realize they left their ovaries behind. Part of growing up, of course, is realizing that there is only so much room in one life, whether you are male or female. You can do one thing wholeheartedly and single-mindedly and give up some other things. Or you can be greedy and grab for something new without wanting to give up what you already have. This leads to a chaotic and crowded life in which you are always late, always overdue, always behind, but rarely bored. Even so, you have to come to terms with limitations; you cannot crowd your life with occupations and then expect to do each one as well as you might if it were all you had to do. I realize this when I race out of the hospital, offending a senior doctor who had offered to explain something to me, only to arrive late at the daycare center, annoying the people who have been taking care of my daughter.

People consumed by ambition, living with ambition, get to be a little humorless, a little one-sided. On the other hand, people who completely abrogate their ambition aren't all fun and games either. I've met a certain number of women whose ambitions are no longer for themselves at all; their lives are now dedicated to their offspring. I hope my children grow up to be nice people, smart people, people who use good grammar; and I hope they grow up to find things they love to do, and do well. But my ambitions are for *me*.

Of course, I try to be mature about it all. I don't assign my friends Nobel Prizes or top government posts. I don't pretend that there is room in my life for any and every kind of ambition I can imagine. Instead, I say piously that all I want are three things: I want to write as well as I can, I want to have a family and I want to be a good pediatrician. And then, of course, a voice inside whispers . . . to write a bestseller, to have ten children, to do stunning medical research. Fame and fortune, it whispers, fame and fortune. Even though I'm not a college freshman anymore, I'm glad to find that little voice still there, whispering sweet nothings in my ear.

QUESTIONS

Reading for Understanding

1. Is this essay about the value of ambition or the harm caused by ambition, or both?

2. What kinds of ambition does Dr. Klass identify? What are her feelings about each kind?

3. Does she agree or disagree with Dr. Gates's attitudes toward big ambitions in his article ("Delusions of Grandeur")?

4. How does her essay apply specifically to women? In what way does it apply to men as well?

Noticing Writing Techniques

1. This is a sort of definition essay, although it also contains analysis and persuasion. In discussing and defining *ambition,* she mentions that in the past, the word has "gotten bad press." What was wrong with the way the word used to be used? How was it used concerning women?

2. Dr. Klass uses her own experience and the example of her college friends to support her ideas. How does this experience strengthen her point? Does it weaken her point not to use other kinds of support?

3. Although her tone is serious and she uses standard English, sometimes Dr. Klass likes to include informal words or phrases to make her writing livelier. What are some examples of colloquial words or phrases in the essay?

Noticing Vocabulary

_____ 1. An *attribute* is a
   A. course of study
   C. trait
   B. state of good health
   D. formal speech praising someone.

—————— 2. A doctor's *residency* is a
   A. place where he or she   B. period of training
      lives near the hospital
   C. series of examinations   D. college of medicine.

—————— 3. *Delayed gratification* means
   A. not getting what you want
   B. being angry because your efforts did not succeed
   C. putting off pleasure now for a long-term goal
   D. having an illness that will not show up for a long time.

—————— 4. To *abrogate* something is to
   A. get rid of it   B. exaggerate it
   C. apologize for it   D. be happy that you have
                                    it.

Writing Topics

1. Write a paragraph giving your own definition of *ambition* and explaining what effect you think it has on people. Review Definition Paragraphs in Unit 2.

2. Write an essay explaining your own *ambivalent* feelings (i.e., feelings that are in conflict) about some social issue or situation. Use your own experience to bring out your conflicted feelings about this situation, concept, or issue (suggestions: marriage, divorce, adoption, religion, the opposite sex, television). Review Essays Based on Autobiographical Examples in the Expository Mode, Unit 3.

Henry David Thoreau (1817–1862)

Often regarded as the ultimate individualist, Henry David Thoreau was one of the great American writers, thinkers, and naturalists of the nineteenth century. Like Perri Klass, he was fond of grandiose dreams, but for him they were never worldly ambitions. Although a Harvard graduate, he cared nothing about making money or achieving status, and he had no wife or children. In this passage from his most famous book, *Walden, or Life in the Woods* (1854), he explains why he lived alone for two years in a cabin near Walden Pond in Massachusetts, spending his time writing, reading, thinking, and fishing.

Where I Lived, and What I Lived For
from *Walden*

We must learn to reawaken and keep ourselves awake, not by mechanical aids, but by an infinite expectation of the dawn, which does not forsake us in our soundest sleep. I know of no more encouraging fact than the unquestionable ability of man to elevate his life by a conscious endeavor. It is something to be able to paint a particular picture, or to carve a statue, and so to make a few objects beautiful; but it is far more glorious to carve and paint the very atmosphere and medium through which we look, which morally we can do. To affect the quality of the day, that is the highest of the arts. Every man is tasked to make his life, even in its details, worthy of the contemplation of his most elevated and critical hour. If we refused, or rather used up, such paltry information as we get, the oracles would distinctly inform us how this might be done.

I went to the woods because I wished to live deliberately, to front only the essential facts of life, and see if I could learn what it had to teach, and not, when I came to die, discover that I had not lived. I did not wish to live what was not life, living is so dear; nor did I wish to practice resignation, unless it was quite necessary. I wanted to live deep and suck out all the marrow of life, to live so sturdily and Spartan-like as to put to rout all that was not life, to cut a broad swath and shave close, to drive life into a corner, and reduce it to its lowest terms, and, if it proved to be mean, why then to get the whole and genuine meanness of it, and publish its meanness to the world; or if it were sublime, to know it by experience, and be able to give a true account of it in my next excursion. For most men, it appears to me, are in a strange uncertainty about it, whether it is of the devil or of God, and have *somewhat hastily* concluded that it is the chief end of man here to "glorify God and enjoy him forever."

Still we live meanly, like ants; though the fable tells us that we were long ago changed into men; like pygmies we fight with cranes; it is error upon error, and clout upon clout, and our best virture has for its occasion a superfluous and evitable wretchedness. Our life is frittered away by detail. An honest man has hardly need to count more than his ten fingers, or in extreme cases he may add his ten toes, and lump the rest. Simplicity, simplicity, simplicity! I say, let your affairs be as two or three, and not a hundred or a thousand; instead of a million count half a dozen, and keep your accounts on your thumbnail. In the midst of this chopping sea of civilized life, such are the clouds and storms and quicksands and thousand-and-one items to be allowed for, that a man has to live, if he would not founder and go to the bottom and not make his port at all, by dead reckoning, and he must be a great calculator indeed who succeeds. Simplify, simplify. Instead of three meals a day, if it be necessary, eat but one; instead of a hundred dishes, five; and reduce other things in proportion. Our life is like a German Confederacy, made up of petty states, with its boundary forever fluctuating, so that even a German cannot tell you how it is bounded at any moment. The nation itself, with all its so-called internal improvements, which, by the way are all external and superficial, is just such an unwieldy and overgrown establishment, cluttered with furniture and tripped up by its own traps, ruined by luxury and heedless expense, by want of calculation and a worthy aim, as the million households in the land; and the only cure for it, as for them, is in a rigid economy, a stern and more than Spartan simplicity of life and elevation of purpose. It lives too fast. Men think that it is essential that the *Nation* have commerce, and export ice, and talk through a telegraph, and ride thirty miles an hour, without a doubt, whether *they* do or not; but whether we should live like baboons or like men, is a little uncertain. . . .

QUESTIONS

Reading for Understanding

1. As a philosopher, Thoreau looks at the purpose of life differently than most of us do. He is concerned not with the quantity of achievement, status, wealth, or power, but with the quality of living, both in his life and in the country. What does he think prevents most people and the country at large from having an "elevated" purpose? What must everyone do in order to raise the quality of life?

2. If Thoreau were writing today, would he have reason to make the same complaints about life in the United States? How might he be impressed by the technological progress we have made? What would he think of our careers, families, and daily life?

Noticing Writing Techniques

1. How is Thoreau's nineteenth-century English different in style, tone, and vocabulary from most writers today? Can you follow his meaning on first reading, or did you have to read it over several times? What does he assume about his readers in order to write as he does?

2. What similes or metaphors does Thoreau use to describe life in his time?

3. Describe Thoreau's sentences and paragraphs. How do they differ from typical sentences and paragraphs nowadays? How do you explain this difference?

Noticing Vocabulary

_____ 1. *Oracles* are
   A. tropical animals   B. messages from the gods
   C. jewels found in India   D. edible shellfish.

_____ 2. The *marrow* of something is its
A. outer surface   B. design and
                                      construction
C. inner substance   D. color.

_____ 3. *Superfluous* means
A. crucial   B. unnecessary
C. large   D. difficult to understand.

_____ 4. *Spartan* living means
A. living in luxury   B. living near the ocean
C. living with animals   D. living with no comforts
   and plants   or luxuries.

Writing Topics

1. Write a paragraph responding to Thoreau's argument that we must live simply and rescue ourselves from "this chopping sea of civilized life." Explain why you agree or disagree with the goal of living simply. Review Persuasive Paragraphs in Unit 2.

2. Write an essay explaining how life has changed as a result of technology during your lifetime. Enumerate some of the ways life has improved, and, possibly, how it has gotten worse as a result of high technology and other changes. Review the Expository Mode in Unit 3.

Ellen Goodman (1941–   )

A well-known syndicated columnist who won the Pulitzer Prize in 1980 for her personal commentaries on social issues, Ellen Goodman has also published several books. *Turning Points* (1979) studies people who made serious changes in their lives, and four later books included collections of Ms Goodman's newspaper columns. The article below appeared in 1990. In it, she looks at the problem of how communications technology threatens to change the way we work and live.

The Cordless Tie that Binds People to Work*

I am standing in the lobby of a large office building when the man beside me starts talking into his briefcase. The fellow looks buttoned up and rational, so

_____
*© 1994, The Boston Globe Company. Reprinted with permission.

I assume if he is hearing voices, they are real ones. There is a phone in his briefcase.

I am sitting at a red light in traffic, when the car beside me starts ringing. The driver picks up the receiver and begins a now common routine. She steers her car with one hand and her business with the other.

I am somewhere over Connecticut on a one-hour shuttle from Boston to New York when my companion sticks his credit card into the chair before us and calls his office to find out if there are any messages. At 22,000 feet, he leaves a phone message in Boston about where to forward his phone messages in New York.

Once upon a time, a sitcom hero named Maxwell Smart used to talk into his shoe, and we laughed. But somewhere along the line, the high-touch gadgetry of the spy films got transformed into the tools of everyday trade. Today there are people within reach of a phone every moment of their lives except takeoff, landing, and a long tunnel ride. The work-world is now an interlocking network of communications and messages, a proliferation of phones, a great babbling overkill of Touch-Tone technology. We live from call-waiting to call-forwarding, from answering machines to voice mail. We are surrounded by cellular phones and portable phones. We even have a little pocket phone to form a "personal communications network."

In theory, this population explosion of phones and their fax-similes has sprung into being to offer mobility and freedom from the office. Indeed, people who take phones to the gym, the restaurant, even the bathroom, swear by the freedom they gain with this telephone tether. But watching my colleagues-on-call, I have become convinced that this network is a tie that binds more and more people to work. The executives who go to the beach with a towel and a telephone aren't liberated from the office: They are only on work-release. The cellular commuters haven't changed the work environment; they have turned every environment into workspace. The new touchable class reminds me of parolees let out of jail after being collared by a tracking device.

I admit to being somewhat phonephobic. One of the great pleasures of life is being out of touch. If I were to devise a home voice mail, it would say: Touch 1 if this is a life-threatening emergency. Touch 2 if you are a family member with a flat tire on a dark corner. Touch 3 if you are a junk phone call and would like to be immolated.

But even by normal standards, we've gone too far. In the work-world, we are increasingly seduced by the notion of how efficient it is to be in constant contact with each other. The phone in all its forms has become a kind of endless meeting that entices us to spend more time communicating than producing. And the operative phase is "more time." The Bureau of Labor says that Americans are working longer hours than we used to. Twenty million or so have bumped the workweek over the forty-nine hour mark. There are no figures that tell us how many of those hours are spent leaving messages for people who left messages to call. Nor do we know how much time is spent responding to questions that we're asked only because of the availability of the instant-information-gratification system. In the constant-contact future, it's easy to see an insidious expansion of work and a more insidious extension of the workplace. In the industrial age, the factory foreman controlled his workers from nine to five. In the information age, workers are always available. Today it is possible to begin work with the first commuting mile on a cellular phone, continue it through a lunch accompanied by a "personal communications network," and end with a bedtime chat into your briefcase. In twenty-four-hour contact, we haven't missed a thing. Except, of course, the time for rumination, the solitude and space for the work we call thinking.

For years the pitch of the telephone company was "Reach out and touch someone." Now we're all tied up, workers of the world united by the Touch-Tone, and we need a new slogan. How about this one: "Let my people off the hook."

QUESTIONS

Reading for Understanding

1. What is the chief problem that Ms. Goodman thinks will result from the new communications technology? Do her examples illustrate this problem?

2. Does Goodman share Thoreau's belief that technology and excessive complications prevent us from improving the quality of our lives?

3. Telephone technology is meant to be a means of better communication, but Ms. Goodman shows that it tends to become an end in itself. Where in the essay does she show this reversal of ends and means?

Noticing Writing Techniques

1. How does Ms. Goodman create humor in her language and examples?

2. Ms. Goodman is an *allusive* writer. What famous statement does she echo in her phrase "workers of the world united"? What well-known line is she echoing when she says, "Let my people off the hook"? What reference does the title of her essay contain?

3. How much of her own personal experience does she use to illustrate her point? What other evidence does she use as well?

Noticing Vocabulary

_____ 1. A *proliferation* of something is
A. a decline in numbers   B. an increase in efficiency
C. an increase in numbers   D. a decline in interest.

_____ 2. A *tether* is a
A. writing instrument   B. machine for lifting
C. shoelace   D. leash.

_____ 3. To be *immolated* means to be
   A. killed   B. rewarded
   C. cured   D. injured.

_____ 4. An *insidious* development is
   A. beneficial in the long run   B. treacherous
   C. too expensive   D. a turn for the better.

_____ 5. *Rumination* means
   A. good nutrition   B. correction of errors
   C. hard work   D. meditation.

Writing Topics

1. Write a paragraph telling about how you use telephones, answering machines, cordless phones, and fax machines. Review Exposition: Classification and Exposition: Cause and Effect in Unit 2.

2. Write an essay in which you agree or disagree with Ms. Goodman's main point. Try to persuade the reader of either the benefits or the harm of the new communications technology to both the workplace and our private lives. Review the Persuasive Mode in Unit 3.

Lester Thurow (1938–   )

Lester Thurow is dean and professor of economics at MIT's Sloan School of Management and author of many books and articles on economic issues, including *The Zero-Sum Society, Economics Explained,* and the book from which the following comparison is taken, *Head to Head* (1992). In the global economy since the fall of communism in Russia, we no longer face a conflict between capitalism and communism but an intense competition among different forms of capitalism, ours and the forms practiced in Europe and Japan. How are workers' lives affected by the differences, and what will be the outcome of this competition?

New Competitors*
from *Head to Head: the Coming Economic Battle Among Japan, Europe, and America*

Economics abhors a vacuum no less than Mother Nature. The economic competition between communism and capitalism is over, but another competition between two different forms of capitalism is already under way. Using a distinction first made by George C. Lodge, a Harvard Business School professor, the individualistic Anglo-Saxon British-American form of capitalism is going to face off against the communitarian German and Japanese variants of capitalism. . . . The essential difference between the two forms of capitalism is their stress on communitarian versus individualistic values as the route to economic success—the "I" of America or of the United Kingdom versus "Das Volk:" and "Japan, Inc."

America and Britain trumpet individualistic values: the brilliant entrepreneur, Nobel Prize winners, large wage differentials, individual responsibility for skills, easy to fire and easy to quit, profit maximization, and hostile mergers and takeovers—their hero is the Lone Ranger. In contrast, Germany and Japan trumpet communitarian values: business groups, social responsibility for skills, teamwork, firm loyalty, industry strategies, and active industrial policies that promote growth. Anglo-Saxon firms are profit maximizers; Japanese business firms play a game that might better be known as "strategic conquest." Americans believe in "consumer economics"; Japanese believe in "producer economics."

In the Ango-Saxon variant of capitalism, the individual is supposed to have a personal economic strategy for success, and the business firm is supposed to have an economic strategy that is a reflection of the wishes of its individual shareholders. Since shareholders want income to maximize their lifetime consumption, their firms must be profit maximizers. For the profit-maximizing firm, customer and employee relations are merely a means to the end of higher profits for the shareholders. Wages are beaten down where possible, and when not needed, employees are to be laid off. Lower wages equal higher profits. Workers in the Anglo-Saxon system are expected to change employers whenever opportunities arise to earn higher wages elsewhere. They owe their employer nothing. In contrast, many Japanese firms still refer to voluntary quits as "treason."

In communitarian capitalism individual and firm strategies also exist but are built on quite different foundations. The individual does not play as an individual. One joins a team and is then successful as part of that company team. The key decision in an individual's personal strategy is to join the *right* team. From then on their own personal success or failure will be closely bound up with the success or failure of the firm for which they work. In the Anglo-Saxon world, company loyalty is somewhat suspect. The individual succeeds as an individual—not as a member of a team.

In both Germany and Japan, job switching is a far less prevalent phenomenon than it is in the United States or Great Britain. Labor-force turnover is bad in communitarian capitalism, since no one will plant apple trees (make sacrifices for the good of the company) if they do not expect to be around when the apples are harvested. In contrast, turnover rates are viewed positively in America and Great Britain. Firms are getting rid of unneeded labor when they fire workers, and individuals are moving to higher wage (higher productivity) opportunities when they quit. Job switching, voluntary or involuntary, is almost a synonym for efficiency.

The communitarian business firm has a very different set of stakeholders who must be consulted when its strategies are being set. In Japanese business firms employees are seen as the number one stakeholder, customers number two, and the shareholders a distant number three. Since the employee is the prime stakeholder, higher employee wages are a central goal of the firm in Japan. Profits will be sacrificed to maintain either wages or employment. Dividend payouts to the shareholders are low.

Communitarian societies expect companies to invest in the skills of their work forces. In the United States and Great Britain, skills are an individual responsibility. Firms exist to promote efficiency by hiring skills at the lowest possible wage rates. Labor is not a member of the team. It is just another factor of production to be rented when it is needed, and laid off when it is not.

QUESTIONS

Reading for Understanding

1. What is the difference between companies' attitudes toward workers in the United States and Japan? What is the difference between workers' attitudes in those countries?

2. What is the main goal of a corporation in the "Anglo-Saxon" economy? What is the main goal of a corporation in Germany or Japan? What group of people is considered most important in each type of corporation?

3. Who is considered responsible for training workers in each system?

Noticing Writing Techniques

1. How does Lester Thurow organize this comparison/contrast essay? Does he emphasize similarities or differences? What are the categories of comparison?

2. Does Thurow show a preference for one system or the other, or does he remain neutral? If he does show signs of partiality, what are they?

Noticing Vocabulary

_____ 1. To *abhor* something is
    A. to love it   B. to prefer it
    C. to hate it   D. to forget it.

_____ 2. A *variant* of something is a
    A. bad example   B. differing example
    C. identical example   D. positive example.

_____ 3. *Hostile mergers* are
    A. sudden increases in prices
    B. price wars between large corporations

C. absorbing of corporations by others

D. firing of top executives in big corporations.

_____ 4. A *synonym* is a

A. word that has a meaning similar to another one's

B. a word that means the opposite of another one

C. a word that has an unclear meaning

D. a word that sounds just like another one.

Writing Topics

1. Write a paragraph describing a job environment where you worked. Explain how you felt about the job, especially whether you identified with it or felt alienated from it. Review Descriptive Paragraphs in Unit 2.

2. Is it better to have an individualistic attitude toward a career, with the full responsibility for your own training and the freedom to change jobs when you want, or a collectivist attitude, with the assumption that it is the company's responsibility to provide job security, benefits, and training, and your duty to remain loyal to the company? Write a persuasive essay explaining and supporting your opinion on this controversy. Show awareness of opposing opinions, and support your opinion with examples from your own experience and that of others you know. Review the Persuasive Mode in Unit 3.

Tillie Olsen (1913–   )

Tillie Olsen was a part of the generation whose lives and careers were profoundly disrupted by the Great Depression of the 1930s. She came from Omaha, Nebraska, and dropped out of school to work, later becoming a writer and activist while writing and raising four children. "I Stand Here Ironing" (1954) reflects the limited, tough-minded view of a mother who has seen hard times and values survival over extravagant ambitions.

I Stand Here Ironing*

I stand here ironing, and what you asked me moves tormented back and forth with the iron.

"I wish you would manage the time to come in and talk with me about your daughter. I'm sure you can help me understand her. She's a youngster who needs help and whom I'm deeply interested in helping."

---

*"I Stand Here Ironing", from TELL ME A RIDDLE by Tillie Olsen. Copyright © 1956, 1960, 1961 by Tillie Olsen. Used by permission of Delacorte Press/Seymour Lawrence, a division of Bantam Doubleday Dell Publishing Group, Inc.

"Who needs help.". . . Even if I came, what good would it do? You think because I am her mother I have a key, or that in some way you could use me as a key? She has lived for nineteen years. There is all that life that has happened outside of me, beyond me.

And when is there time to remember, to sift, to weigh, to estimate, to total? I will start and there will be an interruption and I will have to gather it all together again. Or I will become engulfed with all I did or did not do, with what should have been and what cannot be helped.

She was a beautiful baby. The first and only one of our five that was beautiful at birth. You do not guess how new and uneasy her tenancy in her now-loveliness. You did not know her all those years she was thought homely, or see her poring over her baby pictures, making me tell her over and over how beautiful she had been—and would be, I would tell her—and was now, to the seeing eye. But the seeing eyes were few or nonexistent. Including mine.

I nursed her. They feel that's important nowadays. I nursed all the children, but with her, with all the fierce rigidity of first motherhood, I did like the books then said. Though her cries battered me to trembling and my breasts ached with swollenness, I waited till the clock decreed.

Why do I put that first? I do not even know if it matters, or if it explains anything.

She was a beautiful baby. She blew shining bubbles of sound. She loved motion, loved light, loved color and music and textures. She would lie on the floor in her blue overalls patting the surface so hard in ecstasy her hands and feet would blur. She was a miracle to me, but when she was eight months old I had to leave her daytimes with the woman downstairs to whom she was no miracle at all, for I worked or looked for work and for Emily's father, who "could no longer endure" (he wrote in his good-bye note) "sharing want with us."

I was nineteen. It was the pre-relief, pre-WPA world of the depression. I would start running as soon as I got off the streetcar, running up the stairs, the place smelling sour, and awake or asleep to startle awake, when she saw me she would break into a clogged weeping that could not be comforted, a weeping I can hear yet.

After a while I found a job hashing at night so I could be with her days, and it was better. But it came to where I had to bring her to his family and leave her.

It took a long time to raise the money for her fare back. Then she got chicken pox and I had to wait longer. When she finally came, I hardly knew her, walking quick and nervous like her father, looking like her father, thin, and dressed in a shoddy red that yellowed her skin and glared at the pockmarks. All the baby loveliness gone.

She was two. Old enough for nursery school they said, and I did not know then what I know now—the fatigue of the long day, and the lacerations of group life in the kinds of nurseries that are only parking places for children.

Except that it would have made no difference if I had known. It was the only place there was. It was the only way we could be together, the only way I could hold a job.

And even without knowing, I knew. I knew the teacher that was evil because all these years it has curdled into my memory, the little boy hunched in the corner, her rasp, "why aren't you outside, because Alvin hits you? that's no reason, go out, scaredy." I knew Emily hated it even if she did not clutch and implore "don't go Mommy" like the other children, mornings.

She always had a reason why we should stay home. Momma, you look sick. Momma, I feel sick. Momma, the teachers aren't there today, they're sick. Momma, we can't go, there was a fire there last night. Momma, it's a holiday today, no school, they told me.

But never a direct protest, never rebellion. I think of our others in their three-, four-year-oldness—the explosions, the tempers, the denunciations, the demands—and I feel suddenly ill. I put the iron down. What in me demanded that goodness in her? And what was the cost, the cost to her of such goodness?

The old man living in the back once said in his gentle way: "You should smile at Emily more when you look at her." What *was* in my face when I looked at her? I loved her. There were all the acts of love.

It was only with the others I remembered what he said, and it was the face of joy, and not of care or tightness or worry I turned to them—too late for Emily. She does not smile easily, let alone almost always as her brothers and sisters do. Her face is closed and sombre, but when she wants, how fluid. You must have seen it in her pantomimes, you spoke of her rare gift for comedy on the stage that rouses a laughter out of the audience so dear they applaud and applaud and do not want to let her go.

Where does it come from, that comedy? There was none of it in her when she came back to me that second time, after I had had to send her away again. She had a new daddy now to learn to love, and I think perhaps it was a better time.

Except when we left her alone nights, telling ourselves she was old enough.

"Can't you go some other time, Mommy, like tomorrow?" she would ask. "Will it be just a little while you'll be gone? Do you promise?"

The time we came back, the front door was open, the clock on the floor in the hall. She rigid awake. "It wasn't just a little while. I didn't cry. Three times I called you, just three times, and then I ran downstairs to open the door so you could come faster. The clock talked loud. I threw it away, it scared me what it talked."

She said the clock talked loud again that night I went to the hospital to have Susan. She was delirious with the fever that comes before red measles, but she was fully conscious all the week I was gone and the week after we were home when she could not come near the new baby or me.

She did not get well. She stayed skeleton thin, not wanting to eat, and night after night she had nightmares. She would call for me, and I would rouse from exhaustion to sleepily call back: "You're all right, darling, go to sleep, it's just a dream," and if she still called, in a sterner voice, "now go to sleep, Emily, there's nothing to hurt you." Twice, only twice, when I had to get up for Susan anyhow, I went in to sit with her.

Now when it is too late (as if she would let me hold and comfort her like I do the others) I get up and go to her at once at her moan or restless stirring. "Are you awake, Emily? Can I get you something?" And the answer is always the same: "No, I'm all right, go back to sleep, Mother."

They persuaded me at the clinic to send her away to a convalescent home in the country where "she can have the kind of food and care you can't manage for her, and you'll be free to concentrate on the new baby." They still send children to that place. I see pictures on the society page of sleek young women planning affairs to raise money for it, or dancing at the affairs, or decorating Easter eggs or filling Christmas stockings for the children.

They never have a picture of the children so I do not know if the girls still wear those gigantic red bows and the ravaged looks on the every other Sunday when parents can come to visit "unless otherwise notified"—as we were notified the first six weeks.

Oh it is a handsome place, green lawns and tall trees and fluted flower beds. High up on the balconies of each cottage the children stand, the girls in their red bows and white dresses, the boys in white suits and giant red ties. The parents stand below shrieking up to be heard and the children shriek down to be heard, and between them the invisible wall "Not To Be Contaminated by Parental Germs or Physical Affection."

There was a tiny girl who always stood hand in hand with Emily. Her parents never came. One visit she was gone. "They moved her to Rose Cottage" Emily shouted in explanation. "They don't like you to love anybody here."

She wrote once a week, the labored writing of a seven-year-old. "I am fine. How is the baby. If I write my leter nicly I will have a star. Love." There never was a star. We wrote every other day, letters she could never hold or keep but only hear read—once. "We simply do not have room for children to keep any personal possessions," they patiently explained when we pieced one Sunday's shrieking together to plead how much it would mean to Emily, who loved so to keep things, to be allowed to keep her letters and cards.

Each visit she looked frailer. "She isn't eating," they told us.

(They had runny eggs for breakfast or mush with lumps, Emily said later, I'd hold it in my mouth and not swallow. Nothing ever tasted good, just when they had chicken.)

It took us eight months to get her released home, and only the fact that she gained back so little of her seven lost pounds convinced the social worker.

I used to try to hold and love her after she came back, but her body would stay stiff, and after a while she'd push away. She ate little. Food sickened her, and I think much of life too. Oh she had physical lightness and brightness, twinkling by on skates, bouncing like a ball up and down up and down over the jump rope, skimming over the hill; but these were momentary.

She fretted about her appearance, thin and dark and foreign-looking at a time when every little girl was supposed to look or thought she should look a chubby blonde replica of Shirley Temple. The doorbell sometimes rang for her, but no one seemed to come and play in the house or be a best friend. Maybe because we moved so much.

There was a boy she loved painfully through two school semesters. Months later she told me how she had taken pennies from my purse to buy him candy. "Licorice was his favorite and I brought him some every day, but he still liked Jennifer better'n me. Why, Mommy?" The kind of question for which there is no answer.

School was a worry to her. She was not glib or quick in a world where glibness and quickness were easily confused with ability to learn. To her overworked and exasperated teachers she was an overconscientious "slow learner" who kept trying to catch up and was absent entirely too often.

I let her be absent, though sometimes the illness was imaginary. How different from my now-strictness about attendance with the others. I wasn't working. We had a new baby, I was home anyhow. Sometimes, after Susan grew old enough, I would keep her home from school, too, to have them all together.

Mostly Emily had asthma, and her breathing, harsh and labored, would fill the house with a curiously tranquil sound. I would bring the two old dresser mirrors and her boxes of collections to her bed. She would select beads and single earrings, bottle tops and shells, dried flowers and pebbles, old postcards and scraps, all sorts of oddments; then she and Susan would play Kingdom, setting up landscapes and furniture, peopling them with action.

Those were the only times of peaceful companionship between her and Susan. I have edged away from it, that poisonous feeling between them, that terrible balancing of hurts and needs I had to do between the two, and did so badly, those earlier years.

Oh there are conflicts between the others too, each one human, needing, demanding, hurting, taking—but only between Emily and Susan, no, Emily toward Susan that corroding resentment. It seems so obvious on the surface, yet it is not obvious. Susan, the second child, Susan, golden- and curly-haired and chubby, quick and articulate and assured, everything in appearance and manner Emily was not; Susan, not able to resist Emily's precious things, losing or sometimes clumsily breaking them; Susan telling jokes and riddles to company for applause while Emily sat silent (to say to me later: that was *my* riddle, Mother, I told it to Susan); Susan, who for all the five years' difference in age was just a year behind Emily in developing physically.

I am glad for that slow physical development that widened the difference between her and her contemporaries, though she suffered over it. She was too vulnerable for that terrible world of youthful competition, of preening and parading, of constant measuring of yourself against every other, of envy, "If I had that copper hair," "If I had that skin. . . ." She tormented herself enough about not looking like the others, there was enough of the unsureness, the having to be conscious of words before you speak, the constant caring—what are they thinking of me?—without having it all magnified by the merciless physical drives.

Ronnie is calling. He is wet and I change him. It is rare there is such a cry now. That time of motherhood is almost behind me when the ear is not one's own but must always be racked and listening for the child cry, the child call. We sit for a while and I hold him, looking out over the city spread in charcoal with its soft aisles of light. "*Shoogily*," he breathes and curls closer. I carry him back to bed, asleep. *Shoogily*. A funny word, a family word, inherited from Emily, invented by her to say: *comfort*.

In this and other ways she leaves her seal, I say aloud. And startle at my saying it. What do I mean? What did I start to gather together, to try and make coherent? I was at the terrible, growing years. War years. I do not remember them well. I was working, there were four smaller ones now, there was not time for her. She had to help be a mother, and housekeeper, and shopper. She had to set her seal. Mornings of crisis and near hysteria trying to get lunches packed, hair combed, coats and shoes found, everyone to school or Child Care on time, the baby ready for transportation. And always the paper scribbled on by a smaller one, the book looked at by Susan then mislaid, the homework not done. Running out to that huge school where she was one, she was lost, she was a drop; suffering over the unpreparedness, stammering and unsure in her classes.

There was so little time left at night after the kids were bedded down. She would struggle over books, always eating (it was in those years she developed her enormous appetite that is legendary in our family) and I would be ironing, or preparing food for the next day, or writing V-mail to Bill, or tending the baby. Sometimes, to make me laugh, or out of her despair, she would imitate happenings or types at school.

I think I said once: "Why don't you do something like this in the school amateur show?" One morning she phoned me at work, hardly understandable through the weeping: "Mother, I did it, I won, I won; they gave me first prize; they clapped and clapped and wouldn't let me go."

Now suddenly she was Somebody, and as imprisoned in her difference as she had been in her anonymity.

She began to be asked to perform at other high schools, even in colleges, then at city and statewide affairs. The first one we went to, I only recognized her that first moment when thin, shy, she almost drowned herself into the curtains. Then: Was this Emily? The control, the command, the convulsing and deadly clowning, the spell, then the roaring, stamping audience, unwilling to let this rare and precious laughter out of their lives.

Afterwards: You ought to do something about her with a gift like that—but without money or knowing how, what does one do? We have left it all to her, and the gift has as often eddied inside, clogged and clotted as been used and growing.

She is coming. She runs up the stairs two at a time with her light graceful step, and I know she is happy tonight. Whatever it was that occasioned your call did not happen today.

"Aren't you ever going to finish that ironing, Mother? Whistler painted his mother in a rocker. I'd have to paint mine standing over an ironing board." This is one of her communicative nights and she tells me everything and nothing as she fixes herself a plate of food out of the icebox.

She is so lovely. Why did you want me to come in at all? Why were you concerned? She will find her way.

She starts up the stairs to bed. "Don't get me up with the rest in the morning." "But I thought you were having midterms." "Oh, those," she comes back in, kisses me, and says quite lightly, "in a couple of years when we'll all be atom-dead they won't matter a bit."

She has said it before. She *believes* it. But because I have been dredging the past, and all that compounds a human being is so heavily and meaningful in me, I cannot endure it tonight.

I will never total it all. I will never come in to say: She was a child seldom smiled at. Her father left me before she was a year old. I had to work her first six years when there was work, or I sent her home and to his relatives. There were years she had care she hated. She was dark and thin and foreign-looking in a world where the prestige went to blondeness and curly hair and dimples, she was slow where glibness was prized. She was a child of anxious, not proud, love. We were poor and could not afford for her the soil of easy growth. I was a young mother, I was a distracted mother. There were the other children pushing up, demanding. Her younger sister seemed all that she was not. There were years she did not want me to touch her. She kept too much in herself, her life was such she had to keep too much in herself. My wisdom came too late. She has much to her and probably little will come of it. She is a child of her age, of depression, of war, of fear.

Let her be. So all that is in her will not bloom—but in how many does it? There is still enough left to live by. Only help her to know—help make it so there is cause for her to know—that she is more than this dress on the ironing board, helpless before the iron.

QUESTIONS

Reading for Understanding

1. How have the economic circumstances of the mother caused Emily's life to be what it has been? What does she mean by calling Emily a "child of her age, of depression, of war, of fear"?

2. Why is the mother not willing to come in to speak to the counselors about Emily?

3. What career does Emily have a talent for? What does the mother think about her chances of success? Why? What has held her back from moving ahead in it?

4. What is Emily's attitude toward education and the future? How does it differ from the mother's?

Noticing Writing Techniques

1. What sort of English does the mother use in her speech? Does she sound educated or not? Does she sound intelligent or not? What is the difference, and how does her language reflect the difference between intelligence and education?

2. Why does the author keep mentioning the ironing? What does it symbolize in the mother's life? How does it apply to Emily?

3. What ironic twist is there between the family's and Emily's experience and the talent Emily has? Why does the author stress this ironic contrast?

Noticing Vocabulary

———— 1. *Tenancy* means
    A. a habit of doing something   B. occupancy
    C. persistence   D. courage.

———— 2. *Lacerations* are
    A. links   B. scars
    C. cuts or tears   D. loud noises.

———— 3. To *implore* is to
    A. search for   B. argue
    C. plead   D. reject.

———— 4. *Pantomimes* are
    A. kinds of pancake
    B. clothing worn in the Middle East
    C. games played with racquets
    D. dramatic skits without words.

———— 5. A *convalescent* home is for
    A. the insane   B. recovery
    C. criminals   D. the elderly.

———— 6. A *replica* is a
    A. copy   B. coin
    C. dramatic performance   D. long story about another person.

———— 7. *Corroding* substances cause
    A. a high polish   B. change in color
    C. wearing away   D. sticking of objects together.

———— 8. To be in a state of *anonymity* means that
    A. you are hungry all the time
    B. nobody knows your name
    C. you are ill much of the time
    D. you get along with people.

Writing Topics

1. Write a paragraph telling about some activity you did as a child or teenager that influenced your choice of a career—either something you

did well or something that taught you what you were not good at. Review Narrative Paragraphs and "How-To" Paragraphs in Unit 2.

2. Our career choices are influenced by many factors—incidents in our lives, family values and pressures, famous people we idolize, images we have of different occupations, the abilities we think we possess based on experiences and test results, and the practical possibilities open to us because of economic realities. Write an essay explaining what your career goal is and enumerating as accurately as you can the chief influences that caused you to make that choice. Review the Persuasive Mode: Enumerating Reasons in Unit 3.

Heinrich Böll (1917–1985)

Heinrich Böll was a German novelist and short story writer who looked back on the horrors of World War II and Nazism while asking whether any of the values that caused that disaster might still be present. He strongly opposed militaristic nationalism and found the postwar world in Europe to be suffering from moral emptiness and false values. In this story, which slightly resembles the fantastic tales of Franz Kafka, he imagines a man with an odd profession. What does this story show about work and about human nature?

The Laugher*

When someone asks me what business I am in, I am seized with embarrassment: I blush and stammer, I who am otherwise known as a man of poise. I envy people who can say: I am a bricklayer. I envy barbers, bookkeepers and writers the simplicity of their avowal, for all these professions speak for themselves and need no lengthy explanation, while I am constrained to reply to such questions: I am a laugher. An admission of this kind demands another, since I have to answer the second question: "Is that how you make your living?" truthfully with "Yes." I actually do make a living at my laughing, and a good one too, for my laughing is—commercially speaking—much in demand. I am a good laugher, experienced, no one else laughs as well as I do, no one else has such a command of the fine points of my art. For a long time, in order to avoid tiresome explanations, I called myself an actor, but my talents in the field of mime and locution are so meager that I felt this designation to be too far from the truth. I love the truth, and the truth is: I am a laugher. I am neither a clown nor a comedian. I do not make people gay, I portray gaiety: I laugh like a Roman emperor, or like a sensitive schoolboy, I am as much at home in the laughter of the seventeenth century as in that of the nineteenth, and when

---

*Excerpt from SHORT SHORTS ed. Irving and Ilana Howe, Bantam 1988. Copyright by Heinrich Böll, 1966.

occasion demands I laugh my way through all the centuries, all classes of society, all categories of age: it is simply a skill which I have acquired, like the skill of being able to repair shoes. In my breast I harbor the laughter of America, the laughter of Africa, white, red, yellow laughter—and for the right fee I let it peal out in accordance with the director's requirements.

I have become indispensable; I laugh on records, I laugh on tape, and television directors treat me with respect. I laugh mournfully, moderately, hysterically; I laugh with a streetcar conductor or like a helper in the grocery business; laughter in the morning, laughter in the evening, nocturnal laughter and the laughter of twilight. In short: wherever and however laughter is required—I do it.

It need hardly be pointed out that a profession of this kind is tiring, especially as I have also—this is my specialty—mastered the art of infectious laughter; this has also made me indispensable to third- and fourth-rate comedians, who are scared—and with good reason—that their audiences will miss their punch lines, so I spend most evenings in night clubs as a kind of secret claque, my job being to laugh infectiously during the weaker parts of the program. It has to be carefully timed: my hearty, boisterous laughter must not come too soon, but neither must it come too late, it must come just at the right spot: at the prearranged moment I burst out laughing, the whole audience roars with me, and the joke is saved.

But as for me, I drag myself exhausted to the checkroom, put on my overcoat, happy that I can go off duty at last. At home I usually find telegrams waiting for me: "Urgently require your laughter. Recording Tuesday," and a few hours later I am sitting in an overheated express train bemoaning my fate.

I need scarcely say that when I am off duty or on vacation I have little inclination to laugh: the cowhand is glad when he can forget the cow, the bricklayer when he can forget the mortar, and carpenters usually have doors at home which don't work or drawers which are hard to open. Confectioners like sour pickles, butchers like marzipan, and the baker prefers sausage to bread; bullfighters raise pigeons for a hobby, boxers turn pale when their children have nose-bleeds: I find all this quite natural, for I never laugh off duty. I am a very solemn person, and people consider me—perhaps rightly so—a pessimist.

During the first years of our married life, my wife would often say to me: "Do laugh!" but since then she has come to realize that I cannot grant her this wish. I am happy when I am free to relax my tense face muscles, my frayed spirit, in profound solemnity. Indeed, even other people's laughter gets on my nerves, since it reminds me too much of my profession. So our marriage is a quiet, peaceful one, because my wife has also forgotten how to laugh: now and again I catch her smiling, and I smile too. We converse in low tones, for I detest the noise of the night clubs, the noise that sometimes fills the recording studios. People who do not know me think I am taciturn. Perhaps I am, because I have to open my mouth so often to laugh.

I go through life with an impassive expression, from time to time permitting myself a gentle smile, and I often wonder whether I have ever laughed. I think not. My brothers and sisters have always known me for a serious boy.

So I laugh in many different ways, but my own laughter I have never heard.

QUESTIONS

Reading for Understanding

1. How is it possible for this man to make a living just by laughing? Do you believe that in real life this could be done? What is he proud of in his work? How does his "profession" affect his personal life?

2. Why is the laugher embarrassed about his "profession"? Why does he envy other kinds of workers?

3. If we take this story as more symbolic than realistic, what does it tell us about human nature? About how jobs affect our personal lives? What similarity is there between the laughter's talent and Emily's talent in "I Stand Here Ironing?" How are they opposite?

4. What does the laugher mean when he says, "but my own laughter I have never heard"?

Noticing Writing Techniques

1. This story is about laughing, but is it funny? If so, what causes it to be funny? If not, what makes it so serious?

2. Does the way this story is written make it seem intended to be taken realistically, or does it seem to be a sort of fantasy story? What details tell you that it is realistic or a fantasy?

Noticing Vocabulary

_____ 1. An *avowal* is a
    A. declaration   B. angry statement
    C. question   D. grammatical term.

_____ 2. To be *constrained* is to be
    A. tense   B. relaxed
    C. compelled   D. encouraged.

_____ 3. *Elocution* is the study of
    A. cooking   B. engineering
    C. public speaking   D. tropical medicine.

_____ 4. A *nocturnal* event happens
    A. in the morning   B. on the ocean
    C. in the country   D. at night.

_____ 5. *Infectious* laughter is
    A. loud and enthusiastic   B. catching
    C. quiet and subtle   D. sickly.

_____ 6. The purpose of a *claque* is to
A. applaud a performer   B. spread rumors
C. form a conspiracy   D. organize a mailing
    against a government   campaign.

_____ 7. *Confectioners* make
A. sandwiches   B. breakfast cereal
C. bread and crackers   D. candy.

_____ 8. To be *taciturn* is to be
A. aggressive   B. silent
C. energetic   D. well-coordinated.

_____ 9. An *impassive* expression is
A. friendly   B. confused
C. timid   D. emotionless.

Writing Topics

1. Write a paragraph describing in detail your fantasy job—what you would do for a living if you had the ability, means, and opportunity. Explain in detail what satisfactions you would get from the doing the job. Review "How-To" Paragraphs in Unit 2.

2. Some people live to work; others work to live. Write an essay explaining what place people's jobs should play in their lives. Give examples from types of careers you know about, and explain how people's work enhances or harms their personal life. Review the Expository Mode in Unit 3.

Luisa Valenzuela (1938–   )

Born in Buenos Aires into a literary family, Luisa Valenzuela is a well-known novelist and journalist working in both Argentina and the United States. She has been a strong advocate for freedom of speech and the press in the face of oppressive governments, and her writing often focuses on political issues and women's rights. In the following story, she reveals the ironic twists and treacherous unpredictability of working in countries led by oppressive regimes.

The Censors*

Poor Juan! One day they caught him with his guard down before he could even realize that what he had taken as a stroke of luck was really one of fate's dirty

_____

*"The Censors" translated by David Unger. Translation copyright David Unger.

tricks. These things happen the minute you're careless and you let down your guard, as one often does. Juancito let happiness—a feeling you can't trust—get the better of him when he received from a confidential source Mariana's new address in Paris and he knew that she hadn't forgotten him. Without thinking twice, he sat down at his table and wrote her a letter. *The* letter that keeps his mind off his job during the day and won't let him sleep at night (what had he scrawled, what had he put on that sheet of paper he sent to Mariana?).

Juan knows there won't be a problem with the letter's contents, that it's irreproachable, harmless. But what about the rest? He knows that they examine, sniff, feel, and read between the lines of each and every letter, and check its tiniest comma and most accidental stain. He knows that all letters pass from hand to hand and go through all sorts of tests in the huge censorship offices and that, in the end, very few continue on their way. Usually it takes months, even years, if there aren't any snags; all this time the freedom, maybe even the life, of both sender and receiver is in jeopardy. And that's why Juan's so down in the dumps: thinking that something might happen to Mariana because of his letters. Of all people, Mariana, who must finally feel safe where she always dreamed she'd live. But he knows that the *Censor's Secret Command* operates all over the world and cashes in on the discount air rates; there's nothing to stop them from going as far as that hidden Paris neighborhood, kidnapping Mariana, and returning to their cozy homes, certain of having fulfilled their noble mission.

Well, you've got to beat them to the punch, do what everyone tries to do: sabotage the machinery, throw sand in its gears, get to the bottom of the problem so as to stop it.

This was Juan's sound plan when he, like many others, applied for a censor's job—not because he had a calling or needed a job: no, he applied simply to intercept his own letter, a consoling but unoriginal idea. He was hired immediately, for each day more and more censors are needed and no one would bother to check on his references.

Ulterior motives couldn't be overlooked by the *Censorship Division*, but they needn't be too strict with those who applied. They knew how hard it would be for those poor guys to find the letter they wanted and even if they did, what's a letter or two when the new censor would snap up so many others? That's how Juan managed to join the *Post Office's Censorship Division*, with a certain goal in mind.

The building had a festive air on the outside which contrasted with its inner staidness. Little by little, Juan was absorbed by his job and he felt at peace since he was doing everything he could to get his letter for Mariana. He didn't even worry when, in his first month, he was sent to *Section K* where envelopes were very carefully screened for explosives.

It's true that on the third day, a fellow worker had his right hand blown off by a letter, but the division chief claimed it was sheer negligence on the victim's part. Juan and the other employees were allowed to go back to their work, albeit feeling less secure. After work, one of them tried to organize a strike to demand higher wages for unhealthy work, but Juan didn't join in; after thinking it over, he reported him to his superiors and thus got promoted.

You don't form a habit by doing something once, he told himself as he left his boss's office. And when he was transferred to *Section J*, where letters are carefully checked for poison dust, he felt he had climbed a rung in the ladder.

By working hard, he quickly reached *Section E* where the work was more interesting, for he could now read and analyze the letters' contents. Here he could even hope to get hold of his letter which, judging by the time that had elapsed, had gone through the other sections and was probably floating around in this one.

Soon his work became so absorbing that his noble mission blurred in his mind. Day after day he crossed out whole paragraphs in red ink, pitilessly chucking many letters into the censored basket. These were horrible days when he was shocked by the subtle and conniving ways employed by people to pass on subversive messages; his instincts were so sharp that he found behind a simple "the weather's unsettled" or "prices continue to soar" the wavering hand of someone secretly scheming to overthrow the Government.

His zeal brought him swift promotion. We don't know if this made him happy. Very few letters reached him in *Section B*—only a handful passed the other hurdles—so he read them over and over again, passed them under a magnifying glass, searched for microprint with an electronic microscope, and tuned his sense of smell so that he was beat by the time he made it home. He'd barely manage to warm up his soup, eat some fruit, and fall into bed, satisfied with having done his duty. Only his darling mother worried, but she couldn't get him back on the right road. She'd say, though it wasn't always true: Lola called, she's at the bar with the girls, they miss you, they're waiting for you. Or else she'd leave a bottle of red wine on the table. But Juan wouldn't overdo it: any distraction could make him lose his edge and the perfect censor had to be alert, keen, attentive, and sharp to nab cheats. He had a truly patriotic task, both self-denying and uplifting.

His basket for censored letters became the best fed as well as the most cunning basket in the whole *Censorship Division*. He was about to congratulate himself for having finally discovered his true mission, when his letter to Mariana reached his hands. Naturally, he censored it without regret. And just as naturally, he couldn't stop them from executing him the following morning, another victim of his devotion to his work.

QUESTIONS

Reading for Understanding

1. What does this story say about the effect of government censorship and dictatorial control? Does the author glorify or condemn those who support such governments zealously, as Juan does?

2. What is his motive for working as a censor? How well does he do at the job? Does his relation to his job change?

Noticing Writing Techniques

1. What is the meaning of the twist at the end? Why does the author predict it at the beginning of the story? What attitude toward life does this ending reveal?

2. Would you call the author's tone serious, sympathetic, harsh, or ironic? Is it a combination of attitudes?

3. Why does the title refer to the censors rather than the censor? Why does the author go into such detail about Juan's job, when his letter to Mariana was more important to him than the job itself?

Noticing Vocabulary

_____ 1. A *confidential* source is
A. given in good faith
C. secret
B. hard to read
D. from the government.

_____ 2. An *irreproachable* act is
A. above criticism
C. hard to understand
B. harmful
D. deserving of
punishment.

_____ 3. To put someone in *jeopardy* is to
A. give them good luck
C. put them in danger
B. win them money
D. keep records of them.

_____ 4. A *consoling* idea is full of
A. warning
C. profit
B. excitement
D. reassurance.

_____ 5. To have an *ulterior motive* is to
A. have a noble purpose
C. have religious belief
B. have a hidden intention
D. be stingy.

_____ 6. A *conniving* person is
A. scheming
C. intelligent
B. generous
D. forgetful.

_____ 7. A *subversive* act is one that
A. seeks to win friends
B. seeks to improve technology
C. seeks to support the government
D. seeks to undermine the government.

Writing Topics

1. Write a paragraph telling about an experience of yours or a friend's that had a surprise ending. Review Narrative Paragraphs in Unit 2.

2. Many people believe that it is a precious American tradition to protect all speech and writing from censorship. Some speech and writing, however, is painfully offensive to one group or another and may incite violent response. Therefore some people believe that speech codes should be enacted in schools and colleges preventing students from offending one another's feelings and that some censorship should be practiced in society to prevent hate groups from gaining strength. What is your opinion? Write an essay stating and supporting your beliefs on this issue. Review the Persuasive Mode in Unit 3.

Alex Thio

By studying sociology, students learn to arrive at their conclusions about social issues on the basis of analysis, evidence from expert studies, and the results of systematic interviews and questionnaires. Reading sociological writing requires close attention to the author's points and to the methods of support he or she uses. In this passage from a leading sociology textbook, the author analyzes the question of whether education really increases earning power.

How Education Raises Our Income*
from *Sociology: A Brief Introduction*

As individuals, Americans tend to value the knowledge and skills transmitted by the schools, not for their own sake but because they hope to translate those skills into good jobs and money. As one study indicates, many students are attracted to college because of job and career considerations. Sixty percent of the college students and college-bound high school students in the study agreed that one must have a college education in order to make it in a career today (Widrick and Fram, 1984). Does education really enhance the individual's opportunity for social mobility?

The answer is no, according to a number of critics in the 1970s. Sociologist Randall Collins (1971; 1979) argued from the conflict perspective that formal education is often irrelevant to occupational achievement. Whatever training is needed comes more from work experience than from formal education. Even highly technical skills can be learned on the job. In 1970 about 40 percent of the practicing engineers did not have college degrees. Only 20 percent of the jobs available in the 1970s truly required a college education. For the most

---

*"How Education Raises Our Income" from *Sociology: A Brief Introduction* by Alex Thio, Copyright © 1991. Reprinted by permission of HarperCollins College Publishers.

part, education seems to provide credentials rather than skills. In effect, a diploma or degree certifies to employers that the holder is employable. It gives them a place to start screening potential employees, and those who have the right educational credentials are likely to make the "first cut" in competing for a job.

More blunt than Collins, social critic Caroline Bird (1975) blasted college education for being the "dumbest investment you can make." She estimated that if a Princeton freshman in 1972 had put the $34,181 needed for four years of college into a savings account earning 7.5 percent interest compounded daily, then at age 64 he would have $1,129,200—which is $528,200 more than a college graduate could expect to earn between 22 and 64. According to Bird, college is not only a waste of money but also a waste of time because colleges do not prepare students for jobs. "The plain fact," she argues, "is that what doctors, nurses, lawyers, journalists, social workers, broadcasters, librarians, and executives do all day long isn't taught in classrooms."

But those criticisms are far off the mark. First, Bird underestimates the value of college education. The estimated lifetime earnings for college graduates as reported in government documents, from which Bird got her information, do *not* include various fringe benefits, periodic savings, and investments in stocks and bonds. These can be substantial when added up from age 22 to 64 (Burkhead, 1983). Second, she ignores the fact that a bird in the hand is worth two in the bush. After only four years of college education, a person can have an income every month for the next 42 years. But Bird's hypothetical freshman has to wait empty-handed for 46 years before he can get the money from his savings account. Third, both Bird and Collins gloss over the fact that most doctors, engineers, and other professionals can hardly do their jobs competently if they have not gone to college at all. While it is true that on-the-job training can enhance professional achievement, that training will be more beneficial if that individual has received the appropriate college education in the first place.

More positively, functionalist theory suggests that education serves a useful function by upgrading prospective workers' skills—human capital—which in turn boosts earnings for individuals and promotes economic growth for society. There is growing evidence to support this view. As the figure above shows, education and income are strongly related. In 1989 the average college graduate, for example, made $43,952, whereas the high school graduate earned $25,910. Economist Dan Burkhead (1983) estimates that a 25-year-old man with a college degree can expect to earn within 40 years $365,000 more than a man with a high school diploma can. A 25-year-old female college graduate also can expect to earn within 40 years $144,000 more than a female high school graduate. Another economist, Anne Young (1983), finds that higher education is not only a gateway to the most desirable jobs and career advancement but also provides considerable advantages in a sluggish economy, as demonstrated by the consistently lower-than-average jobless rates among college graduates. In analyzing the relationship between education and income from 1950 to 1970, sociologists Richard Wanner and Lionel Lewis

How Education Raises Our Income

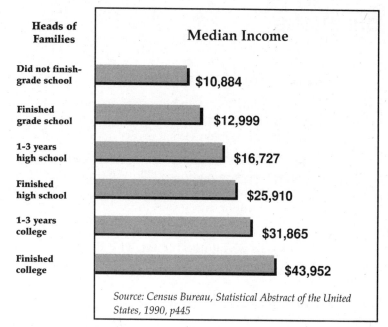

Heads of Families

Median Income

Did not finish-grade school — $10,884

Finished grade school — $12,999

1-3 years high school — $16,727

Finished high school — $25,910

1-3 years college — $31,865

Finished college — $43,952

Source: Census Bureau, Statistical Abstract of the United States, 1990, p445

A major function of education is to enhance the individual's opportunities for social mobility. Thus the more education people have, the bigger their earnings are.

(1982) conclude that "the overall trend is toward a stronger relationship." Most importantly, sociologists Pamela Walters and Richard Rubinson (1983) find that the expansion of education in the United States since 1933 has contributed to the nation's economic growth. The reason is that educational expansion can increase worker productivity, develop more productive or labor-saving technology, and create a stable political climate.

REFERENCES

Bird, Caroline. 1975. *The Case Against College.* New York: McKay.

Burkhead, Dan L. 1983. *Lifetime Earnings Estimated for Men and Women in the United States: 1979.* Current Population Reports, Series P-60, No. 139. Washington, D.C.: U.S. Government Printing Office.

Collins, Randall. 1971. "Functional and conflict theories of educational stratification." *American Sociological Review,* 36, pp. 1002–1019.

———. 1979. *The Credential Society: An Historical Sociology of Education and Stratification.* New York: Academic Press.

Walters, Pamela Barnhouse, and Richard Rubinson. 1983. "Educational expansion and economic output in the United States, 1890–1969: A production function analysis." *American Sociological Review,* 48, pp. 480–493.

Wanner, Richard A., and Lionel Lewis. 1982. "Trends in education and earnings, 1950–70: A structural analysis." *Social Forces,* 61, pp. 436–455.

QUESTIONS

Reading for Understanding

1. According to the author, what do the critics say who believe that education does not improve earning power? What evidence do they give for their opinion? What errors does the author say such critics make?

2. What kinds of support does the author use to show that education *does* improve earning power? Do you find this support convincing? Do you expect your college education to improve your earning power as much as the author says it should?

3. If college education does improve earning ability, what are some of the reasons why it does? If not, why not?

Noticing Writing Techniques

1. Notice that the author uses studies by other sociologists to support his points. He also gives a list of references to supply details about these articles and books. This is a procedure you will use in writing research papers. The form used in this selection is the one used for the social sciences, called the APA style, named for the American Psychological Association. Another form used in the humanities is the MLA style, named for the Modern Language Association.

   What effect does all this use of source references have on you as a reader?

   Why do you think the APA style requires the author to mention the year of publication for every reference mentioned in the paper?

2. Some people say there is no such thing as objectivity—that every writer shows a bias of some sort. Sociologists, however, are supposed to be as objective as possible. Is Prof. Thio objective in this passage, or do you think he reveals his personal bias? If you think he has a bias, what is it?

Noticing Vocabulary

_____ 1. *Transmitted* means
   A. translated into another language
   B. passed from one person or place to another
   C. made invisible
   D. eliminated from competition.

_____ 2. *Social mobility* means
  A. the ability to earn money   B. the right to vote
  C. the ability to change   D. the ability to acquire
     social status   an education.

_____ 3. A person's *credentials* are his or her
  A. ethnic background
  B. proof of professional qualifications
  C. evidence of good health
  D. preferences in food, entertainment, and style.

_____ 4. *Fringe benefits* are
  A. taxes added to small businesses
  B. special advantages for the elderly
  C. unusual skills in reading and writing
  D. extras added to salaries such as insurance and
     pensions.

_____ 5. *Prospective* workers are
  A. well-paid employees   B. future employees
  C. retired employees   D. laid-off employees.

Writing Topics

1. Write a paragraph enumerating some of the benefits of a college education. Review Exposition: Cause and Effect Paragraphs in Unit 2.

2. Write an essay proposing some realistic changes that could be made in high school and college education that would improve students' job skills and their ability to get jobs. Review Problem/Solution Essays in Unit 3.

Poems on Career Options

Robert Frost (1874–1963)

Although born in San Francisco, Robert Frost is often thought of in connection with New England, where he lived much of his life and about which he often wrote. He is, in a larger sense, the quintessential American poet, close to the land and the lives of ordinary working people. He wrote in plain language and often used simple natural settings and objects as metaphors for life's choices and problems, as he does in the following poem, so familiar to most readers that the central

metaphor in its title has become a common phrase
in American speech.

The Road Not Taken*

Two roads diverged in a yellow wood,
And sorry I could not travel both
And be one traveler, long I stood
And looked down one as far as I could
To where it bent in the undergrowth;

Then took the other, as just as fair,
And having perhaps the better claim,
Because it was grassy and wanted wear;
Though as for that the passing there
Had worn them really about the same.

And both that morning equally lay
In leaves no steps had trodden black.
Oh, I kept the first for another day!
Yet knowing how way leads on to way,
I doubted if I should ever come back.

I shall be telling this with a sigh
Somewhere ages and ages hence:
Two roads diverged in a wood, and I—
I took the one less traveled by,
And that has made all the difference.

QUESTIONS

Reading for Understanding

1. Although this poem can be read as an account of a walk in the woods,
   it also has an easily recognizable metaphorical meaning. What do the
   two roads stand for? What does it mean that he looked as far ahead on
   each road as he could?

   What is the difference between the roads? Why did he choose one over
   the other? Why does he sigh when he thinks back on the choice he made?

*From THE POETRY OF ROBERT FROST by Robert Frost. Reprinted by permission of Henry
Holt and Company, Inc.

2. In what way might this be a poem about Robert Frost's life as a poet? How well does it apply to your life? What does it say about all choices in life?

Noticing Writing Techniques

1. How many details in the poem can be read as metaphors and not just as physical details? Are there any details that cannot be seen as metaphors?

2. Explain the rhyme scheme that Frost uses in every stanza. How many stressed syllables are there in every line? Do the regular rhyme and meter make the poem more enjoyable for you?

Noticing Vocabulary

———— 1. *Diverged* means
   A. joined together
   C. ran parallel
   B. went up a hill
   D. went in different directions.

Writing Topics

1. Write a paragraph explaining what this poem means to you. Mention as many details and phrases as you can; if you quote, be sure to put the phrases from the poem in quotation marks.

2. Write an essay telling about an important decision you made. Tell about the circumstances that required you to make the decision, how you made the decision (did you get advice, flip a coin, think it over for a week, etc.), how you felt about it afterward, and what you think of your decision now. Do you look back and wonder about your "road not taken"? Review the Narrative Mode in Unit 3.

Gary Snyder (1930–   )

The key influences on Gary Snyder's life are his growing up in the Seattle area, his closeness to the outdoors, his familiarity with Native American culture, his study of Zen Buddhism in Japan, and his acquaintance with members of the Beat Movement such as Jack Kerouac and Allen Ginsberg. He is imaginatively aware of the unity of all life and of humanity's oneness with the cosmos. In the following poem he evokes the working experience of an ordinary person who, as in Frost's "Road Not Taken," but in a California setting, looks back on his past life.

Hay for the Horses*

He had driven half the night
From far down San Joaquin
Through Mariposa, up the
Dangerous mountain roads,
And pulled in at eight a.m.
With his big truckload of hay behind the barn.
With winch and ropes and hooks
We stacked the bales up clean
To splintery redwood rafters
High in the dark, flecks of alfalfa
Whirling through shingle-cracks of light,
Itch of haydust in the sweaty shirt and shoes.
At lunchtime under Black oak
Out in the hot corral,
—The old mare nosing lunchpails,
Grasshoppers crackling in the weeds—
"I'm sixty-eight" he said,
"I first bucked hay when I was seventeen.
I thought, that day I started,
I sure would hate to do this all my life.
And dammit, that's just what
I've gone and done."

QUESTIONS

Reading for Understanding

1. How would you describe this man's job itself? How difficult is it? What pleasure might he get from it?

2. Why might he have continued to do this work all his life, even though he never thought he would? What does this say about human nature and about people's relation to their jobs?

3. How does nature play a part in the poem?

Noticing Writing Techniques

1. Why does Gary Snyder tell the story from the point of view of another worker who observes the 68-year-old man?

---

2. Which of the five senses does Gary Snyder evoke through his details? Are these mostly pleasant or unpleasant sensations?

Writing Topics

1. Write a paragraph describing a natural scene familiar to you; try to evoke through your choice of details the response of your five senses to the scene. Review Descriptive Paragraphs in Unit 2 and Using Specific Language in Unit 4.

2. Laws prevent most employers from forcing elderly workers to retire at a set age, as long as they can do their jobs competently. Do you believe that people should be allowed to work as long as they want, even if that means that fewer young workers will be hired to replace them? Or should there be mandatory retirement ages? Write an essay supporting your opinion on the question and explaining your attitude toward retirement for yourself. Review the Persuasive Mode in Unit 3.

W.H. Auden (1907–1973)

Born in England and educated at Oxford, W.H. Auden came to America in 1939 and became a U.S. citizen in 1946. However, he returned to become a professor at Oxford from 1956 to 1960, and returned one more time to spend the last year of his life at Oxford. He was influenced by the political activism of the 1930s, the cataclysm of World War II, and the Cold War era. His poetry is often praised for its craftsmanship and keen intellectualism. In the following poem he contemplates the conformist life of a typical "good citizen." The title recalls the many monuments paying tribute unknown soldiers.

The Unknown Citizen*

(To JS/07/M/378
This Marble Monument
Is Erected by the State)

He was found by the Bureau of Statistics to be
One against whom there was no official complaint,
And all the reports on his conduct agree

---

*From COLLECTED POEMS by W.H. Auden Copyright © 1940 and renewed 1968 by W.H. Auden. Reprinted by permission of Random House, Inc.

That, in the modern sense of an old-fashioned word, he was a saint,
For in everything he did he served the Greater Community.
Except for the War till the day he retired
He worked in a factory and never got fired,
But satisfied his employers, Fudge Motors, Inc.
Yet he wasn't a scab or odd in his views,
For his union reports that he paid his dues,
(Our report on his Union shows it was sound)
And our Social Psychology workers found
That he was popular with his mates and liked a drink.
The Press are convinced that he bought a paper every day
And that his reactions to advertisements were normal in every way.
Policies taken out in his name prove that he was fully insured,
And his health-card shows that he was once in hospital but left it cured.
Both Producers Research and High-Grade Living declare
He was fully sensible to the advantages of the Installment Plan
And had everything necessary to the Modern Man,
A phonograph, a radio, a car and a frigidaire.
Our researchers into Public Opinion are content
That he held the proper opinions for the time of year;
When there was peace, he was for peace; when there was war, he went.
He was married and added five children to the population,
Which our Eugenist says was the right number for a parent of his
    generation,
And our teachers report that he never interfered with their education.
Was he free? Was he happy? The question is absurd:
Had anything been wrong, we should certainly have heard.

QUESTIONS

Reading for Understanding

1. This unknown citizen did everything "right." What, then, was wrong with his life or missing from it?

2. This poem was written in 1940; are there many "unknown citizens" today? If so, what details of their lives would be different?

Noticing Writing Techniques

1. Which statements in the poem appear to be praising the unknown citizen but are actually finding fault with him? Why does the poet use this indirect, ironic method of criticizing his way of life?

2. Why does W.H. Auden use verse lines that are flat, unemotional, and almost like prose in their varying length and uneven rhythm? Why does he nevertheless use a lot of simple rhyme?

3. What is the purpose of the rhyming epigraph (the short lines with numbers above the poem)? What might the numbers refer to?

Noticing Vocabulary

——————— 1. A *scab* is a
    A. person defies a strike by working
    B. person who steals equipment
    C. person who heads a union
    D. person who refuses to work.

——————— 2. A *eugenist* is a person who believes in
    A. astrology   B. population statistics
    C. improvement of society   D. joining all religions
        by controlling heredity   into one.

Writing Topics

1. Write a paragraph explaining whether you are a conformist of a nonconformist. Review Definition Paragraphs in Unit 2.

2. Write an essay in defense of either conformity or nonconformity. Explain benefits of conformity (or nonconformity) and the dangers of the opposite. Give examples from recent history, from what you have seen on television, and from your own life. Review Persuasive Essays in Unit 3.

FAMILY RELATIONSHIPS

What exactly is a family? Whom do you consider to be members of your family? Much debate has been waged recently about this matter. Phrases like "the breakdown of the family," "family values," "blended families," "the new family," "alternative families," and "dysfunctional families" occur frequently in talk show conversations, news reports, and editorial columns. Although Americans have always been interested in families, never before has there been such a feeling of crisis surrounding the future of the family in America. We know that the family has changed dramatically in the last two generations, but we disagree vehemently over what the changes have been and whether they are liberating us or destroying society.

Families differ widely, and family patterns differ from one culture to another. Because America is made up of so many subcultures, it is hard to describe "the American family" in any way that would apply to all families in the United States. What seems dysfunctional to one family may seem normal to another; the family values that one cultural group wants to maintain may seem like a breakdown of the family to another group. Perhaps all groups agree that the family, in some form, is crucial to everyone's life—yet there is even a lurking suspicion that for many people family relationships and family loyalty are becoming less important and intense. Most commentators blame our social problems—violent crime, drugs, poor schooling, unemployment, and domestic violence—on the breakdown of the family, and they nearly always insist that solving these problems will be almost impossible without restoring the family unit closer to what it used to be.

To write about the family, then, is to jump into a swirling controversy. We all have some family experiences in common, as well as individual differences. Therefore our purpose in reading and writing about family relations is not to settle the controversy once and for all but to participate in it, to separate myths from realities, to recognize patterns of cause and effect, to compare and contrast experiences, to share common feelings and experiences, and, above all, to learn as much as we can. Learning about families from other cultural groups often gives us a more varied perspective on the family, but it also can surprise us by revealing how much different groups have in common.

Reading the following selections is an experience of unity in the midst of difference, of agreement amid controversy, of one subject seen from many angles. Writing about family experiences also gives you the opportunity to discuss topics that mean a lot to you personally while exploring larger social issues.

Jane Howard (1935–   )

Jane Howard is a journalist, editor, biographer, and college professor. She has written numerous books, among them her autobiography, *A Different Woman* (1973), a biography of Margaret Mead, and *Families* (1978), the book from which the following selection is taken. Do agree with her list of characteristics for the good family?

The Earmarks of Good Families* from *Families*

Each of us is born into one family not of our choosing. If we're going to go around devising new ones, we might as well have the luxury of picking their members ourselves. Clever picking might result in new families whose benefits would surpass or at least equal those of the old. The new ones by definition cannot spawn us—as soon as they do that, they stop being new—but there is plenty they can do. I have seen them work wonders. As a member in reason-

---

able standing of six or seven tribes in addition to the one I was born to, I have been trying to figure which earmarks are common to both kinds of families.

(1) Good families have a chief, or a heroine, or a founder—someone around whom others cluster, whose achievements as the Yiddish word has it, let them *kvell*, and whose example spurs them on to like feats. Some blood dynasties produce such figures regularly; others languish for as many as five generations between demigods, wondering with each new pregnancy whether this, at last, might be the messianic baby who will redeem us. Look, is there not something gubernatorial about her footstep, or musical about the way he bangs with his spoon on his cup? All clans, of all kinds, need such a figure now and then. Sometimes clans based on water rather than blood harbor several such personages at one time. The Bloomsbury Group in London six decades ago was not much hampered by its lack of a temporal history.

(2) Good families have a switchboard operator—someone like my mother who cannot help but keep track of what all the others are up to, who plays Houston Mission Control to everyone else's Apollo. This role, like the foregoing one, is assumed rather than assigned. Someone always volunteers for it. That person often also has the instincts of an archivist, and feels driven to keep scrapbooks and photograph albums up to date, so that the clan can see proof of its own continuity.

(3) Good families are much to all their members, but everything to none. Good families are fortresses with many windows and doors to the outer world. The blood clans I feel most drawn to were founded by parents who are nearly as devoted to whatever it is they do outside as they are to each other and their children. Their curiosity and passion are contagious. Everybody, where they live, is busy. Paint is spattered on eyeglasses. Mud lurks under fingernails. Person-to-person calls come in the middle of the night from Tokyo and Brussels. Catchers' mitts, ballet slippers, overdue library books and other signs of extrafamilial concerns are everywhere.

(4) Good families are hospitable. Knowing that hosts need guests as much as guests need hosts, they are generous with honorary memberships for friends, whom they urge to come early and often and to stay late. Such clans exude a vivid sense of surrounding rings of relatives, neighbors, teachers, students and godparents, any of whom at any time might break or slide into the inner circle. Inside that circle a wholesome, tacit emotional feudalism develops: you give me protection, I'll give you fealty. Such treaties begin with, but soon go far beyond, the jolly exchange of pie at Thanksgiving for cake on birthdays. It means you can ask me to supervise your children for the fortnight you will be in the hospital, and that however inconvenient this might be for me, I shall manage to. It means I can phone you on what for me is a dreary, wretched Sunday afternoon and for you is the eve of a deadline, knowing you will tell me to come right over, if only to watch you type. It means we need not dissemble. ("To yield to seeming," as Buber wrote, "is man's essential cowardice, to resist it is his essential courage . . . one must at times pay dearly for life lived from the being, but it is never too dear.")

(5) Good families deal squarely with direness. Pity the tribe that doesn't have, and cherish, at least one flamboyant eccentric. Pity too the one that supposes it can avoid for long the woes to which all flesh is heir. Lunacy, bankruptcy, suicide and other unthinkable fates sooner or later afflict the noblest of clans with an undertow of gloom. Family life is a set of givens, someone once told me, and it takes courage to see certain givens as blessings rather than curses. Contradictions and inconsistencies are givens, too. So is the war against what the Oregon patriarch Kenneth Babbs calls malarkey. "There's always malarkey lurking, bubbles in the cesspool, fetid bubbles that pop and smell. But I don't put up with malarkey, between my stepkids and my natural ones or anywhere else in the family."

(6) Good families prize their rituals. Nothing welds a family more than these. Rituals are vital especially for clans without histories, because they evoke a past, imply a future, and hint at continuity. No line in the Seder service at Passover reassures more than the last: "Next year in Jerusalem!" A clan becomes more of a clan each time it gathers to observe a fixed ritual (Christmas, birthdays, Thanksgiving, and so on), grieve at a funeral (anyone may come to most funerals; those who do declare their tribalness), and devises a new rite of its own. Equinox breakfasts and all-white dinners can be at least as welding as Memorial Day parades. Several of us in the old *Life* magazine years used to meet for lunch every Pearl Harbor Day, preferably to eat some politically neutral fare like smorgasbord, to "forgive" our only ancestrally Japanese colleague Irene Kubota Neves. For that and other reasons we became, and remain, a sort of family.

"Rituals," a California friend of mine said, "aren't just externals and holidays. They are the performances of our lives. They are a kind of shorthand. They can't be decreed. My mother used to try to decree them. She'd make such a goddamn fuss over what we talked about at dinner, aiming at Topics of Common Interest, topics that celebrated our cohesion as a family. These performances were always hollow, because the phenomenology of the moment got sacrificed for the *idea* of the moment. Real rituals are discovered in retrospect. They emerge around constitutive moments, moments that can only happen once, around whose memory meanings cluster. You don't choose those moments. They choose themselves." A lucky clan includes a born mythologizer, like my blood sister, who has the gift of apprehending such a moment when she sees it, and who cannot help but invent new rituals everywhere she goes.

(7) Good families are affectionate. This of course is a matter of style. I know clans whose members greet each other with gingerly handshakes or, in what passes for kisses, with hurried brushes of side jawbones, as if the object were to touch not the lips but the ears. I don't see how such people manage. "The tribe that does not hug," as someone who has been part of many *ad hoc* families recently wrote to me, "is no tribe at all. More and more I realize that everybody, regardless of age, needs to be hugged and comforted in a brotherly or sisterly way now and then. Preferably now."

(8) Good families have a sense of place, which these days is not achieved easily. As Susanne Langer wrote in 1957, "Most people have no home that is a

symbol of their childhood, not even a definite memory of one place to serve that purpose . . . all the old symbols are gone." Once I asked a roomful of supper guests who, if anyone, felt any strong pull to any certain spot on the face of the earth. Everyone was silent, except for a visitor from Bavaria. The rest of us seemed to know all too well what Walker Percy means in *The Moviegoer* when he tells of the "genie-soul of the place which every place has or else is not a place [and which] wherever you go, you must meet and master or else be met and mastered." All that meeting and mastering saps plenty of strength. It also underscores our need for tribal bases of the sort which soaring real estate taxes and splintering families have made all but obsolete.

So what are we to do, those of us whose habit and pleasure and doom is our tendency, as a Georgia lady put it, to "fly off at every other whipstitch?" Think in terms of movable feasts, for a start. Live here, wherever here may be, as if we were going to belong here for the rest of our lives. Learn to hallow whatever ground we happen to stand on or land on. Like medieval knights who took their tapestries along on Crusades, like modern Afghanis with their yurts, we must pack such totems and icons as we can to make short-term quarters feel like home. Pillows, small rugs, watercolors can dispel much of the chilling anonymity of a sublet apartment or motel room. When we can, we should live in rooms with stoves or fireplaces or anyway candlelight. The ancient saying still is true: Extinguished hearth, extinguished family. Round tables help, too, and as a friend of mine once put it, so do "too many comfortable chairs, with surfaces to put feet on, arranged so as to encourage a maximum of eye contact." Such rooms inspire good talk, of which good clans can never have enough.

(9) Good families, not just the blood kind, find some way to connect with posterity. "To forge a link in the humble chain of being, encircling heirs to ancestors," as Michael Novak as written, "is to walk within a circle of magic as primitive as humans knew in caves." He is talking of course about babies, feeling them leap in wombs, giving them suck. Parenthood, however, is a state which some miss by chance and others by design, and a vocation to which not all are called. Some of us, like the novelist Richard P. Brickner, "look on as others name their children who in turn name their own lives, devising their own flags from their parents' cloth." What are we who lack children to do? Build houses? Plant trees? Write books or symphonies or laws? Perhaps, but even if we do these things, there still should be children on the sidelines, if not at the center, of our lives. It is a sadly impoverished tribe that does not allow access to, and make much of, some children. Not too much, of course: it has truly been said that never in history have so many educated people devoted so much attention to so few children. Attention, in excess, can turn to fawning, which isn't much better than neglect. Still, if we don't regularly see and talk to and laugh with people who can expect to outlive us by twenty years or so, we had better get busy and find some.

(10) Good families also honor their elders. The wider the age range, the stronger the tribe. Jean-Paul Sartre and Margaret Mead, to name two spectacularly confident former children, have both remarked on the central importance of grandparents in their own early lives. Grandparents now are in much

more abundant supply than they were a generation or two ago when old age was more rare. If actual grandparents are not at hand, no family should have too hard a time finding substitute ones to whom to give unfeigned homage. The Soviet Union's enchantment with day care centers, I have heard, stems at least in part from the state's eagerness to keep children away from their presumably subversive grandparents. Let that be a lesson to clans based on interest as well as to those based on genes.

QUESTIONS

Reading for Understanding

1. Howard talks about families we are born into and other family-like groups as if there were no important difference between them. Do you agree that substitute families and family members can take the place of families made up of blood relatives?

2. Which of the ten points characteristic of good families do you agree with and which do you disagree with? Are there any traits she left out? Could any of the traits she lists be characteristic of bad families?

3. Are any of the traits she lists likely to diminish or be lost in our society the way it is?

Noticing Writing Techniques

1. Does Howard's method of listing ten points help you understand her ideas and organization? Does it make the essay more or less interesting?

2. What examples does Howard use to make her points? List as many as you can. What points does she support by using long quotations?

Noticing Vocabulary

_____ 1. *Messianic* means
   A. related to sports   B. bringing salvation
   C. communicative   D. disorderly.

_____ 2. *Gubernatorial* means related to
   A. laws   B. chemistry
   C. medicine   D. a governor.

_____ 3. *Dynasties* are
   A. rules pertaining to politics
   B. families that rule for generations
   C. schemes for taking over a business
   D. patterns for organizing businesses.

———— 4. *Temporal* means pertaining to
    A. time   B. money
    C. religion   D. music.

———— 5. To *exude* means to
    A. escape arrest   B. detect
    C. give off   D. disappear.

———— 6. A *tacit* agreement is
    A. discussed publicly   B. advertised in the newspapers
    C. silently understood   D. settled by a third party.

———— 7. A person who is *flamboyant* is
    A. a show-off   B. timid
    C. trained in the arts   D. argumentative.

———— 8. *Fetid* bubbles are
    A. dark   B. bad-smelling
    C. steaming   D. sticky.

———— 9. A *smorgasbord* is a varied display of
    A. flowers   B. tools
    C. foods   D. wines.

———— 10. An *ad hoc* committee is one that
    A. is set up for a temporary purpose
    B. has been in existence for a long time
    C. has a large membership
    D. is made up only of high-ranking individuals.

Writing Topics

1. Write a paragraph explaining how your family (or family-like group) fits one of Jane Howard's criteria for a good family. Review "How To" Paragraphs in Unit 2.

2. Write an essay listing a number of the traits of bad families. Review the Expository Mode in Unit 3.

Ella Taylor (1948–   )

Ella Taylor is a sociologist, professor of cultural studies at the University of Washington, and author of many articles on television and film. The following reading is part of her book, *All in the Work-Family: Family and Workplace Imagery in Television* (1990). Here she looks back on the family sitcoms of the 1980s as a reflection of attitudes about the family in American society.

TV Families*

Like *All in the Family, The Cosby Show* has attracted an enormous amount of attention from critics and public interest groups, as well as a huge and devoted audience, but there the similarity ends. The robustly working-class Bunker household was never a model of consumer vitality, nor did it aspire to be. If Archie was dragged, kicking and screaming, into the seventies, the Huxtables embrace modernity with gusto. From grandparents to the disarmingly cute Rudy, this family is sexy and glamorous. Surrounded by the material evidence of their success, the Huxtables radiate wealth, health, energy, and up-to-the-minute style. *The Cosby Show* offers the same pleasures as a commercial, a parade of gleaming commodities and expensive designer clothing, unabashedly enjoyed by successful people. And Cosby himself is a talented promoter of the goods and services, from Jell-O to E.F. Hutton, that finance his series.

Given the troubled condition of many American families in the eighties, *Cosby* must be palpably compensatory for many of its fans. Week after week, the show offers what family comedy in the fifties offered, and what most of us don't have, the continuity of orderly lives lived without major trauma or disturbance, stretching back into an identical past and reaching confidently forward into an identical future. Two generations of Huxtable men attended "Hillman College" and met their wives there, and although Cliff's eldest daughter chooses Princeton, the next goes for Hillman too.

But where the TV families of the fifties casually took harmony and order for granted, the Huxtables work strenuously and self-consciously at showing us how well they get along. Not that much happens on *Cosby*. It's a virtually plotless chronicle of the small, quotidian details of family life, at the heart of which lies a moral etiquette of parenting and a developmental psychology of growing up. Every week provides family members, and us, with a Learning Experience and a lesson in social adjustment. Rudy's terrified playmate learns to love going to the dentist. Rudy learns to stop bossing her friends around. Theo learns not to embark on expensive projects he won't complete. Sandra and her boy friend learn to arbitrate their bickering over sex roles. Denise learns to cope with bad grades in college. Even Cliff and Clair, who despite high-powered careers as physician and lawyer respectively, have all the leisure in the world to spend "quality time" with their kids, teach each other parenting by discussion as well as by example. The show's endless rehearsal of mild domestic disorder and its resolution suggests a perfect family that *works*. The family that plays, sings, dances, and above all, communicates together, stays together.

Didacticism is nothing new in television entertainment. *All in the Family* was stuffed with messages of all kinds, but on *Cosby*, moral and psychological instruction are rendered monolithic and indisputable. Unlike the Bunkers, for whom every problem became the occasion for an all-out war of ideas, no one ever screams at Huxtable Manor. True, beneath their beguiling mildness there lurks a casual hostility, in which everyone, Clair and Cliff included, trades insults and makes fun of everyone else. But there's no dissent, no real difference of opinion or belief, only vaguely malicious banter that quickly dissolves into sweet agreement, all part of the busy daily manufacture of consensus.

Undercutting the warm color and light, the jokey good humor and the impeccable salutes to feminism, is a persistent authoritarianism. The tone is set by Cosby himself, whose prodigious charm overlays a subtle menace. If the pint-sized Ruby gets her laughs by aping the speech and manners of adults, Cliff gets his laughs—and his way—by turning into a giant child, and then slipping his kids or his wife their moral or psychological pills with a wordless, grimacing comic caper. A captivating child, undoubtedly, with his little vanities and his competitiveness, but he's also quietly coercive: Father knows best, or else. The cuddly, overgrown schoolboy becomes the amused onlooker and then the oracle, master of the strategic silence or the innocent question that lets one of his kids know they've said or done something dumb, or gives his wife to understand that her independence is slipping into bossiness. In Huxtable-speak, this is called "communicating." Cliff practices a thoroughly contemporary politics of strong leadership, managing potential conflicts with all the skill of a well-socialized corporate executive.

There's none of the generational warfare that rocked the Bunker household every week. And this family doesn't *need* the openly authoritarian "tough love" that's cropping up more and more in recent TV movies, because parental authority has already been internalized. The kids put up a token display of playful resistance, then surrender happily to the divine right of parents whose easy knowledge of the difference between right and wrong irons out the inconvenient ambiguities of contemporary life. Indeed, since the Huxtables are a supremely "intact" nuclear family, those ambiguities rarely come up, or if they do, they occur outside the charmed circle and stay outside it. A teenage pregnancy, a drug problem, a worker laid off, occasionally one of the problems that bedevil most families hovers near, casts a brief shadow on the bright domestic light and then slinks away, intimidated by the fortress of Huxtable togetherness. Unlike the sitcoms of the fifties whose vision of the social terrain outside the family was as benign as that inside it, the "world outside" *Cosby* is downright perilous, to the limited degree that it exists at all.

The Huxtables have friends but no discernible neighborhood community, indeed no public life to speak of aside from their jobs, which seem to run on automatic pilot. They inhabit a visibly black world, whose blackness is hardly ever alluded to. "I'm not going to talk about social justice or racial harmony or peace, because you all know how I feel about them," intones the retiring President of Cliff's alma mater, and delivers a limp homily exhorting old alumnae to invite young alumnae to dinner, which earns him a standing ovation from old and young alike—all black. No wonder *The Cosby Show* is number one in the South African ratings. It is, as a Johannesburg television executive remarked complacently on the nightly Hollywood chat show *Entertainment Tonight* last year, not a show about race, but about "family values."

Even *Family Ties* (the white obverse of *Cosby*) whose premise of ex-hippie parents with a pre-corporate, neoconservative son promises some refreshing friction, flattens genuine argument into the stifling warmth of domestic affection. The mild-mannered Keaton father, Stephen, is persuaded by an old friend from the campus Left to start a radical magazine. A difference of opinion leads to Stephen's being accused of copping out, but his wife Elyse assures him that "you're making a statement by the way you live your life and raise your children," suggesting not only that family integrity transcends politics, but that political affiliation is reducible to being nice to other people—especially your family.

This is not to say that the articulation of family trouble so central to seventies television has disappeared from the small screen. Other sitcoms retain the preoccupation with "reconstituted" families, if in watered-down form. "Do I have to be a relative to be family?" a small boy asks his mother in *Who's the Boss?*, a role reversal comedy about two single parents (she the breadwinner, he the housekeeper) living together. "Not necessarily," his mother smiles down at him, "a family means people who share each other's lives and care about each other." An unexceptionable definition, and also virtually meaningless; with the sting of divorce and family poverty removed, single parenthood and stepparenting turn into a romp, a permanent pajama party. Even *Kate and Allie*, which began as a witty comedy of divorce manners and a chronicle of the single life encountered second time around, has slipped into the parenting psychology mold, focusing more on the kids and teenagers' rites of passage than on the adults. Here we see television hedging its bets by nodding in the direction of radical changes in family form and structure, without really taking them on. And the "single woman" comedy so wildly popular in the seventies seems to have little resonance for the eighties; several new shows of this kind, including a new *Mary Tyler Moore Show*, were cancelled in short order. Christine Cagney of *Cagney and Lacey* alone survives as a prototype of the mature single woman, and even she must be balanced with her partner Marybeth Lacey, the harried working mother.

If anything, the locus of family disharmony on TV these days seems to be the nighttime soaps, and nothing else on prime time matches the seething ambiguities and flaring passions of these clans. On *Dynasty* this season, Blake Carrington struggles to contain his wife and his former wife (who collects younger men with a studied casualness only Joan Collins could bring off with a straight face); his son Stephen, whose sexual identity oscillates between gay and straight as the plot requires; his son Adam, who turns out not to be his son at all (so he adopts him); his niece Leslie, who has just discovered her lover is her brother; and, in a grand but wildly implausible burst of televisual affirmative action, his sister Dominique, who's black. Season after season, the soaps' elastic tribal boundaries expand and contract to admit or expel undiscovered relatives, bogus and genuine. But I suspect that soap audiences appropriate these shows in the high camp spirit in which they're offered. This is not "reality," which may be why soap stars invariably collapse into disclaiming giggles when interviewed about the characters they play.

Bill Cosby, in his rare interviews, *never* giggles. The actor takes his responsibilities as an educator very seriously. *Newsweek* reported in 1984 that Cosby had commissioned a well-known black psychiatrist to review every *Cosby Show* script for authenticity. And the actor told the *Los Angeles Times* in 1985 that viewers loved the series because it showed that "the people in his house respect the parents and the parents respect the children and that there is a l-o-v-e generated in this house." Norman Lear in his heyday felt convinced that viewers loved *All in the Family* because it exposed bigotry and addressed "real life" problems. No one really knows much about audience responses to television, but there's probably always an asymmetry between producers' intentions and viewers' readings. It's equally plausible that Bunker fans were as engaged by the rage that imprinted itself on almost every episode of *All in the Family* as by its liberal politics.

Similarly, the Huxtable brand of patriarchal dominance may strike as resonant a chord as the l-o-v-e Cosby cites—testified to by the success of his recent book *Fatherhood*, which topped the bestseller list in 1986. And if Cosby's child-like charm works, it may also be catering to what is most child-like in us, his audience; namely the yearnings for a perfectly synchronized family, or community, that provides for the needs of all its members and regulates itself through a benevolent dictatorship, a family that always was as perfect as it is now, and always will be. That isn't merely infantile; it also signals the political retrenchment that comes from a cultural exhaustion, a weary inability to imagine new forms of community, new ways of living.

QUESTIONS

Reading for Understanding

1. What does the author say is the main difference between family shows of the seventies and those of the eighties? Which does she seem to prefer?

2. What does she find missing from *The Cosby Show?* Do you agree? Do you think she is taking the show too seriously, when it is mainly intended to entertain?

3. How were the soaps of the 1980s different from the sitcoms?

4. Do the sitcoms of the 1990s differ from those of the 1980s? Do Taylor's criticisms of *The Cosby Show* and *Family Ties* apply to today's sitcoms?

Noticing Writing Techniques

1. This article is chiefly based on a number of comparisons. What are the main comparisons Taylor makes? Are they mostly to point out similarities, differences, or both?

2. Taylor is making a very serious intellectual analysis of television programs that are not serious or intellectual in themselves. Is this approach

to light entertainment valid, or should entertainment be discussed only for its entertainment value and not for its sociological meaning?

Noticing Vocabulary

_____ 1. *Palpably* means
A. invisibly
B. slowly
C. obviously
D. with difficulty.

_____ 2. *Compensatory* policies are intended to
A. provide information
B. make up for something wrong or lacking
C. allow for later increases in cost
D. reach back to a previous date.

_____ 3. *Quotidian* details are
A. everyday details
B. details pertaining to health
C. details related to government
D. details that are not noticed by ordinary means.

_____ 4. *Monolithic* means
A. unable to read
B. consisting of one material
C. constructed of wood
D. able to speak only one language.

_____ 5. An *oracle* is
A. a prophet or prophecy
B. a disastrous event
C. a luck event
D. a reversal of fortune, either good or bad.

_____ 6. *Ambiguities* are
A. small rodents
B. one-sided arguments
C. careful observations
D. double meanings.

_____ 7. A *benign* attitude is
A. kindly
B. cruel
C. amusing
D. boring.

_____ 8. A *homily* is a speech containing
A. jokes
B. statistics
C. a sermon
D. a tribute to someone who has died.

_____ 9. *Resonance* means
A. health
B. sympathetic vibration
C. an angry reaction
D. difficulty in understanding.

_____ 10. *Asymmetry* means a lack of
     A. purpose
     C. communication
     B. balance or agreement
     D. adequate funding.

Writing Topics

1. Write a paragraph explaining what you like about your favorite television program. Be sure to choose details that support your main point. Review Descriptive and Expository Paragraphs in Unit 2.

2. Write an essay comparing sitcoms and soap operas of the 1990s with those of the 1980s. Focus on a few of the best known programs from each decade. What overall difference do you find in their social significance? In their entertainment quality? Review Comparative Paragraphs in Unit 2 and the Persuasive Mode in Unit 3.

B.D. Colen (1942–   )

Bombarded with television images of the family, from dysfunctional families exhibited on talk shows to daily trauma in soap operas and flawless intact families on sitcoms, we may get a distorted sense of real families offscreen. In the following article, *New York Newsday* columnist B.D. Colen reminds us that real families are never perfect, but their flaws do not make them "dysfunctional."

What Real Families Are Like*
from *Newsday*, January 14, 1992

Are you the product of a "dysfunctional" family? Was your "inner child" repressed and psychologically abused by the "dysfunction" of the adults who raised you?

To judge by guests on Oprah, Phil and Sally Jessy these days, or by the titles of the latest pop psychology tomes, we are members of "dysfunctional" families, struggling to overcome the child-rearing sins of our mothers and fathers.

Think about it for a minute: Do you know *anybody* whose family wasn't "dysfunctional"? Oh, the goings on at your best friend's house might have looked rosy from your 8-year-old perspective, but now, 40 years later, when your old friend puts away a few and begins to tell you what *really* went on back then, can you believe how bad it was? How bad things were for all your friends and relatives?

Didn't *anybody* live in a happy, fully functional, all-American household?

The answer to that question won't be found in books that could easily be titled "Escaping Your Dysfunctional Past," or "How to Slay the Daddy Monster," or "Growing Up by Growing Down."

Instead, we can seek some understanding of the supposed dysfunctionality of our families by separating the myth of the Perfect Family from the reality of family life.

Virtually none of us grew up in households like those we saw on television. In fact, the reason that those houses peopled by the likes of Cathy and Bud and Ricky and Dave and Wally and Beav and Ward and June and Ozzie and Harriet and Margaret and Jim were so popular, is that they were so relatively calm, safe and loving, totally removed from the reality of the turmoil and difficulties of family life.

Jim Anderson never lost his job. (Come to think of it, did he ever go to work?) Harriet Nelson never forgot to pick Ricky up after school. (Did she know how to drive?) Mom and Dad never fought. Fought? They never even got angry with one another.

But in real families Mom and Dad fight. They occasionally yell. At each other. At the kids. The kids yell at each other—and maybe even at Mom and Dad.

In real families the car invariably breaks down when there's no money to repair it.

In real families siblings sometimes realize that genes and bunk beds are the only thing they have in common with each other.

In real families there is always an aunt, or an uncle, or a cousin, who nobody wants around. Ever.

In real families junior gets suspended from school for smoking dope, sis has an abortion, Dad loses his job and Mom runs off with the next door neighbor. All in a two-month period.

In real families grandma is dating a 28-year-old Hell's Angel and grandpa thinks it's 1937 and he's running a ride at Coney Island.

In real families deciding which house you'll go to for Christmas Eve and where you'll spend Christmas morning is about as easy as deciding who's going to control which section of Beirut.

In real families Mom is required to tell Sis that her skirt is too short and Dad is required to tell Bud that his hair is too long. It's a law.

Does that mean that all families are "dysfunctional"? No. All it means is that functional families are imperfect city states often peopled by warring factions.

There are, of course, some truly "dysfunctional" families, families where people abuse one another, families where substance abuse interferes with normal function, families where the problem is not that love is sometimes misdirected or buried in momentary blizzards of anger, but where there is no love to begin with.

But the vast majority of us come from homes where we were loved. We come from homes where most of our psychological and physical needs were met by parents who meant well, even if they didn't always do well.

What really matters is not how functional or "dysfunctional" your family was, but how functional or "dysfunctional" you are today.

If you're reasonably happy with your life, if you're functioning well by your standards, then forget the rest of it. Just leave it to Beaver.

QUESTIONS

Reading for Understanding

1. What, according to Colen, has caused most people to think they came from dysfunctional families? What, according to him, are most real families like? How are they different form genuinely dysfunctional families?

2. Does Colen have the same opinion of television families that Ella Taylor does?

3. Is he discussing the family as a group of people related by blood or as any family-like group of people?

Noticing Writing Techniques

1. Colen, like many editorial commentators and news reporters, writes many very short paragraphs. Why is this practice common in newspapers but not in most books and specialized magazines? What effect do these one- or two- sentence paragraphs have?

2. Colen uses *hypothetical examples* to support his point. Why does he do this instead of including examples from actual families he knows? Why would statistics not be necessary to make his point?

3. Colen gives a sort of definition of the "dysfunctional" family; do you agree with his definition?

Writing Topics

1. Write a paragraph using a metaphor to describe your family—as a team, a therapy group, a circus, a small corporation, or some other metaphor that fits the interactions of your family. Review Exposition Paragraphs, in Unit 2, particularly "Definition."

2. Some people say that "real" families are only the nuclear units made up of two biological parents and their children. Others insist that any family-like group, which may include stepparents, gay parents, single parents, foster parents, or any collection of individuals committed to living together, should be called a family and given the legal rights of families. What is your opinion? Explain your ideas in detail and give examples from families you know about or ones seen on television. Review the Persuasive Mode in Unit 3.

Judith Wallerstein and Sandra Blakeslee

In their classic study, *Second Chances* (1989), Judith S. Wallerstein, Ph.D., director of the Center for the

Family in Transition in California, and Sandra Blakeslee, a *New York Times* science writer, reported for the first time in a reliable, systematic way the long-term effects of divorce on children. In the following passage they write about one of the most familiar patterns in today's families—the tendency to place the burden of adult roles and responsibilities on children of divorce, thus robbing them of their childhood.

The Overburdened Child
from *Second Chances:*
Men, Women and Children a Decade After Divorce

One of the tragedies of divorce is that the breaking of the marriage bond reverberates into the parent-child relationship. Children are almost inevitably burdened by greater responsibilities and feel less cared for.

Many youngsters, like Ruth Moore and Steve Burrelle, feel burdened for almost a decade. In caring for her mother and young siblings, Ruth was forced to put her development on hold. But she eventually broke free and caught up—by dint of her own efforts and her mother's strengths. Steve, while feeling abandoned by his father, was protected by the heroic efforts of his mother on his behalf and by her example. Although burdened by depression and longing for his father, he was not pressed into taking responsibilities beyond his capacities.

Unfortunately, many youngsters confront far greater problems and pressures than do Ruth Moore or Steve Burrelle. Within such families, the needs of chronically troubled parents override the developmental needs of children—and the children have nowhere to turn for help. After divorce, the burden of caring for a disorganized, alcoholic, intensely dependent, physically ill, or chronically enraged parent falls almost entirely on the child. There is no other adult to buffer the pain or to take charge. In some families the child picks up the vacated role of the departed parent; then, what begins as a temporary caretaking role can go on to last for years, as the parent fails to recover from the divorce.

These pressures can overburden children to the point that they become psychologically depleted and their own emotional and social progress is crippled. Instead of gathering strength from their childhood and adolescent experiences to facilitate the move into young adulthood, these young people are seriously weakened by the demands made on them within the divorced family. In their efforts to help needy and distressed parents, children can and do assume a wide variety of unfamiliar roles, including arbiter, protector, adviser, nurturer, sibling, battle ally, confidant, and concubine. A child can become the key figure who wards off a parent's depression and allays a parent's fear that the world is falling apart. Others become instruments of their parents' rage. .   .   .

A quarter of the mothers and a fifth of the fathers have not gotten their lives back on track a full ten years after the divorce. They are chronically disorganized and, unable to meet the challenges of being a parent, they lean very heavily on their children. Simply put, the child's role is to ward off the serious depression that threatens the parent's psychological functioning and to keep the parent from feeling that he or she is coming apart.

The result for the child is continued suffering and serious derailment of his or her psychological development. The situation causes severe disturbances of the parent-child relationship, with long-term deleterious effects. Like battered and sexually abused children, overburdened children are found in every social class, and their predicament is not temporary. It affects their entire growing up and certainly their attitudes as young adults toward themselves and toward the adult world. Since most children live with their mothers after divorce, women overburden their children more often than men. But men who are awarded custody of their children or who visit their children regularly may also make similar demands. Several children in our study who were visited several times weekly by their fathers over the ten-year period fell into this role of maintaining the psychological functioning of a man who was intensely dependent on them.

These are not role reversals, as some people have claimed. The child does not take on the role of parent. Rather, these new roles played by the children of divorce are complex and unfamiliar. They merit our careful examination, for they affect many youngsters in our time.

Children who end up playing these roles are often those who naturally feel a great deal of empathy. They pity the adults around them and are frightened about losing their parents. Feeling vulnerable, they tend to yield to the parent's wishes and threats. Their sensitivity becomes their undoing, as they assume multiple roles to support the parent's neurotic needs, often over many years.

Children can, and do, provide the needy parent with a magical looking glass in which flaws, wrinkles, and cracks are erased. Paradoxically, and tragically for their development, young children have an extraordinary capacity to fulfill this role. They are able to bolster a parent's self-esteem, to assure the parent that he or she is a good person, to grant indulgences, to forgive.

Unfortunately for the overburdened child, the price is very high. Under the facade of her competency, for example, Gail was preoccupied with fears of abandonment and she suffered night terrors, chronic constipation, social isolation, and poor learning. Because her role in life was to stave off her father's psychological problems, she had no permission to be a separate person with her own identity and feelings. Many such youngsters are under the terrifying impression that their ministrations and their very presence are keeping their parents alive. Within this fantasy, the children alternate between feeling pleasure and excitement at their own power and despair at their own helplessness. To survive, they often become profoundly defensive and emotionally constricted. Or they become adept at manipulating the vulnerability of others to their own ends. They feel separate from their peers—as Gail says, "weird, an oddball who has no friends." They feel less fortunate and are envious of others. As time goes on, these youngsters have trouble sorting out reality.

Although they are keen observers, they do not necessarily make accurate sense of what they observe. The empathy they show to a troubled parent does not necessarily extend to others.

In truth, few children can really rescue a troubled parent. Many become angry at being trapped by the parent's demands, at being robbed of their separate identity and denied their childhood. And they are saddened, sometimes beyond repair, at seeing so few of their own needs gratified.

QUESTIONS

Reading for Understanding

1. According to the authors, how do children become overburdened after the divorce of their parents? What effects does this have on them?

2. Why do mothers more often burden their children this way? Under what circumstances do fathers do it? What kind of children are most likely to become overburdened?

Noticing Writing Techniques

1. Wallerstein and Blakeslee support their arguments mostly by examples of individual families they have interviewed. How effective do you find this method of support? Would you be more strongly persuaded by some additional method of support?

2. This reading is primarily an analysis of cause and effect—that is, the long-term effects of divorce on children. What are some of the ways the authors avoid oversimplifying their subject? Do they consider more than one possible effect? Do they see different effects on different people? Do they correct common misunderstandings people have on the subject?

Noticing Vocabulary

_____ 1. To *reverberate* is to
    A. deteriorate   B. energize
    C. echo   D. cause to lose strength.

_____ 2. *Chronically* troubled by something means
    A. almost killed by it
    B. bothered by it for a long time
    C. having your health affected by it
    D. losing hope because of it.

_____ 3. *Depleted* means
    A. full of ideas   B. careless
    C. talented   D. exhausted.

———— 4. To *facilitate* something is to make it

    A. cheaper   B. faster

    C. more interesting   D. easier.

———— 5. An *arbiter* is a

    A. mediator   B. labor leader

    C. translator   D. manager.

———— 6. A *concubine* is a

    A. student   B. worker

    C. teacher   D. lover.

———— 7. To be *constricted* means to be

    A. taught   B. held in

    C. confused   D. sad.

Writing Topics

1. Write a paragraph explaining why there is such a high divorce rate in our society. Review Cause and Effect Paragraphs in Unit 2.

2. Write an essay proposing some ways of reducing the harmful effects of divorce on children. Review Problem/Solution Essays in the Expository Mode of Unit 3.

Deborah Tannen (1945–   )

A professor of linguistics at Georgetown University, Deborah Tannen has written books that make the general public aware of their own styles of communication and the effects they have on others, especially those of the opposite sex. *You Just Don't Understand* (1990) focuses on the differences between men's and women's styles of communication. In this passage, Deborah Tannen discusses the effect of these differences on family life.

Parents' and Children's Communication Styles*
from *You Just Don't Understand: Women and Men in Conversation*

Children may be influenced by their parents' styles, just as adults are influenced by what they learned as children. Psychologist Jean Berko Gleason studied how parents talk to their young children, and found that fathers issue more commands to their children than mothers do, and they issue more commands to their sons than to their daughters. Sociolinguist Frances Smith observed a similar pattern in a public-speaking situation. Examining the practice sermons of male and female students at a Baptist seminary, she found that when referring to chapters and verses in their exegesis, the men frequently gave the audience orders, such as "Listen carefully as I read Luke, chapter seventeen." The women, on the other hand, rarely uttered imperatives but rather tended to invite the audience to participate, as in "Let's go back to verses fifteen and sixteen."

Given this pattern, Nathan is not far off the mark when he hears "Let's" as equivalent to a command. It *is* a way of getting others to do what someone wants. And yet Diana is also right when she says he should not feel coerced. The difference lies in the fundamentally different social structures of girls and boys, and women and men. In the hierarchical order that boys and men find or feel themselves in, status is indeed gained by telling others what to do and resisting being told what to do. So once Nathan has deciphered Diana's "Let's" as her way of saying what she wants him to do, his next step is to resist her. But girls and women find or feel themselves in a community that is threatened by conflict, so they formulate requests as proposals rather than orders to make it easy for others to express other preferences without provoking a confrontation. Not accustomed to having others try to bend their will simply to solidify a dominant position, girls do not learn to resist others' demands on principle and don't expect others to resist theirs on principle either.

It is not that women do not want to get their way, but that they do not want to purchase it at the cost of conflict. The irony of interactions like those between Diana and Nathan is that the differences between men's and women's styles doom their efforts. The very moves that women make to avoid confrontation have the effect of sparking it in conversation with some men. Insofar as men perceive that someone is trying to get them to do something without coming right out and saying so, they feel manipulated and threatened by an enemy who is all the more sinister for refusing to come out in the open.

These differences in approaches to conflict have many other ramifications in ways of talking as well. In her study of preschoolers at play, Sachs found that when little boys played doctor, "I'll be the doctor" was the normal stance. Boys wanted to take the doctor role 79 percent of the time, and they often got into long arguments about which boy would get this high-status role. Others have found similar patterns. Linguist Elaine Anderson had preschoolers play out doctor-patient scenes with hand puppets. She too found that the boys wanted to take the high-status role of doctor and generally refused to be the patient or baby. The girls wanted to be the doctor only a third of the time; they often wanted to be the patient, the baby, or the mother.

In Sachs' study, in the vast majority of cases, boys told each other what role to take ("Come on, be a doctor"). Girls, on the other hand, usually asked each other what role they wanted ("Will you be the patient for a few minutes?") or made a joint proposal ("I'll be the nurse and you be the doctor"; "Now we can both be doctors'" "We can both be sick'" or "Okay, and I'll be the doctor for my baby and you be the doctor for your baby"). Many of these proposals, in addition to avoiding confrontation or telling others what to do, are creative ways of keeping the girls equal in status.

Do these experimental studies, in which children played in a laboratory setting, accurately reflect how children play in natural settings? Evidence that they do appears in an article written by a father, Rodger Kamenetz, that begins:

> *My daughter Anya, six, and her friend Rosemary, seven, were playing together in Anya's room. The door was ajar, and when I heard some cooing noises, I peeked in and saw that each child was holding a Cabbage Patch doll, cradling it in her arms. "Now you change your baby," said Rosemary to Anya, "and I'll change mine."*

In reading this I was struck by the symmetry of the girls' play. Rosemary was proposing that they both engage in the same activity at the same time. Instead of trying to cast Anya in the low-status role of baby, she reserved that role for the unprotesting Cabbage Patch dolls.

Girls' and boys' different ways of trying to influence each other's behavior reflect—and create—different social structures. In getting ready for their slingshot fight, the boys in Goodwin's study evidenced a hierarchical organization: The leaders told the others what to do. Giving orders and getting others to follow them was the way that certain boys got to be and stay leaders. A command, by definition, distinguishes the speaker from the addressee and frames him as having more power. In contrast, the girls' groups were organized in an egalitarian way; according to Goodwin, "In accomplishing a task activity even among four- and five-year-olds, all participate jointly in decision making with minimal negotiation of status." By framing proposals with "Let's" and "We," the girls implied that their group was a community, and the results of compliance would increase the power of the community, not the individual power of the person making the suggestion.

Furthermore, the boys typically did not give reasons for their demands, other than their desires. For example, a boy who took a leadership role made demands like:

> *"PLIERS. I WANT THE PLIERS!"*
> *"Look, man. I want the wire cutters right now."*

But the girls gave reasons for their suggestions:

> *Sharon: We gotta clean 'em first. You know.*
> *Pam: I know.*
> *Sharon: Cause they got germs.*
> *Pam: Wash 'em and stuff 'cause just in case they got germs on 'em.*

Not giving reasons for their demands, the boys reinforced their orders as moves in a contest. Compliance indicated submission to the authority of the leader, although submission is an act of cooperation insofar as it reinforces the smooth working of the group. But the girls' methods of getting their way worked differently. Not only did they give reasons, but the reasons were for the general good: The bottles should be cleaned so no one would be harmed by germs. When Pam collaborated by echoing Sharon's suggestion and also her reason, she appeared to be participating in the decision making rather than following orders. This does not, however, mean that there may not be a pattern in whose suggestions tend to be taken up, or that someone whose suggestions are frequently taken up may not feel personal satisfaction and gain prestige in the group.

The different social structures that boys and girls maintained went along with the sorts of activities they preferred. Boys particularly liked to play openly competitive games, such as football and basketball. Even for activities that were not competitive by nature, the boys often broke into teams to facilitate competition. Girls were not much interested in organized sports or games. They preferred whole-group activities such as jump rope or hopscotch.

Goodwin found that the boys ranked themselves according to skill at different activities and often boasted and bragged about their abilities and possessions. Like the little boys in Sachs' study, arguing over who would get to be the doctor, the preteen and teenage boys in Goodwin's study argued about status—about relative skill and who had the power to tell whom what to do. The girls argued about their relative appearance, their relationships to others, and what others said about them. Whereas boys boasted that they were better, a girl who acted as if she was better than the others was criticized for "bragging" or "showing off."

Boys not only commanded but also insulted and threatened each other. If they had a complaint about another boy, they tended to voice it in his presence. Girls' complaints, however, were typically voiced in the absence of the accused.

The girls' preference to avoid direct confrontation resulted in behavior that is traditionally thought of in a negative way—talking behind someone's back. Expressing this negative view, one man remarked that girls sacrifice sincerity for harmony. The accusation of "insincerity" is commonplace in cross-cultural communication, because culturally different individuals don't talk in ways that seem obviously appropriate. Sparking direct confrontation by expressing criticism may seem "sincere" to those who believe that confrontation reinforces camaraderie. But in a system where confrontation causes rifts, it would not be "sincere" at all, since directly expressing criticism and sparking a fight would send a metamessage that one wants to weaken the bonds of friendship.

These differences in children's experience result in divergent expectations, assumptions, and attitudes that confuse adult conversations. For example, the following argument arose because the woman expected to hear reasons from a man who was not in the habit of giving them. Maureen and Philip were trying to set a date for a dinner party.

> *Maureen: The only weekend we seem to have free is October tenth.*
> *Philip: That's the opening of the hunting season.*
> *Maureen: Well, let's do it Saturday or Sunday evening.*
> *Philip: Okay, make it Saturday.*

Maureen: Wouldn't you want to be able to hunt later on the first day of hunting?

Philip: (Annoyed) I said Saturday, so obviously that's the day I prefer.

Maureen: (Now also annoyed) I was just trying to be considerate of you. You didn't give a reason for choosing Saturday.

Philip: I'm taking off Thursday and Friday to hunt, so I figure I'll have had enough by Saturday night.

Maureen: Well, why didn't you say that?

Philip: I didn't see why I had to. And I found your question very intrusive.

Maureen: I found your response very offensive!

Since Philip didn't give a reason for choosing Saturday, Maureen assumed he might be accommodating to what he perceived to be her preference, as she might have done—indeed, as she was doing. She wanted to let him know that it wasn't necessary, and she was hurt by his objecting when she was being considerate. To Philip, being asked to explain his reasons feels like having to give an account of his time. He assumes that individuals watch out for their own interests, so her poking around in his interests is intrusive. Her attempts to ameliorate a potential conflict of interests actually sparked a conflict.

Differences in attitudes toward conflict itself show up in daily conversations. Gail hates to argue. If Norman becomes angry and raises his voice, she is deeply upset. "I can't talk to you if you're yelling," she says. "Why can't we discuss this like mature people?" Norman can never figure this out. To him, being able to fight with someone is evidence of intimacy. In contrast, the endless monotonous discussions that she values as a sign of intimacy are anathema to him. They just wear him down, whereas he feels fine after a good knock-down, drag-out fight—which leaves her feeling weary and defeated. He regards such fighting as a form of ritual combat and values it as a sign of involvement, since only those who are intimately involved with each other argue.

Many cultures of the world see arguing as a pleasurable sign of intimacy, as well as a game. Americans in Greece often get the feeling that they are witnessing an argument when they are overhearing a friendly conversation that is more heated than such a conversation would be if Americans were having it. Linguist Deborah Schiffrin showed that in the conversation of working-class Eastern European Jewish speakers—both male and female—in Philadelphia, friendly argument was a means of being sociable. Linguist Jane Frank analyzed the conversation of a Jewish couple who tended to polarize and take argumentative positions in social situations. But they were not fighting. They were staging a kind of public sparring, where both fighters were on the same side. . . .

For boys and men, aggression does not preclude friendship. Quite the contrary, it is a good way to start interaction and create involvement. A woman told me of her surprise when she was a member of a mixed group of students attending a basketball game at the University of Michigan. Although their tickets had seat assignments, the usual practice among students at this university was for spectators to take any seats they found—first come, first served. Following these unwritten rules, the students took seats in the front row of the balcony. Before long, a group of men from Michigan State University arrived, assuming they were entitled to the seats shown on their tickets. Finding people in their seats, they ordered them out. When the University of Michigan students refused to vacate the seats, a loud argument ensued in which the men of the two groups denounced and threatened each other, and the women sank down in their seats. After a while, the visitors settled for the seats adjoining the disputed ones. Then the men who had just been engaged in an angry verbal fight began a friendly chat about the teams and the schools and the game about to begin. The women were dumbfounded. They would never have engaged in such an argument, but they assumed that if they had it would have made them enemies for life, not friends in the wink of an eye.

QUESTIONS

Reading for Understanding

1. Tannen's overall idea is that men and women have different styles of talking beginning in childhood and continuing through adult life. What are the main differences that she mentions in this passage? What do these differences in styles of communication reveal about differences in attitude?

2. What differences does she mention among cultures in their ways of communicating?

3. What effect do parents' styles of communication have on children?

Noticing Writing Techniques

1. Why does Tannen use direct quotations of conversations to illustrate her points?

2. Why does she cite other studies to support her points? What kinds of studies are they?

3. Do you think she shows a bias either toward women or toward men in her description of their attitudes or their styles of communication?

Noticing Vocabulary

_____ 1. *Exegesis* of the Bible means
A. reading aloud   B. interpretation
C. praying   D. translation.

———— 2. A *hierarchical* order means
   A. an orderly progression in time
   B. an organization with a large number of people
   C. an organization based on equality
   D. an organization based on levels of authority.

———— 3. An *egalitarian* method is one based on
   A. equal rights   B. money
   C. rules given by one leader   D. a small elite group

———— 4. *Divergent* expectations are ones that
   A. agree completely   B. are not very intense
   C. lead in different   D. are extremely
      directions   ambitious.

———— 5. To *ameliorate* a conflict is to
   A. intensify it   B. reduce it
   C. bring in new issues   D. settle it.

———— 6. To *preclude* something is to
   A. rule it out   B. make it necessary
   C. make it possible   D. make it more attractive.

Writing Topics

1. Write a paragraph explaining the role of arguing in your family, mentioning whether the men participate in it differently than the women. Review Exposition: Comparative in Unit 2.

2. Write an essay explaining how the cultural background of your family influences the way you communicate—whether you prefer confrontation or avoid it, whether the men communicate differently than the women, and whether families of other backgrounds seem to communicate differently. Review Expository Essays in Unit 3.

Earl Shorris (1936–   )

The author of several novels and books of nonfiction on varied subjects, Earl Shorris paints a portrait in *Latinos* of the many cultures that fall under the category of Latino or Hispanic. In this introductory sketch, he portrays a near-legendary ancestor who stamped her personality on the family for several generations. As Jane Howard wrote, good families have "a chief, or a heroine, or a founder." Earl Shorris' family had Bienvenida.

Bienvenida*
from *Latinos: A Biography of the People*

When Bienvenida Petilon got lost on the subway, her sour daughter Alegre (which means *happy*) was beside herself, for there was hardly anyone in New York who spoke Spanish in those days and Bienvenida did not speak one word of English. Fortunately, that was a gentler time, and Bienvenida, toothless and terrifying, all in black, found her way back to the Bronx and her haven of gossip, coffee, and the Spanish language.

Language held a special place in Bienvenida's life, beginning with her name; as the eighth child and the first daughter, she was called Welcome. She continued the policy with her children by Petilon the fisherman; in addition to the inappropriately named Alegre, she had an olive-skinned daughter whom she named Blanca, the fair.

Although Bienvenida was not old when she came to the United States, she held on to her language and culture as if they were life itself. Indeed, when she died, it was not of illness but of English, for she had been condemned to a nursing home where no one spoke Spanish. Until that time, Bienvenida had determined the language spoken in her presence. She had also done her best to fend off the culture of the new country. According to her granddaughter, Bienvenida never accepted the concept of such things as recorded music. When she heard the voice of a singer on the radio before breakfast, she mused to her granddaughter Sylvia that it seemed strange for someone to be so happy in the morning.

Bienvenida was often an embarrassment to her daughter and granddaughter. If she didn't approve of a suitor who brought her daughter home after dinner or a party, Bienvenida waited at the window for him to come into range, then rained bananas on his head. She filled the rooms of the apartment with the evil eye, black stars, and the misinterpretation of dreams. In the practice of medicine she excelled at the use of garlic, which she hung around Sylvia's neck in clusters before sending her off to school. It was a very long time ago, when New York was still welcoming to immigrants, but even so it must have been very difficult for a little girl with a Buster Brown haircut, a strange Spanish name, and a necklace of garlic to attend a public school in the Bronx.

A generation later, Assistant District Attorney James Sasson Shorris, Sylvia's son and Bienvenida's great-grandson, paced the worn-out floor of a Manhattan courtroom, questioning a witness who spoke only Spanish. In high school James's weakest subject had been Spanish. His mother had met often with his instructor to try to find a way to coach a bright young man in the language one of his ancestors had used to write poetry in the city of Toledo in the beginning of the fourteenth century. She had spent years of evenings cajoling her son into the world of Spanish verbs and vowels, but the effort had been entirely in vain; the assistant district attorney who looked as if he should be working in Madrid or Mexico City spoke to the witness through an interpreter.

The process of assimilation, the core issue of this book, is more dramatic in the Sasson-Petilon family than in most, for they are Spanish Jews, people who left Spain at the end of the fifteenth century, but who so loved the language and the culture that it was their first language 450 years later. Why were James and his brother Anthony, the great-grandsons of Bienvenida and the grandsons of Ernesto and Blanca, the first generation to lose the language?

It might appear to someone looking at the family from a distance that the loss was due to the first out-marriage of either a Sasson or a Petilon in four-and-a-half centuries of living among speakers of foreign languages, but I think there were other reasons. The language really began to lose its grip on the families with the courtship of Ernesto and Blanca, for they wrote to each other in French rather than Spanish, seeking to make something like love out of an arranged marriage.

She succeeded. We do not know about him, because he died suddenly at the age of twenty-eight, but there is no reason to believe that he was not also in love. In French. And Spanish and Italian and Turkish and Greek, and eventually in English. For Ernesto and Blanca the Spanish language fell into equality. Multicultural and multilingual, they did not cling to any one language, but to languages. Ernesto, a romantic, believed Esperanto was the solution to the punishment of Babel. Blanca, being more practical, changed her name to Blanche, and limited her reading to novels in French.

Sylvia, among the first generation born in the United States, was apprenticed to Bienvenida, who knew several languages but lived in Spanish. Although it was uncomfortable being Spanish in schools filled with Goldbergs and Murphys, Sylvia did not abandon the language. On the contrary, she went to Mexico, where she felt so comfortable that she stayed for years, living and working in a Mexican world. Arriving in Mexico, she said, was like coming home.

Her brother, who was much younger and not in the thrall of Bienvenida, limited his Spanish to the few nouns required to get through dinner and dessert. He was a portly Don Quixote in appearance and character, but he spoke with a Princeton accent, drawling the words through a very Spanish nose. His rejection of the language of his ancestors was so complete that it affected the way he chose to make his living; he taught English.

The lesson of the Sasson-Petilon family is one of the axioms of Latino culture: *Las viejitas* rule the world. The language survives for one generation beyond the last little old lady who spoke it, and neither bilingual education nor English-only initiatives can change that. The difference between Sylvia and her brother was Bienvenida, who reached over a generation to speak to her granddaughter. Otherwise, the last Spanish-speaking Sasson-Petilon would have been Blanca.

No other factors appear to have had much importance in the transmission of language. Both of Bienvenida's great-grandsons spent their early years on the Mexican border; James was born in El Paso, Texas. James's parents both spoke Spanish, one like a *chilanga*[1] and the other like a *pachuco*[2] with Alzheimer's. The babysitters who cared for him until he got through the first two years of school spoke no English. He ate tortillas before he ate bread, but he did not ingest the language, not even when he tried.

The last test of Bienvenida's influence came with the 1990 U.S. Census forms. Her granddaughter, Sylvia, identified herself as Hispanic, but her great-grandsons simply checked the box marked white and went on with their lives.

According to some people, mainly on the political right, the progression from Latino to Anglo of the descendants of Bienvenida was inevitable; the melting pot, which excludes blacks, will not exclude Latinos. Perhaps—but I wonder what would have happened to Bienvenida and her family if they had arrived in New York just twenty years ago or even yesterday. Bienvenida would not have gotten lost on the subway, which is a bilingual monster now; the commonness of her language might even have led her to feel, like Sylvia arriving in Mexico, that she was home, and that would have changed everything.

QUESTIONS

Reading for Understanding

1. How was Bienvenida's arrival in New York different than it would have been in recent times?

2. Why was the process of assimilation more dramatic for this family than for most? Does the author seem to favor or oppose assimilation?

3. What were some of Bienvenida's ways of behaving that made her memorable?

4. What was the main way Bienvenida exerted her influence over later generations?

5. What rule of Latino culture is taught by Bienvenida's example?

Noticing Writing Techniques

1. How does the author at the end of this essay return to what he said in the beginning? Why does he do this?

2. Although this essay is mostly a description of a person and a narrative of family experiences, several comparisons occur. What or whom does the author compare and contrast? How do these comparisons add to his discussion of his main idea?

---

[1]*chilanga*, a resident of Mexico;
[2]*pachuco*, a tough guy, a gang member

Noticing Vocabulary

——— 1. A *haven* is a place of
    A. entertainment   B. work
    C. comfort   D. opportunity.

——— 2. To *fend off* something is to
    A. push it away   B. clean it off
    C. argue against it   D. remove a cover from.

——— 3. *Assimilation* refers to
    A. keeping one's culture separate
    B. improving one's status economically
    C. learning the language spoken by one's ancestors
    D. acquiring mainstream culture.

——— 4. A *portly* person is
    A. plump   B. rich
    C. healthy   D. thin.

——— 5. To *ingest,* when used literally, means to
    A. hide   B. eat
    C. dissolve   D. see.

Writing Topics

1. Write a paragraph defining and illustrating the term *assimilation.* You may begin by reading a dictionary definition, but create your own explanation of the term in your paragraph. Review Definition Paragraphs in Unit 2.

2. From your own knowledge and talks with older members of your family, write an essay portraying a legendary figure in your family's past. Try to find out information beyond what you already know; tell about this person's character and actions, and explain his or her influence on later generations. Review Portraying a Person in the Descriptive Mode of Unit 3.

Janet Campbell Hale (1946–   )

A member of the Coeur d'Alene tribe of northern Idaho, Janet Campbell Hale was born in Los Angeles and grew up on reservations in Washington State. She graduated from the University of California at Berkeley and earned her master's degree at the University of California at Davis. She is the author of *The Jailing of Cecilia Capture* and *The Owl's Song.* This selection is from her recent collection of essays entitled *Bloodlines: Odyssey of a Native Daughter* (1993).

Return to Bear Paw*

My grandmother, the one who ran with Chief Joseph, died five years before my birth so I have no memories of my own of her. But I heard a lot about her from both my parents, from my uncle and cousins and sisters who did know her and had memories. My three sisters, who are ten, twelve, and fourteen years older than I, remember a little old woman who liked to joke, who told them Indian stories in our Native language. (She never learned English. They knew Indian as children.) How I envied them. How I wished I, too, had known her, had listened to her stories, had understood the language. I imagined her, though, when I was a child, and she became almost real to me.

My family had a photograph of her taken in old age: She is small and thin, her face very wrinkled, her eyes squint in the sun. Her long hair is white. She wears it parted in the middle and in two braids that hang in front to her waist. She is dressed Indian style. . . .

The Big Sky Country of Montana, the mountainous terrain, the grey, cold weather, the country western music, the motion of the car took me out of myself and my own petty hardships. (I had a cold, I had to eat in diners and sleep in cheap motels.) I had to speak to nine audiences in eight days (as a single mother I needed the money), though I would rather be home. I recognized these as petty concerns as we made our way across the big, big state of Montana. I saw her, my grandmother, the young girl she had been in 1877, more and more clearly. I drew closer and closer to her. She was there when they drove their ponies and cattle across a treacherous river and over two mountain ranges (they sometimes reached altitudes of ten thousand feet). Always (until that last day) they managed to keep ahead of the soldiers. In the last month they had no more cattle herds and only a few ponies.

Their food supplies ran out. Their clothes and moccasins were worn out. They became ragged, cold and hungry and could not stop to hunt or gather food or make new clothes. They wrapped their bleeding feet in rags and continued. They hurriedly buried their dead in shallow graves along the wayside. Soldiers noted scarred trees where hungry Indians had eaten bark and that they left behind a path marked by blood.

I thought of her, the devout Catholic girl she was, swept along with Nez Percé, who were never the friend of the Coeur d'Alene, whose language was not the same or even similar, whose culture was not her own.

I remembered something I heard about Chief Joseph when I was a child of eleven: he, always portrayed as "noble" in books, films, poems (in *Bury My Heart at Wounded Knee*), had actually been a mean person, a wicked man who hated women and treated them very badly.

Whether or not it is true that Chief Joseph was a misogynist and had had a woman put to death because she brought him bad luck, I'll never know for

---

sure. But I didn't doubt it when I heard it at age eleven, and I've read accounts of Indian chiefs of that region (of an earlier time) having wives put to death for the same reason. It could be true. At any rate the Nez Percé, to my grandmother, were strange people with different beliefs and customs. Maybe their leader held women in low regard, as the grandson of Looking Glass told me. They were not in any way *her people*. Except one: they were Indians and all Indians had in common a powerful enemy who had conquered them and would now hold them in captivity and would not tolerate any defiance.

So there she was, a young Catholic Coeur d'Alene, running for her life with Nez Percé (they left a trail marked by blood) from the United States Army (which was commanded by a man who was in fact against the reservation system, who believed Indians should all be killed off lest the government end up supporting "a race of paupers." "The only good Indian is a dead Indian" was a heartfelt sentiment in the America of 1877). And where were they going? To Canada to join the Sioux chief, Sitting Bull. And what kind of a life would she, the little girl who would be my grandmother, have were they to make good their escape? While the Nez Percé were never the friend of the Coeur d'Alene, the Sioux, still polygamous in 1877, were their bitter enemy. The literal translation of the Coeur d'Alene word for "Sioux" is "cutthroat."

The last days of the Great Flight were in September, and that year it was, as it often is, very cold in Montana, maybe as cold as the time of my own journey. I know it snowed in the night while they camped and slept in the Little Bear Paw Mountains. I know the snow fell softly throughout the next day. . . .

The Indians had come far, had suffered such great hardships, were so tired and hungry. There would be time enough, or so they thought, to stop for the night, their last night. They knew of Howard, a good long distance away, and they knew they had completely lost the other, the Cavalry. But they were not aware of a third division, which now came towards them from the east. So they went down there, made their camp in the gulch beside Snake Creek. They hunted, cooked their fresh meat, ate and rested. What did that girl dream of that night as she lay sleeping? Did she dream of the beautiful Coeur d'Alene country that was her home? Did she see the faces of her father and mother? Or did she now dream of her new life in Canada?

The cavalry attacked just before dawn while the Indians still slept. The battle raged as the snow fell, hour after bloody hour, throughout most of the day. When the Battle at the Bear Paw ended, 419 Indians—88 men, 184 women and 147 children—lay dead on the frozen ground. . . .

Chief Joseph of the Nez Percé was thirty-six years old at the time of the Battle at the Bear Paw. His surrender speech was made through an interpreter and recorded on the spot by an army clerk. It would become one of the most famous of American speeches:

> *"Tell General Howard I know his heart. What he told me before I have in my heart. I am tired of fighting. Our chiefs are killed. Looking Glass is dead. Toolhoolzote is dead. The old men are all dead. It is cold and we have no blankets. The little children are freezing to death. My people, some of them, have run away to the hills and have no blankets, no food; no one knows where they are—perhaps*

freezing to death. I want to have time to look for my children and see how many of them I can find. Maybe I shall find them among the dead. Hear me, my chiefs! From where the sun now stands I will fight no more forever."

After it was all over, my grandmother would return to Coeur d'Alene country in northern Idaho. She would live through a smallpox epidemic that would wipe out most of the tribe, begun when the Coeur d'Alene people, no longer permitted to go to Montana to hunt buffalo, were given smallpox-infected army blankets.

She would marry a tall, shrewd Coeur d'Alene man, who would, as a rancher, provide very well for her and the six sons and one daughter they would have together.

She would give birth to my father in the mountains one summer day in 1892 while out picking huckleberries. She would tell him about his birth in the mountains and how she came riding down with the basket strapped to her horse on one side filled with huckleberries and the basket on the other side containing her new baby boy.

My father would go to mission school at the age of twelve, where he would learn English: to read, to write, to speak. He would become a soldier in the United States Army during World War I (though Indians would not be made citizens until 1924). He would marry and have one son. His first wife would die. He would marry my mother when he was thirty-nine years old, and they would have four daughters together.

My paternal grandmother would live to be a very old woman, and she and my three older sisters would know each other very well. She would tell them stories, speaking the old language they would understand as children but forget as adults (and I would never know).

The old woman who survived the Great Flight and the Battle at the Bear Paw and the smallpox epidemic would die peacefully in her sleep in her home in Idaho in 1941.

I would be born five years later in 1946, shortly after the end of World War II. And though I would live on that same Idaho reservation, and then on the Yakima in Washington State, I would grow up knowing only the English language. I would go to college and law school. Eventually I would become a writer. As a writer I would go back to that hard Montana country, and on a cold day in May 1986, I would, at last, return to Bear Paw.

QUESTIONS

Reading for Understanding

1. Why was it important for Ms. Hale to visit the site of the Battle of Bear Paw in Montana in 1986? What connection did the events there have to her family's history? What significance did it have to Native Americans in general?

2. How was Ms. Hale's image of the famous Chief Joseph different from the image of him that most Americans have been given in such books as *Bury My Heart at Wounded Knee?*

3. Why did some Indian nations who had wide differences in culture and were not friendly to one another, act as allies in 1877?

4. In what ways is Ms. Hale different from her ancestors, including her grandmother? What does she seem to share with them?

5. Is there anything in her family's past that she seems sad or angry about? What does she seem proud of?

Noticing Writing Techniques

1. Ms. Hale is telling three stories in this selection—the story of the Native Americans in 1877, the story of her grandmother, and the story of her own visit to Bear Paw in 1986. How does she tie the three stories together?

2. What details does Ms. Hale use to reveal the prejudices against Native Americans and the mistreatment of them? Why do you think she uses these details to condemn such attitudes and actions rather than merely express her own opinion of them?

Noticing Vocabulary

———— 1. A *misogynist* is a person who
   A. hates families   B. loves women
   C. loves animals   D. hates women.

———— 2. A *polygamous* society is one in which
   A. gambling is allowed
   B. people speak more than one language
   C. men may have more than one wife
   D. parents may have many children.

———— 3. A person's *paternal* grandparents are the grandparents
   A. on the father's side of the family
   B. on the mother's side of the family
   C. who raised the person's parents, even if they are not blood relatives
   D. who were most loving and supportive.

Writing Topics

1. Find a photograph of an older relative, someone of your grandparents' generation, if possible. Brainstorm or do some focused writing in which you put down on paper all the descriptive details in the picture and all the personality traits you see revealed in the picture. Finally,

compose a paragraph in which you portray this person for the reader as accurately and meaningfully as you can.

2. Write an essay in which you tie in your family's past with some historical event or situation, such as a time of war, economic depression, revolution, technological change, or other famous event. Do whatever prewriting will help you gather facts and ideas, including interviewing older members of the family. Write a first draft in which you explore the impact of this event or situation on your family; write a final draft in which you tie together effectively the historical situation and the personal experiences.

Andrea Starr Alonzo (1953–   )

Amid all the talk about the fate of the nuclear family, we should also pay attention to the question of the *extended family*—that large crowd of relatives and step-relatives that is defined differently in every culture but which all of us experience in some form. In the following essay, Prof. Andrea Starr Alonzo, a writer of fiction and professor of English at the Borough of Manhattan Community College, describes her own extended family and explains the influence of African family patterns on African-American families.

My Extended Family*
From *Women and Stepfamilies*

Obviously one of the unfortunate prerequisites to any stepfamily is divorce (or death). It is, in any case, painful for all concerned, and if the particulars of the previous relationship, either emotional or legal, are not resolved before the new party enters the picture, it's sure to complicate things even more.

When I met Brandon he was a lonely man who hung out in bars (I was working in one). As a child I was already today's modern woman and I promised myself not to marry until my late twenties. I didn't want to be a child bride; I wanted to experience life first. Then, at twenty-five, when something in me clicked and said it was time to meet Mr. Right, I met Brandon. One slight fact that I had failed to consider in my perfect plan was that at our ages (Brandon is six years older than I) we would certainly by then have a past. My own was fairly uncomplicated—no marriages, no children. Brandon, however, was a different story.

---

*Excerpt from WOMEN AND STEPFAMILIES: VOICES OF ANGER AND LOVE by Andrea Starr Alonzo, edited by Nan Baver Maglin and Nancy Schniedewind. Copyright © 1989. Reprinted by permission of Temple University Press.

One night a couple of months after I was hooked, it occurred to me to ask how a great guy like Brandon could reach his thirties without getting "caught." It turned out that he had, still, a wife and two daughters. In the same breath I was told that the marriage was over, and now he "had a reason to get a divorce." It didn't *sound* like a line then, and I believed it. But here I was, the "other woman." I detested the idea of being in love with a man who was legally bound to someone else even if, as he'd told me, his wife had left him. The fuzziness surrounding Brandon's relationship with his wife (now his ex-wife) and his delayed divorce turned out to be the stormiest issue in our relationship before we married.

Meanwhile, I soon met Brandon's daughters, ages five and ten, two beautiful brown-skinned dolls who had both inherited their father's large eyes. We got along just fine. They never seemed ruffled by the fact that their daddy had a girlfriend, although they had their particular ways of dealing with it. The older one, Myla, was especially protective of her mother's image. She was always careful not to reveal much about her, particularly if it was unflattering. Often I would catch her nudge her sister, Joy, who at five would indiscriminately blurt out anything that came to mind. I respected Myla's way of handling the situation. I, in turn, have always been sensitive enough not to infringe on their mother's sovereign place in their lives.

I did see the children fairly often at first, although there were always hassles about the mother letting them go. Often Brandon would drive all the way to New Jersey to pick them up and return a couple of hours later, long-faced and empty-handed. I would always be heartbroken and furious myself. Intimidated by her tactics, he went to get the girls less and less. Now I rarely see them.

Nevertheless we managed to have lots of fun times together, and as Myla approached her teen years we grew closer. She found that she could talk to me in a way that she never could with her mother. I think she enjoyed having a grown-up for a friend. Myla had a tendency toward sullenness, though, that caused problems later.

We saw how much the girls enjoyed being with their father. He said it was because they witnessed a side of him they never saw at home—a happy side. Since I'd never met the mother, I began to form my own opinions, which naturally weren't good. Especially when I heard of little incidents, such as the time Joy was writing Christmas cards and her mother caught her writing one for me—she snatched it from her and tore it up. I began to want to "rescue" them from that unhappy woman. We even talked of having them come and live with us after we were married.

Finally Brandon got his divorce, and we made immediate plans to get married. Our first son, Jason, was on the way, and we hadn't a moment to waste. I had encouraged Brandon to talk openly with his daughters about all this, and he said he would. When I asked him how they had responded to the news of our wedding, he said, "Fine." When I subsequently mentioned it to them over the phone, I got a completely different reaction. They were shocked and upset (they didn't even know!). This was the first open display of rejection they had ever shown toward me. Not an unreasonable reaction under the circumstances. They, especially Joy, had been hoping for a reconciliation between their parents.

Meanwhile, another wrinkle began to form. I was in graduate school and working odd jobs. I stopped working altogether when Jason was born. We were having money problems, and the child-support money dwindled, then stopped. While this would have made an excellent excuse for the mother, I somehow felt it was really not the basis for the limited visitation. Nevertheless, even though we were broke, I felt that Brandon should have somehow done better by the girls. Not seeing them *and* not paying? There was already a part of me that was guilty for having their father when they didn't. So no matter how broke we were, I would never deny them for us. This became an issue well into our marriage. I used to nag him like crazy to find a way to get them the money they deserved (and us, too, poor thing) and fight for his right to see them. I'd tell him that they'd grow to resent him. He seemed to believe, however, that they would grow up and see the mother as the villain in all this. I doubt it. She's got the upper hand. And she apparently does nothing to uphold their image of their father. She'd tell them that their father wasn't supporting them financially. She told Myla that we were not legally married because they were not divorced. She even pulled a stunt straight out of a soap opera: not long after our first child was born, she had a baby, and she tried to put the word out in the family that Brandon was the father. Thank God this seed of doubt didn't take root.

I guess there are any number of reasons why a man who loves his family would distance himself from them, besides dollars and cents. Not giving financial support breeds guilt and embarrassment. Or, as in Brandon's case, dealing with their mother may be an excruciating experience. Maybe he even subconsciously wants to punish her for denying him his children. The money-visitation issue is really a vicious cycle. Then too, having a part-time relationship with one's children is much more difficult than a full-time one. It's easier not to deal with painful situations; it's easier to put them off. I think the tendency for men to do this is greater than for women. When Brandon does communicate with their mother, it's usually through Joy. He avoids direct confrontation with her as much as possible. He never refers to her by name, always as "the child's mother."

To add to things, Brandon and Myla have a strange relationship. Brandon has tended to outwardly favor Joy, who has a visibly sweeter disposition. As Myla got older, she became moodier. Even so, I could still communicate with her pretty well. As she entered her teens and began to experience discord with her mother, she'd drop complaints about her, which I'd happily lap up. The first antimaternal outburst occurred when Myla's mother made her have her hair cut when she was twelve. I was surprised at this display of anger toward her mother; from there, unfortunately it got worse.

At fifteen, Myla and I had another enlightening conversation. I was braiding her hair, which generally relaxes the tongue, and she began to explain to me her feelings about her father's marriage to me. She told me she was glad her father had married me. I couldn't believe I was hearing this.

"But what about your reaction when we told you about the wedding?" I asked her.

She explained that that was because it happened so suddenly. They hadn't had the chance to adjust to a divorce between their parents. That was a legitimate complaint, I felt. She went on to say that she realized her father was unhappy with her mother, and that she really didn't think her mom was cut out for wife- and motherhood. She was unaffectionate and insensitive. That sounded like an astute assessment of her mother from what I'd heard.

A typically rebellious teenager, Myla became increasingly difficult for all of us to cope with. They reside in an affluent town in New Jersey, and Myla of course wants to keep up with the crowd, which is wealthy kids who are often granted the freedom and money to do as they please. She refuses to understand that her parents can't afford that world. Eventually we began to hear rumors that Myla was smoking cigarettes and marijuana. She began to stay out whenever she wished, and her mother couldn't do a thing with her. Once she even called Brandon to help discipline Myla for getting caught smoking in school. Myla began to be rude to me and show open resentment toward her father. I finally had to give her my first "scolding" about respect for her father, regardless of his shortcomings. I think I did a pretty good job, because she apologized and things were all right between them for a while.

A few months ago, however, she and her father got into the last in a series of explosive fights. She was arguing with her mother when Brandon happened to be there, and he tried to intervene, whereupon Myla locked herself into the bathroom and yelled through the door at Brandon. "Go away! You're not my father! Go back to Anne and the boys. You've never been a father to me, so just get out of my life!" Brandon stopped speaking to her.

When graduation rolled around, I had to urge him to go. "You're the adult," I told him. "You can't afford to miss this milestone in her life by holding grudges. You have to set an example." He went, they kissed and made up, and we're proud of what a fine young lady she's grown up to be. She's still sullen, though.

She had also invited me to attend the ceremonies, but I made the excuse that it was a school day, and I had to get the boys to bed. I really wanted her mother to be able to enjoy this event without any discomfort. She'd earned it. I had long since begun to soften my attitude toward her, despite her acts. A broken marriage, for whatever reasons, is a difficult thing. Yet she had, with or without the help of her husband, put one child through high school and was well on the way to putting the other. They weren't rich, but the children wanted for nothing in the way of material needs or comforts. If she's fallen short on the other part, well, who's perfect? She'd done a good job.

Brandon has been supporting them fairly regularly this year. He and Myla are speaking, and a lot of the rough edges have smoothed out. I admit that there have been times when I've wished that it was just Brandon and me, and that he didn't have such concrete reminders of his life before me. For me, the main thrust of being a stepmother is simply that they are an extension of their father, whom I love. I share some of the excitement, pride, apprehension, and pain of watching them grow. But I have never tried to force my "stepmother" status upon them, whatever that means. It wasn't until a few weeks ago, when Myla accompanied me to the hairdresser's and he asked her relationship to me, when she first heard me identify her as my stepdaughter. I deemphasize that title as much as possible. To them I am simply their father's wife.

My stormy relationship (or lack of one) with Brandon's ex-wife notwithstanding, I believe my tendency to downplay the "step" part of my family is a common trait in black culture. If you ask my Guyanese husband how many sisters and brothers he has, he'll tell you, "thirty-nine." Well, of course many of them are "steps," but they are not labeled that way. I have *never* heard my husband refer to his father's wife as his stepmother, and I seriously doubt if that term ever entered his mind. For one thing, blacks tend to feel their mothers' special place is sacred and cannot be tampered with. I once had a student who said, "As long as I have my mother, I wouldn't call anyone my stepmother."

Another cultural explanation for the lack of distinction between "steps" may lie in an old African tradition that is still prevalent in many parts of the continent: polygamous relationships. In African culture the more wives and children a man has, the wealthier he is. This precept has continued to flourish among blacks in Western civilization. What else would you call a man who has thirty-nine children by four women? And it's common knowledge among them! Of course he couldn't marry them all; it's illegal. And of course he doesn't say (or probably even recognize) that he's practicing polygamy. Technically, he's not, since he's not married to them all. But no matter what we call it, this strong cultural tradition must surely have ramifications in transported Africans.

My husband made me painfully aware of this idea when I couldn't understand (was in fact quite condemning of) his mother for continuing to have children by a man she knew she'd never marry. Similarly, she's in a panic for her eldest granddaughter, nearing thirty, to begin having children before it's too late. Never mind that she can't marry the man (he's already married). To her, marriage is nice, but having children is more important. That's why when Jason was on the way, Brandon's attitude toward marriage was "What's the rush?"

My mother's explanation for "outside" children is closely linked to the African one. She attributes it to the black man's lack of power in Western society. This is by way of justifying her own father's case. She, of course the all-time bourgeois, ignores her "halfs" as much as possible. That must be the white, middle-class thing to do. To the rest of the Jordans, however, Sam, Bud, and Edith are family. Again, though, we see the "children are wealth" principle.

"Outside" relationships and children are nothing new in any society, human beings being what they are. It's how they are treated that's different. For mainstream Americans it was always something to hide. But for blacks, the closer they are culturally to their African roots, the less of a hidden taboo it is when out-of-wedlock parenting occurs. The new wave of divorces has made the multiple family more of an issue for us all. But for blacks, stepfamilies are simply another form of the extended family.

QUESTIONS

Reading for Understanding

1. What was Ms. Alonzo's original attitude toward her husband's ex-wife? How did her attitude change?

2. What did she think about the question of paying child support?

3. How does she think African attitudes toward the extended family influence her sense of herself as a stepmother? How do African attitudes differ from mainstream American attitudes toward out-of-wedlock children?

4. How did her husband's relationship with his daughters change over the years? In what situation did Ms. Alonzo achieve a level of confidentiality with one of his daughters?

Noticing Writing Techniques

1. Ms. Alonzo mentions African traditions for the first time near the end of the essay. Why do you think she does this? Do the early parts of her story sound just like any American divorce, or are there parts of it that are especially African-American?

2. Which parts of the essay are in narrative form? Where do you find cause and effect analysis? Where are there brief descriptions?

Noticing Vocabulary

_____ 1. A *prerequisite* to something is
A. a good result
B. a previous requirement
C. a fringe benefit
D. a previous investigation.

_____ 2. To speak *indiscriminately* is to speak
A. without prejudice
B. carefully
C. carelessly
D. vaguely.

_____ 3. *Sullenness* means
A. liveliness
B. talkativeness
C. friendliness
D. brooding.

_____ 4. An *excruciating* experience is
A. painful
B. pleasant
C. sad
D. puzzling.

_____ 5. An *astute* judgment is
A. silly   B. old-fashioned
C. hurried   D. wise.

_____ 6. An *affluent* town is
A. interesting   B. large
C. friendly   D. wealthy.

_____ 7. *Polygamy* means the practice of
A. a woman having many husbands
B. families having many children
C. a man having many wives
D. a family moving from one home to another.

_____ 8. *Ramifications* of an event are its
A. spreading aftereffects   B. hidden causes
C. inner contradictions   D. costs

_____ 9. *Bourgeois* attitudes are those of the
A. poor   B. rich
C. middle class   D. elderly

Writing Topics

1. Write a paragraph describing a relationship you have with someone in your extended family who is not one of your parents or a sibling. Review Exposition Paragraphs in Unit 2.

2. Write an essay analyzing how your family's cultural and ethnic background has influenced how your extended family is defined and how it functions. Is everyone welcomed equally? Are some people in it more closely linked than others? Are there frequent family reunions? Are the elder members held in special esteem? What is the attitude toward children? Review the Expository Mode in Unit 3.

Brent Staples (1951–   )

Brent Staples is a writer and editor for the *New York Times*. Originally from Chester, Pennsylvania, he earned a Ph.D. in psychology at the University of Chicago. His journalistic writings bring psychological and sociological insight to a variety of social issues, especially those affecting African-American families in big cities. In the following essay, first written for the *New York Times,* he poses painful questions concerning urban violence and family responsibility. When and how can we be our brothers' keepers?

A Brother's Murder*

It has been more than two years since my telephone rang with the news that my younger brother Blake—just 22 years old—had been murdered. The young man who killed him was only 24. Wearing a ski mask, he emerged from a car, fired six times at close range with a massive .44 Magnum, then fled. The two had once been inseparable friends. A senseless rivalry—beginning, I think, with an argument over a girlfriend—escalated from posturing, to threats, to violence, to murder. The way the two were living, death could have come to either of them from anywhere. In fact, the assailant had already survived multiple gunshot wounds from an incident much like the one in which my brother lost his life.

As I wept for Blake I felt wrenched backward into events and circumstances that had seemed light-years gone. Though a decade apart, we both were raised in Chester, Pa., an angry, heavily black, heavily poor, industrial city southwest of Philadelphia. There, in the 1960s, I was introduced to mortality, not by the old and failing, but by beautiful young men who lay wrecked after sudden explosions of violence. The first, I remember from my 14th year—Johnny, brash lover of fast cars, stabbed to death two doors from my house in a fight over a pool game. The next year, my teenage cousin, Wesley, whom I loved very much, was shot dead. The summers blur. Milton, an angry young neighbor, shot a crosstown rival, wounding him badly. William, another teen-age neighbor, took a shotgun blast to the shoulder in some urban drama and displayed his bandages proudly. His brother, Leonard, severely beaten, lost an eye and donned a black patch. It went on.

I recall not long before I left for college, two local Vietnam veterans—one from the Marines, one from the Army—arguing fiercely, nearly at blows about which outfit had done the most in the war. The most killing, they meant. Not much later, I read a magazine article that set that dispute in a context. In the story, a noncommissioned officer—a sergeant, I believe—said he would pass up any number of affluent, suburban-born recruits to get hard-core soldiers from the inner city. They jumped into the rice paddies with "their manhood on their sleeves," I believe he said. These two items—the veterans arguing and the sergeant's words—still characterize for me the circumstances under which black men in their teens and 20s kill one another with such frequency. With a touchy paranoia born of living battered lives, they are desperate to be *real* men. Killing is only *machismo* taken to the extreme. Incursions to be punished by death were many and minor, and they remain so: they include stepping on the wrong toe, literally; cheating in a drug deal; simply saying "I dare

---

you" to someone holding a gun; crossing territorial lines in a gang dispute. My brother grew up to wear his manhood on his sleeve. And when he died, he was in that group—black, male, and in its teens and early 20s—that is far and away the most likely to murder or be murdered.

I left the East Coast after college, spent the mid- and late-1970s in Chicago as a graduate student, taught for a time, then became a journalist. Within 10 years of leaving my hometown, I was overeducated and "upwardly mobile," ensconced on a quiet, tree-lined street where voices raised in anger were scarcely ever heard. The telephone, like some grim umbilical, kept me connected to the old world with news of deaths, imprisonings and misfortune. I felt emotionally beaten up. Perhaps to protect myself, I added a psychological dimension to the physical distance I had already achieved. I rarely visited my hometown. I shut it out.

As I fled the past, so Blake embraced it. On Christmas of 1983, I traveled from Chicago to a black section of Roanoke, Va., where he then lived. The desolate public housing projects, the hopeless, idle young men crashing against one another—these reminded me of the embittered town we'd grown up in. It was a place where once I would have been comfortable, or at least sure of myself. Now, hearing of my brother's forays into crime, his scrapes with police and street thugs, I was scared, unsteady on foreign terrain.

I saw that Blake's romance with the street life and the hustler image had flowered dangerously. One evening that late December, standing in some Roanoke dive among drug dealers and grim, hair-trigger losers, I told him I feared for his life. He had affected the image of the tough he wanted to be. But behind the dark glasses and the swagger, I glimpsed the baby-faced toddler I'd once watched over. I nearly wept. I wanted desperately for him to live. The young think themselves immortal, and a dangerous light shone in his eyes as he spoke laughingly of making fools of the policemen who had raided his apartment looking for drugs. He cried out as I took his right hand. A line of stitches lay between the thumb and index finger. Kickback from a shotgun, he explained, nothing serious. Gunplay had become part of his life.

I lacked the language simply to say: Thousands have lived this for you and died. I fought the urge to lift him bodily and shake him. This place and the way you are living smells of death to me, I said. Take some time away, I said. Let's go downtown tomorrow and buy a plane ticket anywhere, take a bus trip, anything to get away and cool things off. He took my alarm casually. We arranged to meet the following night—an appointment he would not keep. We embraced as though through glass. I drove away.

As I stood in my apartment in Chicago holding the receiver that evening in February 1984, I felt as though part of my soul had been cut away. I questioned myself then, and I still do. Did I not reach back soon or earnestly enough for him? For weeks I awoke crying from a recurrent dream in which I chased him, urgently trying to get him to read a document I had, as though reading it would protect him from what had happened in waking life. His eyes shining like black diamonds, he smiled and danced just beyond my grasp. When I reached for him, I caught only the space where he had been.

QUESTIONS

Reading for Understanding

1. Whom or what does Brent Staples blame for his brother's death? How did he try to prevent it?

2. How does he relate the Vietnam War to his brother's story?

3. How was Brent's adult life different from Blake's? What does the author mean by saying that Blake had embraced their hometown, Chester, Pa., when he actually lived in Roanoke, Virginia?

4. How do you account for the fact that these two brothers followed such different directions in their lives?

Noticing Writing Techniques

1. Staples often writes for newspapers. In what ways is this essay typical of journalistic writing? How would it be different if he were writing about his brother's death in a psychological study? In a drama? In a letter to another family member?

2. Why does Staples end with a description of his dream? How do you interpret the meaning of the dream?

Noticing Vocabulary

_____ 1. *Light years* are
    A. great periods of time   B. easy stages in life
    C. great distances in space   D. years measured by
                                      astronomy.

_____ 2. *Mortality* means being subject to
    A. sin   B. death
    C. growth   D. time.

_____ 3. *Paranoia* causes a person to feel
    A. silly   B. calm
    C. affectionate   D. suspicious.

_____ 4. *Incursions* are acts of
    A. generosity   B. exploration
    C. invasion   D. friendship.

_____ 5. To be *ensconced* is to be
    A. invited   B. imprisoned
    C. rewarded   D. settled.

_____ 6. *Forays* are
  A. raids   B. small animals
  C. flights   D. caves.

_____ 7. *Terrain* refers to
  A. waves on the ocean   B. landscape
  C. large buildings   D. psychological
                                 mechanisms.

Writing Topics

1. Write a paragraph explaining what you think Brent Staples should have done when he became worried about the dangers of his brother's way of living. Review Persuasive Paragraphs in Unit 2.

2. Sometimes two people raised in the same family turn out very differently. Write an essay in which you describe and compare two people in your immediate or extended family who are very different. Then explain what caused their differences. Review Comparative Paragraphs in Unit 2 and Expository Essays in Unit 3.

Sherwood Anderson (1876–1941)

One of America's most important writers of fiction and a perceptive commentator on the lives of heartland Americans, Sherwood Anderson is remembered especially for his collection of short stories, *Winesburg, Ohio* (1919). In the following selection from his memoirs, Anderson tells about a reversal in his youthful attitude toward his father, the kind of maturing of attitude that occurs in many young people's lives.

Discovery of a Father* from *Memoirs* (1939)

One of the strangest relationships in the world is that between father and son. I know it now from having sons of my own.

A boy wants something very special from his father. You hear it said that fathers want their sons to be what they feel they cannot themselves be, but I tell you it also works the other way. I know that as a small boy I wanted my father to be a certain thing he was not. I wanted him to be a proud, silent, dignified father. When I was with other boys and he passed along the street, I wanted to feel a glow of pride: "There he is. That is my father."

But he wasn't such a one. He couldn't be. It seemed to me then that he was always showing off. Let's say someone in our town had got up a show. They were always doing it. The druggist would be in it, the shoe-store clerk, the

---

Discovery of a Father by Sherwood Anderson. From The Reader's Digest. Copyright 1939 by The Reader's Digest. Copyright renewed 1966 by Eleanor Copenhaver Anderson.

horse doctor, and a lot of women and girls. My father would manage to get the chief comedy part. It was, let's say, a Civil War play and he was a comic Irish soldier. He had to do the most absurd things. They thought he was funny, but I didn't.

I thought he was terrible. I didn't see how Mother could stand it. She even laughed with the others. Maybe I would have laughed if it hadn't been my father.

Or there was a parade, the Fourth of July or Decoration Day. He'd be in that, too, right at the front of it, as Grand Marshal or something, on a white horse hired from a livery stable.

He couldn't ride for shucks. He fell off the horse and everyone hooted with laughter, but he didn't care. He even seemed to like it. I remember once when he had done something ridiculous, and right out on Main Street, too. I was with some other boys and they were laughing and shouting at him and he was shouting back and having as good a time as they were. I ran down an alley back of some stores and there in the Presbyterian Church sheds I had a good long cry.

Or I would be in bed at night and Father would come home a little lit up and bring some men with him. He was a man who was never alone. Before he went broke, running a harness shop, there were always a lot of men loafing in the shop. He went broke, of course, because he gave too much credit. He couldn't refuse it and I thought he was a fool. I had got to hating him.

There'd be men I didn't think would want to be fooling around with him. There might even be the superintendent of our schools and a quiet man who ran the hardware store. Once, I remember, there was a white-haired man who was a cashier of the bank. It was a wonder to me they'd want to be seen with such a windbag. That's what I thought he was. I know now what it was that attracted them. It was because life in our town, as in all small towns, was at times pretty dull and he livened it up. He made them laugh. He could tell stories. He'd even get them to singing.

If they didn't come to our house they'd go off, say at night, to where there was a grassy place by a creek. They'd cook food there and drink beer and sit about listening to his stories.

He was always telling stories about himself. He'd say this or that wonderful thing happened to him. It might be something that made him look like a fool. He didn't care.

If an Irishman came to our house, right away Father would say he was Irish. He'd tell what county in Ireland he was born in. He'd tell things that happened there when he was a boy. He'd make it seem so real that, if I hadn't known he was born in southern Ohio, I'd have believed him myself.

If it was a Scotchman, the same thing happened. He'd get a burr into his speech. Or he was a German or a Swede. He'd be anything the other man was. I think they all knew he was lying, but they seemed to like him just the same. As a boy that was what I couldn't understand.

And there was Mother. How could she stand it? I wanted to ask but never did. She was not the kind you asked such questions.

I'd be upstairs in my bed, in my room above the porch, and Father would be telling some of his tales. A lot of Father's stories were about the Civil War.

To hear him tell it he'd been in about every battle. He'd known Grant, Sherman, Sheridan, and I don't know how many others. He'd been particularly intimate with General Grant so that when Grant went East, to take charge of all the armies, he took Father along.

"I was an orderly at headquarters and Sam Grant said to me, 'Irve,' he said, 'I'm going to take you along with me.'"

It seems he and Grant used to slip off sometimes and have a quiet drink together. That's what my father said. He'd tell about the day Lee surrendered and how, when the great moment came, they couldn't find Grant.

"You know," my father said, "about General Grant's book, his memoirs. You've read of how he said he had a headache and how, when he got word that Lee was ready to call it quits, he was suddenly and miraculously cured.

"Huh," said Father. "He was in the woods with me.

"I was in there with my back against a tree. I was pretty well corned. I had got hold of a bottle of pretty good stuff.

"They were looking for Grant. He had got off his horse and come into the woods. He found me. He was covered with mud.

"I had the bottle in my hand. What'd I care? The war was over. I knew we had them licked."

My father said that he was the one who told Grant about Lee. An orderly riding by had told him, because the orderly knew how thick he was with Grant. Grant was embarrassed.

"But, Irve, look at me. I'm all covered with mud," he said to Father.

And then, my father said, he and Grant decided to have a drink together. They took a couple of shots and then, because he didn't want Grant to show up potted before the immaculate Lee, he smashed the bottle against the tree.

"Sam Grant's dead now and I wouldn't want it to get out on him," my father said.

That's just one of the kind of things he'd tell. Of course, the men knew he was lying, but they seemed to like it just the same.

When we got broke, down and out, do you think he ever brought anything home? Not he. If there wasn't anything to eat in the house, he'd go off visiting around at farm houses. They all wanted him. Sometimes he'd stay away for weeks, Mother working to keep us fed, and then home he'd come bringing, let say, a ham. He'd got it from some farmer friend. He'd slap it on the table in the kitchen. "You bet I'm going to see that my kids have something to eat," he'd say, and Mother would just stand smiling at him. She'd never say a word about all the weeks and months he'd been away, not leaving us a cent for food. Once I heard her speaking to a woman in our street. Maybe the woman had dared to sympathize with her. "Oh," she said, "it's all right. He isn't ever dull like most of the men in this street. Life is never dull when my man is about."

But often I was filled with bitterness, and sometimes I wished he wasn't my father. I'd even invent another man as my father. To protect my mother I'd make up stories of a secret marriage that for some strange reason never got known. As though some man, say the president of a railroad company or maybe a Congressman, had married my mother, thinking his wife was dead and then it turned out she wasn't.

So they had to hush it up but I got born just the same. I wasn't really the son of my father. Somewhere in the world there was a very dignified, quite wonderful man who was really my father. I even made myself half believe these fancies.

And then there came a certain night. Mother was away from home. Maybe there was church that night. Father came in. He'd been off somewhere for two or three weeks. He found me alone in the house, reading by the kitchen table.

It had been raining and he was very wet. He sat and looked at me for a long time, not saying a word. I was startled, for there was on his face the saddest look I had ever seen. He sat for a time, his clothes dripping. Then he got up.

"Come on with me," he said.

I got up and went with him out of the house. I was filled with wonder but I wasn't afraid. We went along a dirt road that led down into a valley, about a mile out of town, where there was a pond. We walked in silence. The man who was always talking had stopped his talking.

I didn't know what was up and had the queer feeling that I was with a stranger. I didn't know whether my father intended it so. I don't think he did.

The pond was quite large. It was still raining hard and there were flashes of lightning followed by thunder. We were on a grassy bank at the pond's edge when my father spoke, and in the darkness and rain his voice sounded strange.

"Take off your clothes," he said. Still filled with wonder, I began to undress. There was a flash of lightning and I saw that he was already naked.

Naked, we went into the pond. Taking my hand, he pulled me in. It may be that I was too frightened, too full of a feeling of strangeness, to speak. Before that night my father had never seemed to pay any attention to me.

"And what is he up to now?" I kept asking myself. I did not swim very well, but he put my hand on his shoulder and struck out into the darkness.

He was a man with big shoulders, a powerful swimmer. In the darkness I could feel the movements of his muscles. We swam to the far edge of the pond and then back to where we had left our clothes. The rain continued and the wind blew. Sometimes my father swam on his back, and when he did he took my hand in his large powerful one and moved it over so that it rested always on his shoulder. Sometimes there would be a flash of lightning and I could see his face quite clearly.

It was as it was earlier, in the kitchen, a face filled with sadness. There would be the momentary glimpse of his face, and then again the darkness, the wind and the rain. In me there was a feeling I had never known before.

It was a feeling of closeness. It was something strange. It was as though there were only we two in the world. It was as though I had been jerked suddenly out of myself, out of my world of the schoolboy, out of a world in which I was ashamed of my father.

He had become blood of my blood; he the strong swimmer and I the boy clinging to him in the darkness. We swam in silence, and in silence we dressed in our wet clothes and went home.

There was a lamp lighted in the kitchen, and when we came in, the water dripping from us, there was my mother. She smiled at us. I remember that she called us "boys." "What have you boys been up to?" she asked, but my father did not answer. As he had begun the evening's experience with me in silence, so he ended it. He turned and looked at me. Then he went, I thought, with a new and strange dignity, out of the room.

I climbed the stairs to my room, undressed in darkness and got into bed. I couldn't sleep and did not want to sleep. For the first time I knew that I was the son of my father. He was a storyteller as I was to be. It may be that I even laughed a little softly there in the darkness. If I did, I laughed knowing that I would never again be wanting another father.

QUESTIONS

Reading for Understanding

1. Why did Anderson as a boy not understand why the townspeople liked and appreciated his father? Why did he feel ashamed of him and want a different father?

2. What was the meaning of their swim in the storm at night? Why did it permanently change his attitude toward his father?

3. How do you explain his mother's reaction to her husband's absences? To their swimming in the pond?

4. Why did his father act in such crazy ways? Why did he not explain himself to his son, even at the time of the swim?

Noticing Writing Techniques

1. What is the symbolic meaning of the swim? Of his father keeping the boy's hand on his shoulder?

2. Anderson quotes frequently. What effect does he achieve by such frequent use of direct quotation? How does it allow you to understand his parents better?

3. What discovery does his title suggest?

Noticing Vocabulary

_____ 1. An *orderly* is
A. a superior officer   B. a radio technician
C. a squad leader   D. an officer's assistant.

_____ 2. An *immaculate* person is

    A. intelligent   B. argumentative

    C. spotless   D. humorous.

Writing Topics

1. Write a paragraph explaining some of the things a member of your family did that made you feel either proud or embarrassed. Review Description Paragraphs in Unit 2 and Portraying a Person in the Descriptive Mode of Unit 3.

2. Write an essay explaining the difference between what some well-known person or group appears to be and what you think it really is—the difference between reality and illusion. Review Expository Essays in Unit 3.

Robert Bly (1926–   )

Robert Bly grew up in Minnesota, attended Harvard University, and studied in Norway and England. First known as a poet of the 1960s his volume *The Light Around the Body*, Robert Bly in the 1980s became a leader in the men's movement. *Iron John*, taking its title from a fairy tale by the brothers Grimm, is a kind of mythical study stressing the need of sons (and, to some extent, daughters) for the guidance of fathers and other men in their lives.

The Hunger for the King in a Time with No Father*
from *Iron John: A Book about Men*

Temperament Without Teaching

When a father, absent during the day, returns home at six, his children receive only his temperament, and not his teaching. If the father is working for a corporation, what is there to teach? He is reluctant to tell his son what is really going on. The fragmentation of decision making in corporate life, the massive effort that produces the corporate willingness to destroy the environment for the sake of profit, the prudence, even cowardice, that one learns in bureaucracy—who wants to teach that?

We know of rare cases in which the father takes sons or daughters into his factory, judge's chambers, used-car lot, or insurance building, and those

_____

*IRON JOHN (excerpted from pp. 96–100), © 1990 by Robert Bly. Reprinted by permission of Adison-Wesley Publishing Company, Inc.

efforts at teaching do reap some of the rewards of teaching in craft cultures. But in most families today, the sons and daughters receive, when the father returns home at six, only his disposition, or his temperament, which is usually irritable and remote.

What the father brings home today is usually a touchy mood, springing from powerlessness and despair mingled with longstanding shame and the numbness peculiar to those who hate their jobs. Fathers in earlier times could often break through their own humanly inadequate temperaments by teaching rope making, fishing, posthole digging, grain cutting, drumming, harness making, animal care, even singing and storytelling. That teaching sweetened the effect of the temperament.

The longing for the father's blessing through teaching is still present, if a little fossilized; but the children do not receive that blessing. The son particularly receives instead the nonblesser, the threatened, jealous "Nobodaddy," as Blake calls him: "No One's Father"—the male principle that lives in the Kingdom of Jealousy.

A father's remoteness may severely damage the daughter's ability to participate good-heartedly in later relationships with men. Much of the rage that some women direct to the patriarchy stems from a vast disappointment over this lack of teaching from their own fathers.

We have said that the father as a living force in the home disappeared when those forces demanding industry sent him on various railroads out of his various villages.

No historical models prepare us for the contemporary son's psychic condition. To understand the son's psyche we have to imagine new furniture, new psychic figures, new demon possessions, new terrors, new incapacities, new flights.

Enormous changes have appeared at the last minute; few of us—fathers or sons—are prepared for such vast changes. I have mentioned so far the young men's father-hunger and the starving bodies of the sons; also the demons of suspicion who have invaded the psyches of young men; and the son's dissatisfaction when he receives only temperament and no teaching. We might look now at the disappearance of positive kings.

The Darkened Father

. . . The demons who have set up a propaganda shop in the son's psyche convince him that his father's darkness is deeper than the son ever imagined. What can be done about that? The son finds out early that his mother cannot redeem his father; moreover, in most cases she doesn't want to. The only one left to do it is the son.

As long as the political kings remained strong, the father picked up radiance from above; and the son tried to emulate the father, to become as bright as he is, to reach to his height. The son perceives the father as bright. Though this may not have been true in reality, we notice that literature as late as the eighteenth century is full of this sort of deference, this reverence for the father, and emulation.

In our time, when the father shows up as an object of ridicule (as he does, as we've noted, on television), or a fit field for suspicion (as he does in *Star Wars*), or a bad-tempered fool (when he comes home from the office with no teaching), or a weak puddle of indecision (as he stops inheriting kingly radiance), the son has a problem. How does he imagine his own life as a man?

Some sons fall into a secret despair. They have probably adopted, by the time they are six, their mother's view of their father, and by twenty will have adopted society's critical view of fathers, which amounts to dismissal. What can they do but ask women for help?

That request is not all bad. But even the best-intentioned women cannot give what is needed. Some father-hungry sons embody a secret despair they do not even mention to women. Without actually investigating their own personal father and why he is as he is, the fall into a fearful hopelessness, having fully accepted the generic, diminished idea of father. "I am the son of defective male material, and I'll probably be the same as he is." Then, with this secret they give up, collapse, live with a numb place inside, feel compelled to be dark because the father is dark. They lose the vigorous participation in political battles, so characteristic of nineteenth-century men in the United States, feel their opinions do not matter, become secret underground people, and sometimes drown themselves in alcohol while living in a burrow under the earth.

Other sons respond by leaping up and flying into the air. The deeper the father sinks in their view, the longer their flights become. More and more evidence comes out in newspapers and books each day about sexual abuse perpetrated by fathers, inability of fathers to relate in a human way, the rigid pro-military stance of many fathers, the workaholism of fathers, their alcoholism, wife-beating, and abandonment. All of this news intensifies the brightness that some sons feel compelled to achieve because the father is dark.

QUESTIONS

Reading for Understanding

1. According to Robert Bly, what is wrong with the way children experience their fathers nowadays? What changes in society have caused this situation?

2. What, according to him, are the two ways sons respond to this unsatisfactory relationship?

3. What images of fathers, according to Bly, appear on the media? What effect do these images have on children?

4. How well does Sherwood Anderson's experience in "Discovery of a Father" fulfill Bly's notion of what a son needs from a father?

5. How important for daughters does Bly think fathers are? What effect does the father-daughter relationship have on daughters?

6. Do you agree with Bly's statement that "even the best-intentioned women cannot give what is needed" for sons? Can you think of examples to prove or disprove his point?

Noticing Writing Techniques

1. As a poet, Bly is interested in mythology, and he tends to think of current problems in terms of myths. What mythological phrases or poetic language do you find in this passage? What does he mean by a "dark" father or a son "flying into the air"? Do you find mythological images persuasive?

2. In addition to poetic images, Bly makes use of historical analysis to support his point. In what passages does he refer to history and what is his point?

3. This essay is partly in the cause and effect mode. What are the two effects that Bly sees of the damaged role of fathers in recent times?

Noticing Vocabulary

_____ 1. *Fragmentation* means
    A. breaking up   B. rapid increase
    C. slow growth   D. slow chemical change.

_____ 2. *Patriarchy* refers to a system of authority ruled by
    A. voters   B. rich people
    C. fathers   D. a king.

_____ 3. To *emulate* others is to
    A. criticize them   B. agree with them
    C. oppose them   D. try to be like them.

_____ 4. *Generic* means pertaining to
    A. an individual   B. a whole group
    C. one sex only   D. both sexes.

Writing Topics

1. Write a paragraph telling about your relationship with one of your parents and what effect it has had on you. Review Cause and Effect Paragraphs in Unit 2.

2. Write an essay analyzing Robert Bly's views and stating whether you agree or disagree with them. Use Sherwood Anderson's "Discovery of a Father" as part of your discussion, and bring in your own experience to support your ideas. Do you mostly agree or disagree with Bly? Do you think he overstates the importance of fathers? Does he neglect mothers and daughters in his analysis? Review the Persuasive Mode in Unit 3.

Poems on Family Relations

Langston Hughes (1902–1967)

Among Hughes's many works of poetry and prose, this short poem stands out in many readers' minds because it sums up in one metaphor a lifetime of wisdom passed on from parent to child. Notice both the language and the physical details.

Mother to Son*

Well, son, I'll tell you:
Life for me ain't been no crystal stair.
It's had tacks in it,
And splinters,
And boards torn up,
And places with no carpet on the floor—
Bare.
But all the time
I'se been a-climbin' on,
And reachin' landin's,
And turnin' corners,
And sometimes goin' in the dark
Where there ain't been no light.
So boy, don't you turn back.
Don't you set down on the steps
'Cause you finds it's kinder hard.
Don't you fall now—
For I'se still goin', honey,
I'se still climbin',
And life for me ain't been no crystal stair.

QUESTIONS

Reading for Understanding

1. What advice is the mother giving her son? Would this advice still be good for a young man or woman? Is it likely that a parent today would give the same advice? How do you imagine the son responding to this advice?

---

2. What attitudes does the mother assume her son must have if she feels the need to tell him her life was no crystal stair?

3. What qualities does she most want to instill in her son?

4. What feeling do you have toward the mother herself? How does the poem make you feel this?

Noticing Writing Techniques

1. What associations and meanings do you get from the metaphor of the crystal stair? Why did Hughes not have her call her life a "bowl of cherries" or some other familiar phrase? What do the other details mean? Are they intended to be taken as parts of the metaphor too?

2. What kind of language does the mother use? Would the poem be different if Hughes wrote the poem in his own educated language?

3. The poem does not use rhyme or regular meter. How does it achieve a sense of rhythm in other ways?

Writing Topics

1. Write a paragraph imagining that you were the son writing a one-paragraph letter in answer to the mother in the poem. You may want to invent a metaphor for *your* life in response to hers. Review Description Paragraphs in Unit 2.

2. Write an essay comparing and contrasting the attitudes and values of your parents' generation with those of your own generation. You may want to interview your mother or father or an aunt or uncle to be sure you have an accurate sense of their attitudes. Review Comparitive Paragraphs in Unit 2 and Expository Essays in Unit 3.

Theodore Roethke (1908–1963)

Theodore Roethke was born in Saginaw, Michigan, and grew up surrounded by the extensive greenhouses managed by his father. He graduated form the University of Michigan in 1929 and taught in many colleges throughout his career. His poetry reflects a psyche troubled by emotional problems and complexities. The following poem is read by different readers in different ways, depending partly upon their own family experiences. Whether you read it as a loving memory of his father or a portrait of abusive behavior, it is

probably most accurate to say that it reflects mixed
feelings and complex memories.

My Papa's Waltz*

The whiskey on your breath
Could make a small boy dizzy;
But I hung on like death:
Such waltzing was not easy.

We romped until the pans
Fell from the kitchen shelf;
My mother's countenance
Could not unfrown itself.

The hand that held my wrist
Was battered on one knuckle;
At every step you missed
My right ear scraped a buckle.

You beat time on my head
With a palm caked hard by dirt,
Then waltzed me off to bed
Still clinging to your shirt.

QUESTIONS

Reading for Understanding

1. What exactly is being described in this poem? Who is involved, where
   are they, and what are they doing? Be sure to get the facts straight before you interpret the meaning of the poem.

2. What feelings does the boy seem to have about what is going on? What
   feelings does the adult remembering this experience seem to reveal in
   the poem? Do you sense more than one feeling being expressed at the
   same time?

3. What attitude does the mother seem to have? What causes her to respond this way to what is going on?

Noticing Writing Techniques

1. Does the author use a simple rhyme scheme? A recognizable rhythm? Does the rhythm of the poem suggest a waltz?

2. Why does the poet use *papa* in his title instead of *father, dad,* or *daddy?* How would any of these words change the feeling suggested? Why does he mention his mother's *countenance* instead of using the familiar word *face?* What does the verb *romped* suggest about the action being described?

3. What physical details are important in the poem? What do they tell us about the poet's father or about the experience?

Writing Topics

1. Write a paragraph telling about a game or other favorite activity you enjoyed doing as a child. Looking back on the activity now, try to explain why you remember it so vividly. Review "How-To" Paragraphs and Cause/Effect Paragraphs in Unit 2.

2. Describe and compare individuals from three generations in your family, such as your grandmother, your mother, and yourself, or your grandfather, your father, and yourself. Try to identify continuities of character traits, attitudes, and values, as well as contrasting traits and attitudes. Review Descriptive Essays and Expository Essays in Unit 3 and Comparative Paragraphs in Unit 2.

INDEX